Harry Boland's Irish Revolution

Harry Boland's
Irish Revolution

David Fitzpatrick

CORK UNIVERSITY PRESS

First published in 2003 by
Cork University Press
Crawford Business Park
Crosses Green
Cork
Ireland

941.50821/2290456

British Library Cataloguing in Publication Data
A CIP catalogue record for this book is available from the British Library.

ISBN 1 85918 222 4

Library of Congress Cataloging-in-Publication Data

Fitzpatrick, David.
   Harry Boland's Irish Revolution, 1877–1922 / David Fitzpatrick.
      p. cm.
Includes bibliographical references and index.
   ISBN 1-85918-222-4 (pbk. : alk. paper)
1. Boland, Harry, 1887–1922. 2. Ireland–History–Easter Rising, 1916–Biography. 3. Ireland–History–1910–1921–Biography. 4. Revolutionaries–Ireland–Biography. I. Title.
   DA965.B65F58 2003
   941.5082'1–dc21
                                               2003012206

Front Endpaper: Jack B. Yeats, 'A Funeral', 1922 (Niland Gallery, Sligo).
Back Endpaper: Jack B. Yeats, 'A Lament', 1929 (Private Collection).
© The Estate of Jack B. Yeats 2003. All Rights Reserved, DACS.

Unless otherwise attributed, all illustrations are taken from photographs in family possession; the author admits responsibility for the sketch-maps.

Typesetting by Mark Heslington, Scarborough, North Yorkshire
Printed by MPG Books Ltd, Cornwall

Contents

Prologue   VII

I   Apotheosis   I

II   Preparation   18

III   Rebellion   38

IV   Intermission   59

V   Celebrity   89

VI   Cavalcade   122

VII   Conspiracy   147

VIII   Takeover   168

IX   Anticlimax   194

X   Enlightenment   225

XI   Compromise   239

XII   Rupture   264

XIII   Remission   286

XIV   Ruin   306

Epilogue   326

Abbreviations   328

Notes   329

Chronology   420

Index   432

Prologue

I

HARRY Boland (1887–1922) was surely the most versatile of Irish revolutionaries. While others specialised in fighting or speech-making, conspiracy or diplomacy, he tried his hand in every department. The eloquent deputy for South Roscommon was also President of the Irish Republican Brotherhood; the American Envoy of the Republic of Ireland was also an arms smuggler; the Joint Honorary Secretary of Sinn Féin was also a staff officer in the Civil War. Quick-witted, hard-working, efficient, generous, attractive even to his adversaries, he soon became indispensable in every organisation or enterprise which engaged his interest. Yet he neither sought nor attained leadership of any revolutionary instrument except the IRB, the fraternity which set out to dominate and manipulate all other republican bodies. Unlike his close comrade and fellow-conspirator, the almost equally versatile Michael Collins, he never translated his indispensability into political or military dominance. Though clear-headed and a shrewd political analyst, he was not an original thinker or a policy-maker. Harry Boland's wide-ranging influence was a testament to his remarkable personal and social gifts, exercised through an ever-expanding network of brethren, Gaelic athletes, and female admirers. Many things to many men and women, he had the gift of seeming straightforward even when compelled to be devious.

Intriguing in its own right, the abundant documentary record of his revolutionary life also allows us to penetrate the inner workings of Irish republicanism. It illuminates the methods by which republican organisers achieved the appearance of unity, and the origin of some of the divisions which emerged so spectacularly in 1922. Harry Boland experienced in extreme form many of the contradictions thrown up by the revolutionary struggle. A republican by faith and pedigree more than intellectual conviction, he advanced many attempts at political compromise. An impassioned advocate of physical force, most of his energy was devoted to propaganda. Tolerant and curious about other cultures and a frequent and appreciative visitor to England, he was often shamelessly Anglophobic. A persuasive advocate of popular sovereignty, his deeper commitment always remained to the inner circle of those claiming 'apostolic succession' from past martyrs. Through disentangling these contradictions within a man of honour and good intentions, we may better understand the origins of hypocrisy and deceit among his less upright contemporaries and successors.

Though he died young during a Civil War which marked the defeat of his unremitting campaign for unity, his life cannot be dismissed as a failure. The cult of Harry Boland as a martyr for the Republic, manufactured within hours of his death and chronicled in the first chapter, does less than justice to his practical achievements. His work as a propagandist and envoy in America, though never securing American recognition of the Republic, was crucial in creating the political conditions for the Peace Conference which generated the Irish Free State. His capacity to persuade rivals to work together, though ultimately unavailing in resolving Irish-American factional disputes, played a vital part in temporarily persuading most nationalists at home that they shared a common cause. Without Harry Boland, the Irish revolution would undoubtedly have been less effective, and probably still more destructive. Yet, despite his prodigious talent, influence, and goodwill, all the institutions that he had fostered in Ireland and America lay fractured and discredited at the time of his death. The dream of universal brotherhood among Irish republicans died with the man who best embodied it.

II

SINCE Harry Boland was a leading participant in every facet of revolutionary activity between 1916 and 1922, both in Ireland and America, virtually every major archive, memoir, newspaper, and monograph for the period contains relevant material. Any bibliography would therefore be at once unwieldy and superfluous. Like many 'secret society' men, he and his closest associates were remarkably casual about revealing and documenting each other's secrets, and thousands of letters received or sent by Harry have survived. The richness and range of available sources is fully set out in the end-notes; but several collections deserve particular mention. The extensive archive assembled by members of the family, and preserved by his nephew and namesake, includes fascinating personal and prison correspondence, reminiscences by Gerald and Kathleen Boland, various keepsakes, and the photographs from which most of the illustrations in this book were copied. Many official documents relating to Harry were consulted in the National Archives, Dublin, and the Public Record Office, London (including recently released files relating to convict prisoners, M.I.5, and individual 'Sinn Féin' activists). At an uncomfortably late stage, it proved possible to incorporate material from the rich holdings of the Irish Government's Bureau of Military History, amassed in the decade from 1947 but released through the Military Archives, Dublin, only in March 2003. The papers of Eamon de Valera, now in the Archives of University College, Dublin, incorporate most of Harry's voluminous semi-official correspondence with American and Irish leaders, including Michael Collins, in addition to his four American diaries and several important personal reminiscences. Although this vast collection was being catalogued, renumbered, and microfilmed throughout the period of my research, I was allowed extensive access to many of the relevant files (whose call numbers, so far as feasible, have been altered in the end-notes to accord with the list released, alas, just after the delivery of my book to the publisher). This superb archive houses many other useful collections, especially those of Richard Mulcahy, Kathleen O'Connell, Ernie O'Malley, and Maurice Twomey.

The National Library of Ireland holds scores of relevant deposits, including the papers of Piaras Béaslaí, James O'Mara, and Austin Stack. Particularly rich are those relating to Harry's dealings with John Devoy and Joseph McGarrity, rival leaders of the Clan na Gael. Additional McGarrity papers were consulted at Villanova University, Philadelphia. Many of the Devoy papers were copied from the collection of Daniel F. Cohalan, in the library of the American Irish Historical Society in New York, which also houses the files of the Friends of Irish Freedom. At the New York Public Library, the collections of Dr. William J. Maloney, F. P. Walsh, and J. C. Walsh proved invaluable. In Washington, the files of various Intelligence agencies in the National Archives provided diverting slants on the activities of Harry and his circle. My research in American libraries and archives was facilitated by generous assistance from Trinity College, Dublin, through the Charles James O'Donnell Lecture Fund, the Arts and Social Sciences Benefaction Fund, and the Department of Modern History.

Among the most illuminating published sources are the recollections of colleagues such as Robert Brennan, *Allegiance* (Dublin, 1950) and Kathleen Clarke, *Revolutionary Woman: Kathleen Clarke, 1878–1972, an Autobiography*, ed. Helen Litton (Dublin, 1991). In pursuit of particular episodes, various Irish, American, and English newspapers have been consulted in the National Library, the British Newspaper Library, the Belfast Central Library, and elsewhere. The many biographies of Michael Collins and Eamon de Valera contain numerous references to Harry, often based on documents cited in this book. Of particular value are the works of Piaras Béaslaí, including *Michael Collins, Soldier and Statesman* (Dublin, 1937), the seminal *Eamon de Valera* (London, 1970) by the Earl of Longford and Thomas P. O'Neill, and Tim Pat Coogan's partisan but intimate portraits, *Michael Collins: A Biography* (London, 1990) and *De Valera: Long Fellow, Long Shadow* (London, 1993). In *Revolutionary Underground: The Story of the Irish Republican Brotherhood, 1858–1924* (Dublin, 1976), Leon Ó Broin provided an essential guide to the labyrinth of conspiratorial Dublin inhabited by two generations of Bolands. The same author's *In Great Haste: The Letters of Michael Collins and Kitty Kiernan* (Dublin, 1996; 1st edn. 1983) incorporates Harry's contribution to a fascinating triangular relationship.

Selections from his official correspondence in America appear in the indispensable *Documents on Irish Foreign Policy*, i (1919–1922), ed. Ronan
Fanning et al. (Dublin, 1998). F. M. Carroll's *American Opinion and the
Irish Question, 1910–23* (Dublin, 1978) is the most thorough survey of the
political context of Harry's mission in the United States. Like all scholars in
a crowded field, I have spent much time following up the citations of other
historians and biographers, whose work is always acknowledged in cases
where the original document was not consulted. I am particularly indebted
in this respect to Jim Maher's pioneering study, *Harry Boland: A Biography*
(Dublin, 1998). *Harry Boland: A Man Divided* (Dublin, 2000), by Andrew
Brasier and John Kelly, includes a few useful documents not otherwise
accessible. Of course, my reading or interpretation of shared sources often
departs, significantly or trivially, from that of other scholars. In such cases, I
have desisted from drawing attention to our points of difference.

III

EXCEPT for apparently deliberate or revealing oddities, I have somewhat
regularised punctuation, capitalisation, and spelling in extracts from
unpublished documents, in order to avoid needless distraction. This applies
even to proper names, since many revolutionaries veered arbitrarily between
several versions of their names in both Irish and English. In such cases, I have
chosen the most common contemporary form in either tongue, even when
odd (thus, Seán McKeown rather than MacEoin, Piaras Béaslaí rather than
Pierce or Percy Beasley, Seán Ó Murthuile rather than Seán Ó Muirthile or
John Hurley, Harry Boland rather than Enrí Ua Beolláin). Code-names, when
used in correspondence, are given in the end-notes, likewise in their most
common spelling (thus, Gould rather than Goold for Collins). American
spellings within quotations have been retained. Diary extracts have been
regularised by the addition of weekdays, and irrelevant passages within a
day's entry have been omitted without notice. Minor editorial glosses appear
in square brackets within extracts. Where two or more copies of a document
survive, as often applies to official correspondence, only one location is
normally cited. Full citations are given only for the first reference to a
publication or archival collection within each chapter. Biographical notes are
restricted to fairly obscure but significant or interesting figures, other
individuals being supplied (where practicable) with a brief identification in
the index.

IV

I am grateful to several scholars, especially former students, who supplied copies of documents or alerted me to relevant sources. These include Marcus Bourke, Marie Coleman, Eugene Coyle, Brian Hanley, Peter Hart, Frank Bouchier Hayes, Jim Kirwan, Fearghal McGarry, Patrick Murray, Eunan O'Halpin, and Rory Sweetman. Various correspondents were kind enough to send information in response to my appeals to the press. William D. Corbet, Seamus Helferty, Noel Kissane, and Commandant Victor Laing were among the many indulgent archivists and librarians who eased my task. For help with illustrations, I am indebted to Brendan Dempsey (TCD), Paddy Farrell (Independent Newspapers Ltd.), Joanna Finegan (NLI), Sandra McElroy (National Museum of Ireland), Willie Nolan (UCD), and John de Vere White. At Trinity College, Louise Kidney responded calmly and efficiently to my often outrageous demands, notably upon the communal printer. Under the wise direction of John Horne, and his predecessors David Dickson and Aidan Clarke, the Department of Modern History remained a safe haven for scholarship. Sara Wilbourne, Caroline Somers, and their beleaguered colleagues at the Cork University Press, showed a patience borne of long experience in dealing with academic authors. Harry Boland, jun., suggested that a biography of his uncle should be written, made available an important family archive, and (with his wife, Nóirín) pampered me during my work in their home. Jane Leonard read two entire drafts of the text, spotted innumerable errors and infelicities, uncovered many pertinent sources through her unique filing system, and cajoled me into writing this book rather than merely talking about it. Our daughter, Julia Dorothy, arrived in the middle of chapter IX (inappositely named 'Anticlimax'), but generously allowed me enough time off to complete my task. This book is dedicated to Jane and Julia, with my love.

Apotheosis

JUST after nine o'clock on Tuesday evening, 1 August 1922, Harry Boland succumbed to the Irish Civil War, then in its fifth week. A coroner's jury attributed his death to 'shock and haemorrhage resultant upon a gun shot wound'. This had been sustained at about two o'clock on the previous morning at the Grand Hotel in Skerries, a fishing village nineteen miles north of Dublin. Boland, identified on his certificate of death as a merchant resident at 15, Marino Crescent, Clontarf, died in St. Vincent's Hospital, then at the corner of Leeson Street and St. Stephen's Green. He was thirty-five years old.

The fatal shooting of Ireland's least hated and most lovable 'Irregular', while reportedly 'resisting arrest' by a nocturnal raiding party, was an embarrassment rather than a triumph for Michael Collins and his new 'National' army. The torrent of republican protest and innuendo following Harry's killing forced the army on the defensive, as indicated by a laboured apologia in its official journal:

> During times of war and civil disturbance, persons in revolt against the Government, when once made prisoners by the military authorities, are liable to certain well-defined risks, where any effort is made to escape. . . . The Irregular propagandists seem desirous, however, of creating a code of warfare entirely their own, under which an Irregular, once taken prisoner, has a right to escape, when and where he likes, without any danger to himself.[1]

Republican lawyers wrought rhetorical havoc at the Coroner's Inquest on 3 August, making 'speeches about murder and that sort of thing' and causing Collins to bemoan having left such devil's advocates at liberty. Yet, as his Intelligence department pointed out, their projected arrest had been postponed in order to avoid the even worse outcome of inflaming 'possible feeling re their connection with Inquest'.[2] The military censor failed to suppress a damagingly accurate report of these proceedings in the *Dublin Evening Mail*, allegedly because 'General [Piaras] Béaslaí was out' when a messenger called with the proofs, there being nobody else in the office capable of handling so sensitive an issue. The editor was severely chastised; yet a similar report appeared without interference in next morning's *Irish Times*, another post-Unionist newspaper without suspected republican sympathies.[3] Though more successful in restricting press coverage of the public ceremonies of mourning, the authorities made no attempt to interfere with the massive funeral procession, so enabling Harry to join the venerated 'Fenian dead' in public imagination. Despite intermittently draconian censorship, a compliant press, and widespread popular acceptance of the nascent Free State, the Provisional Government and its army could not neutralise the emotional charge of such a death. 'Martyrs' like Harry Boland restored dignity and passion to a campaign which, to most contemporaries, seemed bereft of political logic and without democratic sanction.

Republican propagandists instantly took advantage of Harry's death to dramatise the inhumanity and vindictiveness of their opponents. On 2 August, a bulletin issued by Erskine Childers reported that 'big-hearted Harry Boland, gallant, generous, dauntless, has followed his friend and comrade Cathal Brugha' (who had died of bullet wounds on 7 July). Childers asserted 'that, both by incitement and direct order, the Free State troops are being authorised to adopt the most cowardly of the tactics of the Auxiliaries – the shooting of unarmed men on one of three craven pretexts: "failing to halt", "attempting to escape", or "resisting arrest"'.[4] Harry's intimate friendship with Collins made his killing a potent symbol of the 'conflict of brothers' or 'war of friends', inviting its depiction as the tragic outcome of personal treachery rather than as a mere casualty of war. Constance de Markievicz was reported to have heard Harry prophesy on 17 July that 'I expect Mick will get me "plugged". I know too much about him.'[5] Another account extemporised on this theme:

> Harry Boland is dead. One of Ireland's truest children has gone to his eternal rest. Beannacht Dé lena anam [The blessing of God upon his soul]. Some time ago in conversation with a friend he said: 'I'll be done in. I'm sure of it. I know too much about them and their treachery, particularly about ——.' He has been done in. Enough said.[6]

The melodrama culminated three weeks later, when Collins was himself killed in curious circumstances. The *New York Times* reported that 'Americans who have recently arrived here from Dublin declare that the attempt to kill Michael Collins' was, in part, 'a measure of reprisal against the shooting of Harry J. Boland by Free State soldiers'.[7]

Already on 5 August, one of Harry's old colleagues in the American campaign had observed that 'the dead walls tell us he was murdered', a fact confirmed by the *New York Times*: 'On the walls of Trinity College and other public buildings is the inscription in white paint: "Harry Boland Murdered", while handbills pasted on telegraph poles by the irregulars assert that Boland was shot by Free State troops when he was unarmed.'[8] An emissary for the Clan na Gael reported that 'almost every wall in Cork was covered with such inscriptions' as 'Harry Boland was murdered by the I.R.B.'[9] In Wexford, a Franciscan friar declaimed at Mass on 6 August that 'your prayers are requested for the Eternal Repose of the soul of Harry Boland murdered in Dublin'. Among the faithful who presumably ignored this injunction were a painter, a housewife, and a Military Intelligence officer, whose testimony eventually reached the Commander in Chief. Collins, acutely conscious of the potency of Harry's ghost as a republican inspiration, induced the Provisional Government to protest to the Bishop of Ferns and the Franciscan Provincial that the accusation of murder was 'absolutely unjustified' and liable to create 'a very serious and very regrettable impression'. The Bishop passed the buck to the Provincial, who anticipated that the excitable Fr. Mathew would 'be prudent in his choice of words in future, and will cause no further trouble to your Government'.[10]

Crudely printed leaflets reinforced the republican view that Harry was the innocent victim of betrayal and oppression:

> Commandant Harry Boland is wantonly slain when in custody by armed troops of the Provisional Government.
>
> Harry Boland shot trying to escape. Black and Tan method and the old excuse. ... Harry Boland is shot down because he stood faithful to his Oath to the Irish Republic.
>
> Harry Boland's reward ... is to be murdered by a former comrade at the bidding of Churchill.
>
> Brugha and Boland gave their lives for the old cause which will never die.
>
> Heads up! Into the Empire over the dead bodies of Cathal Brugha and Harry Boland.
>
> The power that killed Cathal Brugha and Harry Boland is the power that killed Tone and Padraig Pearse.[11]

These early interpretations of Harry's death were endlessly reiterated in republican propaganda and martyrologies, such as the 'List of Republicans deliberately sought out and murdered by the King's forces' which was later assembled for the abortive 'Leabhar na Aiseirghe' ('Book of the Resurrection'). The first of seventy-one names so classified was that of 'Comdt. Harry Boland, T.D.'[12]

Harry's rapid apotheosis was not accomplished by accident. From the moment that the dying man began to receive visitors at St. Vincent's Hospital, the process of translating personal confidences into republican propaganda had been under way. Various accounts of Harry's 'last words' to his sister and mother, along with their vain attempts to secure a meeting with his imprisoned brother Gerald, spread quickly and appeared in obituaries in both Ireland and the United States. In their simplest reported form, his parting words conveyed unalloyed kindliness: 'His last words, "I forgive everybody", were a final index of the character of the man.'[13] In another widely circulated version, the act of forgiveness was more specific and tinged with menace: 'Mother a comrade of my own from Lewes Jail shot me but I forgive him. I am going to Cathal

3

Brugha.'[14] Kathleen Boland remembered a similar utterance when, just before Harry's unsuccessful operation, she asked who had shot him:

'I'll never tell you Kit,' he said. 'The only thing I'll say is that it was a friend of my own that was in prison with me that fired the shot. I'll never tell the name and don't try to find out. I forgive him and want no reprisals. I want to be buried in the grave with Cathal Brugha.'[15]

Kathleen's account was widely reproduced in republican obituaries, though one well-informed insider believed that Harry 'told his mother and sister who the man was who actually shot him'.[16] These moving if inconsistent reports of Harry's dying injunctions reinforced his posthumous saintliness, as did the publication of several high-minded letters written, in mid July, to American friends 'from the Dublin mountains'. Joseph McGarrity quickly recognised their value as propaganda, informing Austin Stack that 'his letters to me will be Historic documents and indeed they are a terrible indictment against his opponents. I will send you copies. One has already been published in the *New York American* and the Irish Papers here.'[17]

Within a day of the death, Stack (then in charge of 'Accounts and Records' on the Dublin staff of the IRA)[18] had devised a plan for disrupting the forthcoming Coroner's Inquest:

The Inquest on Harry will be a hush up affair if the F.S. [Free State] people can manage it. We should have a strong man as leading Counsel. I dare say Healy is out of reckoning, but if he took up the case I know he would do it well. Then there is Paddy Lynch. After Healy I know of none better. Perhaps there is. If so the best man should be retained. An adjournment should be insisted upon for production of Joe Griffin and all other material witnesses, including the men who effected arrest. If this be not granted the lawyers on our side should I think leave Court at once.[19]

Neither Tim Healy (Parnell's betrayer) nor Patrick Lynch (de Valera's execrated opponent in East Clare) accepted the brief, but the republicans found a ready vessel in Michael Comyn, KC, who in tandem with his brother James sabotaged the proceedings as Stack had envisaged.[20] Michael Comyn had performed a similar function at Cathal Brugha's Inquest a few weeks earlier, though on that occasion he had contented himself with a verbal protest against the Coroner's refusal to extract 'material witnessess' from Mountjoy Prison.[21]

Having failed to have the Skerries raiding party brought over to identify the body and elucidate '*who* killed him and *how he was killed*', Michael Comyn declared that 'the men who in the dead of night broke into the hotel and assassinated this noble, gallant, kindly Irishman dare not come here to give evidence according to law'. Comyn brushed aside a counter-proposal by counsel for the

Provisional Government to adjourn the Inquest, if at all, 'for at least three months' since it was 'not prudent or advisable' to seek evidence from the raiding party under current conditions.[22] Instead, Comyn demanded that the body be identified either by Harry's imprisoned companion Joseph Griffin or by his brother Gerald. In a theatrical interlude, he went outside to consult Harry's relatives, only to discover that 'the ladies of the family ... were so prostrated with grief that they could not give evidence'.[23] When the hapless Coroner sought and secured the jury's agreement to reach a verdict based on medical evidence alone, the brothers Comyn withdrew after vilifying the Coroner for adopting 'Black and Tan methods' in order to 'shield the murderers'.[24] With two dissentients, the jury accepted the findings of the hospital surgeon, and the Coroner moved a vote of condolence for a man known to most of those present, observing blandly that it was 'a very sad occurrence for any young man to meet such a death'.[25]

Since his death, Harry's corpse had been 'lying in state' in the hospital, where a guard of honour maintained 'a silent vigil' while 'a constant stream of people passed beside the body', by 'kind permission of the Rev. Mother'.[26] Once the verdict had been delivered on Thursday afternoon, 3 August, the rites of mourning resumed. Stack had already perceived the opportunity for a great public demonstration:

> 'Tis terrible! But no use bewailing the brave. He must be buried in the Republican Plot. Cumann na mBan ought to have charge of funeral arrangements. I suggest Carmelite Church, Whitefriar St. for lying in state ... There must be a firing party and buglers; and if possible bands. His poor mother and Kathleen – I pity them. But we lose too.[27]

Though the Carmelites had provided Harry with extensive practical as well as spiritual support in New York, their grim Dublin headquarters had no strong symbolic or personal associations.[28] According to Harry's successor as Director of Purchases for the IRA, Liam Pedlar, the Carmelites were selected only after 'the pro-Cathedral and another church [had] refused to take his poor body into them'.[29] The Roman Catholic hierarchy had yet to pronounce its general excommunication of subversives, but most of the secular clergy were already deeply hostile to violent republicanism. Less effectively controlled by the bishops, and intrinsically akin to the fraternal networks of underground republicanism, regular orders such as the Carmelites provided ample substitute services.

With minor elaborations, Stack's plan was put into effect. The procession to Whitefriar Street, via Dawson Street, College Green, and South Great George's Street, was scheduled for 7.30 on Thursday evening: 'Public bodies and organisations wishing to march in the Procession will assemble in St. Stephen's Green South and will be allotted positions. Bands taking part will take up position in

Earlsfort Terrace.'[30] The removal prompted 'a remarkable and impressive demonstration of sympathy', with 'large sections of various trades and other organisations assembled'. The coffin was received by four priests, placed 'on a catafalque, around which the people prayed', and guarded overnight by the Cumann na mBan. Requiem High Mass was celebrated by Dr. Patrick Browne, Professor of Mathematics and Natural Philosophy at Maynooth, on Friday morning at 10 o'clock. He was assisted by about a dozen clergy in 'choral dress', and the congregation included Harry's Carmelite ally from New York, Peter Magennis, who had reached Dublin from Rome that morning.[31] The choristers sang the Canticle of Zachary from St. Luke's Gospel, enjoining the Lord God of Israel 'to enlighten them that sit in darkness, and in the shadow of death: to direct our feet into the way of peace'.[32]

The ceremony was followed by a second procession to Glasnevin cemetery via George's Street, College Green, O'Connell Street, Dorset Street, Whitworth Road, and Finglas Road. The mourners reached Glasnevin without apparent disorder, though as they passed College Green (according to a republican report) 'two of Mick's Oriel House spies were standing on the pavement. One was telling the other the names of the various people marching past'; while the second entered the incriminating data in his notebook.[33] In O'Connell Street, a Lancia-load of national troops 'laid down their arms, removed their caps, and stood to attention until the hearse had passed'.[34] The diversion along Whitworth Road was for the convenience of inmates in Mountjoy Prison; but their warders ensured that 'there was not a face to be seen at any of the windows when the cortège, proceeding slowly, passed by. On the route a number of blinds were drawn, and in a great number of places the employés left their business to witness the passing of the funeral.'[35] Over a hundred priests were alleged by the *Roscommon Herald* to have participated, a score more than the clerical retinue for Cathal Brugha; but a more circumstantial report enumerated only thirty-two priests in the procession. No prominent 'Free Staters' were noted among the 'general attendance', which included at least six republican TDs, seven members of the Dublin City Council, the three barristers who had disrupted Harry's Inquest, and female mourners ranging from Sinéad de Valera and Leslie Barry to Maud Gonne MacBride. The ceremony at the Republican Plot was 'very simple', with 'the prescribed prayers', an oration in Irish from Constance de Markievicz indicating that 'there was no more loyal or faithful comrade than Harry Boland', three volleys over the grave, and the 'Last Post'.[36] In Frank Henderson's phrase, he had been accorded 'a soldier's burial'.[37] For half a century, his only memorial in the Republican Plot was a small heart-shaped stone, rudely inscribed 'Harry Boland, 1st August 1922, R.I.P.'[38] His burial ceremony was memorably depicted in swirling oils by Jack Butler Yeats, who mistakenly believed that no permanent record survived except his painting, *A Funeral*, since all cameras had been confiscated at the gate. The isolated redhead in the foreground is said, implausibly, to represent Kevin O'Higgins, the implacable Minister for Justice and Assistant Adjutant-General.[39] The priest was modelled on Fr. James FitzGibbon, a curate serving the cemetery, who was to officiate at the funeral of Arthur Griffith later in the same month.[40] Eight years later, Yeats painted a less representational but equally disturbing scene entitled *A Lament*, contrasting the dour procession to Glasnevin with the gaudy hoardings of inner Dublin.[41]

The records of mourning for Harry Boland illustrate the uncertain boundary between private grief and public commemoration. Authentic grief was a powerful engine of propaganda which even his closest friends and relatives did not hesitate to deploy; while political opponents had to tread carefully when expressing personal regret. Harry's friends were legion on both sides, and many of the messages sent by public bodies and societies were accompanied by private notes from those who had known him well. Dozens of local authorities throughout Leinster, Munster, and Connacht, many of which had supported the Anglo-Irish Treaty, sent resolutions of sympathy to Harry's mother and sister. The Dublin Corporation judiciously approved simultaneous condolences for Harry Boland and Arthur Griffith after Griffith's death a fortnight later.[42] The Leinster Council of the Gaelic Athletic Association incorporated Michael Collins in a joint resolution deploring the loss of 'three distinguished Irish Patriots who have given their lives for Ireland'.[43]

The resentment engendered by civil war made it awkward for advocates of the Free State to attend the funeral or display their grief, however intensely felt. Some opponents of the uprising simply ignored politics and concentrated on personality. Joseph Connolly, a former Irish Consul in the United States who had assumed a neutral stance and thereby provoked bipartisan distaste, wrote that Harry's 'great good nature, his generous disposition and his consistent kindness made us all love him'.[44] James O'Mara, Harry's close colleague as organiser of the American Bond Drive, also refused to allow recent differences to snap the fraternal bond: 'Everyone loved Harry and Harry loved everyone – But in a special way Harry and I were friends – and brothers.'[45] Their mutual friend Seán Nunan, who had decided 'he would not fight either against Mick or De V.', recalled wistfully that Harry used to call him 'little Brother', affirming that 'he died as he lived, good and clear and straight, and true to his principles'.[46] But Maurice Collins, an old comrade from the IRB and the GAA, could not conceal his unease: 'I can assure you that although Harry and I differed in our views at the moment, ... it made no difference to me as regards the friendship I had for him.' This message, among others received from those deemed to have betrayed the Republic, was marked 'not answered'.[47]

Patrick McCartan, a would-be conciliator strongly attached to Collins, had visited Harry in hospital and lamented his fate: 'Poor big-hearted good-natured Harry to be shot by his own friends.' He deplored the distortion apparent in both official and republican accounts of the shooting, remarking sympathetically that 'Harry was so anxious for peace and associated so much with Mick that he was suspected by some of his own side.' McCartan believed that 'everybody who was opposed to him is very very sorry for him and no doubt Mick is the worst of all for with all their quarrels they loved each other'. With blinding lack of insight, he reported to Joseph McGarrity in Philadelphia that the papers had given the funeral little space, and that 'this day week he will be entirely forgotten except by his poor mother'. McCartan felt unable to send a wreath because of an incident at Cathal Brugha's funeral, and did not attend Harry's: 'I was anxious to go but feeling is pretty tense and some fool might make a scene which would get into the press and shame all of us.'[48] Yet he expressed his regret without inhibition in his own newsletter, recalling 'the old days' when Harry had 'stood shoulder to shoulder' with Collins and the brethren: 'Who is it who does not remember how Boland was in everything, was everywhere? We were all in the one lot then.'[49]

The response to Harry's death by his closest friend and chief antagonist, Michael Collins, was a matter of much speculation and rumour. While Harry lingered on his deathbed, *The Fenian* offered a perceptive prediction: 'Now you will hear over public house bars proclaiming [*sic*.] to the bystanders how poor Mick's great heart was rent with grief at this as they proclaimed it was rent at the shooting of Cathal Brugha. Crocodile tears indeed.'[50] It quickly became common (if anecdotal) knowledge, validated by countless repetitions· with minor variations, that Collins had responded to the news by bursting into Fionán Lynch's bedroom and 'weeping uncontrollably'.[51] By 3 August, an American newspaper had already picked up the rumour that Collins had 'wept on hearing of Boland's death'.[52] Collins's celebrated correspondence with his fiancée, Kitty Kiernan, suggests a more circumspect and contorted reaction:

Last night I passed Vincent's Hospital and saw a small crowd outside. My mind went into him lying dead there and I thought of the times together, and, whatever good there is in any wish of mine, he certainly had it. Although the gap of 8 or 9 months was not forgotten – of course no one can ever forget it – I only thought of him with the friendship of the days of 1918 and 1919. They tell me that the last thing he said to his sister Kathleen, before he was operated on, was 'Have they got Mick yet?' I don't believe it so far as I'm concerned and, if he did say it, there is no necessity to believe it. I'd send a wreath but I suppose they'd return it torn up.[53]

The same sinister rumour soon reached the ears of McCartan, who remarked enigmatically that Harry's reported utterance was 'impossible for he was not responsible for what he said when I saw him but if repeated it will have the same effect as if he had said it'.[54]

Kitty Kiernan's letters likewise suggest that personal and political divisions had tarnished the trust that she had once felt for Harry, and also that her responses were conditioned by fear of disapproval from Collins: 'I see poor Harry is knocked out. Will I write to him? (Diplomacy.) I wouldn't do so without asking you.'[55] The prospect of the funeral threatened further tension: 'As for [her brother] Larry, he was just going up to town to-day to see him. He will motor up to his funeral, I think, and if I get a seat I'll go for the day to see you. .... I'll wire you if I go up. It's very undecided yet. You wouldn't think it right for me to go to his funeral? I sent a wire to his mother; also I'll send some flowers, tho' they're not much good to him. He had my rosary beads: I have his.' Just as Collins denied yet half-believed the tale of Harry's malicious query, so Kitty attested yet half-renounced her trust:

> I realise I have lost a good friend in Harry – and no matter what, I'll always believe in his genuineness, that I was the one and only. I think you have also lost a friend. I am sure you are sorry after him. ... When I think of the little whispering into my ear – *always*, when H. was saying good bye, he'd say 'Don't worry, Kitty, M. will be all right etc.' He seemed sincere saying that, and it used to make me happy, and then he'd say, 'Ah I know how to make you happy.'[56]

Though Kitty missed the funeral, the Kiernan family sent a message of 'sincere and deepest sympathy on the death of our dear friend, Harry'.[57]

If Harry's death led many of his political adversaries to seek solace in pure sentiment, it invited republicans to translate personal affection into patriotic fervour. He had been 'a great man' and Ireland's 'bravest son'; 'one of her bravest and best'; one of the 'best fighters' in the Dublin Brigade whose 'fearlessness and ... light-heartedness appealed to all our men'; 'a most endearing companion and a fearless soldier'; an inspiration to 'future generations for the Republican ideal he lived and died for'.[58] His colleagues in the IRA hastened to draw positive consequences from his death. The redoubtable Liam Lynch intoned that 'such sacrifices consecrate the cause, and inspire and encourage others to uphold their traditions and the principles for which they died'; while Leo Henderson of the Dublin Brigade reassured Kathleen Boland that 'the death of men like Cathal Brugha and Harry will bring fresh life and energy to the course of freedom and will hasten the end of the supremacy of duplicity and political ambitions'.[59] Reared on the rich rhetoric of *Speeches from the Dock*,[60] Harry's admirers were not stuck for words to celebrate his beatification:

> When the present strife is over and the scales have fallen from the people's eyes, and Right rises again triumphant over Might, the names of Cathal Brugha and Harry Boland will shine forth among the noblest of that long list of Irish martyrs who have given their lives for the sacred cause of an Irish Republic.[61]

In the United States, where Harry's political interventions had sometimes proved profoundly divisive, he was remembered with appreciation by most Irish-American factions. John T. Ryan, an arms smuggler from Buffalo known as 'Jetter', was unusually succinct: 'These are sad days. Poor Harry! After all he had done for the Old Homestead!'[62] Even John Devoy, the 'Old Man' whose authority he had so relentlessly undermined, expressed a certain condescending affection for his antagonist:

> Boland worshipped De Valera as a fine dog adores his master, and obeyed his orders implicitly, never questioning his motives. He had bulldog courage and was blunt, and even brutal of speech, and in the carrying out of his orders he was ruthless and thorough. He was not a man of intellect or fine feeling, was wholly devoid of political judgment, and his idea was to crush and demolish every man who stood in his Chief's way. His allegiance to De Valera was the allegiance of the Irish clansman of old to his Chief. ... He often differed with De Valera privately, and sometimes bullied him, and in such cases he always won – for De Valera, in spite of his stubborn and unyielding exterior, is a weak-willed man – but Boland always fought for him and would sacrifice his best friend for him, for De Valera owned his soul.[63]

Peter Golden of the Irish Progressive League observed that Harry's death was 'a great personal loss to his thousands of friends throughout the United States, for Harry was loved and admired in America ... by Ireland's friends', though 'hated and feared by Ireland's enemies'. He was always calm and sure, and never got 'rattled'.[64] Peter Magennis, the influential Carmelite who had collaborated with Harry in New York, remembered him as 'a boy in face and form and manner; in soul he was as yet unsullied, for his clear grey eye told the tale of the past, and to gaze on him was to love him with that mystic holy love that one thinks of when one recalls the Leader who died in 1916'. Unlike the self-conscious Pearse, however, Harry had 'jumped into Irish-American life as if he were specially intended by Providence to occupy a place therein'.[65] Another clerical collaborator was less sententious when cabling his condolences: 'Hundreds of thousands Harry's heartbroken friends mourn his loss to you Ireland then they will hold Collins his Green and Tans responsible for murder of gentle patriotic Irishman. Father Shanley.'[66] Devoy's former *bête noire*, Dr. William J. Maloney, drew a different political lesson from Boland's death: 'Cable Collins lament Boland express detestation civil war deny right of any American to furnish money or material for fratricide publish cable. Maloney.'[67]

Harry's death had a dramatic impact on McGarrity's henchman Luke Dillon, who held the key post of Treasurer in the Clan na Gael Reorganized. Hitherto unwilling to support either side in the Irish conflict, he swept into 'Irregular' waters on a wave of emotion:

Cathal Brugha and Boland's murder is the result of Treachery and perjury to the Irish Republic. Their blood is on the hands of Collins and Griffith. Our people here have no sympathy with Traitors or West Britains [sic.].[68]

McGarrity himself was perhaps the most deeply affected of Harry's American associates, having 'lost my dearest friend'.[69] He had 'loved Harry', and after such an act of 'cold blooded butchery' he could no longer contemplate 'neutrality' in the Irish conflict as urged by Maloney and McCartan: 'If there was any neutrality in the organisation here Cathal's and Harry's death wiped it out. ... My efforts as mediator was [sic.] a miserable failure.'[70] As Mary McSwiney's brother Peter told her after a trans-Atlantic visit, 'Harry's death has gone far to converting all the people in America who had been inclined to go Free State.'[71] Harry's directive influence in Irish-America was still more potent in death than in life.

McGarrity viewed the demise of Harry Boland and Cathal Brugha as a much needed opportunity to reinvigorate his faction of Clan na Gael, through memorial meetings and even a mock funeral. Setbacks were encountered: an associate in Chicago begged 'to be excused' from organising such a funeral since the city was 'tied up with a Street Car Strike', and took the opportunity to resign from the Clan's governing body in order 'to devote all my time to my own business'.[72] Instead, an elaborate ceremony was held in McGarrity's Philadelphia on Sunday, 6 August. No less than 150 priests were solicited to offer prayers 'for the repose of the souls of my two dead friends'.[73] The police were asked to permit a 'memorial funeral procession', numbering at least 1,000, 'in memory of Honorable Harry Boland and Honorable Charles Burgess, who recently died in Ireland'. The name Burgess was presumably deemed more likely to encourage official co-operation than its Gaelic equivalent, Brugha. The procession to the Metropolitan Hall, where an ex-army chaplain was to deliver a memorial service, would be accompanied by two gun carriages, draped, and 'a small Pipers' Band, with muffled drums to sound taps along the line of parade'. The police duly offered protection and a mounted escort, on condition that no music be played in the vicinity of churches and that the national flag be displayed in accordance with police regulations.[74] The police escort was bolstered by companies of 'Irish Volunteers' and American ex-servicemen.[75] McGarrity claimed that the procession was 'three miles long, four deep and closely massed', and that even a lukewarm press had acknowledged 'that 5,000 to 10,000 people clamored for admittance when the hall was already filled'.[76]

The 'memorial service' had a distinctly secular tone, adopting fierce resolutions 'calling on the Irish race throughout the world to unite in avenging the death of Harry Boland and Cathal Brugha and to continue the fight ... until "the last vestige of British power and authority is driven from the shores of Ireland"'. A highlight was the production of a recent letter from Harry to

McGarrity, promising that all would 'turn out all right for Ireland'.[77] As hoped, the euphoria of this event was sufficient to induce most of the 200 delegates attending the subsequent Clan convention to repudiate the IRB, on account of its support for 'the so-called Free State pact'. Belying the Clan's clandestine reputation, 'cheers for the Republic and its bodies and defenders were audible two squares away from the meeting Hall'. More letters from Harry were unveiled at the convention, which agreed that copies of these 'Historic Documents' should be 'read at all Camps'.[78]

In New York, where McGarrity's faction had so far failed to extinguish the hostile influence of Devoy and Judge Cohalan, an indoor 'mass meeting' in memory of Harry Boland was arranged for the following Sunday at the Lexington Opera House. This provoked an open letter of protest from the Friends of the Irish Free State, warning that the meeting was designed to support 'the misguided youths now fighting the Provisional Government of Ireland, and to collect funds to continue the struggle over there in direct opposition to our policy as a neutral country'. The letter ended limply with a request that 'if you really know what the people of Ireland want, tell us'.[79] Subsequent reports blaming Collins for Harry's death inspired a correspondent in the *New York Times* to extol Collins as 'the bravest of the brave and the truest of the true', Harry being dismissed as 'generally an impulsive man of little powers [*sic.*] of discrimination when left to his own judgment, hence exhibiting extraordinary changes of attitude'.[80] Nevertheless, over 3,000 mourners overflowed the hall, hissing the memory of Arthur Griffith, celebrating that of Harry 'as a gallant Irish man who laid down his life for his country', relishing further readings from his letter of 13 July, and thus tending to revive the faltering appeal of Clan na Gael Reorganized.[81]

Harry's apotheosis was crowned by the composition of numerous odes by doggerelists such as McGarrity:

> A dismal Pall hangs o'er Fingall
> There's wail and woe.
> A Hero bold in death is cold
> And lying low.[82]

Not content with celebrating Harry's Requiem Mass at Whitefriar Street, Dr. Patrick Browne added his voice to the chorus:

> But who could have thought of the midnight stand,
> The secret raid, and the murderer's hand?
> We brought you home and laid you to rest
> In Glasnevin's earthly bed;
> Your body in soldier's clothes we dressed,
> And we can't believe you're dead.[83]

Peter Golden's collective tribute to the republican dead had the distinction of spurning rhyme:

> 'Aye, 'twas today, so many years ago,
> 'They killed poor Harry Boland,
> 'Poor Harry – well I knew the splendid lad;
> 'I fought beside him all through Easter Week.'[84]

Other memorials in verse included an anonymous 'In Memoriam', printed in Dublin with instructions that it be sung to the air, 'She is Far from the Land';[85] a melodramatic handbill entitled 'In memory of Cathal Brugha and Harry Boland and their many brave comrades who have fallen in defence of the Irish Republic';[86] and an 'Ode to Harry Boland' by 'Countess' Markievicz, sung by the author to piano accompaniment at a commemorative concert held at Dublin's Theatre Royal on 5 October 1924. The programme ranged from 'Eileen Aroon' and 'The West's Awake' to Masefield's 'To-Morrow', along with 'Little Mary Cassidy' from Harry's colleague in America, Joseph Begley, and 'Comrades in Arms' from the Mountjoy Glee Singers.[87] Equally evocative of his memory were the 'In Memoriam' cards exchanged between republicans each August, and the 'real photographs' and picture postcards which proliferated in 1923.[88] Through words, music, and pictures, the sense of his personality was celebrated and perpetuated among his intimates, and manufactured for those who had never known him.

The cult of Harry Boland as martyr had spread rapidly and widely in both America and Ireland, providing valuable rhetorical and emotional thrust for the republican campaign of subversion, resistance, and dissent against the Irish Free State. The high-flown phrases of versifiers and orators were plucked ready-made from the familiar idiom of sentimental Irish nationalism. They were also echoed, as already indicated, in the private and spontaneous tributes of Harry's friends as they tried to give acceptably solemn form to their grief and dismay at his death. Yet these exalted images jostled with more humdrum memories of his 'genial smile' and 'the hearty grip of his hand'; of 'cheerful, smiling, boyish Harry'; of a soldier who 'was so earnest and yet so gay, so brave and yet so considerate for all who were not so great of heart as himself'.[89] As Leo Henderson remarked in a letter sent surreptitiously from Mountjoy Prison: 'There was no-body who knew Harry, with his cheerful smile and good humour and his kind true heart, and did not love him.'[90] Love, above all else, was the quality which Harry's memory evoked.

No lover could have been more shattered by Harry's death than Eamon de Valera, unless perhaps his Irish-American secretary. According to Kathleen O'Connell, with whom he travelled from Fermoy to Clonmel soon after hearing the 'awful news', the beleaguered ex-President was 'broken-hearted and sad. On that long journey we never spoke a word. ... Oh the loneliness and the thought that H. was gone forever. He was in my thoughts all day today. May God have mercy on his poor soul is all that I can say. Cathal gone and now Harry – when will be the end!'[91] In an earlier draft of her diary, she had written that 'he felt it terribly, crushed and broken. He lost his most faithful friend.'[92] Just as the Requiem ceremony was beginning at Whitefriar Street, de Valera wrote his last letter to Harry through the medium of Mrs Boland:

> I feel I am privileged as one to whom Harry was more than a brother. To think that Harry is being buried and to think that I cannot be even at his funeral. He would have walked from the ends of the earth were it possible for him, to come to mine. Gentle, womanly, loving, loyal, generous Harry – Harry strong and brave ... When my turn comes Harry, more than all others I want to meet you.[93]

Ten days later, his wife informed Kathleen Boland that 'Dev is in an awful state about Harry. He says he could write and write about him – he thinks of his wit, his good humour – all – connected with their friendship. ... Dev seems to be thinking of Harry all the time.'[94] On 10 September, he told Joseph McGarrity that he was

> beginning to 'feel like one who treads alone some Banquet Hall deserted', etc. ... Loyal, generous, big souled, bold, forceful Harry – Harry of the keen mind and broad sympathies. Incapable of the petty or the mean. Typical of the best in the Irishman, Harry was fit for anything. Since I have heard of his death, I have lived with him more intimately than when he was alive. His stories, his snatches of song, his moods – how can any one get any idea of what he was who did not know him?[95]

Harry's death inspired de Valera to despatch a spate of uncharacteristically long and impassioned letters, whereas 'when Harry was alive I never felt it necessary to write to any of our old friends, knowing that he would do it and give all the news'.[96] De Valera was bereft as a widower missing his essential helpmate, lamenting like McGarrity that 'Harry's death has deprived me of the dearest friend I had on earth'.[97] He wrote repeatedly to Mrs Boland as if a dutiful son-in-law, reassuring her that 'like all the best men he loved his mother and was always talking about you when we were alone'.[98] Harry's optimistic spirit warded off despair in the dark days after the republican ceasefire: 'There are so many of the best gone that the future has little attractions [*sic.*] for me. If Harry were here, however, I believe I could with a bold heart "start again at the beginnings, And never breathe a word about the loss". How often he used to quote this poem of Kipling's for me! It is well to be able to believe that we will all meet again.'[99] De Valera was still doting on Harry's wraith in October 1924, when he addressed the commemorative gathering at the Theatre Royal:

It is always an effort for me to think of Harry Boland as dead. Subconsciously my feeling about him is as of one who has but gone a short journey and is expected to return at any moment. If he were to dash in here as I write, it would scarcely surprise me, – and oh! what joy if only it could be so. What work there is for him to do. ... How sensitive he was, how kind, how gentle, how faithful, and loving, and loyal, how high his standards of honour, and how devoted to the good and the true, only those whose privilege it was to be his constant companions can understand. To most, he was Harry Boland, the dashing athlete and the impetuous fighter. To us, he was Harry Boland, the generous and soft-hearted, one of nature's noblest gentlemen. ... Harry, we miss you sorely now. That great heart of yours, bold as a lion's, and soft and gentle as a woman's, has been stilled, and that mind that knew how to execute as well as design, is removed from us.[100]

Though less lyrical in its expression, the sense of loss within Harry's immediate family was immeasurable. His mother informed de Valera that 'he never hurt a human being in his life, and from being 16 years of age has practically kept the home going'.[101] His death was a financial as well as personal disaster, since Harry's reported personal estate amounted to only £657 7s. including bank deposits, an insurance policy, and household effects valued at £5.[102] The weekly allowance of £3 paid by Collins to Mrs Boland had terminated at the New Year, and despite intercession by Min Mulcahy (wife of the Minister for Defence), she failed to secure four months' arrears of salary which Harry had waived when envoy to the United States.[103] When told the sad tale, de Valera exclaimed:

It is just like Harry not to take his salary and never say a word to me about it. If ever the American funds are settled, I will see that the settling of that debt will be the first charge on the funds – that is if I am alive.[104]

Meantime, Kate Boland appealed to the generosity of Harry's closest American ally, McGarrity, stating that 'he was everything to me – for not only his bright self, but he practically kept the house going'. On receipt of a cheque for £50 from Clan na Gael, she felt that 'my darling son Harry (God rest his pure soul) is still looking after me, when he has left such true friends to look after his heartbroken mother'.[105] She received a further £150 from the Clan when threatened by a legal action arising from the subletting of Harry's tailoring business during his absence in America. This was 'a Godsend for I know you would not wish me to return [it]'.[106] In retrospect, Harry seemed the ideal son, protecting his mother from beyond the grave. Yet, as her daughter remarked in January 1925, Kate Boland was 'not getting over Harry['s] death at all, she always is speaking of it'.[107]

Harry's adoring sister Kathleen, long active in Cumann na mBan, followed the example of dozens of bereaved republican women by campaigning in the United States. Travelling at the suggestion of Harry's close American associate, Mary McWhorter, she visited 28 states in 14 months 'and collected an awful lot of money. I have forgotten the figure.'[108] The receipts were directed to supporting republican dependants, and her fellow-campaigners included Linda Kearns, Hanna Sheehy-Skeffington, and (initially) Muriel McSwiney. Kathleen's heart-rending accounts of Harry's deathbed drama had already been widely reported in the United States, and handbills for meetings at which she spoke identified her as the 'sister of the late Hon. Harry Boland, U.S. Envoy of the Republic of Ireland, murdered in bed by the British Provisional soldiers'; 'sister of the martyred Harry Boland'; or just 'Harry's sister'.[109] She received a ready welcome from Harry's associates throughout the United States, repeatedly reminding her listeners that her brother had been shot, executed, or assassinated.[110] Her oratory seems to have been touchingly simple: 'No man in Ireland is so admired as President de Valera. He is the most wonderful man, I think, in the world, but I know the most wonderful in Ireland.'[111] Yet she was not without guile and inside knowledge of clandestine republicanism, and a Clan organiser recollected in 1925 that she was one of only two visitors who had desisted from branding 'secret societies as wanting in loyalty to the Republic'.[112] Her spell in America coincided with the incarceration of her fiancé, Seán O'Donovan, whose application for nuptial leave from Mountjoy Prison had been refused by the Provisional Government on 11 August.[113] As Kathleen drily recalled: 'When I returned I was asked to go again but I wouldn't. I got married then.'[114]

No evidence survives of the response to Harry's death of his restless younger brother, Ned, who was 'on the run' in August 1922 and could not visit the hospital until after Harry's death (though he attended the funeral).[115] But the effect on Gerald, the elder brother, was profound and lifelong. Annie Traynor, whose husband had been Gerald's superior officer in command of the IRA's Dublin Brigade, wrote on 2 August that 'I knew Harry was his idol, and he would have gone through fire and water for him at any time.'[116] From Mountjoy Prison, Gerald sent his mother a message of solace:

You may yet see our Darling's dream realised and he would not say the price was too heavy. ... Is not our loved one's lot much grander than his one time friend's, who did not survive him one month. How uncertain we all are of life. I suppose Mick dreamt of being head of the Empire some day but God willed otherwise. I hope you will have no difficulty over our Darling Harry's affairs. Don't neglect to press the claim for his arrears.

Having urged God to strengthen his mother to bear her heavy cross, Gerald admitted that 'I don't bear up too well myself. Sometimes I think my heart will burst.' A few days later, he reflected that 'it is much better to live a short life, full of honour and glory than drag on to old age like a worm'.[117] As Gerald's disillusionment with de Valera's movement eventually set in after decades of loyal service, compromise, abuse, and disappointment, this insight became all the more pertinent.[118] Harry's youthful example seemed to set a standard to which Gerald, and especially his colleagues, aspired in vain.[119]

Republicans had wasted no time in raising Harry Boland to their pantheon of martyrs, reconstructing his last hours as a tragic drama in which he was stricken down by his closest friend, only to triumph in death through his dying words of forgiveness and his appearance of unshaken idealism. Harry's apotheosis was more smoothly achieved than most, since his luminous personality and reputation for good-natured sincerity were easily translated into the qualities expected of a saint. The warmth with which he was remembered by so many of his opponents demonstrates his personal appeal and the durability of the intricate webs of friendship that he had helped to fashion. Yet behind his vitality and bonhomie there was an undeniable ruthlessness, forcefulness, and even menace, betokening less saintly attributes. By dissecting the astonishingly rich record of his short life, I hope to restore due complexity to a twice-told and superficially simple soldier's tale.[120]

Who and what was Harry Boland?

II

Preparation

WITH the birth of Henry James Boland in Dublin on Saturday, 27 April 1887,[1] his migratory family could at last feel unequivocally Irish. His father James, mother Catherine, and brother Gerald were all natives of Manchester, while sister Nellie had been born in the United States.[2] Henry (commonly called Harry) began life at 76, Phibsborough Road, in a modest terrace between the North Circular Road and the Royal Canal.[3] A short stroll across Royal Canal Bank led to the Mater Misericordiae Hospital and Mountjoy Prison, both of which were to have unhappy associations for the Boland family. Behind the terrace, on the west side of Phibsborough Road, was Dalymount Park, then a wilderness inhabited in common by Bohemian soccer players and sheep, which Harry and Gerald made a point of mounting and falling off.[4] There were several public houses in the block, including a haunt of advanced nationalists known as 'the Hut', where Jim Boland was often found near the end of his life.[5]

Harry's mother was the daughter of a blacksmith named Philip Woods, who had emigrated to Manchester from the Cooley peninsula in County Louth.[6] Though reared on a farm, he had worked in a smithy before settling in Manchester, where he became foreman smith with Fairbairn & Co., engineers.[7] A reputed ancestor had made pikes for the United Irishmen and survived 1798, despite being scourged and dragged along the road between Carlingford and Dundalk, after leading his pursuers a merry chase until one was tricked into plunging over a cliff.[8] When flogged, he had 'held a piece of lead clenched between his teeth to stifle any cries of pain'.[9] With his ingenuity, pugnacity, and pluck, this James Woods became an irresistible rôle-model for the younger Bolands, providing a pseudonym for Harry in the United States and also for Gerald when he visited Russia on a clandestine mission in 1925.[10]

Jim Boland, born in Manchester on 6 October 1856, was thirty when Harry arrived.[11] His own parents were both Famine emigrants from Connacht: Patrick Boland, a pavior from Cams in the parish of Fuerty in Roscommon, and Eliza Kelly from Newbridge, near Mountbellew in Galway. According to family lore, both lines of descent were rich in rebel associations. Eliza's first cousin was Thomas J. Kelly (1833–1908), the American Civil War veteran who deposed James Stephens from the Fenian leadership and created mayhem in Lancashire, before being arrested only to be rescued from a prison van in Manchester on 11 September 1867. Patrick reputedly belonged to the IRB in Manchester, and his ten-year-old son Jim may have been a scout for the party that murdered

Sergeant Brett in the course of rescuing Colonel Kelly.[12] Jim adopted both of his father's professions, becoming an IRB activist as well as a pavior (who helped lay Manchester's tramlines). He first settled in Dublin in about 1880 as a foreman with Worthingtons, a firm then under contract to pave the streets of Smithfield.[13] By 21 October 1882, when he married Catherine Woods at St. Kevin's Roman Catholic Church in Harrington Street, he had acquired the dignity of a 'paving overseer' and already shared an address with his bride at 4, Carlisle Terrace (in nearby Portobello by the Grand Canal). His weekly earnings from Worthingtons were assessed at £3, placing him a cut above the common labourer.[14] The two Mancunians seemed ready to embark on a life of humble respectability in the grimy and rather stagnant setting of late Victorian Dublin.

This prospect was almost immediately blotted out when Jim Boland found it prudent to flee to the United States because of his links with the Society of Invincibles, the Fenian faction responsible for the Phoenix Park murders of 6 May 1882.[15] While his active participation in this sordid conspiracy is unproven, Jim was a close associate of several key suspects, including Joe Brady, a colleague at Worthingtons.[16] Two informers indicated at a subsequent trial that he was a member of the IRB's Dublin Directory in late 1882, without demonstrating that he belonged to the more or less autonomous Invincibles.[17] When the Invincibles again came under scrutiny in 1889, another informer named Jim as a member, stating that he had given orders to Brady and that he was implicated in an attempt to murder a Crown Solicitor at Baggot Street Bridge.[18] His alleged associate in this conspiracy later used Jim as an intermediary in a trick designed to trap a representative of *The Times*, when that newspaper was busy soliciting evidence to incriminate Parnell and his colleagues in the crime at Phoenix Park.[19] Like many of 'the fellows' at Worthingtons, Jim was apparently questioned at Dublin Castle immediately before his departure for New York.[20] A warrant for his arrest was issued on 25 January 1883, whereupon 'all the Tram Companies' in Manchester were searched in the vain hope that Jim had fled to his home city.[21]

Encouraged by favourable references from Worthingtons and the Dublin Corporation, Jim secured a post in charge of centrifugal machinery in the engineers' department of De Castro & Donner, a sugar-refining company in Brooklyn. The Chief Engineer, when supplying a further reference on 8 September 1885, stated that Jim had been 'a steady, energetic, reliable and trustworthy workman' during his three years in that position.[22] In the United States he consorted with organisers of the Clan na Gael such as Parnell's ally, John Devoy, who got to know him 'very well' when he 'had to take refuge in New York for a while during the Invincible troubles'.[23] His period in the United States may have been interrupted, as he is alleged to have participated in meetings of the IRB in 1883, which led, by some accounts, to the formation of the GAA.[24] Jim Boland was not merely a restless migrant, but an 'itinerant' maintaining contact between the clandestine cells of republican conspiracy to be found in every centre of Irish settlement.

Even more active as a peripatetic Fenian was his younger brother John Patrick Boland, whose base remained in Manchester. In 1887, Jack was allegedly paid by the IRB's Supreme Council to organise the brethren in Ulster and to arrange for shipments of dynamite from Liverpool. Jack, whose movements under a plethora of aliases were reported in minute detail by detectives and informers, was a man of 'slight active' make and 'very dark' complexion, 5 feet 7 inches in height, who 'holds his head erect and walks with a quick pace'.[25] When in Dublin he often visited his brother's house in Phibsborough Road, and was remembered by one Dublin housewife in the year of Harry's birth as 'a "Gent." who spoke with an English accent'.[26] Next year, in February 1888, the brothers celebrated Jack's arrival from Manchester with an epic pub crawl, beginning at six o'clock in the Royal Oak Tavern near Kingsbridge, with further calls to the National Club in Rutland (now Parnell) Square, the Ship Hotel in Lower Abbey Street, and a hairdresser and perfumer across the way.[27] After a few hours at home in Dalymount Terrace (presumably enlivened by the presence of nine-month-old Harry), and 'a short delay at Dunphy's Public house', Jim deposited his brother and a friend in Rutland Square at 11.15. An hour later, being 'greatly under the influence of drink', they were arrested, detained, and fined 5s. each, before proceeding to McCarthy's in Pill Lane to drown their sorrows.[28] They remained under 'close observation' from the tireless detective force, the G Division of the Dublin Metropolitan Police. When arrested, the self-professed journalist from South Kensington had but a single penny on his person, along with a notebook teeming with the names of contacts around Leitrim.[29] Jack Boland's night out set an excellent negative example for would-be conspirators and secret agents. Such incidents lowered Jack's standing among Dublin Fenians, who looked on his extravagant habits 'with suspicion'; whereas Jim retained 'a good many followers and stands very well with Mr [Louis J.] Lawless and other officials of the Corporation'. Yet Jim, loyal to the last, promised to 'make it hot for some of the G men from the way in which they treat his brother when he comes to Ireland'.[30]

In June 1888, Jack extended his mission to the United States and met John Devoy, who long afterwards dismissed him as having been 'no good'.[31] On his temporary return from America a year later, Jack 'associated very little with the Fenians of the City, and kept within doors at his brother's residence the most of the time'. Detractors accused him of failing to honour debts, and of being 'a low mean puppy, without a particle of gratitude, and a dirty skunk'. When a prominent Fenian denounced Jack as an informer, the faithful Jim 'attempted to assault him, and took off his coat to fight him in Nagle's Public House during the Horse Show Week'.[32] Jack's low reputation was confirmed by a Dublin Castle informant, who alleged that a Clan na Gael inquiry had unmasked him as a double agent:

John Boland was drawing £16 a month for a long time from a British Consul in America for his information; and at the same time £30 a month from Secret Societies in America, the latter sum for carrying out crime in the United Kingdom.[33]

For good measure, Tim Healy identified John P. Boland as 'one of Jenkinson's spies' in 1891, implying that he had received money from Dublin Castle as well as the Consulate, the IRB, and Clan na Gael.[34] By contrast, when Harry himself was acting as the IRB's envoy to Clan na Gael in 1921, he displayed unqualified pride in recollecting that his uncle had held 'precisely the same position that I hold now, 25 years ago in America'.[35] Whatever the true sources of his supplementary income, Jack Boland seems to have made good use of the mobility afforded him by his 'very lucrative appointment' in an international publishing house, to promote Irish revolutionary activity with English and American assistance.[36]

After returning to Dublin in 1885, Jim Boland had resumed his work as a pavior with the Dublin Corporation, which now employed 'direct labour' rather than contractors. His efforts were rewarded in March 1891, when Louis Lawless, the Deputy Borough Surveyor, recommended his promotion from foreman to overseer.[37] He was also a leading figure in the Paviors' Society, whose President, Edward Hart, was ejected in June 1891 under a cloud of innuendo that he had given information to detectives. Jim and a fellow-overseer warned Hart that the paviors would not work with him, and summoned him to defend his conduct before Jim's ally Lawless. Hart accused Jim and his colleague of using 'threatening, abusive, and insulting words, with intent to provoke a breach of the peace', but failed to sustain these charges when Lawless denigrated Hart's own record while describing the overseers as 'first-class men'. Dublin's chief detective dismissed Hart as 'a garrulous, crotchety old chap' and suggested that 'the bandying of words between Hart and Boland was mere chaff'. But he also drew a significant connection between this 'workmen's dispute' and the struggle for ascendancy among Dublin conspirators: 'No doubt Boland is desirous of having all the paviors in his hands.'[38] His political activity within the Corporation reached well beyond the paviors, as he exploited his influence in the workforce to campaign on behalf of Fenian candidates in other departments. Such efforts were often futile: the 'Dynamiter' O'Donovan Rossa did not after all return to Dublin, in 1894, draped in glory as City Marshal and Registrar of Pawnbrokers; and another conspiratorial protégé, Patrick Tobin, failed by a single vote to become Superintendent of the new Fish and Fruit Market in 1892.[39] Even so, the Corporation provided Jim Boland with a solid social base for his wider political enterprises.

Like many artisans struggling for a comfortable living in the Dublin slums, he moved restlessly from one rented home to another, occupying at least five addresses between 1886 and 1892. After a brief spell in a south-side tenement off Whitefriar Street, the Bolands lived for a couple of years in a tiny terrace-cottage in Inishfallen Parade, a stone's throw to the east of Mountjoy Prison, before moving westwards to Harry's birthplace in Phibsborough Road. By 1892, the family had twice migrated to other terraces in Phibsborough, without any detectable improvement in the quality of housing.[40] Indeed, a police report in April suggested that the Bolands, like Dublin's economy, had entered recession: 'James Boland was not so bumptious as he usually is. He looked somewhat seedy, and I believe that his funds are very low. Recently he has changed to very humble lodgings at Phibsboro.'[41] If conspicuous riches were the main source of malicious rumour in the Dublin underworld, as the police often suggested, then Jim Boland should have seemed beyond reproach.

Despite the growing demands of his family, augmented by Harry a year or so after the return from New York, Jim became more and more deeply embroiled in conspiratorial nationalism. In November 1886, he was observed in a group of nine prominent Fenians gathered by the cenotaph for the 'Manchester Martyrs' after the annual procession to Glasnevin.[42] As the nationalist movement fractured after Parnell's removal from the parliamentary leadership in December 1890, Jim emerged as one of the most notable Parnellite organisers in the city. With Parnell's desperate appeal to 'the men of the hillsides', the term 'Parnellite' became synonymous with advocacy of 'advanced nationalism'.[43] This term embraced various combinations of political protest, Gaelic games, and other less benign exhibitions of 'physical force'. Jim was prominent in the attempt to reorganise the GAA as a Parnellite body in July 1891, inducing a would-be national convention to pledge its support for 'the movement in progress for the release of our brothers now suffering in English jails for political offences'.[44] In March 1892, he was elected President of the Dublin County Committee, the 'only unit of the entire Association to come out as a body for Parnell' and one of the few to remain active in the 1890s. In the following two years, as Dublin's delegate on the Central Council, he campaigned against dissidents who had, after all, emerged among the 'Dublin Gaels'.[45] Jim was the Eoin O'Duffy of his generation, unremembered as a player but fabled for his 'organisational' skills.

The link between games and politics was manifest at Parnell's funeral procession on 11 October 1891, when Jim and seven colleagues headed a contingent of 2,000 Gaels each wielding a camán (hurley), draped in black. The Dublin County Committee contributed a wreath, chillingly inscribed 'an eye for an eye and a tooth for a tooth'.[46] A month later, Jim helped organise another public funeral, for that 'well known Connacht athlete and Nationalist' Patrick William Nally, from Balla in Mayo. Nally, a former member of the IRB's Supreme Council with whom Jim had conspired in Manchester, had died in Mountjoy Prison while undergoing ten years' penal servitude for his contribution to the 'Crossmolina Conspiracy' of December 1881.[47] Jim applied his organisational acumen and overseer's influence to packing the Coroner's jury with paviors, who duly returned a verdict of wilful murder against Queen Victoria (so causing 'a great sensation').[48] The Bolands revered Nally's memory: Jack was 'practically engaged' to Nally's sister (improbably named Bébé) and when in New York presided over the conspiratorial 'Nally Club'; while Jim became chief organiser and Secretary of the P. W. Nally GAA club in Dublin.[49] This club was unashamedly political in its aims and membership: 'In view of the fact that the Gaelic Athletic Association was founded for the preservation and fostering of our national aspirations as well as our national pastimes, we do not hold it to be absolutely essential that all candidates for membership should be hurlers or footballers.'[50] When the club opened the 'Gaelic Season' for 1892 with an event at Clonturk Park, Superintendent Mallon noted that 'the five members of the Dublin IRB Directory were present, and acted as umpires and collectors of gate money'.[51] Jim was among them. Remarking on the club's revival after three years of subsequent public inactivity, Mallon declared that 'it was the Nally Gaels who were suspected of having committed all our Dublin outrages'. Such an encomium might have brought solace to Jim Boland on his sickbed.[52]

Though never an orator or elected politician, Jim achieved some public prominence as the key organiser of a succession of memorial events for Parnell, Nally, and the Manchester Martyrs who had rescued Colonel Kelly. Police reports confirm his energy and ubiquity in raising subscriptions, entertaining visitors, and convening committees to arrange public processions or meetings. Except in the GAA, Jim was a back-room manager, nominating or seconding the secretary of an organising committee rather than seeking office himself. His reticent approach was illustrated in June 1894 by the prelude to a Dublin reception for O'Donovan Rossa, then on a 'begging mission' in Ireland. An 'informal meeting' was first arranged, issuing a circular signed by Jim, Patrick Tobin, and three other 'honorary secretaries pro tem.', who summoned a second meeting to appoint a reception committee. Three of the five were retained as secretaries, Jim preferring to second the motion for their appointment and withdraw himself from public view. A visiting 'exile' who acted as intermediary, having met Rossa in Cork, asked a correspondent to 'tell my friend James Boland to look after my interests as I will want all I can get when I arrive'. Indispensable behind the scenes, Jim joined the procession but not the brakes on which the reception committee sat, remaining only 'a very few minutes' in the Imperial Hotel when Rossa was treated to supper.[53] Like many able organisers, Jim worked most effectively when out of the limelight.

Such reticence, though largely attributable to his preferred style of organisation, was encouraged from 1892 onwards by a whispering campaign typical of the venomous relations between nationalist factions in the decade of the 'Split'. Hitherto at the hub of all Fenian and Amnesty demonstrations, Jim declared that he would 'have nothing more to do' with a torchlight procession planned for New Year's Eve: 'The cause he assigns for taking this step is, that he and his brother have been accused of giving information to Government.' Ever cynical, the police interpreted this as a disingenuous appeal for 'a renewed expression of confidence', the 'real cause' being Jim's inability to account for £30 contributed to the Nally Memorial Fund.[54] His name was absent from the committee of the Irish National Amnesty Association elected in February 1893; and he 'took no part whatever' in the unusually vast Parnell Anniversary Procession in October 1894.[55] The Parnellite press lamented his absence through illness from Glasnevin on 25 November 1894, 'Decoration Day' for the memorial to the Manchester Martyrs: 'In former years [he] was one of the chief organisers of these demonstrations, as indeed of every other good National work in the city.'[56] The pavior from Manchester had become a Dublin institution, arousing praise and malice in equal measure.

Jim Boland's conspiratorial career had long been traced with attentive interest by Dublin Castle and the police, who classified him as a 'B' List Suspect along with celebrities such as Michael Davitt, John O'Connor, James O'Kelly, and Fred Allan (proprietor of the *Independent*). This entailed unremitting surveillance with ciphered reports of his comings and goings – a mild régime by comparison with that imposed on John Dillon, William O'Brien, and other 'A' List Suspects who were to be 'shadowed' continuously.[57] Gerald Boland's account suggests that Jim eventually attained 'A' status: 'One of my clearest recollections is that of a detective on watch at our house, day and night. Everywhere my father went he was followed.'[58] Informers with pseudonyms such as 'Richmond', 'Alpha', and 'Nero' sent frequent reports of meetings involving Jim and his associates, sometimes using sub-agents who were not immune to contemplating a change of paymaster. As one wrote in a mutilated letter pasted into Jim Boland's notebook:

> I am sorry I haven't got a master that is just what I am looking for, to earn an honest livelihood which I had formerly but gave up foolishly enough to please certain parties and believe me you would have never been tormented by *Nero*. I should like to know the Gentleman but of course it is a State secret.[59]

Jim Boland was a familiar figure in a Dublin underworld characterised by intrigue and betrayal, in which every conspirator seemed to his brethren a potential turncoat.

In September 1886, Jim Boland was allotted 59th place in a list of 63 'dangerous Fenians' in the Dublin Metropolitan Police District: 'This man was a leading Invincible but evaded arrest although there was a warrant issued for his apprehension. He left Dublin and did not return until last year. ... He is a very clever and dangerous fellow and seems to be as active now as ever.' He was of medium make and 5 feet 8 inches tall, with black hair, dark eyes, a sallow complexion, and a 'heavy dark brown' moustache. His closest Fenian associates were also in public employment, being John Clancy (sub-sheriff) and James

Cooke (sanitary inspector).[60] Six years later, he had risen to second place among twelve 'prominent Dublin Fenians', and was returned as Chairman of the IRB's Dublin Directory.[61] His high Fenian office was no fantasy of some inventive detective or informer: as Harry informed the Clan na Gael Reorganized in March 1921, his father had eventually joined the Supreme Council as Centre for the Province of Leinster.[62] His activities as a Parnellite organiser included a trip to Manchester to promote the Amnesty movement in October 1891, when he reportedly tried 'to get his brother, Jack, out of the country, as he suspected that the latter was engaged in Dynamiting, of which he disapproved, at present'. Jim, in the uncharitable view of his detective adversaries, was 'an arrant coward [who] works Fenianism through his position under the Corporation'.[63]

Yet Jim himself was strongly suspected of proposing or organising a series of outrages, including explosions at the office of the anti-Parnellite *National Press* in October 1891, the detective office in Exchange Court on Christmas Eve 1892, and the Four Courts on 6 May 1893 (the eleventh anniversary of the Phoenix Park murders). His brother Jack reportedly 'furnished the money and some of the explosives from America', while Jim 'got it done in Dublin'.[64] When he heard of the 'Boland bomb' which had rocked the *National Press* soon after Parnell's funeral, Michael Davitt wrote sympathetically to Tim Healy that 'in my opinion it was this Dublin edition of Red Jim McDermott[65] who planned, if he did not carry out, the devilish design'.[66] The attacks on the detective office and the Four Courts were both devised 'by a more or less uninstructed person' using a crude but effective 'infernal machine' (a tin box filled with a high explosive such as dynamite or gun-cotton). The first of these exploded when picked up by a detective (Patrick Synnott), who died from his horrific injuries, whereas the second was lobbed over the railings and did little damage except to 349 panes of glass.[67] Jim Boland was also implicated in the murder in November 1893 of Pat Reid, wrongly believed by his own faction of the IRB to have acted as an informer; but the only outcome was a police interrogation and a desultory inspection of 9, Phibsborough Avenue. The visitors informed Kate Boland that their only object was 'to search the house, "don't you know, ma'am; of course we know there is nothing in it"'.[68] Jim was never prosecuted for any terrorist offence, being either innocent or astute enough to avoid incrimination.

By October 1894, when Harry was a street-wise seven-year-old, his father was an habitué of the National Club, an inveterate schemer among Corporation workers, and a prominent leader of the 'Invincible' faction which was still vying for control of the fragmented 'physical force' movement. Though the police distinguished between Jim's group and Fred Allan's new Parnellite secret society, the American-based Irish National Brotherhood, Jim and his closest associates seem to have joined its Supreme Council and worked closely with Allan against the followers of James Stephens.[69] Yet he remained on good enough terms with the 'Stephenites' to be invited to join the Old Guard Benevolent Society, a Fenian body aiming 'to form a bond of United

Brotherhood in promoting the indestructible rights of our Race to Self Government' and headed by John ('Shehan') O'Clohessy.[70] Jim was indefatigable in arranging concerts and raffles, ostensibly for 'charitable causes' such as prisoners' relief, and concocting dark plots which may have existed only in the minds of police informers. He was said to have become chairman of a committee 'on Invincible lines' which met in his house in mid October and provided funds for mysterious Parnellite missions to London, perhaps with the purpose of assassinating the Home Secretary or the Chief Secretary for Ireland.[71]

Before the end of October, however, Jim Boland's conspiratorial career was abruptly terminated by his removal to the Richmond Hospital with a serious brain disorder, ascribed by his descendants to the delayed effects of another fracas in a newspaper office about three years earlier. Following a Healyite takeover of *United Ireland*, Jim and 'a few Fenians' had invaded the office and assaulted the staff, in the course of which Jim's head was struck (according to conflicting anecdotes) by an iron bar, a policeman's baton, or the leg of a chair. In yet another account, Jim developed concussion after being hit by a stone near Broadstone Station, as he defended Parnell from assailants before his last journey to Wicklow. The outcome was a large lump and an undetected fracture of the skull, which may have caused an abscess to develop.[72]

During his illness, Jim was visited by numerous friends and Fenians. These included John Nolan (the suspected murderer of Pat Reid), who, on his return from America, 'expressed his intention to visit James Boland to-day although Boland's children are ill with scarlatina and he himself at the point of death'.[73] Fred Allan was 'knocked about ... at the news' of his comrade's illness, but hinted that hospitalisation might be opportune: 'You know what I said to you last time I saw you about being about at night tho' I'm afraid you did not mind me. But really, Jim, your good wife deserves that you should give more consideration to your health than you do, apart from the loss you'd be to the whole of us.'[74] An informer's report confirmed that Jim, along with his brother Jack, had been 'suspected by some of their followers' of being police spies, and that their lives were at risk. 'Richmond' went so far as to assert that Jim 'had attempted suicide on more than one occasion' while in the state-funded Richmond Hospital, as a result of which he was transferred to the more attentive care of the Sisters of Mercy at the Mater.[75]

John Mallon's spies were no less attentive, as the Assistant Commissioner reported on 6 November: ' "Alpha" visited him on Sunday and he was scarcely able to speak. ... On last night Boland's wife was very rough with "Alpha" and the others and threatened all sorts of exposure, however they believe she knows nothing and in the event of his death there is not a scrap of compromising matter in or about the place.' The Invincible meetings had become 'very dull without Boland', though his likely successor as faction leader was 'more dangerous than Boland as he is more steady and I think he is more intelligent'.

Six days later, Mallon could not deduce 'his real state as one day we find him in bed and the next sitting by the fire'.[76] By 1 March, a team of doctors pronounced his 'condition very critical', though a few days later there was renewed hope that their ministrations 'may yet pull him through'.[77] On 11 March 1895, however, the death was announced of James Boland, a 'clerk' aged thirty-eight years, the certified cause of death being a 'cyst of brain'. Mallon reflected that 'it will be interesting to observe the effects of his death on the rowdies of Dublin. ... He has been their leading spirit since 1885.'[78]

The public response to his death demonstrated his influence in a wide range of Parnellite organisations. Allan's *Independent*, noting that he had been 'born among the enemies of his race', remarked that 'his political work was always carried out in so quiet and modest a fashion that it was only amongst his immediate associates in Dublin that his sterling work was properly known and appreciated'. He was better known for his service with the GAA, his 'numerous striking social qualities', his 'charitable work', and his feat in winning the Royal Humane Society's medal in 1882 after 'jumping off the Metal Bridge' to save a life. News of his death was rushed by special messenger to Allan in Rathgar, and a meeting of friends (including organisers of the Irish National Brotherhood) was immediately arranged in the National Club.[79] In preparation for the funeral, further meetings were convened at the same club on the following night by the Dublin County GAA, the P. W. Nally club, and assorted 'friends and admirers' including representatives of the Amnesty Association, the Monuments' Committee, the Paviors' Society, the Workmen's Club in York Street, the Old Guard Benevolent Society, the GAA, and, notably, the Central Council of the Liquor Trade for Ireland. A great many names in the published report were underlined in red by detectives, signifying their Fenian notoriety. The well-wishers included John MacBride, a medical student from Mayo who was soon to organise an Irish Brigade in the Transvaal. The only prominent politician to participate in these preparations was the conciliatory Parnellite, Patrick O'Brien, MP, whose 'dash and daring' had recently been redirected from the 'physical force movement' to the Home Rule Confederation of Great Britain.[80] It was agreed that Jim's remains be buried along with his mother's in a site to be acquired at Glasnevin, and a Dominican was engaged to perform the Requiem Mass, the curate at Phibsborough (Fr. Michael Ivers) having declined to bestow absolution upon an unrepentant Fenian. Corporation managers were asked to allow time for workers to attend the funeral, and the civic flag was flown at half mast.[81] A 'foot contingent' of about 1,500 mourners followed the open hearse, draped in a green flag, and 'at the graveside the crush was very great'. Among that crush were three Members of Parliament, eight city councillors, and an impressive parade of brethren including James Stritch, his fellow overseer for the Corporation, Fred Allan, and Arthur Griffith.[82]

Further misfortune afflicted the family in November 1895, when Jack Boland died in Liverpool after returning from another mission to America. He had evidently been acting as an emissary of the 'home organisation' in trying to reunite the Clan na Gael, fractured since 1881 by vicious conflict between the devotees of Alexander Sullivan's 'Triangle' (the 'Dynamiters') and those of John Devoy (the relatively mild 'Kickers'). The Triangle included a Louisville lawyer and Civil War veteran named Michael Boland, who was implicated in the murder in 1889 of Devoy's associate, Dr. Philip Henry Cronin, and accused of squandering funds intended for the relief of prisoners' dependents.[83] Jack Boland's assignment as envoy, so his niece Kathleen was informed during her American tour of 1922–3, included an investigation of Cronin's murder on behalf of John Devoy.[84] By 1895, however, Jack was closely aligned with William Lyman, Devoy's opponent, Sullivan's successor, and the chief instigator of the Irish National Brotherhood. One of Harry Gloster Armstrong's[85] network of informers in New York confirmed that J. P. Boland was 'an important man in the Organisation and had acted as an envoy on behalf of the Organisation in America and England'. In 1894, he became President of the new Nally Club, Camp 197 of the National Brotherhood, which met twice monthly at Clarke's Lodge Rooms at the corner of 31st Street and 8th Avenue. When the Brotherhood launched its front organisation (the Irish National Alliance) in September 1895, the informer was introduced to John MacBride by Jack Boland, and had productive chats with P. J. Tynan (the leading Invincible), O'Donovan Rossa, and John Groves from Omaha (who had accompanied Jack to Dublin to propagate the National Brotherhood in October 1894). This narrative of infiltration culminated in the agent's election as Camp President after Jack's unexpected demise.[86]

Jack's death in Liverpool was variously ascribed to enteric fever, typhoid fever, or (according to the ever-melodramatic 'Richmond') self-administered poison. Fearful of being murdered as a suspected informer, and having noticed an acquaintance boarding the vessel on arrival, Jack allegedly 'went down through the ship and poisoned himself'. These suspicions led to a 'row' in the National Club, between factions associated with Patrick Tobin and Fred Allan, over arrangements for the funeral.[87] The police reported that 'there was very little sympathy, and the funeral was small. Only a few of the I.N. Alliance were present. None of the I.R.B. followers of Fred Allan attended.'[88] Even so, as Allan's newspaper reported, the party accompanying the coffin from Liverpool was met at North Wall by the Isles of the Sea Band, which accompanied the procession to the Carmelite church in Whitefriars Street, where Jack's nephew would lie in state a quarter of a century later. Those at the graveside at Glasnevin included old Boland allies such as John MacBride and James Stritch, as well as that personification of Yeats's 'romantic Ireland', John O'Leary. Patrick Tobin, Vice-President of the GAA, cast the 'last spadeful' and 'expressed the great grief which had been occasioned to the many friends of the deceased young Nationalist'.[89] Jack's friend Bébé Nally was devastated by the news from Liverpool, cabling Kate Boland her 'deep and heartfelt sympathy. Cannot believe you mean it is Jack Boland you found dead.' Though absent, she sent a wreath: 'He loved his God with true man's pride, / For Ireland lived, for Ireland died.'[90] For the time being, the formidable Boland influence on 'advanced nationalism' had been extinguished, to the dismay of the brethren and the relief of their adversaries in Dublin Castle.

Jim Boland's generosity towards needy republicans had been reciprocated shortly after his death, when two funds were raised to save Kate Boland and her five orphans from destitution. Their plight might have been worse, as Jim had continued to receive £2 10s. per week from the Corporation throughout his eleven-week illness, an act of grace that provoked some 'quibbling'.[91] Fred Allan, Patrick O'Brien, and other leading Parnellites such as William Field, MP for Dublin (St. Patrick's), agreed to organise a public appeal at a meeting (in the writing room at Glasnevin) on the day of the funeral. The fund was inaugurated next afternoon in the City Hall, by permission of the Lord Mayor (John Dillon's Parnellite cousin and solicitor, Valentine Blake Dillon). The organisers, predictably based at the National Club, pointed out that 'his slender purse was always open to help those of his fellow Nationalists who were struck down and reduced to penury in Ireland's cause'. Contributors included the Council of the Young Ireland League (represented by Arthur Griffith), the United Labourers of Ireland, scores of Corporation workers offering anything from 6d. to £2, an anonymous 'admirer', and John E. Redmond, MP.[92] The Old Guard Benevolent Society called upon its members to support the family of this 'true and sterling Nationalist'.[93] The month-long appeal raised just under £300, supplemented in June by the profit, if any, from a mini-tournament of four hurling and football matches organised by the GAA at Clonturk Park.[94]

Most of the proceeds were devoted to acquiring a tobacconist's business for Kate Boland at 28, Wexford Street. In a busy working-class district later known as 'the Dardanelles',[95] the shop was half a mile north of Portobello, where the Bolands had set up their household thirteen years earlier. Kate secured useful advice from a well-wisher working for Gallaher & Co. of London: 'You will find it not hard work but very confining – if the committee decide on a tobacco shop, I am entirely at their service. ... I will be able to get you credit from all the best people that work Ireland say for pipes' purchase etc., cigars and cigarettes and also tobaccos.'[96] Her adviser helpfully pointed out that cigarettes and pipes were more profitable for retailers than tobacco; but Kate hedged her bets, soliciting 'a trial of her stock of pipes, tobaccos, and cigars' when advertising in the nationalist journal *Shan Van Vocht*, founded in 1896. Patriotic smokers were particularly encouraged to patronise the 'widow of the late James Boland'.[97]

Gerald recollected that Kate 'barely made a living there', as 'she could not refuse the poor, whether they had money or not'.[98] Conditions were cramped, since the house, though featuring five front windows and eight rooms, also contained four families in 1901. Kate's share was three rooms for her household of six.[99] Even so, she had aquired two resident shop assistants and also a second shop in Great Brunswick (now Pearse) Street, which Gerald briefly took over after leaving school in September 1900.[100] In 1907, she gave up the business and moved closer to Portobello, sharing another eight-roomed house in Lennox Street with a commercial traveller and his family. Now elevated from tobacconist to self-styled 'bean an tighe' (woman of the house), in 1911 she boarded a fireman and a butcher as well as her family in five rooms.[101] At last, in 1914, she secured an entire house in the far more elegant if faintly sinister surroundings of 15, Marino Crescent, the Clontarf birthplace of Bram Stoker in 1847.[102] On amicable terms with her Baptist landlord and loyalist neighbours, she had exchanged urban squalor for a measure of suburban gentility.[103]

When Jim Boland died in 1895, he left five children ranging from ten-year-old Nellie to the infant Edmund.[104] Harry, the middle child, had yet to reach his eighth birthday. In February 1896 (through the intervention of Patrick O'Brien), his elder brother Gerald became a boarder under the Christian Brothers in the O'Brien Institute for Destitute Children.[105] The family's removal south of the Liffey enabled Harry to be consigned to the custody of the same order in Synge Street, a block away from Wexford Street. According to family lore, Harry left Synge Street abruptly after being beaten by a Brother; yet by 1915 he had recovered enough interest in his not-so-alma mater to subscribe to the Past Pupils' Union of the Christian Brothers.[106] Harry's schooling was eventually resumed with the help of Thomas and Anna Tynan of Mountrath, Queen's County (now Laois), family friends who apparently secured his admission as a boarder in the Preparatory or Junior Novitiate of the 'De La Salle Brothers' at nearby Castletown.[107] These Brothers of the Christian Schools taught a small group of novices, scholastics, and aspirants such as Harry. Junior pupils were admitted between the ages of thirteen and fifteen years, 'in order to test their vocation, and to prepare themselves for the Novitiate proper'. Each aspirant was required to display 'a gentlemanly appearance, without any apparent deformity', along with 'a sound judgement, ... a docile and sociable disposition, detachment from worldly goods and interests, zeal for the glory of God, for the salvation of children, and for his own perfection'.[108] Those in the Junior Novitiate were taught French as well as English, arithmetic, and algebra, enjoying 'weekly walks; occasionally a whole day's outing', and summer swimming in the Nore.[109] Harry, then in his thirteenth year, was not among the 70 boarders enumerated for the census in March 1901, when 4 youthful 'principal directors' presided over a staff of 9 teachers and 4 stewards in a substantial mansion with 24 rooms and 36 front windows.[110] His brief experience of secondary schooling probably began in the following autumn, when Gerald was already in the workforce.

Once out of school, both Gerald and Harry hastened to learn a trade. Having tried and abandoned shopkeeping, Gerald joined the Midland and Great Western Railway Co. at Broadstone, through the customary intercession of Patrick O'Brien. Moving to the company's drawing office in about 1903, he spent seven years attending evening classes in the Kevin Street Technical Schools before finding employment with the Dublin Corporation in 1907.[111] Harry, two years his junior, worked briefly in Manchester before entering the tailoring department of Todd, Burns & Co. of Mary Street, one of Dublin's largest department stores.[112] His employers advertised themselves long-windedly as 'silk mercers, shawl men, linen and woollen drapers, tailors, hatters, boot and shoemakers, upholsterers, carpet warehousemen, cabinetmakers, haberdashers, hosiers, glovers, jewellers, lacemen, outfitters for emigration purposes, and for family and general mourning'.[113] The management and workforce were mainly Catholics, but not exclusively, with directors ranging from John Boyd Dunlop, Scottish inventor of the pneumatic tyre, to Matthias McDonnell Bodkin, a former nationalist MP who had bitterly opposed Parnell.[114] The tailors of Dublin belonged to a ramshackle aristocracy of labour, equally eager for the respectability betokened by their bowler hats and the camaraderie of the bar. As a Relieving Officer for the North Dublin Union complained in 1906:

> Tailors give us more trouble than all other classes of men in Dublin. They earn good wages, but the most of them spend their money on drink. The ordinary labourers were much better towards their families. ... The system of drinking in the tailors' workshops in Dubin is scandalous. They drink all their wages. I have repeatedly gone to workshops to follow a man up, but as soon as I arrive he disappears, and trots from one shop to another.[115]

Harry became a cutter and made many close friends in the firm, which eventually also employed Kathleen and Edmund.[116] His prison correspondence after the Rebellion of 1916 evokes a busy and convivial workforce, rather than a den of debauchery as depicted by the Relieving Officer. Harry never lost his keen sartorial eye, or his liking for a pint of plain.

By 1898, Harry and Gerald were already regular attenders during school holidays at children's classes in the Workmen's Club, York Street, one of the nationalist societies which had staged Jim's funeral. They learned 'The Rising of the Moon' in Irish, using phonetic transcription, and Gerald memorised every verse in Songs and Ballads of '98, compiled by Denis Devereux (a member of the club).[117] Gerald's first nationalist organisation was the Celtic Literary Society in Abbey Street, the haunt of Arthur Griffith and William Rooney.[118] It may have been for that audience that he inscribed an earnest essay on 'the United Irishmen', affirming that 'there are some to whom their memory is an inspiration ... to fight the way to human liberty all over the earth'.[119] Kathleen remembered Gerald dragging 'my youngest brother [Edmund] and myself to the Gaelic League in Upper O'Connell Street, but I am afraid we were so naughty that the teacher, Miss O'Brien, had to put us out'.[120] Harry's participation in the Gaelic League is undocumented. His experiments with the

Irish language, while imprisoned after the Rebellion, suggest that this was a recent enthusiasm.

The IRB was another matter. Both brothers seem to have been enrolled in a 'Circle' known as the Joseph Holt '98 Club in January 1904, when Gerald was approached after a hurling match by the referee, Michael F. Crowe.[121] They were introduced into the IRB by their father's old associate James Stritch, who was also Branch President of the Irish National Foresters at 41, Rutland Square. Meetings of this ever expanding Circle were held either in Stritch's house at 51, Mountjoy Street, or in the Foresters' hall.[122] The Foresters, nominally a friendly society with romantic nationalist precepts and picturesque fraternal rituals, were notorious as a front for 'the Organisation'. Thinly disguised Fenian bodies proliferated at the same address, including the Wolfe Tone and United Irishmen Memorial Committee which claimed thirteen affiliated clubs in 1910. This association promoted 'the complete independence of Ireland' by encouraging 'the union of Irishmen of all creeds and sections in working for the freedom of the country', and aimed to 'inculcate the spirit of self-sacrifice and self-reliance, by which alone true liberty can be attained'.[123]

The Joseph Holt Circle soon had Gerald as its Secretary and Harry as Treasurer, with Charles J. Kickham (the novelist's nephew) as Centre. Edmund 'could not stick the apparently aimless way we kept meeting, so he left'. Gerald remained a member until 1916, but with decreasing zeal:

> I never liked the I.R.B. although for a while, like all the rest, I thought I was a great fellow to belong to an Oath Bound Secret Society whose object was to establish an Irish Republic. What I got sick of was the sneaking into a meeting every month and later every fortnight and doing nothing only meeting and paying our shilling. I did not like the practice of infiltration which went on continuously into other organisations.[124]

Though coloured in hindsight by the lukewarm response to the Rebellion of many Dublin brethren (including Stritch, Kickham, and Crowe), Gerald's negative assessment accurately reflected the posturing hypocrisy of many 'secret society men' in a period when insurrection seemed out of the question. Harry, by contrast, seems to have relished the very practices which Gerald later deplored, becoming an expert infiltrator with cloak and dagger ever at the ready. His work as a tailor and cutter involved visits to firms in cities such as Belfast, Manchester, and London, enabling Harry to extend his conspiratorial as well as mercantile networks. In Belfast, for example, he met IRB contacts at the tailor's shop of Danny McDevitt, known to a wide range of socialists and republicans as the 'Bounders' College' or the 'Bolshevik Club'.[125] Like his father, Harry used his daytime trade as a vehicle for exerting political and conspiratorial influence.

Before 1916, that influence was most effectively applied within the GAA, in which Harry became even more notable as an administrator than as a player. His skill as a hurler was sufficient to earn him a place in several championship teams, beginning with service as full back in a Middle League victory for Rathmines in December 1906. He first played in an All-Ireland senior final in April 1909, when Dublin tied with Tipperary, only to lose without Harry's participation in the replay.[126] Not for the last time, he suffered at the hands of an Irish-American combination in July 1911, when a visiting hurling team defeated Dublin at Jones Road (the site of Croke Park).[127] In early 1914, presumably when the Bolands moved from Lennox Street to Marino Crescent, Harry switched allegiance from the O'Donovan Rossa Club in Rathmines to the 'Faugh-a-Ballagh' Athletic Club based at Clonturk Park, Drumcondra. This very successful hurling team, which shared its war-cry (otherwise 'Clear the Way') with the Royal Irish Fusiliers, won the Dublin senior hurling finals in May 1914 and June 1915 with Harry in both teams.[128] In his last competitive match, in Tullamore on 19 March 1916, Dublin lost narrowly to Leix in the final of a tournament devoted to the long-projected Wolfe Tone Memorial, an IRB enterprise. Despite 'unfavourable' weather and slow play, this was reportedly a 'great' contest.[129] Yet six years later he might still be observed at Croke Park, playing an impromptu game of rounders: 'The boy-heart was still his – a little heavier, perhaps, because it had grown bigger!'[130]

Elected to the Dublin County Committee in December 1907, Harry emulated his father four years later by becoming its Chairman, having easily defeated two rival candidates. His key colleague, as Secretary and Treasurer, was Mick Crowe, the referee who had beguiled the Boland brothers into joining the IRB in 1904. Though seldom available for practical administration after 1916, Harry retained formal control until his death.[131] As a senior organiser, though never a member of the GAA's Central Council, Harry was well placed to consolidate his alliances with Gaels on and off the field. Like Crowe, he became a notable referee, presiding over his first All-Ireland hurling final at Dungarvan in 1912, and a senior football final in 1914.[132] He also refined his tactical skills at the GAA's annual convention in March 1913, pushing through motions which improved the flow of the game by restricting free hits and limiting the size of all hurling and football teams to fifteen players, and compelled county teams to distinguish themselves by displaying approved colours.[133]

More significantly, he belonged to the small band of IRB organisers who 'realised the potentialities of the G.A.A. as a training ground for Physical Force' and set out to place their County Committees under the brethren's control. Though James J. Walsh claimed that this strategy had been invented in Cork, with Harry and Mick Crowe as mere imitators, it had been anticipated in the GAA's infancy by conspirators like Jim Boland.[134] As a detective had observed in 1886, the GAA aimed 'to improve the physical condition of Nationalists in case of a future fight for Independence', its meetings being 'constantly used to cloak Fenianism'.[135] Harry drew no clear distinction between his labours as an organiser for the GAA and the IRB, taking advantage of a visit to London on athletic matters to entice Michael Collins, Secretary of the Geraldines club, into the Brotherhood in November 1909.[136] Six months earlier, Harry had induced the Dublin County Committee to postpone all games in order to support the unveiling of a monument to John O'Leary, formerly President of the Supreme Council: 'Mr John O'Leary was a patron of the Association, and he made many sacrifices for Irish freedom during the course of his life.'[137] The GAA provided the Brotherhood with a fertile recruiting field, a powerful propaganda instrument, and a source of patriotic fervour which the conspirators hoped to activate whenever the orgasmic moment of insurrection came.

The long-predicted climax seemed less remote after 1913, when the IRB began to drill in preparation for an open organisation of Irish Volunteers, just as the Orange Institution had anticipated the creation of the Ulster Volunteer Force. As Gerald recalled: 'Jim Stritch got the Foresters to build a large Hall at the back of 41 [Rutland Square] and the I.R.B. men started to learn foot-drill and simple military movements, in anticipation of the formation of Volunteers to counter the Carson organisation.'[138] As a member of B Company, 2nd Dublin Battalion, Gerald shared his drills with Arthur Griffith.[139] He took soldiering seriously, saving up 'to get a gun' and purifying his mind and body by renouncing meat, dairy products, alcohol, and tobacco.[140] Harry was selected to represent the Holt Circle on the Provisional Committee of the Irish Volunteers in November 1913, but declined to act because of his preoccupation with the GAA.[141] He nevertheless joined F Company, 2nd Battalion, which drilled on Thursday evenings in Fr. Mathew Park, Clontarf.[142] Other members of the company included future Volunteer leaders such as Oscar Traynor, Frank Henderson, Charles Saurin, Harry Colley, and Gearóid O'Sullivan.[143] There was even a Protestant – Arthur Shields of the Abbey Theatre.[144] Traynor's enrolment followed the Howth gun-running of July 1914, which persuaded him to 'break with' football since 'I saw that there was something serious pending'.[145] This episode also militarised Kathleen Boland, who invited the Volunteers scurrying along the laneway behind Marino Crescent to throw their German weapons into the garden for safe-keeping.[146]

The outbreak of war in Europe created an unbridgeable gap between those nationalists who viewed England's difficulty as Ireland's opportunity, and those who hoped for Anglo-Irish reconciliation through shared sacrifice in a common battle against despotism and oppression. The great majority, including some of Harry's family circle and comrades in the GAA, initially took the second standpoint. Kate and Kathleen Boland, when writing to Harry in prison after the Rebellion, referred to at least three connections who had taken the colours: a friend's brother who had been 'killed at the Front'; a doctor who was 'out at the front' yet seemed 'a very nice sinsible [sic.] young fellow'; and a certain Michael who was 'still at the front, made permanent Lieutenant'.[147] Perhaps from the last, Harry received a graphic pencilled account of life in the trenches, evoking the 'loud hissing which is the sound of the gas leaving the cylinders', the sentry banging his gong 'like blazes when he sees gas coming over', the men 'making tea and frying bacon for breakfast' and cooking their dinner on braziers 'well supplied with coke and kindling wood'. After twelve exhilarating days 'in the line', Michael and his men had been sent 'into reserve in a ruined town behind the lines', where they sheltered all day long in cellars to avoid the shelling:

> It was a rat-like existence. All this time we had neither a wash [n]or a shave. The cellars are full of rats and mice and occasionally a bit of the house used fall on them when the house was struck by a shell. ... There is a fine piano in one and so far it is untouched. The only inhabitant of the place is a cat who starts the most mournful wailing every night. In one of the cellars there is a human corpse with a pick stuck into his back and right into the ground. In another there is a man and a woman who were probably killed by the gas as this town is only 300 yards from the front line.[148]

Accounts like this ensured that the Great War was more than a source of abstract horror to those who deplored it. The elements of drama, excitement, and camaraderie by the campfire may also have whetted Harry's appetite for battle in another cause.

When the Volunteers split over John Redmond's appeal to them to fight the Axis powers 'wherever the firing line extends', F Company voted in favour of Redmond by a majority of 80 to 50. Harry belonged to that minority, along with fellow-hurlers and brethren such as Jack Shouldice and Maurice Collins. The dissidents managed to retain possession of Fr. Mathew Park for drilling, but membership sank to a dozen before recovering to 25 or 30. Henderson and Traynor eventually became Captain and 1st Lieutenant of this rump, but Harry Boland held no office in the company.[149] The company roll book for early 1916 suggests that he was an infrequent attender at the weekly meetings in Foresters' Hall, attending on only two out of nine recorded occasions, though keeping up to date with his weekly subscription of threepence. He presented himself on 24 February and 16 March, but missed the last four musters before Easter Week. Harry was not among the company élite who subscribed for a rifle or revolver, though he doubtless played a man's part in consuming the bread, cake, butter, tea, sugar, jam, and fruit which fortified the Volunteers on drill nights. As excitement intensified, company attendance recovered to a peak of 46; and 44 members of F Company were among the 1,600 Volunteers who took over College Green, without interference or disturbance, for a massed review on St. Patrick's Day.[150] Eoin McNeill and his Commandants, including Patrick Pearse and Eamon de Valera, inspected his forces to the accompaniment of national airs from a pipers' band, stationed near King William's statue.[151] The gulf within nationalism was illustrated that evening at St. James's fountain, where the RIC band livened up a pro-War rally addressed by William Field, MP. Jim Boland's old Parnellite associate, while admitting 'past misgovernment', declared 'that this was a fight for Fatherland and Freedom, Christianity and Civilisation', in which 'the democracies of Great Britain and Ireland were united in the resolve to resist the foreign invader'.[152] Harry was evidently present at neither of these meetings. Along with 'a big Bank Holiday crowd', he had spent St. Patrick's Day at the Baldoyle Races, as his hurling friend 'Mossie' Collins reminded him a year later: 'I and Celia and Con [O'Donovan] went to the Baldoyle Races last Sat. Do you remember last Patrick's Day? Didn't we, in company with Mick Dwyer, lower a few half pints?'[153] Less than six weeks before Easter Monday, few members of either the Volunteers or the IRB knew whether or when the leap would be attempted from cheekiness to rebellion.

Harry's first public intrusion into politics beyond the GAA had occurred on 5 June 1915, when he was co-signatory of a circular calling for a 'representative conference' against Conscription to be held at Harry's childhood haunt in York Street, the Dublin Workmen's Club and Total Abstinence Association. The four sponsors, all 'acting in their individual capacity' yet giving affiliations, were William O'Brien of the Trades Council, Mícheál Ó Foghludha of the Gaelic League, Alderman Tom Kelly of the Corporation, and 'H. Boland' of the GAA. The circular asserted that 'the opinion of the Irish people is strongly opposed to Conscription, but such opposition to be effective must be organised without further delay'.[154] William O'Brien recalled that the resultant anti-Conscription committee 'met for some months in 41 York Street, with Seán P. Campbell as Secretary'.[155] Although the protest lost its impulse when Ireland was exempted from the first Military Service Act of January 1916, it provided Harry with valuable contacts and political experience outside the involuted circles of conspiracy and Gaelic athletics.

On 8 September 1915, Harry served as best man when Gerald, returned as an engine fitter, married Annie Keating, a 27-year-old farmer's daughter, at St. Kevin's Catholic Church in Harrington Street. This event left Harry, still living in Marino Crescent, as the main breadwinner for the family. At twenty-eight, he could yet play the gay bachelor with gusto, if with reduced resources. He had a vast circle of friends, a devotedly dependent family, some public repute through the GAA, and at least a casual involvement in the anti-War movement. Yet he had done nothing to suggest unusual abilities, except perhaps as an organiser of small societies on the fringes of nationalist politics. In this respect, he closely resembled the father and uncle that he had scarcely known, and whose feats and beliefs he therefore revered with the unquestioning eye of a child. His pursuit of nationality, like theirs, relied on conspiracy, manipulation, and sociability within a trusted élite, whose views, as in the 1890s, were at odds with those of most Irishmen. He too had plotted Ireland's liberation in the 'backwoods' and 'the dark rooms of secret societies'.[156] He too was a favourite figure in the bars, clubs, and hotels of the inner city, where the illuminati could reassure each other over a bottle of stout that they shared the key to Ireland's future. He too despised the old men who dominated the Home Rule movement, while revering Fenian veterans as the custodians of an arcane wisdom and an uncompromised cause. There was nothing in Harry's record, outlook, or upbringing to suggest that he might become one of the foremost spokesmen for a great popular movement. His career after 1916, like the history of Ireland itself, could scarcely have been anticipated in his wildest dreams.

III

Rebellion

UNLIKE most Volunteers, Harry Boland had been forewarned of the insurrection which belatedly erupted on Easter Monday, 24 April 1916. In his elder brother's words, 'as we were both I.R.B. men we knew what was on foot'. Gerald had chosen his wedding day in September 1915 to inform Annie that, having been responsible for introducing Harry, Ned, and many others into the Organisation, he 'could not possibly shirk the fight if it came'. Gerald (1st Lieutenant of B Company) became aware of the general mobilisation scheduled for Easter Sunday at least two days earlier than Oscar Traynor, his counterpart in Harry's F Company. Traynor, a bluff compositor who had lost patience with the cloak-and-dagger antics of his former brethren, remained in the dark until Thomas MacDonagh addressed officers of the 2nd Battalion on Holy Saturday. Gerald, though increasingly disillusioned with the Brotherhood, remained enough of an insider to assist Joseph Mary Plunkett in distributing arms around the city on Thursday, 20 April. On the morning of Easter Sunday, the substantial arsenal stored at Marino Crescent was removed to Fr. Mathew Park in Philipsburgh Avenue, Clontarf, 'to be handed out to the assembled Volunteers' of the 2nd Battalion.[1]

Despite this flurry of activity, Harry did not allow the incipient Rebellion (or 'Rising') to interfere with his work for the GAA, whose annual congress had likewise been scheduled as usual for Easter Sunday. This coincidence suggests that the organisers, though often also brethren and Volunteers, were not privy to the machinations of the shadowy 'military committee' which had plotted the Rebellion without reference to its ostensible superiors in either body. Nevertheless, rumours of an outbreak probably foreshortened the congress, which re-elected all officers unopposed, approved all reports, and shelved most controversial motions (such as an attempt to ban trotting at Croke Park). Harry was one of several speakers who bemoaned the death of Frank Brazil Dineen, the former sprinter, President of the GAA, and IRB Centre for East Limerick, who had expired on Good Friday while composing his weekly column for *Sport*. By 2.30 that afternoon, after some 'private business' which may have touched on public events, the small band of fifty-five delegates had dispersed.[2] Harry's exertions on behalf of the Dublin County Board were interrupted by Gerald's arrival with news that Professor Eoin MacNeill had 'countermanded' the mobilisation order, following the interception of the *Aud* with its indispensable cargo of German arms. As Gerald recalled: 'I had arranged to tell him

[Harry] what was happening. When we were told to go home, but to keep in readiness for a sudden mobilisation, I went to the City Hall and told Harry that it was all off.' Assuming that 'there would be no more about it', Gerald returned to the Crooksling Sanatorium near Brittas, south-west of Dublin, where he had recently become land steward.[3] As on St. Patrick's Day, when the Volunteers had flaunted their strength in College Green without major disturbance, it seemed that the oft-rumoured Rebellion had come to nothing.

Harry, under the influence of fellow Gaels in the IRB who had followed Pearse in repudiating MacNeill's authority as Chief of Staff, reportedly thought otherwise. His sister Kathleen recollected the following conversation after Harry's return from the GAA convention on Sunday afternoon:

> [He] said to my mother, 'I have to go out. The other boys are going.' She asked, 'Who are they?' He replied, 'Jack Shouldice, Frank Shouldice and many others.' She replied, 'Go, in the name of God! Your father would haunt you if you did not do the right thing.'

Harry wondered how his mother would manage, but was reminded tartly that she had survived when in worse circumstances after his father's death. Despite this strong parental injunction, Harry evidently did not venture forth until Monday afternoon, long after MacDonagh's semi-successful attempt to remobilise the Dublin Brigade and Pearse's proclamation of the Irish Republic outside the GPO.[4] An enigmatic passage in his sister's memoir hints that Harry, like many future combatants on both sides, spent Easter Monday at the Fairyhouse horse-races in Meath. Since Fairyhouse is 14 miles out of Dublin, and the last race was scheduled for 4.40 p.m., punters would scarcely have reached the city before dusk.[5]

Harry's delayed mobilisation may also be attributable to the confusion aroused by contradictory instructions from rival Volunteer factions. As Traynor recalled, F Company was summoned to Fr. Mathew Park early on Monday morning, and instructed by Captain Thomas Weafer (E Company) to escort a load of explosives and ammunition across the Liffey, to Jacob's biscuit factory in Peter Street. While in the park pavilion, vainly awaiting the lorry's arrival, the officers were addressed by a 'rather excited' young lady:

> [She] told them that she had been instructed by The O'Rahilly[6] to ask the [commanding] officer to demobilise all Volunteers and send them to their homes, as a small body of men had disobeyed orders and had taken possession of some buildings in the city. This led to an almost heated discussion as to, firstly, the veracity of the order, and secondly, our right to demobilise if any unit of the Volunteers were in action. It was eventually agreed that a short demobilisation would take place while enquiries were being made, and all the Volunteers were instructed to stand-to in their homes.

According to Frank Henderson, Captain of F Company, this suspension lasted for only about half an hour, while Weafer secured sanction for action from James Connolly in the GPO. After a friendly curate had administered confession and blessed those still at the park, the 'rearguard' of twenty-five men began its march down Philipsburgh Avenue to Fairview Strand and Ballybough.[7]

Chaos still prevailed, as members of the 2nd Battalion were arbitrarily dispersed around the city by various officers or drawn into roving bands of rebels by chance. Traynor eventually found Henderson with a section of the 2nd Battalion (including parts of B, E, and F Companies) marching south along Ballybough Road with the lorry-load of arms, having already 'been in action'. A second party had previously been despatched to St. Stephen's Green, as directed in the original orders for mobilisation on Easter Sunday.[8] Along with other units from the 2nd Battalion, they were sent on to Jacob's factory and joined there by Gerald Boland, who had scoured the city in search of B Company after hearing of the Rebellion in Crooksling.[9] Harry was not with either party, having attached himself to a unit headed by Vincent Poole of the Irish Citizen Army (whose expertise in guerrilla tactics had been acquired at the receiving end while serving the Empire in South Africa). As Traynor recalled: 'It appears that Boland, in his anxiety to get into action, reported to the first unit he met, which happened to be Poole's, at the corner of Poplar Road [Row] in Fairview.'[10] Harry was accompanied by his younger brother Ned, who had recently worked his way home from Rio de Janeiro as a British merchant seaman.[11] Poole's party had occupied the Wicklow Chemical Manure Factory, and made sporadic sallies against soldiers setting up an armoured train on the Great Northern Railway, which passed over the 'sloblands' to the east of Fairview. Harry and three companions were supplied with gelignite by Poole, who told them 'to dig a little hole in the ground under the tracks, to place the gelignite in it as he demonstrated for us, cover it again with soil, light the fuse and clear out'. They carried out these instructions with alacrity, yet 'the job was a failure'.[12]

Harry Boland, Harry Colley, and other Volunteers decided to abandon the irascible Poole and his Citizen Army comrades when they heard that Frank Henderson had seized Gilbey's wine depot in Fairview Strand (turfing out the mother and daughter who resided there). Henderson was delighted at the arrival of the two Harrys, who 'were a great help to our men, both by force of example and by their cheerfulness'. Henderson had doubled back from the main party bound for the city, along Ballybough Road, in the hope of preventing 'enemy' reinforcements from reaching central Dublin by road and rail. Like Poole's unit, Henderson's men made ineffectual attempts to disrupt the railway with gelignite.[13] In solidarity with her brothers, Kathleen visited Gilbey's to offer her services, delivering several consignments of ammunition as well as provisions.[14] Another account indicates that Harry did not reach Gilbey's until Tuesday morning, thereupon assuming command (presumably in

Henderson's absence). Under his direction, Kathleen's rations were augmented by 'commandeered' bread, along with a live sheep 'which was killed, cooked, and devoured by Gilbey's starving garrison'. His party also captured a musketry instructor from the Dollymount training camp on Bull Island, Sergeant Henry, who remained in Harry's custody throughout the day. The garrison's morale was fortified by a message from his redoubtable mother: 'Dear Harry, God bless you. You are out to win.'[15]

On Tuesday evening, Harry's section of F Company was summoned by James Connolly to the beleaguered GPO. Having cheekily travelled across the battle-field by cab, Harry, with his uniformed captive, faced an unexpected obstacle on arrival. Traynor and Henderson had been instructed to propel the Volunteers and their prisoners across Sackville (now O'Connell) Street. The spectacle of British army uniforms proved irresistible to some of their comrades:

> As this single file of Volunteers and British soldiers were doubling across the road, fire was opened on them from the Imperial Hotel which was occupied by our own men. In the course of this firing James Connolly rushed out into the street with his hands over his head, shouting towards the Imperial Hotel.[16]

Though 'a couple of our men had been wounded' during this brief attack, Harry escaped the indignity of either shooting or being shot by his colleagues. Reassured by Connolly that 'it's all a mistake', F Company gratefully surren-dered custody of Sergeant Henry and his fellow-prisoners to the O'Rahilly, before submitting to an address from Patrick Pearse. The new arrivals were divided into three groups of about twenty men, commanded by Frank Henderson, his brother Leo (Captain of B Company), and Oscar Traynor. These units were despatched respectively to Henry Street, the Imperial Hotel, and the block bounded by Middle Abbey Street, Lower Sackville Street, and Prince's Street. This included the Metropole Hotel, Eason's stationers, and Manfield's recently opened boot warehouse. While Ned reinforced the trigger-happy garrison at the Imperial, Harry accompanied Traynor to the Metropole.[17]

Harry's arrival in the vestibule was greeted by a storm of abuse from Captain Poole, who accused him of deserting his command in Fairview and even 'raised the butt of his rifle in the course of the argument'. Traynor pointed out that Harry, being present, could not be deemed a deserter, declared that he (Traynor) was Poole's superior officer in the post if not in rank, and sent Poole upstairs to check for undiscovered guests cowering in their bedrooms. Poole soon produced another victim, whom he had instantly recognised as 'a British officer and a spy' when this seeming civilian answered Poole's order to quick-march by stepping out with his left foot. On further enquiry, the 'spy' was released after producing a watch presented to him by grateful pupils at Portora Royal School in Enniskillen. Traynor then embarked on the rather bizarre task, assigned by Connolly, of excavating a series of zigzag holes 'through each of the houses until I got to the corner of Abbey Street', each just large enough to allow a single man to crawl, if necessary, towards the dubious sanctuary of Sackville Street. By Wednesday night, the tunnel to Manfield's was complete, and a small detachment comprising Harry, Vincent Poole, and Tom Leahy (E Company) did their best to prevent the Crown forces from advancing across Lower Abbey Street into Sackville Place. Traynor recollected that their rifles became overheated through continuous use, allowing Poole to deploy his sergeant's savvy by demonstrating that the glowing barrels could be cooled with oil drained from sardine-tins.[18] A participant remembered 'heavy rifle fire in Abbey St. direction. Kept rifles loaded for H. Boland at window. No sleep. House burning fiercely.'[19] Under such conditions, it seems extraordinary that an intrepid friend visiting Marino Crescent was able to report 'that he had left Harry in Manfield's in Abbey Street and that he was in great form'.[20] Thursday, 27 April, was Harry's twenty-ninth birthday.

By early Friday morning, the fires raging around Sackville Street had engulfed the top floor of the Metropole, and Traynor (then in Manfield's) evacuated the block in response to an order conveyed by Seán Russell, his second-in-command. Once again, the chain of authority had failed: 'Pearse appeared very much surprised by our appearance and asked why we had retired' without orders from GHQ. Traynor returned crestfallen with his men to the inferno; but by late evening, as roofs caved in and the heat became unbearable, Traynor was again in Manfield's planning his exit:

Harry agreed that another hour would be about as long as we could occupy our present position. At this time the heat was terrific and there was also the danger of the building collapsing. Harry was all for dropping into the street and fighting our way to a new position. Vincent Poole, who was an employee of the Sewers Department of the Dublin Corporation, suggested getting down a convenient manhole and making our way through the sewers to the Four Courts. The pros and cons of this suggestion were being excitedly discussed when I was informed I was wanted at the Prince's Street door. . . . I was to evacuate the position which we were holding and retire to the G.P.O. as quickly as possible.[21]

With Traynor, Harry formed the tail of the bedraggled party which dashed across Prince's Street to the GPO, only to find the building largely empty. In their haste to be gone, the leaders had forgotten the Metropole contingent until 'at the last moment' Seán McDermott remembered to order their recall, using Frank Henderson as his emissary. Pearse and the 'rearguard' were already at the corner of Henry Street and Henry Place when Harry, closely followed by Diarmuid Lynch, narrowly avoided self-immolation by dashing out of the abandoned building at 8.40 p.m. 'Terrific explosions' had caused at least three casualties among the loiterers, and Harry spent his last moments in the GPO helping Lynch to dismantle the remaining 'bombs and explosives'.[22] They found 'near chaos' in Henry Place, until Tom Clarke reasserted authority with his revolver and ordered a group including Traynor, Poole, and Harry to break into a shop in nearby Moore Street. Their task was to hack out a tunnel from house to house until every intervening wall had been smashed between Henry Place and Parnell (once Great Britain) Street. Tom Leahy, the boilermaker who assisted Harry in this enterprise, remembered 'the untiring enthusiasm' and 'never stop attitude' of the whole party, and 'the cheerfulness of Harry until his hands were bleeding from blisters from using the heavy hammer and tools'.[23] Harry's time off from hammering was spent behind a diversionary barricade at the corner of Moore Street and Henry Place, where he 'showed amazing courage. He fired away by himself for a long time.'[24]

By Saturday morning, according to Traynor, the tunnellers had reached their goal:[25]

I was discussing our situation with Harry Boland when Dermod [Diarmuid] Lynch appeared on the scene and called for volunteers for a bayonet charge. Harry and I volunteered with a number of other men. Our instructions were to charge and take the barricade at the end of the street and, having done so, force our way on towards Williams & Woods,[26] keeping the route open as we went along. I can remember saying to Harry Boland 'Well, this looks like the end for us.' His reply was typical of Harry, for he said 'The only thing that is wrong about this order is that it should have been given long ago.'

In preparation for the charge, each man received a valedictory portion of pear. Then two further orders were received: first, to abandon the bayonet charge and rest; next, as they awakened, to surrender. When the rebels lined up for their last march down Sackville Street, Traynor looked upon his work with grotesque satisfaction: 'I was very proud as I looked at the spot where the Metropole and the other buildings had been, because all that was left of that fine six storied building was a lone gable end at the corner of Prince's Street.'[27] Traynor's wreckers had done their bit. By 10.30 p.m., General Lowe and his staff had accepted the surrender of 450 rebels at the Parnell monument. Staff Captain Harry de Courcy Wheeler of Robertstown House, County Kildare, walked down the ranks with his field notebook, jotting down eighty-four names, including Michael Collins of 16, Rathdown Road, and Harry Boland of 15, Marino Crescent.[28]

Harry had had a 'good Rising'. He had survived unscathed, apart from blisters, captured a hostage, and evidently killed nobody. Admittedly, he had suffered a succession of indignities arising from disorganisation and inept leadership.

Having missed the start and joined the wrong unit, he had been fired on by his comrades, accused of desertion, implicitly rebuked for obeying an order to retreat, primed for a suicidal mission only to be ordered to surrender, and assigned the inglorious tasks of smashing, tunnelling, and (had Poole prevailed) sewering. Yet his energy, pugnacity, optimism, and good cheer had heartened his comrades in Gilbey's, Manfield's, and Moore Street. Never an officer and spurning uniform, tailor though he was, Harry had shown himself to be a courageous if reckless fighter.[29] He had justified his membership of the team, without emerging unmistakably as a leader. As in the GAA, his spirited performance in the field provided useful yet scarcely sufficient preparation for a subsequent political career.

By contrast, his elder brother had had a rather frustrating experience in Jacob's factory. The chosen building had so little strategic importance that it was virtually ignored by the Crown forces and suffered only superficial damage during Easter Week. Gerald therefore had little to do, except when sent on a raiding party to Dublin Castle by his father's friend 'Major' John MacBride, whose military reputation rested on his controversial command sixteen years earlier of one of the 'Irish Brigades' supporting the Boers. Gerald and a companion reportedly silenced a machine gunners' nest in the Bermingham Tower. Gerald failed to enter fully into the Easter spirit, sympathising with the horde of looters who swarmed around the biscuit factory, and urging MacBride to disperse the garrison before it was surrounded. Reckless to the last, MacBride scoffed at his advice, though some Volunteers melted away before the 'Major' and his titular Commandant, Thomas MacDonagh, eventually surrendered as ordered by Pearse.[30]

Gerald, like Oscar Traynor, Frank Henderson, and Michael Collins, was among the thousands interned in Britain without trial. A party of 308 internees, including Gerald Boland, a fitter of 9, Vincent Street, South Circular Road, was despatched on 2 May from Richmond Barracks to Knutsford Detention Barracks in Cheshire.[31] There he met Traynor, who told him 'of the heroic conduct of my two brothers Harry and Ned'.[32] As a protective eldest brother, jealous of his precedence in the family, Gerald seemed rather uneasy when writing for the first time to his mother about Harry's sudden seniority:

> I heard about poor Harry. I wish to God it was not he as I think you will admit I could stand more than he, though I might not be quite as brave in action. Still he will bear himself like a man I well know, no matter what comes his way.[33]

On 11 June, he called to mind his 'dear father, oh wouldn't he like to have been in that scrap. Well he saw it all in spirit I'm sure, and was proud of his boys, if the dead are capable of pride.' He recalled his separation from Harry during the Rebellion with a twinge of guilt: 'I tried to get across town to find where Harry was, but had to go back again.'[34] Harry seemed omnipresent, for 'all his friends here are asking for him, several were with him up to the last of the fight, and often talk about him'.[35] This continued after Gerald's removal to the Frongoch Prisoners-of-War Camp near Bala in North Wales, where inmate no. 1,051 and his neighbours often chatted about Harry: 'Every time I get a letter, scores of fellows ask, any news of Harry, there should be a letter now?'[36]

Harry's revolutionary promotion had been assisted by an incident which led to his being court-martialled rather than merely interned. Unlike most subordinate Volunteers, Harry was identified as a serious offender – by Sergeant Henry, his prisoner from Bull Island. The Sergeant's humiliation had continued after his release from the GPO, when he and a soldier had 'sought refuge in the [Coliseum] theatre, and there they stayed unaware of the fact that the fighting about the place had ceased'. After five days without food, they were finally liberated from the smoking ruins by Francis Ridgeway, managing director of Bewley's Oriental Cafés.[37] This galling experience gave a sharp edge to Henry's denunciation of his tormentor. Kathleen recalled Harry's characteristic anecdote:

> He picked out Harry, saying, 'He who laughs best, laughs last.' Harry replied, 'Yes, chum, I am laughing! I am not whinging as you were when I took you prisoner.'[38]

Harry's self-possession was to serve him well during his confinement. Even before his trial, he had been chosen by his cell-mates in L 5, Richmond Barracks, as their spokesman in dealing with the military: 'We selected Harry Boland and no better selection could have been made. Harry was gay and happy and full of life and vitality. He was good-humoured and kindly and at the same time was a rock of sense and shrewdness.'[39] As Gerald later told his brother: 'I met a lot of fellows who were in Richmond with you and they all said you kept them alive.'[40]

On Tuesday, 9 May, Henry James Boland, a tailor's cutter aged twenty-nine years, was sentenced by a Field General Court Martial to ten years' penal servitude for 'taking part in armed rebellion and waging war against His Majesty the King'. By grace of General Sir John Maxwell, General Officer Commanding-in-Chief the Forces in Ireland, his sentence was remitted by five years. Unlike fifteen of his colleagues, he thus escaped execution. Several of his associates in the GAA such as Jack Shouldice, Con O'Donovan, and Thomas Ashe had received commuted sentences of death, while Austin Stack was among the 'lifers'.[41] The relative lenience of Harry's sentence suggests that he had not been identified as a ringleader, an impression confirmed by the only available record of his trial:[42]

Evidence that he held up soldiers at Dollymount and handed them over to rebels. In defence stated he was unaware of Rebellion. Mobilized and had to obey orders – was more interested in G.A.A. Denies he attempted to cause disaffection.[43]

After sentence, the convicted prisoners spent a week in Mountjoy Prison, where Harry was visited by his mother. Ever resourceful, she reportedly exclaimed: 'Wasn't it an extraordinary thing to arrest you, and you only coming from the races!' Harry: 'Ah, no, mother. I was not coming from the races. I went out to strike a blow against the bloody British Empire.'[44]

The Empire struck back by consigning Harry and most of his fellow felons to the grim confines of Dartmoor Prison in Devonshire, Harry sharing a chain with Eamon de Valera as the party left Mountjoy. Along with Shouldice and O'Donovan, they were among the first batch of a dozen convicts to reach Dartmoor.[45] The rather bemused Governor at Dartmoor (Major E. R. Reade) sported 'a huge waxed moustache' and strutted about with a sword-bearing chief warder (Tom Stone). Reade did his best to treat the rebels as ordinary convicts. This entailed withholding privileges for a lengthy probationary period, allowing only one outward letter and one visit every four months, and enforcing silence when the prisoners mingled for exercise, work, or meals. The first month was the worst, as the new arrivals had no occupation apart from making naval coal sacks, being confined to their cells except for two brief spells of daily exercise.[46] Kathleen maintained that Harry 'spent most of his time in the punishment cells, as he was so lighthearted he could not obey the rigid rules of silence, etc.' This disposition was confirmed by Harry after his departure from Dartmoor, when he recollected that 'the silence rule was awful, especially to a Chatterbox like me'.[47] Robert Brennan remembered Harry's 'cheerful voice' outside his cell intoning 'The Green Isle's Loved Emblem', and making so eloquent a case for defying the rule of silence that he was finally exempted from his task of polishing the banister.[48] Harry was unusually adept at ingratiating warders, so that even the 'officious' Stone became strangely 'enamoured' and even 'highly honoured' when the Irish charmer approached him. Harry attended happily to his sewing machine as he made bags and doubtless banter with Brennan and the singer Gerald Crofts, under the indulgent eye of Warder Geraghty.[49]

The Irish convicts showed no initial inclination to challenge authority by systematic defiance or subversion. Having anticipated death, they accepted their incarceration as an appropriate sacrifice, and strove to be respected as men of honour. After visiting Dartmoor on 29 May, Eardley-Wilmot of the Prison Commission sent a remarkably positive report on the thirty-five Irish prisoners:

> I questioned each man in his cell, and encouraged him to talk. I was struck by their demeanour which was always respectful and courteous. Their

attitude was almost dignified. ... They were drawn from all classes – shop assistants, small tradesmen, labourers, two or three farmers from Galway, students, civil servants, journalists, clerks – and amongst them was a doctor, a Professor of Mathematics, and a writer of fiction – no corner boys nor criminals.

Wilmot was particularly taken by the co-operative, even obsequious demeanour of 'the Mathematician, de Valera, son of a Spanish father':

A few days after my visit when the prisoners were being unlocked for exercise a new arrival was being let into the Hall – Professor M[a]cNeill, one of the Sinn Féin leaders. De Valera, seeing him, gave the words of command 'Volunteers, attention, eyes right!' The prisoners paid no attention, and de Valera was put back into his cell. When before the Governor under report he explained that he had had a disagreement with this leader and wishing to make the *amende* he had acted as he did on the spur of the moment. He was very sorry and prepared to undergo any punishment the Governor thought proper. I mention this incident to show the attitude of these prisoners to their own Authorities on the one hand and to Prison Authority on the other.

By late June, another thirty Irish convicts had arrived, including a dozen short-term prisoners 'of the corner-boy type'. But the Governor reported that 'they all seem perfectly contented and in fact grateful for their treatment'.[50] After all, they had been granted the compliment of a court martial and rigorous punishment, with all the cachet that this entailed in nationalist Ireland.

Though not yet systematically disruptive, the Irish prisoners spared none of their persuasive powers to secure concessions which might render their captivity productive. De Valera, Robert Brennan, and Thomas Ashe each petitioned for a fountain pen, ink, and paper, in order to pursue abstruse mathematical problems, write a novel, or create (as Ashe proposed) 'a record of my best ideas, received through reading, or developed through self-thought'. All such requests were eventually refused on the principle that 'ordinary rules' should apply to the Irish, not being deemed prisoners of war.[51] Even so, de Valera and others were allowed to accept books for study; and Harry asked his mother to send 'Fr. O'Growney's five books and the Christian Brothers' Aids to Composition, as I want to look up my Irish'. She duly requested the Governor to allow her the 'favour' of sending her son 'Father Growney's simple lesson in Irish, with grammars and simple Mathematics'.[52] But the 'mathematic book' never reached Dartmoor, so confirming Gerald's contempt for 'the hypocrites' who had denied Harry his books despite parliamentary promises of civilised treatment.[53] The Irish prisoners at Dartmoor were unusually diligent in seeking 'extra diet' on various grounds, though their applications were mostly unsuccessful. Nearly half of the sixty-five Irish convicts requested more food between mid August and mid October, compared with only 8 per cent of 'ordinary' prisoners.[54] For several months, they worked within rather than against the regulatory system, hoping to use their comparative advantages in education, respectability, and demeanour to secure comforts denied to coarser inmates.

The restriction of correspondence from Dartmoor prevented Harry from sending his first letter home until 15 September, though the Governor had previously despatched several pro forma messages indicating that convict 'q 90' was in his 'usual' health.[55] That first letter reassured his mother that Harry had 'never felt better, also I am reconciled to my lot although it is not very pleasant to be confined to prison'. He promised that 'I can come through this ordeal in good style and rest assured that I will return as gay as ever'. He sent businesslike messages to colleagues at Todd's and in the GAA, along with chirpy greetings to friends. Harry's extraordinary capacity to chirp and cheer, and his awareness of that gift, are evident in a message to his sister:

> I trust you are all singing and dancing. I would be sorry to think that you were in the dumps because your brothers are away. Now Kathleen, keep smiling and enjoy yourself and tell all my friends that I am A 1. If you are very good I will bring you back a parrot or a monkey so keep your pecker up.[56]

The response from Marino Crescent eventually reached Harry after six weeks, on 25 October. Already, Harry and his comrades had joined the company of republican martyrs:

> We were so glad to hear our darling was in good health and spirits under such very trying circumstances and that all your fellow prisoners are well, carrying the Cross cheerfully like the brave men they are. It appears extraordinary that you should be in jail, you, Harry, that never injured anybody through the whole course of your life, but all the good you have done for your home and everyone who was in trouble. 'God's will be done.' So you are suffering your purgatory here for a little while. 'No Cross no Church.' So, dear son, continue to lift your heart to God and you will come through manfully.[57]

Shortly after his trial, Harry's virtue had been rewarded by the delivery to Mrs Boland of 'a handsome present' by 'Mr. [Bill] Duggan', the rumbustious colleague at Todd's who later became his business partner. The family letter, compressed as required onto a single foolscap sheet, bore warm greetings from friends, relatives, and internees. As Kathleen observed, 'hundreds of the boys ask about you in the camp' [Frongoch]. There were also snippets of GAA news, often in the stilted style of sporting journalism: 'I can assure you that you are greatly missed in G.A.A. circles in Dublin, and I hope you will soon be back again, to put a bit of extra steam in. I hope you are practising "Kevin and Kathleen" for the big night.'[58]

Among the contributors was Harry's youngest brother Ned, who had avoided incarceration despite his pugnacity as a sniper in the Imperial Hotel. When that garrison was abandoned, he had fought for several hours in Cathedral Street before accepting the invitation of a considerate priest to deposit his gun in the vaults of the pro-Cathedral. He evaded arrest by the same gambit which his mother vainly deployed on behalf of Harry:

> When the British officers came and cross-examined them, Edmund, who had a week's beard on him and was black from the grime and smoke of the burning Imperial Hotel, and smelled of gunpowder, said he had been at Fairyhouse races and had not been able to get home.[59]

Ned was the first to visit Harry at Dartmoor. As he recalled in the family letter:

> I won't try to tell you how tough it was for me to leave you behind on that day I was with you; those 40 minutes went by like seconds, we had so much to say to each other. We had a few good laughs all the same, hadn't we, Har, and we'll shortly have a few more, please God, with nobody to stop us either. You looked in great form too and seemed to have grown stronger. I got a great look at you crossing the square.

Ned promised to send a batch of photographs of Harry's family, hurling team, and pet dog, assuring his brother that 'Paddy's growing a great terrier and is wishing for you back again.'[60]

Harry's delayed response indicates his excitement at the reunion after four months of isolation, and also his playful relationship with a brother eight years his junior:

> Your visit acted as a rare tonic to me. You brought such good news from home that I felt really happy. When the Governor told me you were coming I was all agog, and when I heard your 'Basso Profundo' outside the visitors' box, it was like a breath from the hills. I did not find my voice for some time, and in the joy of your presence I quite forgot a number of queries I had to ask you. Here they are. No 1. Were John Connolly and John Doyle, Geraldines, killed? No 2. Who did ye beat in the final? No 3. Who are the new Co. Dublin officers? No 4. What teams won All Ireland Finals?

The arrival of the photographs was equally momentous:

The photos created a sensation in Dartmoor. I have had several offers for Kathleen's hand on the strength of her photo. I could not see my way to close the bargain as they were all long-sentence men. As for Ena [Shouldice], tell her I had to hide her photo as I was afraid it would be stolen, so many admirers had she, both Warders and Convicts. You have no idea how they brighten up a cell. I have built a shrine and worship and commune with ye all, so if your ears are red especially on Sundays from 2 o.c., you will know that your Convict brother is talking to you and all at home as you sit down to dinner, and I get great consolation in seeing your photos on my table.[61]

Harry's letters, far from evoking a brutal and inhumane régime at Dartmoor, testify to his success in domesticating a harsh environment and getting on easily with his captors.

On 16 October, peaceful coexistence was abruptly interrupted by the impetuosity of Eamon de Valera, who had been noticed throwing an 8-ounce loaf of bread into the cell of John McArdle. McArdle 'caught the loaf as he would a cricket ball and put it on the shelf', but surrendered it on demand to a warder. Instead of apologising for his offence, as in the case of MacNeill's reception, de Valera 'added that he had other loaves in his cell that he had intended distributing in the same manner that night', and boasted that this was 'not the first loaf he had supplied to another prisoner'. In characteristically parental mode, he preferred to stint himself in order to sustain his flock, who had not received 'sufficient diet after their arrest and the authorities seemed to forget they had been fighting for a week'. De Valera compounded his defiance by refusing to pick oakum while temporarily in solitary confinement, and Major Reade detected 'hints of a sympathetic strike (labour) on de Valera's behalf'. Reade concluded that he was 'a real firebrand and fanatic. ... He is decidedly a "Personality" and the others seem to look up to him as their "leader".' Fearing that any hunger-strike by de Valera would have a 'bad effect', he recommended his removal to Maidstone in Kent, a 'star-class' prison impervious to Irish idealism. On 27 October, de Valera was removed in chains, along with his 'two Lieutenants', Dr. Richard Hayes and Desmond FitzGerald ('a poet-visionary, and decidedly bitter').[62] Harry Boland was not yet conspicuous enough to attract unfavourable notice as a potential ringleader of resistance.

Such incidents fuelled the dual agitation for an amnesty or, failing that, 'political status' for the Irish prisoners. This campaign contributed to the release of Gerald and the remaining internees on Christmas Eve, and the slightly earlier decision to concentrate the Irish convicts in a single prison with a uniquely relaxed system of discipline. On 13 November, it was agreed to bring together and segregate all those undergoing penal servitude (in Dartmoor, Portland, Wakefield, and now Maidstone), and to apply 'a considerable relaxation of the Progressive Stage System in the matter of letters and visits'. Well-conducted Irish convicts would now be allowed monthly letters and visits; 'the privilege of association and conversation' could be conferred 'as an award for good conduct on certain days, for a limited time'; and notebooks might be permitted 'for the purpose of study or literary work'. The Irish were exempted from the usual prohibition of 'all composition relating to prison life and conditions and to political matters', though any notebook containing objectionable matter would be withheld upon the prisoner's discharge.[63] The Home Secretary's announcement encouraged the convicts and their supporters to believe that they were to be treated with the respect due to 'political prisoners', though no such category existed in law. As Kate Boland wrote early in the New Year:

> Everybody thought when you were moved from Dartmoor, that you were to be made political prisoners. I need hardly tell you, my dear Harry, how disappointed we are. Most likely when Parliament assembles early next month there will possibly be some enquiries concerning all our dear ones, in prison cells, and with God's help you will soon be eating one of Kathleen's well cooked dinners again.[64]

On 14 December, Harry celebrated his relative freedom with a lightly coded message to Ned:

> Here I am in Lewes Gaol alive and kicking. Arrived last night after a journey of 12 hours along the Channel and South Coast, a glorious run. It was good to be out in the world again. I left Dartmoor without regret and there was many a dry eye as the train moved off.[65]

In fact, Harry's journey to Sussex was spent in chains, rumours of which soon appeared in the Irish press and 'filled the People with indignation'.[66] This punishment resulted from the prisoners' collective refusal, instigated by James Lawless and Seán Etchingham, to promise not to escape on the way to Lewes. Had the Catholic chaplain received such an undertaking, the prisoners would have been allowed to travel without chains in civilian clothing.[67] By mid March, Harry was emboldened to give a less sanguine account of the journey:

> My eight months up at Dartmoor was an experience to be ever remembered. I was like the D——d Greyhound when I left for Lewes. The twelve hours journey along the English Channel was not very pleasant: I was chained up like a dog.

The prisoners had ventured 'a bar of "God Save Ireland" when we got to Lewes Rly. station, just to show we were still game'.[68]

According to John Devoy, Harry was punished for 'mutiny' on his arrival at the prison and taken to his cell, handcuffed to another convict. When the two warders 'indulged in some impudent talk', Harry 'instantly smashed one of them on the head with his handcuffs (risking the breaking of his own wrists) and gave the other a violent dig of his knee in the stomach, rendering both unconscious'. Once subdued, he was told by the Governor that 'we've tamed tougher men than you, and we'll certainly tame you'. This utterance aroused Harry's racial pride: 'You can tame all the blasted Englishmen you like, but, by C——, you'll never tame me.' When accused of 'lack of dignity' by the more fastidious de Valera, who had been spared the humiliation of chains on his own journey to Lewes, Harry allegedly replied: 'To hell with dignity when we're dealing with Englishmen.'[69]

Despite this inauspicious beginning, the genial Governor (Major R. A. Marriott) worked hard to avoid confrontation and unrest at Lewes. Marriott discussed geology with the historian MacNeill, and allowed de Valera to bring in a mathematical treatise by Poincaré.[70] Patrick Fahy recalled that 'in striking contrast to Dartmoor, there was an air of cheerfulness around', fostered by a 'sympathetic' Governor, Chaplain, and Chief Warder. The 123 Irish convicts chatted freely at exercise, elected de Valera as their Commandant, pursued their nationalist education as freely as the internees had done at Frongoch, and sewed mailbags or made doormats without initial protest.[71] As leader of the cleaning squad, Harry again achieved supremacy over the warders, supplanting Warder Gallop in command and brazenly dispensing extra loaves supplied by comrades on kitchen duty. He regularly purloined the Chaplain's newspaper, which he read thoroughly before passing it on to his fellows.[72] He contributed to a clandestine newspaper in Irish and English, edited by Patrick Fahy, of which only one issue was circulated.[73] In his rather handsome prison notebook, Harry inscribed a bizarre mixture of cutter's patterns, nationalist ballads, adages, exercises in Irish, and draft letters. Despite his inclusion of political matter, usually semi-concealed by empty sheets before and after an offensive passage, the notebook was not confiscated on his departure.[74] The Governor was an 'appeaser', preferring to bend the regulations rather than precipitate conflict.

This became clear on 6 March 1917, when Thomas Peppard and Richard Kelly (both labourers brought over from Portland) were reported for 'laughing and talking in the shop after caution'. Peppard was dismissed with a warning, while Kelly was confined to his cell for a day on the dreaded 'No. 2' diet. That afternoon, all Irish convicts refused to work, despite the Governor's advice that this was 'an unwise action for their own interests, and unfair to their friends in Ireland, who had succeeded in ameliorating their lot in prison'. Even the prospect of a discussion in parliament next day failed to placate the prisoners, several of whom accepted Marriott's invitation to speak. MacNeill declared that 'one man being punished meant all being punished'; John Quinn (a middle-aged linotype operator out of Dartmoor) enviously complained that 'it was always the Portland men and the younger men who were being punished'; Thomas Ashe 'had no fault to find with the officers, but it was the system he objected to'; and de Valera 'said if the man was brought back to the shops they would go back to work'. Marriott responded by claiming that he had only intended Kelly 'to have No. 2 diet for his dinner, and would release him to go back to work'. The Governor informed the Prison Commission that the Irish convicts had acted 'as one man', and that 'in this case there were apparently no ringleaders. The action was spontaneous.' Any attempt to punish insubordination would provoke 'mutiny' which could not be suppressed except by an armed guard (which, significantly, had not been supplied).[75]

Though 'strongly' disapproving of Marriott's 'surrendering his authority', the 'Directors' at the Prison Commission excused him from 'official blame' since Lewes was 'not being governed under ordinary rules'. They sought and secured the Home Secretary's approval for 'strong measures' to restore convict discipline, including 'immediate withdrawal of privileges' after insubordination, 'cellular labour' and enforced silence after any 'concerted action', and distribution of 'the whole body in small parties throughout all the prisons of England and Wales' in response to any hunger-strike.[76] Meanwhile, additional staff and one of His Majesty's Inspectors of Prisons, aptly named Farewell, were despatched to Lewes. Inspector Farewell found 'some reasonable grounds' for the claim that 'the talking rule has been intentionally relaxed' and that the situation had 'drifted'. He too tried to placate the convicts, recommending that the restraint of conversation be eased, and justifying the official policy in discussions with de Valera, MacNeill, and Eamon Duggan. His placatory approach persuaded them to postpone further protest until the Home Secretary had responded to further petitions.[77]

The mild concessions offered by Sir Herbert Samuel, on 19 April, did not restore harmony at Lewes. Harry was briefly deprived of privileges, such as letter-writing, when he and Dick King were discovered stealing bread from the kitchen table. When sentenced to three days' confinement in a punishment cell, he allegedly told Major Marriott that 'if any ten of your men can put me in a solitary cell, I'm willing to go', whereupon the Governor allowed him to confine himself in his own cell. When applauded by Brennan, he replied: 'Go away, don't interrupt my thoughts. I've started the contemplative life.' He embarked on a mini-hunger-strike, crying 'Get thee behind me, Satan' when the Chaplain offered him chocolate. By early May his punishment was at an end, and he promptly initiated a campaign of torment against the warder who had reported his offence, snatching loaves or kippers from one side of the tray while the warder delivered the permitted rations from the other side.[78] Harry made light of his ordeal when resuming communication with his mother:

You heard of my lapse from the path of probity, a sin against the seventh Commandment. Unlike my Great Ancestor who ate the apple the cause of my downfall was a very tempting loaf with a nice brown crust, such a loaf as I had not seen since I left home. As I was not 'cast in a foundry' I could not resist. Result fairly caught and duly punished, all of which has passed and gone and leaves me as of yore, In the Pink.[79]

Even so, Kate Boland's commiseration for her victimised son knew no bounds:

Such a relief to get your cheerful letter after being deprived of the little pleasure of writing for some weeks, for such a slight offence. It seems a cruel thing to leave bread about where men are in a constant state of semi starvation and not allowed to touch it, and to one like you, Harry, who would share your last crust with your fellow man.

Ned's response was jauntier: 'It's a hell of a pity you didn't get a chance to scoff [gobble] the cake before being nabbed, but better luck next time, old sport. You may see some of those swine starving yet, before the Hun is finished with 'em.' Kathleen drew out a political moral: 'It is a great shame to lock you up for such a trivial thing. But, of course, we cannot expect justice from England, that would be impossible. However, with God's help we will soon be independent of her.'[80] A week or so later, Kate Boland was all the prouder of Harry's defiance after a visit from Councillor William Partridge, a leading trade unionist who had been released from Lewes because of illness:

He told me about the bread, and your consequent punishment, and your hunger strike for 3 whole days. Your robust health cannot last with such treatment – and you have been in 'Clink' again, for a day, for daring to speak out of your turn, God help you: it is cruel treatment to give our noble sons, because they hold different opinions and love their own dear land for which they have freely given up their lives and liberty. One would have thought 15 men, who were shot after *surrendering*, would have satisfied their vengeance, without keeping our loved ones as convicts, but it's a case of 'Might conquering Right'.[81]

Though intermittently truculent or defiant, Harry was usually pragmatic enough to take advantage of whatever comforts were permitted. On arrival at Lewes, he reminded Ned 'that three visitors are allowed at the one time', and suggested that a colleague from Todd's, if in London on business, should 'drop a line to the Governor asking permission to visit me, as Lewes is only half hour's run from London'.[82] There was doubtless a tinge of irony in this observation from his close friend Maurice Collins: 'I and all are so glad that the Governor and Warders are so nice to you. Of course ye cause no trouble, and altho' been [*sic*.] convicts in name, the authorities know otherwise.' Collins developed the theme in his next letter:

What a fine regular life ye have – such regularity, and the food fairly good – if not in quality, it's a good thing to have it in quantity. I'd love to be with ye. No fear of an Omadhaun [amadán: fool] like me to be sent over to happy England. The cells must be nice. What a treat it must be to have one to yourself. A high life. I can't afford a room to myself and there you boys are, enjoying the blessings of a highly civilised nation and having the best of times.[83]

Yet Harry, in a coded message to his 'governor' at Todd's, used a cutter's analogy to indicate that his relationship with authority had been tolerably smooth until the episode of the stolen bread:

No doubt life is made up of straightness and crookedness. I have had easy in the scye mostly, barring a few knots on my th[re]ad during the basting under. The finishing left much to be desired – a snubbed X order.[84]

When drafting a letter to the Captain of the Faughs, he remarked that 'this place is not too bad, altho' the food is scarce. Things are looking bright for us now and maybe [I'll] see the County Final.'[85] Harry did not blame the prison system for his peckishness: 'No doubt you are aware of the shortage of food in England. We together with all in England have suffered a reduction. It is very hard on us, our diet not been [sic.] very luxurious. However even as it is, it is better than Dartmoor where I was half starved.'[86] Even his mother, ever sensitive to reports of Harry's degradation, passed on an encouraging message from the ailing Councillor Partridge after his early release from Lewes: 'He tells me the Governor is a perfect gentleman, which consoled me a little, for if a Governor wishes he can make his prisoners suffer according to his disposition.'[87] Harry's correspondence testifies to humanity as well as severity on the part of prison officers, and to co-operation as well as defiance in his own dealings with them.

Harry's breaches of discipline, though sometimes resembling a refractory schoolboy's cussedness, belonged to a broader political campaign. The immediate object of that campaign was to secure either an amnesty or recognition of the convicts as prisoners of war, with the ultimate aim of further eroding British authority in Ireland. Mrs Boland marvelled at the Government's pig-headedness:

One wonders at a powerful country like England stooping to such things, by keeping our breadwinners prisoners, it is like the things done in Russia, and England was always looked up to as such a free country. We were led to believe that your removal to Lewes meant that you would be treated as prisoners of war, or else as political prisoners, so that we could send food and clothing to our beloved ones. I hear the Broad Arrow is all over your clothes and even your hair is cropped to form the Broad Arrow. We know you don't mind that as you are suffering for the Holy Cause of Ireland. We expected such different treatment from Mr. Lloyd George, he being a Welshman, but it seems at present we are doomed to disappointment.

Mrs Boland exclaimed 'with the Prophet, "How long! Oh Lord! How long!"', and asked God to 'bless you and all the gentlemen of Ireland, who are in "dungeons vile"'.[88] In early May, she reiterated that 'you should certainly be treated as political prisoners or else prisoners of war, which you are, but [for] the mere Irish, anything is good enough, "Don't cher know"'.[89] This rather limp conclusion followed a stern warning from Harry against pleading for mercy:

> Dear Mother, I absolutely forbid any appeal to be lodged on my behalf. I prefer to stay here for my term, aye even for life, rather than express any regret or ask any favour from the Champion of Small Nations. Tell Mr [George] Gavan Duffy I am grateful, but firmly refuse to appeal.[90]

Harry and his fellows preferred to wait for their captors' nerve to break.

In the aftermath of the Home Secretary's indecisive statement of 19 April, de Valera sought direction from 'home' as to whether a work-strike should be initiated on the issue of recognition. Sinn Féin's positive response was signalled by a telegram to Harry announcing the death of an uncle, which prompted the often unsympathetic Catholic Chaplain to propose a Requiem Mass for the fictitious deceased. The resultant campaign of progressive disruption was launched on Whit Monday, 28 May.[91] Cabinet's response three days later was to procrastinate:

> The Home Secretary reported that there had been a slight mutiny among the Irish prisoners in Lewes Prison. It was decided to make no announce-ment of an amnesty until immediately before the assembling of the [Irish] Convention. In the meantime the Home Secretary should take steps to disperse the ring-leaders so far as possible.[92]

After much anguished debate among the Prison Commissioners, another Inspector was despatched to Lewes on 5 June to begin the process of removing small parties to other institutions, in descending order of notoriety. De Valera returned to Maidstone, with Thomas Hunter (Commandant of the 2nd Battalion) in a separate car. Ashe, FitzGerald, Quinn, and Vincent Poole (the fiery Corporation labourer who had denounced Harry in the Metropole) were among those selected for removal before Harry. Finally, on Wednesday, 6 June, the 'rather truculent' Harry Boland was despatched to Maidstone in the fifth batch, along with Eamon Duggan. Their last hours in Lewes were uproarious:

'The shouting and singing can be heard beyond the prison walls; as much of the shouting is in Gaelic, it sounds like howling.' As Inspector Winn reflected: 'It is quite an experience in prison life to have howling going on, punctuated by crashing of bed boards against the doors, and window smashing.'[93]

Most of the leaders 'went as quiet as lambs', though 'Ashe made a formal protest against the cuffs and chains'. Even Vincent Poole, from whom trouble had been feared, confined himself to 'a few protestations' in deference to his companion Seán McGarry ('a man quite opposed to Poole's methods').[94] Duggan 'said that if removed he would have to be carried, but offered no resistance when the time actually came'. Only Harry was belligerent in transit, as Winn reported just after his departure:

> Boland said that he had done nothing criminal, and as long as he was degraded by being treated as a criminal, he declined to obey the orders of the Authorities. He resisted violently on being handcuffed, and had to be carried to the car, glorying in the fact that it took more than 3 men to carry him. Once in the car he seemed to accept the situation, but made some remark as it drove off.

His escort later reported 'that Boland tried to attract attention while passing through Lewes, but no one seemed to take any notice, and he was quiet all the remainder of the way. On arrival at Maidstone, he said he "would make a fight for it", and would not obey orders, and the Principal Warder reported to the Governor the kind of men he had to deal with.'[95]

Harry's motive in seeking attention from passers-by was to alert them to a piece of lavatory paper which he had succeeded in throwing out of the open motor car. This contained a letter in ink to his mother, prefaced by a touching appeal: 'Friend – Send on this note to Mrs. Boland, 15 Marino Crescent, Clontarf, Dublin, Ireland and earn the prayers of her son who asks this favour of you.' The letter depicted the prisoners as innocent victims of an arbitrary power:

> My dear Mother – I cast this note in the lap of the Gods in the hope that some good angel will send it to you. I am on my way to some other prison in irons. Just left Lewes after a terrible time there since last Whit Monday at 8 am, when our leaders presented our demand to the prison authorities asking that we be treated as prisoners of war, refusing to do any work or obey any orders so long as we were treated as criminals. We then marched to our cells in a soldierly manner. We got no answer to our request, and we were not allowed from our cells, not even to Mass on Sunday, or did we get any exercise except what we could take in our narrow stuffy cells. We waited patiently and quietly for exactly one week; and so, on Monday night, each man broke 3 panes of glass in his window. As a result of

broken windows, our leaders were removed on Tuesday midday. We then were left behind, wrecked our cells and broke all the glass which was left. The noise was terrific and we are all being sent to other prisons. We have sworn to do no work or to obey any orders whatever until the Government treat us as soldiers. We fought a clean fair fight and should be treated as honourable men, not as criminals. Dear Mother, do not worry too much. With God's help I will keep my health. My spirits are high. Good-bye, give my love to dear sister, brothers and aunt. Pray for the good soul who directs this to you. You won't hear from me again till my time comes. Your loving son, Harry.

An angel duly appeared and forwarded Harry's explosive message to Marino Crescent with a curious covering note: 'This letter was picked up in the street by my daughter and as I, too, have two sons doing their bit, it is with pleasure I forward it to you as the writer wishes.'[96]

Harry's sensational account of the confrontation was immediately taken by Kathleen to the Irish National Aid office in Exchequer Street, where it was examined by Michael Collins and Michael Staines.[97] Collins was already adept at converting prisoners' grievances into emotive political issues, having fallen foul of Gerald in Frongoch when he concocted a collective testimonial grossly exaggerating the maltreatment of the internees.[98] On 10 June, Harry's letter was read out at an amnesty meeting in Beresford Place, Dublin, contributing to an ugly riot in the course of which a police inspector was fatally struck by a hurley.[99] Like James Boland three decades earlier, Harry had discerned that first-hand stories of prison brutality, whether true, false, or misleading, could become a powerful engine for political change. The campaign for an amnesty was not immediately effective; but, on 16 June, Harry, de Valera, and twenty-six other Irish convicts at Maidstone were transferred to Pentonville Prison in preparation for release. His Majesty the King, after due consideration, had declared himself 'graciously pleased to extend Our Grace and Mercy unto the said prisoners and to pardon and remit unto them the remainder of their sentences'.[100] That evening, Harry and many of his released companions sailed for Dublin. His contribution to the party was a performance of 'M'anam a Dhía, But There It Is'.[101] The second phase of Harry Boland's rebellion thus came to a close.

Before examining how he coped with freedom and celebrity, let us look more closely at the character and preoccupations of Convict 'q 90'. His incarceration in Lewes Prison had provided ample opportunity for adapting to novel circum-stances, reflecting on his happy-go-lucky past, and peering into an uncertain future. During this enforced intermission in an otherwise busy and active life, Harry's correspondence and jottings gave free play to his lively mind and unbroken spirit. Preserved ever since by the Boland family, these personal testaments make possible an intimate portrait of the man within the rebel.

IV

Intermission

CONVICT Boland's correspondence with family and friends of both sexes offers insight into many of his worlds, ranging far beyond the walls of Lewes. Prison life, treated with appropriate discretion in order to avoid suppression or seizure of letters, was nevertheless a recurrent theme. Instead of harping on his woes, Harry treated imprisonment as a challenge to his physical and mental prowess. In a letter to Bill Duggan, he reflected that prison life was 'dull, drab and monotonous, yet it has its compensations and can be made cheerful. It's all a question of Temperament.'[1] Harry fortified his temperament with uplifting maxims such as those transcribed in his prison notebook:

'Tis better to have fought and lost than never to have fought at all.

Tho' my body moulders here my spirit is still free.

'Tis not bars that make the prison, bars and bolts no terrors have for me.

The hour that saw her sons in chains, that hour saw Ireland free.

Better a has been than a never wasser.

True happiness can only be found within oneself.[2]

As he told the hurler Paddy Hogan: 'I carried out your motto at Easter Week and kept my head down and heart up, since when I have kept both up very high.'[3]

Harry's self-discipline and natural buoyancy survived the rigours of imprisonment and, unlike many inmates of Lewes, he remained healthy throughout.[4] He reached Lewes in surprisingly robust condition, slightly overweight for a man of 5 feet 8 and a half inches: 'During my stay in Dartmoor I put on 1 lb weight. I weigh 11.11, which leaves me in good form. I have not been troubled with a cold since I left home and my spirits correspond to my health.'[5] After a month at Lewes, he was 'in the pink of condition. I am very fat and heavy, the regular hours agree with me A 1.'[6] Following his period on 'no. 2 diet', his three-day 'hunger-strike', and ample exercise, Harry eventually shed the reserves he had stored over the winter: 'I am in great form, never better, no superfluous flesh, just 11.5: no fear I'll get fat here.'[7] As he explained to Paddy Hogan of the Faughs, prison had done wonders for his fitness:

59

I won't under the circs. apologise for me absence from the team, anyway I was not worth my place. I was very stale and lazy. If you could only see me now you would be satisfied that I am fit. I feel ten years younger, after my twelve months' regular living away from all vices, etc. I would be in better form than ever after a few weeks' practice, so keep a place in the second team.[8]

A month after his arrival, Harry wrote that 'I have left the workshop and am now working about the prison, a nice change.'[9] He professed to be delighted with the convict's daily routine and his growing expertise in household chores: 'I will be very handy about the house when I do come home. I can scrub, wash, sew, hand and machine paint, whitewash, etc., etc. I am going to be a dressmaker's labourer or navvy's clerk on my return.'[10] He amplified this theme in a letter to the friend at Todd's whom he termed 'the Sage', Tim O'Mahony:

I was working a sewing machine while in Dartmoor. I have a better job now sweeping up the prison. I will be quite domesticated when I come out. I can scrub, black lead, use a sewing machine, etc., so if you meet a fair maid or widow who is on the look out, say a word for me some time early in 1920.[11]

He was still reciting the litany of his uxorial qualifications when writing to his mother in May:

I can't look a duster or floor cloth straight in the face, every brush trembles as I approach. Keep your eye out for any Young Woman who wants a handy General Servant for a Hubby. I can scrub, sew, machine, blacklead etc. I would only want one evening off each week and if she's very nice I would not ask any wages only my keep, for 'pon me Sowl I have become so lazy that I fear I will not be able to work again.[12]

Prison was beginning to make a 'new man' of Harry Boland.

Like many prisoners, Harry took advantage of the relatively liberal régime at Lewes to further his truncated education and refine his skills. By mid January, he had finally received the books requested at Dartmoor: 'I got cutting books, also Arithmetic and Geometry. You will be glad to know that I am studying while I may.'[13] Nearly two months later, his notebook celebrated the receipt of an essential tool: 'Pen arrived March 6th 1917, Lewes Gaol. H. Boland. An Beolanac.'[14] But the available equipment was never adequate for technical drawing, as Harry explained to Tim O'Mahony:

I find Lewes more congenial [to] study than Dartmoor, and I beguile the time in my cell by a little work. I have some cutting books and a Mathematical work; I have a pencil and book provided by the

Government. The book is not suited to diagram drawing; if you send me a sketch book and a good drawing pencil I will pray ... [passage erased]. I describe circles with the lid of my salt cellar. 'Necessity is surely the Mother of Invention.' To sweep a segment of a circle I must take the lace from my boot, so you may be sure my work is not very artistic, and would not pass your censorious eye, unless you admired my perseverance.[15]

O'Mahony responded to this appeal, as Kate Boland reported:

He is sending the book on ladies' tailoring etc., also drawing book and pencil which Kathleen had bought, but Mr. O'M. will change for different kind. K. tried all the shops for pencil sharpener, but could only just get a penny one which I shall send along.[16]

In the absence of a measuring rule, Harry marked out a rough substitute (of much reduced scale), using a fragment of postcard from Frongoch which is still preserved in the notebook.

The irrepressible cutter celebrated his achievement in doggerel, his metre expanding as he warmed to the theme:

> 'Necessity is the Mother of Invention.'
> Witness my scale, rule, and square!!
> I asked Director if 'twas his intention
> A pencil, compass, and a rule, to spare
> To me, who was so anxious for the study
> Of problems sartorial, ere my brains got muddy.
> When I had asked this mild request, as simple as could be,
> He flew into a passion. 'Look here young man' said he
> 'We cannot let you have these things to take into your cell
> 'Tis not a convalescent home so you can go to h——.'
> So out I went without a word, I thought it very hard
> Until some friend from Ireland sent me a nice post card.
> So now you see I've made a rule I also made a square
> It may not be quite accurate, if so I do not care.
> It helps me pass the lonely hours in a useful way
> In drafting and in study while I'm waiting for the day.[17]

Harry's patterns were indeed inelegant by comparison with his neat and disciplined calligraphy. His earliest sketches were adorned with rueful annotations such as 'December 30th in my lonely cell' and 'for Ned if I get home again, December 30th. 1916, Lewes Gaol'. His designs embraced Inverness capes and cloaks, Raglan overcoats, vests, trousers, shirts, and even a 'hunting frock' for a sportsman with a 40-inch chest and 33-inch waist. Doubtless reflecting his experience at Todd's, one of Dublin's few predominantly 'Catholic' department stores, most of the drawings were for clerical costumes and vestments. He devoted a whole page to a 'full Roman Soutane cape detach over sleeves', and by mid February he was experimenting with 'leggins', 'pantaloons', and a 'frock, clerical, silk faced'. He sketched two 'tonsure frock coats' for priests of different dimensions, the second for a 'Corpulent Gentleman'. The most outrageous pattern showed a clerical vest for an unidentified monstrosity requiring an 18-and-a-half-inch collar, 46-inch breast, and 52-inch waist: 'Extra erect figure, short necked. Keep neck well up and shirt stand to collar.'[18] Harry's sartorial imagination knew no bounds.

His literary taste, as developed at Lewes, exhibited a similar blend of the sacred and profane. The 'R. C. Library' at Lewes, presumably maintained by the prisoners' Chaplain (Fr. O'Loughlin), was well stocked with works suitable for pious nationalists. Harry's extracts from the catalogue reveal something of his historical and literary interests. In addition to the *Irish Monthly* and the first fifteen pamphlets issued by the Catholic Truth Society of Ireland, he listed six biographies (of St. Patrick, Cardinal Wolsey, Archbishops Oliver Plunket and John MacHale, Fr. Thomas Burke, OP, and Thomas Davis); three books of verse (Gerald Griffin's *Poems*, Cardinal Newman's *Dream of Gerontius*, and *Songs of the Glens*, probably of Antrim and by 'Moira O'Neill'); three historical works (Barry O'Brien's *Irish Memories*, Fr. H. W. Cleary's *The Orange Society*, and Cardinal Moran's *The Catholics of Ireland under the Penal Code*); two novels (*The Croppy: A Tale of 1798* by the Banim brothers, and Rosa Mulholland's *Wild Birds of Killeevy*); two polemics (a study of socialism, and *Ireland's Vindication: Refutation of Froude*, by Fr. Burke); and two religious tracts (*The Sermon on the Mount*, perhaps as expounded by St. Augustine, and Fr. Gerald Molloy's *Geology and Revelation*).[19] These preferences suggest that Harry was more conventional in his Catholicism than Gerald, who had written from Knutsford that 'we heard mass for the first time this morning and although not very orthodox in my beliefs, it was one of the greatest joys of my life; we could scarcely fit in the chapel'.[20] Harry's piety was reinforced by his sister Kathleen, who sent him a prayer book in Irish to be shared with his close friend and fellow-Faugh, Jack Shouldice.[21]

Harry's prison reading was not restricted to worthy religious and national tracts. In addition to the textbooks on arithmetic and geometry, his mother sent a new history of the GAA.[22] Ned supplied two books by Rex Beach,[23] and promised a diet of bush ballads from Australia:

> I'm sure you would love to have a copy of [Adam] Lindsay Gordon's and a few others. You could learn them in your *cell* and let us have them in your inimitable style when you get back home, 'The Man from Snowy River', etc. etc. I'll send them along anyhow at the earliest opportunity.[24]

The notebook records several of Harry's favourite poems and recitations, beginning with a triplet from Byron's 'The Giaour':

> For Freedom's battle once begun,
> Bequeath'd by bleeding Sire to Son,
> Though baffled oft is ever won.[25]

Harry also transcribed Kipling's 'If', that classic compendium of manly British virtues, nicely juxtaposed with Pearse's 'The Wayfarer', along with a medley of adages, proverbs, and edifying extracts. Despite his posthumous reputation for having 'scarcely ever read a book', Harry was clearly an eager and retentive reader.[26] Snippets of remembered wisdom and literature helped 'q 90' to transcend his grim habitat and keep his 'heart up'.

Lewes, like 'Frongoch University', provided ample opportunity for crash courses in Irish culture. As Harry told 'the Sage' from Todd's:

> Your Irish teacher is here in good health and sends his regards to you and all yours; he hopes you are keeping up your Gaelic. We have classes during exercise. We are fortunate in having plenty of good teachers and we are working away while walking round our exercise ring.[27]

In his first letter from Dartmoor, he had requested Fr. O'Growney's five volumes of lessons and the Christian Brothers' *Aids to Composition*, which probably reached him in Lewes.[28] Harry's notebook contains a series of Irish lessons and transcriptions, carefully inscribed in unreformed Celtic script. These include prayers such as 'An Salbhé Regina' and the Apostles' Creed ('Cré na n-Aspol'), doubtless transcribed from Kathleen's manual, along with pages of meticulously copied prose extracts, vocabulary, phrases, and Gaelic names.[29]

More energetic Gaelic exercises were also tolerated by the indulgent Major Marriott, as Harry informed the Captain of the Faughs: 'By the way, we have a Hurling team here. We hope to play Dublin Frongochs if released, so look out for some Hurling of a sort.'[30] His mother learned that he had 'been appointed Captain of the Lewes Hurling team, a very high honour. Colours Brown and White Arrows. We will be useful in a standing position. I will not be able to run 50 yds. but we'll do our best altho' the match may never come off. Yet we take great pleasure in talking of it.'[31] He was less bashful when writing in otherwise romantic vein to Cait Fraher, the daughter of a prominent Gael from Dungarvan, County Waterford:

> By the way, I am Captain of the Lewes H[urling] Club. We have challenged the Dublin men who were interned during Easter. My team is represented by Galway, Wexford, Cork, Kerry and Dublin; and, after a few good feeds, we hope to be in good form and to play the men who were interned from Galway and Wexford, so we hope to have a good trip to Wexford and Athenry. Is it not a great honor to be Capt. of such a team?[32]

The loyal teamster had tasted leadership at last.

Harry relished his moments of indirect contact with the world outside, more frequent in Lewes than in Dartmoor. It is noteworthy that after his tantalising meeting with Ned in September, he discouraged further family visits. As he wrote to his mother:

> I do not want a visit, it is so far and the fare is so heavy that it is not worthwhile for 40 minutes, with a Warder between us. You may be sure that I am O.K., so don't worry about me. After Dartmoor I can stick anything in the prison line.[33]

His only recorded visitor at Lewes was 'Mr.' Morrison of Todd's, a senior colleague rather than an intimate friend whose business often took him to London, and who brought him 'very cheery and welcome' news.[34] More lasting satisfaction could be secured, at a lower monetary and emotional cost, from letters, gifts, and photographs. The photographs originally sent to Dartmoor continued to console him at Lewes: 'They brought me back to you all, and I often have a chat with you; so when you feel your ears burning, remember it is me [sic.] who is talking love to you far away.'[35] Gerald, whose first child (Enda) had been born during his absence in Frongoch, promised 'a photo of the little fellow' and hoped, in return, that 'you will give him his first suit of trousers'. Kathleen, in less sentimental mode, sent 'a photo of the Plunkett Convention, knowing you would like to see it'.[36]

Gifts and comforts were less readily permitted, Kate Boland being disappointed to learn from the Governor that parcels of food and tobacco, unlike books, could not be delivered.[37] Harry had no treats such as those lavished by relatives from Manchester on his brother Gerald in Knutsford:

> They brought me a complete change of under clothing, brush and comb, tooth-brush, blacking brush, soap, vaseline ointment, 2 scissors, 24 combs for the other fellows, 5 looking glasses, a razor and brush, writing-pad and paper, a fountain pen and ink, 2 caps, 2 collars, not to mention all sweets and fruit and food.[38]

One form of fodder, if not food, was permitted at Lewes: 'I suppose you got lots of cards and shamrock on St. Patrick's Day. Every one of your friends got to hear you could get shamrock and cards and were all going to send cards to the heroes.'[39] This dispensation was not renewed at Easter:

> We are surprised you did not get Easter card from home, as Edmund, Kathleen, Auntie, Mrs. Tracey and self sent one each in envelopes all written on the back, also W. Whelan, Kit Doran, a likeness of A. Griffiths [sic.], 'S. F. Aboo' printed on it. Edmund's was grand, representing Ireland as a strong young man, standing on a rock.[40]

But Harry was permitted an uplifting offering from Cait Fraher, whose rosaries he found 'very beautiful and acceptable to me coming from you. I will always remember you in mine, knowing you are praying for me. The little ones are very nice, every one admires them; and I tell them that they reflect the taste and beauty of the Server.'[41]

Letters, as that faintly unctuous extract suggests, were indispensable in maintaining personal intimacy as well as exchanging information. Harry was diligent in modifying his style to suit the temperament and susceptibilities of each recipient: considerate and reassuring in writing to his mother, playful with his siblings, hearty with fellow athletes, pious and high-minded for Cait Fraher, intellectually curious and word-conscious when addressing the Sage of Todd's. He had the gift of writing as he spoke, and of evoking a conversation rather than a monologue. The replies suggest that his carefully personalised letters were appreciated, especially by those to whom they were not addressed. Since each letter was widely circulated, individual recipients were not confined to the particular style which Harry deemed appropriate for them. Thus his mother, while applauding his dutiful manner when writing to herself, could relish the more flippant missives to Kathleen or Ned. As a friend reported:

I saw your last letter to Eamon, and it was brimful of humour. None other could write in such a strain but Harry, and indeed such notes have a great effect on your dear Mother. To hear her laughing wd. do you good.[42]

Likewise, the news-laden letters addressed to his mother were neither private nor confidential:

I read your 'Mother's' letter for a good many of the boys, and indeed all expressed their keen appreciation of the Governor's letting out so much news. Tom Smyth, Luke O'Toole, Con, Mick Dwyer and a good many more were listening as I read it at Croke Pk. We then adjourned to Peter Leech's, and sat in the same corner where you and I often supped together and will, D.V., in a short time again.[43]

The threat of censorship only added to the fun, for Harry and his friends vied with each other to outsmart the presumed dimwits trying to interpret their codes and obscure allusions. As Maurice Collins observed:

The Censor has my sympathy, wading through this, but being a thorough good hearted man like all Englishmen, he will only deem it a pleasure. Good-bye now with all the love of my heart. Your broken hearted wife, Mossie.[44]

The writer, a prominent Gael who had recently married and set up a billiard saloon and tobacconist's business at 65, Parnell Street,[45] had been wounded at the Four Courts and interned at Stafford and Frongoch. Brotherly love had not restrained him from kidnapping the Quaker Bulmer Hobson when he tried to prevent the Rebellion, an act which drew censure even from Seán McDermott.[46] Harry, however, deemed him 'the best hearted fellow I ever met, as straight as a die, a real man; who, when the great test came, threw everything to the winds and stood for Ireland'. Collins, like himself, was a veteran of the IRB who had lost his job after the Rebellion. As a former civil servant who had spent four years in London, he too was intimately familiar with the hereditary enemy.[47] Good old Mossy clearly enjoyed masquerading as Mrs Harry Boland. Despite frequent lapses into unmistakable masculinity, his affectionate salutations and valedictions achieved their object. Harry recounted the outcome to Ned:

> My cup of happiness was complete when Mossy's love letter arrived. It created quite a sensation. The officer who distributes the letters asked his assistant if Boland was married! The assistant swore that I was not, but it was of no avail, for said the gent in charge, here's a letter which begins, 'My darling Husband', and signed, 'Your Heart-broken Wife'. I was called up and pleaded not guilty to the charge, protested that I had been thro' many trying experiences, had been knocked down by a tram, [had] been very nearly drowned, had been robbed in my time, had been tried for my life etc., so I thought I had enough trouble without taking charge of another man's daughter. At last I convinced the officer that altho' [we] were not bound by marriage, we were united by a bond, friendship, tried and true.[48]

Seldom has the romance of male bonding been celebrated with such artless gusto.

Another correspondent with whom Harry communicated in riddles was Tim O'Mahony, his 'Governor' in the tailoring department at Todd's. Their veiled exchange had begun at Dartmoor. O'Mahony protested that his 'interrogative' had been ignored, while Harry indicated that an attempt to smuggle messages had foundered:

> Alas our boasted telepathic sympathy's failed, at least on my [pa]rt. I rung you up from Dartmoor some 500 times praying a reply to that allegorical document I sent you, I tried all my powers of concentration in vain, at last I had to appeal to the ordinary channels and ask Governor to write to you. Then the Censor or *Censless* fell in love with your dear old 'Mahogany' and froze on to the photo and letter.[49]

Another passage suggests that O'Mahony's query may have carried a double meaning: 'Tell Mr O that the pattern he asked for together with several others he will find in my drawer. I have no idea where key is but give him permission to open same.'[50]

These allegories and cyphers drew upon a long-standing friendship, not between equals such as Maurice and Harry, but between a 'Sage' and his acolyte. To nobody else would Harry have written thus:

[We]ll, Tim a gradh [love], I am in good [form] and feel like your old f[ri]end 'Mutius Scaevola of the fiery hand'. 'Nuff said.' 'The one bright spot' that shines thro' the gloom of prison.[51]

O'Mahony would have instantly unscrambled the parallel between Scaevola's penance after failing to kill the invader of Rome, and Harry's ordeal by imprisonment after the Easter surrender.[52] It was for O'Mahony that Harry elaborated his tortuous analogy between shirt-making and survival as a convict.[53] O'Mahony was evidently Harry's intellectual idol, whose performances he remembered with awe:

It is about 6.30 p.m. I fancy I am with you again in the dining hall, listening with open mouthed wonder to 'the words of learned length and thunderous sound'.[54] Many a grand chat we had. Surely I hope we will have a great many more. Your motto should be Ubique [everywhere]. You could give us Horace, Virgil, or W. R. Lynham [W. F. Lynam], *The Lives of the Saints*, or *Saturday Night in Monto*, in fact I never met your equal.[55]

If O'Mahony had had a few days in Dartmoor, he 'would have written such a malediction on it that would be an ornament to English art [and] letters. Also I feel sure you would never have written a recantation.'[56] Harry drew 'on my memory for many a good story told by you, and I often give the boys a few at exercise. The Blue ones are appreciated very much.' When pondering the collapse of Redmond's Home Rule movement, he imagined his friend in full cry:

Poor John E. has reaped the harvest of English promises, Dead Sea fruit. 'But yesterday he might have stood against the world.'[57] 'But today, ah that vas another day.' A combination of Shakespere [*sic.*] and M. O. L. T. How would these lines meet John's case? He did not get the fur coat after his whoring.

In conclusion, he assured O'Mahony that 'for yourself you stand very near me always. I shall treasure the time spent with you as the happiest days of a happy [?life].'[58]

Harry's correspondence, for the most part, celebrates the warm friendships, sunny gregariousness, animal spirits, and conventional values of an attractive but unremarkable pre-revolutionary 'bhoy'. But Harry also emerges as the unfailing support of his family, especially when compared with the genial but feckless Ned, or the dutiful but married Gerald. Though edgy about the repercussions of losing his job, Harry held no grudge against his employer:

I was glad to know that Gerald got his job back in Crooksling. I knew he would not lose it. There should be a good job for Ned with the Rebuilding [of Dublin]. I know you will be on the qui vive. I am better off here as my job could not be held for me under the circumstances.[59]

Kate Boland responded that 'if you don't get back your own old position it will be your own fault. Anyhow, your abilities will secure you a position anywhere.'[60] But O'Mahony and his colleagues had ensured that Harry, like Gerald, remained on the payroll after incarceration, so cushioning the loss:

I can never hope to repay you for all your kindness to Mother during the trouble. When she told me at Mjoy [Mountjoy Prison] how you had brought my salary every week, it took a great load off my mind and gave me heart to face the ordeal bravely. I thank you from my heart. I hope some day to thank all the staff personally for their kindness.[61]

There was little risk of destitution at Marino Crescent, as Kathleen had become a branch manager for her firm and therefore a 'very important person', while relief was supplied by the Irish National Aid Association and by 'a handsome present' from the Faughs. Harry thanked the Gaels effusively for their 'very great kindness to my Mother', but was assured that 'it was considered a duty and that was enough'.[62] He reflected smugly on the spirit of mutual support embodied by National Aid: 'Ours is a great country, always ready to help national ideas and support the dependents of those who fight for Her.'[63] The ledgers of the fund show that Kate Boland received unusually generous weekly payments amounting to £85 5s. between August 1916 and September 1917, including a Christmas bonus.[64] It was scarcely necessary for his mother to offer further reassurance: 'Don't trouble about us feeling the "Pinch", Harry. Would that you were enjoying the same comforts and freedom, you, my dear son, whom we have to thank for all.'[65] By comparison with the 'pinch' of 1895, her losses were indeed trivial. As Harry remarked, 'I seem to be much more useful to you in prison than I was at home.'[66]

While Harry remained the ideal supportive son throughout his imprisonment, Gerald's relationship with his mother had suffered a setback which tested Harry's skill as a conciliator. During the troubled period of Annie's pregnancy and delivery, while Gerald fretted in camp, relations between Annie and Kate had soured. Gerald was anxious that his mother should visit his wife, who required 'care' but was 'too shy' to visit her mother-in-law. By June 1916, he thought all was well: 'I'm so glad that you have at last broken. Forgive me for being so cruel to you but I think you will understand how I felt. ... Well Mother you're a real brick and no mistake about it, that is if your letters really represent your feelings, and I think they do.'[67] Three months later, he realised that they did not:

I am very sorry to know you are keeping that horrible letter, and shewing it around. I thought you would consider me a little more than this. .... I know she doesn't mean a word of it. Now mother you, yourself, often said things to every one of us, without exception, and you were sorry and really never meant it, but no one of us ever asked you to humiliate yourself by apologising, so for God's sake burn that letter now.[68]

This dispute may account for the rather guarded references to Gerald, and especially his wife, in Harry's correspondence.

Ever the diplomat, Harry tried first to avoid the problem and then to solve it. In reporting Gerald's success in preserving his post at Crooksling throughout his internment, his mother wrote rather testily: 'Yes, Gerald got his back money, £108, and the wife and baby is going out tomorrow, unless she changes her mind.' Ned's response was warmer: 'Gerry's in fine form and got all his back time, some check, too, 108 jimmyos, nice little present, eh Har! His Mrs. is going to live in Crooksling from now on. The kid is as big as a bullock and very like his *Da*.'[69] Harry submitted his mother to a brief homily: 'I hope you are more reconciled to Gerald's marriage now. The *best* son ever born to woman he sure is, and you must repay by taking joy in his Wife and Son.'[70] Kathleen followed his advice, at least in part: 'Gerald is looking very well, he is nice and sunburnt. The little boy is a real Boland. A lot of people say he is rather like you. I suppose we will be making him Chairman of the County Board one of these days.' Kate Boland remained slightly cool, observing in the same letter that 'I don't expect Gerald can contribute his portion this time, dear Harry'; but the next letter presented a common front, with messages from the entire family.[71] The peace-maker had evidently prevailed.

Central to Harry's political, social, and imaginative life, as exposed in these letters, was the GAA. While at Lewes, Harry was re-elected as County Chairman by 'the Gaels of Dublin'.[72] Harry pondered the implications of his lofty estate:

They have re-elected me Chairman, a very high honour for a convict. I am afraid my hurling days are over, as I am very fat and soft. However I can stand on the side line and growl about the 'decay of Irish youth', and an odd time I'll get garrulous and swing my stick or bottle and shew 'how finals were won'.[73]

Maurice Collins assured him that 'the G.A.A. is not in a bad way, despite the Goat's intervention. They won't allow excursion trains for the matches on Sundays, altho' the race meetings could have as many as were wanted. The reason offered to us was to save the coal – moriah.'[74] On Easter Sunday, 8 April, Andy Harty had 'the pleasure of remembering you to the members of the Annual Congress. Though we had a great many strange faces this time, it was a small convention (about 60) and things passed off very quietly. The agenda was the smallest we have yet had, but the spirit of those present was all right.'[75] Despite cancellation of Dublin fixtures because of 'snow and rain', the tournament in support of National Aid had raised respectable sums in the provinces:

> Taking all in all, things are going fairly well with the Association in Dublin. The weather has been bad and attendances small, but the matches were all right. . . . Under the circumstances it is very satisfactory. It is far better than I expected.[76]

Harry would have read between the lines that the Association was in serious disarray.

Harry did not allow imprisonment to shield him from the sordid underside of Gaelic politics. He was kept up to date by key organisers such as Maurice Collins, Paddy Hogan, Andy Harty, and also Luke O'Toole, the longest-serving General Secretary of the GAA. The factionalism endemic among Gaelic athletes had been intensified by the fragmentation of nationalism prompted by the Great War and the Rebellion. Clubs unhappy with Dublin's dominance of the Association, and with the IRB's dominance of the Dublin County Board, formed a rival body centred in County Limerick, which had some success in disrupting the GAA between 1915 and 1919.[77] The dissidents included brethren at odds with the cabal which had plotted the Rebellion, as well as Redmondites and 'clericalist' opponents of secret societies. Harry was bombarded with news of the Limerick 'seceders', the treacherous Kickhams, the split in the Dublin Commercials, and the unpatriotic feats of the Hibernian Knights:[78]

> The latter are very unpopular, owing to Jack Kelly having put on the Khaki, Easter Week, and drove a van with ammunition. The public wouldn't allow him on a field with Gaels, and at the moment the spirit is high.[79]

Maurice Collins assured him that the rules of the Association would be defended against all challenges, and furthermore 'that the honour of the Gaels who have stood by the Association will not be jeopardised, and that the Assn. stands now, as it always did – for the preservation of our National Pastimes and for fostering the spirit that [Wolfe] Tone left us'. He warned, however, that the incumbent Leinster Chairman showed no sign of stepping aside after his deplorable absence from the Rebellion:

> I suppose [John J.] Hogan will go forward again as Chairman. The b——y hypocrite. The scoundrel. Where was he when he was wanted? His excuses would make a dog vomit. I know him. He remained at Dufferin Av. and

never knew a bit, Harry. What an innocent child. He is almost ashamed now to lift his head.[80]

Ned reported rather guardedly on a dispute involving Mick Crowe, the Limerick referee who had introduced both Gerald and Harry to the IRB before likewise losing face through his inactivity at Eastertide:

Regarding O'Toole and Crowe, I do not know of any deflection from the rules, but of course the last Convention was held in private so I am not exactly in the Know, Har; but I believe that the less said of Mick C. the better, he's hardly the stuff that gold is made from.[81]

Better news came from 'the famous Rockwell College', where de Valera had first taught mathematics, and which had 'at last decided to adopt the Games of the Gael. I saw a letter from the President last week to that effect, it's a good healthy sign anyhow, Harry.'[82]

Each letter transmitted hearty greetings to or from a catalogue of Faughs and Gaels, along with comments on fixtures or results. As Harry explained to his old hurling Captain, Paddy Hogan: 'I follow the fortunes of the Faughs with a very keen interest. I get the results a week or so later and Ned keeps me in touch in his letters from home.'[83] These rather tedious recitals of names and scores were interspersed with wistful asides, conjuring up the cosy camaraderie of a chosen people. As Maurice Collins exclaimed: 'Oh what days, Har, we spent together going to the matches.'[84] Harry wrote in similar vein to Hogan: 'Believe me, Paddy, if I do not see you 'til 1920 I will always treasure the days spent with the Faughs as the happiest days of my life.' He allowed his imagination free play in embroidering reports of a game against Collegians:

I am glad to see Bob Mockler has as good a free Pack as ever, his fame has even penetrated Prison Walls. Hard luck the goal was disallowed. I notice you had hard luck in striking the cross bar in the last minute. I could see ye attacking fiercely with that determination for which the Faughs are famed. In my mind's eye could I see Tim [Gleeson] and his mouth going up and down with excitement. I can fancy the Boss swallowing his Cigar when ye took the lead, and I can hear the litany from dear old Tim as the Students drew level. It seems to me that ye had hard luck. Ye will meet again. God grant, may I be there to cheer ye.[85]

As ever, Harry contrived not merely to be read, but heard and felt as a physical presence by his readers.

If hurling was at the heart of Harry's competitive fantasies, he did not neglect other distractions. He urged O'Mahony to call into Maurice's new billiard saloon in Parnell Street and 'mesmerise the marker with your famous run thro' the side cush[ion] from Baulk, and before he recovers give him a lesson in screwing in from the centre spot. When he's brought round again, you might give him a lesson in gravitation in your approved style.'[86] Ned challenged him to a round on his release: 'Mossy is doing a roaring trade, no getting in to the Billiard Saloon. I must play you 50 when you come home, Har, your hand should be as steady as a rock.'[87] Maurice Collins himself suggested other diversions: 'A game of "Nap" is held at Luke's every Sunday night now. We are having a wee game here next Sunday. Try and be home for it.'[88] Even more alluring was the prospect of gambling on horses at the Baldoyle races, as they had both done on St. Patrick's Day in 1916: 'Of course I don't want, Harry, to make your teeth water, but my dear boy, all those happy days will return soon again.'[89]

Gaelic happiness was the distillation of a heady cocktail of sport, drink, song, and story. Harry had plenty of wise advice to offer from liquorless Lewes. He hoped that Bill Duggan would not 'burn himself again, 12 months in Dartmoor would suit him A 1'; and later expressed pleasure 'that dear old Wm is off the ra[?cke]t. The last time I saw Bill he was "game ball".' As for himself, he was 'on rations, I do not drink. ... You know the belly is a vital spot.'[90] In contrast, his correspondents regaled him with alcoholic memories and anticipations:

Do you remember the last night we had at 15 [Marino Crescent]? What a drunk; but what it will be when we all meet again. It will be 65 [Parnell St.] this time. How many bottles did I lower that night? ... I am off the 'beer' like yourself since the New Year, see what good example can do. This is my annual retreat, as you know, and indeed I badly wanted it, as since August last the pace was very hot.

We all had a 'wee drap', and your and Jack's health, and all the boys' was heartily drunk. The 'toasts' were too numerous. We were to see your Mother on Sunday evening, but as 'Charlie' was banged off to Swords in a car and the rest got into 'good form', it was unavoidably postponed till y'day.

Mick Kennedy's always asking for you, and wants me to tell you that he has got a special bottle in pickle for you on that *Eventful Day* when the 'Boys come Home'.[91]

Harry was however warned that 'stout is 4d. a bottle now and as you are aware a "bob" won't make a fellow sing v. much'; and that '6d. the pint is a bit thick, eh? *Black Cocoa* is much more economic.'[92] Wartime shortages and excise duties were threatening the very essence of Gaelic culture.

Harry, like several of his comrades, was a notable singer of sentimental nationalist ballads. Jack Shouldice was advised 'to keep practising "Galway Bay" for our reunion when the boys come home', while Maurice Collins recalled offering 'Hugh O'Donnell Roe' on the night of the great 'drunk' at no. 15.[93] Harry's party pieces included 'The Felons of Our Land', fondly remembered by his mother as 'one of your favourite songs, which I fervently pray we shall soon hear you sing again'. Likewise, Ned: 'Do you ever give a bar of that old song, "The Felons of our Land"? It's quite in keeping now, Har, "A Felon's Cap's the noblest crown an Irish head can wear." Anyway, you'll not wear it much longer, for out you'll have come.'[94] Harry was a serious enough performer to recognise superior talent in others, such as the 27-year-old 'shopman and singer' Gerald Crofts whose voice enlivened the exercise yard at Lewes.[95] Crofts was more compelling as an entertainer than as a rebel, since 'some affliction to his hands' forced him to wear woollen gloves at all times and prevented him from taking arms.[96] Harry's notebook contains a tribute 'to Gerald Crofts', contrasting the 'fields of Youth' that he personified with the dreary prospect of 'Old Man's Town':

> And surely here in England's jail
> To sing the Songs of Innisfail
> God sent a blessing rare to us
> A blue eyed fair haired Orpheus
> To cheer our sorrows, God's own Herald
> Eternal Blessings on you Gerald.[97]

Gaelic brotherhood entailed moonlit walks and quiet yarns as well as games and carousels. As Harry reminded Tim O'Mahony: 'Do you remember our trips to the Bull Wall in the good old times, my moonlight swim and the great chats we had, how we settled our ideals and benefited the world thereby? Dreams, Dreams, yet how lovely.'[98] But brotherly love was only one facet of the social and emotional world of a Gaelic athlete. Girls joined Gaels in parties and excursions, and hurlers often teamed up with their comrades' sisters. Harry pursued at least two sisters of prominent hurlers, while Kathleen eventually married a brother of one of the athletes in Lewes. Games provided the entrée to a busy social scene, clubbishly exclusive yet internally democratic, in which high-minded, firm-bodied youngsters could flirt, marry, or simply find easy comradeship.

Nostalgia for these unofficial 'Gaelic pastimes' suffuses Harry's correspondence. Kathleen recalled good times with Maurice Collins and his bride Celia:

> They are always talking of you and the grand day in Glendalough, and say it won't be long before you shall be with us down there again, D.V. I was not on that line since, and it brought back that happy morning on the station, everyone in good spirits, you the brightest of the lot, and waiting for the train at Rathdrum Station, all so happy and not a care in the world. Such changes in a short time.[99]

Harry too dwelt on his memories of Maurice and a previous girlfriend when writing to Cait Fraher:

> When we met at Richmond Barracks after the Surrender, we reviewed our many joyous days throughout Ireland. We spoke of Dungarvan, how Moss drove the Ass and Car round the square, how you brought the luck of the lawn[?] to him; and, in turn, of our Evening Service that never to be forgotten Sunday when we lost Maurice and Selina. We spoke of all this and wondered if we were ever to see again our friends.[100]

Marriage did not prevent Maurice himself from recalling the visit to Dungarvan with glee: 'Do you remember our last night there [?with] Miss Ryan and you mesmerising her, and then wound up by measuring noses. Our beautiful walk at night ... I was so hot, according to you, and how did you know was the innocent question. Oh – Har, what a lovely answer. The girls are as fond as ever of you, and if you have to do the round of them when released, you'd be better off in Lewes.'[101] For Harry and his circle, the GAA was shorthand for youth, happiness, friendship, and romance.

Despite his obvious talent for friendship with both sexes and his apparent predilection for housework, Harry sensed that women were always liable to spoil the Gaelic idyll. He was appalled to learn 'that Faughs are going to start a *Camog* team, would you believe it? Tom [Hogan] will be in his *alley* there all right, also Andy [Harty].'[102] He issued a solemn warning to the team's Captain:

> I dread the result of the Camog team. I speak from experience when I say that Camogie and Hurling teams are incompatible. I well remember the Rathmines days. We had a fine team till some one introduced the Camog. Then the fun started. We had all the boys carrying the girls' sticks and teaching the dears how to play camogie, etc. Result: no Hurling practice. Eventually the Camogie prospered. The Hurling declined. What few escaped matrimony were useless for Hurling. I cannot imagine Tom or John Connolly carrying out the Camog to the Park. He might carry the bottle[?] or the gloves. So, Paddy, beware of the Camogie. Don't let the Camogie league get a hold of this or it will go hard with me. It is a very nice game for girls, no doubt, but only for girls.[103]

As this homily implied, the ultimate threat to Gaelic brotherhood and joyous youth was not camogie but marriage. Rumours of marriage invariably prompted jocose comments:

> By the way, I hear that Watty is to marry Bess? I know, it's like the measles, the later you get it the worse it is. 'God help me when my turn comes.'

> It was a false alarm about Tom [Hogan]. He has no sign of settling down now. I believe the business is off altogether.[104]

Maurice Collins was almost apologetic in specifying his own motives for marriage:

Well, Harry, all I can do is to thank you and Jack [Shouldice] most heartily for your good wishes to Celia and self. Hadn't she the pluck of a 'Buck Cat' to marry such a fellow? It was to be did, I suppose. I cdn't have managed in my own, and as things have turned out it was best, to have acted as I did. I was game for anything, as you knew, before this.[105]

Harry was more enthusiastic when discussing this match with Cait Fraher: 'Mrs. Mossy is a lovely girl in every way. Maurice is very happy, every one who writes to me tells me he is more in love with his wife every day. An ideal couple.' Yet he could not resist recalling Maurice's disappearance with Selina on that 'never to be forgotten Sunday', or from noting that Selina too had 'joined the Army of Benediction. Tell her I wish her every joy from God to grace her wedded life, and that all her troubles may be little ones. Selina [erased: was] is a great sort.'[106] As his friends paired off and his own thirtieth birthday loomed, Harry meditated with pathos, if not originality, upon the imminent end of his well-spent youth:

> The fields of youth are filled with flowers
> The wine of youth is strong.
> What need have we to count the hours?
> The summer days are long.
> But soon we find to our dismay
> That we are drifting down
> The barren slopes that fall away
> Towards the foothills grim and gray
> That lead to Old Man's Town.[107]

Despite such misgivings, Harry was on the lookout. He was delighted by the attention he received from dozens of female admirers at Todd's, in addition to the lithe legion of Gaelic camp-followers. In return, he did not fail to send messages to 'all in the Counting House', as well as the particular favourites whom he termed 'my Sister of Charity', or alternatively his 'true Sisters of Mercy "to comfort the sorrowful"'.[108] He asked Ned, 'if handy to Todd Burns', to 'drop in and give them all my kind regards. Tell my four Lady friends how I blushed as you read their letters for me.' Ruminating upon recent marriages, he exclaimed: 'Great Bhoys. We stand a poor chance, when our time is up we shall be passed the freshness of youth. We might get some one to take pity on us. Anything going for you in the "Coortin' line"?'[109] Whatever Ned's prospects, Kathleen indicated that pity aplenty would be lavished on those lucky enough to have been convicts: 'There will be a great rush for all the heroes when you return. All the girls will want you, so I want to make sure of one of the noble boys, as they will be getting swelled heads from all the *hommage* they receive.'[110]

Meanwhile, Harry showed a particular interest in two women with impeccable Gaelic pedigrees. Ena (Christina) Shouldice hailed from Ballaghadereen, County Roscommon, but was working in 1916 at the Telegraph Office in Amiens Street. Her father had been a police sergeant, and her brothers Frank and Jack were civil servants until their incarceration in Stafford and Dartmoor respectively. Her own dismissal from the postal service was considered after the Rebellion; but, 'in spite of her anti-English sentiments and rebel connexion', she was merely transferred temporarily to Sligo. With her rural ties, urban experience, and genteel aspirations, Ena seemed tailor-made for Harry. However, she had several other suitors and was engaged by May 1916 to Alex McCabe, a teacher from County Sligo who represented Connacht on the IRB's Supreme Council.[111] Ena and her brothers often stayed in Marino Crescent, and were treated as part of the family. She sent 'smokes' to Lewes, which were not delivered, but Harry found her letter 'a treat, her description of the motor trip was classical'.[112] The Boland women assured Harry that Ena was 'looking splendid' and 'looking fine', while Ned reported that 'Ena has just got back from the Easter holidays, and need I say how well she looks'. Indeed he did not, since Harry's 'shrine' displayed the photograph which had caused such a sensation among 'both Warders and Convicts'.[113] He continued to relish her letters ('teeming with wit'), and undertook to 'write soon and thank her for prayers and as there is great virtue in a Sinner's Prayer will say an odd one in return'.[114] Ena and Kathleen may have been expressing more than sisterly affection when they discussed their imprisoned brothers during a Gaelic League excursion in early summer:

All the Keating Branch went for a trip up the mountains on Sunday. We were at the top of the Three Rock Mountain, it was very pleasant. Ena and I were thinking how much you would have enjoyed it, and were thinking of you locked up in your cell at 4.30, when you should only be enjoying yourselves.[115]

Ena's feelings would be put to the test when Harry visited Roscommon after his release.

Cait (or 'Cauth') Fraher from County Waterford also belonged to a prominent family of Gaels, though her father's service was with the IRB rather than the RIC. Dan Fraher of Dungarvan was a founder and long-standing Treasurer of the GAA, becoming Jim Boland's close ally in the Fenian faction and Harry's Godfather.[116] The Frahers and the Bolands often stayed at each other's houses, and Harry was kept up to date with Cait's development. Kate Boland described her as a 'lovely girl, grown tall and graceful, and I feel to have known her all her life, such a nice open manner, and her father is such a fine character'. Kathleen, who probably had other partners for Harry in mind, simply reported that 'Cait Fraher is in good form and is always asking about you'.[117] Harry's own attitude towards Cait may be judged from the uncharacteristically stiff letter which he drafted in his prison notebook, ostensibly to thank 'dear C.' for her 'beautiful and acceptable' rosaries. After this peroration, he set the romantic mood with a celebration of birdsong:

'Tis a glorious evening, such an evening as you often get in Dungarvan in May. The birds are singing an everlasting paen [sic.] of joy pouring out from their mouths, the melody of heaven rejoicing in their freedom. One thing our gaolers cannot do, they can't stop the birds singing, or stop the sun from shining, and so we poor prisoners are cheered by the lovely songs of birds, and the sun which creeps into my cell about 7.0 p.m. So, my dear, you see I am facing west, and often I watch the sun sink in the west. My heart goes with it, and in fancy I see again all those dear to me in my western land. I know they are thinking of us and praying that God may lighten our load, and surely all those good prayers of good girls and women are heard for me here.[118]

Remarking that his exacting mother had been 'quite captured' by her charm, he proceeded to imagine Cait's presence through her letter: 'It was just as if I heard you talk in your sweet Southern accent.' After a brief swagger about his own lack of 'superfluous flesh' and his captaincy of the Lewes hurling team, he returned to more exalting matters:

To the fair ladies who sent their love, I'll return to the full. I note with joy that the Nuns are included, splendid women. Their heroism in Dublin during Easter was marvellous. One incident will shew you what truly Irish hearts they have. We were engaged at a barricade, and during a lull in the fight, a mother came in blustering and tried to bring one of our boys home. He tried to comfort her, but in vain; when one of our Angels came and told the mother that she should be proud to have her son fighting for his country, and pointed out how wrong it was to try to bring him home. She succeeded, and so rendered us a great service. Other incidents showed the devotion of our saintly Irish women and priests, which I hope to tell you when the day comes.

The shamrock that Cait had sent him for Patrick's Day was still in his book, and he hoped 'to keep it for aye'.[119]

It was probably to Cait that 'An Beolanach' addressed two stanzas to his 'own dear Girl', happy 'that I can call / This treasure mine, yes mine, in all / That I may offer'. Whether she received this tribute is unknown:

77

Her form divine, her face so fair
Her modest eye and glorious hair
Her shapely foot and lovely arm
Her winsome smile and melting charm
Her carriage proud as any queen
Yet gentle she of happy mein
Her laugh and voice are as the linnet
Her every look has music in it
With teeth like rows of shining pearls
And rose bud mouth has my Dear Girl.[120]

Harry's year in prison had clearly failed to isolate him from friends, family, or his familiar worlds of work, play, and romance. He had used correspondence and imagination to reinforce these bonds and make his presence felt, as well as missed, at home. Imprisonment also conferred full membership of the new revolutionary élite on those, like Harry, who had been at the fringes of the conspiracy until their conviction. It created a further bond of brotherhood among the ex-convicts, and excellent opportunities for those blessed with social and political nous. Harry's letters suggest that he flourished in the closed society of Lewes. His correspondence refers by name to no less than thirty-eight convicts, nearly one-third of the total. Though many of these were already known to him through the IRB or the GAA, he made further alliances and connections while in prison. An example was Robert Brennan, soon to become Harry's close colleague in reorganising Sinn Féin. Whereas most prisoners were simply named in catalogues of good wishes, his new acquaintance featured prominently in a letter to O'Mahony:

[Henry] O'Hanrahan and Jack Shouldice send regards, also one of whom you often spoke, your friend of the Press table at Croke Park. You and Eddy met and spoke to him at many matches. Bob Brennan is his name, he comes from Wexford Town.[121]

Harry's circle differed strikingly in profile from the rest of the Irish convict population. Their mean age (thirty-three) was nearly five years older; they were more likely to have been awarded death sentences; more had been sent to Portland than to Dartmoor; and most were clerical or professional workers rather than tradesmen, shopkeepers, farmers, or labourers.[122] Harry himself was thus atypical of his own circle at Lewes, being a 29-year-old tradesman who escaped a capital sentence and was placed in Dartmoor. His upward mobility within the republican élite was presumably helped by consorting with his superiors in age, class, and revolutionary seniority. A notable absentee from this exalted circle was the prisoners' Commandant, Eamon de Valera. If Harry's veneration of his future 'Chief' began in prison, he kept uncharacteristically quiet about it.

Censorship did not seriously interfere with the transmission of political comment or news, partly because its main purpose was to inform Military Intelligence about republicanism rather than to keep republicans uninformed. Major Frank Hall of M.I.5, an Old Harrovian from Narrow Water, County Down, was entrusted with the task of reading all letters by convicts, providing explanations of any stoppages, and filtering out or copying selected passages. It was deemed 'particularly useful, in case of future claims for release, to preserve photographs of those letters which admit the writer's share in the Rebellion or acknowledge the justice of his sentence'.[123] Harry's letters were evidently never stopped and few passages were excised, but the censor would have found several unabashed admissions of his share in the Rebellion and adherence to its aims.[124] These included three messages directed to colleagues at Todd's. He endorsed the 'bloody sacrifice' in a letter to Bill Duggan:

You know, of course, I was not unprepared for this – 'tis often I told you that the day was coming. It was inevitable. Ireland had sunk so low that nothing but blood could save her, and it was freely given that she might live.[125]

Even so, Mary O'Keefe would be 'sorry to know that her tall friend was killed during the fight. Tell her he died like a Soldier. I used often joke her about him, God rest him.'[126] Harry showed no such respect for those killed by the rebels, such as the five defenceless members of the Irish Volunteer Training Corps who had been gunned down outside Beggars' Bush Barracks after their Easter Monday route march. He jested that Mr Morrison from Todd's had 'it in for me over his pals the G.R.s who distinguished themselves at Easter by h[?idin]g'.[127] The rebels had nothing to be ashamed of:

'Tis wonderful how the knowledge that one is suffering in a good cause lightens the load and makes even the dungeon bright. Thomas Davis's 'Nationality' tells how 'It gently shines thro' prison bars and sweetly sounds in caves', and so it is with me. I have no regret, and glory that I was associated even in a small way with the men of Easter Week. We don't fear to speak of Easter Week and we never shall[?].[128]

The letters express an exalted patriotism sustained by an unshaken belief in Ireland's destiny. As he told his mother: 'We all believe that we are of service to Ireland whilst here and knowing this we care not.'[129] He elaborated the point in high-flown rhetoric for Cait Fraher's benefit:

All are supremely happy, conscious that we have done no wrong, that we have vindicated the right of Ireland to her place among the nations, and knowing that the Irish nation is behind us, that we are as it were the soldiers in captivity of the New Ireland; and altho' our enemy seeks to degrade us by dressing us in the garb of felons, and treating us as they do their long sentenced criminals, they really degrade themselves.[130]

Though contemptuous of the 'enemy' in its conduct towards Ireland, Harry gave little hint of revulsion against the English people or their culture. After all, his enthusiasm for Irish-Ireland coexisted with an addiction to Kipling, and he maintained close contact with relatives and friends in Lancashire. In dreaming of the 'New Ireland', he did not allow racism to fortify his national pride. With Tim O'Mahony, he reflected upon their speculations before Easter Week: '[?What] was that prophecy you read out for me at Xmas Eve 1915? You remember the one [co]ncerning Ireland. We have seen the first part verified. I hope to see it consummated ere I return and, if so, those years will not have been in vain.'[131] The first anniversary of the Rebellion intensified his sense of exaltation: 'We had a Requiem Mass for Our Dead on Sunday last. Our Chaplain preached an oration, very beautiful, gave us all much joy.'[132]

Such sentiments were fortified by the relentless admiration and optimism of those writing from Ireland:

You have a clear conscience and God has blest you with brave hearts to bear the Cross, for Ireland's sake.

You are all suffering for a noble cause, so you may well feel proud.

You will enjoy your freedom more when it comes, knowing you have done your duty.

God bless and help him [Jack Shouldice] to keep up his health and spirits, and all the brave noble men who are suffering persecution for their country's sake.[133]

Whereas Harry never mentioned the executed leaders by name, his family joined zestfully in the sentimental cult by which their memory was sanctified. Kathleen attended a 'Mass for Éamonn Ceannt this morning at Church St, there were a great crowd at it all wearing black armlets with the colours, it is splendid sight'. She also sent Harry 'a little memory card ... of all fallen Volunteers'.[134] Her mother had previously composed a short sermon on Patrick Pearse, prompted by a photograph of Gerald's infant Enda:

Did you get small picture mounted on pin of the late proprietor of College of that name, God rest him? If ever saint lived on earth, it was He, and in time to come he will be canonised as Joan of Arc who was burnt at the stake for a witch; for next to God, we must love our country.[135]

Harry, through his rebellion and imprisonment, had been raised to the company of heroes, but not yet of saints.

His immersion in the ideals of Pearse and Pearse's models is obvious from 'Dublin Resurrexit', a salvo of rhyming couplets which 'q 90' evidently inscribed while still at Lewes. Having recalled John Mitchel's 'passionate curse' on the 'genteel dastards' of Dublin, and 'the foul disgrace of Emmet's death', he exclaimed:

> Oh! as the years have o'er thee rolled
> I prayed some great deed would yet be told
> To make the blood flow warm and fierce
> Thro' Erin's veins again. Oh Pearse
> 'Twas you with voice with pen and sword
> Who never faltered but gave the word
> To strike again tho' all hope had flown
> For Redemption comes by Blood alone.[136]

During the year of Harry's enforced absence, the very success of Pearse's strategy of bloody sacrifice seemed to make further such insurrections superfluous. Though slow to develop any alternative military strategy, those at home regrouped their fragmented forces in readiness for nothing in particular. Harry's informants made almost no reference to the military reorganisation which followed the release of the internees, except that Frank Shouldice sent his 'regards to F. Co.'s reps.' at Lewes, and Andy Harty sent a message hinting that the fickle Mick Crowe had been reappointed as IRB Centre for Limerick.[137] Harry received no decipherable news of the IRB's reconstruction, even though Gerald had refused an invitation from his adversary at Frongoch, Michael Collins, to join the reconstituted Supreme Council.[138] Nor was he alerted to the reorganisation of F Company 'early in the New Year', when another Lewes prisoner (Patrick Sweeney) was appointed *in absentia* as 2nd Lieutenant to Frank Henderson and Oscar Traynor.[139] Nevertheless, Harry looked forward in verse to a renewal of some form of military struggle against British rule:

> Oh keep your swords and rifles bright
> We yet have work to do
> For England strives with all her might
> Our country to subdue.
> Her terrors fail: she tries the smile,
> Conventions packed right through
> Be on your guard and watch awhile
> We still have work to do.[140]

Meanwhile, propaganda and politics dominated republican activity, and Harry followed with keen interest the amnesty campaign, the collapse of the Home Rule movement, and the mushrooming of Sinn Féin.

The closure of Frongoch raised the prospect of an early amnesty for the convicted rebels and raised morale at Lewes:

It was great news that Gerald arrived home safe and sound for Xmas. We heard on Xmas Eve that the Camp was broken up and all released. I am sure ye were delighted to have him home again. Frank's letter gave us a good idea of the fun they had at camp.[141]

Frank Shouldice had 'a pretty good time' on his return, but warned Harry that ex-prisoners faced problems of adjustment:

It felt a bit awkward at first *not* having to get up at 6 a.m., and being compelled to wear a collar and appear a bit civilized, but after a week or so I succeeded in suffering on in bed till 11 or 12 (and more'n that sometimes) and am now more or less civilized again![142]

The Government's refusal to extend clemency to the remaining convicts perplexed those at home: 'I hear all the Deportees are to come back. Everybody, *even Unionists* and Nationalists, are surprised at the authorities keeping you all prisoners so long, and asking the sense of it, unless to keep the bitterness here.'[143] However, as popular support for Sinn Féin expanded, an early amnesty seemed to Gerald inevitable: 'I don't think they can hold you much longer. The prospect of 80 Irish prisoners being returned for Irish constituencies will be too much of a sickener.'[144]

Kate Boland was alarmed by the mental state of one 'mere boy', fresh from Wormwood Scrubs: 'He looks well but appeared to me quite *dazed*, and it upset me wondering would you be like that. He spoke so low as though afraid of his own voice, I presume after the intense silence of the prison.'[145] There were more encouraging reports of 'six of the Athenry boys' who had been released early from Lewes and 'all looked in *Pink*. They told us that you were in great form, and as big as a house. You would find it hard to imagine they had just come from jail, they are a good *Ad* despite all the rotten treatment they are giving you.'[146] Yet, as she ruminated upon the state of the remaining convicts, Kate Boland came close to despair:

Poor Ena has just called and has heard that Jack is fading away, though keeping up his spirits. I suppose none will be released until their constitution is wrecked. I hear Gerald Crofts is being released a wreck also. God look down on you all and spare you – oh, it's dreadful. Mother.[147]

Harry's circle despised the veterans of the Irish Parliamentary Party and their attempts to salvage Home Rule from the wreckage of Easter. As T. P. O'Connor and Major William Redmond prepared for another futile attempt to secure for

Ireland 'the free institutions long promised to her',[148] Maurice Collins kept his tongue firmly in cheek:

> Now we are faced with a peculiar dilemma, we must have Home Rule, whether we like it or not. The Mother of Parliaments are to decree so on Wednesday next, at least so the *Daily Mail* and *Westminster Gazette* tell us. We are a peculiar country. Some of us wants Home Rule, others Colonial Legislatures, others Separatists, and so on, in fact it is good to be a member of such a community.[149]

A fortnight later, Collins contemplated the possibility of future American intervention at a peace conference, followed by a political settlement. Giving the term 'Hun' distinct meanings for Harry and the censor, Collins drew an analogy between the likely outcome of the Great War and the fight for Irish freedom. The comparison implied that a political compromise was the probable outcome of both conflicts:

> Without Ireland, the war can't be won, H., and win we must. Of course we may consent to a peace, but not at the moment. We have the Huns on the 'Run', and as long as that continues we can't dream of talking of peace. Then we haven't lost hope that America will defend the 'small' nationalities. If she doesn't, our faith and trust in America has been in vain, just as Sergeant Johnny Redmond['s] had been in Messrs. Asquith and Lloyd George.[150]

Harry, like many socialists but few republicans, was alive to the social and political opportunities created by the Great War, horrific though it was. When reminding O'Mahony of 'the great chats we had, how we settled our ideals and benefited the world thereby', he reflected: 'And how near that ideal, present events are forcing the classes. Rlys., mines and all sources of wealth are now, in the hour of danger, taken over for the Common Good. How many times have we done the same in our dream talks.'[151] Less sceptical than Maurice Collins, he expressed touching confidence in the power of a peace conference to deliver Irish freedom:

> My idea of a free and independent Ireland – not a paltry Home Rule or Colony but Ireland absolutely sovereign. How tenacious Ireland is to that idea notwithstanding all the attempt to barter her soul away. She stands to-day as ever passionately demanding her freedom and I feel sure she will get it ere the war ends, as all the nations are pledged to the rights of small nations. If this be granted then under God to the men who died in Easter Week let the credit belong.[152]

Yet Britain seemed unaccountably indifferent to the inevitable course of history. As the Government struggled to counteract international outrage at its administration of Ireland, Harry gloated over its embarrassment in early May:

> The Huns are 'quare wans'. They seem to rule the Land, Sea, and Air just now, it is very hard on Poor John Bull. ... Yes, 'The mills of God grind slowly yet they grind exceeding small'[153] and England is about to reap the harvest she sowed in blood and tears in Ireland. The Irish brought their vengeance with them, and England feels it to-day in America, feels it in Australia, where the Irish vote defeated Conscription, and kept Australia away from the Empire Conference,[154] and God be praised feels it worse of all in Ireland. What a figure England cuts to-day with all her prate of freedom, filling the jails of Ireland with men, aye, and women because they dare sing their National Songs, deporting others without charge or trial, and keeping 120 here in Lewes as *Convicts*, the last spasm of the Tyrant. I feel certain that Ireland's Star is up, and that New Zealand traveller when he has sketched St Paul's can plane over to Ireland and see the oldest nation in Europe come into her own again. And all the Sea Divided Gael shall join in one grand Alleluia at the Resurrection of Caitlín Ní Hullachain [*sic.*], and the blood of all who died for her from 1130 to 1916 shall flow through her veins in never ending life. And is it not a grand thing to feel that, be it never so small a manner, we gave a helping hand in the glorious work.

The forthcoming nationalist conference in the Mansion House would be an 'eye opener to many', and victory in the by-election for South Longford would 'give Ireland a very strong hand at the Peace Conference'.[155]

In the same month, the IRB's Supreme Council decided to organise support for Irish participation in the anticipated post-War settlement, Dr. Patrick McCartan being its first 'emissary' to the United States.[156] On Sunday, 3 June, as he awaited removal to Maidstone, the prospect prompted Harry to compose a reverie on 'Ireland at the Peace Conference':

> What is that? Proudly flinging its folds to the sun
> And guarded by men both stalwart and bold
> Why comes to the gathering nations among
> This banner unknown of Green White and Gold?
> Say is it the sign of some new race arose
> From the chaos of battle and slaughter untold
> Who snatched at the victory while fighting their foes
> And come with their colours of Green White and Gold?

Far from it, as the poet explained: his nation was 'both glorious and old', though 'scourged, outraged, degraded, forlorn and cold'. Ireland would bring to the assembled powers her 'right / to nationhood supreme', and a just settlement would surely follow.[157]

Ned was even more optimistic in predicting Ireland's future: 'Did you hear of the big Revolution in Russia? Czar and all the crowd "hopped it" first thing. Looks good.' He looked forward to further setbacks for the Allies: 'America's getting a bit too hot for their fancy, also we at home. The German U Boats were all round the Irish waters last week, and there is a rumour afloat of Harland's and Wolfe's [sic.] being shelled in Belfast. That's bringing the War nearer home.' By mid May, Ned's tone was euphoric:

> The country is just grand now, Harry, that little Scrap on Easter Week was Heaven sent, for it saved the country from the 'Traitors and Tricksters'. They are well on the run now, and we will see to it that they're kept on the run till ould Ireland's free from the Centre to the Sea, eh Har. As you say, the nation is indeed behind you to the last *man*, even the A.O.H. and U.I.L. are turning up trumps to the call of Freedom. So you may well be proud of all your sufferings, for the Cause is great, and is going to win, and we are going to win, sure as night follows day.[158]

Ned's apocalyptic tone, redolent of heady evenings in Leech's or Vaughan's, should have quelled any lingering doubts in Lewes about Ireland's ability to win freedom.

Harry and his comrades were heartened by the widespread sympathy for their cause even among former opponents, which seemed to justify their temerity in rebelling without popular support or prospect of victory in 1916. As Harry remarked to Bill Duggan: 'There are quite a number of people turned Sinn Féin since our Clatter and thus we did accomplish the Resurrection of the old [?myth].'[159] Gerald confirmed that sentiment was changing, even at the Crooksling sanatorium: 'The majority of the patients are our way. Of course, there are a few wrecks from the War, some of whom are all for the Empire.'[160] The focus of political excitement was the by-election campaign in South Longford, where Joe McGuinness from Lewes was put forward by Sinn Féin with the slogan 'put him in to get him out'. McGuinness, a 'rather diminutive' fiddler and draper aged forty, had no obvious credentials except his birthplace and enthusiasm for Gaelic games, since he did not belong to the IRB and had received a sentence of only three years for his modest part in the Rebellion.[161] His nomination by a committee of separatists had initially been opposed by most of the prisoners, who feared that their republicanism would be compromised by seeking election to the House of Commons. Thomas Ashe and Harry were the only prisoners who conceded from the first that such decisions should be left to the 'Home Organisation'.[162]

Harry's correspondence makes no reference to this debate, but confirms the critical significance of the campaign for Sinn Féin's emergence as a political force. Its election agent was Dan McCarthy, a prominent Fenian and Gael who was to become President of the GAA between 1921 and 1924. Andy Harty informed Harry that 'Dan Mack is very cagey. Same as ever if not worse. He is a marvel, away at Longford working for McGuinness for last fortnight. Of course he was in Roscommon also.'[163] By early May, the Bolands were 'anxiously looking forward to Wednesday next, to S. L'ford, though it will be a miracle if Mr. McGuinness wins as there are such terrible odds against him – 20 M.P.s, Messrs. Dillon, Devlin, etc. etc. all telling the old people they will lose the Old-Age Pensions, etc. if Mr. McGuinness is returned, and several hundred police sent down fully armed'.[164] Kathleen's perspective was characteristically prayerful: 'Ena and a good many girls I know have made novenas that Mr. McGuiness may get in, so if prayers have any effect he will surely get in. There is great excitement about it. There's a lot of soldiers' women paid for to throw stones at our people. One or two ladies were hit, Countess Plunkett and Mrs. T. Clarke were hurt but are recovering. The police looked on while they were throwing them and never offered to stop them.'[165] Ned, by contrast, was aggresively confident:

> Well, Har, there's great gas over here with the S. Longford Election, and before this letter gets you, Joe McGuinness will be an M.P. You can congratulate him for me right now. The Party are making a hell of fight for they know[?] it's their last kick. They are sending money round like snuff at a wake, and of course they are well supplied with funds (of course you know who from); but they can take both themselves and their rotten money to blazes, for they're going to be blotted out. Even their own 'Hibs' are turning over. They fired J. D. Nugent out of his own hall in Longford, and it's nearly time too. The party emblem now is a green flag and a Union Jack. Joey Devlin is doing a lot of flag wagging too, also all his 'separation allowances' *women*. All the boys back from deportation in England are gone down to Longford to help to win the fight for freedom.[166]

McGuinness's narrow victory on 9 May, when he upset Patrick McKenna by fewer than 40 votes after two recounts, was scarcely definitive. Even so, as Gerald reflected: 'Sth. Longford is an affair of the most far-reaching importance as it endorses our action in Easter Week and, to use the hackneyed MP's expressions, gives us a "Mandate" to press Ireland's claim for an independent Republic before the Powers of Europe.' Like many veterans of the Rebellion, Gerald had largely reconciled himself to adopting the tactics, though not the principles, of the despised Home Rulers:

> On the whole, electioneering is a bad business, such rotten things are done, but unfortunately it seems the only way of getting the voice of the nation, at least the only recognised way. The franchise is so limited that it is only the opinion of a small percentage. If all the people in Sth. Longford had

votes, the result would have been 4 to 1 in our favour. I believe Dan McCarthy won the election. He demanded some votes which had gone astray, and would not be put off till they were produced. 150 stray votes were then discovered which put McGuinness in.[167]

Provided that enough votes with the right marking were 'discovered', their provenance did not matter. Kathleen was sure that Harry would be as delighted as herself, and reported that McGuinness's wife 'was in a state of excitement as we all were. I suppose you heard we had our flags out of all the Irish houses of note, all that day.' Ned was predictably exultant:

You must have had some div*arsion* when you heard the result of the Longford Election, did you convey my congrats to the new M.P. as I told you? Tell him I backed him and won a couple of bob, and drank his health on the head of it too. It's a pity you were not there to join us, but as John E. [Redmond] says, the 'Day is not far distant'. Of course his day is done; the country has awakened at last and given him the Order of the Boot. We are going to run all '*Convicts*' in future for all elections and, of course, will sweep the boards with same. You will be the next on the list, so prepare.[168]

Harry himself remarked to Cait Fraher that 'South Longford has shewn the world, that Ireland honours the felons'.[169] Even before their release, often against their inclination, the prisoners were being transmuted into politicians.

The prisoners were well aware that, on their release, they would face formidable problems of adaptation to the 'New Ireland'. Harry's native city remained in ruins. A former colleague at Todd's exclaimed: 'Poor Dublin you would hardly recognise it now. They have not started to rebuild yet. Some of the shops have little temporary structures erected on the old site, like what they had at the exhibition in 1907.'[170] A few months later, this was confirmed by a returned internee: 'Well, Harry, this old town of ours is certainly a bit shook. I hardly recognised O'Connell St. on my arrival, there is so little of it left from the Pillar down to the bridge. Some earthquake!!'[171] The Rebellion had worsened the wartime stagnation of the city's economy, despite Harry's hope of future employment for Ned in 'the Rebuilding' and his confidence in the economic benefits of rebellion: ' "Bis" should be moving soon in Dublin as the Housing and Rebuilding Scheme goes on. When the builders are busy it means general prosperity.'[172] He learned from Maurice Collins that 'things are very quiet, and a good deal of unemployment. If the breweries are closed a lot more of it must follow.' His mother confirmed that 'trade in Dublin is at a standstill', viewing the economic future with maternal pessimism: 'No work, not commenced to rebuild yet, and prices of food and all necessaries of life enormous prices, God help the Poor! I don't know how they exist, or [what] will be the consequences, but the "Darkest hour is that before the Dawn".'[173] Such bleak reports did not dissuade Harry from yearning in comical vein for his home town. He told Tim O'Mahony that his letter had come 'like a "breeze from Ballybough", I don't mean [Fai]rview, altho' the perfume of the Sloblands to me now would be the sweetest that ever ble[w. I] would gladly exchange the ozone of the Sussex Downs for dear old Anna Liffey at her worst.'[174]

The moment of homecoming was a recurrent theme for Harry and his correspondents. When still in Dartmoor, he had wallowed in the prospect of an outdoor reunion with his sister and friends:

> We are going to [have] a picnic on our release in return for all the prayers. So I hereby invite all your friends and the children of M[?]. We will hire Thompson's charabanc and make Glendalough again. We may let Father McDonnell [sic.][175] come if he agrees to go with the driver. We will live that never-to-be-forgotten day of last year again. Gosh, that was some day. The drive, the boat, the saint's bed, the wish, the jarvey and the songs. And then, the railway trip home. We were a happy party and we will be again, D.V. I won't be the Poor Lone Boy next time so keep an eye out for me.[176]

Kathleen responded to this reverie in kind:

> We shall have a fine time when [you] come home, God sent it may be soon. Anna, Celia and Ena say they will have a gala time, as many 'Clatters' as you like. There is a rush on the invitations to the picnic, it will take all the Char a Bancs in Thompson's to hold all the friends. Ena says we are getting into training for you and Jack. So you will want to keep in good form to do some of our walks and we shall not have you breaking the rules by going home in the tram.[177]

In May 1917, Kathleen was still contemplating their reunion: 'As Ena often says, there is never true joy without sorrow; so we will, please God, be all happy together again, and will feel more gay, if possible, knowing you done your duty as an Irishman for Ireland's holy cause.'[178] In drier vein, Gerald hoped that 'you will spend a little time with me among the mountains when you come home, and we can have a few talks about our experiences'.[179] Maurice Collins was 'anxiously awaiting to hear of your homecoming and won't we have a Clatter. When I think of the past and the rattles we used to have, it makes me sad; but then look at the honour and glory of it all and one becomes as proud as a bantam cock.' Soon, they would once more be 'doing Howth, Lucan or Bray on Sunday evenings', and having 'a damn good Clatter' about matters 'that are impossible, at this time, to hope'.[180] Harry himself reminded Bill Duggan of 'the Yarns we had coming back in the train', looked forward to seeing the County Final with Paddy Hogan, hoped for 'a swim with Maurice long before 1920', and urged Cait Fraher to 'bring me up to see the good Nuns who are praying for us, when I do come home'.[181] On 17 June 1917, Harry came home at last.

V

Celebrity

ON Sunday morning, 17 June 1917, a crowd of well-wishers assembled at Dublin's North Wall to welcome Harry and the heroes, only to learn that they had been diverted to Kingstown (Dún Laoghaire). The crowd therefore rushed to Westland Row in time to meet the train bearing many of Ireland's future rulers. Among those present were Kathleen Boland and Ena Shouldice, the glamorous Gaelic Leaguer who had figured so prominently in Kathleen's letters to Lewes. In an unguarded letter which never reached her brother in New York, having been intercepted by the censor, Ena celebrated the return of Jack Shouldice and his comrades. The public welcome had been simply 'immense, nothing like it seen in Dublin before':

> When the convict train got in to Westland Row everyone lost their heads. We were carried off our feet. I expected to see old Jack with drawn face, sunken eyes etc. but he actually looked as if he were returning from a picnic, brown and plump. He and a few more looked miraculously well but the majority were haggard and ill.[1]

The lads from Lewes lost little time in putting to the test Kathleen's prediction that 'there will be a great rush for all the heroes when you return'.[2] Harry's first day of freedom was predictably sociable. After breakfast at Fleming's Hotel in Gardiner's Row and a visit to the Mansion House, where he was photographed with the Lord Mayor (Laurence O'Neill), Harry brought a score of his ex-convict brethren to celebrate their liberation at Marino Crescent. These included Thomas Ashe, the melodious Gerald Crofts, and Jack Shouldice.[3]

When Jack returned to his home town in North Roscommon, he did not travel alone. As Ena wrote: 'I got special leave when I heard Harry Boland – a fellow prisoner of Jack's – and his brother and sister were coming down to B. [Ballaghadereen] with Jack!' The local reception of the ex-convicts was 'splendid for B. Better than John R. [Redmond] M.P. in his heyday! Local band, procession, torchlight – and tar barrels and illuminations, speeches etc.! J. doesn't like all the fuss he gets – but he has to stick it for propaganda work. He's in the pink and so are all of us D.G.' Their visit was a heady mixture of politics and festivity: 'Jack is home just three weeks and for the most part he and Harry B. have been holding meetings and forming Sinn Féin Clubs all over the district! You wouldn't believe J. could stand up and make a speech. Well we heard him and it wasn't bad.' The house party ended on 10 July, Jack having 'proceeded to Ennis Co. Clare for de Valera's election: another convict! He is expected to be returned. If so it will be the third!'[4]

All was well, for two days later Harry received a telegram from a second devotee in Ballaghadereen, a Mrs Condon: 'Hearty congrats up Erin valour virtue and honour embodied in de Valera and Harry Boland'.[5] The coming of the heroes had renewed a fierce competition in republican hospitality between the Shouldices and the Condons, who in Ena's opinion tended to 'put it on thick'. They had 'an air of condescension' which made the policeman's daughter prickle:

> Besides they're not sincere and are only pro Irish because it suits their game. There's no stability in them. They're among the higher fry at present, entertaining Count Plunket[t], Countess Markaveiz [*sic*.] and so on. All those rebels who come west are 'copped' at once by them and 'taken in'. We are barely noticed. Not that we want it – but one hates to see others reaping the good sown by themselves. Bridie is engaged to an officer in English army. If she were Irish she'd give him up same as I did five years ago. And it's still a struggle to keep it down!![6]

Being truly Irish and relentlessly female required sacrifice, which in turn fostered seething social and personal grievances.

Though Ena, unlike Jack, had retained her post in the civil service after the Rebellion, she was restive and preoccupied. For much of her working life, she had been pursued around the Telegraph Office in Amiens Street by a Superintendent Doyle, who had his 'position' but 'no soul – nationality or anything'. Ena was fed up: 'He is too old and I don't care much for him at all. He's kept at it so long (five years!) and a few times last summer [when] I felt desperately lonely and miserable I was inclined to favour the idea – but when I was myself absolutely couldn't bear to think of it. I'm weary refusing and snubbing him but he's like India rubber – rises again every time just as tho' nothin' happened!!'[7] The advent of Jack's comrade suggested a way out of the Superintendent's clutches:

> You may probably hear of my Engagement soon to Harry Boland, one of the Bolands at the Crescent. You didn't see him as he was in with Jack. I rather liked him before the Rebellion – used to go to dances etc. with Jack and crowd. He has nothing at present – but will get back his job in Todd's as a cutter – soon. He doesn't want to go back, however. Wants something better. There's a few to go over [to America] and he may be one – but it's not fixed up. If it comes off you will meet him. He's a bluff hearty fellow – has a very bad temper tho'! and isn't quite as refined as I would like. He's a wee bit rough. Anyhow I can't get what I really want – it's not in my

sphere here – and people have told me I'm too hard pleased – and I better not go on refusing each one. There were a few others – I don't know whether I told you – none of them were much to look at or ever had anything!! If I was once settled perhaps I should be content. I'm really afraid to go on with it fearing H. would not understand me – or be kind enough always. He rushed me into promising him and now I feel nervous.

From Ena's genteel perspective, marriage to a Boland had other drawbacks: 'Am not struck on the rest of the family. The female portion are not too refined.' Then again, Ena was strangely enamoured of

that blessed Englishman whose face you didn't like – always has come back on three or four occasions when I had such an offer and thought I was happy. I was quite happy for first week or two after H. and fixed it up and now I find this Englishman disturbing my peace once more and imagine no one understands me like him. He was altogether more refined than anyone I've known and maybe that's the reason I can't forget him. Of course I'd never marry an Englishman – but there are plenty of Irishmen I wouldn't marry either. Anyhow if all goes well and I'm fairly happy – it may come off this time next year. His mother isn't aware of it yet. She has other views (£. s. d. ones) for H. and I fancy she won't be pleased. It's all on the laps of the Gods anyway.[8]

Their engagement lapsed, but Harry's friendship and collaboration with the Shouldices was unimpaired. By December 1918, Ena was working with Harry at Sinn Féin headquarters, while Jack, who unlike Harry had just secured a wife, spent three weeks 'sprinting' with his old comrade on the election trail.[9] No harm done, so.

Harry's involvement with Ena Shouldice had evidently not deterred Cait Fraher's family in Dungarvan, for in early October 1917 he was presented with a fulsome address in Irish signed by her father Dan Fraher and other officers of the local Sinn Féin club. Along with Count Plunkett and the Liverpool Irish Irelander, Piaras Béaslaí, he was extolled as one of the 'leaders of the Gael who suffered much for Ireland', enduring the severest laws and punishments to remain 'still undaunted to work for Ireland'.[10] According to Kevin Boland, Harry courted Cait during 1918 with sufficient enthusiasm to achieve a formal engagement.[11] Early in the same year, however, he met another stylish, spirited, and worldly lass while staying at the Greville Arms Hotel at Granard, County Longford. Catherine Brigid Kiernan, then twenty-six, was one of four famously nubile sisters who held court in their brother's hotel, entertaining and captivating myriad visiting Sinn Féiners and Volunteers.[12] To judge by the tone of her earliest surviving letter, dated 3 February 1919, their friendship was still casual enough:

Dear Harry – Will yourself and Mick [Collins] come down here for the weekend? Maud's friend is here, and we wld. all like to see you again. You can look up the trains yrself and I suggest that you shld. come on the 1.30 Saturday, it arrives about 4 o'c. The remnants of the trains go to Edgeworthstown. So just send a wire to say what train we are to meet you [sic.]. Please don't disappoint! Le grad [with love] – Kit Kiernan.[13]

On the day of writing, both men were otherwise preoccupied in the vicinity of Lincoln Prison, so Kit probably was disappointed.

Michael Collins, the former financial clerk who had left London shortly before the Rebellion, was already entangled with Kit's younger sister, Helen. Though Harry had reputedly shepherded his fellow Gael into the London IRB eight years earlier, Collins was not one of the Frongoch internees who figured in his prison correspondence. Over the next two years, however, they recognised their own strengths in each other and joined forces in an irresistible combination. Their friendship became a symbol of republican brotherhood in practice. Within a few weeks of his release, Harry was hotly defending Collins against Gerald's impression from Frongoch that he was 'a braggart and a bully'. Robert Brennan, who was staying with the Bolands, used this episode to dramatise his own perhaps retrospective distrust of Collins, embroidering the tale with Gerald's impersonation as he 'strode about the room boastfully, heaving his shoulders and tossing his head'. Harry, three years older than 'Mick', sagely responded: 'Never mind, he's young. He'll get over it. He's a great fellow.' Brennan considered Harry to be far superior to Collins in both intellect and 'political acumen', surmising that Harry was 'courting Mick so as to form a link between the I.R.B. and Dev, to whom he was already devoted'.[14]

Even those who supported Collins after the 'Split' over the Treaty, such as Piaras Béaslaí, recognised Harry's ability and the power of the bond between them:

In prison and afterwards, ... his daring spirit, pugnacity, energy and enthusiasm began to bring him to the front. He was a hard worker, a stubborn fighter, warm-hearted, generous, unselfish, sociable, intensely human; in many respects, a man after Collins's own heart, and having much in common with him. He lacked, however, the judgment and sagacity that lay at the back of Collins's fierce energy and impetuous manners. His friendship with Collins had already begun; but it was not until the following year that it ripened into an ardent attachment.[15]

Batt O'Connor, a wealthy builder of 'safe houses' who worshipped Collins, noted their shared lack of affectation:

A warm friendship had sprung up between him and Harry Boland. They were about the same age, and they were both high-spirited, unconventional and of convivial habits. While he always got on well with men, Michael Collins was naturally shy in what is called society, and the gay, irresponsible, easy-mannered company kept by Harry was congenial to him.[16]

Still diffident and quiet-spoken with strangers, the young Collins left a favourable impression even upon police observers. In August 1917, his description was '28 years, 5 ft. 10 ins. high, well built, square shoulders, dark brown hair, round face, clean shaven, pale complexion, wears grey tweed suit and brown trilby hat'. By March 1919, he had reportedly grown an inch, elongated his face to an 'oval', developed a 'fresh complexion', and acquired a fawn overcoat. The active youth of that period was scarcely recognisable in the sagging figure observed not long before the Truce of July 1921, when Collins's true age was thirty:

Height about 5 ft. 8 ins. Broad and heavy in build. Weighs 12 or 13 stone. Must have been a powerful man a few years ago; now heavy in movement and greatly out of condition. Coarse, pale face and heavy jowl. Clean shaven. Looks like a publican. Eyes, stern; and have a purpose in them. Over hanging eyebrows. Except for the eyes he is now quite unlike earlier photograph. Looks about 40. Now wears a moustache (October 1920). Age, 35.[17]

Revolution had evidently taken its toll.

In the heady days before the terror of 1920–1, however, Collins and Harry had helped each other to keep fit while 'on the run'. When hiding during 1918 in the Dublin Distillery, which was managed by Diarmuid Lynch's brother, they 'played games' on the concrete floor and 'engaged in many wrestling matches'. With Luke O'Toole's blessing, they would often take exercise at Croke Park, where 'Harry and Mick had the whole playing pitch on which to exercise with the camán'. According to their fellow-fugitive Seán Ó Murthuile (John Hurley), 'they were both of that buoyant, spirited, reckless type that made for happy companionship'.[18] Yet their games were sometimes cerebral, for Béaslaí 'vividly' remembered Harry's performance as an angel's advocate, when the two desperadoes debated 'the relative efficiency of moral and physical force':

Boland, the most pugnacious of men, on this occasion championed pacifism, only passive resistance to evil and the triumph of the spirit over brute force. He maintained that the greatest man was the man who gave up his life in resisting evil without using force against it. When Collins caustically remarked that he should be the last man to preach a doctrine so contrary to his practice, Boland retorted with spirit that he knew he was unable to live up to his ideal, but that did not prevent his regarding the man who could as his truest hero.[19]

For devout rebels such as Harry, the life and death of Christ provided an awkward and unsettling precedent.

While Harry basked in the glamour of the returned convict, his family supplied a variegated supporting cast. Ned remained restless and unpredictable, sending enigmatic scrawls from exotic locations as he pursued adventure and riches as a merchant seaman. In a typical undated missive, despatched in care of the Dennis Lumber Co., via Cape Horn, he announced that 'I have reached the good old West Coast after a great hike and many adventures across the grand old Continent of Americkey.' He had just come down from Oregon, where 'I was working at my old game with a bunch of Government Surveyors, laying out roads for the Indians, and their squaws and papooses.' He was thinking of moving on to China, or Japan, or 'maybe a flying visit to Dear Old Dublin', for 'the wanderlust is strong upon me still'. A postcard from Alexandria reassured Gerald that mines and torpedoes held no terrors for Ned: 'How's Crooksling looking, also the Mrs and family, any addition? Well Jer this is where you should have a look at, it's grand the East. We just got safely through from Canada. *Fritz* sends his compliments.'[20]

Kathleen stayed in Marino Crescent as the supportive unmarried sister, guarding Harry from capture, passing on messages, storing weapons, and fulminating against British misrule. In late 1918, the postal censor observed that her letters to Con O'Donovan (a veteran of Lewes and inmate of Usk) were 'intensely hostile and sarcastic' in tone, 'denouncing in bitter terms the project of Conscription in Ireland'. As she told O'Donovan:

> John Bull I am sure does not know what on earth to do with you Irish hottentots, you are really a thorn in his poor old side. And now Con a cara he thinks he will clear the earth of the wild Irish by Conscription. But seriously he forgets that there is a just God in heaven and he shall look after our little Ireland and her people will continue to live when every other filthy Freemason gang will be gone west.[21]

For Kathleen and her comrades, untroubled by guilt or doubt, Ireland's battle with Britain was an uncomplicated struggle between virtue and evil.

Gerald was preoccupied after his release with building a family and career. As a 'full member' of the Amalgamated Society of Engineers in 1917, he had attained some seniority as well as a decent salary from the Dublin Corporation.[22] Kevin, the second of his six children, was born in October 1917, others following in December 1920 and May 1922. In due course, their dates of baptism were inscribed in a Bible which Gerald had filched from Belfast Prison, having been rearrested and court-martialled in June 1918 for illegal drilling.[23] Gerald had rejoined the Volunteers, eventually becoming Commandant of the 7th Dublin Battalion just before the Truce of July 1921.[24] After his conviction and removal from Mountjoy to Belfast, on 22 June 1918, he became involved in a protracted campaign of disruption and window-breaking, which resulted in the withdrawal of the privileges normally allowed to Irish prisoners in consequence of previous confrontations. Gerald was sentenced to a fortnight's solitary confinement on bread and water, but within three days had been let off without the nuisance of a hunger-strike. As at Frongoch, he refused to make extravagant claims of personal maltreatment, though he did report having heard 'some frightful screams' from fellow inmates, and noted that several of those attending Mass in handcuffs were 'in a filthy condition owing to not being able to use their hands when nature called'.[25] With typical stoicism, he wrote to his mother in August that 'I don't want anything in the clothing line; I never use overcoat or hat, and this suit will do till the winter sets in, when I will have to send for my blue one as it is much warmer; I will have to manage a new one when released.' Once again, Gerald could not escape the celebrity of his younger brother: 'I had a visit from two priests to-day who wanted to know where Harry was; they both knew him.'[26] Gerald remained in Belfast for his full term, doggedly declining to embellish the atrocity stories which his brother was circulating with such effect on Sinn Féin's behalf.

Harry, unlike Gerald, had lost his post in the course of his prolonged incarceration. Since revolutionary prestige did not as yet carry any income, Harry set about securing a livelihood. Six weeks after his release, he informed the Irish National Aid Association that he had not been reinstated at Todd's: 'If your Committee made a request to my late firm I feel sure they would meet you. I am ready and willing to resume as soon as possible.' Better still, he would appreciate help in setting up on his own:

I am depending solely on your Committee. I had some few pounds before Easter Week all of which has gone to keep the home. I had hoped to establish a business of my own some day. I also understand that your Association are prepared to advance money on guarantees. I think I could satisfy you that my chances and connections would be a good investment if you so desire. ... I must thank you for your good work for the dependents of the Men of Easter Week. The one sorrow I had during the early stages of my imprisonment was for the helpless ones at home. It lightened the load when I knew they were being looked after by you. I will always consider it my duty as long as life lasts to help any one who may have suffered for the cause of Ireland.[27]

According to a less polished draft of this letter in his prison notebook, Harry's 'few pounds' had 'very naturally disappeared' during his incarceration, justifying a disarmingly breezy request for aid: 'I understand you are prepared to assist any man who desires to start in Biz. As I have a very big Connection Lay and Clerical I would have no fear of failure.'[28]

By September, Harry had selected 'a suitable house' in Middle Abbey Street, at £150 per annum: 'If your Council would assist me in starting I could get going at once.' He had discussed the requisites with Fred Allan, his father's ally and fellow-conspirator who had emerged from political oblivion to help organise Irish National Aid after the Rebellion. When pressed for detail, Harry estimated his initial expenses at £125 for 'fitting up, lighting, and workshop accessories', along with £300 for stock, 'as the price of woollens has now gone very high'. His future success was assured by his established networks of influence and clientage: 'I have a very large connection including a Clerical one as I have been working the several Colleges of Maynooth, All Hallows and Holy X. Again I am President of the Co. Dublin G.A.A. and am well known throughout the country in connection with the G.A.A.'[29] The rather unsatisfactory outcome was a grant of £200 from an American Relief Fund administered by Irish National Aid, but restricted to the support of convicted rebels and their dependents. Harry deemed the grant 'altogether inadequate' to cover his initial rental, shop-fitting, and stock, requesting a supplementary grant or loan of £100 which was refused after his failure to attend the appropriate sub-committee.[30]

Nevertheless, Harry's 'tailoring and outfitting business' was launched on a ten-year lease within three months of his release.[31] No. 64, Middle Abbey Street was one of the few buildings in the vicinity not in ruins after the Rebellion. From his window across the road, Harry could look nostalgically at the site of the Metropole Hotel.[32] His link with the old firm was maintained by acquiring the gregarious Bill Duggan as his manager or partner, and by emblazoning his letterhead with the words 'H. Boland (late cutter, Todd, Burns & Co., Ltd.), Merchant Tailor'.[33] All that remained was to persuade his 'very big Connection Lay and Clerical' to pick their way to his door through the rubble of post-Rebellion Dublin. According to an American associate: 'Harry had gone through a struggle in his own mind when he decided to go in with Sinn Féin. He had a tailor shop and probably a nice little business.'[34] In fact, his success as an independent tailor was always threatened by economic factors as well as by his growing preoccupation with politics. Undaunted by his previous rebuff, he requested a further 'American grant' of £150 in February 1918. Though 'just holding my own after four months' trade', having accumulated 'a much larger stock' in response to brisker demand, he was under pressure to repay his substantial debts to the manufacturers who had supplied him with wool on short-term credit. In a final if grudging act of benevolence, he was awarded a further £50.[35] Since Harry also supplied clothing required for other beneficiaries of the fund, Irish National Aid had made a significant contribution to launching and developing his business.[36] Similar benefits were secured by other entrepreneurial ex-convicts and brethren such as Jack Shouldice and Seán McGarry, though humbler heroes like Thomas Peppard had to be content with small hand-outs. Eamon de Valera, a father of five who had surrendered his teaching post to campaign full-time for a Republic, received a much larger sum;[37] while his long-suffering wife Sinéad was offered 'all necessary financial assistance' in establishing 'an Irish Kindergarten'.[38]

Among Harry's other sponsors was the GAA, which put on a benefit match for the Dublin County Chairman on 11 November. Three thousand people watched Dublin defeat the All-Ireland football champions, Wexford, by two points.[39] Harry received £140, which was also invested in his new business.[40] He had lost no time in reasserting his influence among the Gaels, testing his fitness as a referee in mid August, and pressing Dublin's leading Catholic secondary schools to emulate Rockwell College by promoting native games. He joined deputations to Blackrock and Castleknock Colleges, urging that they should 'again take up' Gaelic football, 'both from its intrinsic value and from the National point of view'. The deputation to Blackrock 'explained that the introduction of hurling and Gaelic Football did not mean that the college should abandon Rugby', despite the GAA's notorious ban on players indulging in 'foreign' games which had undermined the former Leinster College League. Blackrock's President was 'quite pleased with the explanation', while Fr. Murphy at Castleknock felt that hurling, but not football, might be accommodated.[41]

Despite Harry's apparent tolerance of divided loyalties among sporting schoolboys, he was otherwise prominent among the 'exclusionists' for whom Gaelic purity mattered more than popularity. In March 1918, he and Jack Shouldice induced Congress to censure the Central Council for its negotiations with the Government in 1916 over gate tax and excursion trains, during which Luke O'Toole had allegedly discovered that General Sir John Maxwell was 'a fine manly fellow'.[42] Three months later, Harry attended a special meeting of the Council which unanimously rejected further attempts to secure match permits from Dublin Castle and laid plans for 'Gaelic Sunday', 4 August, when unlicensed matches were held without interference throughout the country.[43] Gaelic games had become a mere tool of republican politics, providing a cover for meetings of brethren and a source of funds for prisoners and their dependents. Harry was the referee at one such football match on 6 April 1919, when Tipperary avenged their loss in the previous All-Ireland final by defeating Wexford. The *Independent* deemed it 'a poor affair compared with the final. It was spoiled by the wild methods of the players, which we think might have been checked early in the game, and not allowed to develop into roughness, which was unedifying. Frees were given by Mr. Boland in large measure to both sides.'[44] Indulgent at first, yet coercive when challenged, he was later to attract similar criticism as a referee of political disputes in Irish-America.

Harry's relentless subordination of sport to politics brought him into unexpected collision with Jack Shouldice at the annual congress held on 20 April 1919, just before his departure for America. When Shouldice opposed the undiscriminating expulsion of civil servants who had recently been required to swear an oath of allegiance to the Crown or face dismissal, Harry responded grimly that 'the G.A.A. owed its position to-day to the fact that it had drawn a line between the Garrison and the Gael'. With support from Dan Fraher and Maurice Collins, he routed the advocates of moderation by 50 votes to 31.[45] His militancy was rewarded by nomination against the incumbent President, Alderman James Nowlan of Kilkenny, but Harry withdrew from a contest for reasons not immediately revealed and allowed Nowlan to preside for his nineteenth year. Despite this show of respect for the old guard, Harry became petulant when the congress failed to impose a limit of two years on senior officers, and walked out with his supporters after accusing his opponents of an 'exhibition of jerrymandering'.[46]

Harry's increasing influence over the GAA reflected his rapid promotion within the clandestine body which controlled so many of the Gaels' inner councils. The execution of the IRB's military committee had left many gaps in its leadership, enabling Michael Collins and his Frongoch cronies to establish a 'provisional governing body' in early 1917. Its President was Thomas Ashe, still incarcerated at Lewes. After Ashe's death on hunger-strike in September 1917, he was succeeded by another Lewes veteran (Seán McGarry), with Collins as Secretary and his acolytes occupying all key positions.[47] Though not yet a member of the Supreme Council, Harry played a key part in the elaborate obsequies for the late President, arranging for Batt O'Connor and Maurice Collins to dress Ashe's body in uniform prior to burial.[48] When McGarry was arrested for his part in the alleged 'German Plot' in May 1918, it was Harry who took his place as (acting) President after being co-opted to the Supreme Council. With Collins as Treasurer and his fellow Corkonian Seán Ó Murthuile as the new Secretary, the Supreme Council was more like a bunch of likely lads on the prowl than the representative governing body of a political organisation. Harry's presidency was curtailed by his departure for the United States after a year in office, though according to one member of the Supreme Council he remained President *in absentia* until at least 1920.[49] His immediate successor was reportedly Patrick Moylett, a shadowy businessman and go-between from Mayo.[50] Meanwhile, Collins continued as Treasurer until 1921, when he finally assumed titular direction of the Brotherhood.[51]

During the period of Harry's and Collins's ascendancy, the IRB seems to have lost much of its sociability, becoming little more than a network for distributing instructions, organising Volunteer companies, and acquiring arms. Denis McCullough, the powerless President of the Supreme Council in 1916, doubted that any Circle meetings were held after the following year: 'The thread that ran through them holding them together were the intelligence strings from Collins's hands.'[52] Though far smaller than in Parnell's time, the reorganised IRB probably expanded its membership after the Rebellion. By 1918 there were 350 Circles with about 4,000 brethren, and three years later 864 were enrolled in 26 Dublin Circles. Membership of Collins's McDermott Cumann veered between 20 and 40, though Harry's old Circle (the Holts) had shrunk to only 22 members by late 1921.[53] While Gerald Boland joined de Valera and Cathal

Brugha in calling for the organisation's disbandment as an anachronism, Harry helped to transform it into an efficient instrument of central control.

Like most separatist leaders of the period, Harry defied easy classification as a conspirator, soldier, or politician. In addition to his prominence in the GAA and the IRB, he was to become a key organiser for Sinn Féin. It is perhaps surprising that so enthusiastic and intrepid a fighter assumed no formal rôle in the Irish Volunteers, reorganised after August 1917 by Lewes veterans such as de Valera, Ashe, and Diarmuid Lynch, along with Richard Mulcahy and the ubiquitous Collins. The Convention of the Volunteers which elected de Valera as President, on 27 October, did not appoint Harry to either its National or its Resident Executive.[54] Nor did he play any recorded part in his old F Company or in the 2nd Dublin Battalion after the Rebellion.[55] Yet Harry's reputation and fraternal influence enabled him to assume military command at will. This was apparent during the violent by-election campaign in South Armagh, which resulted in Dr. Patrick McCartan's emphatic defeat by the Home Ruler, Patrick Donnelly.[56] In Newtownhamilton, Harry's party was attacked by Unionist missiles, one of which penetrated the hat of Joe McGuinness's brother Frank:

> Mr Boland asked the sergeant of police to clear the street of the stone throwers, but he replied that he had only three constables, and one of them had been injured. Mr Boland then said he would clear the street himself, and, marshalling 60 local Volunteers, marched them four deep on to the square, where he addressed them, and said if the police did not keep order they must see that it was kept. The stone throwing ceased when the Volunteers lined up.[57]

Reports of this incident confirmed the ostensibly defensive function of the Volunteers, while highlighting the impotence of the police.

On the night of 17 May 1918, most separatist leaders including de Valera, Griffith, and McGarry were rounded up on the plausible if undocumented supposition that they were plotting with the German enemy. Though Collins had secured the list of suspects and advance notice of the raids (conveyed by a message left at Harry's shop), most of his colleagues either failed to receive the warning or preferred to court popular sympathy by soliciting further incarceration. Collins, Harry, Eamon Duggan, and Seán Ó Murthuile were among those who decided, after meeting with the Volunteer Executive at Rutland Square, to go 'on the run'. Harry initially ran straight home, secure in the knowledge that no. 15 had already been raided. Following the deportation of over seventy suspects to England, however, he embarked on ten months as a fugitive in company with Collins and Ó Murthuile, their first 'safe house' being on the south side of Richmond Road, Drumcondra. Since the property backed onto the Tolka River, opposite Holy Cross College and the Archbishop's house at Clonliffe, getaway could be accomplished by raft.[58]

Being on the run did not preclude frequent visits to Marino Crescent, where his mother had installed a stepladder and table upstairs, to facilitate egress through the skylight. Kathleen recounted a raid shortly after the round-up, during which Harry, Jack Shouldice, and two other Volunteers escaped in their pyjamas while Kathleen delayed the chivalrous 'G-men' by pleading for time to dress and then showing them over the basement. The fugitives scampered along the roof-valleys to the north end of the Crescent, where they plunged through the skylight of no. 26, occupied by the family of John McGrath, a journalist on the *New Sunday World*. Though unsympathetic to Sinn Féin and with sons in the forces, the McGraths sent a daughter to collect clothes from no. 15 and so allow a decent retreat. Samuel Jennings, the Bolands' Baptist neighbour and landlord, also declined to incriminate the family when questioned after the raid, stating that 'Mrs. Boland is a decent woman; she pays her rent regularly; and I knew her husband. Outside that, I want to know nothing about them.' Though appreciative of these tokens of neighbourly solidarity, Kathleen observed darkly of the landlord that 'he may have had ulterior motives'.[59] Protestants, like the 'filthy Freemason gang' who ruled Ireland, could not be trusted.

The legend of Harry as Ireland's Houdini, a rôle later appropriated by Collins, spread rapidly during his year on the run. As Seán McEntee wrote from Gloucester Prison, Robert Brennan had arrived with 'a budget of most interesting news and has held us breathless while he tells of the hair breadth escapes of a certain young man called Henry'.[60] Initially, he used a theatrical disguise while cycling about the city, but abandoned it when told of an onlooker's response: 'I saw a man passing on a bicycle, with a false moustache and spectacles with no glass in them. I wonder who he was.'[61] As Collins had already worked out, the most effective disguise for a fugitive was often transparent lack of disguise. A 'Waterford Ex-Internee' recollected that Harry had 'entered Belfast Jail to see his brother and Austin Stack, undisguised, and in the face of Secret Servicemen, military and police, merely adopting an assumed name'.[62] By mid 1919, John Devoy was publicising Harry's exploits for the benefit of American sympathisers:

> The story of this part of Boland's career beats anything in fiction and shows the possibilities of outwitting the British Government in Ireland by skill and audacity. On one occasion while the chase after him was hottest, he was put for concealment in a room with Field Marshal French in the Dublin Mansion House. When French learned this later he was furious, but he could do nothing but gnash his teeth.[63]

Harry, like the cheeky Celtic heroes of the Christian Brothers' magazine, *Our Boys*, had shown how to outmanoeuvre might with mother wit.

Equally noteworthy, if less dramatic, was Harry's growing prominence in Sinn Féin, the former fringe party which by late 1917 had become a mass movement with branches (cumainn) in almost every parish. His initial appeal as a politician, like that of de Valera, arose paradoxically from his lack of political experience. The rising élite were at pains to declare their purity of principle, abhorrence of hypocrisy, and innocence of the corruption associated with their 'Constitutionalist' adversaries. It might have been Harry of whom Collins wrote in November 1918: 'I'm having a quiet laugh "within myself" at the political eagerness of some of the "I'm only a fighting man" fraternity. I think I'm entitled to that.'[64] Harry's early success as a Sinn Féin organiser was assisted by the simplicity of his speeches, which matched his reputation as a courageous rebel without political finesse. During his first visit to Roscommon with Jack Shouldice on 1 July 1917, they were greeted at Strokestown by a procession headed by 'a Sinn Féin flag, which paraded the village singing disloyal songs'. To a background of 'seditious cries' and 'disorderly' scenes, Harry 'spoke in praise of the Rebellion of Easter 1916, referred to the Courtmartials and prison treatment of the rebels, and attributed their release to fear on the part of the Government [of] a general strike in English prisons'. A month later, he warned those joining Sinn Féin that 'there is no use in your doing so unless you are prepared to follow the example of those of Easter Week in Dublin and go the whole way'. The people of Drumlish were urged to 'wait for the opportunity of England's difficulty to again strike a decisive blow for victory, and to combine, drill and be ready for that eventuality'.[65]

The struggle for independence could not, of course, be separated from the greater international conflict, the outcome of which remained unpredictable. In Lanesborough, he asked: 'Why should we fight for the bloody Saxon? All Germany wanted was freedom of the seas and she had won [this]. Ireland was the only barrier to such freedom as she was the western fortress and all ships that went to America had to pass her shores.' Harry concluded that they should press on against the English 'cowards' for an Irish Republic, declaring that 'they did not want Colonial Home Rule or any other kind of Home Rule, that they must get their independence and clear the English out of the country'. Harry's view of the Rebellion and his own rôle was clarified at another meeting in Frankford:

> I am here to take the place of Tom Ashe (arrested). I am one of the men who did a man's part in Easter Week. ... It was said that he went out in Easter Week to beat the British Empire. We were not so mad as to think that 860 [sic.] of us could do that. We went out to kindle anew the fires of patriotism, to demand the rights of the Irish people.[66]

Since the most promising forum for that demand was the eagerly awaited post-War conference, Harry was at pains to deny that this would entail compromise: 'They were not going to the Peace Conference as beggars or suppliants – they were going as belligerents (cheers).'[67] His scribbled notes for a speech in

September 1917 suggest that he was becoming a confident stump orator. After a few references to Lord Hugh Cecil and international affairs, he jotted down 'arrests, trials, naked arm of force, organise'.[68] Simple and unqualified, yet leaving ample room for future refinement of terms such as 'independence', 'victory', and 'rights', Harry's rhetoric echoed that of the young de Valera.

On occasion, Harry spoke not from rough notes but from laboriously inscribed scripts, one of which illuminates his view of the historical roots of the current struggle.[69] This lecture set out to refute the common view that Easter Week was 'the action of thoughtless revolutionaries who were imbued with the spirit of the unrest [?] and warfare that convulsed the world at that period and who endeavoured to snatch the freedom of Ireland from the chaos of the World War'. Instead, he sought 'the source of the Insurrection' in the American and French revolutions and the succession of Irish risings initiated by the United Irishmen. In words anticipating his adulation of Michael Collins in 1920, he celebrated Theobald Wolfe Tone as 'a true revolutionary with a genius for organisation, a soul that never quailed and a spirit brave and noble'. He recalled Pearse's oration at Bodenstown in 1915, concluding that Tone was indeed 'the father of [the] Irish Republic'. The history of Irish nationality since 1798 was a continuing struggle between the uncrushed 'spirit of Ireland, the spirit of Wolfe Tone', and the disastrous strategy of compromise epitomised by Daniel O'Connell. The nineteenth century amounted to a catalogue of lost opportunities, despite 'the marvellous spread' of the Fenian Brotherhood and the advent of 'that wonderful ill-starred patriot Charles Stewart Parnell'. Though admiring Parnell's 'cold pride', 'withering condemnation of English rule in Ireland', and 'utter contempt of the English Parliament', Harry regarded the decision of the 'revolutionaries' to co-operate with the campaign for Home Rule as their 'great mistake'. This had encouraged further compromise with Parnell's less dedicated successors, until the centennial celebrations of 1798 and the Boer War revived the republican movement and created 'a virile body of men who were working in every Irish Ireland movement in an unobtrusive way sowing the seeds of revolt in the minds of the young men'. Having secured arms in imitation of Carson, the leaders had prepared for revolution in the context of an inevitable war between Britain and Germany: 'They had a clear cut idea of what would occur and it filled their hearts with joy when on August 1st [*sic*] 1914 England declared war.' For Harry, the Rebellion of 1916 marked the culmination of a consistent and practical strategy inaugurated in 1798 and frustrated hitherto only by treachery, misfortune, and misjudgement. It remained to complete the predestined victory of the Republic. Tendentious as history, this analysis bristled with a quality which the 'New Ireland' craved and which Harry had in abundance – certainty of ultimate success.

Even more important in Harry's political ascent than this quality of infectious optimism was his intimacy with the revolutionary inner circle. When Sinn Féin sought to ensure 'unity of intention' with the Volunteers, in case of 'drastic action' to release republican prisoners, it was Harry who was 'empowered to act and confer with Mr Mulcahy as representing the I.V. Executive'.[70] Such eminence within Sinn Féin had not been achieved without opposition. Many separatists outside and even within the Brotherhood resented the Supreme Council's attempt to impose an Executive Committee, dominated by often obscure conspirators, upon the delegates who assembled at the Mansion House for the crucial convention (Ard Fheis) of October 1917. Though the IRB's 'ticket' was mainly the work of Collins and Diarmuid Lynch, who hoped to emulate the organisation's success in grabbing control of the Gaelic League in 1915, Harry was presumably implicated.[71] Following protests from the floor and an agreement between de Valera and Griffith to share the leadership, the conspiracy collapsed. The rout of the IRB was compounded by 'an adroit move' by the Chairman, Eoin MacNeill, 'who announced that he had been told that police had surrounded the building. This caused Collins to withdraw accompanied by Harry Boland.'[72] Collins had the humiliation of coming equal last (with 340 votes) among the 20 men and 4 women elected, while Harry gained tenth place with 448 votes.[73] Since the Executive Committee had no functions, except as one element of a governing body (Ard Chomhairle) which met but once a quarter, the election was a mere beauty contest. Secure in the middle rank of the separatist élite, Harry resumed his work as a speaker and organiser, accompanying 'the chosen Leader of the Irish Race' as he inspected the customary bands, banners, triumphal arches, and mounted guards of honour.[74]

The statutory extension of Conscription to Ireland in April 1918, though never implemented, provoked a crisis which seemed likely to result in renewed coercion followed by further rebellion. The consequent campaign of resistance created an unprecedented show of nationalist unity, as Sinn Féin collaborated with Labour, and even with the reviled 'Parliamentarians', in the Mansion House Conference and Committee. Within Sinn Féin, however, the crisis greatly strengthened the militant influence. In preparation for the expected arrest of the leaders, Sinn Féin's Standing Committee agreed to set up a substitute body to carry on its weekly business, including both Harry and Michael Collins.[75] Among the first to be arrested, a fortnight before the revelation of the 'German Plot', was Harry's old comrade Austin Stack, the Kerry footballer, Lewes veteran, and IRB leader who also acted as joint Honorary Secretary to Sinn Féin. Having been nominated by Stack as a substitute, Harry took over his crucial office on 17 May, the very eve of the swoop which removed more than half of Sinn Féin's leadership. Apart from Fr. Michael O'Flanagan, the turbulent curate from Roscommon, he was the only officer to avoid arrest.[76] His secretarial work was shared with Alderman Tom Kelly, whose socialist leanings were invaluable in cementing the alliance with Labour. In the absence of most of the separatist leaders, 'moderate' as well as revolutionary, Harry's whirlwind presence became indispensable to Sinn Féin's organisation and morale. According to Robert Brennan, the Director of Elections:

During this period, though he was very much on the run, Harry came bustling into the office nearly every day, if only for a few minutes. Sometimes he was disguised as a priest and he loved the masquerade. He was always in the highest of spirits and his coming in was like a breath of fresh air. He had a desk but never sat in it for more than a minute or two.[77]

For his adoring colleagues of both sexes at 6, Harcourt Street, he personified the uncrushed 'spirit of Ireland'.

During his year on the Standing Committee, Harry attended three-fifths of its meetings, missing almost none during the General Election campaign of late 1918. By comparison, Michael Collins was an irregular and rather testy participant, attending less than one meeting in five and frequently inveighing against Sinn Féin's incompetence in his letters to the imprisoned Stack.[78] Yet one of Collins's chief adversaries insisted that he was 'the real master of the new Executive', Harry serving merely as his 'hourly companion and faithful adherent'.[79] Harry was an indefatigable committee-man, dealing at a single meeting with issues as diverse as prisoners' dependents, propaganda, and 'communications'.[80] It was Harry who arranged bail to extract Béaslaí from Belfast Prison, and Harry who kept McGarry, his imprisoned predecessor as President of the Supreme Council, informed of Sinn Féin's doings.[81] His triumphal tone is audible in the statement circulated by Sinn Féin for declamation at public meetings throughout the country on 15 August: 'A race that is pre-eminent for coolness, daring and ingenuity is rapidly turning against the crude and clumsy enemy every weapon that is used against her. We have at last emerged into the full sunlight of national consciousness, and no power on earth can drive us back.'[82] While making Sinn Féin's voice heard, Harry worked equally hard to silence opponents such as Colonel Arthur Lynch, the repented 'traitor' whose recruiting meetings for an 'Irish Brigade' to fight alongside the French were systematically heckled and disrupted under the direction of Collins, Ó Murthuile, and himself.[83] When Sinn Féin secured the platform after one of these confrontations, it was Harry (disguised in a 'jet-black moustache' but recognisable from his left wink) who rescued the speaker from the advancing police by bouncing him over the massed bodies of the hecklers.[84]

Harry worked hard to maximise unity among those supporting 'self-determination', while avoiding compromise within Sinn Féin on its republican commitment. On 20 August, he proposed 'that as it is evident that the English government are anxious to compromise Sinn Féin on the question of Dominion (or Colonial) Home Rule, it be an instruction from this Ard Chomhairle that no conversations take place between intermediaries of the English Government and representatives of Sinn Féin on the question'.[85] At this period, Sinn Féin's vitality had been sapped by a combination of complacency and coercion, leading Collins to remark that the Ard Chomhairle 'was not a very impressive gathering. The attendance was poor and most of the things lacked any great force.'[86] In his report to the Ard Fheis two months later, Harry had to admit that 'since the arrest of the leaders S.F. work had been confined to organisation, election propaganda, and food', but claimed credit on behalf of Sinn Féin for blocking Conscription. Both Harry and Tom Kelly were confirmed in their posts as Honorary Secretaries, receiving fulsome acknowledgement from Fr. O'Flanagan (the acting President) as men 'who stepped in as volunteers' and 'came into the gap of danger' after the arrest of the elected officers. Michael Collins advanced half-way up the order of those elected to the Executive Committee.[87] The meeting made a show of defiance by marching to College Green to protest against the physical deterioration of Stack and other prisoners in Belfast. For the time being, the IRB's control of Sinn Féin seemed secure, as Collins indicated to Stack: 'You will have heard from Boland what the Ard Fheis did! If anything warrants it our old idea will be carried out with a slight variation.'[88]

Despite the growing militancy of Sinn Féin's propaganda, Harry hoped to make the Mansion House Committee the foundation of a national front for 'self-determination'. Just after the Ard Fheis, he and Collins visited Tim Healy, causing the ageing casuist to reflect that 'all the Field Marshals in that army are just beyond their teens and are full of the balmiest strategy'. The 'Secretary on the run' had 'demanded I should attend the Mansion House meeting – one of them said to proclaim self-determination and the other added "a provisional government". ... All perfectly sincere and self-sacrificing and piteous.' Healy resisted their 'little game' to manoeuvre the Home Rulers into forming an alliance on issues unconnected with Conscription, and John Dillon also 'secured a loophole for not acquiescing'.[89] Healy identified his visitors only in 1922, when he found Harry 'a joyous soul' who chuckled that 'we knew d—— well we could not bluff you then, but we hoped to fool the Lord Mayor and Dillon!'[90] Laurence O'Neill did indeed provide the Mansion House for the meeting held on Armistice night, receiving gracious thanks from Harry for his 'many good turns' to the prisoners and his hospitality.[91]

The occasion was somewhat spoiled by other festivities marking the Armistice, during which (as Kathleen alleged) '800 drunken soldiers' and 'things' called WAACs 'broke into the Mansion House, Sinn Féin offices, Liberty Hall, a convent in Clarendon Street and private houses – when they went to Harcourt Street, the boys, 30 of them, ran them down like a lot of sheep'.[92] In fact, those who invaded no. 6 were students from Trinity College, who exchanged 'some blows' with those defending the hall before they 'were forced out, and, forming up, marched along Stephen's Green into Grafton street, cheering and singing'.[93] During this fracas, 'Harry Boland would dart out of the crowd, lay one of them out, and as suddenly be lost to view'.[94] Michael Collins was attending a 'staff meeting' and unable to join the fun; but he exulted in the claim that his cronies had cut their knuckles to such effect that 125 servicemen were wounded and at least 4 killed as they celebrated the coming of peace.[95] Since many of the celebrants were presumably Irish patriots, who had followed Redmond and Dillon in adopting the struggle against German tyranny as Ireland's war, the prospect for a united nationalist front seemed remote indeed.

Nationalist unity was scarcely conceivable without the co-operation of forces such as the Labour movement and the Catholic Church. Harry, with his long experience of investing the clergy, made several attempts to solicit clerical support for Sinn Féin's demands. When the Standing Committee decided to seek the reinstatement as a practising priest of its Vice-President, Fr. O'Flanagan, Harry was among the deputation sent to plead his case (unavailingly) with the Bishop of Elphin in August 1918.[96] Three months later, he and Tom Kelly addressed a rather peremptory letter to the aged Archbishop of Dublin, recalling the united campaign against Conscription:

> Now that the Peace Conference is about to decide our destiny, we claim from the Catholic Hierarchy, for the same reason, a similar assistance in the work of securing the Independence of our country: firstly, by placing the case of our prisoners before the Vatican; secondly, by declaring for Independence as courageously and as clearly as they declared against Conscription; thirdly, by endorsing the growing unity of the Irish people.

This appeal was followed by a prolonged and rather naive exposition of the case for national independence and clerical intervention. After discussing the matter in person with Archbishop Walsh, Kelly left Harry to attend to the undisclosed 'subject-matter of it', which five weeks later he had still failed to do as 'unfortunately he had to leave town'.[97] Though increasingly favourable towards Sinn Féin, the Hierarchy was never unambiguously to endorse the republican programme.

On 14 August, Harry had been assigned the equally daunting task of defusing Labour's challenge at the forthcoming General Election. The chief advocates of a separate Labour Party were William O'Brien, incoming President of the Irish Trades Union Congress, and Cathal O'Shannon, the militant editor of *Irish Opinion: The Voice of Labour*. As a left-leaning tradesman who had collaborated with his fellow-tailor O'Brien in the campaign against Conscription in 1915, Harry seemed an ideal intermediary between Sinn Féin and Labour. His partners in this enterprise were O'Shannon and Tom Kelly. Having been Sinn Féin's most effective allies in the continuing struggle against Conscription, Labour's leaders expected the reward of several uncontested seats in Dublin and beyond. Harry's dual task was to placate resentful Sinn Féin activists in working-class constituencies, and to persuade Labour candidates to accept the separatist pledge of 'abstention' from Westminster. After a month's manoeuvring, Harry 'reported that his efforts to bring about a conference with Labour were fruitless. He understood that Labour intended to contest some fifteen seats and to declare for abstention from the English Parliament but not as a principle but as an expedient.'

The Standing Committee prevaricated, deciding 'to go ahead with our programme leaving it open to adjustment should occasion, and opportunity arise'.[98] On 23 September, the ratification of candidates in sensitive constituencies was further postponed after Labour had at last presented its detailed demands to a deputation including Harry.[99] He continued to press for a compromise allowing the selection of candidates acceptable to both parties, and was accused of contriving the withdrawal of a Sinn Féin candidate for Dublin's Harbour division in deference to Labour.[100] After a protest from the combined Dublin constituency executives, matters were brought to a head on 7 October by demanding an unqualified pledge of abstention from Labour candidates seeking Sinn Féin's sanction, though Harry continued to affirm that 'they could not afford in this election to antagonise Labour'. Early in November, a special Trades Union Congress responded to both internal and external pressure by withdrawing all of its candidates, and Sinn Féin decided to contest every seat without formal reference to Labour.[101] Harry was unstinting in his praise for Labour's patriotic self-sacrifice, joining Tom Kelly and Eoin MacNeill in public tributes on Armistice night.[102]

Harry's part in these parleys was ambiguous. The Dublin executives feared that he was a tool of Labour, whereas Labour protagonists suspected that his purpose was to reinforce Fenian control of all electoral nominations and 'make Labour representation as difficult as possible'.[103] Despite Harry's undoubted inclination towards elements of socialism, his correspondence with Cathal Brugha confirmed that his first commitment was to the Republic. Brugha, whose uniquely narrow pursuit of that ideal had impelled him to resign from both the IRB and the Standing Committee, had little sympathy with Labour. He felt it 'a pity that Labour people have not the intelligence and patriotism to let their class claim wait until we have cleared out the enemy'. Yet he was concerned to gather that Sinn Féin had failed to 'arrive at an understanding' with Labour before the names of Sinn Féin candidates were announced.[104] Harry replied rather irritably that the negotiations with Labour had 'dragged' as a result of a wave of strikes and 'the apparent apathy' of Cathal O'Shannon, the Labour leader and member of the Standing Committee through whom the negotiations had been instigated. He suspected 'that Shannon delayed our meeting until Labour had definitely committed themselves to enter the field', admitting that 'Shannon outmanoeuvred us'. Harry's response was intricate but problematic:

We decided to buck them up, and we asked the Comhairli Ceanntair [constituency executives] to nominate their men, having an agreement with them that in the event of our Executive deciding that Labour should get certain seats, their candidates would be withdrawn. The arrangement did not work out as happily as we hoped. Several individuals got busy on the matter and circulated around Dublin the rumour that we were selling the pass to Labour.

The resultant 'mild revolt' had been resolved, and Harry correctly predicted that 'Labour will stand down by the pressure within their own ranks. ... We are all of us anxious to placate Labour as we know that we will require their aid in matters of greater importance than the General Election, but all our actions will be governed not by expediency but by principle.' In his reply, on the day of Labour's withdrawal, Brugha exclaimed: 'Could not be better. We'll go ahead now.'[105] Harry's manipulation of his colleagues in both Labour and Sinn Féin had, after all, been justified by the outcome. Though ineffectual as a unifier, having failed to divide the electoral spoils with Labour just as he had failed to harness the Home Rulers to 'self-determination', Harry had revealed some of his hidden steel as an enforcer. There was no room for a second separatist party in his New Ireland.

Harry and Collins were widely credited with manipulating the entire selection process in order to ensure the IRB's domination of the nascent republican assembly.[106] Even before his temporary appointment as chief election agent on 21 November, Harry had become chief broker in the allocation of seats. In a vain attempt to overturn the nomination of 'Sceilg' for Louth, a local opponent asked Harry to suggest 'to Mick Collins [that] a move should be made from your end to influence him to withdraw in favour of somebody, whom you or Mick would suggest'.[107] Austin Stack, writing from Belfast Prison, recommended several candidates to Harry, who did not always accept his proposals and rather resented his 'lecturing'. Stack warned against nominating de Valera for the Falls division of Belfast, but Harry supported the majority of the Standing Committee who believed on the basis of a local poll that he could defeat 'wee Joe' Devlin on his home pitch. De Valera was routed by the Hibernian leader in that constituency, though returned for both East Clare and East Mayo. Despite his differences with Harry, Stack remained cordial in his own mannered way: 'I hear you are getting quite fat. Stop it. Fond love. Thine own – Aoibhistín.'[108] One of those who objected to Harry's machinations was Tom Clarke's widow, Kathleen, who was nominated by the Clontarf executive while incarcerated in Holloway Prison. She later learned that Harry had urged the local Chairman to withdraw her nomination in favour of Richard Mulcahy, reassuring the subsequent executive meeting 'that literature was already out for my election in Limerick, and that I was sure of being elected there'. Yet Harry, according to Kathleen, was aware that another nomination for Limerick City had already been ratified.[109] His persuasive power could foster mistrust as well as admiration, even among those like Kathleen Clarke who stayed close to him to the end.

Secretary Harry was an administrator, a diplomat, a fixer, and, above all, a propagandist. His preference for robust, plain speech appealed to journalists, and he quickly became adept in using the press to propagate the republican demand. In November, for example, he and Seán T. O'Kelly explained to a group of American editors at the Shelbourne Hotel that the republicans were not pro-German but pro-Irish, with a 'long-standing sympathy for France'.[110] It was Harry who proposed at the end of September that a common 'Manifesto to the Irish People', drafted by himself, Tom Kelly, Fr. O'Flanagan, and Robert Brennan, be issued on behalf of all Sinn Féin candidates for the General Election.[111] Each man submitted a draft, the revised document being an amalgam of disputed ingredients.[112] Harry's draft was characteristically lively, denouncing the Irish Party's 'policy of whine' and asserting that Conscription was the 'logical outcome' of its endeavour 'to harness the people of Ireland to England's war chariot'. Sinn Féin was 'not a political party', but 'the natural successor of that great body of the Irish nation, that never through the long and bloody struggle, surrendered the right of Ireland to absolute independence'. Sinn Féin was 'a new name for the United Irishmen' and their successors, whose spirit generated the 'heroic sacrifice of 1916' which had 'undone the evil of 80 years'. The organisation sought 'a mandate ... to place Ireland's claim to self determination before the world', and so decide 'whether the seven century struggle for Nationhood shall be consummated in a glorious Freedom, or whether our Nationhood shall be manacled to an Alien Government'.[113] Harry contributed several such ringing declamations, one of which he himself deleted with the annotation 'anticlimax'. Though traces of Harry's colourful rhetoric survived, the published document was less histrionic in its style and more specific in its programme (Harry, in his excitement, had forgotten to denounce Partition).[114]

Harry had been among the first batch of candidates ratified by his own Standing Committee when, on 12 September, he was selected for the constituency including grandfather Boland's birthplace, South Roscommon. Press reports revealed that the challenger to John Patrick Hayden, the incumbent newspaper proprietor who had first been returned as a Parnellite in 1897, was 'on the run'.[115] When Dan Fraher's Dungarvan Sinn Féin club sought permission to nominate this 'brave Irish soldier' for County Waterford, Harry modestly replied that he was 'altogether unsuited for the constituency as I am not an Irish speaker'. His recommendation of Cathal Brugha, 'one of the greatest men in the movement and an Irish speaker', was acted upon.[116] Harry had also been provisionally adopted for Clontarf, his home constituency when resting from the run, before giving way to Richard Mulcahy when the negotiations with Labour collapsed.[117] Like de Valera in East Clare, eighteen months earlier, he entered the campaign in South Roscommon as an outsider preoccupied with national issues rather than local loyalties.

In the spectacular tradition of Irish rural elections, Harry deployed bands, banners, and mounted escorts to tickle public interest, sending out a decoy wearing a 'rebel' hat to divert attention when he needed privacy before addressing the townspeople of Roscommon on Sunday, 24 November. Already a practised politician, he 'returned thanks for the hearty reception' in Irish, before declaring in English that 'the two greatest events of Irish history were the Rising of 1916 and the North Roscommon Election, last year (cheers)'. He represented a movement, not a party: 'We are not looking for prolonged political power. We believe in new times new men and new ideas.' Having lauded little Denmark for its economic success in the absence of colonial exploitation, he added primly that 'I do not like to discuss these questions from a material point of view. I for one would rather see Ireland with a crust in her mouth standing erect, proud and free, than fat and sleek and prosperous, a beggar and a slave (cheers).' Of the '137,000' Irishmen who had served in the Great War, he exclaimed: 'Peace to their bones! they are now lying in unhallowed graves in France and Flanders and every other battle front.' Distancing Sinn Féin from the defeated Germans, he stated that 'we went out in Easter Week not to fight for Germany, but to fight for Ireland (cheers). Not as rebels, but as Insurrectionists, for we spoke for a Nation, and if we thought well of it, we were quite justified in allying ourselves with our enemy's enemy. ... Was America wrong to ally herself with the Yellow Japanese?' Confident that American influence would assist the Irish cause, he declared that 'Wilson won it [the War] in order that America might spread and expand. ... America hated German militarism, but she hated English navalism too. Don't say America won the war for humanity; she won it that America and every other power could sail the ocean as they pleased without hindrance.' Remembering on this occasion to discuss Partition, he cried: 'Is it Ulster, our Ulster, to be handed over to the seed of Cromwell, the Bristol tanners, and the English Clubs? Ulster, our Ulster, the Ulster of the Gaelic tongue of Patrick and of Bridget and O'Neill? Never! Never! Never! (cheers).' Having bitterly attacked the Irish Party for refusing Sinn Féin's invitation 'to let the Mansion House Conference put forward Ireland's claim and let there be no election', he nevertheless claimed the legacy of constitutional nationalism when thanking the chairman: 'Mr. [Michael] Finlay had proposed the present Member twenty years ago. The Party complained that the people had deserted them. Well, no; the Party had deserted Ireland and the people had remained true (cheers).'[118]

Hayden, who had never faced a contest in his two decades as a parliamentarian, did his best to revive the rusty machinery of the United Irish League and mobilise the parish priests against the upstart, whom he described as 'only a tramp tailor'.[119] Hayden claimed support from all parish priests but two in the constituency; though one of these retorted that 'of the 28 priests in the Constituency 22 are voting for Mr. Boland'.[120] The extensive reports of Hayden's orations in his own newspaper avoided all criticism of his unnamed opponent's 'personality', instead reciting the achievements of the Irish Party while colleagues reminded younger voters that Hayden had been 'in prison as often as any other man'. He expressed confidence 'that upon the closing day the green banner will float triumphantly over this constituency', and that Roscommon would vote 'in favour of the old policy, the old party, and the old leaders'.[121] Hayden ridiculed Sinn Féin's policy as impracticable, claiming that an Irish Republic was 'impossible to realise, unless it could be enforced by an army and navy equal to that of Great Britain', and that no intervention could be expected from a Peace Conference 'dominated by Great Britain, France, America, and Italy'. If, as he had heard, Sinn Féiners would not go to Parliament if elected, 'how were social reforms to be won? How were Irish interests to be safeguarded?'[122] A 'voter', possibly Hayden himself, submitted a rhyming dialogue to his paper:

> I would ask you, Mr Boland, if elected, will you stay
> From attending to our business in the Commons o'er the way?
> Where our taxes will be trebled by Lloyd George and Bonar Law,
> Who, for all your bogus risings, do not give a single straw.
> 'Friend,' he says, 'the House of Commons is no fitting place for me,
> I'm too advanced a rebel for that quarter, don't you see;
> But to South Roscommon's business I'll attend without a stint,
> When we form our new Republic and our Irish Parliament.'[123]

Hayden's supporters also deployed graffiti such as 'Don't vote for the tailor', embellishing the slogan 'Vote for Boland' with a jeering reference to the supposed effeminacy of his avocation ('The ninth part of a man'). Republican wits responded in kind: 'Don't vote for the nailer'; 'Hayden can't see the other eight'.[124]

After a campaign enlivened by increasingly bitter exchanges and systematic heckling of Hayden's meetings, such objections were brushed aside by the majority of voters. Henry Boland, merchant,[125] was credited with 10,685 votes, compared with 4,233 for the perplexed Hayden. In Castlerea, Harry's electoral appeal proved overwhelming among women, voting for the first time, and illiterates, who were required to declaim their preference in public before the presiding officer. The *Roscommon Herald* gloated that all but one of eighteen illiterates in one booth had supported Harry, including a woman whose husband had declared for Hayden, in defiance of her husband's choice: 'Oh no, I'm for Sinn Féin, and I must vote for Boland.'[126] The polling was marred by 'rowdy scenes' at one booth, when 'a crowd of Mr Hayden's supporters attacked some Volunteers, tore down Sinn Féin flags and bunting and trampled on them. A dispatch to Strokestown brought out reinforcements of Volunteers, who put the Party men to flight.'[127] In Roscommon town, the returning officer managed to disperse 'a crowd of lads armed with ashplants and hurleys' as they surrounded the booths. Almost every ballot box was accompanied to the courthouse by a 'Sinn Féin guard', one of whom insisted on policing the policeman in the storeroom until removed after protracted negotiations between the candidates, the returning officer, and the High Sheriff.[128] Such displays of force, as Gerald later observed, undermined Sinn Féin's claim to a democratic mandate: 'The General Election of 1918 was not a free election, because the Irish Volunteers, as they were called, took control and in numerous cases prevented candidates from going forward for decision. The Volunteers were not soldiers in the accepted sense but armed citizens and more politicians than soldiers.'[129]

Sinn Féin had not only outgunned the Party but outsmarted it, instructing its many counting agents to 'be very much alive' to 'sharp practice and trickery', while not objecting to 'votes for our Candidate *even if they are bad*'.[130] Harry and his team had learnt all too many of the devices practised by the despised 'politicians' of the Home Rule movement. At the declaration of the poll, Harry spoke as smoothly as any parliamentarian, commending the returning officer for 'a very orderly' election, extending the hand of friendship to the Sheriff ('if he was hot, I was hot'), dissociating himself from any 'personal' remarks uttered by his supporters, and identifying all Home Rulers as supporters of 'Ireland's claim to self-determination'. His predecessor phlegmatically interpreted the Party's defeat 'as the passing away of a great movement, to be succeeded by another'.[131] Harry Boland, MP, emerged from the courthouse to be carried shoulder-high to his party's headquarters, his victory being marked by speeches, a torchlight procession, bands, and house illuminations.[132] As one 'Dublin Socialist' observed just after the poll, Harry was now taking 'second place to de Valera. He travels all round Ireland addressing meetings and organizing the rebels.'[133] The local hero had become a national figure.

During the fortnight between the election and the declaration of the polls on Saturday, 28 December, Sinn Féin had been preparing to celebrate its victory nationwide. With typical flair, Harry asked Hanna Sheehy-Skeffington to provide the committee rooms of the Irish Women's Franchise League so that his party could 'announce the results of election on the screen'.[134] The outcome matched Harry's optimism, as 69 Sinn Féiners secured election for 73 out of Ireland's 105 seats in the House of Commons. Among its deputies almost one-third were veterans of Lewes, another third having been incarcerated elsewhere following the Rebellion.[135] Harry and his fellow-selectors had ensured that the new parliamentary party would be a living memorial to Easter Week. Immediately after this mandate had been secured, a journalist from the Conservative *Daily Mail* visited no. 6, noting the windows broken on Armistice day, the Sinn Féin bank on the ground floor, and the 'bundles of literature' and prisoners' comforts cluttering the office at the back of the building. He was taken upstairs by 'a young woman with short hair, smoking a cigarette', who introduced him to the Director of Organisation (Seán T. O'Kelly), and also to 'a pleasant young Irishman, intense, enthusiastic – fanatical, if you will – aflame with love of his country'. For two hours, Harry expounded 'the essence of Sinn Féinism' in front of a portrait of de Valera and a bust of Count Plunkett. He declared that 'Ireland is a nation, geographically, historically, ethnologically', that she had 'nothing to say to England, her hereditary foe', and that she wanted 'to run her own country herself and has had enough of foreign domination'. Harry and O'Kelly 'referred with pride to their wonderful organisation', and promised to carry on 'an active propaganda till they had converted a majority in Ulster to their doctrine'. Their 'ramifications' were 'world-wide', and, until Britain relented, they would mobilise the Irish vote in America and the Empire to 'act as a constant thorn in the side of Great Britain'. Harry explained that 'he liked many Englishmen but hated England – by England he did not mean Scotland or Wales'.[136] Such was the ambitious strategy which Harry would soon do so much to implement.

The use to which this interview was put made Harry wary of such discussions, as he indicated to a rally in Longford in early January. He had been approached by 'a representative of the Ministry of Information', anxious to know 'the meaning of Sinn Féin, and we put it to him fairly straight and solid. We saw an article then in the "Daily Mail" insisting that Ireland must be granted Dominion Home Rule (laughter). Well, we are not going to be taken in.' Eager to reject all suggestion of compromise, Harry expounded Sinn Féin's contingent diplomatic strategy with unsurpassed clarity:

> We are going to the Peace Conference to have our claim heard along with the Hottentots, the Jugo-Slavs, and the rest, and if we fail we will try the other remedy of building up from within our own nation, of getting ready for every difficulty of England to advance our claim to freedom. ... We must have independence first, and inter-dependence afterwards (hear, hear). ... We have declared for an Irish Republic, and we are going to bend all the energies of Ireland towards that end (hear, hear). If we do not get it, we have other methods. All the English papers are anxious to know what they are. There is a great inquiry to know what we are going to do. Well, we will tell them at the right time (hear, hear).

Despite the playful but unmistakable hint of violence, should diplomacy and propaganda fail, Harry remained hopeful that the post-War settlement would transform Ireland's prospects: 'I am not a prophet, but I am a student of international politics, and we know England's power at present has been built upon holding the balance of power in Europe – but now America has the "strong hand".'[137] But for the gaming metaphor, the happy-go-lucky sportsman of three years earlier was scarcely recognisable in the grave 'student of international politics' of 1919.

The election was still under way when the Standing Committee agreed to convoke a new assembly of the successful candidates, 'Dáil Éireann'. The arrangements were made by a sub-committee chaired by Seán T. O'Kelly and dominated by brethren such as J. J. Walsh, Piaras Béaslaí, Collins, and Harry.[138]

Harry's reputation for dealing effectively with Labour ensured that he played a key part in persuading its representatives at the International Socialist Congress, in Berne, to advertise Ireland's case for independence.[139] He also 'undertook to look after' the Dáil's Democratic Programme, which was to be Labour's reward for its co-operation. Though preoccupied with other schemes and an irregular participant in the consultations with Labour, Harry cobbled together 'a series of handwritten notes' by Labour leaders and 'other friends', which provoked 'a long and sometimes heated discussion' on the eve of the Dáil's inauguration. By 1 a.m. the sub-committee had lost patience, and the sheaf of notes was 'thrown at' O'Kelly, who finished drafting the document three hours later while Harry and Collins relaxed with the brethren in another room at O'Kelly's house in Ranelagh. In the course of revision, all socialist elements were deleted from Labour's drafts except those which echoed the insipid collectivism of Pearse's 'The Sovereign People'.[140] Despite this setback, William O'Brien and his Labour colleagues spoke at the inaugural reception given on 21 January 1919 by Cathal Brugha, as acting Speaker of the Dáil. O'Brien noted that the reception was 'not very impressive, room terribly cold'.[141] Among those marked absent from that first day's official proceedings were 'Énrí Ó Beóláin' and 'Mícheál Ó Coileáin', though for the benefit of the press other deputies answered to their names. They had both left that morning for England to prepare for the rescue of de Valera, Seán Milroy, and Seán McGarry from Lincoln Prison.[142]

This escapade had been initiated by de Valera, who secured an impression of the Chaplain's master key in late November and made several over-subtle attempts in Irish, English, and Latin to alert those at home to the significance of a Christmas card from McGarry, depicting a large key drawn by Milroy. The fourth message, sent on 10 January, resulted in the production of three keys by Gerald Boland, one being retained by Harry while the remainder were delivered to Lincoln in a cake. Political sanction for the rescue was evidently provided by a meeting of republican deputies on 14 January, which set up a 'special committee' with 'full executive powers with regard to steps to be taken to secure the release of the prisoners'.[143] Collins and Harry were soon poised for action in Manchester, 60 miles to the west of Lincoln, where they stayed with Harry's aunt. But the rescue, first planned for 24 January, was twice delayed when Gerald's keys, and then a substitute set embedded in a second cake, were found to be defective.[144] Meanwhile, evidence of Harry's mission proliferated as indiscreet messages poured in and out of Lincoln. The prison censor perused at least three letters to the effect that 'Kamerad was in M.', or that 'we had a distinguished visitor in Manchester yesterday, H. B.'[145] De Valera suggested postponing the scheme after the arrival of these letters, but Harry and Collins correctly surmised that the demoralised prison authorities would fail to act on such evidence.[146] Harry himself was allowed to deliver a third cake containing blanks, and persuaded the Chaplain to convey a coded message from McGarry to a priest visiting the prison from Manchester. In a letter smuggled to de Valera,

Harry set out four alternative 'parole messages as the parole stunt is the only one the Chaplain will carry'. 'I have applied for parole' would indicate readiness to 'reach the back gate outer wall at 6 p.m. on Tuesday, January 28th'; whereas 'I will not apply for parole' meant 'the Job is off'. Harry was 'satisfied that our part of the work is very easy. The coast is safe and clear. No guard. No trouble. ... Do not worry about the key to the back gate as we have a ladder and will use it on the signal from you. ... I hope to see your curly head coming over that wall on Tuesday. Slán leat [goodbye to you].'[147]

The masterminds in Manchester soon learned that McGarry would not, after all, 'apply for parole': the blank key in Harry's cake had a slot in the centre which was incompatible with the prison locks. The Irish reputation for a sweet tooth was confirmed by the arrival of a fourth cake, laced with files and a slot-less blank.[148] On 31 January, after three weeks of farce, a usable key was prepared by the imprisoned locksmith and Mayor of Kilkenny, Peter de Loughry. At 7.40 on the following Monday evening, 3 February, the three prisoners progressed without hindrance to the outer wall after a signal from Harry, who almost spoiled the operation by proving unable to switch off the torch. He was obliged to hide it, still alight, in his pocket. A further crisis occurred at the outer gate, when Collins broke Gerald's key in the lock while trying to open it from outside. Understandably reluctant to test out the rope ladder, de Valera pushed the shank out with his own key, turned it, and emerged to make a successful getaway in a fur-lined coat supplied by Harry.[149] Safe and warm in America, Harry would still recall his frustration during the long vigil with Collins, 'waiting for the President to make up his mind to come out, and then to make up his mind after he got out'.[150] Arm in arm, doubtless relishing the fraternal masquerade, Harry and his towering sweetheart mingled with the trysting soldiers and their girlfriends scattered across the field outside the prison. The group of five was picked up by a car outside the Adam and Eve Inn and driven to Worksop in Nottinghamshire, where a second car set off with Harry and the prisoners for Manchester while Collins took a train to London.[151] While in Manchester, Harry made arrangements for preserving the multitude of keys associated with the escape.[152] When news of the escape reached the press on Tuesday afternoon, republican propagandists instantly embroidered and adjusted the tale to suggest an unmitigated triumph of Irish ingenuity over English oppression and obtuseness. It only later emerged that de Valera's 'great fear' was that he would be released before having the opportunity to escape.[153]

De Valera's escape had not been noticed until 9.30 on Monday night, when the remaining prisoners aroused suspicion by being 'inclined to disregard the usual summons' and scattering in all directions. Next morning, a warder found footmarks and a well-constructed rope ladder in the field. There was evidence of tampering with several locks, one of which could have been removed and used as the basis for a key by 'at least two skilled mechanics' among the prisoners. An inquiry was conducted by Inspectors Winn and Farewell, who had struggled so patiently with Harry and his comrades to restore control at Lewes Prison in 1917. They concluded that signals in Morse code could have been picked up from windows on the north-facing hall staircase or in a lavatory to the east, and that the key might have been 'made to a drawing' and supplied from outside. The report exonerated the administrators, attributing the mishap to shortage of staff and the 'peculiar liberty of treatment permitted to these men'.[154] Desultory efforts were made to trace the fugitives, and Lincoln was festooned with handbills offering 'a reward of £5 for information which will lead to their capture'.[155] The mystery of de Valera's escape and disappearance became a matter of worldwide speculation, and 568 readers of one illustrated magazine entered a competition to 'find de Valera' somewhere among the squiggles on a sketchmap of Ireland, Britain, and France.[156] Harry pandered to public curiosity by appealing to a crowd outside the Gresham Hotel for information as to his whereabouts ('We all know where he is not; he is not in jail'), and then declaring enigmatically that de Valera 'was strong, happy, and perfectly safe'.[157]

The escapade was widely discussed in the censored correspondence of other Irish prisoners. Paul Cusack, a Granard draper who attired his stylish cousins, the Kiernan sisters, wrote from Lincoln wondering 'where our fugitives are. ... This place is not the same without them, especially De V. who helped us all so well, all the time.'[158] Cusack and his comrades were much diverted by Seán T. O'Kelly's picturesque assertion, to an interviewer in Paris, that the escape had been engineered with the help of ballad-singing gardeners and Sinn Féin sirens, who had used their womanly graces to distract the guards from the creeping fugitives.[159] Cusack found the tale 'absurd and more like a cinema plot from Mexico than anything else. If Dev sees it he will be amused, particularly about the singing part, as poor man, he doesn't know one note from another.'[160] The escape generated interest, envy, and emulation in other prisons. From Reading, Frank Thornton remarked that 'Cahill has gone away, I daresay he is in Berne by this time. I hope he will do some good.' Writing to a convent in Yorkshire, an internee in Birmingham Prison enquired: 'Is Lincoln anywhere in your country up there in the north? It will be more well worth a visit in the future ... because of its recent leap into the limelight. We here seem to be the tamest of all at present.'[161] Encouraged by their triumph at Lincoln, the brethren in Dublin prepared for further exploits. In Gloucester, Robert Brennan received a message from Harry inscribed in dried saliva and revealed by a spilt bottle of ink: 'We want to arrange Griffith's escape. You are to come out on parole on account of your father's illness so we can fix up plans.' Brennan secured his parole, but the conspiracy was frustrated by the premature release of the remaining Irishmen in English prisons, following the death of Pierce McCann in Gloucester Prison's hospital on 6 March.[162] The game was transferred to Mountjoy, from which twenty prisoners decamped in late March despite their success in securing 'chops and steaks for dinner' and 'eggs for breakfast' from a placatory Governor.[163] As the prisons emptied and such antics grew tedious through repetition, Sinn Féin's propagandists concentrated on alerting the world, initially through the Paris Peace Conference which had assembled on 18 January, to Ireland's claim for self-determination.

Though de Valera was the campaign's chief advocate, Harry played an essential part in its formulation. De Valera's first performance after his clandestine return to Dublin, on 20 February 1919, was to conduct an 'interview' to be published simultaneously by some 700 newspapers served by the United Press of America. Since the Chief still lacked confidence in his command of the spoken word, he placed severe restrictions upon the unfortunate journalist Ralph F. Couch, who had been driven in blindfolds to the meeting. According to a statement drafted jointly by Harry and de Valera, the interview consisted of 'one comprehensive question the reply to which Mr de Valera wrote with his own hand' and 'slightly amended' on the following day. To Harry's draft preface, which explained that 'the Irish cause stood to gain by publicity', de Valera added that 'it was for this reason he took the risk'. He went on to list documents necessary to amplify the 'interview' into a Sinn Féin leaflet, instructing Harry to 'pay attention to the paragraphy and get fairly good paper'.[164] A few days later, Harry shepherded de Valera to his old haunt in the Dublin Distillery, and thence (having uttered 'a plaintive curlew's call') through a side gate to the house of the unsuspecting Archbishop Walsh at Clonliffe. In a gate lodge supplied by Walsh's secretary, Fr. Michael Curran, de Valera was left to develop his ideas into a statement of Ireland's case for the Peace Conference.[165] When eventually published on 12 March, the interview aroused controversy by explicitly condoning violence as a last resort: 'If the Paris Conference fails to take steps to extend self-determination to Ireland, violence will be the only alternative left to Irish patriots. This will mean something like continued revolution, until Ireland's rights are recognised. We hope to avoid violence, but if we must fight again to regain our rights we shall not hesitate.' It was Harry who was left, rather unconvincingly, to repudiate 'Mr. Couch's impressions', and to assert that 'such headings as "Violence is the Only Alternative" must be laid on Mr. Couch, not on de Valera.'[166] Already, Harry's new persona as the faithful dogsbody and silver-tongued apologist was under construction.

When George Creel visited Dublin in late February, to assess the Irish claim on behalf of President Wilson, he was introduced to the separatist leaders at 'a secret rendezvous' through the mediation of their old antagonist, John Dillon:

Of the twenty-odd men that stood before me, the two that stay clearest in my memory were Mike Collins and Harry Boland, then like brothers. . . . For all their implacability, the Sinn Féiners were far more reasonable than the Irish-American group in Paris. Even while contending that it was

President Wilson's right to urge consideration of Ireland's case by the peace conference, they listened without interruption to my insistence that it was a meaningless gesture that could only have dangerous consequences.

Touched by 'the disappointment in every face' as he explained the futility of this strategy, Creel promised to pass on their request that Wilson 'bring personal pressure to bear on Lloyd George that would force him to [show] some regard for English pledges'. Though nothing came of this undertaking, Wilson having already circulated senators with the first draft of a Covenant for the League of Nations before Creel could act, his response gave credence to Sinn Féin's belief that Ireland could benefit from Britain's formidable debt to its wartime ally.[167]

During his brief participation in the First Dáil, confined to four days in early April, the deputy for South Roscommon was unusually trenchant in his denunciation of a League dedicated to defending the imperial interests of the victorious powers. Observing with mock sympathy that 'President Wilson had enough to bear without having this covenant of the League of Nations fathered on him', he called for denunciation of a scheme 'built up by the British Government and by the Cecils' and therefore 'evil to Ireland'. The repented Home Ruler Laurence Ginnell warned against 'repudiating President Wilson until he knew he was guilty'; and Collins, on behalf of the Dáil Ministry, gained approval of a diplomatic resolution expressing readiness 'to enter a World League of Nations based on equality of rights, in which the guarantees exchanged neither recognise nor imply a difference between big nations and small'.[168] Otherwise, Harry confined himself to insisting that all documents be issued in English as well as Irish, attending to the interests of prisoners and internees, and seconding the nomination of Collins as Secretary for Finance.[169]

Meanwhile, he redoubled his effort as an Honorary Secretary of Sinn Féin, attending all but two of the Standing Committee's eleven meetings during what turned out to be his last ten weeks in Ireland.[170] Brushing off a suggestion 'that the local people be first consulted', Harry pushed through a motion to contest a by-election for North Londonderry, in which the Sinn Féiner scored scarcely 30 per cent of the poll.[171] His distrust of decentralisation narrowly prevailed when it was agreed, contrary to a sub-committee's recommendation, to subject Sinn Féin's 'organisation abroad' to 'control from Headquarters in Ireland'. Yet Harry, always alert to the value of front organisations, was among the instigators of the autonomous Irish Self-Determination League of Great Britain, whose appeal extended beyond republicanism and Sinn Féin.[172] He also contributed to practical projects such as 'social ostracisation' of the police and co-operative acquisition of land.[173] He even had to deal with a courteous request from the self-designated 'traditional enemy', in the person of T. C. Kingsmill Moore of Trinity College and 'the Phil', to 'expound the Sinn Féin views and policy to the two American officers who bring this note'.[174] His work was only mildly inconvenienced by the reiterated presence of detectives outside no. 6, whom he 'used to confound' by his cheeky greetings: 'Hallo, Bruton; Hi there, Wharton.'[175] Versatility was essential for organisers of revolutionary Sinn Féin.

Harry, like Collins, was indefatigable in arranging relief for distressed activists and receptions for ex-prisoners.[176] The most spectacular of these was to have been a rather tardy civic welcome for de Valera by Dublin's Lord Mayor, Laurence O'Neill. When the ceremony announced for 26 March was proscribed by Dublin Castle, separatist leaders were divided on the issue of cancellation. The advocates of defiance included the Fenian civil servant and historian Patrick Sarsfield O'Hegarty, who declared that 'a withdrawal would be as fatal to the morale, and I believe to the success of Sinn Féin, as was the Clontarf withdrawal to O'Connell's Repeal Movement'.[177] Less predictable was the response of the red-bearded maverick and poet Darrell Figgis, who (according to one account) neatly reversed the usual pattern of debate within Sinn Féin by stoutly opposing Collins's prudent injunction that the demonstration be abandoned. Collins, though also fearful of the analogy with Clontarf, had submitted to de Valera's insistence that such a confrontation be avoided. This led to an extraordinary outburst of mutual affection among the wrong-footed brethren, witnessed by Robert Brennan at no. 6:

> After the meeting, Mick and Harry Boland came to my office and Mick indulged in sulphurous language about Figgis. Then he and Harry had a bout of their customary horseplay. Harry was standing with his back to the fire and Mick shouldered him aside. Harry retaliated and soon they were engaged in a vigorous rough and tumble, giving evidence of the great reserves of surplus energy both of them had. The incident itself was an indication of Harry's attachment to Mick, because he disliked having his clothes tousled while, at that time, Mick gave little attention to his clothes.[178]

A week later, decorum was restored when Harry joined the Lord Mayor at the Mansion House to welcome the Chief as he alighted, without fanfare or public notice, from a tramcar.[179]

Harry's confrontation with Figgis was resumed on 8 April, when both contested the election for Honorary Secretaries at Sinn Féin's extraordinary Ard Fheis. Although admitting to 'a lamentable lack of duty on the part of the clubs' in paying their dues, the ruling cabal retained control. Figgis was heavily defeated by Harry and the imprisoned Austin Stack. Figgis attributed this outcome to a militant takeover, celebrated by further horseplay:

> As I left the hall, the Convention over, I was suddenly stopped by a strange sight. Behind one of the statues with which it is surrounded stood Michael Collins and Harry Boland. Their arms were about one another, their heads bowed on one another's shoulders, and they were shaking with laughter. They did not see me. Their thoughts were with their triumph.[180]

Ó Murthuile, however, interpreted Harry's re-election as an impartial tribute to his 'success in the job'.[181] There is indeed evidence that the IRB had yet to secure its stranglehold over Sinn Féin. In nominating a substitute upon his departure from Ireland, Harry proposed another Fenian from Lewes, Con Collins. This appointment was first approved and then overturned by the Standing Committee, which selected the suffragist Hanna Sheehy-Skeffington instead. Michael Collins snarled that 'the position is intolerable – the policy now seems to be to squeeze out any one who is tainted with strong fighting ideas or I should say I suppose ideas of the utility of fighting'.[182]

Harry's growing preoccupation with international affairs reflected the decision of the Supreme Council to send him as its 'envoy' to the American Clan na Gael, the Fenian fraternity whose practical co-operation was considered essential for the success of the separatist campaign. His task was to reassert 'home' control over Devoy's organisation, and to settle the conflicts which were already tearing apart the Clan and its front organisation, the Friends of Irish Freedom. Harry's appointment was suggested by Collins (as Treasurer of the Supreme Council), though Ó Murthuile later claimed that some of his colleagues 'were sceptical about his ability to handle such a situation as we felt would present itself when he began dictating to the Clan na Gael'.[183] Collins supplied him with a scrap of typescript stating that 'the bearer Mr. Énri Ó Beolláin has full authority to act in every capacity on behalf of the [Supreme] COUNCIL. He has been acting Chairman of that body since the general round-up in May last. He is visiting you in his official capacity.'[184] De Valera, using the Dáil's letterhead, declared that 'the bearer, Énri Ua Beoláin, is a special envoy of the Elected Government of the Irish Republic to the United States of America. His acts may be regarded as official. His formal credentials follow.'[185] The Dáil sanctioned expenditure by the 'American Delegation' on 2 May and, a fortnight later, approved an advance of £250 for Harry's outgoings.[186] His departure was kept secret until Sinn Féin's indiscreet announcement, in mid May, of the appointment of his substitute as Honorary Secretary. Collins was disgusted: 'Our own people give away in a moment what the Detective Division has been unable to find out in five weeks.'[187]

On 17 April, Harry assigned his tailor's business and tenancy in Middle Abbey Street to Bill Duggan, without taking the precaution of informing his landlord and thereby protecting himself against Duggan's creditors. The Boland family continued to frequent the shop, which was used over the next two years as an address for clandestine messages, and a store for guns, ammunition, gelignite, and home-made 'eggs' or Mills bombs. Poor Duggan 'hated Volunteers in the shop', but the redoubtable Kathleen 'managed to terrorise him into silence'.[188] On Easter Sunday, 20 April, Harry played a notable part in the GAA's annual congress, and three days later he attended Sinn Féin's Standing Committee for the last time until 1920.[189] Soon afterwards, the adoring office staff farewelled their 'gayest spirit' – 'boyish, indomitable, full of laughter and at the core of it all a hidden toughness'. 'Fitz' (Anna Fitzsimons) typed him a copy of the Dáil's Declaration of Independence for insertion within the heel of a cannily designed sea-boot, and the staff gathered for a 'sad lunch' to mourn his departure.[190] By evening the farewell had become maudlin, as Collins was reminded a few months later: 'Your remarks to him at Vaughan's on the night of his American wake, he often repeats: "I'm a poor lonesome whore".'[191] Harry and Seán Ó Murthuile then proceeded to Manchester, diverting themselves *en route* by making a British soldier in their compartment 'as happy as possible', before removing his rifle at Chester Station. Ó Murthuile recalled that 'Harry acted the part of a wounded man in perfect style after I had placed the rifle in the leg of his trousers', enjoying free tea dispensed by 'some sympathetic ladies' before consigning his prop to Dublin.[192] After a brief stay with his ever hospitable aunts, he used the IRB's extensive network of agents in Liverpool to secure work as a stoker, evidently on the *Royal George*, a Cunard liner bound for New York on 4 May.[193] Harry Boland's American adventure was under way.

Cavalcade

WHEN Harry Boland landed at New York on Friday, 16 May 1919, the dapper tailor had been transformed into a grimy stoker. Under the supervision of a Galwegian named O'Flaherty, he had spent his twelve days at sea 'sweat[ing] over a coal shovel' in the engine room of the *Royal George.*[1] He was perhaps relieved rather than insulted when, like other Irish envoys without maritime experience, he was 'disrated for incompetency'.[2] Using a false identity card, he was ushered through customs by two agents of the Clan na Gael, and spent his first night in America with Diarmuid Lynch, an old associate from the GPO, Dartmoor, Lewes, and Sinn Féin headquarters.[3] Lynch, a naturalised American deported from Ireland in 1918, had become National Secretary to the Friends of Irish Freedom, the most formidable of the Clan's front organisations. Lynch 'gave him an account of the position in America, including the differences of opinion which had arisen between a few of the leaders on some matters of policy' – notably over the American preference for 'self-determination' rather than 'recognition of the Irish Republic' as the most expedient slogan for American consumption. Harry dismissed this contention as 'a tempest in a teapot'.[4]

Harry was introduced next day to the cantankerous President of the Clan na Gael, John Devoy, and his closest colleague, Daniel Francis Cohalan, an American-born judge and political fixer who dominated the strategy of the Friends. According to Devoy, who admittedly was a very deaf 76-year-old, Harry 'informed them that it was Michael Collins and he who insisted that the Republic must be made the Mandate in the General Elections of 1918, and that when Collins and he rescued De Valera from Lincoln Jail and they informed him of the fact, he told them that if he had been out he would have opposed this, believing that they would be beaten at the polls, but seeing that they had won the elections he was then satisfied'. They advised Harry that the sole source of dissension among Irish-American activists was his volatile precursor as the IRB's envoy, Dr. Patrick McCartan. The evening was spent in Devoy's hotel, chatting about the exploits of Jim and Jack Boland, Harry's political education being resumed next day over Sunday dinner with Lynch. His hosts found him 'most friendly and reasonable all through'.[5]

The warmth of this posthumous account, scarcely diminished by Devoy's subsequent bitterness against de Valera, echoed his first article on the 'Irish Republic's new envoy', published five weeks after Harry's arrival:

Mr. Boland is a splendid type of the new generation of Irish Nationalists. He is essentially a fighting man, both physically and mentally. He inherits his fighting qualities. His father was a Fenian, well known to the editor of this paper, and he brought up his son in the old fighting spirit of Fenianism.

Harry had 'had many hair-breadth escapes and some physical encounters, but was never captured' during his year on the run, showing 'skill and audacity'. He was 'keen of eye, alert and physically very vigorous. His vigour is inherited, his father having been a powerful man, but it was increased by constant outdoor exercise' on behalf of the GAA.[6] At his first appearance before the Friends of Irish Freedom, he made an equally strong physical impression on that organisation's Carmelite President, Peter Magennis. Harry shamelessly exhibited himself as rugged Irish youth personified, sneering 'that grey-haired representatives and men unused to hardships can find no place in the present movement in Ireland. The man who represents Ireland must be capable of fatigue and hardship, of long fasts and of rapid and unprovided for journeys. He must be able to fight and to run. He must be able to spend eight or ten days at a time in the hell-holes of the great American liners.' Magennis recalled that 'as he held up his hands to give them his parting advice we saw how swollen and broken and coal-pitted they were', in keeping with his pronouncement that 'the day of the white shirt and well-starched collar amongst Ireland's representatives has been adjourned'.[7]

Though Harry would soon revert to his customary spruceness, the *New York Times* also depicted the new envoy as a blunt man of the people:

> Boland is of medium height, powerfully built, and rather soft-spoken except when Great Britain and a free Ireland are concerned. Then his broad thick hands close, his chin is thrust forward, and he isn't soft spoken at all.[8]

Harry was still a novelty for the American press, though he had outlined the circumstances of his passage for the New York *Call*, a socialist journal, on 6 June. This was the first intimation of his illicit entry to reach the Bureau of Investigation, which with characteristic imprecision reported that he had 'disappeared from Ireland about the end of May 1919'.[9] Without serious impediment or harassment, Harry had joined the legion of unauthorised immigrants for whom America was the revolutionary front line.

Harry was at first preoccupied, not with propaganda or public display, but with penetrating the labyrinth of Irish-American politics and winning the confidence of its leaders. His purpose was to prime the existing networks of Irish organisations, both secret and open, for mobilisation in support of a future public campaign to be conducted, as it turned out, by de Valera. The 'Chief'

duly arrived, also under O'Flaherty's supervision, on Wednesday, 11 June.[10]
Harry later enjoyed recounting the seaman's impressions of his rebel charges, as
unwittingly addressed to him during a later voyage:

> At Sea. Come up out of Engine Room, meet O'F., who asks me if I know
> Harry Boland. Answer – 'I heard of him.' 'Well,' says O'Flaherty, 'I
> brought that guy out to America in the *Royal George*.' 'That so.' 'Yes;' and
> 'then I brought out de Valera who came in stoke hold. Of course "meself"
> and Bob done his work. One day Second Engineer finds de V. idling. "Pick
> up yer slice," sez the 2nd, "Go and —— yerself," sez de Valera.' Good for
> you, O'Flaherty, I appreciate your talk. Know you and thousands like you
> would do the work with joy.[11]

As a fugitive who was disqualified, despite his birthplace, from receiving an
American passport,[12] de Valera followed Harry's example by lying low for a
week or so. His clandestine arrival surprised not only the American and British
authorities, but also Harry. According to the Fenian bos'n who had arranged de
Valera's passage, 'Harry Boland nearly had a fit when he found whom we had
on board. He knew nothing about his coming over. In fact, no one in New York
knew about it.'[13] A British Intelligence report claimed that 'some of the more
extreme sections fear he [de Valera] has gone over to put a check on Boland at
the invitation of the more peaceable party'.[14]

Harry's first intimation of his leader's arrival was a note delivered at 9.30 on
Wednesday evening:

> Rather unexpected this! Will tell you idea when we meet. Am anxious to
> travel to Rochester tonight – hope it can be arranged. Want to see you
> before I meet anybody. I learnt a number of things since you left dealing
> with the matter you came to investigate. If you are watched here better not
> come to see me but travel to Rochester tomorrow or as soon as you can. I
> hope your experience did you as little harm as mine has done to me. Till
> we meet. E. de V.[15]

At 11.30 p.m., de Valera was delivered to 'Phelan's back room in Tenth
Avenue', where he met Harry and his closest ally in the Clan, the Philadelphian
liquor merchant Joseph McGarrity. McGarrity, who had alienated his Clan
colleagues by employing McCartan as editor of his newspaper, the *Irish Press*,
was a relatively junior member of the Executive. This breach of Clan protocol
affronted Devoy, even though he too was soon summoned to 'Boland's very
plain lodgings' to meet de Valera, who was busy 'washing up and putting on
clean clothes'.[16] Overnight, Harry had become de Valera's valet, shepherd, and
manager instead of acting as an envoy in his own right. Over the following ten
days, he briefed his Chief on Irish-American factionalism, took him to

Rochester to meet his mother and stepfather (Catherine and Charles Wheelwright), 'left Rochester hurriedly, to escape newsmen', and prepared him for public exposure at a reception in the Waldorf-Astoria Hotel on Monday, 23 June.[17] Harry's management of de Valera's American cavalcade was under way.

Notoriously gauche in manner and convoluted in thought and speech, de Valera had become an object of fascination for smooth-tongued, gregarious Harry since the romance of Lincoln Prison. If Collins was his soulmate, de Valera was his antithesis. Each recognised complementary qualities in the other. After two months in America, de Valera told Arthur Griffith that 'I have got a bad reputation here as being "a very stubborn man". Harry is liked by everybody.'[18] A few weeks later, Harry boasted to brother Ned that 'I am going on stump with De V. I have had great success as a speaker. De says we are "an ideal team". The Chief addresses himself to the people's head, while I get into their hearts with my "dope".'[19] An unusually sympathetic observer, James K. McGuire of New Rochelle, interpreted de Valera's clumsiness as the mask of 'a gentle, brave, kindly, noble-souled, determined idealist, like Desmoulins, St. Just and the guillotined Girondists who died to make a new world and succeeded; but a most difficult man to fit in in the most selfish, self-centred, materialistic great country in the world'. McGuire, Treasurer of the Clan, instructed the haughty Judge Cohalan to handle him gently: 'Do not *raise* De Valera's hand *high* and hurt it when you shake hands with him or any other underfed man and speak to him not *at* him.'[20] Yet Cohalan, like Devoy and many other Irish-Americans, found de Valera arrogant, prickly, and pig-headed, a reputation which Harry laboured in vain to mollify.

His diary gives an affectionate but not uncritical impression of an extraordinary personality:

3 Dec. Wed. New York. De V. talks all night, no one else.

16 Dec. Tues. Washington. Chief entertains filing expert for 2 hours to dissertation on correct filing system.

18 Dec. Thurs. Washington. Busy day shopping for de Valera. ... Chief raids book store, 2 hours in store, emerges, 16 books on Ireland.

31 Dec. Wed. Washington. Go to bed early and am awakened by the passing of the old year, to the usual accompaniment of bells, bugles etc. Find de V. writing to wife. 'His first duty' in the New Year.

7 Jan. Wed. New York. Arrive 3 o'c., no room save one. Sleep with de V.

26 Jan. Mon. New York. Very, very busy packing ten bags for Washington. Chief is a 'terrible man' for bags, books and notes. Each trip we take, no matter how short travel, enough books etc. to fill a room. As usual, nearly miss the train.

25 Feb. Wed. New York. Chief not in good form, nervous indigestion. O'Mara prescribes dry toast.

23 Mar. Tues. Washington. Chief arrives full of pep, does not want to go for rest. I threaten to strike if de V. does not go. Result, all well.

25 Mar. Thurs. Washington. De Valera calls off holiday. Nunan and Boland raise hell of a row. De Valera surrenders. Chief can only receive rest by working. Works day and night, his mind never rests.

8 Apr. Thurs. Washington. Go to train. God speed, feel lonely for Chief.

5 May. Wed. Washington. Poor de V. is very lonely for home and children.[21]

Even Harry's managerial talent was tested to the limit by the idiosyncrasies of his prize exhibit.

By mid 1919, Irish-America was already swarming with emissaries, gun-runners, fund-raisers, and propagandists from home, most of whom had been fugitives in Ireland before slipping illicitly into the relative immunity of the United States. As one neglected wife wrote to an American friend in the following year: 'You have a great number of mysterious Irish men over there now. I know hardly a man among my intimate friends who is not either in America or somewhere unknown here. ... The on-the-run system here does better work than all your American divorce courts.'[22] The most prominent of the brethren who had preceded Harry were Liam Mellows, who had escaped from Galway after the Rebellion in the habit of a Sister of Mercy, and Patrick McCartan, the Tyrone doctor who had compensated for an inconspicuous Rebellion by embarking on a series of lurid adventures in America and eventually Russia. Like Diarmuid Lynch, these two emissaries had been elected to the Dáil in their absence. Both had absconded from internal 'exile' in England, and both had been charged in New York with possession of forged papers but released on bail.[23] Mellows was the bonny baby of the 'mission': '5 ft. 3 ins.; fair, fresh complexion; grey eyes, thin face, regular nose; medium make; very fair hair; clean shaven; gold rimmed glasses; weight 128 lbs.'[24] In McCartan, however, the RIC detected a brooding and uncomfortable presence:

Has restless small brown eyes, has a habit of looking in a shifty way from side to side and downwards when speaking to anyone; ... keeps his lips usually apart, showing his teeth, one of which, a double tooth, has gold filling visible; thin, long jaws, and the movements of his mouth cause wrinkles on his cheeks; keeps hands in trouser pockets, peculiar gait, takes long steps and looks shaky at the knees when walking, turns in his toes slightly; constantly smokes cigarettes, and fingers are usually stained with nicotine.[25]

Harry worked easily with the jaunty Mellows ('fresh as paint') but initially found McCartan a more prickly colleague. McCartan suspected that his dispute with Devoy and Cohalan over 'recognition' had led to his recall, and that Harry, with his superior authority as President of the Supreme Council, had been sent to replace him. In fact, the new envoy presented him with new credentials from the Dáil which confirmed McCartan's responsibility for pursuing 'recognition', Harry at first being formally responsible only to the IRB. McCartan continued to regard himself as redundant, but his departure was postponed on de Valera's insistence.[26] Harry informed de Valera on 4 June that 'McCartan is in hot water with Judge [Cohalan], Seán Fear ['the Old Man', Devoy] and New York. He has held out all the time for Recognition and has had tips [sic.] with these men. I hope to use "the oil can" here, anyway do not worry, as all will be well. The Doctor and I are working together and he will do as I think best.' Of Mellows, he wrote that 'Liam is outside the Council [of the Friends]. He has fallen foul of the same men and has been cold-shouldered. Liam hates America and will go home. Let me say I am satisfied that he has done great good notwithstanding his been [sic.] outside. He is very popular with the people.'[27] Far from resenting or supplanting other envoys, Harry preferred to harness them to his own well-oiled American 'chariot'. As Mellows observed: 'We are all thrown very much together – An Árd, Dr., Seosamh, Enri and Mise.'[28]

His closest collaborators in the United States were men like Seán Nunan and James O'Mara, who had previously worked with him at Sinn Féin's headquarters and relished his inspirational approach to office management. Nunan, a puny Londoner with Limerick origins who had become intimate with Collins since their internment at Frongoch, proved to be 'cool, careful, with a good head for business'.[29] He relished the Brotherhood and his nights of wild talk and 'mountain dew' with the 'alarmers' of Vaughan's Hotel, where Collins and Harry used to hold court.[30] He reached New York less than a fortnight after de Valera, who had tried to keep him in Ireland 'after hearing from Harry Boland about the rigours of firing a ship'.[31] Nunan reported proudly to Collins that 'I was not disrated for incompetency like Harry', giving the lie to de Valera's fear 'that I would not stand the hardship of the journey'.[32] Like many new arrivals, he spent his first night at the Carmelite priory with Fr. Peter Magennis, whose presidency of the Friends of Irish Freedom ended soon afterwards upon his appointment as 'General' of the Order in Rome. Harry hurried from Philadelphia with McGarrity to meet and brief their 'little Brother'.[33] The future Secretary of the Department of External Affairs joked and pranked his way across America with Harry, who succeeded at least once in discomfiting him during a train journey with de Valera. Warned by Harry that there was no ticket for him and that he must either climb under the seat or be put off, Nunan chose the former. When the conductor was shown three tickets and enquired after the third passenger, Harry observed that 'for some reason he's hiding under the seat'.[34]

James O'Mara, who like Nunan had once served as Director of Elections for Sinn Féin, was less obviously a kindred spirit. The 46-year-old bacon curer and provision broker from Limerick had represented South Kilkenny as a Home

Ruler from 1900 until his resignation in 1907, once noting with striking candour that he 'was not connected with Easter Week Rising 1916 – too suicidal'. With stores in Canada and Dublin and a vast income by republican standards, he continued to '*beware* public men and public life – business and only business means liberty, comfort, safety'.[35] Yet he accepted Sinn Féin's nomination for his old constituency in 1918 and became a Trustee of the Dáil's first external loan, before donning 'an old slouch hat' and pursuing 'the stoke-hold route' to New York. An acute Irish-American considered that 'in business ability' and other qualities, O'Mara was 'the ablest of all those who came out from Ireland' – despite his appalling dress-sense and 'defects of temperament' which made him 'hard to put up with'.[36] Even John Devoy acknowledged that he was 'a very level headed man with a long business experience'.[37]

Yet O'Mara's impatience with less competent colleagues led to reiterated disputes, resignations, and retractions, requiring frequent interventions from the emollient Harry:

6 Mar. Sat. Philadelphia. J. O'Mara resigns. Fearful blow.

7 Mar. Sun. Philadelphia. O'Mara's decision very severe blow. Cannot hope to secure his like again.

8 Mar. Mon. Philadelphia. O'Mara arrives from Ohio, looks very upset. I have long chat with him, use all my persuasive power.[38]

Much of O'Mara's spleen was directed against the mission's other representative of business, the Corkonian Diarmuid Fawsitt who had been appointed as the Republic's 'Consul' in New York.[39] He was as liberal as O'Mara in his announcements of resignation:

2 Dec. Tues. New York. Fawsitt wants to go home, seems to me very childish, won't stay and finish the job.

14 Feb. Sat. New York. Fawsitt back from Ireland, fine work. I lose a dollar on Fawsitt['s] safe return.

17 Feb. Tues. New York. Fawsitt to open new offices. Great fellow.[40]

In a characteristically robust exchange, Fawsitt protested 'against the inattention and incivility which you have meted out to my letters to you of recent date', drawing an equally icy response from O'Mara: 'I resent the tone of your letter and repudiate the allegations therein.' Within a few weeks, civility had returned and both men had withdrawn their threatened resignations.[41] Such conflicts and tantrums were endemic in the feverish atmosphere of the Irish mission, where versatility was valued more than any pedantic demarcation of functions, and Harry's 'oil can' was crucial in securing reconciliation.

Of all the envoys, Harry himself was the most versatile. As we shall see, he meddled in every aspect of the republican campaign, from propaganda, fund-raising, and lobbying to arms procurement and clandestine military organisation. His diplomatic and administrative skills were in demand at every level from representing the Republic to resolving office feuds. Yet, for much of his first year, he adopted the modest title of 'Secretary to the President'. Far from being a misnomer, this reflected the humdrum character of much of his work, ruefully chronicled in his diary:

> 3 Oct. Fri. Pittsburgh. Seán [Nunan] and I lost in crowd, had to look after luggage, and reached the hotel before parade.
>
> 14 Oct. Tues. Valparaiso. Leave by auto for South Bend. Blow out. Seán, Chief and I get out and get under, fix burst [?], arrive South Bend.
>
> 1 Jan. Thurs. Washington. Get back to Shoreham in time to secure tickets and rush for train to New York. Manage tea and toast for party.
>
> 5 Jan. Mon. New Haven. Nearly miss train. Manage to scrape in, no tickets, arrive O.K. Crowd to meet Chief. I struggle with baggage.[42]

Harry presided over the volatile staff of several offices, mostly run by domineering Americans or Canadians (such as Katherine Hughes) who some-times resented talented emigrants like de Valera's future secretary (Kathleen O'Connell):[43]

> 18 Feb. Wed. Washington. Office again. Clear up. Miss O'Connell very good girl, could not manage without her.
>
> 6 Apr. Tues. Washington. I am at office all day, invite Miss O'Connell and Miss Rosser. Miss Hughes objects to staff been [sic.] invited. Girls out for Miss Hughes' blood. Boland retires and leaves the fight 'tween em.[44]

Devoted though he was becoming to de Valera, Harry was clearly exasperated by his interminable petty demands for service and attention. In late January, he told Collins sardonically that 'the President requires a personal servant' who would attend him 'all the time and give the little attentions necessary – (believe me it is the hell of a job!)'. He explained that 'for the past few months, I have been with the President all the time, looking after him personally, travelling from place to place, speaking with him, and generally doing the work of a valet. The President feels that I could be employed more usefully by being a free lance.'[45] In fact, de Valera never ceased to regard Harry as an essential personal accessory.

As in the preceding campaign to secure popular support for Sinn Féin in Ireland, every organiser was expected to double as an orator and public performer. From the first, Harry was keenly aware of the need to keep up appearances, requesting lavish expenses as 'I have to do the heavy when I come out, dress suit etc.'[46] Within a week of de Valera's unveiling at the Waldorf-Astoria on 23 June, Harry and his fellow-envoys had embarked on an arduous series of meetings and receptions ranging from Boston and New England to Chicago and San Francisco.[47] The idea of a cavalcade, on the lines of a royal visit, evidently came from the Clan. As Devoy told Cohalan on 24 June: 'It looks as if they had changed their minds a bit and come round to our way of thinking about a series of big meetings. Harry was enthusiastic for it last night and wanted a meeting this evening to discuss it and make arrangements.'[48] At the first monster meeting, in Boston's Fenway Park, Harry enjoyed a 'magnificent reception' as a rebel who had been condemned to death and as a former Director of Elections for Sinn Féin (both inflated claims).[49] With uncharacteristic lack of plámás, he announced that he was 'astonished on visiting America to find that the people of this great country have not an intelligent idea of the actual situation in Ireland and the aspirations of its people'. After explaining that Redmond's party had become 'more English than the English themselves', and that 1916 was 'not a rebellion, but an insurrection of a people who have ever claimed their right to freedom', he read out Sinn Féin's extraordinarily convoluted Constitution to a perhaps bemused audience.[50]

The sheer excitement of his new life was obvious in his first letter home, largely devoted to de Valera's sensational impact and his 'great success' in playing 'the Lincoln of Ireland' to American audiences. Harry's own achievement was quieter but crucial: 'I have secured a good name from the American journalists and gain some news every day. I feel at home at this work and am gaining every day some new stunt which will be of service to me.' He had also 'become an "Orator" and the people like to hear the story of Ireland'.[51] Harry spoke forcefully at many meetings, but missed out on de Valera's first visit to California following a recurrence of influenza in July. By early September he was at ease with American crowds, mixing banter with fierce assertions of the republican demand. In Rocky Glen near Scranton, Pennsylvania, he denounced Partition with scant regard for Unionist preferences: 'Ulster belongs to Ireland, every inch of it. Not as much as would "sod a lark" can be claimed by England.' Having pumped up the 'Irish blood coursing through their veins', this 'eloquent orator' appealed for all Irish-Americans to contribute 50 cents apiece to the forthcoming Bond Drive:

Immediately there were shouts of 'We'll contribute more than that!' And the crowd roared when Sec. Boland shouted back to the spectators: 'And we'll accept all of it, too!'[52]

Throughout his stay in America, Harry relished the buzz of roaring crowds, receptions from mayors and governors, motorcades, airlifts, banners, banquets, and balls. Heady with universal adulation, he could confront with optimism the intractable problems that beset the mission from without and within.

The campaign was initially centred in New York with brief sallies elsewhere, often requiring no more than an overnight stay. On 1 October, however, Harry inaugurated his new diary with the headline, 'Grand Tour of America'. The plan for a cavalcade moving from city to city around the United States had been devised well in advance by Charles N. Wheeler, a Protestant without Irish blood but 'an experienced man, having accompanied different Presidents of the United States in their campaigns'. Harry submitted the draft itinerary for the 'approval' of Cohalan, who responded graciously that 'on the whole it is very well done' while urging more attention to the South.[53] On 30 September, Harry boasted to his mother that 'everywhere we go, we meet with great receptions, and I have developed great power of "oratory". I am going on the great tour which opens to-morrow in Philadelphia, and I will have visited every state in the Union ere I return.'[54] In writing to the well-travelled Ned, Harry could not restrain his excitement at the prospect, while dutifully claiming that he 'would rather 1 hour in Ireland just now than all this very wonderful trip'. As he travelled from Albany to New York along the Hudson, through 'the land of Fenimore Cooper, Natty Bumppo and Chingachcook',[55] he ticked off the delights to come:

I am about to go on tour from New York thro' Penna, Ohio, Michigan, Indiana, Illinois, Kansas, to Denver, Col.; from thence N.W. to Salt Lake, Butte, Seattle, Tacoma, along the Pacific Slope to Frisco and Los Angeles, then through the South to Florida, and home to N.Y. thro' the South. I often think of your trip, and can fancy some of your journeyings.

After four months in the United States, he felt 'very pleased with America' and its people:

There is something very breezy about the people here that is a delight to me, and I have had the opportunity of meeting all classes from the Governors of States, Mayors, millionaires, down to the poorest class. It is a treat to travel thousands of miles through this land and not to see a high wall with broken glass on the top to keep out the plain people, no hedges or iron railings. It's grand, to let the eye wander round to the very horizon, unimproved by any relic of feudalism.

With a foreigner's unselfconscious condescension, he remarked that 'the "Coloured Gentleman" who is guard of this carriage is a cheerful soul. I have a regard for the Coon, they are always smiling and happy.' After a homely reference to the Leinster hurling semi-final, he assured Ned that he had 'enjoyed writing this, as I feel very near you and all at home'.[56] Practised in the art of migration, Irishmen like Harry switched effortlessly between wanderlust and nostalgia, relishing their exile.

The tour began in McGarrity's Philadelphia, where the organisers spent nearly $7,000 on supper for 613 guests at the Bellevue Stratford Hotel, along with the hire of bands performing at the station, banquet, veterans' parade, and Opera House, and $10 for Harry's taxi:

> 1 Oct. Wed. Left New York for Philadelphia 10 a.m. Raining. Met by thousands at North Phila. Mounted escort of 300 motors all decorated. Went to Independence Hall where Mayor's Deputy welcomed de V. in the name of City. Visited Barry's monument.[57] Banquet in evening. Spoke at Banquet.

> 2 Oct. Thurs. At Philadelphia. Spent the day easily. Evening parade of City to Opera House, great welcome and procession 2 miles long. Hall full and overflow of 30,000. Spoke at two meetings. Phila gave great send off.[58]

The sheer thrill of conquering America rippled through the spare prose of his diary as it recorded the 'Grand Tour', sometimes with a sidelong glance towards posterity. Even his spelling veered towards American style:

> 3 Oct. Fri. Pittsburgh. If cheers and parades mean anything we have won. Wish we could translate cheers etc. into deeds. Bed.

> 5 Oct. Sun. Youngstown. Cosmopolitan crowd. Banquet in evening. 2 speeches. Hell of a life. Note – Boys at home more capable to organise than any I have met here so far.

> 6 Oct. Mon. Akron. Banquet at 6, meeting in Armoury, packed, 5,000. Bad form, stale, so is de V. ... Leave for Cleveland 9 o'c. a.m. By auto. Fed up banquet.

> 7 Oct. Tues. Cleveland. Official visit to Mayor, Freedom of City. Central Armory [sic.] packed, huge overflow. Horse police and motor escort. ... Boland not well, did not speak. Mayor Davis. Aeroplane.

> 15 Oct. Wed. Notre Dame. Wonderful greeting. War Cry U.N.D. [University of Notre Dame], Rah Rah Rah, de Valera, de Valera, de Valera, then Boland, Nunan, Republic. Meet old friend Clark – Bro. Albans [sic.].[59] Enjoy spirit of boys. De V. speaks well and long. Off to St. Mary's girls. Small boys best at War Cry. De V. secures half holiday for kids.[60]

De Valera's propagandist triumph was the outcome of methodical preparation and relentless lobbying, with Liam Mellows inspecting and reporting on each local committee in advance. Harry served 'as an additional speaker and co-ordinator of the Friends of Irish Freedom and Clan-na-Gael officers where problems arose, such as which of the local men should introduce the President, who should be on the platform with him and other details'. In the words of Seán Nunan, also on tour 'as a kind of aide-de-camp': 'Harry was perfect in this regard, both because of his own cheerful disposition and his status as representative of the I.R.B. to the Clan-na-Gael.'[61] In his advance reports, Mellows dealt with everything from baggage arrangements to local references suitable for inclusion in speeches.[62] He also alerted Harry to the problems awaiting the delegation in each city, such as 'a bad mess' in Fort Wayne, due to 'very poor organization, though good people'.[63] Despite this warning, Harry observed that the meeting at Fort Wayne was disastrous: 'Neglect to see programme. Result, chairman calls me first. Chief follows, does fine. Resolution not put, double crossed. De V. in hell of a wax.'[64] Harry often expressed dissatisfaction with local arrangements, remarking that 'Columba [recte, Columbus, Ohio] and Cincinnati were very poor. I feel that we are not getting at our people as we could do if proper attention were given to organisation.'[65] Nevertheless, after 'ten days on the road', Harry deemed the tour a 'wonderful success. The Chief has made a great impression everywhere. . . . We have had many expressions of good will from all classes and creeds here and De V is exploding all the Anti-Irish propaganda.'[66] His letters home bristled with confidence:

I am now a hardened speaker and am quite at home speaking to 30,000 people.

The journey so far has been a great success and we hope it will continue. In every city we have had official recognition.

We have put Bunker Hill back on the American map, and we have been the rallying ground of all good lovers of Liberty.[67]

The cavalcade seemed irresistible.

The tour's highlight was a visit on 18 October to the Chippewa Indian reserve in Wisconsin, at the invitation of 'the Chief and Headmen of the tribe'. Apart from offering welcome relief from the incessant round of railroads, receptions, and banquets, this adventure symbolised the broader fraternity of the Irish with other 'Oppressed Peoples'. As Mellows had previously explained, 'the Indians venerate the Chief, as a person holding the same ideals regarding Ireland as they hold regarding their own rights'. Arrangements had been assisted by Fr. Gordon, one of 'only two Indian priests in America' and 'a most enthusiastic Sinn Féiner'. The agenda had all the elaboration of a royal protocol, with a 'Memorial Mass for Indian Soldiers who died in the Great War', an official welcome at which de Valera would 'smoke Pipe of Peace', and presentation of a wampum belt, the 'most precious gift in their power'. Ever alert to the value of a good story well promoted, Mellows had also arranged 'for the moving picture men to take the scenes at Reserve'.[68] All went well, as Harry informed his mother:

The party had a wonderful day at the Indian Reservation. De Valera is now a Chief of the Chippewa Nation, his Indian name is 'nay nay ong a ba' which means 'the Dressing Feather'. We had the pleasure of seeing the native games and dances, fed on venison and wild rice and other delightful Indian dishes. Five Chiefs of the tribes made speeches in their native tongue and offered presents of beaded work to De Valera. An Indian interpreter then translated their speeches into English and I was back again reading Fenimore Cooper. We had to drive 34 miles to the Reserve thro' the pine forests of Wisconsin and I never enjoyed a day so much.[69]

Having all but missed the train to St. Paul, he spent the next two days there and in Minneapolis, banqueting, giving a 'rotten' speech, visiting the 'Seminary and Military College', 'shopping for Indians', and getting 'roses etc. for Nunan'.[70]

Within a week, to his chagrin, Harry had been abruptly detached from the party in order to assume a less agreeable duty in New York:

> 24 Oct. Fri. St. Louis. 21 Guns, for de Valera. Parade of city, 5 speeches today. . . . I am ordered back to New York to see to organisation of Bonds. I had looked forward to seeing the Rockies and California. ''Tis but in vain etc.'[71]

While de Valera spent the next six weeks circling the country from Seattle to New Orleans and on to Washington, Harry's tour ceased in the 'wild west town' of Kansas City.[72] Thereafter, he spent most of his time within the triangle of Chicago, Washington, New York, and Boston. Though his wings had been clipped, he still yearned for the stimulants of travel and public display. The return of de Valera, reluctant tourist though he was, gave Harry an excuse for sight-seeing in Washington:

> 11 Dec. Thurs. Chief and I take a fine walk thro' Park, walk around Washington Pillar. De V. won't go up. Stroll round lake and admire Lincoln Memorial, Jack Barry's monument, Sherman, La Fayette, Grant and all America's heroes, Army and Navy dept., and home to work. Fine day.
>
> 21 Dec. Sun. Spend very pleasant day walking. Visit Soldiers' Home, Catholic University, Rock Creek National Cemetery, and admire St. Gauden's wonderful statue over Adams' grave.[73]

In New York, too, there were moments of innocuous recreation: 'Chief and I ramble round New York, attend Mass for Dr. [Thomas Addis] Emmet and play truant on Fifth Av. bus.'[74]

Harry continued to attend meetings in the north-eastern states, rushing from town to town to deliver de Valera, and sometimes to 'harangue the crowd' himself:

> 22 Jan. Thurs. New York. Arrive very tired 6.30 a.m. Go to bed for few hours, shopping, leave 7 o'c. Chief speaks at Richmond Hill, Flushing,

Jamaica, Astoria, and winds up at F.O.I.F. Ball meeting. Wonderful performance. 5 meetings in 5 hours, 70 miles driving in snow.[75]

In Boston, he made an impression in his own right: 'Harry Boland was the principal speaker and he got a tremendous reception, had the pleasure of speaking with him after the meeting. We all love him and of course our President is our idol, and dear little Shaun Nunan too is much admired.'[76] For the most part, however, his involvement in de Valera's cavalcade was now vicarious. When his Chief embarked on another tour of the south-eastern states in March, Harry attempted to co-ordinate arrangements from Washington while Mellows, again the advance guard, fretted about the incompetence of local organisers ('the priests are as *thick* as the rest – and ignorant').[77] Harry, the mission's indispensable anchor, would never complete his 'grand tour' of the American continent.

Though outwardly an instrument rather than an architect of the Dáil's political strategy in America, Harry was capable of political analysis which was at once logical and robust. When writing to de Valera in early June, he declared 'that the policy of backing America during the War has given wonderful power to the Movement', ensuring that 'the League of Nations will be smashed and the Irish will have been the pioneers in the killing'. This raised 'wonderful possibilities for Ireland', as Democrats and Republicans alike vied for Irish-American support. Describing himself as the 'Director of International Bluff', Harry urged de Valera to 'send on at once how you can spend £1,000,000 pounds', observing that 'as I must shew what our Constructive Programme is I invented one: splitting ranches, draining rivers, oil, coal, etc., etc.' His own public rôle should be that of a loyal representative rather than a policy-maker: 'Do not say anything that would give the impression that I asked you to do things on my advice. Let the appeal for money and *bonds* come as from you, blood out of a turnip.'[78] Even after de Valera had arrived to assume personal control, it is likely that Harry's influence on policy remained significant. Devoy later maintained that, blindly loyal though he seemed in public, he 'often differed with De Valera privately, and sometimes bullied him, and in such cases he always won'.[79]

The rationale of the campaign, throughout Harry's first two years in America, was the belief that American recognition of the Irish Republic could be secured through propaganda and political lobbying. For Harry, as for Collins, this strategy was always secondary to the domestic battle. Collins, though initially delighted with Harry's success in raising money and teaching 'USA Pressmen things they never dreamt of', insisted that 'our hope is here and must be here. The job will be to prevent eyes turning to Paris or New York as a substitute for London.'[80] Likewise, Harry hoped 'that we can accomplish much in America in the way of creating favourable public sentiment, yet finally we can and must fight it out in Ireland, backed up by the public opinion of America'.[81] Meanwhile, the changing political context forced the envoys to adopt a succession of expedients in their pursuit of international recognition.

Even before Harry's arrival, the possibility of winning a hearing for the Irish case in Paris was remote, being formally eliminated just before the signature of the Versailles Treaty when Clemenceau, President of the Peace Conference, emphatically rejected the American Senate's request for a hearing.[82]

Thereafter, the campaign concentrated on exploiting the prevalent fear that Congressional ratification of the Treaty and participation in the League of Nations would lead inexorably to an Anglo-American alliance. Through an intricate sequence of dubious alliances and disingenuous 'reservations' concerning the Treaty and the Covenant, Irish-American lobbyists and politicians contributed significantly to the Senate's rejection of the Treaty in both November 1919 and March 1920.[83] Initially, Harry aimed merely to have 'a reservation inserted in the League of Nations in favor of Ireland. This is the most to be hoped for from official America. Some time ago it looked as if the League of Nations would be defeated, but now the prevailing sentiment seems to be "Peace at any price".'[84] Outright rejection still seemed uncertain in mid October, when Harry recorded a discussion in Detroit: 'Wonderful interview with Henry Ford, extraordinary man. De V. and Ford hot and heavy on League of Nations. Ford fanatic. Bad League better than no League, holds de Valera, being very positive.'[85]

Subsequently, all major Irish and Irish-American factions became embroiled in the broader campaign to subvert Anglo-American co-operation by rejecting both the League and the Treaty:

> 3 Nov. Mon. New York. [Charles N.] Wheeler and I to late supper. Good news in paper. Treaty in bad way. Wheelerism – Ireland's fight, against the world. Come over here and smash England's League. Big Bully etc.

> 19 Nov. Wed. New York. Treaty, dead. Great news for Ireland. England has now to reckon with an united Race. We can now go ahead with direct Irish appeal for recognition.

> 22 Mar. Mon. Washington. Great joy over dead Treaty. Irish Reservation was very clever move on Democrats' part. Now we know where we are. Sorry the Treaty did not pass so that England would have to 'deny her own child'. Our Washington work aided considerably. Gore spoke in great style.[86]

Harry's admiration for this 'clever move' was not shared by Warren Gamaliel Harding, the Republican Senator who was soon to succeed Wilson as President. As Harding observed to Frank P. Walsh: 'The insincerity of it was made manifest when sixteen Senators, who pressed the Irish reservation, refused to vote for the Treaty after it was incorporated. I had the satisfaction myself of casting a favourable vote after the incorporation was made.'[87] As Harry reflected: 'What a "queer" thing is American politics. I will have the light Italian hand finely developed if fate ordains that I remain here.'[88]

With the issue of ratification suspended, if not finally resolved, the only promising route towards recognition was through the party conventions which were to nominate presidential candidates in mid 1920. In January, Harry told Collins that 'our political aim is to secure if possible as a plank in the platform of the candidates for the presidency the recognition of the right of the people of Ireland to the principle of national self-determination'. With touching naiveté, he added that 'if we can secure this, we will of course have committed the candidates to the recognition of the Irish Republic'.[89] Though anticipating 'a very stiff fight', he had 'great hopes' of recognition, 'if not from this Administration, then from the next'.[90] President Wilson, incapacitated by a stroke in September 1919, was largely irrelevant to the Irish campaign, though just after Christmas Harry secured an introduction to his secretary from George Creel, the Paris negotiator whom he had met in Dublin in February 1919.[91] In preparation for the conventions, Harry worked tirelessly to lobby influential Congressmen, relying heavily for tactical advice on Washington veterans such as Frank P. Walsh and John E. Milholland:

> 15 Dec. Mon. Washington. I go to House, find Mason, go to House with him, guest. Uncle Joe [McGarrity], Cohalan[?] and Congressmen Newton, Flood, Porter and others bring Mason to Chief. All well.

> 9 Jan. Fri. Washington. Spend all forenoon at Capitol. Meet Gallavan, Flood and a dozen other Congressmen, re de Valera's appearance before House.[92]

Though resulting in nothing more substantial than sympathetic resolutions and publicity, such contacts enabled Harry to build up a network of powerful allies and to develop a more sophisticated insight into the American political labyrinth.

Without broader public support for the Irish cause, even the finest 'Italian hand' was bound to fail. As in Ireland, Harry proved to be a shrewd and effective organiser of propaganda. His aim was to appeal to American, as well as Irish-American sentiment. By 1920, there were scarcely a million natives of Ireland in the United States, and many of the three million natives of America with Irish parentage were no longer self-consciously 'Irish'.[93] It was therefore essential to ensure that 'prominent citizens of other than Irish descent should have a place' on the innumerable reception committees for Presidential visits.[94] Irish propagandists were urged to exploit the deep-seated Anglophobia of many Americans devoid of Irish blood, including returned servicemen: 'It is extraordinary the bitter feeling these men brought back, gathered by them from their personal contact with the Britishers in France.'[95] In order to reach beyond Irish-America, Harry took pains to publicise de Valera's cavalcade and the Irish cause through the popular press. His proven ability to seduce journalists was extended to proprietors, paramount among whom was the model for *Citizen Kane*, W. R. Hearst:

15 Jan. Thurs. New York. Lunch with 'Nation' staff, very interesting – Oswald Garrison Villard.[96] ... Good day's work for Eire.

24 Feb. Tues. New York. Wm. Randolph Hearst. Like his manly face and eyes. I had visualised as a forceful, aggressive type, found him quiet, thoughtful and very fine[?] towards Chief. Agreed to aid us.[97]

Though élite journals such as the *New York Times* remained largely impervious to his charm, Harry's alliance with Hearst ensured sympathetic press coverage for the Irish campaign throughout the Union.

Harry's finesse as a tactician was evident in the links which he forged with an astonishing range of radical groups dissatisfied, for reasons unrelated to Ireland, with Wilson's administration. His most obvious potential allies were other organisations seeking extension of Wilson's principles of self-determination to nationalities unrecognised by the victorious powers. Harry was prominent in Dudley Field Malone's League of Oppressed Peoples, formed at New York's Lexington Opera House in late September 1919.[98] He also collaborated with anti-colonialist lobbies such as the Indian Friends of Freedom, potential partners in any general rising across the British Empire. The flavour of that collaboration is suggested in his diary: 'Chief in bed all day. Gets up for Indian dinner. ... Dinner great, speeches, Russia very popular. Rajahs, Presidents, Revolutionists etc. and the usual Canon J. W. Morse.'[99]

An even closer link developed with Ludwig Martens, American representative of the still unrecognised 'Russian Socialist Federal Soviet Republic'. Martens presided over a 'Society of Technical Assistance to Soviet Russia' and a 'Russian Soviet Government Information Bureau' with 35 staff.[100] The Bureau received substantial consignments of gems from Russia and money from international well-wishers,[101] which were handled by his deputy, Santeri Nuorteva.[102] Just before Harry's arrival, Martens and McCartan had 'formed a sort of mutual admiration society', based, in McCartan's words, upon 'that sense of brotherhood which a common experience endured for a common purpose can alone induce'. While sedulously avoiding any endorsement of Bolshevism, McCartan argued that British intervention in the Russian Civil War justified wide-ranging co-operation in these two anti-imperial struggles.[103] According to the Bureau of Investigation, one of Harry's first engagements in New York was to visit Martens in his office on 40th Street, shortly before a raid which paralysed the Bureau's public functions without terminating its illicit dealings.[104] The relationship flowered during early 1920:

9 Jan. Fri. Washington. Had lunch in Capitol restaurant. Dine with Millholland [John E. Milholland], [Rossa] Downing, Santeri Nuorteva, Martens, McBride, Sol Levison, P. Hand and ladies. Fine Soviet.

27 Jan. Tues. Washington. Meet Martens, Nuorteva and Miss Paul, Miss Pulitzer, John Millholland, Senator Hardwicke etc.

3 Mar. Wed. Washington. Call on Millholland, meet Martens, Nuorteva, Hand, Raymond Robbins, Philip Francis, Senator Hardwicke, Georgia. Very pleasant evening. Bolshevists in great form.[105]

Culmination followed in April, when Harry demonstrated his trust in Russian good faith by lending $20,000 to the Russian representative in the expectation of eventual mutual recognition, to be negotiated by McCartan in Russia. On 9 April, Harry provided the Dáil with suggestions as to McCartan's mission; a week later, Martens presented him with a receipt for the loan, 'to be repaid on demand and return of security rendered'.[106] The intervening transactions were recorded in several cryptic diary entries:

11 Apr. Sun. New York. Nuorteva in trouble owing to Senate report. Make ap[pointment] for Credentials for Pat [McCartan], get them at midnight, all correct.

14 Apr. Wed. New York. Meet Nuo[rteva] who asks me to aid him. Visit O'Mara, wait for him till midnight, put proposal to him – enter a new line of ladies' ornaments for security. Reflect on the saw, Uneasy lies the head that wears the Crown.

15 Apr. Thurs. New York. Meet old Nuo[rteva] and make him happy. Have my eyes filled with Security. Jas. [O'Mara] satisfied.[107]

The 'security' was a selection of four 'Crown Jewels' that were only identified as paste some three decades later, when the Soviet government grudgingly repaid the loan (without any interest) in exchange for the worthless treasure.[108] Meanwhile, the glistening jewels had remained a symbol of two unfinished revolutions, long concealed in Marino Crescent by Harry's doting mother and sister.[109]

In addition to fraternising with spokesmen for other suppressed nationalities, the Irish envoys sought collaboration with organised Labour and the suffrage movement. As in Ireland, Harry proved particularly adept at winning the confidence of trades unionists and feminists, many of whom were happy to pool resources in pursuit of disparate legislative goals. Within five weeks of his arrival, Harry had induced the American Federation of Labor to espouse recognition of the Irish Republic, rather than mere self-determination, at its conference in Atlantic City.[110] Though utterly ineffectual, this gesture raised hopes of more practical collaboration over the next two years. In April 1920, Harry contracted an unexpected *mariage de convenance* with the formidable Dr. Alice Paul, Quaker organiser of one of the most efficient lobbies on Capitol Hill.[111] Hoping for future assistance from suffrage lobbyists, Harry briefly threw himself into the current campaign to secure votes for the women of Delaware:

15 Apr. Thurs. New York. Get a call from Women's Suffrage to aid in Delaware.

17 Apr. Sat. Washington. Meet Miss Paul and agree to go to Wilmington.

18 Apr. Sun. Washington. Go with Rossa Downing to Wilmington. Meet McNabb, Mulvena, Mulrean. Talk and argue in vain attempt to secure their vote for Suffrage. McNabb an eloquent Dempsey. Arrive Washington 7.40, weary of it all.

19 Apr. Mon. Washington. Attend Women's H.Q. Report to Miss Paul.[112]

In reporting his futile meeting with the three Delaware Congressmen to Judge Cohalan, Harry urged him 'to take the matter up personally with them' and pointed out 'the advantage to our cause of securing the good opinion of the leaders of the Suffrage movement who can be of great assistance to Ireland in her fight for Recognition'. Adopting the hyperbolic American style, Harry asserted that 'four ardent Irish-Americans can enfranchise thirty-five million American women'.[113] Cohalan's lukewarm response infuriated the Republican journalist John E. Milholland, one of Harry's closest allies and tactical advisers.[114] Affirming that 'the women can win out in Delaware' and that 'Irish Republicans can have the full credit', he stated that 'the propaganda for the Irish Republic must depend for its success largely upon the appeal which it can make to all people who desire the widest possible extension of liberty' – including women. McNabb, the leading opponent of suffrage in Delaware, was a former prize-fighter who (according to the ever emphatic Milholland) 'only understands strong language':

> You should send for him to come to you – you know how to make him come. Don't go to him, don't ask him to do this, *order him* to do it. You are Boss of his people. He knows it. He will obey and if he does not – put a candidate in the field against him immediately – a red hot Irishman, and a Democrat, of course.[115]

Milholland's attempt to mobilise the 'Boss' failed, and Cohalan ridiculed the notion that Congressmen such as these would allow 'their racial affiliations' to influence their position in American politics.[116] Nevertheless, within four months universal suffrage had been enshrined in the Constitution, allowing Harry and the Irish mission to claim some of the credit.

Since the Irish demand for independence aroused deep suspicion in many Americans, energetic counter-propaganda was required to refute the widespread belief that Irish nationalism was both sectarian and un-American. Despite their belated expressions of support for America's intervention in the European War, the most prominent Irish-American leaders were not easily forgiven for conspiring with the German future enemy between 1914 and 1916. Harry and his comrades faced the even more formidable challenge of justifying their furious opposition to the Allied cause and to Conscription in Ireland, which, like American War fever, had peaked in 1918. This was achieved by expressing admiration for Wilson's War-aims, while denouncing Ireland's exclusion from his principle of national self-determination. Such casuistry did not impress the American Legion, which used its extensive influence among War veterans to disrupt Irish meetings and oppose civic receptions for de Valera. Harry's reaction to one such confrontation in April 1920 was typically forthright: 'Chief in Columbia, S. C. The Legion have protested his visit. Seems to me, the American Legion are a rotten "bunch", strike-breakers, arbiters of America's music, intolerant lot.'[117] In response, local committees often welcomed the envoys with military bands and parades of Irish-American ex-servicemen. In Newport, for example, de Valera was 'met by 200 veterans of the late war and a parade of about 200 motor cars all decorated with American and Irish flags', in preparation for his reception by the Governor of Rhode Island.[118] Even so, many loyal Americans remained justifiably sceptical of Irish and Irish-American patriotic credentials.

Equally damaging was the venerable assumption that Irish nationalism was a cloak for papal aggression, a threat to religious toleration, and therefore inimical to American ideals of liberty. This was the view, not merely of the Loyal Orange Institution of the United States, but of many American evangelical Protestants of all political persuasions. In Pittsburgh, so Mellows informed Harry in late September, 'a strong Orange element' had dissuaded the Mayor from offering de Valera an official reception. He suggested that the President should confound his opponents by discussing 'the Ulster Question' and 'the Religious Bogey', adding 'a word to the wise – this part of the country strongly prohibitionist!'[119] A few weeks later, Mellows reported from Springfield, Illinois, that the local organisers considered a Protestant speaker essential to counteract 'anti-Catholic prejudice' and to 'get a number of non-Catholics to attend meeting'. Mellows again urged both de Valera and Harry to 'lay stress on the non-religious aspect of the Irish case in your addresses'.[120] The problem was exacerbated in November by the arrival of an 'Ulster Delegation' whose aim was to mobilise American Protestant opinion against de Valera's programme and, by a neat turn of phrase, to proclaim Ulster's right to self-determination. During its twelve weeks in North America, the delegation of six clergymen and a prominent Orange MP visited twenty-four cities, typically preaching against popery from fourteen pulpits each Sunday and addressing political rallies across the northern and eastern states. The Ulster cavalcade, though modest by Harry's standards, won significant press coverage for the anti-republican case. The delegates also secured expressions of solidarity from influential American politicians such as Vice-President Thomas Marshall, a Democrat, and Governor Calvin Coolidge of Massachusetts, a future Republican President.[121] The mission was effective because its local organisers were drawn not merely from Orange Lodges and Scotch-Irish societies, but from all the major Protestant churches and a plethora of 'loyal' associations promoting the League of Nations and a closer Anglo-American alliance. Like Harry, the Ulster delegates reached beyond ethnic loyalties to leave an imprint in American domestic politics.

The Irish envoys were alarmed and irritated by this counter-mission, as Harry noted in early December: 'Boston American, Roche, Ulster delegation. My wrath. Chief very vexed over Roche's article, spends all day worrying and decides to write interview. Does so. Too much attention been [sic.] paid to Orangemen.'[122] Eager to refute the mission's claims that Sinn Féin's cause was sectarian, and that Ulster Protestants had the right to reject Irish nationality, Harry acted promptly to undermine its effect. His allies tried to disrupt meetings in Jamaica and Jersey City as well as in Pittsburgh, though evidently without success.[123] The mission was also greeted by a hastily assembled front organisation, the Protestant Friends of Ireland. That 'great patriotic Ulsterman', John E. Milholland of New York, pointed out that 'the cry of "Derry Walls and No Surrender", as well as "The Boyne Water", represents resentment of foreign domination just as much as "Remember Limerick" or "Kinsale" stir up memories'.[124] As Boland reassured Collins:

> The Ulster Delegation is being looked after by an organisation established here known as 'The Protestant Friends of Ireland'. Many influential clergymen from different parts of America, and prominent men in all walks of life (all Protestants) have banded themselves together into an organisation and are following the Ulster delegation throughout the country. So far they have successfully combated the attempts of these men to foment religious strife in America.[125]

In fact, the Irish mission had great difficulty in recruiting liberal Protestant advocates, and was obliged to seek assistance from local Catholic priests[126] and to import suitable clergymen from Ireland. The titular Secretary of the Protestant Friends was the libertarian editor of the World Tomorrow, the Revd. Norman Thomas, who had discarded his collar soon after joining the Socialist Party in 1918.[127] His Executive Secretary, the Revd. Patrick James Grattan Mythen, was rumoured to have 'studied for the Catholic priesthood and then bec[o]me a convert to the Episcopalian faith', before undergoing further conversion to the American Orthodox-Catholic Church (Holy Eastern Confession), of which he promptly became an Archimandrite.[128] Even so, the presence of non-Catholic speakers at most Irish meetings reinforced de Valera's consistently non-sectarian rhetoric, so helping to allay American suspicion that Sinn Féin was merely a reincarnation of the AOH.

In order to sustain the political campaign in Ireland as well as America, massive fund-raising was essential. Harry's most pressing public assignment in late 1919 was to raise credit for Dáil Éireann through the sale of 'Republican

Bonds', redeemable only after the creation of a recognised and functioning independent state. Imitating a Fenian scheme concocted half a century earlier,[129] the Dáil had authorised the issue of Bonds worth £250,000 (then equivalent to about $1,250,000) a few weeks before Harry's departure for America. In mid August, de Valera was granted discretion to increase the American issue in keeping with the grand manner of his tour, the ceiling being raised first to 5, later to 10, and then, absurdly, to 25 million dollars. In the event, the sum raised from the 'first external loan' was just over $5,000,000, of which half was buried throughout the revolution and the 1920s in various American banks. Despite legal impediments and the uncertainty of repayment, over a quarter of a million Americans were induced to subscribe during 1920.[130] This achievement required not only relentless propaganda and enthusiastic local committees, but also an efficient and businesslike central office capable of co-ordinating local campaigns, handling and accounting for huge inflows and outflows, and evading seizure of funds.

For several months, it seemed beyond the mission's capacity to handle so complex a financial enterprise. The creation of an office under Charles Wheeler, sheltering behind the letterhead of the 'American Commission on Irish Independence', aroused antagonism in Judge Cohalan's Friends of Irish Freedom.[131] The Commission's titular Chairman was Frank P. Walsh, the radical lawyer who with two other envoys had lobbied Wilson in Paris – with notable lack of either tact or success – shortly before Harry's departure for America. The Friends, whose Irish Victory Fund raised $850,000 before its premature closure on 31 August 1919, were understandably resentful of a rival appeal directed primarily towards their own members and subscribers.[132] De Valera's insistence on launching and controlling the Bond Drive, energetically backed up by Harry and his colleagues, further soured the mission's already fractious relationship with its most influential American allies. The latter dismissed as 'preposterous' the 'idea that a loan could be floated on normal financial grounds', acknowledging 'that money might be raised for such a purpose as matter of sentiment but never as a cold financial investment'.[133] De Valera finally accepted that the Bond Certificates could not 'be issued on a purely financial basis', addressing his appeal 'to Americans who love liberty and desire to see it triumph in Ireland, particularly, to Americans of Irish blood'.[134] Despite their doubts and suspicions, the Friends eventually acquiesced in the scheme, temporarily provided Walsh with a rent-free office, and through their branches supplied many of the local organisers.[135] On 1 October, after three months of preliminary manoeuvring, Walsh publicly recommended the issue of Bond Certificates 'in the name of Liberty', promising redemption in the form of 'Gold Bonds of the Republic' one month 'after the Republic has received international recognition and the British Forces have been withdrawn'.[136] The main purpose of the 'grand tour' which followed was to advertise the Bond Drive in advance of its intended flotation.

It was Harry's misfortune to assume effective management of the scheme, while Walsh offered little but his name on the Commission's letterhead. By contrast with Michael Collins, who directed the 'internal loan' with meticulous efficiency, Harry had neither the experience nor the temperament to handle the even more intricate 'external loan'. His diary became a record of frustration:

22 Oct. Wed. St. Louis. Fear that Bond has not been properly organised.

23 Oct. Thurs. St. Louis. No arrangement yet made for banks. All anxious to start on Drive. I fear start as no proper organisation to handle sale.

24 Oct. Fri. St. Louis. Walsh and McSweeney arrive, have long chat on Bond issue. I am ordered back to New York to see to organisation of Bonds.[137]

Edward F. McSweeney, the Boston financier whom Judge Cohalan had recommended to manage the Bond Drive, was equally nonplussed. Having met de Valera, Harry, and their staff at the Waldorf-Astoria Hotel, he had already 'concluded that there was no adequate systematization of the work, and no clear or definite idea of the handling of the mass of detail necessary for such a campaign as had been worked out during the War by the Red Cross, the United War Drive, the Liberty Loans, etc.' While on the train to St. Louis, he drafted a scheme to rectify the current absence of campaign literature, of a banker, and, indeed, 'of any organization'. He recommended nationwide preparations leading to a launch in March instead of November (the current unattainable deadline), with a substantial initial outlay and a goal of $20,000,000. De Valera's response was 'decidedly unfavorable', as he wanted rapid results without any 'elaborate organization'. Frank P. Walsh 'had little to say', while Harry restricted himself to moaning about the failure of the Friends of Irish Freedom to pay over nine-tenths of the Irish Victory Fund, as allegedly promised. The decision to place Harry in charge of the Bond Drive meant that McSweeney heard no more until after the arrival of James O'Mara, who reinstituted McSweeney as national organiser and implemented a scheme similar to that which de Valera had previously rejected.[138]

Meanwhile, Harry's misery was unabated:

4 Nov. Tues. New York. Very uneasy on Bond organisation, no idea of detail shewn by Wheeler, Elder etc. 'Where do I get off?' Bond Bond Bond.

6 Nov. Thurs. New York. Office not yet ready. I am very much upset at present position of Bond – no system. Cannot take up affairs. Callaghan quits and sends Elder who is all right in his own way. I fancy we will have to scrap present plan.

8 Nov. Sat. New York. Bonds by day and night. Bonds will be all right! Bonds not yet in sight. Talk Bonds all day rave Bonds all night. I had better stop.[139]

The nightmare was relieved later that month, when to Harry's profound relief James O'Mara took control: 'This month should see the end of indecision. I have hopes that Bond Drive shall be accomplished in time. O'Mara in command guarantees success. Seán [Nunan] goes as O'Mara's sec. I take up my old job as sec. to Chief who is in great form, bursting with energy and determined to carry out Loan, cum [sic.] weal or woe'.[140]

Though no longer Harry's personal responsibility, the Bond Drive remained a moral and material burden for the mission and a source of acute anxiety for Collins as Minister for Finance. No subscriptions were received until mid January, when the oft-postponed Drive was finally launched, yet huge expenses were incurred during the preliminary campaign. After much haggling, the Friends had agreed to lend Walsh's Commission $100,000 towards 'the preliminary expenses in connection with the President's tour and the Irish Republican Bond-Certificate issue'.[141] This loan seems to have been the only major contribution to the Bond Drive from Diarmuid Lynch's Irish Victory Fund, leaving the mission with substantial unfunded general expenses including $1,125 in Harry's name and $750 for de Valera's personal outgoings.[142] Lynch had also given Harry $110,000 'for An Dáil', not all of which had been delivered by the New Year.[143] Much of the envoys' animosity towards Devoy and Cohalan arose from the refusal of the National Council to act on its undertaking that one-quarter of the Irish Victory Fund 'be sent to our friends in Ireland to carry out the necessary work of sustaining the Irish Cause and defending it against English attacks'.[144] Collins was clearly worried by the delay in transmitting the eagerly anticipated American bounty, though relieved to learn that Harry 'had definitely decided on a general plan of action' with 'invaluable' support from O'Mara. He was also gratified to learn that the campaign would be self-supporting, if not immediately remunerative, and 'that you do not require any more assistance from Ireland on the Bond Issue'.[145]

Even when Bond revenue began to accumulate, subterfuge was required to avoid its being traced and possibly seized in either America or the United Kingdom. Despite the substitution of 'Bond Certificates' for plain 'Bonds', the legality of the issue remained dubious. State Department officials advocated 'a firm policy against the sale', in order 'to prevent our territory being used to further rebellion against a friendly nation', notwithstanding the qualms of 'politicians on the eve of the election'.[146] It is therefore not surprising that O'Mara and his associates took elaborate measures to conceal their first payment of $200,000 to the Dáil. The Bond-money, deposited in cheques payable to de Valera, was laundered by withdrawing it from two banks in such a manner that the payee's 'identity could not be traced', depositing the cash in a third bank, and securing a draft purporting to be a gift from the Carmelite Fr. Denis O'Connor in New York to Bishop Fogarty of Killaloe.[147] Such were the dodges to which Harry and his fellow-envoys were driven in order to finance the Irish revolution. The flow of funds was sluggish and intermittent, leading

Collins to remind Harry in mid May that 'we could do with a great deal more money quickly', including at least a million pounds for the National Land Bank and fisheries.[148] By the end of the year, however, scarcely a million dollars of Bond-money (£200,000), one-fifth of the total subscribed, had been smuggled over to the Dáil.[149] During his first year in the United States, Harry had contributed massively to every aspect of the public campaign for self-determination, as a speaker, propagandist, negotiator, organiser, and fund-raiser. Yet, when he made his first visit home in May 1920, none of the mission's goals had been attained. The cavalcade was not yet over.

Conspiracy

HARRY Boland's primary assignment in the United States was clandestine. Throughout the mission, his public work as an envoy and organiser alternated uneasily with his conspiratorial duties on behalf of the IRB. His principal objective was to take control of the Clan na Gael, in order to pursue an ambitious revolutionary strategy which only gradually unfolded. From the first, however, he set about securing arms, and money for purchasing arms, through associates in the Clan. Though little is known of Harry's initial dabbling in the American arms market, intercepted correspondence confirms that this enterprise was central to his mission. Three quirkily coded letters were addressed to James P. Flood of Granard, a prominent Volunteer officer and election organiser for Sinn Féin,[1] by an unidentified Irishman posing as a student at Fordham University.[2] When Harry reached New York, the writer was already trying to buy 'foodstuff' (arms) on behalf of the 'Irish Retailers' Association' (whose prosperity was essential 'in order that your Syrup Federation [Sinn Féin] may succeed'), and had been trying to 'make arrangements for transferring some of this foodstuff across'. He claimed to have authority from 'William' and 'Patrick' (Mellows and McCartan), and advised Flood that 'Michael Collins would be the best salesman to speak with'.[3] Just before Harry's arrival, the writer warned that 'Kathleen's money' (the Irish Victory Fund) was in danger of passing into the wrong hands, and that the 'Friends' were conspiring to send McCartan home and 'win over' Mellows by offering 'a large job to him'.[4]

The third letter, sent on 26 May, casts a unique perspective on the new envoy:

> I'm glad you've taken up business and you want me to state a contract in re certain stocks you wish to buy in this country. ... However, I shall give all particulars to your *cousin* Harry who has come up from the country and is in New York presently. ... Only half dozen altogether know he's come home. ... Well I told your cousin that he would let you have 5,000 or 6,000 of these stocks in which you say your manager has opened up a new line of business since the Armistice.[5]

Though ultimately responsible for these arms shipments, Harry was too preoccupied with other worries to intervene directly 'for at least 3 months', and seemed to lack the calm efficiency of Michael Collins: 'You needn't look much to cousin Harry to look after this line of business – besides he's much too busy about other things and may be sent – in fact will – by his Aunt to Australia soon as his health is much broken down. He's as anxious looking as a *Manx* cat.[6] If it was only your brother Mickel was here. Is Mickel still engaged to Helen Kiernan or was he ever?[7] Talk things over with him.' This cryptic account suggests that Harry, though at the heart of the arms-smuggling network, preferred to avoid direct personal involvement. His indispensability as an organiser and publicist made it prudent for him to act as a Godfather rather than a 'salesman'.

Within six months of Harry's arrival, he was thought by American Military Intelligence to have 'at last succeeded in his mission to America, and has obtained supplies which may be expected in Ireland any day. . . . It is because of this information that the British have been watching American shipping and crews arriving in Irish ports.'[8] For once, the rumour was well founded. On the previous day, Collins had urged Harry to take the initiative by procuring and delivering arms on his own terms: 'It is quite useless to make any distinct arrangement at this side. The vigilance is greater than ever. The difficulties of secrecy are greater than ever. What must be done – I feel nothing else is practicable – is to make the purchase at your end, and when this has been done take the next step.'[9] Such illicit operations involved elaborate preparations, incorporating Consul Fawsitt's ambitious plan (never fully realised) to buy 'a one-half interest in four ships for trade between Ireland and the Continent – ships which would not otherwise be put on these routes'. The American shipping line, Moore & McCormack, did eventually arrange for their vessels to call at Irish ports, so facilitating the trans-Atlantic despatch of arms consignments.[10] This topic figured increasingly in the coded correspondence between Harry and Collins, using their *noms de guerre* as brethren (James Woods and William Field). Collins's early references to the 'supply of munitions' included receipts for specimen automatic weapons and instructions for transmission. Numerous 'messengers' were to bring small quantities to specified safe houses in Dublin, including Maurice Collins's billiard saloon in Parnell Street. In addition, Harry was expected to spare no expense or trouble in securing 'large quantities': 'We suggest that articles such as machine guns, rifles, rifle grenades with the special ammunition used for discharging these, small flame-throwers, small guns such as one inch guns, be purchased in whatever quantities they can be got.'[11] These transactions were invariably arranged and financed through the Brotherhood, without reference to Cathal Brugha as Minister for Defence. Surprisingly, the implicit conflict between Harry's responsibilities to the Dáil and the IRB did not materialise until mid 1921.

Harry's most daunting challenge was to mobilise Irish-American resources of money, manpower, and goodwill, without surrendering the Dáil's claim to ultimate authority. His experience as a Sinn Féin organiser in Ireland provided poor preparation for a campaign demanding partnership with established interests, in which the envoys could ill afford to appeal to the mass of Irish-Americans over the heads of their existing spokesmen. Far from being a spent force like the Irish Parliamentary Party, Cohalan's movement had a coherent and plausible political strategy, a formidable battery of organisations, and the proven capacity to publicise the Irish cause, raise money, and influence Congressmen. Furthermore, the leaders of the Clan na Gael and Friends of Irish Freedom could not be discredited as compromisers or closet Home Rulers, since they were no less intransigent than de Valera or Harry in pursuing the republican ideal and castigating British misrule. This harmony of outlook encouraged Harry to believe that Devoy, in particular, could be induced to submit to de Valera's better judgement. In his first report home, Harry stated that he had 'seen many groups since my arrival' and that 'all here are working hard for us and all that is required is co-ordination'. It was 'most opportune that I got here at this moment as I may be able to harmonise the little differences that have arisen on policy, finance etc.' Ten days later, he boasted of having 'applied "the oil can" and got the disputants together', asserting that 'the house is divided and I saved the situation ... and earned the good will of all for avoiding split.'[12]

His faith in the essential decency of Irish-American ex-gunmen and ex-Dynamiters never wavered, being expressed in outpourings of fraternal sentiment. While recuperating from exhaustion in Atlantic City, New Jersey, he was reinvigorated by the company of local Fenians: 'McCarney, Gallagher and Laverty aged 60, 76, 73 respectively, all gold and a yard wide, never lost the faith. ... Get sound advice from the three Far Downs,[13] enjoy and appreciate the grand old men.'[14] As he told Ned:

> I have met all the survivors of '67, John Devoy, Col. Richard [sic.] O'Sullivan Burke,[15] and some of lesser note, but all of them are as fierce to-day as in '65, and are sure that they will live to see America recognise Ireland's Republic. The pride of these old men in Young Ireland is very wonderful, their views are fresh, and they can speak of '67 as of yesterday. We have been most attentive to them and they appreciate our regard for them. They are very proud to have lived to witness the day that the people of Ireland voted for the Republic, and so justified the men of '67.[16]

Harry's warmest feelings often followed a fight: 'Attend F.O.I.F. and join issue with J. D. [Devoy] on resolution. Have a free for all row and find every thing ends well. Lynch went off like a soda water bottle. ... Old Man [Devoy] and I square things up.'[17] All would be forgiven in the moment of victory:

> Met Boys. Very satisfactory, everything conceded. Have very pleasant time with Old Man, speaks of old times. Irish Emigrant Aid Asso., '56, Emmet Monument Asso., Pluck Plodge Bridge Dodder, [Queen] Victoria's visit '48, Peter Langan, Dr. Kane, Kilkenny, Stephens' walk, first subscriptions to Fenianism, in M. Doheny's office Centre St. New York. Corcoran, Col.

[Thomas J.] Kelly, Roche, few others turned out pockets, 80 dollars Joe Denieffe. Could listen all day to the old stories.[18]

Even when thwarted by Devoy, Harry remained oddly tender towards his adversary: 'John Devoy out for trouble, hopes to bring de Valera to heel for Cohalan. John my son you have your hands full. Shall America dictate? That's the question. I have no fears of the result. Sorry the "Old Man" is firing the balls for Cohalan.'[19]

For a revolutionary sentimentalist like Harry, Devoy and Cohalan represented two familiar republican types, the honest Fenian manipulated by the devious politician. As a former Grand Sachem of the Tammany Society in New York, Cohalan had the potential to become either a dangerous opponent or a valuable ally for an inexperienced Irishman dabbling in American politics.[20] When referring to the Judge in his diary, Harry exhibited wariness rather than either warmth or venom:

31 Oct. Fri. New York. Long talk with Judge, on situation, and come away easier in my mind. Have learned that [Senator William E.] Borah intends to support and introduce resolution in favour. Judge promises all aid possible. He is not satisfied with Bond arrangement. I am, and fear more trouble.

11 Feb. Wed. Washington. Judge Dan F. Cohalan calls to [Irish National] Bureau, not on me. 'Tá rath lé Tac nidh' [there is a reason for everything]. Go to Washington Irish National Club, give a talk on Ireland. Fear we will have trouble here yet with our vain friends, hope not. What is to be will be. Boland a Fatalist.

10 Apr. Sat. New York. Call on Cohalan re Olympic Games,[21] sit on the bench with Judge. Quite a change from the dock.[22]

At Christmas, their relations were cordial enough to induce Harry to 'pray that the New Year may bring you in full measure all the blessings of God', an invocation which the Judge found worth preserving.[23]

Yet retrospective reports suggest a clash of temperament which was always liable to erupt into conflict. When travelling to Ireland in August 1921, Harry told a radical priest of his 'first interview with Cohalan', which he portrayed as a dramatic confrontation between incompatible programmes:

Boland said: 'If we get the guns and ammunition we need, we will write Ireland's name on the front pages of the papers in blood.' And Cohalan replied: 'The Irish Republic doesn't exist. Ireland will never get anything, but the day is coming very soon when England and America will go to war. Then in the treaty between England and America, America will annex Canada, and then Ireland will get her freedom.' ... Boland said: 'Well,

Judge, before your dream comes true, thousands of men will have died on the hillsides of Ireland without a gun to protect themselves with', and he left.[24]

The conflict was personalised in Kathleen Boland's account of a public meeting at which Cohalan, as chairman of the reception committee, drew attention to Harry's humble origins:

> Cohalan asked him publicly at what university he had graduated. Harry, who realised that the question was intended to humiliate him, promptly replied, 'q. 90, Dartmoor Prison, for Ireland!' The applause was tremendous and Cohalan never forgave Harry.[25]

Though coloured by the public slanging match which followed the initial attempt to resolve factional differences, these anecdotes probably convey authentic incompatibilities of class, temperament, and policy between the Judge and the Rebel. These tended to obscure the deeper affinity between two conspirators and manipulators for whom the end would always justify the means.

In his tussle with Devoy and Cohalan, Harry's chief ally was Joseph McGarrity of Philadelphia. Though without rebel or political experience in his native Tyrone, McGarrity had scarcely reached America in 1892 before joining the AOH, through which he was initiated into the Clan na Gael. Having made his name by rioting against an American production of that reputedly immoral play, J. M. Synge's *The Playboy of the Western World* (1907), he was elected to the Clan's Executive in 1912 and played a key part in soliciting German support for rebellion in Ireland.[26] By 1918, the turnover of his wholesale liquor business exceeded $125,000, upon which he contrived to avoid paying a single cent in tax.[27] Already at odds with Cohalan and intimate with McCartan (who edited his weekly newspaper, the *Irish Press*),[28] McGarrity consistently asserted de Valera's right to direct the Irish-American campaign and control its funds. A devout Catholic with five children and another on the way, he appealed to Harry as a family man who was also pugnacious and outwardly robust, with his square chin, high forehead, grey-blue eyes, greying hair, dark complexion, and solid physique.[29]

Their friendship was that of true brethren, spontaneous, unquestioning, and founded on mutual trust. It therefore offered welcome relief from the usual tactical alliances:

> 2 Oct. Thurs. Enjoyed meeting [Liam] Pedlar and the old Guard – Luke Dillon, Joe McGarrity – Great Soul.
>
> 1 Nov. Sat. Long talk with Joe McGarrity, love him more and more.
>
> 11 Jan. Sun. Meet many good people at Joe's. Baby generally admired. Speeches, songs and joy.[30]

27 Mar. Sat. Meet Joe McGarrity, talk away the night, discuss recent events. Joe very happy.[31]

The introduction of nation-wide 'prohibition' on 17 January 1920 had a depressing effect on the liquor merchant, though McGarrity soon reapplied his acumen to real estate. He also succumbed to a prolonged and debilitating illness:

9 Apr. Fri. Poor Joe McGarrity very sick, the strain of the past year tells heavily on him. Let me here repeat what I have often said before, that McGarrity is far and away the best Irish man here.

29 Apr. Thurs. I call on McGarrity, find Joe very, very ill, cannot see him. Doctors say Joe will not recover for a year. Terrible loss to us. I have no doubt that Joe's breakdown has been brought on by overwork.[32]

In McGarrity's absence, Harry lacked an essential lever for activating his American brethren in the Irish cause.

The struggle for control of Irish-America was prolonged and convoluted, and it would be superfluous to burden this biography with yet another chronicle of its tactical twists and turns.[33] As psychological melodrama, however, it reveals the emotional intensity with which Irish-American politics was conducted, and the tendency of all parties to personalise political disagreements and impute sinister ulterior motives to opposing leaders. In public, some attempt was made by both sides to restrict the torrent of personal abuse. Though prominent in the early battles over the Irish Victory Fund, Harry seldom attended meetings of the Friends of Irish Freedom after his first six months in America.[34] When he did so and enjoyed 'the courtesy of speaking' as a visitor, he was at pains to deny any 'intention of interfering with the work of the Friends of Irish Freedom', leaving McGarrity to fight his corner and swap insults with Lynch, Devoy, and Cohalan.[35] Behind the scenes, he never stopped interfering and suffered accordingly. As Seán Nunan wrote to Collins in early September: 'I thought at one time that we had some politicians at home, but believe me, they are nothing to the brands out here. Harry's hair is falling out with worry.'[36] At this period, Devoy still considered that de Valera was the creature of 'Harry's manipulations', rather than the reverse, concluding that 'Harry is the man to get at first.'[37] Yet Harry himself was the dupe of 'the little handful who are working might and main to sow distrust and create dissension', especially the enigmatic Dr. William Maloney of New York. Maloney, a neurologist with Ulster forebears who had lost the use of a leg following gunshot wounds at Gallipoli in June 1915, subsequently became an eloquent advocate of Irish self-determination.[38] Never fully trusted even by de Valera or Collins, he was repeatedly denounced as a British agent by Devoy.[39] In private, however, Devoy admitted that he had no evidence for the accusation: 'Even if he is not a British agent, he is an outsider.'[40]

Devoy's insinuations 'upset Harry terribly', leading to an emotional encounter at which de Valera, for once, seemed 'straight' and sincere. This led Devoy to expect that 'the air will be cleared and that it will be plainer sailing in future'.[41] Despite recurrent tensions, this prediction was temporarily fulfilled. Buoyed by his qualified success in winning the Friends' lukewarm support for the Bond-Certificate campaign, and eventually securing more than expected of the Victory Fund, Harry remained sanguine into the New Year. In late January, he gave Collins a balanced account of the residual differences without imputing base motives to his opponents:

> Judge Cohalan and Mr. Devoy have all their lives been strong and active supporters of the Irish Republic, and I want to say right here that to-day they stand exactly as they always stood. ... These men felt that we were interlopers and they look with disfavour on the taking of so much money from America. ... The Bond has been 'knocked' in private, and the talk is going around about this group of young men from Ireland who are running things in America.

Devoy, being a 'poor old man' and 'very, very deaf', was 'at the mercy of those who whisper in his ear'; while Cohalan, though 'a very able man and a sincere lover of Ireland', exhibited 'an intolerance for the opinions or ability of others' and, 'to put it bluntly', was 'a little envious of De Valera'.[42]

Within a month, Harry had abandoned moderation when writing to Collins in his brotherly persona as 'Woods' to 'Field'. Cohalan had degenerated into 'a low down, cheap Tammany Hall politician, who cannot even run straight with his own people', and was a menace to the mission:

> Devoy and Cohalan are prepared to knife every man who comes from Ireland if they attempt in the slightest way to guide the movement for Irish freedom in this country. ... I am compelled to say that these men cannot be trusted; that they have attempted not only to knife De Valera, but seen fit to send one of the rubber stamps to me – a man named [Laurence J.] Rice – in an attempt to take me out in the public press against the President, and to split with him on this interview.[43]

In attempting to win over Harry by accusing his Chief of 'lowering the flag', Cohalan and Devoy had reversed their previous assumption that the puppeteer was Harry. The occasion for this renewal of hostilities was the publication on 6 February of a pseudo-'interview' containing de Valera's notorious suggestion that an independent Ireland should play the part of Cuba under the Monroe doctrine, by undertaking not to provide a base for attacks upon Britain. Despite de Valera's denial that this would entail any surrender of national sovereignty, the proposal enabled Cohalan to turn the tables by affirming that it was de

Valera, not himself, who was willing to compromise the republican ideal.[44] Though Harry initially deemed it 'good stuff', the 'Cuban analogy' aroused genuine and lingering distrust among Irish-Americans, who justifiably viewed Cuba as an American protectorate rather than an independent ally.[45] Harry laboured to restrict the damage, assuring one correspondent that 'the Monroe Doctrine for the two islands cannot come until the British Empire has passed away. The President very carefully chose his words in that interview, when he laid it down that England would be entitled to her national life. He did not say her "Imperial life".'[46]

Harry's response to Rice's approach was characteristically abrasive, further widening the rift. De Valera reported with satisfaction that Cohalan's 'messenger was near finding himself thro' a window of the Waldorf',[47] an account confirmed in Harry's diary:

16 Feb. Mon. New York. Larry Rice attempts to dictate to me as to what I should do: i.e. Quit The Chief. Sorry I did not kick Larry out – done next best thing. Go to Phila, speak to Irish America Club. Up the Republic. Arrive New York, 1.30 a.m. Meet Mac [James O'Mara]. Momentous decision. Chief on edge.

17 Feb. Tues. New York. [Eugene F.] Kinkead, Frank P. Walsh, J. K. McGuire, Bourke Cockrane all stand up with Chief. Out of evil cometh good, 'we will clean the Augean stable yet'.[48]

20 Feb. Fri. Washington. Walk over Potomac. Final decision Cohalan, in open if possible. Return to office, must leave again for New York. Some journeyings this week, to be sure. 'Tis in vain for soldiers to complain.

21 Feb. Sat. New York. I go to Cohalan with letter. Painful silence, walk back to office. Chief very upset and dispirited.

22 Feb. Sun. New Rochelle. Spend evening with J. K. [McGuire], discuss pros and cons of situation and decide plan of action. The more I see of this scandalous affair the more disgusting it becomes. The Rice attempt on me was most dastardly. Cohalan an evil for Ireland.[49]

The stage was set for confrontation, but not yet in public. Assuming as ever that political control was best assured by achieving dominance within the Brotherhood, Harry grappled first with the Clan na Gael.

The struggle for control of the Clan had been under way since his arrival, when with McGarrity's connivance he had supplanted Devoy as the conduit of all 'communications' from the IRB. Harry justified his decision on historical grounds: 'Having read through the mass of correspondence dealing with the '80s in Ireland I am learning the lesson of history, as I am convinced and the officers of the organisation here are convinced that in practically every gathering of the Clan there is a British agent, so I discuss our business with very few, and in many cases with no one.' He recognised, however, that 'the Old Man' had 'resented my arbitrarily taking charge of them immediately I arrived here'.[50] Since Harry's motive was to use his control of communications as a 'big stick' against recalcitrant Clansmen, their resentment was understandable.[51] Devoy's distrust was deepened in autumn 1919, when Harry reportedly urged the Clan's convention 'to merge the organization in the Friends of Irish Freedom'.[52] His motive was presumably to counteract infiltration and prepare the way for a more secure secret network under reliable direction.

The contest came to a climax on 19 March on the second floor of New York's Park Avenue Hotel, where Devoy had convened a supposedly secret meeting of his leading supporters in the Clan, to challenge de Valera's authority. Despite Devoy's attempts to conceal the scheme from all but his trustiest allies, McGarrity's network of spies secured copies of his correspondence through John A. McGarry, whose desire to avoid an irrevocable split had caused him to face both ways on the Clan's Executive.[53] The evidence suggesting that Devoy and Cohalan were plotting 'to ruin the Chief' was duly passed on by McGarrity to de Valera and Harry, who had ample time to prepare their counter-attack and secure further Intelligence from other agents.[54] After energetic manoeuvring on both sides, Harry decided to confound Devoy's caucus by confronting it with the unwelcome presence of de Valera, whose advertised visit to Chicago had been cancelled without Devoy's knowledge.

The outcome, as reported by Harry, was a melodramatic victory for Ireland's envoys:

18 Mar. Thurs. New York. Deputation wait on Chief, suggest Devoy's proposal, giving Americans sole charge. Chief adamant. Result, no change. Hear of Caucus. Ask Joe [McGarrity] to stay over and go. Great old Joe agrees. Chief leaves tomorrow for Chicago.

19 Mar. Fri. Joe calls me, advises that Chief attend meeting at Park Avenue as Dan [Cohalan] has called a very representative crowd together. Cable to Ireland. Bishop Turner [of Buffalo], Judge Goff, J. T. Maloney. Historic scene, Cohalan hoist by his own petard. De V. refuses to budge, emotions all, cheers, curses, challenges, shrieks and final blessing. Chief magnificent. M. J. Ryan, chair, cad. Joe great. My spilling the letter finished the job. Dirty attempt to break Chief fails miserably. Bubble burst, and ends up in Bishop Turner blessing all while they all are on their knees. Very dramatic. Jas. O'Mara cool and calm, Boland crying, de V. shaken, Devoy and Cohalan licked.[55]

McGarrity's less telescopic diary gives a vivid account of Harry's robust debating style. After McGarrity had shamed the meeting into inviting de Valera to venture forth from the more luxurious Waldorf-Astoria to defend himself against attacks by Cohalan and Devoy, Harry overrode the chairman's attempt to keep his Chief waiting outside by shoving past the doorman and ushering in de Valera midway through an opponent's speech. De Valera seemed 'under a great strain', his teeth 'set', while he defended 'his Cuban interview' against misreadings and endured repeated interruptions, though himself 'always courteous and respectful'. Harry then named McGarry as the recipient of letters revealing a plot to send de Valera home, 'a discredited man'. This drew 'a weak denial' from McGarry before de Valera, 'waving his hand' towards McGarrity, 'said: "Get those letters"'. The audience became quite excited, and I fumbled in my overcoat as though going to produce the letters.' Although the relevant letter did not in fact support Harry's charge, the threat to expose the Executive's undoubtedly indiscreet correspondence was sufficient to provoke an exaggerated display of unity. The meeting ended with cheers for de Valera, Cohalan, and Devoy, and an exhausting round of handshakes.[56]

Harry's opponents took a different view of the proceedings. John P. Grace, the Mayor of Charleston in South Carolina and Cohalan's fervent admirer, remarked 'that President de Valera was that day revealed to me as either labouring under some psychopathic condition or that the evil spirit himself had taken hold of the Irish movement'. For ten hours, he and his supporters had offered a deplorable 'exhibition of intolerance and ingratitude'.[57] Devoy's recollection of the meeting was equally damning if less histrionic:

> Boland, under the stress of great emotion, was making a No Surrender speech, broke down in the middle of it, burst into tears and had to retire from the meeting room in order to compose himself. He returned in a more peaceable mood, resumed his speech, accepted personal responsibility for many of the misunderstandings which had arisen, and then urged De Valera to yield for the good of the Cause. De Valera at once yielded and the whole crowd knelt down, with Bishop Turner of Buffalo standing over them, and the bargain was solemnly ratified – that De Valera was to be recognized as the spokesman of Ireland ... and that the elected officers of the Irish organizations were to be left in unquestioned charge of affairs in America. Before many days had elapsed De Valera broke the solemnly ratified Treaty and resumed his war on the Irish organizations in America.[58]

By a miracle of collective self-deception, both factions momentarily convinced themselves that this display of pseudo-unity signified victory. In reality, they remained locked in a mutually destructive conflict with no clear solution.

In reporting the outcome to Collins and the IRB, six days after the meeting, Harry showed none of the euphoria expressed in his diary:

> You will be glad to know that the crisis has been safely passed. Last Friday we had it out before a group of 60 selected men, and as a result the air has been cleared. ... Anyway, there is now no fear of a split, altho' I am very,

very far from securing the objective you and I so often debated. American-Irish leaders will never accept the proposal from Ireland that will give the home men the least control. ... It is practically impossible to harmonize the two points of view.[59]

Writing to Harry on 26 March, Devoy also expressed guarded optimism rather than triumphalism. While praising his former adversary as 'a fine fighting man' and offering 'to do all I can to help you out', Devoy continued to 'regret the differences as much as you do'.[60] Harry Gloster Armstrong, the Consul-General from Cavan who had once tracked Jack Boland and the 'Dynamiters', confirmed that 'an understanding was patched up' which left de Valera's American future undetermined and Cohalan as anxious as ever 'to remain the leader of the Irish at this side and to consolidate the Irish and German vote for electioneering and propaganda purposes'.[61] The Friends of Irish Freedom, true to their tradition as a respectable front for the Clan na Gael, tamely cited the agreement reached at the Park Avenue Hotel when declining de Valera's request for a special meeting in Washington, the main issue having already been 'settled to the satisfaction of all who participated'.[62] In the Friends, as in the Clan, the issue of Irish control remained an irritant, but not, for the time being, a focus for open conflict.

Having concluded that Devoy's faction would never submit to dictation from Ireland, Harry prepared nonetheless to dictate. A logical corollary of his policy after March 1920 was therefore to split the movement which he had previously aimed to unify. Before asserting supremacy over the Clan, he secured unqualified backing from the IRB's new Supreme Council elected in November 1919, in which Collins remained dominant as Treasurer.[63] On 5 March, Collins had affirmed that 'at every stage, no matter what difference was reported, and no matter what fault was found, and no matter what rumours were put out by certain people, your other colleagues and myself have unfailingly endorsed your actions and words even when these were not known to us'. Yet Collins's promise of continuing support for the Council's 'representative' carried a veiled warning: 'If at any time it ceases you yourself will be the first to be told. You know me as far as this is concerned.'[64] A fortnight later, Harry was informed that his 'authorisation' had been renewed by the new Council, with implications revealed in a package of despatches sent on 26 April. This contained an ultimatum for the Clan's Executive, to be presented at Harry's 'own discretion' in case of 'any further difficulties', along with a memorandum which 'certainly should not be used now but it can as certainly be used if trouble recurs'. The Executive would be asked for a written declaration as to whether it regarded 'the Organisation in the U.S.A. as a subsidiary of the Organisation at home, or whether it regards the Clan na Gael as an independent Organisation'. The Supreme Council's own desire was for:

an Organisation of Irishmen, in whatever land they live, bound by the same obligations, drawing their inspiration from Ireland, and having the purely Irish aspect as the first object of their existence. .... In operation this would mean direction from Ireland on big issues, accepting the policy and measures of the home Organisation even when it directed a course which might be considered as opposing the local interests of the subsidiary Organisation abroad.

In particular, the IRB would require an extensive supply of munitions, along with an annual subsidy of £20,000.[65] The Clan na Gael would thus be reduced to a collecting agency, with Harry as manager and Collins as supremo.

The renewal of Harry's 'authorisation' as an envoy, with plenary power to subjugate the Clan, demonstrated that his relationship with Collins was unimpaired after nearly a year of separation. In his diary, Harry often reflected rather enviously on the feats of his resourceful friend in Dublin:

1 Nov. Sat. New York. Get news from home, important. Field in rare form.

25 Jan. Sun. New York. Find welcome visitors with mails from home. Miceál sends interesting story from Quinlisk.[66] Miceál has had wonderful escapes, hope his luck will continue. I give it to Miceál. Great man.

31 Jan. Sat. New York. Go to Laurette Taylor, hear of round up. Miceál gone too, very awkward, seems to me that the raid is for municipal councillors. All get very sad at news, feel so far away, yet are thankful that we are here to carry on Bond. Will go over. An Irish Republic will live for ever. Seán [Nunan] and I mope home together. Chief and Jim [O'Mara] sad.

20 Feb. Fri. Washington. Great news. Miceál not arrested. Best of news. Hurrah.[67]

Their remarkably informal 'official' correspondence is a testament to the possibility of mutual trust and brotherly love among politicians. Though warning Harry not to be 'so communicative', Collins himself made little attempt to conceal delicate transactions despite his intermittent use of code-names.[68] Harry's despatches were far from confidential, as Collins indicated on 25 August: 'All your messages were duly elaborated to a great many of our mutual friends at Croke Park yesterday. It is a long time since I was there and it was quite pleasant to meet some of them. I may say that I sadly miss last year's exercise there.'[69] Nostalgia as well as self-interest may have influenced Harry in his first attempt to persuade Collins to join him, when he wrote on the following day that 'the organising of this Bond issue is a tremendous undertaking, and it is my judgement that you are now wanted here'.[70] Collins responded firmly that 'at present, and for the purpose you outline – no – it is quite impossible, although some of my close colleagues are not in agreement with me on this'. He added enigmatically that 'there is still only *one* thing that would take me away, and when the time comes for that, I'm off without delay'. Yet, when the matter was discussed two days later by the Dáil Ministry, 'opinion was divided, but I must say it was in favour on balance of your suggestion'. Collins pointed out 'that there are other reasons (for instance, communications, Volunteers, etc.) why I should remain here', but admitted that the case for his removal had been strengthened by an almost miraculous escape from arrest when detectives entered his room but failed to recognise him. He managed nevertheless to resist these pressures, and by early October assumed 'that all thought of *my* going on account of Loan is done with'.[71] If reunion were to occur, Harry would have to make the journey.

Meanwhile, intimacy was maintained through visits by Collins to Marino Crescent, 'personal' requests for Harry to procure books by earlier revolutionaries to satisfy Collins's lively interest in Irish history,[72] and the exchange of fraternal jocosities. The once elegant envoy was mercilessly teased for his sharp sartorial style in the 'New World': 'I believe you were a rare sight in a check suit, check bow, *check hat* and Club shoes!' Collins's imagination was further tickled by Seán Nunan's startling depiction of Harry's Great White Chief, whose partiality for dour quasi-clerical garb was to become notorious: 'The G.W.C. and Harry have now discarded their check suits and now appear in Palm Beach suits, what are known as "real nifty suitings".'[73] Collins could not resist alluding to his own amorous adventures, while warning Harry not to 'pay very much attention to the tall stories ... regarding myself. This is absolutely necessary with regard to a very pleasant lady named Mrs. O'S.' In similarly cryptic vein, he wrote that 'I'm having a —— time. No rest either way now.'[74] To the irritation of Seán Ó Murthuile, who preferred official correspondence to adopt his own bureaucratic manner, Harry could not resist flirting with Collins in mid-despatch: 'That film of yourself and [Diarmuid O'] Hegarty selling Bonds brought tears to my eyes, Gael Boy! You are some movie actor. Nobody could resist buying a Bond and we having such a handsome Minister for Finance.' Harry would stray from de Valera's triumphs, and the misdeeds of Devoy and Cohalan, to speculations about his hero: 'Judging by the expression on your face when you were shaking hands with J. J. [Walsh], you were saying something nice to him.'[75] Collins gushed rather less, though boasting shamelessly of 'escapade[s]' which were 'too long and too thrilling to tell in a letter'.[76] He would add to the effect by assuming the jaded tone of an old soldier: 'The worst of it is that these things cease to be exciting. They simply come to have the same effect as unwelcome callers – the effect of making one lose one's temper and get behind with work.' But Collins, too, looked forward to a fraternal reunion, possibly on the run in Ireland: 'One little matter remains. Instructions have now been issued for your arrest as well as the arrest of the President. Therefore, we may have tennis together again.'[77]

Other old associates were equally jocular when writing to Harry. On 12 July 1919, the Secretary to the Ministry addressed 'H. Boland, Esq., T.D., Envoy of the Elected Government of the Irish Republic', with mock solemnity:

> Your credentials are ready for a long time with the exception of the Seal. The freedom of Ireland and the Channel Tunnel are both immense undertakings, but they appear to be of very much less magnitude than the manufacture of the Seal. . . . I believe, however, we will get this masterpiece next week, and I will then have your authorities sent over.[78]

Michael O'Flanagan, Harry's normally earnest fellow-officer in Sinn Féin, also adopted a sardonic tone when recounting his restitution to priestly functions in the diocese of Elphin: 'At last about 3 weeks ago the Bishop told me to go to Roscommon but omitted to make place for me there. It took ten days to get Fr. Murray promoted to Sligo. . . . Wasn't it grand of the old man to send me to Roscommon to hold the fort for you till you come back?'[79] Robert Brennan, when forwarding a document from Sinn Féin headquarters, wrote playfully that 'things have gone splendidly since you left – that may not seem complimentary but you know what I mean'.[80] Harry's inimitable secretarial contribution was acknowledged in August 1919 in a report by the substitute Honorary Secretaries, who remarked that de Valera's mission had 'been a colossal success, the labours and triumphs of which are shared by Mr. H. Boland, our absent Secretary, whose progress we watch with pride and pleasure'.[81] As a visitor from Manchester reported, 'Dublin hadn't half the attractions it had whilst you were there and particularly no. 6 [Harcourt Street]'.[82] In the offices and hostelries of rebel Dublin, Harry's aura lingered on.

America offered ample alternative pleasures for a gregarious visitor, and Harry did not allow official duties to interfere unduly with his social life. Though the interminable succession of banquets and balls eventually palled, it provided an outlet for his surplus energy:

> 8 Oct. Wed. Cincinnati. Visited K. of C. [Knights of Columbus] Dance and warmed 'em up.
>
> 8 Dec. Mon. New York. I have a date with de Valera and O'Mara, to dinner at F. P. Walsh's. Celia and I go to *East is West*. F. P., De V. and Mrs. W. also retire to Waldorf. Boland nicks it to dance. *Hurrah*.[83]

In keeping with his persona as a bluff Gael innocent of social graces, Harry was inclined to deprecate his performance as a lady's man: 'Call at 565 Park Avenue, make arrangement for [Irish Counties] Ball tonight. Frank P., Mrs. Walsh, Celia, Virginia, James, Aine, go to Ball. Judge, Mayor, Frank P., La Guardia, Boland. Boland parades the floor, leading the march. Feel embarrassed.'[84] Yet, when reminiscing in 1955 with Harry's partner, de Valera gave a different impression:

'Poor Harry! I remember how he enthused about leading the Grand March at the New York Ball (or was it the Grand Parade?) with you!'[85] Rumours of romance were rife in Dublin, probably accounting for Collins's characteristic comment that 'I am very glad to hear that you are having luck in my line'.[86] When Seán Nunan assured him that 'I'm doing my best to steer a straight course for Harry, but his fatal beauty and mellifluous voice make it difficult', Collins voiced his appreciation for 'your efforts in regard to Harry' while hoping that Nunan himself would escape the fate of the 'strong swimmer' (who, one supposes, drowned when saving a beginner).[87] A former fellow-convict asked Harry for confirmation that 'Seán Nunan has solved the colour question by marrying a negress', and hoped that 'even if you do come back with a Yankee heiress – and we will be disappointed if you don't – you will not forget the time you had to steal bread in Lewes Prison'.[88] So the banter went on, leaving proof of revolution's glamour in every package of official despatches. Terse though it was, Harry's diary also carried a sexual charge, as in his distillation of Louisville, Kentucky: 'Dark and bloody soil, lovely women, fast horses, strong whiskey.'[89]

Harry's evenings were often spent at shows, his enjoyment being influenced by the company as well as the content:

31 Oct. Fri. New York. Skating, with Miss Mc. Quite a relief from the political worries to the hallow-e'en party. Leave lady at home and turn in. Find Pat [McCartan] in bed. Give him the dope and talk hours away in bed.

20 Dec. Sat. Washington. Go for good walk with O'Connell and dine at University Club. Witness performance of *Sunrise at Poli*, then to Child's for Griddle.

22 Dec. Mon. Washington. Finished up work in office and spent evening at theatre, *Bitter Ale*. Good old ignorant English stuff.

4 Jan. Sun. New York. O'Mara, Seán, Chief and I go to movies, very dull show.

4 Feb. Wed. New York. Attend Irish Literary Society with Chief. Poems, music, drama, Ireland.

6 Feb. Fri. New York. Go to Metropolitan Opera and meet Caruso with J. K. McGuire.

26 Feb. Thurs. Washington. Go to movies, forget Chief, Cohalan and Devoy.

14 Mar. Sun. Washington. Chief and I have great walk around Basin, go to movies, thence to meeting.

3 May. Mon. Washington. Liam, girls and I hear [Verdi's] *Rigoletto*.

10 May. Mon. New York. Chief and Seán go to show. Scandal. Boland takes lady to *Golddiggers*, very enjoyable play, and company.[90]

Harry's appetite for pleasure extended equally to quiet evenings with friends and raucous gatherings with Irish-Americans:

2 Nov. Sun. New York. I go to F. P. Walsh home, spend very pleasant evening with Celia, Virginia and James. Some kids.

26 Nov. Wed. Atlantic City. Walk to inlet, take car to Longport, have good breeze, then dine at Breakers. Go to Avoca and have champagne. Escorted home by Harry [McCarney] and Lavery and bottles for me.

1 May. Sat. Washington. I dine at Miss [Kathleen] O'Connell's with gusto. Marie and Rose, just like home.

9 May. Sun. New York. Ap[pointment] for [Carmelite] Priory 1 o'c., late as usual. Very enjoyable day and dinner. Seán [Nunan], Father Metcalfe and I indulge at target.[91]

Ever the soul of the party, he would round off a long evening with 'a five-minute reminiscent talk with a bit of humour', or a medley of rebel songs winning 'rounds of applause from the guests'. In Manchester, a party including the Governor of New Hampshire and assorted mayors was regaled with 'Out and Make Way for the Bold Fenian Men', a parody of 'Mary had a Little Lamb' as sung by the Volunteers on route marches, 'The Mangy British Lion, Ha! Ha! Ha!' and an adaptation of 'The South Down Militia'.[92]

As in Ireland, games and fights provided essential relaxation for this exuberant envoy. Seldom satisfied when a mere spectator, he was 'most disappointed in display' after accompanying Nunan to Jersey City 'for fight'.[93] As a participant, he concentrated on urban amusements such as gambling and shooting:

24 Nov. Mon. Atlantic City, for a few days. Salt water baths, Skee Ball, Rifle Shooting.

2 Jan. Fri. N.Y. Attend Mass and funeral to Brooklyn, Holy X, with Judge Cohalan and J. K. McGuire, after which I spend a few hours with J. C. Lee, who gave me a good hand for home. Ten five[?] up. N.Y. – Free City.

19 Jan. Mon. Leave Chicago for New York. ... Play Fan Tan,[94] win 1 dollar, very enjoyable day on train.

21 Mar. Sun. New York. Have great fun at Jim and Seán, ramble back to Wolcott [Hotel]. Poker, first game of cards since left Ireland.[95]

Running for trains provided some physical exercise, as did occasional tussles with de Valera – ever eager to be acknowledged as one of the lads. When introduced to Dr. Maloney, 'de Valera was genial and told how he had beaten Harry Boland that morning at hand-ball, and how in Lincoln Jail he had surprised the young fellows there by outrunning them'.[96] Their rivalry extended to wrestling: 'Chief, who is tireless, never seems to grow weary. Indulge in wrestling bout for which I am sorry.'[97] Harry found few opportunities for team games such as hurling, apart from an 'exhibition game' following a rally at Chicago's Gaelic Park.[98] He soon became conscious of his declining fitness: 'I have grown lazy and soft, have not had an opportunity to have a walk since I came. Trains, motors, etc. is the order here, and we all feel the want of exercise badly, which reminds me that Dublin has again won the Leinster Hurling and defeated Wexford in Semi Final. I must write to Luke [O'Toole] and Andy [Harte].'[99] Memories of hurling provided a wholesome antidote to the enticements of the saloon and the dance-hall: 'Go to Ball, dance. Oh for a Good Hurling Match.'[100]

Under intense pressure by day and night, Harry suffered recurrent break-downs throughout his period as an envoy. Only two months after his arrival, he withdrew from de Valera's party bound for San Francisco to prepare for the Bond campaign. Before long, he was 'laid up at the Carmelite Priory' in Middletown, New York, after an attack attributed to 'an aftermath of influenza, which he had in Dublin'.[101] Writing tongue-in-cheek to McGarrity, he paid tribute to the controversial neurologist who tended him: 'If Maloney is as brilliant a spy as he is a doctor, then England has a very able man working for her. I sincerely hope he did not put it over on me whilst I lay sick. It would be very serious if I came under his "Hypnotic influence" like you did, you poor simple fellow.'[102] Bamboozled by Bonds and factional struggle, he broke down again four months later and renewed his expressions of admiration for Maloney.[103] Maloney's cure was to despatch him far from Manhattan, on this occasion to the rather down-market resort of Atlantic City, New Jersey, where he fraternised for three days with that trio of 'grand old' Fenians. The salutary effect of the sea air was subverted by energetic socialising, and on his return to New York, Maloney had to order him 'off smokes'. However, apart from a 'very bad cold, slight fever' on April Fools' Day, he avoided further collapse during his first year in the United States.[104]

Gregarious though he was, Harry had predictable moments of loneliness. At Christmas, he turned down McGarrity's invitation to join 'just a little family party of ourselves' in Philadelphia and dined in New York with another displaced revolutionary. This was Muhammad Mahmud (Pasha), an Egyptian product of Balliol and future Prime Minister whose expulsion to Malta in 1919 had sparked an uprising in Cairo.[105] As Harry noted: 'Mahmoud Pasha and I eat Xmas dinner at F. P. Walsh's hospitable home, 565 Park. Go to *Irene* and enjoy show, back to Waldorf and 675. Play Fan Tan, win dollar, enjoy very happy time. Call on J. D. [Devoy] and Father O'Connell.'[106] Despite these diversions, he sent a tear-jerking letter to an admirer in Dublin, who 'read and re-read it many times. . . . I am sorry your Christmas was so lonely, but we were with you in spirit – we spoke of you continually. . . . Please God 1920 will not draw to a close without us seeing you, and hearing these lovely stories you have promised to tell us around the fire, and that is something wonderful to look forward to (now Harry *please* don't say "It's a habit the poor girl has") – I really mean it all.'[107] He remained in touch with at least one 'Miss F.',[108] and also with Kitty Kiernan of Granard. During the first 'grand tour', he sent her 'a card from Ohio in remembrance', without specifying precisely what memory he dwelt upon:

> I often think of you, and your happy family, and the pleasant times I had with you. I suppose ye will all have forgotten me by now. Anyway keep a warm corner for me in that gay heart of yours. My regards to Maud, Chrys and 'the Parisian Rose' [Helen Kiernan], not forgetting Larry, Mr and Mrs Paul Cusack, and all friends. I will pay you a visit early next year D.V., and I will give you all the story.[109]

If America provided adventure and excitement, Ireland signified enduring friendships, a captive audience for exotic tales – in short, home.

Another force tugging Harry towards Ireland was his family, which remained heavily dependent on his earnings and influence. Looking after the relatives of envoys was a major preoccupation of the revolutionary Dáil, which on Arthur Griffith's motion granted the Bolands an annuity of £156 while Harry remained 'in America on official work for the Dáil'.[110] This modest pension and Kathleen's income were evidently sufficient to maintain the household at Marino Crescent, and fear of poverty was no longer a theme of family correspondence. Other worries remained, as Kate Boland indicated in July:

> About the same time peace was being signed in France, military and police raided No 6; and, 2 weeks ago, my house was raided by 2 G. men and 1 S. [Scotland] Yard man. However, their visit was not so terrible, as it took place in the middle of the day, which was an improvement to the middle of the night. The search was fruitless, Thank God.[111]

Ned, restless as ever, still had no regular job, despite reiterated attempts by Harry to arrange employment for his younger brother through Collins and Diarmuid Fawsitt, the irascible Consul in New York. In early July, Ned reported thus: 'Well, Har old-timer, that job never showed up yet, and it's looking as if I will have to get moving again. I never heard from Collins since, and as you know the[re's] little or nothing doing in this little old Burg of ours.'[112] Ned pursued the idea of American 'agencies' through 'a namesake of ours in New York, Bill Boland'; Kate agreed that 'it would indeed be a good thing to get some agencies, as Edmund is tired being so long idle', praying that 'Mick' would 'soon fix him up'; and Harry promised that he would be placed 'on the list' of the trade bureau which Fawsitt was about to open.[113] Ned arrived in New York in late October and shared dinner and 'yarns' with Harry, but evidently outstayed his welcome: 'Neds won't go home, wants to winter in South.'[114] Even in America, Harry could not escape his responsibility as head of the Boland household.

Of all the factors urging return, the strongest was his inevitable frustration at missing out on the revolution in Ireland. Harry's very first despatch, addressed to de Valera scarcely a fortnight after his arrival, expressed disappointment at the need to prolong his mission: 'Boland must remain here for some time as he is in with everyone and can smoothe the ruffled etc. Ergo, he must remain incog[nito] no longer, so look out for "A Couch Splash", "The Man Who Blindfolded Me", etc. Boland regrets this as he hoped to be home by the end of June.'[115] A month later, he told his mother that 'the only trouble I have in my mind is that I may be wanted in Ireland. England is evidently in a very bad temper and may use the mailed fist even more strongly than at present. I will never forgive myself if anything happens while I am away.'[116] Harry's sense of envy, guilt, and exclusion was doubtless intensified by the obvious impatience of his Dublin colleagues with the often petty if insoluble disputes engulfing the American mission. As Collins sneered in a letter to Nunan: 'Oh yes, I am fully aware of all the little troubles you have had in the New World, but the little troubles here are so absorbing that one is inclined to forget them.'[117] In moments of nostalgia, Harry recalled his former heroics and perhaps yearned to re-enact them:

5 Dec. Fri. Newark. I visit jail, renew glimpses of the moon.

4 Apr. Sun. Washington. Had to decline invitation to speak at Easter Week celebration owing to my illness of last week. Chief gone to New York to speak and attend John McCormack's concert. I go to High Mass and quietly spend the day walking. Visit the F.O.I.F., address meeting and ruminate on 1916 – the friends who died, not in vain.[118]

Above all, he wished to reassert his old indispensability as the organiser who knew everybody, picked up every story, remembered every connection, and deployed his knowledge to control vast networks of scattered activists. By returning to Ireland, he hoped to ensure that his ideas and methods remained at one with those of Collins and the Brotherhood.

Harry used his diary not only to record events and appointments, but intermittently to ruminate about his American enterprise. On New Year's Eve, he wrote that 'the year has been one of great adventure for me and has given me 365 days of real experience. I feel that Ireland's cause has made wonderful progress. Hope the year we are entering in will see the triumph of Ireland.' Two months later, he exuded confidence in the prospect for independence:

The Treaty is nearly finished and a grand healthy anti-British sentiment is abroad. Ireland is fighting magnificently and Russia is victorious. We are confident that the future is ours. Ireland is now out in the sun and can never go back into the shadows of English Imperialism. We will yet place that crown on her 'dear dark head'. March comes to us like a lion in snow and frost. We go forward confident in our cause, having accomplished more in our few months than ever had been dreamed of by our late leaders. $300,000 to Ireland and ten million in sight and Recognition not impossible. The gallant men in Ireland carry on cheerfully knowing that 'The very subtlest eloquence injured man can shew is the pathos of a pike head the logic of a blow.'

At the end of April, there was still more to celebrate:

The wonderful courage of the people at home, the many striking victories of the Volunteers, the driving in of the British Garrison and the loss of 'Morale' suffered by England. Add to this the sentiment in America. The Bond Drive guarantees us funds for a long fight, and a long fight it must be. All depends on the people at home. We must link up the race all over the World for the final struggle. Enter, May.

Then, on the day of his departure, Harry focused sharply on Ireland itself:

Look back at New York and contemplate the forces there that are interested and working in Ireland's cause. I feel more and more convinced that Irishmen in Ireland must themselves win this fight, as the leaders in America have not and in the very nature of things cannot have the same viewpoint and spirit of the men at home.[119]

Already, the American campaign seemed a mere side-show, incapable of delivering freedom through propaganda and international pressure alone.

The summons, when it came, was urgent. On 12 May, he met '[Jim] McGee, home to be fixed up'; next day, he noted that 'O'Mara, Chief and I spend few hours on details, for word has come to be off. Call on Barney [Downs], home, meet Boys.'[120] A more extended account reveals that Harry's travel arrangements were discussed at a midnight meeting in Murphy's Cellar, a basement dive on the corner of 56th Street and Third Avenue. It was decided to place him as a messman in an engineer's room, equipped with a false passport in the name of Barney Downs, bos'n of the *Lapland* in which de Valera had sailed to New York. Harry was to pose as 'a poor painter, his mother was dying, property to be attended to, no money'. After careful rehearsal, he was escorted aboard the same boat bound for Southampton which, two crossings later, was to return him to New York.[121] His journey is best evoked by his own words:

14 May. Fri. New York. Late bed, early rise, go to work in dishabille. Get through easily, report 3 o'c. 'Now blow wind float billow and swell barque the storm is up and all is on a hazard', for tomorrow we go.

15 May. Sat. New York. At Sea. Go aboard at seven a.m. Bid Seán [Nunan] adieu and set out for Holy Ireland. Feel very confident and happy,

throw off my Waldorf airs and clothes, and get back to Mother Nature and hard manual toil. . . .

16 May. Sun. One Day Out. Get to know my messmates, tough bunch. Have easily dropped into Fo'castle manners and customs. Wonder if all the lies I am compelled to tell will count against me in the final tot. Get a big fright when I discover a big G. Man looking over my shoulder.

17 May. Mon. Second Day at Sea. Pass a very uneasy day, find what I consider are four Irish detectives on board. Decide to try 'em out. Discover after investigation that they are indeed policemen, but from China on their way home to Co. Clare. For this relief much thanks. . . .

20 May. Thurs. Five days out. Feel fine and dandy, hard work, good food and coming nearer Ireland every day. Have a very good report to make to Dáil Éireann and gallant news for the I. R. Army. Get on very well with my mates.

21 May. Fri. Sixth Day at Sea. I can quite understand how men who follow the sea grow to love their good ship. One wakens each morning to hear the Chug Chug of the mighty vessel pounding away, go up and watch the giant ship dashing her way thru' the foam and steadily working on.

22 May. Sat. One week at Sea. The crew are in great form. All hope to see land tomorrow night. I enter a Sweepstake as to the hour on which we drop anchor. I feel very, very well. The work and sea breeze have made a new man of me, and the hope of seeing Ireland is ever of great joy to me.

23 May. Sun. Towards the close of this Sunday evening we sight the low lying hills of France, take Pilot up, and steam right into Cherbourg Harbour. Frenchmen come up and take off passengers and mails. My Nigger Mate wins the Sweep. I am glad of it. Steam off.

24 May. Mon. England. Rise 5.30 and go up on deck and find we are safely at anchor in the Solent. Now for the final test. 8 a.m., go alongside. 12.30, all passengers off. 1.30, Boland off safe and sound, all anxiety over. Now for 'The one bright spot'.

25 May. Tues. England. Send a very good friend across to warn the people at home that I am in England. Go off to the races and enjoy day. Wonder how many days I will have to spend in 'Merrie England'. Very quickly find my land legs again.

26 May. Wed. England. Get word from Miceál Ó Colieán to proceed as per his instructions, so that I may enter my own land in safety. Call to see dear old N. K. [Neil Kerr].[122] Am delighted to bring him home from hospital and feel that he is equally glad to see me.

27 May. Thurs. England. Hear that Ned has just left for home the day before I got here. Mother and all will get a great surprise when her rambling boys get in together. Go aboard, turn in to bed to dream of Ireland and all the tried friends I hope to meet tomorrow.[123]

VIII

Takeover

As the ferry steamed towards Dublin's East Wall, Harry Boland looked forward with joyful confidence to rediscovering Ireland after his year in America. His diary recorded the last stages of the homeward journey:

> 28 May 1920. Fri. Dublin. Wake up as we pass Ben Eadair [Howth]. Gaze long and lovingly thro' the clear morning at the old familiar spots. Follow the line from Sutton to the Crescent. Can see my own home, and am not a bit uneasy. Come with good news to my comrades who are doing such magnificent work. Find no one to meet me and decide to take a hack as far as the East Road and then walk to the Crescent. Arrive home, and am warmly greeted. Find Mother, Kathleen and Ned are in great spirits. I enjoy myself round the old home and feel very happy.[1]

Ned had only just preceded him, having sent a characteristic postcard from Barcelona to announce that he was 'rolling Home, thro' Paris'.[2] But Harry's arrival was unexpected, his plans concealed from all but his closest associates in America and in the IRB.[3]

Any hint of anticlimax was quickly brushed aside as Harry basked once more in the glamour of Michael Collins:

> Then Joe [Hyland][4] calls to bring me to Mick in a fast auto. Micheál comes to meet me and in a second I have the hand of Ireland's ablest man – one who combines wonderful ability with a courage and heart that knows not fear. A Genius for organisation, strict disciplinarian, and master hand in this struggle. After the first greeting, we get down to biz. I put before him the exact situation in America, and he electrifies me by his description of the wonderful work that has been accomplished in Ireland during our absence. Arrangements made for my meeting Cabinet. Spend the day with Micheál and Batt [O'Connor]. Am looking forward to greeting many old friends tonight.[5]

One of Harry's first ports of call was the office of the brilliantly effective *Irish Bulletin*, where several of his closest comrades in Sinn Féin and the IRB were now based. As Robert Brennan recalled: 'He breezed into Mount Street and gave us all a lively account of how he had been twice smuggled across the

Atlantic. He had arrived only that morning and the first man to meet him was Michael Collins.' When Anna Fitzsimons hazarded 'that the first thing he said to you was come and have a ball of malt', Harry half-confirmed the rumour in stage-American: 'You said it, babe.'[6]

Harry's childlike delight in rejoining Collins and the Brotherhood persisted throughout his four weeks in Ireland. Meetings and outings with Collins thrilled him, regardless of their ostensible object:

2 June. Wed. Dublin drive to Greystones with Micheál, meet Mrs. de Valera, who is very, very well, trusting to see her husband soon. All the Chief's children are looking fine. Mrs. de V. is a very wonderful and very brave woman, and is quite prepared for what ever may come. Enjoy the drive thro the lovely Glen o' the Downs back to Dublin, where I meet the Executive[7] and many old friends. Am very busy just now. Find my visit very opportune, and the story I bring gives great heart to all those concerned in the movement. Get out my old bike again and pedal away.

Best of all was an idyllic excursion on the following Sunday:

6 June. Sun. Micheál and I with Ned take a run to Howth, cross to Ireland's Eye, eat barnacles and plan out the future. In Micheál Collins, Ireland has the man of a generation. Able, intrepid, with a genius for organisation coupled with a scrupulous attention to detail, he stands out as the greatest force of the movement.[8]

Harry did not mention that they were accompanied by a goggle-eyed Liam Lynch, Commandant of the Cork No. 2 Brigade, who 'had the honour of being out in Ireland's Eye a few Sundays ago with Harry Bowland [*sic*.] and Ml. Collins TDE. He gives glowing accounts of America. . . . There is great hopes of we winning through this year, anyway it is only a matter of time.'[9] Even without Collins, a houseful of brethren had stirred Harry's heart on the previous day: 'Spend the day at home, happy as can be. Mother looks fine and Kathleen is great. Meet the Parson [Diarmuid O'Hegarty], Seán O'Murthuile, Austin [Stack], [Seán] McGarry, Gearoid [O'Sullivan], and many other good men. Feels like a cool plunge after my twelve-month away. All are cheered with the news I bring.'[10]

After the seething ill-will of Irish-America, the simple verities of revolutionary brotherhood epitomised Harry's ideal of home. His fraternisation with the boys on the Supreme Council was appropriately harmonious, despite the growing misgivings of its Secretary, Ó Murthuile. During these meetings, 'no fresh powers were given him' to deal with his opponents in the Clan na Gael. 'In fact', according to Ó Murthuile, 'he did not ask for any, and he had no suggestions to offer as to the solution of the difficulty other than that the Supreme Council should call Devoy to order.'[11] He used his visit to discredit the version of events offered by another 'visitor' representing Cohalan's faction, sternly rejecting the suggestion that de Valera be recalled before he could provoke an irrevocable split. When Kathleen Clarke supported this proposal, 'Harry got wildly angry with me and said, "He is not leaving the USA until he finishes the row, no matter how long it takes".'[12] The key purpose of Harry's visit was to consolidate his authority in America by revitalising his influence at home, and he was equally impatient of opposition in both quarters.

Yet 'home' conditions had changed radically during his year of absence, as symbolic defiance and sporadic coercion gave way to increasingly systematic campaigns of terror by both parties. His return coincided with the reorganisation of Dublin Castle and the Crown forces, the mobilisation of the 'Black and Tans', the extermination of the Dublin detective force by Collins's notorious 'Squad', and the first experiments with 'flying columns' and large-scale ambushes by the IRA. Through letters, despatches, and press reports he had of course become aware of the intensified coercion, to which his mother referred in a letter sent to America just after his departure. Confirming that 'the mothers of Ireland are suffering persecution', she observed that 'the knocking and breaking into houses in the middle of the night, and police and soldiers fully equipped for war, was a most awful experience, but Thank God it has eased off this last few weeks'. Many close friends from the GAA and Lewes were in trouble, as Kathleen Boland had discovered:

> She went to London with Mrs. [Celia] Collins and Con [O'Donovan], where our noble men were dying in Wormwood Scrubs Prison. Seán O'Donovan was released after 21 days' hunger strike, more dead than alive, and is now lying in a London hospital after undergoing an operation, through hunger and having to lie on a concrete floor in a basement cell. Just 2 weeks today since he with others were released. Maurice Collins, also, did 20 days and the men say he was so cheerful that he kept them up wonderfully.

Seán O'Donovan's brother Peter had gone on hunger-strike in Cork, 'but Thank God was released after 10 or 12 days, the prison officials not being quite so brutal here as in London. One poor fellow had his artificial teeth knocked down his throat, and his comrade going to his assistance was knocked down and recd. a black eye. Kathleen saw him in hospital. His eye was still black. Wasn't it brutal? And they had then been 7 or 8 days without food. Such noble Heroes!'[13]

Outraged tales of martyrdom were nothing new, and did not prepare Harry for the increased aggressiveness and ferocity of the IRA and the Squad. As he reflected after his first week at home: 'Coming back after twelve months' absence am struck by the fact that when I left Ireland, "I was on the run" – now I find that I may go my way in Ireland without fear, for the boot "is on the other fella". The police are now on the run, with a vengeance.'[14] Despite this reassuring discovery, he remained apprehensive enough to travel with an automatic revolver, and also to hastily dump this with an acquaintance in Stillorgan when a party of 'Tans' approached.[15] Collins noted his comrade's disorientation with mocking amusement: 'Yes, we have had a fortnight with the visitor, and there is some new aspect to discuss every day. It surprises him how much he has got out of touch during the time he has been away. He is pretty pleased with everything.' Collins assured Nunan that 'it would amuse you to see how meekly he accepts the position of visitor. In fact he is beginning to tire of his holiday already and is anxious to get back to work.'[16]

His refresher course in revolutionary politics ranged from chats with the brethren to formal meetings with the Dáil Ministry. These he recorded with pride:

1 June. Tues. It's just fine to find oneself amongst old friends again. Spend a very happy day. Meet the Cabinet of Dáil Éireann and make my report. Am very happy to find that the Leaders and the Irish People are not relying on America, but on their own determination to be free.

7 June. Mon. I find great delight in calling on old friends and enjoy their surprise at seeing me. Meet the Cabinet and deliver my report. All are very pleased with the progress in America. I am deeply impressed by the wonderful work being accomplished here.[17]

Harry, in his excitement, had evidently fallen behind with his diary and confused the sequence of events, as the relevant meetings were held on Monday, 31 May and Saturday, 5 June. At the first meeting, the Ministry agreed to reinforce the American mission with a regular secretary for de Valera and two 'clerk-accountants' to restore order to the Bond Drive. These were required to 'satisfy M. C. re Accountancy Qualifications and Sceilg [J. J. O'Kelly] re Irish Language'. In the event, the linguistic tests applied by the President of the Gaelic League proved insuperable: 'Reported can't get men knowing Irish. Get other.'[18] On 5 June, a special meeting of the Ministry was called to hear Harry's report and defence of a series of proposals by de Valera. The Ministry agreed to recommend sending a 'delegation' to Russia immediately, with the significant caveat that no demand for Russian recognition of the Republic should be made until after a formal demand had been made in the United States. De Valera was firmly instructed to maintain his base in the USA rather than returning home or moving on to South America, options raised in Harry's report. The Ministry declined to transfer Robert Brennan and Erskine Childers to America (as Director of Propaganda and 'Ambassador' respectively), while agreeing to establish an international Consular service with its headquarters in Washington. With revolutionary abandon, it was decided to allocate a million dollars each to the Department of Defence and de Valera (who was granted 'discretionary powers' in applying this sum 'to secure Recognition'), and to arrange for immediate transmission of £500,000 (almost $2,500,000) to Ireland.[19] Though the conflict with Cohalan was discussed at a subsequent meeting, the Ministry had evidently accepted Harry's remarkably sanguine account of the mission's achievements and prospects.[20]

Politics was not Harry's sole preoccupation during his Irish 'holiday'. Three days after his arrival, the news had reached Kitty Kiernan in Granard through her cousin Paul Cusack. With becoming diffidence, she proposed a meeting:

Can you imagine how excited *I'd* be – I guess you must be some youth now (and I am the same old Kitty). Paul gave me no details only that he met you. I was stunned, you might have sent me a card. I got yr. nice notes from the other side, many thanks. Didn't know yr. address or I wld. have written. I was glad you remembered me. I spent a dull week last week in town, nobody interesting enough! – I hope you found Mick well. I never see him. Everybody here is in great form. We shall soon lose Chrys and Helen [her sisters], and the happy home will be broken up.[21]

A fortnight later, Harry was back with Mick in Joe Hyland's 'fast auto', bound for Granard. Though Helen Kiernan was now otherwise engaged and presumably no longer available to Collins, he consoled himself by accompanying Harry and Kitty to a dance.[22] Harry, at least, made rapid romantic progress during this visit to 'Granard's Ancient Moat', and immediately afterwards felt 'hungry to see you again ere I go on the great hike'. Kitty's company seemed all the more enticing after a session with Sinn Féin's rather unctuous Vice-President in Roscommon:

I have just left Fr. O'Flanagan, having spent the last few hours with him. I need not say how truly wonderful my few days' holiday were to me. I feel, however, that I treated you rather unfairly in keeping you from your slumbers. Do say that you are now recovered. If I could only be with you I would indeed try to make you happy. It may be that I will come back soon again from overseas. Please God it may be our lot to win the fight so long waged for freedom. If so, we can all feel proud of our generation. ' 'Tis but in vain for soldiers to complain.' Yet I long to be in Ireland, more so than ever that I have hopes to win the girl I love best in all the world.[23]

By such devices, Harry tried to ensure that his presence would be felt at home, however long he might remain in America.

Just before returning to the fo'c'sle of the *Philadelphia*, Harry cabled his 'goodbye and best love' to Kitty,[24] and finally revealed his presence in Ireland to the press. Cagily claiming to have 'just returned to Ireland', he boasted of the American triumphs of de Valera and his 'Envoy Extraordinary', recalling the huge crowds and gubernatorial receptions, the successful campaign against the League, his 'great hopes' of inducing the Democratic Party to support recognition, the mission's rebuttal of British propaganda, and the Bond Drive. Harry was particularly proud to have brought back into use the sinister third stanza of 'The Star-Spangled Banner', affirming that the blood of Loyalist traitors had 'washed out their foul footsteps' confusion' [*sic.*].[25] The mood of his diary was as sunny on departure as on arrival:

> 23 June. Wed. Bid good bye to Dublin once more. My Mother comes to Abbey St. with Dan Fraher. I await word from Mick, eventually Joe comes to escort me. A hasty goodbye to all my people, and run out so that I may not witness the tears of my dear loved Mother, the best in all the World.

> 24 June. Thurs. Get away safe and sound. Meet Neil K[err] who is to come with me to port of embarkation. Am anxious to meet Con [O'Donovan?] so that there may be no hitch. Spend the day in train across England. View London and the Thames. Wonder how long it will take Ireland to win out!

> 25 June. Fri. Everything looks well for my journey. Will know at 10 a.m. tomorrow. Spend the day with sailors round the Docks. Drink more beer than I care for, yet keep O.K. One more fence to cross and then for de Valera again.

> 26 Jun. Sat. At Sea. Have successfully accomplished my journey so far without a hitch. Am now at Sea, steering West, and feel very happy. Am aboard a Free Ship flying Stars and Stripes, well out of reach of John Bull. Feel the breeze good.

> 27 June. Sun. At Sea. Working hard. Am very happy. Have couple of stowaways here, keep their hearts up and arrange to feed them. Very rough weather on edge of 'Bay o' Biscay O'.[26]

The sometime Envoy Extraordinary was ready to resume duty in America.

His return to New York, after 'a very uneventful journey',[27] was without fanfare:

> 5 July. Mon. New York again. Go ashore three o'clock. Call up Wolcott [Hotel], no one in. De Valera in San Francisco. Walk up to Park Avenue. Frank P. [Walsh] and family in Kansas. Proceed to the Good Carmelites where, as ever, I am most kindly received. Meet Jas. O'Mara, talk long. Am very, very tired.[28]

De Valera, whom he met three days later, was equally jaded after his futile and ham-fisted attempts, while deprived of Harry's tactical finesse, to induce the major Party conventions to pronounce in favour of recognition:

> 9 July. Fri. Chicago. Chief and Pedlar come to Edgewater Beach Hotel. I spend all the morning talking of home to De V., who is looking very tired

after his strenuous months in Chicago and San Francisco. De V. is very happy with news from home, is longing to get back to wife and children. He is full of vigor and intends to carry on.[29]

Though less thrilling than those in Ireland, the latest sequence of reunions unleashed the customary fraternal endearments. Harry enjoyed James O'Mara's 'company to the full' on the train to Chicago, and was delighted to find Frank P. Walsh 'fit and well, as usual full of vigor and fight'.[30] Seán Nunan, who like Collins on an earlier occasion had pictured himself as 'a poor lonesome ——' after Harry's departure, reported that 'Harry looks fine and has great yarns. They make me all the more anxious to get back again.'[31] Instead, he and Harry decided to settle down as a bachelor couple in New York, as Kitty Kiernan was informed in mid September: 'Seán Nunan and I are on the look out for "digs". We are sick of hotel life and hope to have a little home of our own very soon where we can chat and smoke of an evening.'[32] By early November their search had been successful, though the Italian owner was due to resume occupation a month later. As Harry told 'Mike' Collins: 'Seán and I, with [Gilbert] Ward, have secured a little apartment in West 51st Street and it is a happy change for us from the hotel life. ... It is a great change for us to shop in the evening and get our own meals. Seán is a great cook. I suppose you are leading the usual life – no rest – no fixed abode.'[33] Unexpectedly, Harry had discovered the delights of domesticity amidst Manhattan's most notorious 'speakeasy belt'.

As before, Harry was never too busy to relax, whether spending 'a very pleasant day on the sands' in Atlantic City, losing $25 to O'Mara at billiards, enjoying a 'pleasant evening' and dinner with Kathleen O'Connell and the office-girls in Washington, or playing a 'game of ball' with the Carmelites.[34] Harry resumed his avuncular relationship with Kathleen O'Connell in the Washington office, enjoining her to be a 'good girl' and a 'good sweet child till I see you', asking her to send on his white hat, and hoping that she was 'not lonely' in his absence.[35] Further diversion was generated by the arrival of Joseph Begley and Gilbert Ward, whose appointments as de Valera's secretary and O'Mara's 'clerk-accountant' had been arranged during Harry's visit to Ireland.[36] Harry continued to relish the occasional colourful experience out of town:

> 23 July. Fri. Seán and I start for Albany, en route for Sehnectady per the Night Boat. Enjoy lovely trip up the Hudson. Our friend the Nigger says 'it's the real' – so it is. Nunan and I explore the boat and are amused at most of the passengers. Searchlight works along the banks.[37]

Harry never lost his zest for America, or his ability to convert the Irish mission into an extended and boisterous holiday.

He proved to be an eager tour-guide when James O'Mara's wife and their daughter Patricia arrived in New York, taking them to Chinatown and the

Bowery to show 'what New York could do to those who did not make the grade'. As Patricia O'Mara recalled: 'Off the three of us went and we saw the Chinese light their joss sticks; and we ate in what I happily imagined to be a dive while Harry described to us the Chinatown of San Francisco, and how much more real and more eastern and lurid it was than this more make-believe Chinatown.' Since Harry had missed out on all three of de Valera's visits to California, this version of reality was also make-believe. A week later, on 21 August, he escorted Patricia to Coney Island, 'in a sightseers' coach with a megaphone blaring and a rough and giddy crowd around us. It was a thoroughly plebeian expedition.' While Terence McSwiney languished on hunger-strike in Brixton Prison, Harry and Patricia ate hot-dogs and practised marksmanship with repeating rifles and revolvers.[38] Harry's factional adversaries professed to deplore his 'plebeian' habits, and Devoy delighted in spreading scurrilous rumours:

> I hear that Dr. Gertrude Kelly[39] and her crowd are very angry at De V. for sending Boland out again and are talking bitterly of his vulgarity and bad manners. Some Leitrim men who are waiters in one of Shanley's restaurants[40] say that before he went back he came into the place where they work with a disreputable looking woman, both drunk, and made a scandalous exhibition.[41]

An actor of many parts, Harry slipped easily between the elegant envoy and the street-wise debauchee.

Another facet of Harry's personality was expressed in his letters to Granard, which he pictured as a haven of peace. After posting 'many letters and cards' without response, he sent Kitty Kiernan a parcel of 'autograph photos' and a querulous note beneath the imposing letterhead of the 'Elected Government of the Republic of Ireland (American Delegation), Office of the President':

> I have been very busy since my arrival and fear that I may not see Ireland again for some considerable time. The heat here is very intense and most uncomfortable. I envy you in the coolness of Granard and the quietude of your peaceful home knowing nothing of the cares and worries attendant on such work as mine.

He prayed for 'a little line', expressed gratitude for her brother's hospitality during his 'never to be forgotten trip', and promised to send an appropriate gift: 'I am going West again very soon, and will send you on an Indian bag made from deer skin and beadwork which will go just fine with your delightful style.'[42] This sally had the desired effect, prompting a cable and 'a nice long letter' (since lost) which encouraged Harry to adopt a cheerier style, discard his letterhead, and sign off as 'H' rather than 'E. Ua Beolláin'. Talk of holidays stimulated a slightly saucy reflection: 'I wonder did you ever think of "the Mimber" as you meandered along the Shannon, thro' South Roscommon. The Mimber meanwhile was wondering how it came that he had not had even a wee post card from Miss Kitty and was very miserable and lonely in consequence.'[43] A few days later, as he prepared for a fortnight's tour of Virginia, the 'Middle West', and New York State, he relished the thought of his beloved dutifully marooned in Granard: 'I am sure you and Mopsie [Maud Kiernan] are very good girls to mind the house the while the remaining members of the family were disporting themselves at the Show.[44] I feel sorry for Kitty yet I am sure you have made up for it (the Show) since.' The 'really delightful' Fall weather in Washington reminded him, inevitably, 'of the glorious days I spent in Granard last time'. The climax adopted Harry's most elevated style, as used in his letter to Cait Fraher from Lewes Prison: 'Remember me to all, may God bless you, and don't forget the "wee prayer" for God knows I need all the prayers I can get said for me.'[45] An ocean separated the Granard socialite of his prayers from the 'disreputable looking' alleged consorts of his New York nights.

At this point, all correspondence between Harry and Kitty ceased for six months, despite a catastrophe in Granard which shattered Harry's idyll of 'the quietude of your peaceful home'. On 5 December, he received a letter from Collins congratulating him on having 'more or less abandoned hotel life' and speculating quizzically on his new domestic circumstances: 'With the company I wonder if it is so much quieter after all. It may be a question of coming events simply!' Collins went on to refer indirectly to the Volunteers' murder on 31 October of District Inspector Philip St. John Howlett Kelleher, RIC, while drinking with members of Sinn Féin's North Longford Executive and a priest in the Greville Arms. The hotel had been burned down in reprisal, and Kitty briefly apprehended: 'The Granard thing was pretty dreadful. It appeared in the papers to-day that one of the girls was arrested. It seems it was not actual arrest, but just a sort of restraint – but I have no details yet. I don't know which of them it is. Paul [Cusack], you will have seen, has been arrested, so has Larry [Kiernan].'[46]

Harry delayed his 'kind enquiries' about the incident until the following spring, whereupon Kitty responded with an oddly jaunty account:

I wrote you a long letter early in October. I wonder if you ever got it. Funny, in that letter I told you all about our new D.I. etc. ... I was often wondering why you hadn't written or if you had heard of Granard's fate. I too had an exciting time. The military treated me extra[?], gave me a dance when I was leaving!! Don't be shocked, shall tell you all details some day if I am lucky enough to meet you again.

The belle of the hotel professed herself reconciled to reincarnation as a petty shopkeeper: 'We are still carrying on buis [business] in Granard, couldn't tear ourselves away! We have a flat here and are fairly comfy, and business is going on fairly well, of course *no* Hotel. So Kitty *shld*. have a rest, but instead, they have made me a shop (walker) girl, and now, behold me, behind a counter in a little shop!! We are all there together and running it ourselves.' Despite these reverses, and Harry's silence at the critical period, she reopened their long-distance flirtation: 'How is Seán [Nunan], is he still with you? Hope you haven't got too many lady visitors to yr. digs. You never tell me those things, or the nice little evg's (or is it nights?) you have, you think you must have some diversion now that there are no bars!!!'[47] The tenuous link had been restored.

Meanwhile, the mission operated much as before, its members constantly on the move between cities and between assignments, alternately collaborating, quarrelling, and carousing. Yet the character of the campaign was changing, as populism gave way to systematic organisation and intrigue. After a year on the road, the mission's orators, and probably the American public, had tired of monster meetings at which the same simple message was declaimed in every city. In any case, Harry, like de Valera, had lost much of his appetite for public performances. In early August, he told McGarrity that, 'as to your suggestion re meetings, we are so busily engaged now fighting each other that it is very difficult to get concerted action for such a purpose'.[48] A week later, he informed Arthur Griffith that 'the Chief has abandoned the idea of touring South America. ... The President has definitely decided to retire from public speaking here, and has taken active management of the foreign affairs.'[49] The few major rallies organised during the second half of 1920 relied upon visiting stars to provide the sparkle required for extensive press coverage. A flurry of demonstrations had greeted the arrival of Daniel Mannix, the Catholic Archbishop of Melbourne, whose translation from Maynooth to Australia had transformed the prickly scholastic into a pulpit-thumping Irish republican. The British Government's decision to deny him access to Ireland, ostensibly to visit his elderly mother, offered irresistible opportunities for damaging propaganda when Mannix reached New York a fortnight after Harry:

18 July. Sun. New York. Archbishop Mannix arrives. Chief and His Grace attend Madison Square Gardens. Fifteen thousand people inside cheer de Valera for twelve minutes. De V. makes slashing speech. His Grace delivers a wonderful speech. Many thousands outside hold overflow. Everything passes off, O.K.[50]

After Mannix's departure, the mission lacked an oratorical focus until the arrival in December of Mary McSwiney.[51] Lionised since the death on hunger-strike of her brother Terence, formidable in her own right, the schoolmistress from Cork was quickly identified as the most suitable substitute-orator for the departing de Valera. When Harry was told of her proposed schedule, he protested that 'Miss McSwiney is a woman, and this is a schedule for a horse.'[52]

He accompanied her to a few of the forty states that she visited, sometimes with other members of her family: 'Off on tour of New England with McSwiney, party'; 'A great meeting, Miss McSwiney wonderful speaker.'[53] Fresh-voiced advocates like Mannix and Mary McSwiney momentarily restored the illusion that recognition of the Republic could be secured by charisma, amplified through a megaphone.

After de Valera's abject failure to induce either major Party to endorse recognition, there was little point in pursuing that demand in Washington pending the inauguration of the new President and Congress in March and April 1921. Despite the conviction of a key adviser that the 'Third Party' would get nowhere,[54] Harry and his colleagues found some solace in securing its rhetorical support in mid July:

> 10 July. Sat. Chicago. We are busy at work on the Third Party's Convention, find ourselves bereft of all the big wigs, so fall back on the faithful rank and file. I meet John FitzPatrick, Labor leader.[55] A two fisted upstanding Irish American.

> 11 July. Sun. Third Party will have a trying time in evolving from the different groups that go to make up the Progressive forces – 'Committee of 48', 'Single Taxers', 'Labor', Constitutional Party, 'Veterans of the World War' etc. We arrange for De V. to go before the Convention.

> 12 July. Mon. Chicago. Very interesting watching the Party emerge from the trials of the different groups. Labor sends Ultimatum to all other groups. De Valera speaks in Convention, well received.

> 13 July. Tues. Chicago. Third Party endorses Platform, calls for Recognition of the Irish Republic, and further demands an embargo of Munitions to England and Poland. We have not much hope of victory, yet find Ireland will be made an issue, thereby forcing the big Parties to take notice.[56]

The big Parties did not take notice, and no further attempt was made at representative level to secure recognition during de Valera's sojourn in America. Indeed, he was to depart without fulfilling the instructions agreed by the Dáil Ministry in early October: '[President] to stay in U.S.A. Issue that Cabinet have instructed him to stay in U.S. until he has presented formal demand for recognition. Write him that this should not be done before new Congress and President come into office.'[57] Meanwhile, the mission suspended its ambitious sally into 'high politics'. As Harry reflected on 4 August, after a 'long chat' over lunch with John E. Milholland: 'I can plainly see that if we get deep into American Politics we will be skinned, so keep clear.'[58]

Harry was now free to pursue the still more ambitious conspiratorial strategy which he had so often discussed with Collins and the brethren. Just before his lunch with Milholland, he had revealed his vision to McGarrity with noteworthy candour:

It is obvious that left to ourselves in Ireland we cannot hope to win final victory without tremendous loss, but granted a world-wide organisation built on the lines of the Parent Body with the same methods of attack and the same willingness to sacrifice I feel assured victory is certain. Our dream is a world-wide organisation pledged and controlled from Home working in concert and with single purpose along clearly defined lines with a plan of campaign whereby we can meet the enemy not alone in Ireland but all over the globe. Thus only can Britain be shewn the power of Ireland. Many will say that it is not feasible to so organise; you I am sure will not say so. It may be our work to travel this country and take care of the clubs on this side. To Australia, Canada, South Africa, India, Egypt, and Moscow our men must go to make common cause against our common foe. I am not alarmed at the new 'Coercion Bill'. The more Coercion the better for Ireland. We go ahead for the final show-down.[59]

At a dinner given for Laurence Ginnell and his wife in New York, Harry and his fellow guests betrayed similar elation as they discussed 'plans for the future, such as the corruption of all British shipping, a suggestion that all British embassies [sic.] in this country be destroyed at a certain time, and plans to cause a general disturbance'.[60]

Harry's grandiose scheme for global revolutionary organisation, absurd in its pretensions yet menacing in its practical implications, was to guide his conduct over the following year. His first priority was to create a suitable organisation, whose precise functions were not immediately revealed. As Harry advised Collins: 'There is no reason in the world why our home organisation should not be the basis of a world movement, with the same obligations, constitution and name of course. This will entail hard work, but would not require a huge membership – say selected men in important places, always having a represen-tative of the Home Body here to co-ordinate effort.' He hoped to send a 'representative' to Australia and also 'link up Canada with home, and thus we have our dream realised'. The first practical test of trans-Atlantic co-ordination was prompted by the threat that Mannix would be prevented from leaving America for the United Kingdom: 'My first effort was directed along the water-front in New York when it was rumored that the *Baltic*'s crew would strike if Dr. Mannix was allowed a passage on the ship.'[61] The outcome was recounted in his diary:

27 July. Tues. Atlantic City, where I meet the Chief re Archbishop Mannix's departure. His Grace takes up Lloyd George's challenge and intends to go ahead.

28 July. Wed. New York. Arrive midday. Look up good friends and arrange to fix the Mannix journey so that, if he should be prevented from travelling, we can hold up all vessels in the port. Longshoremen and Firemen with His Grace. Delighted with results.

31 July. Sat. New York, aboard the *Baltic* for cooks' meeting. Cooks wisely decide not to protest. Go with Chief to Archbishop, thence to boat. A wonderful send off for the Archbishop. De Valera causes a mild sensation among the *Baltic* crew and officers. The Longshoremen hammer Mr. Shaw when he hissed His Grace.[62]

Catholic outrage was refuelled when the *Baltic* was intercepted before reaching Queenstown (Cobh), Mannix being removed by destroyer to Penzance and prohibited from crossing the Irish Sea. Harry exploited the issue to renew his shaky alliance with the Friends of Irish Freedom, to whom he introduced a delegation of Longshoremen which left the meeting with a promise that $15,000 would be donated to the 'Mannix MacSwiney Marine Protest Committee'.[63] Although by 8 August the protest was 'breaking up', Harry boasted to his Minister for Defence that 'the Mannix incident gave us an opportunity to test the spirit of the men along the New York docks, and their response was magnificent'.[64] This experiment in co-operation was the first fruit of an earlier discussion of strategy, following Harry's experience of the 'Progressive' forces uneasily united in the 'Third Party':

14 July. Wed. Chicago. Jas. O'Mara, Chief and I discuss future. Agree that direct help can only come from Labor, so will bend all our efforts to build up an alliance with Labor, so that in the event of England's attempting war on our people we can rely on Direct Action here against her.[65]

In America as in Ireland, Harry used his affinity with working men to manoeuvre organised Labour towards revolutionary action in the republican interest.

The proposed Russian alliance was crucial to the dream of internationalising the Irish revolution. A month after his return to America, Harry remained optimistic: 'I am in great hopes that the Russians will yet settle with the World on a just basis. Wish our men were in Russia. May go myself if others hang back.'[66] It was that 'brave boy' McCartan who was eventually sent to Moscow to negotiate mutual recognition and other more practical forms of co-operation.[67] Yet Harry was active in preparing for this mission, as he informed McCartan in early August:

Liam will give you 'the dope' so that you may go on your way prepared. ... The work you are about to undertake is of the highest importance to Ireland. It is obvious that the future of Europe will be determined by the outcome of the present Russian–Polish affaire. Up to date the stand taken by Russia is all to our advantage and I pray that you will find on your arrival the same warm welcome that was promised some time ago.[68]

On 29 October, Harry presented Ludwig Martens with a second loan of $20,000, this time without securing any jewels, on the understanding 'that the equivalent of the above sum will be made available for the duly accredited Representatives of the Irish Republican Government at Moscow'.[69] His enthusiasm was not shared by George Gavan Duffy at Foreign Affairs, whose hope was fulfilled 'that the Cabinet will be very slow to act upon the power conferred on it'.[70] When de Valera finally supplied the credentials which enabled McCartan to set out from New York for Moscow, on 29 December, the Russian Government had lost interest in any Irish alliance. As McCartan later complained, 'Russia had no longer need of our friendship' following the collapse of the Allied invasion and the rapid movement towards an Anglo-Soviet trade agreement.[71] McCartan, when eventually admitted to Soviet Russia, received politely negative responses from the Commissariat of Foreign Affairs and Santeri Nuorteva, with whom he had drawn up a draft treaty of friendship in New York. He left with no treaty, no promises of material assistance, and no memories of hospitality to justify Harry's investment of another $20,000 on behalf of American Bondholders.[72] Ireland was not, after all, to ride the wave of the international proletarian revolution.

After Harry's return from Dublin, the Anglo-Irish conflict and consequent carnage had rapidly intensified. For men like Harry and Collins, the descent into political and social anarchy was a source of exhilaration rather than regret. As Collins wrote in 'a personal note' to his comrade on 15 October: 'Everywhere here the situation is growing more and more exciting. Probably we are in for a very rough winter – whoever will survive it. But my belief is that at the end of the winter the enemy's grip here will have relaxed: considerably.'[73] In his diary, Harry jotted down the most spectacular incidents:

25 Oct. Lord Mayor MacSwiney dies, R.I.P.

21 Nov. Dublin raids. Croke Park.

22 Nov. Dick McKee, Peadar Clancy, Jim [recte, Conor] Clune murdered in prison, R.I.P.[74]

Under such circumstances, massive acquisition of arms was all the more essential to the revolutionary strategy. By mid July, Harry was 'convinced that we can be best employed in supplying the sinews of war for home. I am in great hopes that "the Hardware" can be got and landed. This then is the main work for me.'[75] Despite the arrest of a messenger carrying 'letters and Hardware', which made 'things awkward for us', he remained sanguine about future shipments.[76] Before long, he had secured 'quotations from G.' and sent 'urgent request to Field for first class man to handle all his Business'.[77]

In early August, he informed Brugha, as Minister for Defence, that 'the Chief has agreed that Liam and I go ahead on your work. We have already secured quotations for wholesale editions, and think we can secure transportation; that is if ye are prepared to accept delivery.' Liam Mellows would be sent to Dublin to complete the arrangements, and Brugha was reassured that the American delegation had 'not forgotten your views in certain contingencies for a world action'.[78] When writing to Collins in confirmation, Harry reported that 'all agree that Charlie's dept. is the most important' and enclosed a .303 silencer 'which you can try out'.[79] A fortnight later, Harry had 'decided to go right ahead' with 'the big project', with the assistance of the faithful bos'n, Barney Downs ('easily our very best man').[80] Undeterred by 'a run of bad luck' as more carriers were arrested, Collins agreed that Harry proceed with his first major consignment of unspecified 'hardware' (which was to 'lie off the coast' instead of being sent 'right in').[81] This scheme was eventually aborted by Brugha, who 'did not consider the cost of transport satisfactory' and complained that Mellows 'had no particulars regarding prices of goods'. The blow was only slightly cushioned by a letter in Irish giving Harry authority to spend $20,000 from the Defence budget.[82] Such was Harry's preoccupation with munitions that James O'Mara, when instructed to advance the President's 'secretary' $50,000 for arms, had ruled in mid September that 'now that Mr Boland and Mr Mellows are employed in definite work in a special department of the government – their salaries should be paid from and chargeable to the funds allocated to this service'. De Valera, wily as ever, responded that 'as the "drive" will end in a very short time it is not worth while making any special analytical division of the expenses. That can be done later.'[83] It never was done, and Harry's status as a gun-runner remained unofficial.

Collins was relentless in his hunger for new weapons to test, expressing partic-ular interest in a 'repeating gun' used by the New York police. Harry replied that the 'riot gun' was 'made in the Government factories for the police but I will do my best to secure one and send you as a sample', a promise which was promptly forwarded to the American Secret Service after an arrest in Ireland.[84] The New York police had two types of riot gun – a single-action, six-shot Remington 'pump-gun', and a new device capable of firing 100 shots in six seconds which was 'not for the exclusive use of this Department'.[85] This miniature sub-machine-gun, still being developed by General Marcellus H. Thompson's Auto-Ordnance Corporation, was a weapon superior to anything comparable in the British light armoury. Harry's ambitious attempt to outgun Ireland's oppressor did not, however, materialise until the New Year. Though the main justification for acquiring American arms was to fortify the IRA at home, Brugha was also intent on extending the terrorist campaign to Britain and beyond. After initial opposi-tion from Griffith, the Ministry had agreed to a campaign of industrial sabotage in Britain, while referring Brugha's complementary plan to assassinate the British Cabinet for adjudication by de Valera. Despite Brugha's urgent requests for de Valera's sanction and for Harry's advocacy of this 'extended system of doing business', the scheme was shelved.[86] The most dramatic element of Brugha's proposed 'world action' would not be put to the test for over sixty years.

Without massive funds, such enterprises could not have been contemplated. Throughout 1920, Harry kept a watchful eye on a bewildering variety of financial appeals designed to pursue the American campaign, support the Dáil's civil and military programme, subsidise the covert operations of the IRB, or relieve distress in Ireland. The ever-widening rift between the mission and its ostensible allies in America generated a plethora of 'relief' funds, ostensibly devoted to aiding victims of repression and economic deprivation at home. Many of these originated with organisations outside Harry's control, making it tricky to ensure that the money would be monopolised by approved republican beneficiaries. When Harry learned that at least $3,000 claimed by the IRB had been turned over to McGarrity for lending to an 'Irish Relief Fund', he requested an immediate report to ensure that the money would be recovered by the brethren.[87] As usual, he attempted to mediate between competing groups, warning O'Mara that any dispute between the White Cross and Dr. Maloney's nascent American Committee for Relief in Ireland would be 'disastrous'. He was even 'inclined to overlook many little defects in the collection and administration of the money in view of the great possibilities of the movement'.[88] Meanwhile, 'the Chief [was] working on a big scheme at present whereby we hope to secure the support of the Knights of Columbus for the relief of the devastated areas of Ireland', so harnessing to the cause a 'wonderful organization' with 'plenty of money'.[89] This partnership fell through, but Maloney's Committee for Relief was duly launched in New York just after Christmas.[90] These initiatives undermined a simultaneous attempt by the Friends of Irish Freedom to instigate 'one general fund for the relief of the victims of English brutality in the devastated Irish cities and towns', further souring relations between Harry and Diarmuid Lynch.[91] Even so, Harry continued to solicit Judge Cohalan's support in an abortive scheme to resettle resigned and dismissed policemen in the United States.[92]

The most ambitious money-spinner was, of course, the 'External Loan' or Bond Drive, which under O'Mara's direction sold Bond Certificates amounting to over $5,000,000. Harry himself contributed $100, for which 'little Brother' Nunan signed the receipt.[93] While money flooded in, it trickled out so slowly that in mid August Collins accused Harry of having 'misled us very seriously in this connection. The figures which have now been sent from U.S.A. are nothing short of being disastrous.' His rebuke was only slightly mollified by a handwritten personal note: 'No chance of the hurling.'[94] Harry replied that about $3,000,000 was 'available for despatch to Ireland', but that de Valera was not yet satisfied that those at home could 'safeguard the money'. Collins, clearly irritated, asked Harry to 'tell him our chief way of safeguarding it up to the present has been by spending it – that is to say, by investing it in land', and chastised O'Mara for sending drafts which could not be drawn on Irish banks.[95] By the end of the year, less than $1,000,000 of Bond money had reached Ireland.[96] Meanwhile, Harry and the brethren tightened their control over the funds still in America. In mid November, Mellows joined O'Mara and de Valera as an American Trustee; four weeks later, the Trustees transferred the balance to a multitude of deposits under various names, including those of Harry, Nunan, and McGarrity. About $1,500,000 was placed in deposit accounts, and a similar sum invested as a 'reserve' in American Liberty Bonds. The effect was to empower Harry and McGarrity together to withdraw money from any cash account, though O'Mara retained the keys to three safe-deposits containing Liberty Bonds. All the nominal beneficiaries pledged their 'honour' to surrender the funds on demand from the Trustees.[97] The Trustees planned to withhold substantial sums for the American campaign over the following year, including $50,000 each for Harry's Washington office, Fawsitt's Consulate, and the Committee for Relief, $100,000 for the nascent 'Recognition Association', and $200,000 (later raised to $250,000) towards raising a second loan.[98] Like their Irish-American adversaries, so often execrated for spending most of the Irish Victory Fund in America, the envoys themselves had grown reluctant to surrender their hard-won assets to those 'at home'.

During and after Harry's visit to Ireland, the unresolved conflict with Cohalan and Devoy flickered on, periodically reignited by vicious exchanges in rival Irish-American newspapers and clashes in branches of the Friends of Irish Freedom and the Clan na Gael. Though Harry delayed acting upon his authority to serve an ultimatum upon the Clan, Devoy soon picked up 'a rumor' that he was 'going to "reorganize" the Clan or start a rival organization'.[99] In mid July, the incessant sniping induced the conciliatory James K. McGuire to announce his imminent resignation as Chairman of the Executive: 'I have visited some 30 towns in the past two months and wherever I go our people are sick, sore and disgusted.'[100] At this point, Harry decided to force the issue by asking Devoy to convene his Executive to consider unspecified 'communications from the Home Body'. As always, he prepared methodically for the coming struggle:

21 July. Wed. New York. Meet Joe McGarrity and Hugh Montague, discuss dispute. I go to New Rochelle to James K. McGuire and lay proposals from Ireland before him. I fear serious opposition from Clan in our efforts to secure an organisation controlled from home, and directed in all matters of policy from home.[101]

He showed at least some of 'the letters' to McGuire, who promptly passed on their substance to Devoy: 'The organization has changed its Constitution and made itself part of the Republic. They want us to do the same, and the implication is that if we don't do so they will cut us off.' When Harry tried to cool the dispute with 'a *very diplomatic* reply', Devoy remarked that this was 'just as if written to an enemy Government', and soon provoked the resumption of mutual abuse.[102] On 3 August, the two 'had a shake hands' on the sidewalk but 'did not talk of anything'; two days later, Devoy called a meeting of the Executive for the 15th; and four days before that meeting, Harry condescended temporarily to 'ignore your vile charges against me out of respect for your work in the past and your advanced age'.[103] Both factions seemed poised for an irreparable split when Harry confronted the Clan's Executive once again in New York's Park Avenue Hotel.

Instead, Devoy's Executive agreed, up to a point, to accept dictation from the Dáil and the IRB, as demanded in the 'questions' which Harry had secured from the Supreme Council before his visit to Ireland. It was resolved 'that on all subjects regarding the policy and interests of the Irish Republic, the wishes of the President shall be respected and followed'; that plans would be devised 'to extend the active work on the part of this organization along the lines directed by the Envoy from Ireland'; that two representatives of the Clan would be sent to Ireland to discuss differences, while a committee of three would urge unity upon local conventions; that 'all future newspaper controversies' should be silenced; that Devoy should publicly retract his denunciation of de Valera's 'lowering of the flag'; and that Harry should 'secure correction' of a passage in the Dáil's minutes criticising Devoy.[104] McGuire, who devised the terms of settlement, had spent seven hours with Devoy and discerned that 'the heart of the great veteran was breaking'. He informed Cohalan that

Boland, working under great difficulties, made a lasting and most favorable impression on all present. His review of the conditions in his country and his give and take style, running all the gamut of Irish emotions and the evidence of the real fighting man that enkindles the spirit of our people, the human side – all in all profoundly affected those present. He has grown greatly in a year. Revolution is the only process by which such types are suddenly developed.[105]

Yet the agreement, unanimous though it was, rapidly unravelled. When reporting it to Cohalan, Devoy added significantly that 'Harry admits that what was done yesterday will amount to nothing without your approval'. Devoy also implied that more than one key member of the Executive was disingenuous in his acquiescence: 'Murphy's reasons are entirely Corkonian.[106] He believes the very defects of the resolutions are the best feature. They give us the chance, he thinks, of tiding over the difficulty and winning later on. I have drafted a circular with that idea in mind.'[107] The phrasing of Devoy's apology and the circular prompted further dispute, and Diarmuid Lynch complained that 'verbal exchanges are worthless, and the written resolutions are all on one side'.[108] A dispirited Devoy told Harry that he was 'used up' and inclined to retire: 'I saw Kickham preside in meetings of the S. C. [Supreme Council] when he was wholly deaf and very nearly blind, and we had to convey the proceedings to him by the deaf and dumb alphabet on his fingers, but there was nothing big going on then.'[109]

In late August, Harry remained convinced that the Executive was 'sincere' in its 'desire for harmony', while warning Collins that 'there has been no change of heart on the part of Devoy'. Harry exulted in having assumed 'control of the machine that has dictated policy to the F.O.I.F. and manipulated all the acts of that body since its inception'. Over the next month, however, he concluded that 'one man, the Judge', had 'practically vetoed' implementation of the settlement, and that 'things remain much as they were during the Chicago business'.[110] According to McGarrity, Cohalan had approached virtually the entire Executive during the fortnight following Devoy's apology, and had 'induced a number of them to refuse to abide by the agreement'.[111] This seemed to vindicate Harry's assumption that the Executive, the power behind the Friends of Irish Freedom, was itself controlled by the outsider Cohalan. Harry, being himself a conspirator reliant for his authority on an outsider (de Valera), intuitively understood the texture of power in Irish-America. Devoy's sleep was spoilt by the incessant tension, and by late September he was intent 'on a final showdown'.[112] Meanwhile, the IRB's Supreme Council had sanctioned Harry's actions, while deploring the extension of the dispute to 'the public press'.[113] As the climax approached, Devoy recounted another rumour: 'The latest news com[ing] out of a tailor's shop – a very appropriate place because Boland is a tailor – is that Harry has a letter from Mick Collins, which he is to let loose whenever he thinks it is needed, "cutting off Cohalan and Devoy from everything". We'll have to take refuge in Greenland or Teria [sic.] del Fuego. God save Ireland.'[114] Harry's 'excommunication' of the Clan was about to be proclaimed.

On 22 October, Harry circulated the press with a letter denouncing Cohalan and dismissing the Executive as 'powerless'. On the advice of de Valera, whose much trumpeted self-denying ordinance in leaving the Brotherhood had never prevented him from gaining access to its most shady secrets, Harry identified himself as the envoy by signing the press release: 'Speaking with full authority in the name of the Supreme Council of the Irish Republican Brotherhood, I hereby announce that the Clan na Gael organization is no longer affiliated with the Brotherhood.'[115] For the third time in a half-year of conflict, Harry had exploited the latent menace of a sheet of paper (this time the letter of excommunication supplied in April by Collins) in his relentless pursuit of supremacy over the American brethren. Devoy, his spirit rekindled, savaged his opponents in the *Gaelic American*: 'Lord High Executioner Boland swings his axe on Clan-na-Gael ... carrying out the plans made at the British Embassy two years ago to "disrupt the Irish movement in America and destroy Cohalan".' Ever the sharp debater, he maintained that Cohalan, not being a member of the Executive, 'has no influence on its action and seeks to exercise none'. As for Harry, he had been 'a good fighting man in Ireland, but he is wholly unfitted, mentally and temperamentally, for the task that has been assigned him. ... His bumptious self-assertiveness and swaggering bad manners are repulsive to self-respecting men.'[116]

In private, Harry was bombarded with letters from flabbergasted Clansmen, calling on him to 'rise above petty jealousy' and to withhold his 'poisoned arrows'.[117] Usually brisk in his response to such pleas, Harry admitted that one letter had 'touched me deeply'. Writing on the 'anniversary of Allen, Larkin and O'Brien', one of 'Rossa's Skirmishers' who had belonged to the Clan for forty-six years protested at being designated as 'an outlaw or traitor to the Irish cause'. He alleged that 'at my Mother's knee I became familiar with Emmet's story and sacrifice, and at the age of 11, I began to contribute my mite to the Fenian movement'. The veteran observed that 'the Cause seems to have become popular and the Old Guard are not wanted. Well I suppose we must bow to the Superior Judgement of the New Comers but if there is any attempt at a compromise in the way of an English Protectorate or otherwise, the Clan-na-Gaels will stand like a stone wall against it.' Though nearly blind and without earnings for twenty years he had 'stood the Acid Test' by buying a Bond, but would never contribute another cent. Harry, abashed, could only express his 'sincerest regard for men of your type' and compose a rambling apologia.[118] The contest for the allegiance of the rank and file was to be bitter and prolonged.

By excommunicating the Clan through the press, Harry had perjured his sworn obligation to conceal the secrets of the Brotherhood from the uninitiated. Even though such obligations are routinely breached by members of all secret societies, he owed Collins an explanation. Without 'full publicity' he could not have reached the members of either the Clan or the Friends, the *Westminster Gazette* having been approached 'so that you [Collins] would be in possession of the letter'! Harry's long-awaited cable ('formally ended partnership to-day') was delivered to 'Field and Co.', through Eamon Duggan's office in Dame Street, only just before the announcement in the *Gazette*. When the Supreme Council met on 18 November, it unanimously agreed that 'the publication of the letter was a mistake', having a 'bad effect here', offering 'a lever to opposition in U.S.A.', and setting a potentially 'ruinous' precedent. Yet it was 'prepared to take into consideration the situation in which you found yourself', and 'practically everybody' had accepted 'the inevitability of the steps taken'.[119] Ó Murthuile, ever a stickler for fraternal proprieties, considered Harry's action 'preposterous' and proposed his recall, but the faithful Collins ensured that this was 'turned down'.[120] The envoy, though no longer on speaking terms with those he had been assigned to inform, remained.

Long before the formal break, Harry's allies and opponents had been grouping for the expected battle. On 23 June, while McGarrity was advising Philadelphian Clansmen of 'the disgraceful and criminal conduct of Brother Devoy', the local council of the Friends had pledged its 'unqualified and continuous support' to 'Judge Cohalan and his associates'.[121] Immediately after the 'excommunication', Harry mustered his allies on the Executive and beyond. On 4 November, he told Collins that he was about to establish a new body, 'and judging from letters to hand we will have little difficulty in building up a genuine organization along the lines so often discussed between you and me'.[122] A week or so later, all accessible 'Camps' were sent a circular announcing the expulsion of five of the Executive's eight members, and ordering all local Secretaries to sever connection with these traitors and send membership lists to Luke Dillon, an elderly ex-Dynamiter in McGarrity's Philadelphia.[123] Dillon's switch further shook Devoy, who charitably decided that the defectors had been 'deceived by falsehoods' and assured Dillon that 'I could not be unfriendly to you, even if you broke my head.'[124] Dillon's circular was rapidly followed by a personal message from Harry, promising friendly Clansmen that 'I shall be happy to co-operate with you in mapping out a program of work befitting the Home Organization.'[125] Meanwhile, Devoy reasserted the authority of the old Executive and advised brethren that 'a line should be drawn with a pencil through that part of the Ritual instructing new members which refers to the close ties between this Organization and the one in Ireland. When the old relations are restored, which we hope will be soon, the pencil erasure can be rubbed out.'[126]

A serious setback for Harry's faction was the decision of James McGuire, Chairman of the old Executive, to withdraw from the fray:

> I have a horror of all Irish-American organizations as a result of 30 years' experience with them and would not join another one. The rivalries of individuals for leadership or control of our organizations are the curse and the bane of the movement. In the old days of the Clan na Gael, the Ancient Order of Hibernians, the Land League, the Irish National League, etc., three-fourths of the efforts put forth were fighting fellow members instead of fighting England. In every case there has been a boss or a clique dominating and the struggle against the caucus and dictatorship has resulted in paralysis of the hopes and aims of pacific but earnest men.

Noting that several 'ambitious disturbers' had already joined Harry's bandwagon, he observed that 'any new organization made up of "old timers" will be bound to be factional and barren of good results'. As for de Valera, though 'unexcelled' in his 'devotion to principle', he was 'a most lamentable failure' as a negotiator and seemed 'lacking in decision, changeable, unsteady'.[127] Bereft of McGuire, Harry was all the more reliant on the less sagacious advice of the ailing McGarrity, who was to become Chairman of the 'Clan Reorganized'. Ever optimistic, Harry assured Collins that there were 'thousands of fine young Irishmen here' to provide the necessary 'new blood' for 'an organization modelled somewhat on the lines of the one at home for the same definite purpose'. His postscript was more sombre: 'The fight is up and we must bear it.'[128] The prospect of success brightened in mid December, with the 'splendid news' of McGarrity's recovery, an event which persuaded Mrs Mary McWhorter of the AOH that 'right will prevail against the devil himself'.[129]

The battle for control of the brethren was re-enacted with even less pretence of secrecy in the Friends of Irish Freedom. Harry's allies traced Cohalan's every move and mood, Dr. Maloney using his network of clerical contacts to ascertain the Judge's views and intentions. Yet Cohalan's opponents were by no means united among themselves. Maloney himself was unhappy with de Valera's 'political bluff', warning that 'we lose all non-Irish support by war threats'.[130] McCartan was also losing confidence in his leader's judgement: 'My experience of him and Harry is that they come to a conference not knowing what they want; have an unconscious contempt or seem to have such for opinions of others.' The mission had lost its way in the morass of in-fighting: 'O'Mara if you remember only wants 100 men and the Chief wants to organise the 20,000,000 [supposed Irish-Americans]. Here are two extremes and neither seem[s] to know where they are going or what they want.'[131]

Ignoring such murmurs, Harry and de Valera pressed ahead with their attempt to outmanoeuvre Cohalan within his own movement:

16 July. Fri. New York. The F.O.I.F. row is growing very nasty in New York. Black Jacks and Hat Pins have replaced argument. 'Gaelic American', 'Irish World' and 'Irish Press' are lashing the fires.

19 July. Mon. New York. Diarmuid Lynch resigns Dáil Éireann – finds himself unable to agree with de Valera and colleagues, so quits Dáil É., with deep regret that he should have chosen Sec. F.O.I.F. to Dáil É. Diarmuid proved himself a good man when the call came. I am really sorry for him and Mrs. Lynch.[132]

By resigning from the Dáil in response to its explicit denunciation of Devoy and Cohalan, the National Secretary of the Friends had aligned himself irrevocably with de Valera's opponents. Lynch was appalled by the short-lived settlement between Harry and the Clan's Executive, and 'disappointed' that Devoy had not discussed with Cohalan 'the question as to how far the "agreement" is to affect the policy of the F.O.I.F.' Though he expected that 'the position of the Race in America will be seriously jeopardized and perhaps ruined' upon publication of the resolutions of 15 August, he could see no clear way forward: 'If the policy of the Friends is to be different from that of the other organization, the members of the latter will find themselves in an impossible position.'[133] The only logical option was to reverse the Clan's surrender and meanwhile to muster the Friends for a future tussle with the unwanted 'Visitor', as de Valera was designated by his detractors.

This strategy led to yet another emotional but inconclusive confrontation on 17 September, when 162 members of the National Council and 63 observers congregated at the Waldorf-Astoria Hotel. De Valera having walked out in a huff while Mayor Grace of Charleston 'dwelt on the importance of keeping the movement on an American basis', Harry was left to represent his Chief. Rather than trying to win over the National Council, he requested 'all of those who wanted to help the Irish Republic to meet him in that room at noon the following day'. Bishop Michael J. Gallagher of Detroit, Fr. Peter Magennis's successor as President of the Friends, warned the Council against taking 'a stand from which it may appear that we take orders from a foreign potentate'; Judge John W. Goff urged 'Mr. Boland not to do something now which might be regretted all the days of his life'; while Devoy, momentarily the peace-maker, proposed that de Valera be pledged their 'continued and earnest support in his efforts to secure Recognition'. Mutual animosity was soon revived by Harry's sneer that 'one word from the man who sits back holding the strings while his puppets dance will settle this whole difficulty'. Even so, the meeting disbanded with a lukewarm commitment that the organisation should extend 'all its resources' to de Valera's campaign, the phrase 'as far as possible' being inserted to general acclamation.[134]

Devoy felt 'our end of things was very badly mis-managed' but that 'we came out all right in the end'. He took solace from the remark of a 'ship man who ran home between trips' that 'he found a strong feeling everywhere among the common people that Harry is not fit for the job and that the delegation has made a mess of things here'.[135] Though a hundred delegates of disparate views attended the additional meeting convened by de Valera, the public session reportedly 'had no life in it at all'. The Chief gave the only speech, which was 'very mild' and provoked only one interruption, upon which Bishop William Turner of Buffalo 'grasped the Presidential biceps and hustled their owner from the salon' for his own safety.[136] Both factions accepted that the final battle for the Friends must await the outcome of the primary struggle within the Clan.

Scarcely a fortnight after the Clan's excommunication on 22 October, the National Council heard that a score of its members had subscribed to a telegram calling for a meeting in Chicago, 'for the purpose of forming a new organization'.[137] In mid November, de Valera launched the American Association for the Recognition of the Irish Republic, pledged by its Constitution 'to uphold the existing Republic of Ireland and to co-operate with the Irish people and their accredited representatives in their efforts to secure official recognition by the Government of the United States'. Though Devoy's resolution at the Waldorf-Astoria had already bound the Friends to do likewise, the creation of a new body enabled Harry, on behalf of de Valera, to control the workings as well as the rhetoric of the open political movement.[138] The advent of the Association failed to destroy the Friends, but helped reduce its regular membership by nearly three-quarters to 26,350 during 1921, with an equally drastic loss of 'associate branches' belonging to other Irish-American bodies.[139] Though most of its eventually huge membership had never been Friends, the Association's organisers concentrated initially on seeking adherence from national officers, local branches, and state conventions of the Friends. Harry himself attended the Pennsylvanian state convention in late November, having responded to the rather tepid suggestion that, if de Valera could not be secured, 'maybe we could get Boland'.[140] The Association's first Director of Organisation was a Canadian-born journalist, Joseph Cyrillus Walsh, who was asked by de Valera to match the membership of the Friends within a year. Walsh's alternative proposal to plan for a million members had an unexpected effect on the myopic Chief: 'It was the first and only time I saw a real flash of light in his eyes.' Before long, however, Walsh found himself starved of money and embroiled in a bitter dispute with the 'exceedingly offensive' James O'Mara, which he endured with help from the sagacious Harry: 'You go ahead J. C. and do the best you can with him, and don't do anything decisive without seeing me first.'[141]

The creation of a vast new body demanding recognition was superficially at odds with the admitted impracticability of interesting American politicians in this issue pending installation of the new Republican administration in spring 1921. Its political justification, as Harry put it to de Valera just before the presidential election held on 2 November, was to prepare for the future:

> America must make peace, and my opinion is that no matter which Party wins on Tuesday next there will be either a League of Nations or an International Court of Justice. Therefore, the force of Irish-American opinion should be organized and definite plans laid immediately for the conducting of the campaign to secure that in any international agreement to which America may commit herself Ireland must be recognized in that agreement.

Claiming that, with full support from the Friends, 'we could have secured recognition' already, Harry suggested that in future 'there must be a final authority, one who will clearly lay down a plan of campaign in the coming struggle'. To Collins, he declared that 'I am convinced that we can bring sufficient pressure to bear in Washington so as to secure a square deal for Ireland.'[142] Buoyant as always, Harry believed that no goal was unattainable provided that the right men, answerable to himself, were firmly in control of every political instrument.

In asserting his own authority, Harry invariably presented himself as de Valera's faithful mouthpiece, thereby appropriating his mandate as a democratic leader. So long as de Valera remained in America, however, Harry's freedom of action was curtailed by the Chief's often unpredictable interventions. Once back in Ireland, his capacity for practical interference would be sharply reduced. Throughout 1920, de Valera had shown signs of impatience with his American exile, his inability to achieve the mission's declared goals, and his perpetual immersion in bruising personal conflicts. The arrival of his wife Sinéad had temporarily alleviated the presidential solitude, as Harry told Kitty Kiernan in September: 'Mrs de Valera is here now and has made a fine impression on every one, "the Chief" is a new man as a result, and we are all very happy to have her here."[143] But the benefit was short-lived, and after her tearful departure Sinéad regretted the visit: 'It was such a big mistake to go for such a long journey for such a short stay.'[144] Harry probably agreed, as he had hoped to make typically ingenious use of her continuing presence to conceal de Valera's own departure when writing to Collins in August:

> The G. S. [Great Statesman] has taken my view of things over, and is in hopes of seeing you all very soon. I think I can arrange an easy method of travel. If so I will accompany him and have as many with me as is necessary to ensure safety. ... Of course it will be at least a couple of months yet, so do not halt Jane [Sinéad]. In fact we could use her visit to camouflage the issue. I am not giving this to the Cabinet.[145]

By early December, de Valera had decided to follow her to Ireland; whereas, so Harry told Collins, 'circumstances have arisen here which compel me to remain some time longer'.[146]

The Chief's last supper with his apostles occurred in room 228 of the Waldorf-Astoria Hotel on 10 December. After settling the essential matter of access to bank deposits, those present made speeches, shook hands, and received souvenirs such as a leather card-case and undeveloped films. McGarrity observed that 'Harry Boland stood gazing at the parting scene and was much more deeply affected than any one in the room'. Returning after midnight, Harry, who 'looked bad and undoubtedly felt bad', told McGarrity that the Chief was now safely aboard the *Celtic*.[147] De Valera had presented him with a diary and a photograph, inscribed in Irish 'to the man who did the work, to Harry, to that rascal, you', recollecting 'our friendship and camaraderie'.[148] With a letter delivered from the ship by Barney Downs, de Valera enclosed a 'farewell message' to the American people, to be published only after his emergence in Ireland, and enjoined Harry to 'keep up the mystery part here as long as you can'. Harry was to 'represent us here till a permanent appointment is made by the Cabinet', and should 'be careful of the words you use in "interviews" – words are really important things in politics'. After various other superfluous instructions, he wrote 'Good bye Harry. ... May God direct and bless everything ye do.'[149] Evidently uncertain of the Almighty's capacity to control his volatile representative, de Valera had meanwhile taken the precaution of advising Seán Nunan that 'your soberer judgement may often be needed to modify Harry's impetuosity. Don't fail to "insinuate" it when you find it necessary.'[150]

Harry dutifully amused himself for the next three weeks by misleading innumerable journalists, declaring that 'the President was resting in the country', simulating de Valera's answers to written questions, announcing that 'the persons whose guest he is and I are the only ones who know where he is stopping', promising that the President would 'come out of retirement here on Christmas Day', claiming that reports of his arrival in Europe were 'a joke', and (after his return) denying 'most emphatically' that de Valera was on his 'way to England or Ireland'.[151] His masquerade was brilliantly successful, since British Intelligence in America, having repeatedly passed on false information about various rumoured return journeys, announced on 20 December that 'we now know practically for certain that de Valera is somewhere in the vicinity of New York City'. On the same day, the Government decided, in any case, 'that de Valera should not be prevented from landing in the United Kingdom if he arrived', as he did a day or so later.[152] Though Harry's campaign of subterfuge had therefore been redundant, neither he nor de Valera was aware of the fact. It was 'with a distinct appearance of elation that Harry Boland, De Valera's secretary, walked into the rooms of the American Commission of Irish Independence' on New Year's Eve, and 'announced that the Sinn Féin leader had landed on Irish soil, presumably earlier in the day'.[153]

With de Valera safely removed, Harry seemed in control of every facet of the American mission. He had broken with his Irish-American competitors and instigated a new brotherhood complete with a new front organisation under his own thumb. He and his closest allies controlled almost every fund, and his elaborate schemes for purchasing and despatching munitions were no longer subject to Brugha's critical scrutiny. Armed with de Valera's authority to act as his substitute, he could prepare for a political and diplomatic campaign for recognition; unhindered by critics or opponents within the Clan na Gael, he could pursue the even wilder dream of global organisation and revolution. Yet, on Christmas Day, Harry Boland's diary had marked the festival in trembling characters: 'Alone in Wolcott Hotel'.[154]

Anticlimax

HARRY Boland began his year as Ireland's ambassador with a declaration of war. Having informed the American press that de Valera and Griffith were in principle prepared, 'as the representatives of the Irish nation, to meet the representatives of England to draw up a peace treaty between the two nations', he quickly dismissed current rumours of 'peace talk' as 'mere British propaganda'.[1] On 5 January 1921, he told a meeting in Philadelphia that 'Eamon de Valera did not return to negotiate for peace with the English or with any English agent. He returned to take his place at the head of the Irish republic, for which we of Ireland will fight until the last red blooded man of our country has died.' As Joe McGarrity noted, this declaration seemed 'presidential', being to the 'same effect' as a statement by de Valera published immediately afterwards.[2] On his return to New York on 6 January, Harry chose Madison Square Garden to unveil his long-cherished 'dream' of Ireland's future strategy in the absence of an acceptable settlement. Apparently tipsy with excitement, despite prohibition, he assured 5,000 auditors that 'I have been privileged to stand by and have been honored in my day – I had the proud honor to stand by – I glory in one thing alone – and that is that we in Ireland to-day are standing up with red blood in our veins.' Belying his inflammatory tone, he added:

> I say calmly and deliberately: that if Britain does not stop her campaign of murder in Ireland, then, by the living God, we will preach, we will preach to our millions scattered all over the world, A RACE VENDETTA! and demand an eye for an eye and a tooth for a tooth (loud applause). ... We cannot lose if our people all over the world take up the fight, and everywhere you see anything English, by God! strike it! (loud applause).

England was 'a monster', her Empire belonging 'to the ninth circle in Hell'; whereas the Irish were 'a race of heroes'.[3] Irish-Americans should respond in kind: 'My God! with the Irish race so strong in America, how can they see their kin murdered by the British? If I had my way, I would tell them to rise up and tear down everything British in America.'[4]

Harry's decision to give public utterance to his fantasy was predictably counter-productive. Even Mary McSwiney, normally matchless in her intransigence, hastened to assure the crowd that 'she did not want the United States to go to war on Ireland's behalf'. The *New York Times* decried Harry's 'passionate exhortation that they start in this country the same sort of warfare that other men who talk less and do more than he now are carrying on in Ireland'. It appeared that 'this man Boland' hoped to 'involve us in war with the other branch of the English-speaking race', notwithstanding its 'close and cordial amity' with the United States. The newspaper urged the State Department and Department of Labor to 'take cognizance' of such threats from an apparently 'undesirable alien' who was rumoured to have reached America unlawfully as a stowaway.[5] J. Edgar Hoover, soon to take over the Bureau of Investigation, asked the State Department for 'such information as you may have in your files upon Harry J. Boland, reported to be Secretary to de Valera'.[6] An anonymous 'Daughter of the A. R.'[7] sent a newspaper drawing of Harry to the State Department and advised it to 'handle this foreigner without gloves'.[8] A prominent fellow-traveller, Oswald Garrison Villard of the *Nation*, dissociated himself from what the *New York Times* termed 'Bolandism, or Bolandery', declaring that 'American interest in self-determination for Ireland does not imply hostility to England'.[9] By appealing to the visceral Anglophobia of an embittered fraction of immigrants and their descendants, Harry had risked squandering the goodwill of liberal America.

For once, he was quick to admit the miscalculation, at least to his diary:

7 Jan. Fri. New York. Full blast in papers against my speech.

8 Jan. Sat. New York. In very bad form. Fear I have made an error, in my speech. Time some man spoke out.[10]

In a subsequent address, he renewed his verbal assault on the 'Imperial British Government' for inflicting 'every abomination on our people', including 'the torch!! the lash!! the pincers!! the bullet!! the torture!! [inserted: the rape!!], in vain! They have desecrated the Tomb, and violated the Host.' On this occasion, however, he added that 'Ireland yearns for peace – peace with honor', maintaining that his earlier reference to a 'race vendetta' had been 'sadly misquoted':

I should indeed be sorry to even suggest to those of our race in America any action that would offend against the laws and institutions of your country; we seek from you your great influence in Ireland's behalf to be given as you deem proper.[11]

In mid April, he was still hoping 'to put myself right' by 'again bringing up my speech in Madison Garden' when addressing a convention in Chicago, since 'the report of that speech may have created an unfavorable impression amongst many of our friends'. On the advice of Seán Nunan and James O'Mara, he let the matter rest.[12] To de Valera, he admitted having 'let my heart run away with my head', only to be chided that he should 'never allow the enthusiasm of an American audience to swing you off into thinking you are addressing our own people in Ireland'.[13] Apart from these tactical reflections, neither de Valera nor Harry recorded any misgivings about advancing Irish freedom through a 'race vendetta' in America.

Meanwhile, as Washington awaited installation of the new President and Congress, the mission renewed its campaign for recognition of the Irish Republic. Harry's diary summarised the strategy: 'Frank P. Walsh will mobilise Friends in Congress. O'Mara will direct organisation.'[14] Harry had appointed Walsh as the mission's 'Legal Counsel' in mid January, at the staggering annual salary of $75,000 in return for his full-time commitment to 'this work'.[15] Walsh undertook to 'represent the Government of Ireland, in all matters in which it may be concerned, before the Departments of the United States Government; Committees of Congress; Courts of Law; any Council or Association of Nations that may be hereafter established; and any other body or agency'.[16] Though not himself a Congressman, the new Counsel made systematic if ineffectual attempts to muster support through allies such as John E. Milholland, who invited him for a consultation at the end of February:

> I'll have a nice little dinner in waiting, and after it's all over we will adjourn upstairs for what may prove a historical [sic.] pow-wow. I have strengthened our combination tremendously since we sampled the flesh pots of the Shoreham [Hotel].[17]

Walsh's papers include a pencilled 'diagram of Counsel's strategy', showing 'lines of pressure' reaching from the 'Irish Rep[resentative]' through Walsh to nine unidentified Congressmen, whose influence would secure Ohio, Illinois, and Massachusetts for the Irish cause. These three states, it seemed, would converge to force through favourable resolutions.[18] In his diagrammatic approach to politics, Walsh resembled Harry's mathematical mentor, de Valera.

James O'Mara, the mission's 'Fiscal Agent', had also been given general direction of the American Association for the Recognition of the Irish Republic. He too became engrossed, if briefly, in Washington politics, and was advised by Walsh to exploit the expertise of Eugene F. Kinkead, a recently retired Major in American Military Intelligence who had followed Dr. Maloney's trajectory towards total immersion in the Irish cause. According to Walsh, the Corkonian ex-Congressman was 'probably the best posted man in your organization in regard to Washington affairs. He should be the starting off of your Irish lobby.' Walsh recommended formation of a 'national legislative committee' of 'at least from two to five, high class, understanding men, preferably former members of Congress, or men with political influence and sagacity, so that this would be a continuous effort at the Capitol'. As a model, he cited Alice Paul's National Woman Party, which had conducted 'the best canvass I have ever known to have been made of Congress'. Miss Paul had 'trained ... a band of women ... whose duty it was to keep in everyday touch with the House and Senate', making daily and sometimes hourly reports to headquarters.[19] As before, Irish organisers felt an affinity with suffragism which owed more to its methods than its merits.

Harry's own approach to lobbying was no less methodical, as his diary confirms:

> 9 Apr. Sat. Washington. Frank P. Walsh – discuss … Senate resolutions – fine. Sens. La Follette No. 1, Norris 2, Borah No. 3. Dáil address. Marley and Evans live pair. Many resolutions for House Reps.

> 7 May. Sat. New York. Ring up Frank P. Walsh, urge resolution re entrance of America to Councils of Allies. Mary McSwiney rings me up saying Friends think we should approach this from American angle – I decide on Irish angle – fed up with pussyfooting.

> 16 June. Thurs. Washington. Try to secure resolution in favor Seán McKeown.[20] Meet Senators David J. Walsh, Ashurst, and Dohoney. Norris to speak Monday.[21]

Harry had become an old hand in American politics, with shrewd advisers and excellent connections on Capitol Hill.

As the new administration edged towards ratification of the peace treaties and re-engagement in diplomacy, Harry and his advisers renewed their campaign to incorporate Irish independence in the belated post-War settlement. A sympathiser interviewed President Harding to seek 'his good offices in the matter of peace' in Ireland, and was reassured to learn that Harding had thrice impressed the 'importance of settling the question' upon Sir Auckland Campbell Geddes, the British Ambassador in Washington.[22] Harry believed that three 'questions of first importance to Great Britain' could 'be made of great concern by Irish-American opposition. We are not losing sight of our opportunities.' These issues were the conditions for repayment of Allied War Loans, Lloyd George's attendance at the forthcoming Washington Disarmament Conference, and the proposed Anglo-Japanese Alliance. If America could be induced to make its continued support for British interests conditional on an Irish settlement, Lloyd George would surely be compelled to cease 'his abominations in Ireland'.[23]

The Congressional campaign was accompanied, as always, by propaganda through public meetings, distribution of leaflets, and the press. Despite his indiscretion over the 'race vendetta', Harry still risked occasional forays into inspirational oratory. On 7 March, 'Ireland's Houdini' addressed 2,000 'sons of Erin' assembled at Chicago's Orchestra Hall to celebrate Emmet's 143rd birthday. He was greeted by 100 Irish-American ex-servicemen in khaki, flanked by the Tricolour and the Stars and Stripes, being entertained by renditions of 'The Foggy Dew', 'Danny Boy', 'A Battle Hymn', and 'A Soldier's

Song'. Harry proclaimed that 'Ireland is the weapon with which God wills to strike down the last remaining empire', already 'rampant' with unrest on the part of '350,000,000 foes of England'. Even if the United States could not 'see its way clear to recognize the Irish republic it might at least stand neutral and let the fight be fought to a finish between Ireland and Britain'.[24]

As an orator, Harry neither secured nor sought so much public attention during 1921 as Terence McSwiney's sister Mary (otherwise Máire, Marie, or Min). Widely worshipped in America as the reincarnation of a dead saint, she had long since discarded all pretence of diffidence. When discouraged from tackling the new President in person, Mary McSwiney protested that 'my only desire to go to Washington was to size up Harding and see if he was open to conversion as he and his Executive could do what we want immediately if they were so minded'. After discovering that she could hold American audiences 'in the hollow of her hand', 'Queen Mary' had developed 'a good opinion of herself' and shamelessly invited O'Mara to picture her 'as a star turn in a Music Hall'.[25] The schoolmistress from Cork, severe and censorious though she might seem, was positively flirtatious in her correspondence with Harry. Writing in late January from Columbus, Ohio, she revealed that 'Catherine Flanagan and Miss Madden the State Secretary of Ohio are discussing the respective merits of yourself, Liam Mellows and the various other attractive specimens of our race that they have met. The result is disastrous to my letters. This makes the third time that Catherine in a beseeching tone urges me to send you her love, in fact threatens dire things to me if I don't – so there it is, x x x x' Faced with questions from the Ohio public about 'your vendetta speech', she could only promise Harry to 'write myself into a proper vendetta frame of mind before I answer that'.[26]

A fortnight later, 'Min' deployed both force and charm to extort extra money and staff for her publicity campaign, then engulfing Fort Wayne, Indiana. She informed James O'Mara that she was 'writing to Harry also and telling him I want *money, money, money*, spent lavishly for *two months*'. Her tone with Harry was gentler: 'Write to me like a good Boy – tell me you will be a brick and shell out generously.' Half a million dollars should suffice to purchase recognition of the Republic in time for Easter Monday, 28 March, which was also 'Terry's birthday'. Even if recognition were not secured, he would 'only be throwing a sprat to catch a salmon as the result of all the organising would result [*sic*.] at least in a bond drive of 20 million dollars'. Despite such grandiose delusions, she believed herself to be perfectly level-headed: 'The "Joan of Arc" and "Idol of the Irish people" stunt nearly did for me, but Thank God for the sense of humour and proportion anyhow that He has given me.' She reminded Harry that she was 'not writing you because I love you but because I want work done'.[27]

Mary McSwiney had indeed become the mission's star advocate, and F. P. Walsh confirmed in April that 'outside of the President, she is undoubtedly our greatest propagandist'.[28] Her admiration for Harry, expressed unstintingly in a letter praising his performance at the Chicago convention of the American Association, was therefore a significant asset.[29] When she expressed concern after the Truce that de Valera might condone a compromise, Harry worked hard to win back her confidence through a seemingly candid confession: 'I fear that my experiences during the past few years has [sic.] resulted in my becoming vague and unsatisfactory in my speech and actions. There was a time, not long ago, when I was very direct and honest both in thought and speech. Now I am so cynical and doubting in my dealings with people that I must be careful that I deal with you in the manner you deserve – frankly, honestly and without reserve.' As for 'compromise: do not worry yourself in writing to de Valera under this head. There can be no compromise between Ireland and England and there will be none.' In reassuring her that Devoy and Cohalan were no longer a menace, he hazarded a rare excursion into Latin: 'They *dare* not openly attack de Valera. "Magnum veritas est veritas pravelabit." I hope I have the quotation correct,[30] if not I know you will understand what I intend to convey.' Peace with Britain was possible; but, if not, 'final victory is not far off' and 'the honor of our nation will be upheld by the men [inserted: and women] chosen to represent the people'. Ever solicitous, Harry urged her in conclusion to 'be careful to take a long rest after your visit to the dentist'. She duly thanked him for his 'real nice letter' and expressed 'relief' at his repudiation of compromise: 'I do not know why but, in Philadelphia, you gave me the impression that you thought there might be a settlement.'[31] Harry's honeyed words had set her mind, for the moment, at rest.

The manufacture and circulation of propaganda continued without remission, primarily through J. C. Walsh's 'Benjamin Franklin Bureau' in Chicago until its absorption into the new American Association. The Bureau, obscurely so named in honour of Franklin's pledge to the 'good people of Ireland ... that means will be found to establish your freedom', aimed to organise societies supporting recognition and to induce 'elected representatives' to underwrite the pledge. Its broader purpose was to educate 'public opinion on the subject, through the activities of such associations, through social and communal clubs, through the press, through the activities of public speakers, the circulation of literature, etc.'[32] As the mission became ever more entangled in American domestic politics, the focus of propaganda shifted from Irish-America to influential groups of potential allies. One of Harry's appeals was circulated to no less than 118,000 Protestant clergymen as well as 19,000 priests, generating just 144 responses.[33] The Bureau devoted nearly $12,000 to buying the advocacy of 'intelligent people' such as attorneys, professors, and teachers, since 'with some of these people it's our only mode of entry'.[34]

Wealthy sympathisers were courted with even greater assiduity, despite their compromising tendencies. As Harry boasted to Collins: 'Immediately the Peace feelers were sent out, I got busy. First waited on the Millionaire group, John D. Ryan, Nicholas Brady, E. L. Doheny, and Judge Morgan J. O'Brien;[35] secured a promise from them to go to London if invited by the Dáil to act in an advisory capacity. They are not very strongly republican, fearing that it is not likely England will let go without another try to strangle us.'[36] He also exploited the mission's marriage of convenience with William Randolph Hearst, for whom the Irish cause remained a pawn in his press crusade against an Anglo-American alliance. Harry suggested to O'Mara that 'we might ask Hearst to open a campaign for American recognition of a "State of War"; ... this could be followed up by our Minister of Defense placing an order for several million dollars worth of munitions from American firms, thus putting the issue up squarely to the Administration'. O'Mara was justifiably sceptical of this proposal, pointing out that 'even the Geneva Conference and Hague Conventions apparently have no machinery to enforce their rulings'.[37] Like most of the mission's interventions in American politics, this bold and ingenious scheme came to nothing.

Harry's growing infatuation with 'the Millionaire group' coexisted uneasily with his long-standing desire to forge radical alliances. In mid April, he met a representative of 'Young Scotland looking for money and support. Regret cannot aid.'[38] He continued to dabble in 'Indian affairs', and tried unavailingly to induce the American Federation of Labor to promote a 'boycott on English goods' at its annual convention in mid June.[39] Despite Russia's rapid if tempo-rary retreat into post-revolutionary prudence, and its desire for a trade settlement with Britain, Harry remained optimistic that Dr. Patrick McCartan would induce the Soviet Government to ratify the treaty of mutual recognition previously drafted in America. Having visited Ludwig Martens (the discredited Russian 'Ambassador') in late January,[40] Harry acted as intermediary between Martens and John A. McGarry, the Clansman who had been sent to Mexico to make arrangements for McCartan's Russian visit. In this capacity, Harry acquired a new pseudonym, 'Mr Cowe', playing upon the bovine connotations of the syllable 'bo' in both Irish and English.[41] McCartan kept in touch with both Harry and McGarrity, sending his 'regards to all old friends' and alluding coyly to 'a peach' of a Swedish girl who had been 'useful' to him in Stockholm while he awaited admittance to Russia.[42] As the prospect of ratification receded, Harry postponed acting on the Dáil's instruction to reinforce the Russian mission with Donal O'Callaghan, Terence McSwiney's successor as Lord Mayor of Cork, who was under threat of deportation after entering America illegally.[43] Yet de Valera still maintained that Russian support was crucial to the Irish cause, to the extent that Harry himself 'should proceed after the Doctor, to work up that centre which will soon be for us the most important in Europe'.[44] McCartan also believed that it was 'possible to do business, as most of the [Soviet] Directors are keen on his goods', and he did not abandon the futile quest until June.[45] The dream of linking Ireland with global anti-imperialism was surprisingly slow to fade.

The main instrument in raising public support was the American Association for the Recognition of the Irish Republic, initially under the direction of Joseph Cyrillus Walsh. Walsh's vision of a vast organisation, propelled by another expensive propagandist crusade, received only lukewarm support from Harry and especially O'Mara. As Walsh protested in mid January: 'Your striking out of my working plan all provision for speakers and literature seems to me to devitalize any campaign to secure a million people pledged to recognition.' Walsh cited his previous discussions with de Valera, in which they had agreed to seek 'a very large membership' through 'intensive organization, with meetings and literature'; concentration on districts outside 'the great Irish centers'; and inclusion of 'non-Irish speakers'.[46] After his return to Ireland, de Valera no longer expected to achieve the Association's ostensible objective, believing that the only chance of American recognition was the eruption of 'a crisis in which America's own interests are involved and when it might be convenient to hit England through us'. He envisaged the Association 'as the machinery through which our Mission would be relieved of any direct responsibility for political and propaganda work, either as regards execution or financial support'.[47] Though self-supporting, it must also be subservient, for de Valera was apprehensive that a great populist body might become ungovernably democratic, particularly if a 'general convention' were permitted to establish 'a bogus National authority'. He therefore proposed an indirect system for appointing a 'Directorate' after consultation between state representatives and the mission's 'Secretariat', naming the officers of his choice. Control, as he explained to Harry, would be 'directly and nominally in the hands of the Directorate but really our envoy's will would always prevail. ... His veto or in a positive form his sanction for all important acts could be arranged for in the Constitution or agreement.'[48]

The case for central dictation was bolstered by simmering disputes within the Association, especially in New York, where Harry's intervention had failed to resolve 'noisy and bitter' confrontations between clerical and secular factions. Echoing Devoy's contempt for priests in politics, Harry concluded 'that priests should not be officers' – an opinion which he put into practice at the convention.[49] Having 'succeeded to a great degree' in bringing 'harmony out of chaos' in New York, he admitted to O'Mara that he had met his match in New Jersey: 'Never again will I assume the rôle of peacemaker!! The Jersey affair is very nasty, so nasty that I am out of it.' O'Mara drew the lesson that conciliation was insufficient: 'Sorry you burnt your fingers on the peacemaking job. Afterwards we might in consultation and where necessary compel peace not by offering mediation but on your old plan of trust the people and organise them.'[50] Despite such setbacks, Harry remained buoyant as ever, reporting on 14 April that 'the movement has spread like wildfire and has a paid-up membership of one-half million'.[51]

A few days later, as 5,000 delegates assembled in Chicago for the first national convention, Harry set about asserting his personal supremacy over the

Association, as urged by de Valera. He neither promoted nor secured the election of de Valera's choice for President (Judge Goff), but ensured that the Judge chaired the convention, overriding O'Mara's objection.[52] Though retired from the Supreme Court and racked with rheumatism, Goff's 'white hair framing his ruddy cheeks gave him an air of quite exceptional distinction'. J. C. Walsh observed with horrified fascination the tactics whereby unamenable candidates and priests were excluded from office:

> Boland and O'Mara decided that none of these would do, and as they could have combined their forces and done as they pleased two measures were adopted. Mr Boland's I.R.B. cohorts were busy in the corridors working against these men. One stumbled upon groups in which suspicions were being ventilated. It seemed to me entirely ridiculous. ... O'Mara's method was that of the Black Jack. Those he stunned made him no more trouble. ... The upshot was that control of the organization by the men from Ireland was not endangered by the election of any of the men who did most in building it up.[53]

Harry's experience as a Sinn Féin officer and convention-fixer had provided excellent preparation for his work in the American Association.

O'Mara's wife Agnes saw things differently, noting that 'trouble was hatched and slate put up by Massachusetts and Illinois and New York' before Harry's arrival, while the O'Maras were relaxing in the Edgewater Beach Hotel. With Harry's help, 'things were straightened out' before the convention opened, 'peace arranged', and elections held which 'all went splendidly'. Inexplicably, the peace-makers were not universally applauded:

> Splendid success of convention due mainly to Harry and Jim who averted dangerous influence. Harry gave lunch to Irish Mission. Big row at end. Very unfortunate. Tasteless handling of situation by [Laurence] Ginnell and Min McSwiney led to slight soreness on Harry's part and open resentment on Jim's. He lashed at M. McS. and sad scene ensued. Too bad for Harry's party. Various troubles through day. J. C. Walsh resigned. However all made peace by night.[54]

Harry's own account made no reference to such mishaps:

> 16 Apr. Sat. New York. Leave for Chicago with Kinkead, Donal [O'Callaghan], Fawsitt. Am wondering how the convention will work. Great gathering of the race assured. Joe McGarrity and Harry hope to make valuable connections.

> 17 Apr. Sun. Chicago. With Donal Oge to Chicago Beach. Meet Jas. [O'Mara], Rossa Downing, John Hearn and discover slate are up against trouble. Jas. and I in harness.

18 Apr. Mon. Chicago. Fr. Cahill and John Harrigan out to rule. Jas. O'M. on the war path.

19 Apr. Tues. Chicago. Wonderful gathering, fine spirit. Our slate wins. Moran – troublesome. All's well that ends well.

20 Apr. Wed. Chicago. McWhorter, Linus Moran, John Hearn – Treasurer. Col. Reilly's men done great work, everything as we would wish.[55]

Harry's report to de Valera celebrated the 'greatest convention ever held in America' and praised the zeal of O'Mara, who had 'flooded the country with organisers'.[56] Despite sniping from the Friends of Irish Freedom and demands for economy from de Valera, the American Association soon became the largest and loudest of all Irish organisations in the United States. Yet the rigid application of central control through Harry and O'Mara always threatened to stifle enthusiasm, and just before Harry's return to Ireland in August de Valera received a disheartening report: 'I have to inform you that the first bloom of enthusiasm has faded from the face of the A.A.R.I.R. Many internal differences have sprung up, and these will grow – especially in idleness. Membership is at a standstill.'[57]

Throughout 1921, the attempt to remobilise popular support was undermined by disputes over money. When de Valera first raised the issue of a second Bond Drive, O'Mara expostulated to Harry that 'a new Loan cannot be put on until the Relief has ceased working – I am as you know laying the lines for it. Please convey above to de Valera – politely.' In fact, de Valera had already reached the same conclusion and suggested the alternative of a levy on members of the American Association.[58] The American Committee for Relief in Ireland continued its attempt to reach beyond the usual pool of political sympathisers, while spoiling the market for explicitly political appeals. Though eventually successful in winning support from the Friends of Irish Freedom, its relationship with bodies such as the Mary McWhorter's Celtic Cross remained fractious.[59] The American Committee displayed some propagandist flair, arranging with the National Committee of the Motion Picture Industries to hold benefit performances in 50,000 cinemas during St. Patrick's Week, all proceeds being devoted to Irish relief.[60] For once, under pressure from de Valera, Harry preferred to avoid overt intervention in this organisation. He advised Frank Walsh to 'proceed very cautiously as the American Committee for Irish Relief [sic.] have adopted the "non-political, non-sectarian, humanitarian" attitude to such an extent that I think it would be disastrous if we should officially interfere with their work'.[61] Harry accepted its subsequent alliance with the Irish White Cross (whose supposedly apolitical organisers included James Green Douglas, a Quaker draper from Dublin), and was confident by mid April that 'Relief will be O.K.'[62] He continued to meddle privately in the allocation of these funds, urging in August that the $4,500,000 raised by the American Committee 'should be thrown into Ireland and vigorous reconstruction begun', despite the reluctance of the Irish White Cross to accept further transfers.[63] Yet, as expenses mounted and the mission's business diversified, the necessity became acute for a political fund under his own direct control as envoy.

In the absence of a second Bond Drive, the Dáil Ministry responded to O'Mara's request for 'discretionary power to expend funds' by endorsing an emergency loan from the American account of up to $200,000 for organisation.[64] De Valera, dubious of any but his own capacity for discretion, informed Harry that, from June onwards, all expenditure 'not definitely provided for in the estimates of the permanent establishment is to be regarded as special and *must be made provision for by a special vote*'. He insisted that 'we have to cut down considerably our American establishment', laying down a schedule for progressive retrenchment of offices and staff. Harry himself should be replaced by O'Mara as the Republic's envoy in Washington, prior to his proposed despatch to Russia. Setting aside the delicate question of his own future, Harry promised to 'live within our appropriations' and proceeded to impose a levy through the American Association's convention, while warning the delegates 'that Erin would soon ask its sympathizers in the United States for another huge loan, possibly for $100,000,000'.[65] O'Mara, openly disgusted by de Valera's pronouncement, abruptly returned the money previously allocated for the second Bond Drive to the Dáil's American account, 'the issue of the loan' being 'too remote'.[66] O'Mara rejected the 'most unacceptable terms' of his proposed appointment as envoy, and his wife interpreted de Valera's offer as a 'plan to provoke Jim into resignation' and to 'move H. and others away so as to have absolute direction direct [*sic.*] here from other side through F. [Fawsitt], only person remaining and very much persona grata with Chief'.[67]

The outcome was indeed O'Mara's resignation, despite heartfelt appeals from Frank P. Walsh, to whom the 'blow seem[ed] insurmountable', and Harry, who 'very deeply' regretted an action that had placed him 'in a very embarrassing position'.[68] Though dissociating himself from O'Mara's criticism, Harry exhibited some fellow-feeling when reporting the crisis to de Valera: 'Should O'Mara decide to remain on and you appoint him representative I suggest you do not instruct him as to how Bond money should be raised or personnel of his staff. He resents lectures.'[69] Yet J. C. Walsh believed that Harry had himself connived in a plot against O'Mara:

> What would have hurt him most would be the knowledge that Boland was party to the bludgeoning. O'Mara was fond of Boland: 'Don't tell me that Harry is in this thing. I don't want to believe that.' I prefer to think, myself, that this was one of many instances in which, with extraordinary loyalty, Boland subordinated his own judgement and obeyed the orders of his Chief.[70]

Harry's pencilled farewell message to O'Mara, affectionately rendered in a Limerick accent, sits uneasily with Walsh's analysis: 'Why did you lave me alone for to die? B.'[71]

Despite further pleas, retractions, resignations, and acrimonious exchanges, O'Mara resigned 'again in a very nasty mood' on 9 May, rejected Harry's 'final appeal' three days later, and had his resignation as a Trustee accepted by the Ministry on 25 May.[72] Within a month James had been replaced by his estranged brother: 'Meet Stephen M. O'Mara, Mayor of Limerick, Trustee of Dáil Éireann, arrives to take Jim's place as Fiscal Agent. Jim gone away to Toronto.'[73] For an annual salary of $12,000 (less than a sixth of the Legal Counsel's takings), Stephen was to act as agent for the Dáil Trustees and the Minister for Finance and as 'an Envoy of the Government in such matters as may be specifically entrusted to you'. He was to raise 'a new Loan of probably twenty million dollars', if obtainable, using the $250,000 previously allocated for initial expenses. As 'an Envoy', he was also expected to 'co-operate' with Harry ('our chief political representative in the United States'), to 'assist' in reorganising the American Association, and to work for 'a more formal and regular system in the accounts and finances of the Diplomatic Mission'.[74]

Since the mission had outgrown the Dáil Ministry itself in its capacity to raise money, if not to release it for use in Ireland, de Valera's desire to control the American budget is scarcely surprising. In late April, he told Harry plaintively that

I wish that before big enterprises are started over there, formal authority for the expenditures were first asked for. I quite understand the necessity for spending money if we are to get more money, but you will get no money at all if the impression grows that the money subscribed is spent anywhere except here in Ireland. People here too are getting restless about it.[75]

When defending the expenditure of nearly $1,500,000 in the United States, de Valera rather limply explained to the Dáil 'that a large proportion of it was really chargeable to world propaganda'.[76] His anxiety was shared and perhaps inspired by Collins, who pointed out that 'it would be every bit as easy for us to abolish discretionary powers there as it is here, and if we don't do it the spoon feeding is going to go on, and the worst of it is that probably discretion won't be used at all'. Collins advocated 'unification' of fiscal control, adding that 'between ourselves I may say that I have a very nervous feeling about our American accounts'. When de Valera expressed his full concurrence, ascribing the problem to inadequate 'communications', Collins denied that these had ever caused 'the slightest difficulty'. He hinted that the problem arose from the excessive freedom allowed to previous emissaries: 'Do you remember the remark I made yesterday about advice and suggestions? – the very same thing applies. I have not the slightest doubt that the new envoy [Stephen O'Mara] has, fully, the spirit of the thing in his mind.'[77]

Despite this change of personnel, the American accounts presented by Collins in August were both opaque and discouraging. At the end of June, the unallocated American balance still exceeded $1,600,000 (over £300,000), compared with a balance of scarcely £250,000 'at home'.[78] Not a cent had yet been raised through the proposed second Bond Drive, now restricted to $20,000,000, which Harry had resuscitated and recommended to the American Association in late May. While ostensibly leaving it up to the National Directorate to decide whether and when such a loan should be initiated, Harry appealed 'to the Association to get down to work to build up an organization that will be prepared, when the time comes for the raising of the new Loan, to raise it overnight'.[79] Eventually launched in mid October, the new Bond Drive was to fail miserably, raising less than 1 per cent of the sum originally proposed by Harry at the Chicago convention.[80]

The mission, as ever, was riven by feuds and disputes, spoiling the relative external calm prompted by the break with Devoy and Cohalan. Early in 1921, Harry lost his close ally, Liam Mellows, who was 'very glad to have shaken for ever (I hope) the dust of the soul-less place off my feet' and 'curse[d] the day I ever went across'.[81] He whetted Harry's appetite for home by reporting 'a great day at Fairyhouse [races] – wish you had been there', and assured him that 'not all the goold [sic.] in California would drag me back again – "Oh, NEVER, NEVER, NEVER!"'.[82] The 'Consul' Diarmuid Fawsitt continued to irritate Harry, responding to a request for 'the immediate despatch' of money to Ireland by proposing to attend to it 'at my pleasure'. As Harry observed to James O'Mara: 'Gee what a ——.'[83] Fawsitt, always on fractious terms with O'Mara, was equally anxious to leave America and advised de Valera that 'it is not to be expected that my associations with my colleagues here will be very cordial; this makes a change both desirable and necessary, for the good of all concerned'. His object had still not been achieved when Harry returned to Ireland in August, carrying a Fenian Bond from the 1860s which de Valera had left with Fawsitt as a keepsake.[84] By then, Mary McSwiney was also eager to return to Ireland, indignant that she had not been allowed 'a voice in the acceptance of any new status' resulting from Stephen O'Mara's reorganisation of personnel.[85] Frank Walsh, the Legal Counsel, was irked by James O'Mara's attempts to draft him into political work, insisting 'that it would be a most severe handicap to my activities, to either be a member, or take a leading part in the meetings of any Irish organization'. The sole exception to his self-denying ordinance remained the American Commission on Irish Independence, a 'skeleton organization' supplying an 'American name' whenever required by the Irish representatives, whereupon 'that organization should be resurrected for the occasion, operating under my name as chairman'.[86] In the absence of a master-plan, demarcation disputes continued to generate resentment and bickering between members of the mission.

Harry's capacity to resolve such conflicts was diminished by de Valera's insistence that he describe himself as a 'Special Envoy' rather than the

'Permanent Envoy'. Nearly three months after his Chief's return to Ireland, Harry was told that 'you may be needed at any moment elsewhere' and that 'we ... have not despaired of succeeding in getting a suitable person' to act as Ireland's permanent representative. This notably dismissive assessment of Harry's diplomatic ability was followed by an equally condescending appreciation of his worth as a dogsbody: 'I wish you were here, Harry. I badly want an assistant not tied to any particular department, but free to deal with these one hundred and one odd jobs that are daily turning up and needing personal attention, but which I cannot really attend to myself.'[87] De Valera's offer to appoint James O'Mara as chief envoy in Washington, though promptly rejected and perhaps disingenuous, further undermined Harry's supremacy. Despite his ruthless takeover of the Irish-American campaign, Harry had yet to secure uncontested authority within his own mission.

Harry's dominance was further subverted by persistent obstacles to his reorganisation of the Clan na Gael as a subservient auxiliary of the IRB. Devoy's refusal to surrender his membership roll had been overcome in characteristic fashion by Joseph McGarrity, back in form after his long recuperation: 'It would be an interesting story to tell how we got hold of the list of all the old members. Larry de Lacy,[88] Tommy O'Connor[89] and myself took a midnight excursion to the *Gaelic American* office and took the list in the only way we were likely to get it.'[90] Even so, the new Executive had no 'complete roster, as in many cases the so-called official lists are quite valueless'.[91] Attempts were made to secure recruits untainted by experience of the old Clan, sometimes using the new American Association as a channel in the same way that many Irish Volunteers had been recruited through Sinn Féin after the Rebellion. At Bridgeport, Connecticut, in early January, McGarrity addressed 600 delegates to the local council of the American Association:

Good sincere types, women above the average at such meetings in education and intelligence. I told them of the friction that led up to the starting of the new organisation, the Park Avenue Hotel Plot against de Valera, etc. Women and men were delighted. Women said they felt like hgng [hugging?] me. After the meeting I organised the men into a Camp of the Clan – 38 new and one old member. Good start.[92]

A few days later, McGarrity gave Harry a report on the Clan Reorganized for transmission to their masters in Dublin. Progress had been slow, with not 'much headway' in Massachusetts, only about 'fifty good men' in New York, opposition from three-fifths of Clansmen in Chicago, and patchy success elsewhere. Only in San Francisco had members transferred 'in a body', being 'a young militant set of men who were disgusted with the old régime' and already in secession.[93] McGarrity's report for the first general conference alleged that 'probably' two-thirds 'of those who took the obligation' were with the Clan

Reorganized, while many hitherto 'active members' had already dropped out because of Devoy's failure to oppose American participation in the Great War. As a result, some Camps were 'mere card parties, the members meeting on Sunday morning, drinking home brew and moonshine and convening when they feel like it'. The Executive concluded that a further year was needed to create 'an organization here appreciably better than the Clan of two years ago', and that no accommodation should be made with Devoy's faction: 'If you ever permit the expelled men to re-enter the organization you will wreck it.'[94]

In his address at New York's Hotel Annexe on 20 March, Harry reasserted his credentials as an envoy and his conspiratorial pedigree. He informed the 187 delegates that

> I have been a member of the Home Organization from the age of sixteen; that before that my father was a member of the Supreme Council in his day, and Centre for the Province of Leinster; that another relative of mine happened to hold precisely the same position that I hold now, 25 years ago in America, and I have the honour of being on the Supreme Council of the Organization.

He regretted that the Clan's former leaders 'had come to regard the organization itself as meaning more to them than the end for which the organization was established', and deplored Devoy's failure to act on a list of British spies within the Clan, extracted from police archives, with which Harry had furnished him in 1920. As for the future careers of such agents, 'we will look after them. Leave the spies to the Intelligence Department that will be built in this organization.' The Clan Reorganized could 'now become an auxiliary of the Irish Republican Army', and Harry guaranteed 'that any man who is prepared to go and who has the necessary training will be given the opportunity to take his place in the firing line'. The conference duly resolved to empower 'the Executive to work in the closest harmony with the home body', to 'take over the financing of all activities of the Defence Department of the Irish Republic in America', and to contribute $100,000 annually to the IRB.[95] After the conference, as Harry reported, 'we had a most wonderful meeting in the evening at the Lexington Opera House. I addressed the overflow off a soap box, not so bad.' The conference had been 'very successful' in achieving his 'objective – namely H.Q. in Ireland', an act of submission to the IRB which gave him 'personal reasons for joy'. He had afterwards met several 'enthused' delegates and despatched a team of Clan organisers around the country, but told O'Mara that 'New York is running true to form, nothing but trouble and "cliques" seeking control.'[96]

The conflict in New York erupted into an ugly riot four months later, when a gang led by Harry's close ally, James (Red) McGee, tried to break up a Fianna meeting in the All Saints' Chapel Hall on East 129th Street. The Fianna, a notoriously violent group of militants of both sexes, were associated with the

O'Leary brothers, whose implacable opposition to American participation in the Great War had set their faction at odds with Devoy and Cohalan. Mgr. James W. Power, an elderly Fenian allied with the O'Learys who had supported de Valera after the break with Devoy, justifiably accused Harry of trying 'to effect a secret control of the American Association'. He blamed the riot on 'the reorganized but misled Clan, who fraudulently call themselves members of the Irish Republican Army' and were under Harry's 'jurisdiction'. Eager to refute the charge that he had acted 'as a brutal dictator', Harry made the astounding claim that 'I neither direct nor control any Irish-American organization' – including 'the re-organized Clan'. His sole intervention had been designed to prevent domination by the O'Learys: 'It became our duty to see that Judge Cohalan was not supplanted by Mr Jeremiah or Mr John O'Leary. ... We have refused our influence to set up another dictator.' Harry's attempt to manipulate the new Clan without overt dictation had failed, and for all his insistence otherwise, he could not 'refuse to be drawn into a factional squabble'.[97] Unity in Irish-American organisations had proven unattainable: at best, he might hope to bully his opponents into a state of sullen acquiescence or withdrawal from the fray.

Harry's pre-eminence among the brethren was reasserted on 12 July, when he addressed a Clan convention in Philadelphia after the audience had risen respectfully for 'several minutes' to cheer him 'to the echo'. Declaring appositely that there would be 'no surrender', despite the recent Truce in Ireland, he alleged that the new body 'had done more for the men on the hills [at] home in six months than the old organization did in the whole of its existence'. He then provoked 'a veritable storm of applause by hoping that the next convention would be in the nature of a thanksgiving'. The delegates agreed to establish a small 'military committee' which would prepare a card index of men, with military experience, who were 'willing to serve when called upon' and to establish and instruct military units. Members in seaports should attempt to recruit customs officers, and 'the friendship of men occupying key positions ought to be cultivated'. Since only 75 Camps had so far been convened, the Clan's membership presumably did not exceed 5,000.[98] This fell ludicrously far short of the strength demanded by Luke Dillon in his explanatory circular to the brethren: 'We need an organization of at least 100,000 to be really efficient as an auxiliary of the fighting men.'[99] Even so, Harry assured Collins that 'great progress has been made since our first gathering last spring', reiterating that there must 'be no truck with the other bunch – they have no conception of the purposes of a revolutionary organization'. His list of the Clan's military projects was impressive in its ambition, if not its practicality:

(1) a secret service;
(2) a military committee to provide exports for Ireland;
(3) provision for sheltering and caring [for] wounded or sickly men from Ireland;

(4) special Camps composed of men in key positions to influence political events in Ireland's favor;

(5) arms and munition dumps throughout the country;

(6) special effort to secure the services of seamen.[100]

At last, the American brethren were being marshalled into revolutionary formation.

The recruitment of fighters for service in Ireland, and potentially America, was central to Harry's conspiratorial strategy. In late January, American Military Intelligence learned that five companies of 'Irish Volunteers' had already been formed in Philadelphia and drilled by ex-servicemen, and that 'many Volunteers are leaving Philadelphia singly or in small groups, bound for Ireland through roundabout channels'. When a Secret Service agent followed up a newspaper notice for a 'drill and dance' organised by the 'Irish Republican Volunteers of America', he was mystified to observe through the window neither girls nor guns, but 'a rough sort of a game, somewhat resembling a football game', played with sticks like 'pool cues'.[101] In late March, Harry told Collins that 'a worthy representative of the Clan' had already been despatched for 'active service' in Ireland, and that 'we have upwards of one hundred men ready, all of whom have seen service and many of them holding high rank in the American Expeditionary Forces'.[102] He offered these to Brugha, who eventually agreed, in late June, to accept a few 'experts' in various fields 'at once'.[103] The project was suspended in deference to the Truce, but Harry promised that 'the twenty-five men will be with you if the "Peace" fails. These men are all members of the C. na Gael, oath-bound, and will be found first "class, o".'[104] Harry's specialists were eventually spurned by the Chief of Staff, Richard Mulcahy, who found 'that we cannot very well succeed in absorbing these men and that we get a very much better return from money spent upon our own men'.[105] Another of Harry's dreams had foundered.

Ever since his public excommunication of the old Executive, Harry's correspondence with 'Field' and the Supreme Council had been fractious. In supporting Harry's 'break' with Devoy, the Council had assumed on the basis of Harry's reports that most members of the Executive would endorse his attempt 'to secure a new spirit in the Clan – to make it the great power lever of the bulk opinion of the Irish masses in U.S.A. – a highly tuned organisation, responsive in every nerve to home needs'. Harry was instructed to make further attempts to win over recalcitrant officers such as James K. McGuire, the former Chairman who had retired in disgust, and to encourage continued contact between Devoy's faction and the Supreme Council.[106] Harry thereupon induced McGuire to send Collins a personal endorsement, affirming that the envoy had 'done his utmost along the lines of national principles without the sacrifice of his convictions, to bring together in harmony all our people'. Stung by Mr Field's officious rebuke, Harry addressed an informal appeal to 'Micheal Ould

Son': 'I cannot quite understand Field's letter and regret very much the tone of it. I would like you to have a chat with the Chief about the whole affair, and particularly publication.' Alluding to yet another of Collins's multiple personalities, each signified by a distinct name, he anticipated the transfer of 'Gould' to America to take control of the mission's finances: 'When Gould arrives he will be in a position, being on the spot, to appreciate the terrible position I was placed in. Tell Field not to be uneasy about the direction of the great public organization.'[107] Seldom has revolutionary schizophrenia been so unambiguously exposed.

Harry's relationship with the IRB was further tested by Devoy's dogged campaign to restore its connection with his own faction of the Clan. In late May, Harry was particularly annoyed by the *Gaelic American*'s assertion that the revolutionary leadership was split between unswerving republicans such as Collins and compromisers such as de Valera and himself. In response to another 'personal' and unofficial appeal from the beleaguered envoy, Collins 'talked the matter over with the President' and produced an affirmation of unity intended for signature by every minister. After its seizure in a raid, still lacking the necessary signatures, this declaration could not be published for fear of admitting the authenticity of other captured documents.[108] Meanwhile, Devoy had summoned a convention of his own faction of the Clan, which met in Boston a few days before the Truce in Ireland. The convention declared 'its emphatic and unalterable opposition to any compromise in Ireland which will destroy the Irish republic', and prepared to issue 'a severe criticism of President de Valera and other Irish leaders'. Delegates were advised that Collins 'was sure to be found in opposition to the reported settlement'.[109] The Military Committee reported that there was no longer any 'practical need of an organized military body', though brethren should give their 'moral support to the units now in existence'. Like its reorganised counterpart, the old Clan decided to create a new 'Military Intelligence Bureau' which would collect information on 'the location and collection of stores and equipment'.[110] The competition for fraternal supremacy was not yet over.

During the summer, Devoy also despatched an emissary named McHugh to induce Collins and the Supreme Council to redress 'the grievances created by Harry Boland's high-handed attitude'. On 22 July, Collins responded by inviting the old Executive to submit its case in detail, and to appoint three delegates to confer with the Supreme Council in September along with delegates of the Clan Reorganized. Though declining to send such a deputation, Devoy expressed willingness 'to resume the old relations with you, ... each supreme in its own field'.[111] Apprehensive of an attempt to merge the two Clans in a single subservient body, Devoy advocated patience as he awaited McHugh's return: 'They recognize they are beaten and leaderless and want to be allowed to climb down easily by absorbing us. There is evidently a tip of that kind from across the water, and I have no doubt there will be something of that kind from

Mick.'[112] McHugh duly reported that 'Mick assured him that D. V. is "playing the game" just as he wants; that there will be no compromise and ... that our men are in absolute control.' Devoy noted that Harry was 'no longer Chairman' of the Supreme Council, having been replaced by an unnamed 'great friend of mine' (not Collins, who had retained the key office of Treasurer).[113] A fortnight later, he was confident that de Valera would be compelled by 'the people' to sustain his 'sudden zeal for the Republic', and told Cohalan that 'we must even act with the fellows here who have been trying to break us up, to make an appearance of union. They are a poor lot, without brains, and will be no match for our trained men in committees and conventions.'[114] Harry, alarmed by rumours that the Supreme Council had recognised his rivals by giving McHugh a receipt for $25,000, anxiously requested a denial from Collins, 'as such action, if true, would leave only one course open to me, and that would be to return home'.[115] This he was soon to do, without having received any recorded response from the many-faceted Mr Field. Mr Woods was no longer the only acknowledged leader of the brethren in America.

The most pressing demand upon Harry's conspiratorial resources was to purchase and deliver arms and ammunition to Ireland. As in 1920, the system for smuggling small consignments through American and British ports proved faulty, causing Harry to deplore the absence of reliable agents in America and the neglect of his 'messengers' on arrival in Liverpool. As he told Collins in mid January: 'I have a great quantity of [Colt] 45 ammunition but am in a very bad way for messengers. ... Practically every man on the job was picked up here by me and in most of them I had to take a chance that I should not have to take, as in my opinion the men should come from Headquarters.'[116] When supplied, this ammunition turned out to fit Colt rifles rather than revolvers, as requested, and had to be cut down. De Valera observed that 'some of the "Young Horse" you sent was unsuitable', and Brugha gave samples of the type required to Harry's messengers.[117] Harry, clearly embarrassed, blamed the error on his intermediary's failure to secure goods in accordance with the invoice, which was 'a damnable thing'.[118] No less than 600,000 rounds had been secured of the redundant ammunition, which took three men a fortnight to pack up.[119] In his first major test as an arms procurer, Harry had been found wanting.

More elaborate and hazardous arrangements were needed to deliver Harry's greatest contribution to the IRA's military campaign. On 13 January, he informed Collins that he had ordered 100 Thompson sub-machine-guns at $225 apiece, and would 'do our damnedest to land them for you as soon as possible'. He enclosed a magazine depicting the amazing power, rapidity, and compactness of these weapons, first issued in 1919.[120] Lieut.-Col. Marcellus Thompson's Auto-Ordnance Company accepted the order from an intermediary acting for George Gordon Rorke, a graduate of Georgetown University and Protestant Friend of Ireland who met Harry on several occasions.[121] Collins responded that the Thompson 'certainly looks a splendid article', adding that

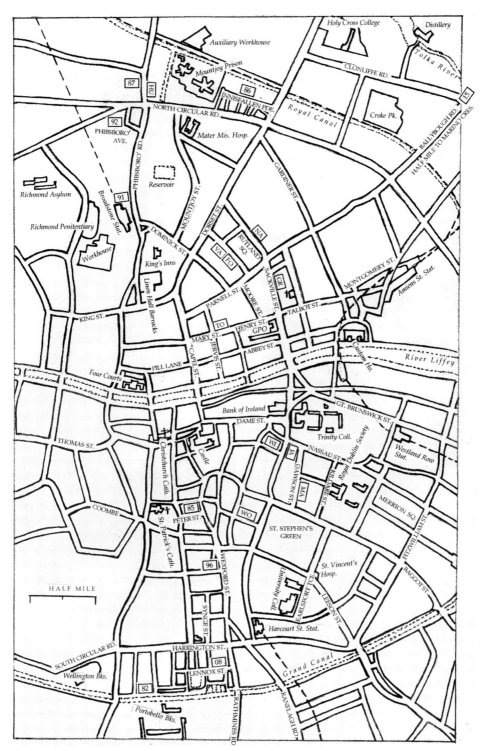

1. Location of Boland households and haunts in Dublin. Households are marked with the first recorded year of occupancy (excluding the century); haunts are marked with the letters FO, GR, HU, JA, NA, TO, VA, WI, and WO (representing Foresters' Hall, the Gresham Hotel, the Hut, Jammet's Restaurant, the National Club, Todd, Burns & Co., Vaughan's Hotel, the Wicklow Hotel, and the Dublin Workmen's Club); certain streets and sites mentioned in the text are also shown.

2a. 'My father himself had to . . . fly away because he believed in a Republic': James Henry Boland, photographed by Lauder Bros., Dublin.

2b. 'I know Brave Dear Mother that you are, that you would rather see me dead than retract one word or shot of Easter Week': Catherine Boland, *née* Woods.

3a. Digging for Ireland: Harry (top right) with his siblings Kathleen, Gerald, Nellie, and Edmund (front), photographed by M. Glover, Dublin.

3b. The new woman: Annie Keating, who married Gerald Boland in 1915, photographed by Lauder Bros., Dublin.

4a. 'I well remember the Rathmines days': Harry and a fellow-Gael named Lecky sport their medals.

MR H BOLAND

4b. In his father's footsteps: a newspaper sketch marking Harry's election as Chairman of the GAA's Dublin Co. Committee, 22 Oct. 1911.

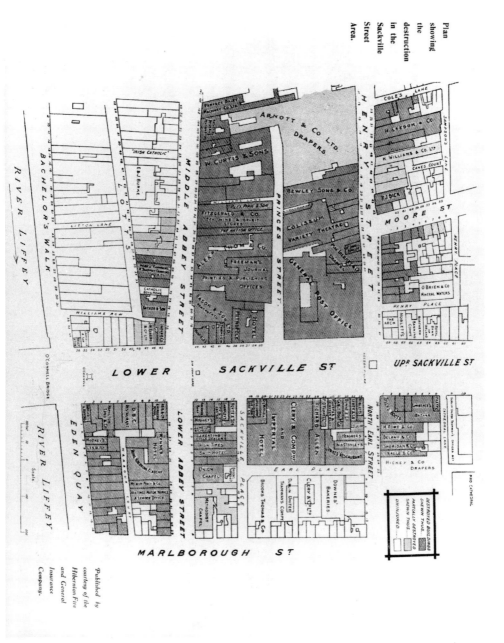

5. This remarkable record of the Rebellion's consequences for property in central Dublin, published in *The "Sinn Féin" Revolt Illustrated* (Dublin, Hely's Ltd., 1916), reveals that Harry's future premises at 64, Middle Abbey St., were 'partially destroyed'.

6a. 'From Fanny to Dear Harry, 2/10/16': postcard addressed to 'q 90, H. J. Boland' by Fanny Cullen, 'a great good girl' from Todd, Burns & Co., who soon afterwards surprised Harry by getting married in Manchester.

6b. 'To the fair ladies who sent their love, I'll return to the full': Harry with unidentified friend.

7a. 'There will be a great rush for all the heroes when you return': Dublin's welcome to the convicts, 17 June 1917. Those on the side-car included (1) Harry, (2) Jack Shouldice, (3) Robert Brennan, (4) James J. Burke, and (5) John J. Derrington. [Reproduced by courtesy of Independent Newspapers, Ltd.]

7b. 'Immense, nothing like it seen in Dublin before'. [Reproduced by courtesy of the National Museum of Ireland]

8. 'He and a few more looked miraculously well but the majority were haggard and ill': the released convicts (including Harry, 2nd from right, middle row) assembled outside Dublin's Mansion House. [Reproduced by courtesy of the National Museum of Ireland]

fuiReann áta cliat

do buaid craod na héiReann i mbáiRe iomána, 1917.

9a. Non-playing champion: Harry (hatless, in wing-collar) with 'the Dublin team that won the All-Ireland final in hurling' against Tipperary at Croke Park, 28 Oct. 1917. *Back row (from left)*: Pat Cullen, Tim Gleeson, and Harry (Faughs), Seán O'Donovan (Collegians), Professor Arthur E. Clery, SJ (UCD), Andy Harty (Faughs), and Luke O'Toole (General Secretary, GAA). Also pictured are Revd. Professor Timothy Corcoran, SJ (UCD) and Bob Mockler (Faughs: seated with moustache).

9b. Apostolic succession: Harry encouraging a junior Gael at Croke Park, 18 Sept. 1921. Kildare, encouraged by their mascot Master Conlan, defeated Dublin by one point in the Leinster Championship final. [Reproduced by courtesy of Independent Newspapers, Ltd.]

10a. 'It was spoiled by the wild methods of the players': a postcard showing Harry (referee) with de Valera (throwing in ball), Croke Park, 6 Apr. 1919.

10b. Wexford, 0–2, Tipperary, 0–1: the match, poor though it was, realised £1,085 for the Irish Republican Prisoners' Dependents' Fund.

11. 'I have secured a good name from the American journalists and gain some news every day': a photograph 'released for publication in magazines or newspapers'.

12a. 'What a 'queer' thing is American politics. I will have the light Italian hand finely developed if fate ordains that I remain here': Harry with unidentified American associate.

12b. 'The pride of these old men in Young Ireland is very wonderful, their views are fresh, and they can speak of '67 as of yesterday': Harry with John Devoy before the breakdown, and his fellow-envoys (from left) Liam Mellows, Eamon de Valera, Dr. Patrick McCartan, and Diarmuid Lynch. They were photographed on the roof of the Waldorf-Astoria Hotel, New York.

13a. 'There is something very breezy about the people here that is a delight to me': Harry on tour (standing), with Mellows (at the wheel) and McCartan (snugly seated).

13b. Playing the aviator: Cleveland, 7 Oct. 1919?

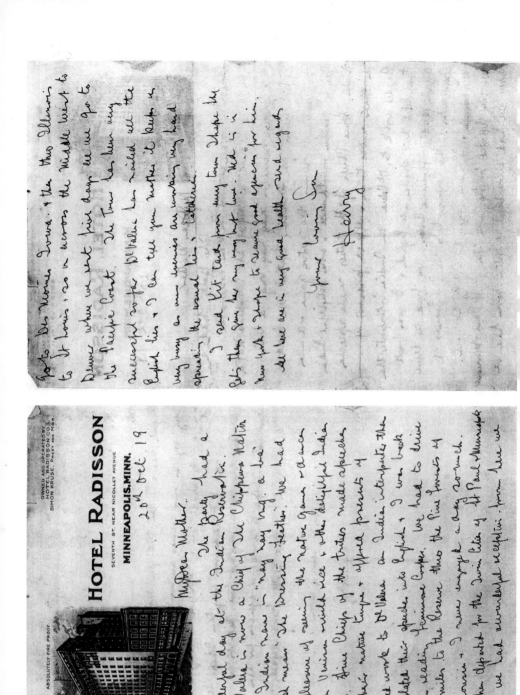

14. 'A wonderful day at the Indian Reservation': Harry's account to his mother, 20 Oct. 1919.

15a. 'De Valera is now a Chief of the Chippewa Nation, his Indian name is 'nay nay ong a ba' which means 'the Dressing Feather': Wisconsin's Indian Reserve, 18 Oct. 1919.

15b. 'We had the pleasure of seeing the native games and dances, fed on venison and wild rice and other delightful Indian dishes': the 'Chief' relaxes, but Harry, Seán Nunan (to de Valera's left), and John Finnerty keep their hats on.

16a. 'Train smash, en route to San Francisco, between Savannah Gorge and New Orleans, with de Valera and party on the train': Harry's own laconic caption for this record of his colleagues' narrow escape, 15 Apr. 1920.

16b. The attentive valet: Harry attending his master, in the garden of Cornelius C. Moore at Newport, Rhode Island.

17a. 'Poor Harry': a photograph stamped 'Óglaigh na h-Éireann G.H.Q., Aug. 1922' and used in posthumous propaganda.

17b. 'I wish you long life and happiness': a montage marking the engagement of Kitty Kiernan and Michael Collins, Mar. 1922. [Reproduced by courtesy of Independent Newspapers, Ltd.]

18a. 'Oh for a Good Hurling Match': Collins, Harry, Eamon Duggan, and Frank P. Walsh (with family) watch a benefit hurling match at Croke Park, 25 Sept. 1921.

18b. 'Mr. Michael Collins, after a few well-chosen remarks, presented the medals to the winners': Harry beside his hero after Dublin, 8–4, defeated Leix, 3–1, in a photograph autographed and misdated by both leaders.

19a. 'The great Crisis has come, and we must face it like men': Harry in Earlsfort Terrace during the Dáil's debate on the Treaty, Jan. 1922. [Reproduced by courtesy of Independent Newspapers, Ltd.]

19b. 'Wandering Statesmen': Harry with Art O'Brien (London), de Valera, Seán T. O'Kelly (Paris), and Count O'Byrne (Rome), shortly before Harry's republican activity led to his dismissal as envoy to Washington. [*Irish Life*, 27 Jan. 1922: reproduced by courtesy of the National Library of Ireland]

20a. The Chief Whip and his assistant: Seán T. O'Kelly and Harry, with Kathleen Boland. [Reproduced by courtesy of Independent Newspapers, Ltd.]

20b. 'Harry alone seemed blooming': outside the Mansion House during Sinn Féin's Ard Fheis, 21 Feb. 1922. [Reproduced by courtesy of UCD Archives: Aiken Papers]

IRISH LIFE

Vol. XXXIX.—No. 2. FRIDAY, MARCH 3rd, 1922. Registered at the G.P.O. as a Newspaper

Photo. "Irish Life."

A PICTURE OF GOOD OMEN
Mr. Harry Boland, Mr. Michael Collins, and Mr. De Valera enjoying a friendly chat.

21. Let us adjourn! [Reproduced by courtesy of the National Library of Ireland]

22. Best of friends?: Harry, Collins and Sinn Féin's Standing Committee at the Ard Fheis, 21–22 Feb. 1922. *Front row (from left)*: Áine Ceannt, Eamon Duggan, Dr. Kathleen Lynn, Arthur Griffith, Eamon de Valera, Michael Collins, Harry Boland, Hanna Sheehy-Skeffington. *Middle row*: Jennie Wyse Power, Desmond FitzGerald, Darrell Figgis, Kevin O'Shiel, Austin Stack, Dr. Thomas Dillon. *Back row*: Seán Milroy, Walter Cole, [*two unidentified*], Paudeen O'Keeffe. [*Irish Life*, 3 Mar. 1922: reproduced by courtesy of the National Library of Ireland]

23. Frisson: the 'Split' takes effect. [Reproduced by courtesy of the National Museum of Ireland]

24a. The mediator. [Reproduced by courtesy of Independent Newspapers, Ltd.]

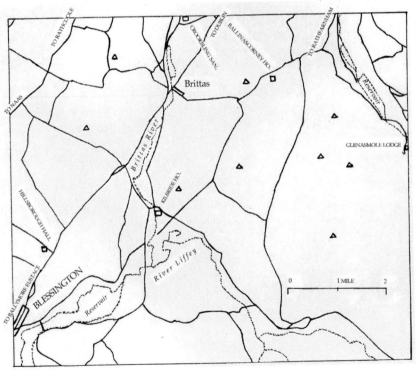

24b. Location of Civil War sites near Blessington, Co. Wicklow.

25. 'A soldier's burial': The Boland family at the graveside in Glasnevin, 4 Aug. 1922. The mourners include Gerald's sons Kevin and Enda in front of their mother Annie (standing back), with Kate Boland (third from left) and (on her right) Jim's unmarried sister, Teresa Anne ('Teasy'). The bearded figure is the republican TD for Longford-Westmeath, Laurence Ginnell.

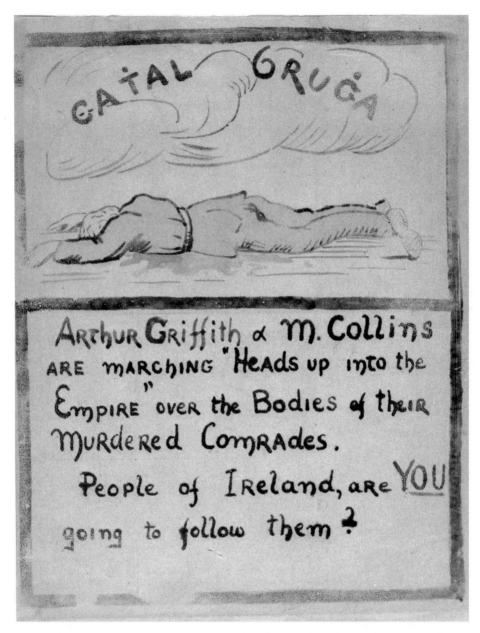

26–29. Civil War cartoons attributed to Constance de Markievicz and her Roneo machine, 1922. [Reproduced by courtesy of the National Library of Ireland]

THE DEAL)--"STAND FIRM, FEAR NOT , BE TRUE , VICTORY WILL BE TO
     THOSE THAT CAN ENDURE MOST ."

THE I.R.A.--" STAND FIRM, HAVE NO FEAR ,WE WILL BREAK YOUR CHAINS.

CUMANN NA MBAN--" WE HAVE PLEDGED OUR WORD TO THE REPUBLIC ,WE
     BEND NO KNEE TO ENGLANDS KING, WE TAKE NO DEGRADING OATH,
     OUR MOTTO IS , 'BETTER DEATH THAN DISHONOUR'. "

FIANNA--IN THE NAMES OF COLBERT AND HEUSTON WE PLEDGE OUR LIVES
     TO THE REPUBLIC "

HARRY BOLAND
assasinated
JULY 31st
1922.

M.C. "What will the MORNING POST
think of me NOW?"

MIDNIGHT ASSASSINS.

The Gang who murdered
HARRY BOLAND
have gone SOUTH to MURDER
Eamon de Valera and
Erskine Childers.

30. 'Sister of the martyred Harry Boland': Kathleen Boland in the USA, inscribed to her brother Gerald, 7 Apr. 1923.

31a. Survivors: Kate Boland with Gerald's sons, Enda (on her right) and Kevin.

31b. 'He was everything to me - for not only his bright self, but he practically kept the house going': Kate Boland at 15, Marino Crescent.

32. Memorial stone and tablet in the
Republican Plot, Glasnevin. [Reproduced by
courtesy of Jane Leonard]

the 'Q.M.G. [Seán McMahon] says they should be got at any price'.[122] A further order for 50 guns was evidently made in mid February, allowing Harry to promise that '150 copies of Col. Thompson' would be 'on hand March 15th'.[123] Harry's third and final order was issued at the end of March: 'O'Rourke [Rorke] arrives re Col. Thompsons. 653 – at [$]225 less 20% – hesitate for long – finally give order at $133,034.40.'[124] Having made this massive financial and material commitment, Harry faced the formidable challenge of storing the weapons as they shot forth from the Colt factory in Hartford, Connecticut, concealing them from the Secret Services, and transmitting them to Ireland.

The guns were safely delivered to a warehouse in the Bronx under the name of 'Frank Williams', usually identified as Harry's Clan associate, Laurence de Lacy from Enniscorthy in Wexford.[125] Transporting the massive cargo by sea was not so simple, particularly because Harry was 'meeting with all sorts of difficulties in seeking employment for Irishmen on the Moore-McCormack line', the shipping firm into which Consul Fawsitt had poured money in the hope of guaranteeing security for the mission's human and material freight. He decided to forward the guns ordered in January and February in several small shipments, before sending 'a full cargo' through 'a new line which I think will be of great service to us'.[126] It seems that 30 sub-machine-guns reached Queenstown in late April, providing valuable firepower for the Cork Brigades, while another 51 guns arrived in Dublin shortly before the Truce.[127] Meanwhile, two American ex-officers 'who are expert in the knowledge of ... Colonel Thompson', Major James Dinneen and Captain Patrick Cronin, were sent to Dublin to demonstrate specimen guns to Collins and his comrades.[128] These arrangements were cryptically recorded in Harry's diary:

30 Mar. Wed. New York. We have now the wherewithal to keep up pressure. Communications are not too good. M. Mc. have given us a raw deal.

7 Apr. Thurs. New York. Take up question of Communications. Decide to invest in Navy. Must deliver goods. Only hope to keep the supplies to Ireland. Will urge Navy on James [O'Mara].

21 Apr. Thurs. Chicago. Dinneen, Pat Cronin off for glory. Great party, pipes, songs etc., early hours.

3 May. Tues. New York. Pat Cronin, Jim Dinneen, 'Aquitania'.[129]

Collins was delighted with the American instructors and their samples: 'They are two good ones and the three attendants are simply splendid – absolutely magnificent.'[130] The Dublin Brigade was less enthusiastic, as its first experiment with the weapons, when ambushing a trainload of troops in late June, was spoiled by the repeated failure of the repeating mechanism.[131]

Harry's worries about 'communications' were compounded by a shipping strike which placed most reliable vessels in dry dock, and his 'navy' was slow to embark. His intention was to make an immediate 'bargain' with the United States Mail Steamship Co., whereby messengers and munitions would be allowed safe passage in return for 'any little courtesy' which Collins might provide. Though coyly pleading with 'Gould' to use his 'influence' to secure 'the good will of Collins' for this scheme, Harry had to wait more than two months for a cautious assent from the Minister for Finance.[132] Meanwhile, the Thompsons accumulated uselessly in the Bronx. At the end of April, he told Collins that it was 'heart-breaking to me to have them lying there', though he remained 'certain' of eventual delivery. Nonetheless, Collins congratulated him on 'a very good job', remarking that 'with the completion of the order which you mention, we should be in a fair way towards winning the war here'.[133]

As news of the Thompsons spread, Harry came under growing pressure to deliver the remaining weapons, 495 of which he proceeded to conceal in the coal bunker of the *East Side*, a steamship owned by the United States Shipping Board, operated by the Cosmopolitan Shipping Co., and chartered by the Irish White Cross to convey coal to Dublin.[134] His chief agent in despatching the 'full cargo' was Liam Pedlar, a naturalised American from Ballynahinch, County Down, who had served McGarrity as a hired 'detective', and his adopted country as a member of the Pennsylvania National Guard, before returning to fight in the Rebellion and serving several terms of imprisonment.[135] As Pedlar recalled, the guns were 'dumped in cases in C[armelite] monastery in cellars. We sewed them up in sacks as legs of lamb.' The continuing strike of New York dockers provided the opportunity for installing a sympathetic crew: 'Jim McGee was in Engineers' Union and was related to all dock workers and he may have arranged plan of getting them on ship. A crew of Irish recruited, completely Irish.' With the Captain's connivance, the vanload of weapons was put on board, and Pedlar ate a celebratory meal with Harry in their shared apartment: 'In bed when a 'phone call came to say "everything is messed" – weapons discovered. I woke up Harry.'[136] Harry's diary was more enigmatic:

11 June. Sat. New York. Liam [Pedlar], Jimmy [McGee] and Co. working hard.

12 June. Sun. New York. Joe McGarrity, Liam Pedlar, H. B. take a few hours' drive. All well so far.

13 June. Mon. New York. A little more and what might have been. A little less and what worlds away. Try to retrieve our fallen fortunes.

14 June. Tues. New York. Eugene Kinkead, James K. McGuire, Joe McGarrity.[137]

Collins was still pithier in his response: 'So disaster befell.'[138]

There is no need to rehearse the melodrama whereby the guns were seized by customs agents, removed to New Jersey on a search warrant by the Hoboken police, retrieved by the federal authorities, and subjected to a prolonged legal tussle.[139] Optimistic as always, Harry immediately set about recovering his precious load by both legal and illicit means, inducing Major Eugene Kinkead to 'pull wires on Jersey' in a bold attempt, with the connivance of Hoboken's Mayor and Chief of Police, to spirit the guns out of police headquarters before federal agents could secure them.[140] Harry himself was fortunate to avoid implication in the attempted gun-running, and no charges were pressed home against his associates despite an unusually effective secret investigation. When reporting to Brugha in July, Harry remained remarkably sanguine:

> The full complement of 653 guns have been secured; the balance is in our hands, save what you have already received; we are confident of securing the return of the guns. ... I am well aware that it is common among men to rail at failure, and I do not expect you be otherwise than disgusted with the mishap. I can only say that we deserved to succeed, and I will (D.V.) land the lot at the first opportunity.[141]

According to a more personal account of the mishap, he was 'satisfied that the enemy could not possibly find them unless someone gave it away', promised to 'explain how the guns were to be hidden on some future occasion verbally', and unavailingly asked Brugha to 'destroy this report'.[142] Despite his confidence, the shipment was impounded until 1925, when the tireless McGarrity gained possession of the rusting Thompsons before eventually exporting most of them in batches to the post-revolutionary rump of the IRA. Although some of the 158 Thompsons which had been ordered in March but not loaded on the *East Side* were successfully smuggled into Ireland in defiance of the Truce, they served no practical purpose until the outbreak of Civil War. Collins and his comrades were never to handle most of the weapons which might have given them military supremacy, however short-lived, over the Forces of the Crown.[143]

Even before the 'disaster' at Hoboken, Harry's lovingly assembled array of 'Col. Thompsons' had projected him towards a bruising collision with Cathal Brugha, ever suspicious of the methods used by his former brethren of the IRB. In early March, Brugha gently asked him to supply 'invoices with all stuff in future *if possible* and let me know how much money you have spent. ... I will give you authority for the spending of any amount you name. If we can get enough goods to keep us going I believe without any exaggeration that we are going to knock —— out of them.'[144] In reply, Harry expressed confidence 'that we can collect a fund here for your department [from] the different public organizations and from people here who would give money freely for your department, when they might hesitate to give it for anything else. ... I will open a special account here, and would hope to pay back to your department an equal amount to the money expended so far, and after that to make this end of your work self-supporting.'[145] Just before paying for the major consignment, he informed James O'Mara that 'we are in want of money and have suggested a "Refugee" Fund to the A.A.R.I.R. with very good results so far', suggesting that the Fiscal Agent might also 'give us a boost'. O'Mara was appalled at the proposal, which would 'spoil' the preparation for a new Bond Drive 'unless you do it through your own group. Besides you have $500,000 available and on hand and appropriated – you and Joe [McGarrity] can sell the U.S.L.B. [Liberty Bonds] in safe deposit.'[146]

Harry's response was to draw funds from both quarters, borrowing the full sum from the Dáil's 'reserve' with a view to repaying the loan through the mistitled 'Refugee Fund'. When expounding this ingenious procedure to Collins, he explained that it was 'purely a matter of book-keeping' as to whether disbursements from his special fund should be made from Ireland or America.[147] He was more circumspect when approaching Brugha:

> I hesitated long before placing this huge order. I was made aware of the fact, however, that if I did not get it in time … I would find it very diffi-cult to secure delivery under a year so I entered into a hidebound contract in the same spirit that a young priest would if told to go out and collect money to build a church for himself.[148]

Brugha, who had earlier enquired suspiciously if he had 'been in communica-tion with anyone on this side regarding this business', was initially 'delighted' by Harry's coup, adding that 'it will not be necessary to send the money here – it is the *stuff* we want. If you wish, however, to send us the auditors' report, you may do so, just to show that everything is in order.'[149] Collins also responded warmly, advising that payments be debited to the special account rather than the 'Defence Vote', but adding pointedly that 'of course this fund is not a Treasury fund, and as such I am in no way responsible for it – particularly as I know the M/D [Minister for Defence] would not like me even to be consulted about it.'[150] All remained well in early May, Brugha being 'glad to hear of the contract' and happy for Harry to 'make the purchases out of this new fund you have started'.[151] De Valera, meanwhile, had expressed his wish in another context 'that before big enterprises are started over there, formal authorisation for the expenditures were first asked for'.[152] He was well aware of the Thompson project, having been involved in preliminary discussions in Cleveland, Ohio.[153] Harry's response assured him 'that expenses of Cleveland enterprise underwritten on this side. To date we have received $15,000.00. Confident that Cleveland will be financed solely by American contributions.'[154]

Such assurances failed to satisfy Brugha when he belatedly learned that 'a considerable sum – between 200,000 and 300,000 dollars – has been drawn out of my vote. Kindly say if this is correct, and if correct, please explain. Now, a chara dil [my dear friend], don't imagine I am taking you to task; but surely a man of your intelligence must realise that our plan of activities here is based upon our having a certain amount of money at our disposal.'[155] Harry was convulsed with righteous indignation when he responded on 19 July:

Am I to understand from your letter of 29/6/21 that you did not authorize me to purchase 650 [sic.] Thompson sub-machine-guns? Where do you think I could get the money to pay cash on the nail for these? ... You are making it very hard for me if you deny me an OK on the purchase. I had to decide in three days as to whether I place the order or risk waiting twelve months, so I accepted certain responsibility feeling sure that the Defence Dept. would welcome such a splendid weapon. Of course, now that the attempt [at] a big cargo has failed, I know what to expect, although I am certain to secure the return of the captured guns. I have had no help or co-operation from your Department; every man carrying stuff from America was originally picked up by me, although I have asked time and again for help to land the tremendous amount of goods we have here.[156]

Two days later, Harry informed Collins that the Refugee Fund had reached nearly $70,000 after three months' work, sardonically suggesting that Collins 'might convey this news to the M.D.' On further reflection, he repeated the news in a separate note to Brugha, adding apologetically that he would 'be more careful in future in doing unauthorized work'.[157] Harry's combination of rage and contrition prevailed upon the warm-hearted Minister, who concluded 'that your liver was out of order, or that you had eaten something that disagreed with you' on 19 July: 'consequently I shall not reply to it in kind. I don't rail at people, and if I ever do, you will not be the man I'll start on.' Instead, he plaintively repeated his previous misinterpretation of Harry's original proposal for a special fund, ending the dispute with a few words of faint praise.[158] As in the case of his excommunication of Devoy's faction, Harry's will had prevailed through a *fait accompli*, leaving his strongest supporters in Ireland baffled, aggrieved at having been misled by empty promises, yet unwilling to repudiate their most energetic American agent. Nevertheless, as mishaps multiplied and resentment mounted, Harry came under increasing pressure to account for his conduct in person.

At home, the fabled solidarity displayed by the republican leaders during 'the four glorious years' was also beginning to disintegrate, as de Valera and Brugha manoeuvred to undermine the supremacy of Collins and the 'Organisation'. Shortly after returning to Ireland, de Valera resumed his attempt to transfer Collins to America, a proposal which Harry – perhaps naively – welcomed and encouraged. On 18 January, de Valera served Collins with 'formal confirmation of the unanimous approval of the Ministry to my proposal ... that the Minister of Finance be asked to proceed to the United States as a Special Envoy on behalf of the Republic'. Collins was charged with a daunting variety of tasks: imposing order on the American finances, opening American agencies for republican enterprises, pursuing the American boycott of British goods, improving communications, executing 'commissions' for the Minister for Defence, organising relief and propaganda, and enticing 'back to our support many of the excellent people in the Clan who have been misled'. In short, he would 'replace Mr. Boland and allow him to return as soon as that can be done without disorganisation or other danger'. De Valera guarded Collins against 'the mistake of thinking that the division began with my advent in America', urged him 'not to be too modest to exploit your fame, or notoriety if you prefer it', and sugared the pill by affirming that we should 'not have here, so to speak, "all our eggs in one basket", and that whatever coup the English may attempt, the line of succession is safe, and the future provided for'.[159]

When reporting the scheme to Harry three weeks later, Collins indicated his persistent misgivings about leaving Ireland and bringing Harry home: 'Now it seems that an old friend of yours named Gould is likely to join you, which will probably have the effect of prolonging your stay still further. ... He is not anxious to leave home, and is making a fight for his view.' Harry replied that Gould would 'indeed be very welcome and will find great openings for his line of business'.[160] On 25 March, he wrote excitedly to O'Mara that 'I expect Gould tonight. Do not mention it to a soul until you hear from him, it will not do to let "Min" [Mary McSwiney] know as yet.'[161] Collins, however, had already decided that the lack of secure transportation rendered it 'impracticable for Mr. Gould to travel just yet. Possibly, however, he will go next time.'[162] Harry was 'disappointed' by the delay, but remained hopeful that his comrade would eventually reach America and devote his expertise in 'communications' to securing shipment of the Thompsons:

> I think it would be a very good stroke for Gould to come. In view of a letter I have written to the Minister of Defence (which I am sure you will have read) in regard to the possibility of receiving a supply of goods from here he will be invaluable. I think it will be very hard for him to be in this country and to remain quiet.[163]

When James O'Mara submitted the last of his many resignations as Fiscal Agent in mid May, Harry declared that 'if he decides to quit, there is only one man to take his place, and that man is Gould'.[164] Collins's objection to being sent to America was fortified on 22 June by 'the discovery in the President's papers of the knowledge that Gould was likely to travel'. Yet, a month later, Harry was still 'looking forward with great joy to chaperone [sic.] the M. F. [Minister for Finance] across this land'.[165] Whereas de Valera's motive in pressing for Collins's removal was probably to eject another rotten egg from his 'basket', Harry was ever more convinced that the American mission could only be accomplished by Ireland's foremost 'genius for organisation'.

As Brugha's campaign against Collins intensified, Harry moved from neutrality towards solidarity with his beleaguered comrade. On 16 May, he regretted 'very much that at this stage of the proceedings there should be the slightest question between Porter and Gould', and confessed to 'some uneasiness' about hints of conflict in their letters to him. He drew a telling comparison between their antagonism and his own internal confusion of priorities as between 'Woods' of the IRB and 'Cowe' of the IRA: 'I understand, of course, the question at issue between you and Porter and am fully alive with the situation, as it is parallel over here as between Woods and Cowe.' Collins clearly felt that Harry had failed to grasp the personal animus inflaming the domestic dispute: 'Indeed there is a question between the two men whose names you mention, and were it not for the forbearance of the writer the thing would be simply a scandal. Boland has received no treatment at the hands of any of his enemies like one of these has received. Some day I'll tell you the real motive ... when, if ever, we have an hour together.'[166]

After his own confrontation with 'Charlie' Brugha over purchasing the Thompsons, Harry left no doubt as to which of his masters was also his friend:

Mick, you're a great pal! Your letter of July 6th, in which you approve my statement on the 'Peace' proposals, arrived together with a short note from Charlie in which he suggests that I had not authority to purchase. I read Charlie's first and felt rotten! Yours gave me a cheer-up for which I thank you.[167]

Harry's unbroken alliance with Collins continued to be expressed in terms of warm camaraderie and mutual admiration. In February, Harry was 'glad to know that you are strong and well and still evading the enemy. I read a report that Mike had been killed, that he was mounted on a white horse directing operations, but I know that he is not likely to do any Joan of Arc business.' He was later reassured that 'things is tough but they've been worse. If they can kill Collins they still hope to win.' In late May, Collins wrote flirtatiously that 'the enemy has run me very closely during the week. It was a question of brushing shoulders. More of this later perhaps – I mean the story not the shoulders.' A month later, he reported 'a couple of the nearest shaves of all during the past few weeks', lamenting that 'they got my private place where you saw me when you were here'.[168] Through his comrade, Harry could experience, if at second hand, the frissons of revolution.

His correspondence with Robert Brennan, the Dáil's new Under-Secretary for Foreign Affairs, confirmed Harry's ability to sustain friendship in the teeth of criticism of his performance as an envoy. In late March, he congratulated Brennan 'on the wonderful manner in which you are handling our publicity', soon afterwards expressing 'very great regard' for his 'unselfish' contribution. These effusions came too late to prevent Brennan from expostulating that

Harry had failed to respond to his last eight letters, and that 'a continuance of this state of affairs is impossible'.[169] In forwarding the complaint to Harry, Seán Nunan remarked sarcastically that 'Bob Brennan must think that the communications service is really by aeroplane', since Brennan's epistolary bombardment had been launched only in late March: 'You tell 'em Bó you've got the kick! Why! he couldn't get a reply by ordinary mail in that time.'[170] Harry defused the dispute in characteristic fashion: 'No doubt you are a great fellah!! The opening barrage of your dispatch of the 7th of April left me gasping for breath here in Washington.' If Brennan wished him 'to report back *in extenso* what we have done regarding each individual item, you will have to use your influence with the Foreign Affairs Department to have a Secretary appointed to the Admiralty, and employ a fleet of fast cruisers between America and Portobello Harbour. ... It is perfectly obvious to me, Bob, that a continuance of this state of affairs is impossible.' In response to this sally, Brennan could offer nothing less than a semi-apology for his 'impatience'.[171] Harry's contempt for bureacratic niceties amongst the brethren had prevailed once again.

Beset by failures in America, reproofs from Ireland, and frustration with his inability to influence the revolutionary movement in a critical phase, Harry's mood fluctuated between an envoy's elation and an exile's dejection. His loneliness was most acute at the New Year, with de Valera departed and many of his associates on holiday:

2 Jan. Sun. New York. Visit James K. McGuire, Mrs McGuire and family. Lonely.

10 Jan. Mon. New York. Much trouble with State Dept. and Donal Oge [O'Callaghan]. O'Mara not yet returned. Feel very lonely and unhappy.[172]

The familiar compensations of American life remained: visiting the Carmelites, watching a fight in Madison Square Garden, listening to the tenor John McCormack, visiting 'Celtic Park Hurling with Donal Oge', spending a 'sweltering' Washington morning with Joe McGarrity 'looking for bathing pool', or attending Seán Nunan's engagement dinner.[173] His thirty-fourth birthday on 27 April was not forgotten, at least by James McGuire's wife Frances, who made and boxed 'a tie for one whom we all like and admire so much'.[174]

Yet the threat of breakdown persisted, and Harry made further visits to Chaquin Falls near Cleveland, Ohio, beginning with a fortnight in the depth of winter:

22 Jan. Sat. Meet Mrs. Phillips and Tom. Begin my rest cure. Am all worn out and need a change.

23 Jan. Sun. Delightful place, kindly people. Nan Ryan [Mrs Seán T. O'Kelly] here pending her return home.

24 Jan. Mon. Walk the town, enjoy the quietude of Halfred Farms and feel new life entering.

25 Jan. Tues. 'Salary Jack' and I go riding.

26 Jan. Wed. Glorious day on 'Salary Jack'.

27 Jan. Thurs. Jas. O'Mara arrives with Frank P. Walsh's proposal. . . . Bank Ac[count]s etc. Ride 'Salary Jack'.

28 Jan. Fri. Jas. O'Mara remains over till Sunday. Mrs. A. Ryan. I go shopping to Cleveland. 2 hours' run on 'Salary Jack'.

29 Jan. Sat. Enjoy a good gallop, had my first jump. Fine.

He returned for three days in early March and four days in July, during which news arrived of the cease-fire at home: '8 July. Friday. Chaquin Falls. Truce declared today, in Dublin. McCready [*recte*, General Sir Nevil Macready], de Valera. Joyous day in Ireland. I am thrown by "Cartridge" taking a jump.'[175] After more than two years of plans, plots, and setbacks in America, the stress and frustration were becoming insufferable.

Further anxiety arose from the vulnerability of Harry's family in Dublin, as raids and arrests multiplied. The house at Marino Crescent remained a favourite resort of gunmen and repository of guns, as Kathleen recalled:

Paddy Daly – he was a daredevil – also brought a bundle of the little American machine guns out to our place in Marino Crescent and stored them in the henhouse at the end of the garden. . . . He was able to come in by the back gate, of which he had a key, and he could come and go without anyone knowing it. He had a motorbike and sidecar which he used for this purpose.[176]

On 11 February, Harry told 'Field' that he was 'most anxious', having 'not heard of my people now since before Christmas'. Thoughtful as ever, Collins replied that he had seen 'your mother and Kathleen recently. I gave them your message alright and they told me they had written to you a few days previously.'[177] Extra reassurance was provided two months later by Robert Brennan, whose wife had recently spent 'a Sunday in the Crescent. They had been landed the day before but it wasn't a savage raid and they were all in good form.'[178]

Harry's attention also turned occasionally to Kitty Kiernan, who played to perfection the part of the girl he had left behind him in Granard. Since the destruction of the Greville Arms in November, she had found solace in a brief engagement to the 'extremely wealthy' Lionel Lyster, who (as she later told Collins) had 'no brains' but was 'young and a good boy and very manly in a way'.[179] When resuming contact with Harry in mid April, she ignored this diversion:

You will be amused to hear yr. other pal, whose photograph you sent me with yr. own, slept in the same house as I was in, one night, but we never met, neither of us were interested! I'm afraid if it had been Harry, things wld. be somewhat different – some night! Goodbye to the good old days when we made things hum at the Greville Arms.

Harry had suggested that she visit him in America, but the prospect seemed remote: 'Yes, I wld. love to take a trip out to see *you*! Maybe when the weather gets fine and peace comes, and I get rich, I might go.' She asked 'if there is any chance of us meeting soon again. Could you not come even on a short holiday?' She expressed interest in Harry's digs and his 'lady visitors', contemplating 'all those fascinating women over the herring pond, have you not fallen a victim?' As for herself, she had just spent five weeks on holiday, enjoying 'a nice quiet rest which I needed, no excitement', while her sisters Chrys and Helen prepared for their weddings. Helen's nuptials prompted a sly reference to her former suitor, Collins: 'By the way, I saw *her* friend and *yrs.*, one day in Dublin in January, he wanted to know if I had heard from you? So of course, I said, cruel Harry that never writes.' Yet, wrote Kitty, 'I *never* forget you, and often say a little prayer for you, and long for happy times to meet you again. Do you remember the lake? It will soon be time to go out there again now, and I know I'd be often wishing you were near me.' Meanwhile, decorum required that she keep her distance: 'Bye bye, dear, this is not a love letter, because you didn't write one. So you will have to be content, with: With fondest love, yrs., Kit. *No Kisses*. !!' 'Mrs Gossip' added a postscript deflating this moment of mock-chilliness before signing off with a heart-sign: 'The night's getting on and I might get romantic and I don't want to. So *cheerie*, o.'[180] The prospect of further dalliance in Granard gave extra spring to Harry's projected return.

Above all, Harry was beckoned home by his sense of exclusion from the climax of the domestic struggle for independence. Ever since mid 1920, the impact of the American campaign had been muffled by the growing expectation of a settlement whereby the Dáil would compromise its republican commitment in return for partial independence. As mediators multiplied and de Valera edged closer to negotiating with Lloyd George, Harry's public statements exhibited a bizarre blend of unswerving republicanism with peace-loving pragmatism, a trick which he was to perfect during 1922. In mid May, after claiming that reports of Sinn Féin's acquiescence in a 'Free Commonwealth of Ireland' were 'wholly false and without foundation in fact', Harry sought reassurance from de Valera that 'I have taken the right course'. Under further questioning, he stated that 'no official negotiations have taken place so far', while indicating that the leaders were 'ready to discuss peace with the Premier of England and his associates' on conditions which they would 'lay down' on meeting 'the British representatives'.[181]

Just before the Truce of early July, he announced that 'the recent offer of peace ... was a matter entirely for the people of Ireland who are in touch with the situation there to decide and intimated that any interference on the part of the Irish in the United States might tend to have a bad effect upon the movement in general'.[182] Collins deemed this a 'splendid' utterance, citing the observation of 'a very interesting and well up friend of mine' that 'Harry's opinion was that he expressed none. Therein lay its excellence.'[183] As the interminable exchange of letters continued between Lloyd George and de Valera, Harry initially avoided comment 'and hid myself from the Press', until provoked by a belligerent resolution from 'Cohalan's puppets' to issue 'a very short snappy statement urging all friends to leave the question to the men on the spot'.[184] When writing to Collins, however, he interpreted the Truce as a victory: 'God! It's great to see the day when our men forced a Truce. No matter what the outcome may be, of one thing we are certain, ye have won Belligerent Rights, and all editorial comment here admits that much. ... De Valera has done great work and has captured the imagination of all. His handling of [Sir James] Craig is delightful.'[185] It was surely time for Harry, as a key member of the inner revolutionary circle, to contribute to that 'great work' in Ireland itself.

The long-awaited summons arrived in Washington on 10 August, as the Dáil prepared to discuss Lloyd George's proposal for a Peace Conference: 'Cable to return, make reservation, *Olympic*.'[186] Harry, informed by Robert Brennan that 'we are negotiating safe conduct and facility to return in your favor for Dáil meeting', cabled that he was 'ready'.[187] On the following day, he alerted Mary McSwiney: 'Cable from Ireland calls me home, sailing Saturday. Will carry your message to the President and advise you immediately upon my arrival. Stephen O'Mara will take charge in my absence. Slán leat [goodbye to you], Harry.'[188] As a farewell gift to Dr. Maloney, his unfailing mentor and neurasthenist, he sent a photograph inscribed 'from Harry to the Doc.', expressing his gratitude 'for many personal services rendered' and 'for the aid, advice and tireless energy given to Ireland during her hour of trial. ... Slán beo [take care], Enri Ua Beoláin.'[189] The Truce enabled Ireland's envoy to travel first-class on the S.S. *Olympic*, a White Star liner and sister-ship of the *Titanic*, instead of taking his customary place in the engine room.[190] The United States Mail Steamship Co., his conduit for clandestine trans-Atlantic enterprises, was taken aback to read in the press that he had chosen a rival line: 'We feel confident that we have your heartiest support and good will in our earnest desire to accommodate the Irish traveling public, and feel that we can rely on your support whenever it will come your way to favor American vessels.'[191] Harry's passport was vetted by his old adversary Gloster Armstrong, the British Consul-General in New York who had despatched so many secret reports of Irish-American intrigues over three decades. As Armstrong informed the Foreign Office:

I saw Boland on Friday, the 12th instant, when the necessary arrangements were being made for a passport to permit him to travel. He seemed very hopeful of the Irish Question being settled and intimated that he was taking with him a number of important documents that would enable the Irish leaders to understand the situation here. Boland, also, probably carried with him a considerable sum of money and rumours to that effect have been in circulation since his departure.[192]

Harry's fellow-passengers included the wife and daughter of F. P. Walsh, who had already reached England, and Mary McSwiney, who had at length decided that no vital decision should be made in her absence: '13 Aug. Sat. New York. Sail for Ireland, *Olympic*. Miss McSwiney, Mrs. and V[irginia] Walsh, Father [Timothy] Shanley.'[193] Harry gallantly withdrew $330 from American funds to cover her ticket to Southampton.[194] Nunan, left behind, ruminated that 'you must have cut a dash up and down the promenade deck in your perfectly good white pants. Did you act the serious diplomat on the trip or the light-hearted attaché? In other words did you jazz and have a bottle of stout?' He wondered if Harry would 'rather travel first class, firing or hash slinging?'[195] Nunan felt 'very lonesome after you', adding that 'Joe McGarrity was a very lonely man when you were gone and so were all your good friends.'[196] As Liam Pedlar sighed: 'How we all miss you here – we are so lonesome. Seán starts off on his little rest tomorrow and then Gilbert [Ward], and I will all be alone.' He could only 'hope that you have not made up your mind not to return'.[197] Stephen O'Mara, left to manage the ailing American Association as Harry's deputy, reminded de Valera that 'H. B. is the ideal man. I trust he will return.'[198] With Harry gone, the mission had lost its driving spirit. As Brennan had once observed, he 'alone could make the necessary co-ordination. He rightly puts in his big punch for all the little ones can specialise in certain departments.'[199]

When opening his diary for 1921 with an epigraph, Harry had self-consciously identified himself with Owen Meredith's flattering depiction of the power behind the throne:

> That man is great and he alone
> Who serves a greatness not his own,
> For neither praise nor Self.
> Content to know, and be unknown,
> *Whole in himself.*[200]

Over the eight months since de Valera's departure, Harry's versatility and skill as an envoy and public representative had achieved wider if far from universal recognition. As a supporter informed the American Association: 'He was left by his President in a very difficult and trying position. He has grown with his responsibilities, difficult as they have been. It is true that he was trained as a tailor and not as a diplomat, but he ... has shown wonderful patience and dignity in his new calling.'[201] As a conspirator and manipulator, however, his once formidable reputation in both Ireland and America had been damaged by repeated setbacks and miscalculations. Harry's return to domestic politics gave him an opportunity to reassert his influence and recover his failing prestige.

X

Enlightenment

ON his return to Ireland in late August 1921, six weeks after the Truce, the not-so-triumphant envoy was greeted by welcoming deputations as well as curious journalists:

> 20 Aug. Sat. Southampton, London. Meet Art O'Brien. Leave for Dublin 8.45 p.m.

> 21 Aug. Sun. Dublin. Arrive 6 a.m. [William T.] Cosgrave, Frank P. Walsh, Donal oge [O'Callaghan], Gresham Hotel. Seán McKeown. Meet de Valera 3 p.m. Mick, St. Enda's. Hand ten thousand to Collins.[1]

The *Irish Independent* noted the contrast with Harry's previous 'flying visit to Ireland in June of last year, the news of the visit being only made public after he had returned to the States'. He informed the paper that Americans had 'heaved a great sigh of relief when the peace *pourparlers* began. The signing of the truce was regarded by the Press as a matter of tremendous importance being a recognition of the belligerents.'[2] He expressed the hope to the *New York Times* that 'the fighting is finished ... and that peace is in sight', adding that he had 'found the leaders in jovial spirits'. Its correspondent reported that 'Eamon de Valera was in exuberant spirits when he met Harry Boland, his secretary, who arrived in the morning from America, and whom he has not seen since he left the United States just before Christmas. Mr. de Valera's manner became as boisterous as that of a schoolboy. His face is usually set in austere lines. Arthur Griffith looked on smiling benignantly.'[3] In a letter to Joseph McGarrity, Harry confirmed that '"the Chief" was very happy to see me again and jumped around like a boy from school'.[4]

Harry's only immediate personal disappointment arose from the debts which his partner had accumulated and failed to settle during Harry's absence from their tailoring business in Middle Abbey Street: 'I know what it means to trust your business to strangers as I have had a rude shock in this regard on my return.'[5] The family welcome was more muted than before, since Kathleen Boland was absent in Connacht throughout his visit, investigating cases of alleged distress on behalf of the White Cross.[6] Such setbacks would quickly have been set aside at Vaughan's Hotel on Monday, 22 August, when Harry attended the wedding of Thomas Bernadine Barry and Leslie Price. Barry, a policeman's son and veteran of the Great War who had gained a fearsome reputation as Commandant of the West Cork Flying Column, included most of the revolutionary élite on his guest-list. Among those photographed on the lawn outside the hotel were Mary McSwiney (grinning indulgently), de Valera (unsmiling, between bride and groom), Collins (head turned coyly downwards), and Harry, dapper in his bow tie, comfortably seated, and rubbing shoulders with a bejewelled Jennie Wyse Power.[7]

The reunion with Michael Collins, though hearty as always, was complicated by the prospect of a man-to-man competition for Kitty Kiernan. Having lost glamorous Helen to a solicitor (Paul McGovern), Collins had transferred his focus to her elder sister. With characteristically forked tongue, he informed Kitty on 21 August that 'Harry is back here this morning. Will that entice you to come to town, to give you that chance to which he is entitled? Do you remember what I said to you about this? I cannot write just now as I am laughing too much at Harry who yarns about things across the Atlantic.'[8] After a week in Dublin, Harry launched the contest in fraternal style by presenting himself unexpectedly at Granard with Collins, Seán McKeown, and Emmet Dalton. Captain Dalton was a congenial novelty in the inner circle, having only recently expunged his previous record of service in the Royal Dublin Fusiliers by joining the IRB and becoming Director of Training in the IRA.[9] The visit filled Harry with optimism:

Hadn't I the cheek of the divil to come to see you last week? – after the rotten manner in which I treated you for the past twelve months. I can never express my sorrow sufficiently to wipe out the reproach of my not having written oftener to you during my American trip. God knows it was not that I had forgotten you! Not a day passed without my thinking of you and the longing of my heart to be with you was such that I could not dare attempt to explain. What a great mercy that you are so forgiving! I could not say a word if you had refused to see me when I called on Sunday last and I can only say I will not offend again.

Thus absolved, he repeated his earlier proposal of marriage, or at least of eternal devotion:

I promise to be so good to you that you will forget my delinquencies of the past, and I will tell you of my love and the great hope that's in me that you and I may go hand in hand thru life. You will remember all I said to you last year. I can only say again that you are the only Girl in the World for me and I will try to prove to you that I love you as a man should love. I know exactly all your emotions and your ways and feel that I could sympathise with you in your sadness and laugh with you in your gladness (I'd better look out or I'll become poetic). . . . Good bye, Sweetheart, write to me and say I am forgiven.[10]

So the cut and thrust of reproach and courtship resumed.

Collins, who a few days earlier had playfully awarded 'the Visitor' a £7 voucher for expenses 'with the compliments of Minister for Finance',[11] initially observed Harry's campaign with wry amusement. As befitted a close friend who was also a practised strategist of seduction, Collins damned his rival with extravagant praise on 29 August, the second night of their visit to Granard. As he informed his 'dear Kitty' two days later, 'I had to talk very very high politics from 10.30 until 2.30 and high politics are very tiresome unless one is in good form. Then to bed, as old Pepys would say, thinking of the previous night when, as I explained to Harry, I stayed up most of the night advocating his claims – isn't that rather nice?'[12] Kitty's temporary withdrawal to Donegal gave Harry an opportunity to make further 'claims': 'I do hope you will enjoy a complete rest among the hills of Donegal. If you see a wee bit of white heather, you might pluck it for me and send it for luck on my Scotch trip.'[13] Her reply was disappointingly mundane: 'I managed to get a bit of heather for you – not so sure that it's the real white heather, but it's the best I could get. ... I am very much looking forward to seeing the American again! and feel sorry that his trip to G. wasn't more pleasant and comfortable last time. But if you give me a chance again, I'll try and make you more comfy and a "whole" bed to yr. self – even in a flat.'[14]

After Harry's return from his 'Scotch trip' as an emissary to Lloyd George, he was to test these promises of improved hospitality by spending another weekend in Granard without the customary retinue of brethren. The latter could scarcely restrain their prurience when they reassembled in Dublin immediately afterwards:

Arrived in town and met 'the bunch' in the Gresham. Gearóid [O'Sullivan] had booked a box for the Gaiety and invited me along, so I went and enjoyed the show O.K.[15] We had a nice supper in the Gresham after the theatre. 'Mopsy', Helen, Gearóid, 'Nuck' Duggan and Mrs, Seán Ó Muirthuile and your humble. Meanwhile many of my pals [?] overtly asked 'How did you (meaning me) get on at Granard?' To all of which I failed to respond. ... Even during the gayest moments of the evening I was all the time thinking of you, Sweetheart, and am certain you and I will be for all time lovers.[16]

Never more alluring than in her absence, Kitty provided essential distraction from the less romantic pursuit of a political compromise, in which Harry quickly became embroiled.

His political re-education under the increasingly discordant tutelage of de Valera and Collins was rapid and intensive, commencing in the Mansion House on the day after his arrival in Dublin. There he renewed acquaintance with de Valera's secretary, Kathleen O'Connell, after an 'important' Cabinet meeting. That evening, 'E[amon] brought H. B. and M. C. home with him. He worked on reply to Lloyd George until the wee small hours of the morning.'[17] Next day, as one of the 124 republicans elected unopposed to the Second Dáil in May 1921, the peripatetic deputy for South Roscommon and South Mayo belatedly resumed his parliamentary career. For a full week he attended private or 'secret' sessions of the Dáil, with a public assembly on Friday 26 August at which de Valera, hitherto merely President of the Dáil, was elevated to presidency of 'the Republic'.[18] Harry's only recorded contributions occurred on that day, after an evening's discussion with de Valera, when he proposed that Collins be approved for further service as 'Secretary of State for Finance'. He also secured election to the Grand Committee, a still-born body designed to maintain the Dáil's business in between plenary sessions.[19] He took no recorded part in the principal business of the session, which was to prepare for the expected Anglo-Irish Peace Conference.

After his nocturnal briefings with de Valera and his excursion with Collins to Granard, however, Harry was sufficiently well versed in the tortuous movement towards a negotiated peace to participate in the impassioned private debate over which revolutionary leader should be allowed to dodge personal involvement in the Conference. On 30 August, as Kathleen O'Connell noted, 'H. B. came out with Chief, remained until next day.'[20] Harry noted the visit in his diary:

30 Aug. Tues. Dublin. With Mick Collins to de Valera. Long sitting to decide as between Chief and Collins as plenipotentiaries.[21]

This was the issue of 'very very high politics' with which Collins hoped to impress Kitty Kiernan, his own appointment being confirmed only after several further meetings at which both leaders protested their unwillingness to serve.[22] Harry also expected to play some undisclosed part in the negotiations, as his own report to Kitty implied:

We had a very fast and pleasant run to town. Mick and I parted at the Wicklow where we lunched. I then visited 'the Chief' and spent the past two days with him discussing the future. I am returning to America at a later date. De Valera is anxious that I remain here pending Peace Conference if and when the Conference takes place.[23]

Less guardedly, he informed Dr. Maloney that 'the Chief is great and was very happy to meet his "Sec." again and is anxious to send me to London!! So do not be surprised if you read that your Little Brother has visited No. 10 Downing St.! Ole John Devoy will take on a new lease of life very soon.'[24] Whether he then expected appointment as a plenipotentiary, secretary, or courier is unclear.

On 1 September, Harry attended an inconclusive meeting of the IRB's Supreme Council, now headed by Collins and evidently divided over the

Ministry's novel espousal of 'external association' between Ireland and the British Empire as the basis for a Peace Conference. This principle, at least superficially at odds with the republican ideal, had been the basis of de Valera's strategy since his awkward confrontation with Lloyd George in mid July:

> 1 Sept. Thurs. Dublin. S. C. Executive[25] debate 'Peace with honor' or War. No decision.[26]

According to the Council's Secretary, Harry also attended a meeting of the full Supreme Council which agreed 'that the influence of the Organisation be directed towards forwarding such a Conference'. De Valera's influence was evident in Harry's reported contribution to one of these discussions:

> At the present time from what I have learned since I came back from America you will not succeed in overthrowing the British militarily. If it is a question between Peace and War, I'm for Peace. If there are negotiations I think 'Mick' should go, and I'll tell you why. In my opinion a 'Gun man' will screw better terms out of them than an ordinary politician.[27]

The alternative that Collins and de Valera should share the burden of representing Irish interests seems to have occurred to nobody. Perhaps at the same meeting, Harry and Collins induced the IRB to endorse his conduct of the Clan na Gael Reorganized, as he triumphantly informed McGarrity: 'You will hear from Field at an early date, all in, as I would desire it to be, and you may rest assured I have been more than vindicated. 'Tis up to you to build up as never before so that we may take full advantage of whatever situation may arise!'[28]

On 4 September, Harry at last had an opportunity to practise in Ireland the oratorical skills that he had developed in America. Along with Ó Murthuile, he accompanied Collins on a motoring expedition into Ulster, where they joined forces with McKeown and the egregious Eoin O'Duffy, the Monaghan surveyor who had become Mulcahy's Assistant Chief of Staff. Every member of the party belonged to the Supreme Council, having been chosen in accordance with O'Duffy's advice to Collins that 'a word from a few of the gudgeons would be better than long flowery speeches'.[29] The visit was marked enthusiastically in Harry's diary:

> 4 Sept. Sun. Armagh. Public meeting with Seán O'M[urthuile] and Micheal Collins. Wonderful gathering. Escort of cars and Thompsons.
>
> 5 Sept. Mon. Clones, Ballybay, Dundalk, Castleblayney, Drogheda. ... Reach Dublin 6 p.m.[30]

The highlight was a mass meeting in the College Grounds, Armagh, where an address of welcome was presented to Michael Collins, MP for South Armagh, by the nationalist majority of the City Council.[31] The party was escorted by over 1,500 Volunteers and auxiliaries, 1,100 Irish National Foresters, 100 bandsmen, 450 cyclists, republican policemen armed with hurleys, and train-loads of supporters from Ulster and the midlands. Although O'Duffy had predicted that 'the meeting will be the biggest ever held in Ulster', the crowd of 7,000 or so compared unfavourably with previous assemblies of the Ulster Volunteers, the Loyal Orange Institution, and the Ancient Order of Hibernians.[32]

In his speech, Harry boasted that Sinn Féin had taken 'up the challenge' of carrying the republican 'doctrine into Ulster', and asserted that Irish freedom had already been 'almost achieved'. As for the Northern parliament, it was 'dying from congenital rickets. (Laughter.)' He looked forward to the imminent triumph of an Irish 'Empire':

They discovered that there was an Empire morally and financially as great, if not greater, than England – an Empire built up all over the world from the emigrants who were driven from the Irish soil. That great Empire was behind them in their present fight, and next January the delegates from that great Empire from all over the world would, if in peace, assemble in Dublin, and if in war in Paris.[33]

Harry indicated that the likeliest outcome of the forthcoming negotiations was peace with honour: 'There was no man in Dáil Éireann who would take peace with dishonour. They could have peace, but the only way to secure peace was to be prepared for war. (Applause.)'[34] This principle worked in Armagh, where the menacing Irish Volunteer presence, in combination with the Royal Black Institution's prudent re-routing of its scheduled procession from a church service to the Protestant hall, restricted the consequent violence to two shoot-ings (one fatal) and a few beatings.[35] The intrepid brethren left Armagh with their honour, and their motorcar, intact. This happy situation was imperilled on the way to Clones, when 'leaden missiles' were hurled at the car by suspected Unionists concealed in a wood, just north of the border near Middletown. Harry and Collins resisted the temptation to deploy 'Col. Thompson', and sped safely to Clones.[36] They 'indulged in endless horseplay, delighted to be together again', and Collins is alleged to have thrown 'the G.S.S.'s boots out of the window' at 3 a.m.[37] The *Irish News* rejoined the party next morning, at St. Joseph's Catholic Hall, 'where they were warmly greeted by many of the leading Sinn Féin and Catholic people' of the town, after which 'Mr. Collins and his friends left for Dublin'.[38]

Following a night in the capital, Harry was on the road again:

6 Sept. Tues. Roscommon. Kathleen, Frank P. [Walsh], Father Finan. Nice reception, great crowd. Leave 10 a.m.

7 Sept. Wed. Athlone. Clonmacnoise and Athlone. I, Frank P., Fintan Murphy, McKeown to camp.[39]

In Roscommon, Harry declared that 'the people of Ireland were anxious to make peace and live in amity with the people of England', but that no deputy would ever sign 'any document that did not secure a lasting and honourable peace'. In Athlone, 'fully two thousand people congregated in the vicinity of the Prince of Wales Hotel' to seek autographs from the visiting celebrities, including two British soldiers who secured McKeown's epigraph saluting these 'friendly Englishmen'. It was McKeown, not Harry, who 'came in for the greatest share of attention'.[40] Harry's ulterior motive in visiting County Longford was to persuade the 'Blacksmith of Ballinalee' to return with him to America, now that Collins was definitely unavailable, in order to prepare Americans 'for the fact that we would not be getting a Republic'. McKeown declined, and Harry was left to defend the Dáil's shifting policy without help from the straightest-spoken of all the 'gudgeons' in the Supreme Council.[41]

On returning to Dublin, Harry regaled Kitty with a selective account of his week's adventures:

Sorry I missed you and M. on Saturday. As a matter of fact we did not leave Dublin until Sunday morning for Armagh, where we had a very strenuous day. ... Michael and party had a very fine meeting at Armagh. We called at Clones, Co. Monaghan on our way home and spent a very enjoyable evening with O'Duffy and Company. We arrived in Dublin on Monday evening at 5 p.m., having motored all the way. I left Dublin on Tuesday morning for Roscommon, and arrived back in town on Wednesday midnight. Some traveller!

He was 'truly happy to have the "official" visit over and done with', but not ready to fully unveil his unofficial activities. He did, however, indicate that 'it may very well be that I shall be in Scotland during the negotiations, and I would very much like to see you ere we go'.[42] On that very day, as Kathleen O'Connell noted, 'M. C. and Harry came at 6.30 to tea and remained until after 11 p.m.' It was perhaps at this meeting that Harry's assignment was determined.[43]

As the sequence of letters about talks and talks about letters stuttered on, while Harry and Collins broadcast their oddly moderate message across the country, alarm grew among diehard republicans. On 7 September, Mary McSwiney told Harry that 'I have been reading your friend Mick's speech in Armagh and don't feel quite pleased with it I must say', being 'much too "safe" on the only point that matters'. She had counted Harry among the waverers ever since their journey home together on the *Olympic*:

I have wondered since I came home if the nonsense you talked on ship-board about 'Dual Monarchy' etc. etc. was spoken from some inside knowledge hidden from the rest of us. I hope not, but if I am alone in Ireland to fight – and I know I won't be – I shall fight to the death against your Dual Monarchies and Government by the Consent of the Governed *within the Empire*. ... If you should be going to London please leave your Dual Monarchy nonsense behind you. Our oaths are to the Republic, *nothing less*. I hope L. G. will make any further parleys impossible.[44]

Indiscreet as ever, Harry passed on her strictures to Collins, whose consequent rebuke prompted further indignation a fortnight later: 'You need not have told your friend Mick that I thought him a compromiser. ... He says he is not and I believe him but I wish people could realise that the Republic means the Republic and nothing less.' She sensed the particular danger of vacillation among those with impeccably republican records, who still had the power to veto any settlement: 'If the "Extremists" won't sanction the Compromise the others won't get it.'[45] Every utterance by key brethren such as Collins and Harry had become a fit object for study and dissection in the feverish atmosphere of Ireland under the Truce.

Though Harry was not among the five plenipotentiaries nominated by the Ministry two days later, his diplomatic prowess was indeed tested by a confidential mission to Flowerdale House at Gairloch on the west coast of Scotland, north of Skye. This was the summer retreat at which Lloyd George conducted his correspondence with de Valera, consulted with his secretariat, and convened skeletal conferences of ministers to give nominal sanction to his Irish strategy. Harry's assignment was to deliver the latest of de Valera's letters to the Prime Minister (accepting his invitation to a conference in Inverness on 20 September), and then to withdraw without any discussion of its contents. Two alternative strategies for publicising the visit had been prepared by Harry in advance, one revealing merely that the letter had been delivered, the other releasing its content at one of two specified hours. The preferred course would be signalled by a telegram reading 'Subject No. 1' (or '2') respectively.[46] His travelling companion was Joseph McGrath, an accountant, also intimate with Collins, who represented North-West Dublin in the Dáil. During the journey to Scotland, Harry was in positive mood, informing his companion that he would soon be returning 'to America to prepare the people for something less than a Republic'.[47] His diary recorded snapshots of their three-day mission:

12 Sept. Mon. Leave Dublin for Scotland with J. McGrath via Manchester and Crewe [*recte*, Crewe and Manchester].

13 Sept. Tues. Gairloch. Meet Lloyd George and Sir Ed. Grigg.[48] Salmon, Sovereign State, Smyrna Turks.[49]

14 Sept. Wed. Inverness. Leave for Crewe 8 a.m. Press mystified. Agree to carry back L. G.'s report to de V. Conference cannot be held. L. G. objects to par. 2, won't call Cabinet.[50]

After waiting for more than two hours, they were greeted by the Prime Minister bearing a salmon in proof of his patience in landing his prey. According to Gerald Boland, 'he told them that they were nice young men, but that he would have preferred to meet a man like Tim Healy'.[51] The emissaries reported to de Valera that Lloyd George had instantly discarded his 'very good humour' on reading the letter, which reasserted the claim made in previous correspondence that his authority was that of one representing 'a sovereign State'.[52] The Prime Minister, who had anticipated a judicious evasion of this principle, exclaimed that 'it won't do, I can't have it, why did he put in the second paragraph? . . . Why could he not leave it at that? I am done, I am done.' As he could not ask the Cabinet to treat with Ireland as an explicitly sovereign state, he proposed that de Valera should be asked either to withhold publication or to take back the letter as if unread, the alternative being cancellation of the proposed conference. After consultation, the emissaries agreed to stop publication (while leaving the letter with Lloyd George), to issue an uninformative communiqué, and to pass on Lloyd George's readiness to accept all but the obnoxious second paragraph as the basis for a conference. Having wired Dublin to confirm 'Subject No. 1', Harry 'explained as best I could with safety on phone from Inverness what had happened'.[53]

Harry's pencilled notes of the meeting convey still more graphically the dramatic force of Lloyd George's protest, and his capacity to win sympathy from his staunchest adversaries. He had 'made more concessions than any British statesman had ever done' and had even 'placed the term Association in his last letter to enable de V. to avail of it to open Conference'. Harry jotted down his exclamations: 'I'm done'; 'No British statesman dare'; 'Protests from sixty supporters'; 'This was Hell'; ' "Celtic Race": he the only man who understood them'. Whereas the emissaries' considered report to de Valera stated merely that they had 'told him we would stop publication', Harry's notes demonstrate that they 'asked time to consider and accepted Mr G.'s proposal to return and submit letter for alteration'.[54] Lloyd George, in his subsequent protest to de Valera, pointed out that he had 'offered to regard the letter as undelivered to me in order that you might have time to reconsider it'.[55] Ministers were informed that 'he (the Prime Minister) had talked very plainly to the two Sinn Féin couriers who came to Gairloch, one of whom was an out and out extremist, and they had both shewed great alarm when it was suggested to them there would be no conference'.[56] Faced with a choice between surrendering to de Valera's convoluted obduracy or to Lloyd George's eloquent pragmatism, McGrath and Harry (perhaps that 'out and out extremist') had chosen the latter.

The outcome of Harry's insubordinacy was his first open breach with the Chief, setting a precedent for de Valera's outrage twelve weeks later when the plenipotentiaries likewise ignored his instructions, yet justified their title, by accepting an agreement that his Cabinet had not in every detail approved.

Under the misapprehension that the emissaries were carrying home his rejected letter, de Valera despatched Robert Brennan to Holyhead to ensure that the document would never re-enter Irish territory undelivered. When told that they 'should not have sent that message', Harry and McGrath 'began to swear' at Brennan and to re-enact Lloyd George's irresistibly persuasive performance. Brennan, a winsome writer but a lifelong apologist for de Valera, attested that when Harry admitted that 'the message was bungled', the President's kindly reply was: 'Don't worry.'[57] He had already rectified the lapse by inducing the Dáil to publish the letter at once in its unexpurgated form, so compelling Lloyd George to 'cancel the arrangements for conference next week at Inverness'.[58] Yet, after a fortnight's further haggling, de Valera submitted a letter of acceptance which omitted the unacceptable affirmation of sovereignty and finally cleared the way for a Peace Conference in London.[59] The outcome vindicated Harry's judgement, but tested his alliance with de Valera to the limit. De Valera's consternation may explain his clumsy withdrawal of Harry's nomination as one of the secretaries to the delegation, when these appointments were debated by the Dáil as the refractory emissaries were returning from Inverness.[60] Yet the jaunty tone of Harry's diary suggests that he viewed the contretemps with more amusement than dismay:

15 Sept. Thurs. Dublin. Meet R. O'B. [Brennan] at Holyhead, Chief at Blackrock. Report written and signed by Joe and me. De V. very mad at non-publication, insists on letter as written – more power to you, de Valera. Conference off.

16 Sept. Fri. Dublin. Go to Navan Races with Joe McG[rath], Austin Stack, Jim Clark.[61] Return to Gresham, meet Collins. Await L. G.'s next move.[62]

Despite de Valera's embarrassing intervention, hope remained for a negotiated peace.

Released from the honour of participating in the conference which opened in London on 11 October, Harry prepared to resume his interrupted mission to the United States. He took time off for two further visits to Granard and a nostalgic excursion to Croke Park for a hurling match on 25 September: 'Leix v. Dublin. McKeown, Collins, Boland.' The smartly uniformed Blacksmith of Ballinalee threw in the ball; Collins presented the medals to the victorious Dubliners; and Harry was photographed standing behind Collins, beaming in his sun-hat (plate 18b).[63] On the following day, he met 'the Chief at Blackrock. Final orders to sail.'[64] His overburdened colleagues in America had been awaiting Harry's return impatiently: Pedlar continued to feel 'very lonesome with you gone and Seán [Nunan] away', while Stephen O'Mara acknowledged 'a great loss to me personally here – I have no one really to consult'.[65] Harry himself, though eager to stay, had been anticipating his recall to America throughout his visit. After just four days in Dublin, de Valera indicated that he might 'have to return to America after negotiations are under way'.[66] By 3 September, as he told Dr. Maloney, he was 'under orders to return to America and may find it impossible to persuade the Ministry to permit me to remain in Ireland so that you may again be troubled with yr. "Young? Brother" coming to you for advice and guidance not to mention mesmerism'.[67] A fortnight later, he was expecting his 'final instructions to stay or go' to be delivered at the Mansion House on 21 September, reflecting that it was 'a quare thing that I have to go away again without my pint and porridge'.[68] He implored de Valera 'to reconsider the question of my returning to America', fearing that 'my usefulness in America is ended' and reminding him 'how bitter is the personal hatred of many Irish Americans to me'. His conclusion was unusually formal: 'Personally I wish to take my place in Ireland in the final phase of Ireland's struggle for freedom.' De Valera was unmoved, emphasising Harry's indispensability in the United States and resurrecting the rustic metaphor with which he had once advocated Collins's removal:

There is a further consideration I am loth to mention. It is unwise to have all our eggs in one basket in the phase about to open. The worst may happen – we must have reserves outside the country, and you have been so closely in touch all through you'll be well fit to head another rally and carry on.

Whether resentment at Harry's display of independence in Gairloch lurked behind this rationalisation is uncertain.[69]

It was not until Friday, 23 September, that the Ministry finally sanctioned his return to America at an annual salary of $10,000 (about £2,000).[70] Harry informed Collins that he had 'no intention of drawing the full salary appropriated to this office and I will, as in the past, draw sufficient to enable me to carry on the work here'. He also arranged that £5 weekly should be deducted for his mother, rather than £3 as before.[71] At last, he was supplied with a set of credentials in Celtic lettering and signed by de Valera, appointing him (in English, Irish, and French) 'as Representative from the elected Government of the Irish Republic to the United States, with all the privileges and authorities of right appertaining to that office'.[72] Six days later, Mr Harry Boland, a 'secretary' domiciled in the United Kingdom and a 'British born subject', secured a British passport valid for two years for travel exclusively to the United States.[73] His departure was as ceremonious as his arrival six weeks earlier:

29 Sept. Thurs. Dublin. Leave Granard for Gresham. Meet Cope,[74] Mick, Liam [Mellows]. Send off by the Fighting Men. Great party, 5 a.m.

30 Sept. Fri. Dublin. Final acceptance of Conference.

1 Oct. Sat. Leave Dublin for Cork. M. Collins and Gerald [Boland] to see

me off. Arrive Cork 11.50. Meet Tom Barry, Donal oge [O'Callaghan], Mary McSwiney, Seán and Annie McSwiney, Barry Egan. Motor to Cobh.[75]

At his farewell supper in Dublin, immediately after another two days of climactic courtship in Granard, Harry was deafened as usual by Collins's party piece (that interminable ballad, 'Kelly and Burke and Shea').[76] Afterwards, he wrote to Kitty in exclamatory vein:

> I have just arrived home! 'Tis 4 a.m. After a joyous and wonderful send off, surrounded as I was by all that is best in our movement!!!, I felt as lonely as an orphan! I am most unhappy, alas! I had your sweet presence before me even when the 'Fizz' and Song was at its height – I had only the remembrance of you and your wonderful smile haunting me.

The festivities had been only slightly spoiled by Harry's decision to share, after all, his most exciting news with Collins:

> I told M. how matters stood atween us; and he, I fear, was most upset. I am not at all sure that I can hope to repeat my impressions of our chat (that is M. and I). I told him as well as I could that you and I are engaged, and further that if he (M.) had not entered into yr. life that I w'd. now have you as my very own Wife. Of course, he was upset and assured me that 'it did not follow if you did not marry me that you would marry him'. Now, Love, let me even at 4 a.m. (having returned to pack my trunk for U.S.A.) say that I want you to come to America at once, at least as soon as you may find it possible.

Harry looked into their future with his customary optimism:

> I told you once what I understood by marriage and named three essentials as necessary and important to happiness. I can quite see that you are rent and torn with conflicting emotions and wonder what is best for you to do as between me and M. Let me offer you an advice! On to-morrow morning (Sunday) after yr. prayers go for a nice walk by the cool roadside and go alone, forget all the romance of having two suitors such as M. and I, ask yourself honestly and fearlessly which of the two wd. you be happier with and which of us you love and feel you could be happy with. Having made up your mind go right ahead and decide to be a one man woman, and may I be the lucky man.

Just to be sure, he took the precaution of mobilising a team of advocates to act in his absence: 'I will ask my Mother to write to you and hope you will come to visit her on your next visit to Dublin. I will also ask Father Shanley to call on you. Of course you will call to see him next week on yr. visit to Dublin for Helen's wedding. Mick will, I have no doubt, press forward his suit as best he can.'[77]

Next day, Harry was again extolling the loyalty of his chivalrous rival:

Mick and I spent the last night together. He saw me home at 2 a.m., and as I had to catch the 7.35 a.m. I bade him goodbye – only to find him at Kingsbridge as fresh as a daisy to see me off. I need not say to you how much I love him, and I know he has a warm spot in his heart for me, and I feel sure in no matter what manner our Triangle may work out, he and I shall be always friends. ... I have now to meet a gang of Corkonians who expect me to call on them ere I leave the Rebel City. So I bid you a fond farewell and, as I can not kiss you with my lips, I do so a million times with the lips of my heart.[78]

This letter again appealed to Kitty to accept his proposal (via a 'wireless' to the *Celtic*), to send her photograph for his 'match or cigarette case', and to join him in the United States despite his pressing state duties:

You will know by now that we have agreed to the Conference, but what may come of it I cannot say. We will know very soon if it is to be Peace or War. If Peace, I will be home in about six months. If War, I shall be in America until Dáil Éireann replaces me, and I would just love to have you come to America where we will spend our honeymoon in perfect bliss!

Despite his misgivings, he left Ireland in buoyant spirits with his reputation and self-confidence only slightly diminished. Yet, as one veteran Sinn Féiner pondered: 'Is Uncle B. crazy again or what is he travelling for?'[79]

Before embarking from Queenstown, Harry spent the first afternoon in October expounding de Valera's plan for 'external association' to the McSwiney family. As Mary's youngest sister Annie recalled three months later:

He said we would have to give up the idea of an isolated Republic for the present anyhow, that it would be such a danger to England that she'd lose every man she had, and every shilling, before she'd agree to an *isolated* Republic, and he said it was only natural after all. ... He said we'd have to have some kind of alliance or association which would satisfy England that we had no desire to ruin her – we only wanted our own rights. ... We discussed what kind of alliance we could have that would satisfy her, but there was *never any* suggestion of compromise on the republican position. It was to be an association of the Republic with England and Canada, etc. And that would be perfectly in harmony with the stainless honour of our Race and the Republic.[80]

In speaking to journalists, Harry concentrated on the forthcoming American Bond Drive, saying little on the situation in Ireland. He assured the *Cork Examiner* that 'the English representatives' at the forthcoming Disarmament Conference could not 'face the American people until they have first made peace with Ireland', without which the Conference would fail just as the League of Nations had failed to win American support. For the *Irish Independent*, the chief 'objects of interest were the two blue Irish terriers indigenous to County Kerry[81] which Mr. Boland was carrying out to the States as presents for friends', and the fact that Harry was observed 'chatting' with the American Consul and Vice-Consul. The latter report alarmed the State Department, which cautioned the Consul against betraying 'a partisan attitude on the part of your office'.[82]

Once on board the *Celtic*, Harry showed 'no reserve in his conversation' with Bishop Phelan of Sale in Victoria, a fellow-traveller with whom he was to share the platform at several mass meetings in the United States. Harry reminisced that de Valera had been alone among his ministers in insisting that the letter delivered to Gairloch should explicitly refer to Ireland as a 'sovereign state'. The 'feeling in the party' was that such an assertion 'would wreck the proposed conference in London'. Harry was also indiscreet enough to state that de Valera's intention in abstaining from the Peace Conference was to leave open the prospect of a non-republican settlement:

> If he went to the conference he could accept nothing less than a Republic, and he knows that a Republic will not be granted. His intention ... is that when the representatives return, having accepted something less than a Republic, he will put that to the Irish people, and if the Irish people are satisfied with it, the idea of a Republic ceases, and the Irish Free State comes into being.[83]

This strategy, seemingly endorsed by the returning envoy, faithfully reapplied de Valera's statement to Sinn Féin's Ard Fheis in 1917 that 'it is as an Irish Republic that we have a chance of getting international recognition. ... We do not wish to bind people to any form of government.'[84] The principle of whether, or under what circumstances, to permit voters to pronounce upon Ireland's constitutional future was to become one of the key sources of contention in 1922. Meanwhile, Harry returned to America not only as the envoy of a Republic, but as the herald of an Irish Free State.

XI

Compromise

THE first to greet Harry Boland when he reached New York on 10 October were special agents from the State Department, masquerading as journalists, who boarded the *Celtic* on arrival and succeeded in interviewing the 'special envoy' in his cabin. There he showed them a 'so-called passport' in a green cover, signed by de Valera and inscribed in French, Irish, and English; but they failed to elicit confirmation that he was also carrying a British passport. Agents Valjavek and Valkenburg then accompanied Harry to the dining saloon, where a physician 'passed subject as physically and mentally admissible'. An immigration official on Ellis Island eventually confirmed that he had indeed presented a British passport properly vised, while the ship's manifest revealed that, under 'nationality', Harry had 'declared himself to be a British subject, and later of the Irish race'.[1]

Harry's arrival, no longer clandestine, was marked with appropriate ceremony by his colleagues:

10 Oct. Mon. *Celtic* at New York. Meet Seán [Nunan], S. M. [O'Mara], [Eugene F.] Kinkead. Address of welcome. All the Boys, Hotel Wolcott.[2]

As he put it to Kitty: 'All my old friends were at the Pier to meet me, and I met with a very hearty welcome. Sunday next I am being welcomed at a great mass meeting in Madison Square Garden, and everything points towards a gathering of twenty thousand people being present.'[3] Meanwhile, he delivered a prepared statement to the waiting journalists in the manner of a diplomat rather than a propagandist: 'What the result of the conference may be I cannot even guess. I do know that Ireland is ready and anxious for peace, and this is equally true of the people of England. I also know that the manhood of Ireland is prepared and ready to defend their country should Britain once more resort to force. ... The final decision rests with England.' By implication, he even looked favourably on Irish membership of a genuine Commonwealth: 'Ireland was not offered equal partnership in the British commonwealth of nations. Canada, Australia, South Africa, New Zealand are free, free to sever their connections with Britain should they so desire, free to control their own fiscal policy, free to build their own navies and to establish their own armies without hindrance from England. The British proposals denied these essentials to Ireland.'[4]

Harry seemed equally moderate and judicious, five days later, when revisiting the scene of his proposal for a 'race vendetta'. Though the crowd in Madison Square Garden was smaller than expected, this was still alleged to be 'the largest and most enthusiastic Irish meeting which has ever been held in that place'. It was followed next afternoon by an even larger meeting in a Brooklyn ball park:

15 Oct. Sat New York. Madison Square mass meeting, twelve thousand extend great welcome. Kinkead v. O'Mara OK. [Amos] Pinchot, Judge [Alfred E.] Tally, Frank P. Walsh, H. Boland all well. . . . Good week's work.

16 Oct. Sun. New York. Mass 11.30. Meeting Clan, reunion Laurel Hall 3.30. Good Brooklyn mass meeting, Ebbet's Field, 5.30, with Frank P.[5]

Harry sent Kitty a platform ticket as a keepsake: 'Had a wonderful welcome last night at Madison Square – was thinking of you all the time and wishing you were with me. Hurry along and enjoy the great Indian Summer in this wonderful land.'[6] John E. Milholland noted his pleasure, remarking to Frank P. Walsh that 'it was a great reception Harry was given, and the very dear boy enjoyed it. Last time he was on the platform with me he proclaimed the "vendetta", you remember, and raised "Ned" generally, but it carried the news of our meeting and our $50,000 collection all over the civilized world, and scared the wits out of "John Bull".'[7] Harry was indeed intoxicated by his own performance as diplomat and orator, magnified by the 'huge acoustiphone' which broadcast his words. He told McGarrity that 'I have changed my mind altogether on the question of my appearing at public meetings, and am convinced that it is absolutely necessary that I be presented with an opportunity to offset the British Dominion propaganda.'[8] Armed at last with his formal credentials of office, Harry even sought, unsuccessfully, to present them at 'an audience' with Charles Evans Hughes, Harding's Secretary of State.[9] After some months off the road, the cavalcade of his first year in America seemed to be rolling again.

As the familiar sequence of Clan reunions, dinners, interviews, consultations, and mass meetings unfolded, Harry remained uncharacteristically on his guard. His initial failure to discountenance the Dominion option had alarmed de Valera, who urged him to 'be careful whilst exposing the fraud that the British have offered Dominion Home Rule to Ireland not to make it appear that Ireland would accept Dominion Home Rule as a satisfaction of her claims. If there should be a breakdown we must take good care that we have not compromised our position so that we could resume again on the old footing.'[10] He instructed Brennan to inform Harry of all English and Irish press reports which 'misrepresented' his speeches. Brennan promptly forwarded a cutting from the *Irish Independent*, highlighting a single sentence from Harry's first speech after his return: 'England, he said, had not offered Ireland an equal partnership within the British Commonwealth.'[11] Harry's response to these reprimands was robust:

Following your instructions, I discussed the British proposals in my speech in Madison Sq. Garden and throughout the country, and my remarks on this question were taken from the *Bulletin*'s analysis of the British offer. I also took the precaution of forwarding copy of my speech to the Under Secretary [Brennan]. I think that the Publicity Dept. of Dáil Éireann should have taken steps to correct the impression conveyed by the New York cable in which one sentence in my speech is reported.[12]

After an appearance at Chicago's Ashland Auditorium on 23 October, the anniversary of Terence McSwiney's death, he gave Kitty a hint of the pressure upon him to avoid further public indiscretion:

I have just returned from a great meeting and all the committee just left me to myself. Seán Nunan and Joe Begley have gone out to 'do the Town'. I have stolen away from the crowd to write to my Sweetheart and to tell her of my love and to ask her once again to come to me. I was the principal speaker at the McSwiney Memorial meeting and 'twas a wonderful gathering. I have to prepare all my speeches carefully now so that I may not prejudice the Peace Parleys.[13]

Throughout the eight-week Peace Conference in London, Harry was largely reliant on reading between the lines of press reports, amplified by rumours, occasional coded cables, and oblique official letters which were at least a week out of date upon reaching Washington. So too were the messages carried by visitors from Ireland, such as James Douglas, who had been instructed by Collins in late October to advise Harry and O'Mara 'that a treaty would be made', which might or might not prove satisfactory to Ireland.[14] Collins's letters made only passing reference to his own part in the negotiations, after conferring for three days: 'This thing is the worst job I have ever been on and the most unsuitable. I suppose we must see it out however.'[15] Harry's mother was equally pessimistic a fortnight later: 'Well, we are all wondering how the Conference will end. Most people are very doubtful and expect it to end like the Convention in Trinity College.[16] God send we may have peace with honour.'[17] Harry's own letters to Kitty were brighter in tone:

The first week of the Conference in London has come and gone, and I am pleased to learn that all goes well so far. We shall soon know how the wind blows, whether the storms of war shall once again rage throughout our country or the gentle breezes of peace shall waft joy to our glorious land.

Now that I am down to my work I am happy and content and I have a very full programme before me and will be going at top speed from this day until I hear the final word from home – God grant we shall soon have won the Freedom of Ireland.[18]

On 9 November, however, Joseph McGarrity awoke from an unpleasant dream in which Harry and he had watched a shipload of 'dear friends of Ireland' drown, after their boat had been deliberately 'run headlong into the wharf or pier with such force that she overturned and sank'. A few hours later, his dream was seemingly corroborated by a cable from an agent in Berlin (John T. Ryan), alleging that 'only great pressure on trustees in L[ondon] and directors at home will save surrender of free title to Old Homestead. All trustees weakening including M. C. Topman [de Valera] stands firm and strong. Correct official from inside.' When McGarrity dictated the cable over the telephone to New York, Harry exclaimed 'He's a liar', and declared that 'to send it to London would be an insult to the men there'. However, he agreed to alert Robert Brennan to the rumour: 'I need not comment further on this. It might be well to put a muzzle on some of your representatives.'[19] This response suggests that his faith in the plenipotentiaries was unshaken.

When accrediting Harry as Ireland's envoy, the Ministry had also recommended a dozen candidates to assist O'Mara and himself in promoting the new Bond Drive in the United States. These included four 'advance guards', among them Fr. Michael O'Flanagan and 'Madame' Constance de Markievicz.[20] On 20 October, Harry misused a 'special telegraphic address' in the hope of securing 'Madame, McKeown and O'Flanagan immediate', stating that O'Mara found it particularly 'necessary to have a man like McKeown, or of his type, here during the Bond Drive'.[21] Doubtless to the Blacksmith's relief, de Valera ruled that 'I am afraid it will be impossible to let McKeown go.' Though Madame agreed to travel, it proved impracticable to get her the Polish passport to which she was thought to be entitled, as she was uncertain of her absent husband's nationality and even of the year of their wedding, and had 'of course' failed to register as an alien in her own land.[22] The only luminary to reach the United States was Fr. O'Flanagan, who was encouraged to make his fifth trans-Atlantic trip by the payment of £100 in advance, provision of a first-class cabin on a vessel of his choice, and suitable arrangements for his 'reception' in New York.[23] This outcome infuriated Stephen O'Mara, who was left to share the oratorical burden with Harry and the turbulent priest. He told Collins that 'coming alone he has the appearance of coming in a representative capacity. This is bad ... owing to his collar.'[24] Despite O'Mara's subsequent warning that 'business [was] in danger owing to your failure send right material', the American delegation was left to fend for itself without imported stars.[25] Though Muriel McSwiney wished that 'heaps more people' could assist the 'excellent' Harry, indeed, that '*every-one* should help him', the mission remained undermanned.[26]

The three linked strands of Harry's political strategy were to allay American distrust of the Anglo-Irish negotiations, to maintain public interest in the Irish cause through a second Bond Drive, and to press American politicians to withhold their support for international naval disarmament in the absence of a satisfactory Irish settlement. On the eve of his return, the Ministry had decided to instruct its American envoy 'not to apply for representation at the Disarmament Conference at present', so ruling out a re-enactment of the Paris fiasco in 1919.[27] As interest in Ireland waned during the Truce, for want of a clear focus for American moral outrage, Harry warned that Lloyd George was likely to 'receive the greatest reception ever tendered to a public man from England' if he attended the forthcoming Naval Disarmament Conference in Washington. Without a strong counter-propaganda, 'we are likely to be lost sight of in the popular demonstrations in his favor'.[28] This prediction was never put to the test, as Lloyd George remained at home.[29]

Harry also drafted two alternative letters to President Harding, the first declaring 'that the Republic of Ireland will not be bound by any understandings, covenants, or contracts which may be entered into by the British delegates', whereas the second revived the demand for Irish participation in the Conference.[30] Neither letter was sent, Harry's appeal for cabled instructions being ignored apart from de Valera's observation that any demand for Irish representation would 'make us ridiculous in the eyes of the world'. Bruised by this rebuff, Harry reported on 27 October that 'we are cudgelling our brains to discover the best method to keep the Irish cause before the American people' at a time when, 'with the negotiations going on in London, all public men here are very chary of taking action'. In order to 'keep Ireland a live issue during the Conference', he proposed opening the Bond campaign in Illinois and Washington, DC, four days after its inauguration. He added sarcastically that 'we presume we will be advised if you consider it necessary to call a halt to our activities'.[31] Despite the Ministry's lukewarm reaction to his strategy, Harry pressed ahead with his customary vigour, lobbying Congressmen, Senators, and the American Federation of Labor,[32] in his vain but heroic endeavour to raise $20,000,000 and manipulate relations between the great powers. His campaign was not an unqualified failure, since Lloyd George's determination to reach a settlement in Ireland was undoubtedly reinforced by his fear of a breach between Britain and America at the Washington Conference.[33]

With perhaps feigned reluctance, Harry began to repay the hospitality so long lavished on him through welcoming banquets and political dinners. As he explained to his parsimonious Chief:

> I am sharing an apartment with Mr O'Mara in Washington and last week we entertained at dinner a group of official people, and I have decided during this Disarmament Conference to do a little entertaining. Personally, I am not favourable to this activity; most people here in Washington agree that it is most necessary so I have at last surrendered.[34]

The culmination of this culinary campaign was a feast for wealthy well-wishers held on 8 December, two days after the signature of the Anglo-Irish Treaty in London:

27 Nov. Sun. Washington. Rock Creek, [P. A.] Drury's house re proposed $1,000 dinner.

28 Nov. Mon. Washington. Leave for New York 1 p.m. Meet Bourke Cockran who agrees to preside at Bond dinner Washington. Dr. Maloney.

1 Dec. Thurs. Washington. Call at Senate, meet Cockran. Arrange with O'Mara on invitations. Drury, Bishop [T. J.] Shahan, Bourke Cockran.

2 Dec. Fri. Washington. Final arrangement for Bond dinner.

8 Dec. Thurs. Washington. Dinner re Bond Campaign. Bourke Cockran, Senator [Thomas] Walsh, other speakers hilarious.[35]

Whereas the first Bond Drive had painstakingly solicited small subscriptions from innumerable 'plain people', valuing their collective goodwill more than their individual wealth, its successor adopted the less laborious stratagem of seducing selected millionaires. The envoy's assimilation into American political culture seemed complete.

Harry's imperturbable optimism could not conceal the mission's inability either to sell Bonds on the previous scale or to assert control over funds raised by other Irish-American bodies. The second Bond Drive, lacking the vast and cumbersome local organisation of the first, was intended to concentrate on one state at a time in order to maximise publicity. Harry believed that 'this working of state by state is altogether the better plan and we feel sure that should war be forced upon the Irish people again American sympathizers will raise the required amount'. The Illinois organisation was 'well nigh perfect', with 'a scheme of organisation comparable only to the Sinn Féin Organisation in the general election'. After a fortnight's campaign, 'they have some $350,000 in bank. ... Fr. Cahill is so confident that he will raise his quota of $1,720,000 that he has wagered a $1,000 bond by the result. Economic conditions in this country are very, very bad, and it is truly wonderful the response we have met with in our appeal.'[36] The priest lost his wager, though Illinois raised all but $70,000 of the paltry $622,720 yielded by the second Republican Loan.[37] Yet Harry's diary suggests that he remained oddly complacent:

12 Dec. Mon. New York. Meet Nicholas Brady who is anxious to secure Bonds of Free State for National City Bank. Nothing succeeds like success.

13 Dec. Tues. Washington. Arrival of Stephen [O'Mara] from Chicago. Half million dollars in bank.[38]

A vastly greater sum, over $5,000,000, had been raised by the relief committees associated with the Irish White Cross, which continued to resist Harry's attempted dictation.[39] His fractious relationship with the White Cross is illustrated by an attempt to secure compensation for the wife of Paul Cusack, the Granard Volunteer, internee, draper, and stylist for the Kiernans. Having raised her case with a leading American organiser in a 'conversation at the Gresham',

Harry scarcely expected that White Cross officials would discover 'some difficulty' requiring the intervention of a 'special investigator'.[40] In late November, he admitted that 'up to date we have not been able to reconcile differences with the White Cross organization here. Our proposals to them were not met in the spirit we anticipated, and as it is imperative that we safeguard our generous friends in America, we have not been in a position to endorse the White Cross.' Instead, he appealed to those raising and distributing relief to switch their connection to Mrs Mary McWhorter's Celtic Cross, which had 'agreed to send all their money through our Fiscal Agent and he in turn will forward it to Ireland to be used ... for the Prisoners' Dependents' Fund'.[41] For Harry and Stephen O'Mara, 'relief' remained a political instrument, undesirable unless raised under their direction and consigned exclusively to approved republicans.

Even within the Clan Reorganized, resentment was sparked by the mission's insistence on controlling and auditing all appeals on behalf of Ireland. During Harry's absence in Ireland, O'Mara raised the ire of a Chicago organiser by demanding a full account of receipts and disbursements at an annual picnic 'under the auspices of the United Irish Societies, which is the public name we use here. ... If O'Mara or any of the rest is going to dictate to us, or deny us the right to raise money in the name of the Irish Republic, we will be unable to give the financial aid that has been requested.' The writer informed Joseph McGarrity that 'a few young men' recently arrived from the IRB had 'been trying to make big fellows of themselves by sending money to Harry Boland' after picnics and matches at Gaelic Park, even daring to suggest that 'the officers of the U.I.S. were grafters and none of the money would be used for Ireland'.[42] On his return, Harry confirmed that 'as a result of the DÁIL decision to stop all unauthorized collection of money in the name of Ireland, you will find it very difficult to take up subscriptions for the Clan through public functions such as dances, concerts, etc. You will have to find some way out of the difficulty.' Clearly confident that such a way could be found when the Republic was in need, he then reminded McGarrity of his promise to present de Valera with a 'suit of clothes (brown)', adding that 'maybe the Pennsylvania A.A.R.I.R. would like to buy a good American motor for the President'.[43]

The Clan Reorganized had collected $106,000 by late October, allowing a steady flow of cheques from the Clan to the 'Home Organisation' through an indulgent banker who allowed withdrawals 'from the other side' on cheques deposited in New York.[44] Just before leaving America, Harry took the precaution of depositing $60,000 of Clan funds in a Washington bank under his own name, with a view to handing it over to the IRB 'when the R.D. [Revolutionary Directory] of the Clan-na-Gael and Mr. Boland are satisfied that the money will be devoted by the Irish Republican Brotherhood towards the realization of an Irish Republic'.[45] The traffic in fraternal funds was not entirely east-bound, for Harry also 'decided in behalf of the home Organization' to present McGarrity with $20,000 in the vain hope of rescuing his *Irish Press* from closure.[46]

Harry's diplomatic dignity did not interfere with his clandestine enterprises, as the IRA and IRB systematically abused the Truce to equip themselves for any resumption of war. Using his playful new *nom de guerre*, 'Toddles', Harry bombarded Brugha and GHQ with price-lists for 'hardware', names of agents in both America and Ireland, and substantial consignments of arms and ammunition. His last day in Ireland had not been solely devoted to emotional farewells: 'While in Cork, I took the liberty of securing a half-dozen names which I have with me; I know from my experience of two hours in the city that there can be no difficulty in getting addresses in Cobh.' He admitted to Brugha that the quoted price of .303 ammunition seemed 'extraordinarily high', pleading 'that our position here does not make it possible to secure estimates from many firms. We can only deal in very limited circles.'[47] When Brugha continued to torment him over the irregular purchase of the Thompsons, Harry assured him that virtually all of his debt had been repaid from the 'Refugee Fund' into the American 'Reserve'. Contributions were still 'coming in steadily although we have decided to close it down'. While most of the guns remained in custody for the time being, he had despatched 106 of the 158 Thompsons ordered in March which had not been seized at Hoboken. Harry reminded Brugha in late November 'that we have been pretty effective in supplying you with materials during the past few months', and that a new system of communications would enable them 'to deliver to you all the material you ask to purchase'.[48]

Throughout Harry's last spell in the United States, he was no longer immediately responsible for arranging the purchase and transmission of arms. During his absence in September, this task had been assigned by Liam Mellows (as Director of Purchases) to Liam Pedlar, now grandly described as the Republic's 'Military Attaché' in New York. He was authorised to spend $50,000 on ammunition, and supplied with an 'elaborate scheme' (devised by Seán Nunan) for packing up 121 Thompsons in bales of cotton waste for delivery to Cork.[49] On 2 November, Pedlar was ordered to 'suspend all operations in connection with the Purchase Department until further notified', in execution of Mulcahy's undertaking 'that during the period of the Truce no attempts shall be made to import munitions into Ireland'.[50] Harry and his colleagues in both America and Ireland shamelessly flouted this agreement. On 19 November, an enigmatic entry appeared in Harry's diary: 'New York. Hearty sails for Ireland on S.S. *Baltic*.'[51] Shortly afterwards, Mellows promised to co-operate in a scheme for sending five trunks on the *Baltic*'s next voyage to Cork, where they would be collected with the help of a friendly sailor by a returned emigrant, Edward J. Hearty of Bridge Street, Dundalk. Each trunk would contain from 1,500 to 1,800 rounds of ammunition, wrapped in 'old clothes lying in his house' in the United States.[52] The story was nicely embellished by Kathleen Boland: 'A Mr. Harty [*sic*], who originally came from Dundalk, was bringing his furniture from America to Cork, as he intended to settle in Ireland. His piano and settee were stuffed full of arms, and the furniture was claimed by Mick's friends in Cork who distributed the arms among the Volunteers.'[53] Harry's negotiations with American shipping lines had at last secured the 'safe ships' needed for the undetected transmission of arms and agents.

Despite lack of enthusiasm at GHQ, Harry sent a trickle of Irish-American Volunteers to reinforce units throughout Ireland. Though most of the ten men listed in despatches to Collins were evidently returning emigrants, they included at least one American citizen, a former captain in the United States army, and several Clansmen.[54] At least ten companies of the Irish Republican Volunteers of America continued to meet in Pennsylvania, their assemblies being openly advertised in McGarrity's newspaper.[55] While in Ireland, Harry had also discussed a scheme for mobilising resigned members of the RIC, whereby 'all abroad could be registered in the event of active support coming over', upon the 'resumption of hostilities'.[56] Though little came of these preparations, Harry was to make much of them during the last day of the Dáil's debate on the Treaty:

No one knows better than my friend, Michael, that there were five thousand men in America ready to come to fight in Ireland, and they couldn't come as a foreign legion because it was against American laws (laughter). MR M. COLLINS: Now you're talking. MR BOLAND: But they were offered, and they came, and they fought. Just as President de Valera got back to Ireland, these men got back, and many of them did get back and they fought.[57]

A handful of Harry's Volunteers may have come and fought, but they conquered nothing.

The spectre of a 'race vendetta' against the English in America seemed embarrassingly anachronistic in this last phase of Harry's American mission. While he was steaming towards Ireland in mid August, his fellow-Gael J. J. Walsh had revived the proposal in the Dáil, urging 'a more active campaign against enemy property in America which he believed would expedite their liberation'. This provoked a flurry of objections from deputies as diverse as Seán Milroy, Kathleen Clarke, and Liam Mellows. Mellows denounced his suggestions as 'all sheer nonsense', ridiculing the misplaced faith in America's '20 million Irish' who were mainly 'Irish of such a kind that they did not recognise it themselves', and pointing out that 'they could not expect more from America than from their own people at home'. Mellows was supported by de Valera:

THE PRESIDENT said the suggested action in America would be wholly impossible and wrong. It would put public opinion against them. They should remember that those who were really in favour of Ireland would not amount to more than four or five millions. They could not judge the feeling of America from the crowd of 20,000 who might attend a special meeting in New York. ... There were limits and narrow limits on which they could operate.[58]

After Harry's return to America, Frank Walsh passed on a letter from a 'Mr. Patrick Lydon, of Louisville, Kentucky, who seems to be a very sensible and spirited old Irishman. I thought it would interest you on account of the elaborate extension of your "vendetta" idea.' Harry enjoyed 'the letter from the Kentucky "feudalist", which I return with thanks. Now, of course, I'm a "constitutionalist". Very sincerely yours, Harry Boland.'[59] The envoy, ever the vendettist at heart, had become a ruefully self-conscious apologist for compromise.

The chief lever of Harry's power remained the Clan na Gael Reorganized, whose relative weakness in New York was counterbalanced by fairly strong support in Massachusetts and Pennsylvania. In late 1921, of the 246 Camps throughout America under McGarrity's control, these three states accounted in turn for 38, 55, and 85.[60] Despite Harry's belief that he had secured unqualified support for this body from the IRB, Collins and the Supreme Council still hoped for renewed co-operation with Devoy's organisation and prevaricated over formalising the alliance with McGarrity. A week after his return, Harry urged Collins to 'hurry along ... letters as per decision of S. C.' Six weeks later, the letters of 'official recognition' for the Executive of the Clan Reorganized were still 'eagerly awaited': they were never to be delivered. The Clan Reorganized and the IRB retained their joint reponsibility for 'communications', but by late November Harry 'thought it advisable not to send materials to the Organization and to charge the Defence Department with any materials collected by Organization'.[61]

As always, the Clan was riven by factions, though Harry's old antagonist Jeremiah O'Leary was eventually outmanoeuvred: 'Jeremiah A. O'Leary retires, endeavours to place onus on me for so doing.'[62] Factionalism, endemic in all secret societies, coexisted with the high-minded pursuit of fraternal unity. When reinforcing O'Mara's prohibition of independent collections on money 'in the name of Ireland or of the Republic of Ireland', McGarrity reminded the brethren that 'the sole and only purpose of our Order is to enable the People of Ireland to make their country independent by physical force'. He also insisted on displaying public solidarity between the Clan and the far larger American Association, implying that any conflicts could be quietly resolved by the Clan in its own favour: 'Districts and Camps are warned that the only rivalry between our Order and the [A.]A.R.I.R. is over our mutual love of Ireland. Where our interests seem to clash, our Order, with its superior discipline and power to direct and claim obedience from chosen leaders, should, when necessary, co-operate with the public association.' Brethren should 'discount all reports of settlement or compromise', recognising that 'Ireland is sovereign, and by our redoubled efforts we will keep her so.'[63] Through their allegiance to a

Republic personified in the mystical unity of initiated brethren, Harry and his comrades imagined that they could transcend the ever more evident tensions and practical disputes fostered by the 'peace process'.

Unlike many of his associates, such as Mellows and de Valera, Harry had never lost his zest for American life. In a rather stilted attempt to entice Kitty to America, he shifted his focus from the pedestrian pleasures of Washington to the thrills of Manhattan:

> I'm going for a ramble thru Potomac Park with Joe Begley. We are alone here, as O'Mara left for Chicago on yesterday and Mrs O'Mara is in New York. Writing of New York reminds me of you, it is a city with a wonderful charm all its own, a city of strong appeal to youth, full of joy and vivacity and, unlike other great cities, there is not that close alignment of poverty and riches which obtains in cities like London, Dublin or Belfast. I know you will love it and I can see you now, either strolling on Broadway doing the shows, or treading the plutocratic Fifth Avenue in open eyed amazement, or, again, enjoying to your heart's content the wonderful roof gardens, with the orchestra dispensing the latest dance music, what time the guests are tripping the light fantastic, men and women old and young, gay and grave, all of them dancing, ever dancing.

In case even this prospect failed to please, he turned back to contemplating Washington once transformed by the forthcoming Disarmament Conference: 'I wish you would come at once and we could then have a wonderful time here during the Disarmament Conference, when the Representatives of All Nations will foregather in this city – the Conference will last two months or more and I do not expect to hear anything final from Ireland for at least two months.'[64]

Meanwhile, Harry failed to resist numerous social diversions:

> 12 Oct. Wed. New York. 11.45 Jacks, Baseball World Series. Columbus Day.
>
> 31 Oct. Mon. Cleveland. Bedford Races.
>
> 4 Nov. Fri. Washington. McSwiney. Ramble with Stephen M. [O'Mara] thru Potomac Park 'Pedestrianisation'.
>
> 19 Nov. Sat. New York. Meet Miss Curran with Joe Begley, agree to give dinner in honor of Joe's engagement!!![65]
>
> 21 Nov. Mon. New York. Arrive 7 a.m. office. Pedlar clears. Secure wines for dinner.
>
> 22 Nov. Tues. Washington. First dinner of Mission. Great success.
>
> 24 Nov. Thurs. Thanksgiving. Washington. Meet Pittsburgh Delegates at Washington. Join fox hunt, 5 hours in rain. Fox shot.
>
> 2 Dec. Fri. Washington. Ride in Rock Creek.[66]

His appetite for physical exercise had revived, as he boasted to Kitty in mid October: 'I'm joining an Athletic Club here and hope to opt into great form again – a few weeks' training will make me slim and fit. I will not rest until I can do the hundred yards in ten and a half, and the mile easy.'[67] Perhaps in need of yet another rest cure as a result, he spent the last weekend of that month in Chaquin Falls, Ohio, though by the Sunday he was back in Cleveland attending a public meeting at the Hippodrome.[68]

In this period, he developed a close friendship with Stephen O'Mara and his family, taking a particular interest in his wife's sister, Kitty O'Brien from Limerick. His letters to Kitty Kiernan included several sly references to her namesake:

> During my absence Mr O'Mara was in charge at Washington and did very well. Mrs [Nance] O'Mara is a very lovely and charming girl and has made a great hit here. She has her sister with her for company and her name is Kitty! and like all Kittys she is lovely. We were out tonight sightseeing and I was thinking how nice 'twould be if you were here.

> Mr and Mrs O'Mara have taken an apartment in Washington and I am to share it with them. This will suit me very well, and I will not be compelled to live in hotels. Of course I will be lonely until I know you are coming, and I will not give you an hour's rest until you have landed here.

> I am sharing an apartment with Mr and Mrs O'Mara and I will be very much more comfortable with them than I have ever been during my American trip. Mrs O'Mara's sister is with her as companion and we are sure to have a good time together. Watch me when you arrive and note what a wonderful dancer I have become?[69]

On 10 December, Harry's diary recorded a poignant moment: 'Play my first golf, with Miss O'Brien and Mary Hearn.'[70] On Christmas night, Mrs O'Mara and her sister were in the party which gathered with Harry, Liam Pedlar, and Joseph Connolly for dinner at the Pennsylvania Hotel in New York.[71] As Harry prepared to leave for Ireland, he received a touching valedictory letter from Kitty O'Brien in Washington:

> Dear Harry, Such a magician as you are! My perfectly beautiful golf sticks are shining at me from the corner, and still I'm not used to them. Jim F. had quite a job persuading me they were mine – I thought he was making some kind of mistake – you kind, kind, kindest man! I simply cannot thank you in any sort of words for all your spoiling of me, and all your thoughtfulness. But this time of course I should be lecturing you – only my lovely golf sticks have so entirely rejoiced me that I'd be an ungrateful brute if I did. But still such extravagance over this good-for-nothing is very wicked. I've been testing all the sticks in the hall and you'll

be glad to hear that they are 'perfect for me'. And with that de luxe bag to carry them in, I certainly ought to look a great golfer, anyway. Please goodness we'll have a game together very soon. I'm going to try my new outfit on the Potomac Links tomorrow with Michael and Jamesie. You never knew how much I loved you – did you, Harry? – until you started going away. What a wet, red-eyed object I was today! Ah well – I'm not the only unhappy female who will weep for the Irish ambassador this week. ... My love and very best wishes to the three of you, and once more, dear Harry, my very inadequate 'thank yous' to the kindest person I know – Yours – Kitty.[72]

His sportive yet sentimental admirer, under the more severe name Kate O'Brien, was to become a much censored novelist and in due course an icon of Irish lesbianism.[73]

Harry's dalliance was doubtless encouraged by his growing frustration with the other Kitty, whose sole communication for two months after his return had been a radiogram sent on 8 October: 'Hope you arrived safely. Writing. Love Kittey.'[74] In his impatience to win her consent, he mobilised his mother and friends as well as his pen. It proved all too easy to convert courtship into another Congressional lobbying campaign. Kate Boland, for whom rejection of her flawless son was inconceivable, had sent Kitty a sadly inapposite letter while Harry was still in transit:

My dear Miss Kiernan, Or shall I call you Kitty? As Harry tells me you are engaged to be married to him, allow me to congratulate you, and to wish you every joy and blessing God can bestow on you both, for a better son never lived than Harry, also a loving brother, and I am confident he will be just as good a husband, for you know the old saying 'a good son makes a good husband'. Well, I feel sure he will be blest in his choice of a wife. Though I've not yet met you I have heard about you, and Kathleen tells me she has met you and I don't wish to flatter you with all the nice things she said about you. Well, dear, I hope to meet you next time you are in town, and sincerely trust you will come up to the Crescent so that we can know each other. Just let me know when you are coming to Dublin in case I might be out, which I would not wish for anything. Harry's auntie and Kathleen join me in love and congratulations, and also hope to see you ere long in Dublin. Very sincerely yours, K. Boland, future mother-in-law.[75]

Four weeks later, Kate informed her son that this 'very nice letter' had elicited no response, having perhaps 'gone *astray*' through Kitty's preoccupation with the wedding of her sister Helen. It was also possible that Harry had chosen the wrong woman: 'Your only fault is you have too much heart, and I pray Almighty God, that whoever you marry will be worthy of you in every way.'[76] Another advocate of dubious value was Emmet Dalton, who told Harry that 'I had a top-hole time at Helen's wedding and it was a huge success – I succeeded in getting "tight" twice that day and since then I have been good occasionally. Your lady looked "top-hole" and spoke of you to me in a most sentimental way – bless her.' As a Secretary to the delegation, Dalton had since been 'throwing my weight about in London. But really I am having a most awfully busy time – what with looking after Mick and arguing with Churchill and [Admiral, 1st Earl] Beatty I am half dead.'[77]

For a few weeks after his return, Harry remained confident that his suit would be accepted and that Kitty would soon join him in America:

I will not go to California until you come, and, as there is a pressing demand for me out there, I put it up to you as a National Question to come at once. Seán Nunan is in bed in the next room and desires remembrance to you. I bid you good night, Sweetheart.

Seán Nunan and all the 'boys' here are in great shape and are, of course, interested in you. I have not dared to tell them of my great hope, and I will spring your coming as a great surprise.

I cannot express how anxious I am to know what way you feel about me and I am hopeful that your letter will tell me that you are very happy and have bought the Ring and further that you intend to wear it. . . . I am going to dinner to-night at Frank P. Walsh's home and I'm sure to be bombarded with all sorts of questions . . . I hope Helen will send me a wee piece of wedding cake so that I may sleep on it and dream of my own sweet Girl: You! I'll never be happy again until I claim you for my very own, you, most elusive of all the 'Restless Sex'. I'm planning all sorts of delights for you when you arrive and we shall be very, very happy, here for a little while, and then home to a Free Ireland to be for ever happy. Write soon and often to me, á lenaibh mo croidhe [child of my heart]. I am ever and always dreaming of you.[78]

As Kitty's silence grew ever more ominous, the tone of Harry's letters modulated from serenity to plaintiveness, culminating in a bewildered screech:

I want you to make up your mind at once. What is the use of hesitating and been [sic.] unsettled in your mind? Here you are facing the Crisis in your life: 'Be Brave and Fear Not.' Don't you know right well that you and I were made for each other? I love you, I respect and worship you, I will be able, D.V., to protect and guard you, and to maintain you, at least in comfort. Knowing your every word and fancy I will, out of the very love I have for you, make yr. life very happy, and we can travel down the path of life together hand in hand in love and truth. If I knew you felt towards me as I do towards you, and was satisfied that I had your love, I would be happy, sublimely so, even if I had to suffer separation from you for years.

Ten ships carrying mail have arrived during the past ten days without a letter for me from you; I'm nearly vexed!

My darling, I have just returned from a great mass meeting. I am now in haste to a dinner with the elect of Cleveland! I have asked Seán Nunan to hold the crowd in the next room so that I may write to say I am thinking of you with love – thirty days today I sailed from Ireland – and not even a line or a postcard from you. God forgive you.

Kitty, Why don't you write to me? Even if you have nothing to say you can at least write and tell me to go to Hell!!![79]

Under this bombardment, Kitty sought and secured solace from Collins, with whom she was in daily, if sometimes fractious, correspondence throughout the Peace Conference. Her letters indicate that the contest was unequal from the start: 'I know how you feel about the Harry business. ... It is wise what you say about H. etc. I haven't written yet. ... It was obvious without my saying a word to him. The conditions weren't the same with our agreement. I told H. I didn't love him, and he was prepared to risk it with the idea that I might grow to love him, and I think I told you all the other little things before.'[80] Harry's attraction lay in his natural talent as a lover and his obvious devotion, which offered a 'splendid foundation' against future neglect: 'Fellows keep young too long, girls get old too quickly (not me!).' As she told Collins, whose constancy seemed more doubtful: 'That's why I even entertained the idea that I could ever possibly marry H., and he knows this too. I may be wrong but I think he is capable of deeper affection (for me) than most men, but he also knows that I don't love him – it's no effort for him to be a great lover and of course no thanks.'[81]

As Harry's pursuit intensified, Kitty's response was retreat: 'If only H. – and his friends – would stop storming Heaven with his prayers, I wouldn't be getting unhappy and such mixed and peculiar feelings. ... When he and his friends *know*, they'll have to stop, and pray for you and me (if they are so fond of me) – you may think me silly, perhaps I am, but there is some queer pressure, and it's *not* Harry's letters but something strange.'[82] The solution, for Kitty but not for Collins, was a formal engagement. For Collins, enigmatic as ever, Harry's campaign had sinister overtones: 'One thing about H. – what you call storming is just what I called "unfair" – and if it is so, I am right. He tried to get every advocate – tried to show that it was so, whether it was or not. I feel sometimes like saying a strange thing about it – tell you some time what it is. Of no importance though.'[83] Whatever personal insight lurked behind this rumination, it is clear that the contest for Kitty was no longer a friendly tussle between brothers but the origin (or perhaps symptom) of a deepening mutual distrust.

Kitty alerted Collins to Harry's every countermove, reporting and sometimes passing on his messages: 'Must really write Harry soon, got this yesterday. Poor Harry, he's getting used to me at last, and seems quite happy now T.G.!'[84] The absent suitor seemed tame and dependable by comparison with the elusive Collins, with whom she shared a secret 'wildness' and expressed a love which was 'there, (no Harry), and only for you'. She veered between exclaiming 'what Bohemianists we are, after all', and yearning for the certainty and respectability of a public declaration.[85] She told Collins that a friend had 'whispered to me when alone that she heard "I was married to a gun", and I said, "and would you believe it?" Of course, she says, "It must be Harry Boland." Her sister heard I was *mared* to you, as you say. I had to smile, and say I never heard that before, although I believe it's a common report.'[86] In retrospect, she believed that her internal commitment to Collins had occurred on the very day of Harry's return to America, after a period of genuine indecision:

> It was later when I realised. I fought it successfully for a short time, then I decided, if it is a question of marriage (two nights before Helen's wedding, on the stairs and the night following it, when you really wanted me), why not marry the one I really love, and what a cowardly thing of me to be afraid to marry the one I really want, and who loves me just as well as any of the others I had thought of marrying.[87]

At last, Kitty expressed some, but evidently not all of these sentiments to Harry in a lost letter which he interpreted with characteristic buoyancy:

> Kitty a Croidhe [dear heart], I'm very happy to have your very nice and very, very welcome letter. I now realise that you have acted exactly right and you will excuse the panicky letters I wrote you. Of course you are right to take a full and deliberate survey of your own heart and mind ere you decide on a matter so vital to your future life, and I for one would not wish to rush you into a contract which is to mean so much to you. ... Looking back on my own actions during the past two months, I'm well satisfied that you were perfectly right in keeping calm and giving careful consider-ation to my passionate proposals – ('tho' you might have written). I agree to wait three months, or just as long as you wish to satisfy your own conscience, and I can only say that I would not be happy unless you were satisfied and confident that you could reciprocate the love I bear you. I have been very miserable during the past few months. Your letter has made me very happy again and I pray you will write to me just when you feel like it. I was prepared to hear the worst from you and now feel like a man reprieved.[88]

The reference to a stay of execution for three months suggests that Kitty, for all her protestations of commitment to Collins, still felt the need for a life-line across the Atlantic. Meanwhile, the Kiernan sisters may have contemplated another romantic realignment, with Maud taking over Harry from Kitty just as

Kitty had inherited Mick from Helen. Not long after sending his ecstatic letter of submission to Kitty, Harry received a warm invitation from 'Mops' in Granard:

> Even though I did not write you, you were not forgotten. I thought of you very often, but somehow I could not write you, as I did not nor do I yet know how things stand; but we are friends, Harry, ain't we? Well, everything in this large city is just the same as ever. The Hotel is nearly ready to live in, so when you come back again we will have somewhere for you to sleep, not three in a bed. ... Helen's wedding went off very well, but we missed your happy face. She is sending you some of the cake, if she has not already done it. George [Gearóid O'Sullivan] is in his usual form, and I believe Emmet [Dalton] has fallen in love again. I hope this will be his final one. ... I suppose you are about fed up with the States. Don't be surprised if I ramble along one day. If the fight starts again I do believe I will go, anyhow I mean to make a trip that way one day.[89]

The merry-go-round whirled on, and it was O'Sullivan, not Harry, who married Maud in the following year.[90]

Kitty's prolonged silence, broken by an unsatisfactory compromise which merely postponed his personal crisis, became entangled with Harry's growing political frustration. Unable to influence his colleagues in Dublin or the delegates in London, and without access to their private intentions, his only contribution as an envoy was to voice support for whatever the Dáil might decide while awaiting a possibly unwelcome *fait accompli*. Once again, the vital decision would be taken by Collins, leaving Harry to save face retrospectively. Collins and Dalton, in their occasional letters from London, avoided detailed comment on the Peace Conference and its likely outcome. De Valera was more communicative, informing Harry on 29 November that 'as things stand to-day it means war. The British ultimatum is allegiance to their King. We will never recommend that such allegiance be rendered. You know how fully I appreciate all that WAR means to our people, and what my misgivings are as to the outcome of war. Without explanation you will understand then that if I appear with those who choose war, it is only because the alternative is impossible without dishonour.' He expected that 'my view will be that of the Cabinet as a whole', and predicted that Harry would 'have a heavy task "keeping our end up" before American public opinion'.[91] Though this letter may not have reached Harry until after signature of the agreement, it offered a handy rationale for any subsequent repudiation.

The Treaty, as signed on 6 December, provided a painful test of the force of republican allegiance when at odds with the popular will, and also of the relative strength of Harry's personal and fraternal loyalties. As the Ministry's American apologist, he felt obliged to voice its policies regardless of his own opinions, so long as it remained united. Even after de Valera's delayed denunciation of the agreement, Harry's public utterances were constrained by his long-standing rhetorical insistence that the will of the people, expressed through the Dáil, was paramount over individual preferences. His deeper commitment to maintaining unity among the brethren, whatever the divisions of public opinion, further discouraged rash declarations. As his two closest mentors became the chief protagonists in the bitter dispute over approval of the agreement, Harry's alignment was affected not only by his admiration for de Valera's intellect and Collins's organisational genius, but by the grievances which had tainted both relationships since his autumn visit to Ireland. With so many vying influences, it is scarcely surprising that Harry's response was contradictory and apparently confused, leading to recriminations from his opponents and energetic attempts at self-vindication.

The entries in his diary, clearly retrospective,[92] helped him to defend and rationalise his conduct:

6 Dec. Tues. Washington. Treaty of London signed 2.50 a.m., to be published tomorrow. Great jubilation here. Go to A[ssociated] P[ress] office at midnight for text of Treaty.

7 Dec. Wed. Washington. Text as published very unsatisfactory. American press favors acceptance. Real friends disgusted. Take wallop at Cohalan and Lynch.

8 Dec. Thurs. Washington. Dinner re Bond Campaign. ... I throw bombshell into party – see *Manchester Guardian*.

9 Dec. Fri. Washington. Hunting, all upset, until de Valera speaks against Pact. Happy again.

10 Dec. Sat. Washington. Cable home, insist on my right to vote.[93]

In short, Harry's diary testified that he had immediately opposed the terms of agreement, once known, promptly expressed his views to 'real friends' and then to Irish-American well-wishers, and made his decision independently of de Valera.

The contemporary record does not fully endorse this account. On the evening of Tuesday, 6 December, Harry gave his unqualified support to an agreement which he had not yet examined in detail, presumably on the assumption that the final draft had been approved in advance by the Ministry (as the instructions to the plenipotentiaries required). Though not in fact hailing the Treaty as 'the freedom that came from God's right hand', as in Sean O'Casey's parody of the speech,[94] he seemed delighted by the outcome:

After centuries of conflict the Irish nation and the British have composed their differences. A treaty of peace has been signed and an agreement reached between the representatives of the Irish nation and the representatives of the British Empire – an agreement which restores Ireland to the comity of nations. The last phase of the conflict was serious and bloody. The determination of the Irish people to be free faced Great Britain with the alternative of an honorable peace or a war of extermination. The agreement will be submitted to the Parliaments of both nations for ratification. ... We feel sure that the agreement reached between Britain and Ireland will be received in America with great joy.[95]

Others were less sure, awaiting not only the full text, but clearer signals from Dublin and from their factional opponents, before pronouncing an opinion. While Harry enthused, Judge Cohalan expressed his 'desire to wait until all the details have been made known'.[96] On Wednesday, after examining the text released at midnight and published in the morning newspapers, Harry was apparently happy enough with the terms to imply that the Treaty amounted to recognition of the Republic. Pointing out that the Bond Certificates might be exchanged for negotiable bonds 'whenever the Irish Republic should have received international recognition', he reportedly declared that 'this condition is fulfilled by the treaty with the British Government'.[97]

Meanwhile, Cohalan's faction had inspected and strongly denounced the agreement, evidently assuming that the compromiser de Valera was its architect and that his vassal Harry was irrevocably committed to upholding it. It was this tactical manoeuvre which prompted Harry's 'wallop' of frustration against Cohalan and Lynch.[98] Harry's response on Thursday night was ambivalent, for the first time hinting at personal reservations: 'If [or] when Dáil Éireann shall have passed [the Treaty] and an Irish Free State shall have come into being, those who will carry on the struggle will not give support or countenance to men who failed so miserably to assist the Irish Republic during its life.'[99] Though anticipating some form of conflict, Harry stopped well short of declaring his own intention to 'carry on the struggle'. On the same evening, he addressed a dinner for wealthy supporters in Washington, at which the only invited journalist was Henry Woodd Nevinson, the celebrated foreign correspondent and English advocate of Irish nationality then covering the Naval Disarmament Conference for the *Manchester Guardian*. Nevinson contrasted the uniformly 'exultant' response of the Irish-American speakers with the 'cooler tone' adopted by Harry and Stephen O'Mara.[100] Harry declared that 'he must be diplomatic and cautious, but still was mainly hopeful'. After his customary account of the quest for Irish freedom from generation to generation, he expressed regret that 'the lesson had not been sufficiently realised by England, who might have acted with a splendid gesture now, for Ireland would never infringe England's liberty. A new era had dawned upon the world, but "we have not closed the door to greater men who may carry the struggle forward to perfect freedom from allegiance". ... He was now returning to Ireland, to cast his vote upon the treaty as conscience might direct.' His speech expressed scepticism and disappointment, but neither urged nor uttered repudiation of the agreement. O'Mara spoke 'in a similar strain', indicating that 'it was for the Dáil to accept or reject, and if the treaty were rejected he would take his place with the men who were still contending for freedom'. Neither envoy contemplated pursuing freedom in defiance of the Dáil, should the Treaty be approved. As Nevinson left the Shoreham Hotel, he heard that the New York *World* had received a telegram 'stating that De Valera had rejected the treaty. There was immediate reaction [of] despondency and extreme disappointment, with fear of a split.'[101] According to his later and perhaps fanciful recollection, the words of the telegram were 'whispered' to be 'Renounce Treaty, De Valera'.[102]

The publication in the Friday morning papers of de Valera's refusal to 'recommend the acceptance of this treaty', in explicit defiance of the majority of his ministers as well as the plenipotentiaries, placed Harry in a still more awkward position.[103] That evening, Harry told an American Association meeting in Philadelphia that Ireland would 'never admit the right of an English king and parliament to make laws for Ireland', and that 'the will of the Irish people is unbreakable; we will suffer extermination before we will bow to the knee of England'. Even then, according to the report in McGarrity's *Irish Press*, he did not indicate that the agreement entailed such abasement, declaring merely that 'we can accept nothing less than independence; we have the right to present the issue to you'. McGarrity himself failed to decode these carefully fashioned ambiguities, in his leading article in the same issue.[104] This refuted the 'deliberate attempt of the American press' to 'make it appear that the citizens of the Republic of Ireland are to give allegiance to King George',[105] and declared that 'if the treaty made is approved and carried into effect, Ireland again becomes an independent sovereign nation. ... Regardless of the exact form that Irish Independence may finally assume, it can be accepted as an unquestionable fact that the battle is won.'

Harry's faction had been wrong-footed not merely by his well concealed change of heart, but by the misjudged initial opposition to the Treaty expressed by Cohalan and Lynch. At their National Convention on the Sunday, the Friends of Irish Freedom had pledged 'support to the element in Ireland which determines to pursue the ideal of a republic, free and independent of all or any connection with England'. Their confusion was manifest in the depiction of de Valera as 'a traitor to Ireland, and with him were condemned all who have been party to the "miserable betrayal" of Irish nationality involved in the Anglo-Irish pact of peace'.[106] It was not until 13 January, a week after the Dáil's approval of the agreement, that the Friends clumsily adjusted to the domestic realignment by denouncing 'external association', while simultaneously endorsing the republican demand yet promising to 'do nothing to interfere with or obstruct' any attempt to place limited government in Irish hands.[107] At the heart of the confusion among all factions was the paradox that de Valera, the suspected moderate with his reiterated disavowal of 'doctrinaire republicanism', had exchanged rôles with Collins, the supposed diehard. It is little wonder that Cohalan, McGarrity, and Harry all miscalculated their initial responses.

More than a week was to pass before Harry came out openly against the Treaty:

14 Dec. Wed. Washington. Cable calling me home too late for decision. Send Cable 1 o.c. As I cannot reach Dublin in time to take part in the Treaty discussions, I must insist on my right to vote. Having no official information I am compelled to take my decision on the text as published here. I desire to record my vote against the Treaty and pray that Dáil will reject the instrument drawn up at London. Acknowledge.[108]

In cables sent two days earlier he had merely declared that he was 'entitled to vote on issue', while affirming that 'no statement [had been] issued by me saving withhold comment until Dáil decision'.[109] In private, however, his opposition was by now explicit, as he explained to Kitty Kiernan on the same day:

It may be that I will be in Ireland as soon as this letter, for the great Crisis has come, and we must face it like men. I do hope to have a chance to vote on the Treaty, if not in person, then I may be allowed to cable; and if the text of the Treaty as published here is correct then I shall vote for its rejection.[110]

In his own correspondence with Kitty, Collins at first expressed sorrow rather than anger: 'All this business is very, very sad. Harry has come out strongly against us. I'm sorry for that.'[111] McGarrity, at last in tune with Harry and de Valera, abruptly reversed editorial direction to announce that Collins's adherence 'to a pact which would not include Ireland's sovereign independence is beyond our comprehension'.[112]

The American Association's National Executive, less easily manoeuvred than McGarrity's Clan and led by an emphatic proponent of the Treaty (the oil magnate Edward L. Doheny),[113] avoided any clear expression of opinion at a meeting, again addressed by both Harry and O'Mara, on 18 December. It resolved ambiguously that 'while their efforts may not as yet have resulted in the complete realization of their hopes, we pledge our continued support to the Irish people'. Harry's speech anticipated defeat in the Dáil, again without addressing the consequences of the Treaty's approval: 'Rejection by the Dáil Éireann of the Treaty between Ireland and Great Britain, creating the Irish Free State, and the possibility of a plebiscite on the matter were predicted today as probable developments of the Anglo-Irish situation by Harry Boland.' He told the Executive that 'it would be an insult to the men who died in Ireland to say that down in the heart of hearts they are satisfied with the treaty, when it was virtually wrung from them by force and duress'.[114]

This chronicle indicates that the 'bombshell' recorded in Harry's diary did not amount to overt rejection of the Treaty, which in fact followed a week later when the lines of division in Ireland were already clearly marked. In his subsequent apologia to the Dáil, Harry proclaimed his consistent adherence to 'external association' as Ireland's minimum demand:

> Now, with that in view, on the Tuesday night on which the Treaty had been signed in London I stepped off the train at Washington, and when I read that the Treaty had been signed I understood that the men who went to negotiate for Ireland had followed out the instructions of their Cabinet, and that the minimum had been achieved. I thereupon issued a statement in which I said that Ireland had come within the comity of nations. On the following morning, Wednesday morning, the Treaty appeared in the American Press; and when I read the terms of the Treaty I was opposed to it.

Harry's account of the Bond dinner provided him with essential proof of the independence of his opposition from de Valera's dictation:

> The men turned up, and we cancelled the Bond Drive, and they turned the meeting into a meeting of rejoicings. Senators were present and they sang hallelujahs; and I, myself, spoke against that Treaty. On the following morning my speech was reported in the *Manchester Guardian* because their representative in America was among the invited guests; that was on record five hours before President de Valera came out against the Treaty.

Harry's careful formulation obscured the fact that Nevinson, while noting his sceptical tone, had not in fact reported his opposition to the Treaty. The actual sequence of Harry's protracted retreat from support into ambiguity gives some credence to Collins's jibe that 'you cannot stand them, Harry, you stood for the Treaty first', lending a hollow ring to Harry's riposte: 'No! and you know it, Michael (laughter).'[115]

Nor did Harry's eloquent defence of the republican credentials of 'external association' allay the justified suspicion that he, like de Valera, had long since abandoned unqualified republicanism. As one Irish anti-Treatyist 'outsider' in New York reflected in late January:

> Harry's horrible blunder in the matter of his benediction of the Treaty by rushing hot foot into the papers with a statement, instead of like Seán T. [O'Kelly] in Paris seeking verification and then denouncing it, merely drove the movement here into the wilderness. It gave the wrong orientation to the over half million organised [Irish-Americans]. ... Even yet no lead has been given. 'Wait for the Dáil', 'Wait for the general elections' is now the

attitude. .... The 'dope' has to be served up, and served quickly. The slogan should not be 'Wait' but 'Save the Republic'.[116]

For those within the revolution's inner circle, such simple affirmations were no longer relevant. Though the debate over the Treaty was construed by most leaders of both factions as a contest between principle and pragmatism, its underlying thrust was a disagreement as to which form of compromise was most expedient.

Harry's embarrassing volte-face was widely noted by the American press, as ever dismissive of the rationalisations offered by politicians for apparent inconsistencies in their conduct. A particularly damning retrospective judgement was offered by the *New York Sun*:

> Though hearty and good-natured, Boland was often the butt of sarcastic comment but no one denied his devotion to De Valera. This was illustrated by one of Boland's last formal statements in this country. De Valera in Ireland had by some mistake been quoted as being in favour of the Anglo-Irish Treaty, and immediately Boland came out with a statement favouring the Treaty. .... It happened, however, that within a few hours De Valera's actual statement was published, in which the Republican leader attacked the Treaty. Immediately Boland came out with a statement so much at variance with his first that it was provocative of many smiles from his friends. Its words were almost the same as De Valera's. Before returning to Ireland, Boland lived at the Waldorf-Astoria, and those who didn't take the hearty Sinn Féiner any too seriously often said that Boland was getting too sleek and rotund in his new environment for any value as a fighting Republican.[117]

For the *Sun*, as for John Devoy, Harry had been reduced to acting as his master's voice.

Such retrospective assessments were unfairly dismissive of Harry's political judgement, which was more sophisticated and more independent than his detractors realised. His delay of a week before publicly endorsing de Valera's repudiation suggests that other influences were at work. For Harry, as for Collins, overt political divisions seemed inconsequential so long as unity could be achieved among the brethren, the charmed circle from which de Valera and Brugha had excluded themselves. In determining his response to the final British draft, Collins was guided as much by the Supreme Council as by the Ministry, the last consultation occurring at noon on 3 December. Having rejected the oath of allegiance, the Supreme Council had deputed Eoin O'Duffy, Gearóid O'Sullivan, and Liam Lynch to draft an alternative oath restricting allegiance to the Irish Free State with a separate reference to the monarch. Fortified by 'the views of the lads', Collins had returned to London and secured a revision of the oath along the same lines. The possibility of united action by the IRB evaporated on 12 December, when the Supreme Council urged ratification of the Treaty, yet gave 'freedom of action' to its members who were about 'to take public action' in the Dáil.[118] It is conceivable that Harry was informed of this fragmentation among the brethren before issuing his first unambiguous denunciation two days later. Yet Harry never abandoned the dream of negating the growing political and military split through the restoration of fraternal unity. His statements and silences during his last month in America were probably conditioned more by pursuit of that ideal than by any hero-worship of de Valera or romantic rivalry with Collins.

Initially hopeful of reaching Dublin before Christmas in order to argue his case in the Dáil, Harry had almost resigned himself to missing the debate when he cabled his demand for an absentee vote on 14 December.[119] His resolve to return was revived by the growing likelihood of an adjournment over the holiday period, as confirmed by a cable from Mellows on 23 December: 'Decision Treaty adjourned come at once to vote.'[120] His departure gave rise to a frenzy of farewells:

23 Dec. Fri. New York. Final arrangements for departure.

24 Dec. Sat. New York. Xmas. Eve. Joe Begley, Liam [Pedlar], Gilbert [Ward], British Consul Armstrong, head spy.

25 Dec. Sun. New York. Carmelites to dinner.

26 Dec. Mon. New York. Goldens,[121] with Mollie Carroll. Banquet A.A.R.I.R. to Bo, Seán [Nunan] and Liam [Pedlar].

27 Dec. Tues. New York. Last day in U.S.A. Police Band, Flag of Ireland at mast. *Panhandle State*, Capt. Ferguson.[122]

Harry had already visited the 'head spy', now almost an old friend, to validate his passport on 20 December, when he 'bitterly denounced Judge Cohalan and his followers, stating they were making difficulties as to the Irish settlement for their own selfish purposes'.[123]

Harry's imminent departure and the crisis in Ireland left the mission in disarray, though he retained the post of envoy and might conceivably return. His closest Irish colleagues either accompanied or soon followed him to Dublin, while Frank Walsh lost no time in redirecting his commitment to other 'oppressed peoples'. As Dr. Maloney remarked sardonically, 'he proposes to specialise in those that can afford to pay for his services, and is thinking of Egypt, Russia, Santo Domingo, and perhaps India'.[124] On St. Stephen's Night, over 100 friends gathered at the Hotel McAlpin to farewell Harry, along with Nunan and Pedlar, at a banquet convened by the American Association of New York. The speakers included old associates such as Milholland and Major Kinkead, along with a Carmelite friar and two judges, one of whom 'drew the contrast of Mr. Boland's arrival in the United States as a coal passer and returning with all the pomp that could be conferred on the envoy of a nation'. In placatory vein, Stephen O'Mara 'said the pact was not quite up to the standard. ... While their lips might breathe a Free State, their hearts will beat for a Republic.' Before delivering the evening's final speech, Harry was presented with 'a silver loving cup, inscribed in Gaelic'.[125] He too was in benevolent mood, describing the Treaty as a 'step forward' while promising to 'criticise' it in the Dáil. He again looked forward to its rejection and to a resumption of war under the former leadership: 'Before the truce was signed 5,000 American citizens of Irish extraction had pledged that they would take up arms with the Irish Republican Army. He knew that they would be ready to back up Michael Collins again, if the Irish people should decide for war.' In a striking premonition, he also drew attention to the limited influence exercised by either the people or the Dáil over those who viewed themselves as trustees for the dead generations: 'But the veterans of 1916 will carry on the fight for a republic, for it is well known that the fight for freedom is handed down in Ireland as if by apostolic succession.'[126] To that end, Harry was accompanied on his voyage by a farewell consignment of ammunition to the value of $25,000.[127]

Next afternoon, Harry and his comrades left Hoboken for Queenstown on the *Panhandle State*, which obligingly 'displayed the new green and white and yellow flag of Ireland beneath the British ensign'. Journalists found him 'in good spirits' but determined to vote against the agreement, 'because in my opinion it will not bring peace between Ireland and England. We are asked by the oath of allegiance to foreswear Irish citizenship, and I for one am not prepared to do that.' He had no objection to 'certain sacrifices' which the delegates had made 'in the interest of peace', confining his protest to 'a moral issue, our Irish citizenship'. He promised that 'any influence I have in Ireland will be thrown behind the President', who, 'more than any other man, is anxious for a just and lasting peace'.[128] In sunny contrast to his previous night's prediction concerning the men of 1916, he promised that 'if the Irish people agree to accept the Free State proposal offered by the English Government then we shall all do our best to carry it out with the idea of the republic still in our minds to be achieved some time in the future'. As the mailship with its thirty-five cabin passengers steamed down the bay, it was escorted by the police boat, *John F. Hylan*, provided by the eponymous Mayor of New York, 'while the police band on the deck played Irish airs'.[129] The passengers were admitted by green cards bearing the arms of the city and wishing the envoy 'bon voyage'.[130] Less privileged admirers followed, as 'a harbor boat crowded with women and children and carrying a band fell in behind and accompanied the ship to the harbor limits'.[131] Harry Boland's American mission was over.

Rupture

ON the night of Wednesday, 4 January 1922, after a week at sea, Harry Boland reached Queenstown to embark on his campaign against the Treaty. His first whiff of Irish life was provided on shipboard by a welcoming deputation from the Urban District Council, and a group of journalists for whom he had 'no message'.[1] So far, he had observed James O'Mara's injunction, sent by wireless to the *Panhandle State*, to 'make no public statement your visit until you ascertain conditions here'.[2] He spent the early morning in Cork City with the veterinary surgeon Seán O'Donovan, a prominent hurler, Volunteer, and hunger-striker who had once tussled with Michael Collins in the Clonakilty schoolyard. By 12.30 he was in Dublin, in time to attend the last phase of the Dáil's angry debate over the Treaty in University College on Earlsfort Terrace.[3] Already repenting of his reticence with the press, he declared that 'the one prevailing thought in the minds of Irishmen in the United States is that the splendid unity that existed throughout the fight for freedom of Ireland must be maintained', the outcome of the ratification debate being a question 'entirely for the Irish people themselves'.[4] Harry's visit that evening to de Valera was noted with interest by his secretary, Kathleen O'Connell: 'Harry, Seán [Nunan] and Liam Pedlar came out to 53 Kenilworth Sq. Seán and Liam went away early, Harry remained until after 11.'[5]

He also met Collins, who sent Kitty Kiernan a guarded report next day: 'Saw H. last night. He was friendly, of course, and very nice. I'm afraid though he was not so nice today, but not about you – I mean not on the subject of you. I'm afraid he wasn't fair in his home coming in what he said about our side today. He's working like the very devil against us, but God is good.'[6] An ugly confrontation had occurred in the Gresham Hotel, after Harry and Seán Nunan had presented Collins with the jewels supplied by the Soviet mission in 1920 as collateral for Harry's largesse in America. Collins, initially punctilious as ever, gave him a receipt for the jewels and associated documents.[7] According to Harry's sister Kathleen, Collins became enraged when he refused to abandon his opposition to the Treaty:

> In the course of the row, Mick took the jewels out of his pocket and threw them at Harry, saying 'Take these back, they are blood-stained.' Harry, who had already obtained Mick's receipt for them, put them back in his pocket and walked out. When he came home to us, he was in a blazing

temper and he showed visible signs of having had a serious struggle with Mick who had been a bit rowdy with him.[8]

This may also have been the occasion when Collins confirmed his conquest of Kitty, eliciting a stiff note from Harry four days later: 'Kitty, I want to congratulate you. M. told me of your engagement, and I wish you long life and happiness. Ever yours, H. Boland.'[9]

When Harry reached University College on Thursday afternoon, 5 January, the protracted and increasingly venomous debate on approval of the Treaty was in its eleventh day and close to climax. Public support for the agreement, as expressed by local councils, clubs and societies, newspapers, and clergymen of all denominations, was yet more overwhelming after the Christmas recess. Harry had to contend with a chorus of approval for the Treaty from his constituents in Roscommon. A curate from Ballinlough declared that 'priests and people and all Sinn Féin Clubs in the parish of Kiltullagh strongly favour ratification'. The parish priest of Kilteevan claimed that 'over 99% of your constituents are also anxious you would vote for it', calling on him to 'speak to your Chief, task him for God's sake not to throw the country into turmoil' by generating 'another and a thousand times worse Parnellite split'. With equal fervour, a 'council representing the electorate of South Roscommon' called for unanimous ratification, deploring 'a contemplated division in the ranks of Ireland's truest and best' which might spoil 'the signal victory of Ireland's 700 years' struggle'.[10] Far from denying the unpopularity of his stance, Harry was to vaunt it when addressing the Dáil, stating that he had 'received scores of letters from friends and constituents – men urging me in the interests of Ireland and of the people of Roscommon to vote for this Treaty'. This fact only highlighted the contrast between his own principled rejection of 'the title of West Briton' and the popular preference for peace through compromise. This was personified by the clerical correspondent who, according to Harry, had once urged electors to 'vote for Harry Boland and the Irish Republic and you will get a good Home Rule Bill'.[11] Already, republicans were sensing the practical inconvenience of the very doctrine of popular sovereignty upon which their objection to the Treaty was premised.

Harry's return to the Dáil was reportedly 'one of the outstanding features' of Thursday's proceedings: 'His entry into the Chamber this evening was the signal for a remarkable scene of enthusiasm. Deputies in attendance rose and loudly cheered their distinguished colleague as he took his seat.'[12] He arrived midway through a trivial discussion of the *Freeman's Journal*, while deputies awaited the outcome of an attempt by Seán T. O'Kelly to achieve republican abstention from the Treaty vote, in return for a declaration that the Provisional Government derived its powers from the Dáil of which de Valera would remain President. Though approved by Griffith, Collins, and influential republicans such as Seán Moylan and Art O'Connor, the compromise was peremptorily rejected by de Valera that afternoon, leading to further inconclusive negotiations throughout the evening.[13] Harry played no recorded part in these negotiations or in the consequent debates. His first intervention, to a private session next day, was a vigorous defence of the IRA against Mulcahy's insinuation that it was 'not strong enough to take a good sized police barrack, because I know something at any rate about the difference in equipment that army had when I left here last October and what it has today'. Harry's polemic was courteously phrased in queries rather than assertions, and prefaced by a disarming apology for 'being a kind of a stranger here (laughter)'.[14]

He was in less placatory mood during the afternoon's public session, when supporting an attempt to give priority to a discussion of de Valera's resignation. With reference to the suppression of the bipartisan agreement reached by O'Kelly's committee but repudiated by de Valera, Collins had accused his opponents of using 'Tammany Hall methods' implemented by 'three or four bullies (applause)'. Harry took this critique to heart:

> I presume the remarks of the Hon. member for Cork were intended for me. I am sorry that he has seen fit to make such a suggestion. I will say this: that I don't know anything about Tammany Hall except this, that if he had a little training in Tammany Hall, and reserved some of his bullying for Lloyd George we would not be in the position we are in to-day.[15]

Harry's admiration for New York's Democratic Party machine was to be noted during a later session of the Dáil by a hostile American observer of this 'jocular, crafty soul not unlike the politicians of Tammany Hall, the resemblance reflecting his profound admiration for an institution against which he would allow no slur of criticism. For, as he explained to me one day, "Between you and me, Tammany Hall has given more aid to the [Irish] Republican cause than any other single body."'[16] Harry's last year or so in the United States had amply vindicated his prediction of April 1920: 'What a "queer" thing is American politics. I will have the light Italian hand finely developed if fate ordains that I remain here.'[17] His undoubted talent as a party organiser was put to immediate use by Seán T. O'Kelly, the self-designated 'Chief Whip for the anti-Treaty side', who enrolled Harry as his 'chief assistant'. As O'Kelly remarked, 'it was helpful that he and Michael Collins kept up their old established friendship all through these difficult weeks'.[18] Since much of that friendship had been expressed jointly through the very 'Tammany Hall methods' and 'bullying' for which they now denounced each other with such vigour, each man was well placed to anticipate the tactics of the other when marshalling allies.

Harry's by-play with Collins preceded his rather incoherent call for 'a vote of confidence' in de Valera as 'President of this Republic', the point of which (as de Valera had indicated) was to enable the leader, once re-elected, to 'throw out that Treaty' and reopen negotiations on the basis of his untabled but widely leaked 'Document No. 2'.[19] The opposition had calculated, correctly, that de

Valera could count on the personal loyalty of a few supporters of the Treaty, making it desirable to ensure that the vote on personalities precede that on principles. De Valera denied that the demand for a vote of confidence was 'a special political manoeuvre' concocted by Harry: 'Mr. Boland came back from America, and then there is talk of Tammany Hall; but I make up my mind for myself, now and always. Mr. Boland didn't know anything about it until I myself told him this morning.' Such 'mean' misrepresentations had made him 'sick and tired of politics – so sick that no matter what happens I would go back to private life'. By this oblique route he withdrew his attempt to resign, allowing the discussion to meander back to the merits of the Treaty.[20] As Harry's diary crisply recorded: 'De Valera resigns, withdraws. Fierce debate.'[21]

If his earlier contributions to the debate lacked clarity, Harry's prolonged critique of the agreement on the Saturday morning was a *tour de force*. As a practised orator, he began by establishing his credentials through a spirited defence of his work in America. While thanking 'the American people for the magnificent support they have given us in the struggle', and trumpeting the success of the second Bond Drive and the appeal for American Volunteers, he reproached Collins for having placed the mission 'in a very embarrassing position in America'.[22] Before Christmas, Collins had fearlessly courted unpopularity in the United States by sneering that Americans had been lavish with offers of money but reticent when asked for 'a thousand men fully equipped', being all too ready with fatuous injunctions such as 'Don't weaken now, stand with de Valera.'[23] Harry responded tartly that 'the cablegram that my friend Michael Collins took such exception to was suggested by me to strengthen his hands, four days before the Treaty was signed'. Having affirmed his own effectiveness and loyalty as the Dáil's envoy, he deployed his familiarity with 'the situation in India and Egypt', as depicted by his fellow-emissaries in America, to refute the proposition that immediate war would result from rejection of the Treaty: 'While I am casting my vote prepared for war, so far as I am concerned I am convinced that there can be no war in Ireland. Allenby requires ninety thousand men in Egypt; India is in flames.' Sliding elegantly from utilitarian to moral arguments, he then tricked Collins into admitting that he did not regard the agreement as 'a final settlement of the question between England and Ireland'. This enabled Harry to contrast his own reliance upon 'conscience' with the hypocrisy of his opponents: 'If this is not a final settlement we have lost the good opinion of the world on the day we sign the Treaty with a mental reservation that it is not a final settlement. ... If I could in conscience vote for that Treaty I would do so, and if I did I would do all in my power to enforce that Treaty', treating 'as a rebel any man who would rise out against it'.[24] In due course, Collins would indeed set aside his 'mental reservation' and treat Harry, without gloves, as a 'rebel'. The defeated rebels would themselves adopt the doctrine of mental reservation in 1927, when Fianna Fáil accepted the execrated Oath of Allegiance to the Constitution and fidelity to the Crown.

The most obvious weakness in the case for repudiating the Treaty was the undeniable weight of public opinion in its favour. Harry's attempt to reconcile his exercise of conscience with the doctrine of popular sovereignty harked back, as so often before, to Pearse's doctrines. He proclaimed that 'this fight for Ireland ... has come down to us in apostolic succession', through the personal connections between the veterans of one campaign and the initiators of the next. He cited his own lineage:

> We picked it up in 1916 and we brought the Irish Republic out of the backwoods, away from the dark rooms of secret societies, and preached the gospel before the Irish people; and we asked them to stand for an independent Republic. Many deputies in this House know that my father himself had to fly from this country and suffer, ... he had to fly away because he believed in a Republic. His son was privileged to stand on public platforms and to ask the Irish [*sic.*] people to subscribe to the Republic.

The revolutionary Dáil had represented 'the real opinion of Ireland and Ireland rallied to us'; once again, if the leaders reunited, 'no demand that you make on the people would be denied. Don't blame it on the wife. If we are prepared to carry on this fight the people of Ireland will support us.' Like a neglected wife, the unguided populace might be unfit to express its 'real' opinions; yet, under strong leadership, its underlying devotion to nationality could be mobilised at will. Unlike many of his colleagues, he did not claim to 'speak for the dead', declaring that 'our concern is with the living and with those who may come after us, and I for one am quite easy in my mind that those who will come after us will deal kindly with the men who vote against this Treaty'.[25] By incorporating future generations in the ambit of popular sovereignty, he enabled adherents of this doctrine to dismiss any temporary preference for the Treaty by the current generation. Harry's classic exposition of national sovereignty as an inalienable right, of which the current generation was merely the trustee, supplied many of the phrases and concepts which de Valera was to develop, more haltingly, during and after the Civil War.

His speech concluded with an eloquent peroration:

> If I could accept that Treaty as a stepping-stone to Irish freedom I would do it; but I know that I would not be doing an expedient thing for Ireland, but doing what, in my opinion, would forever debar Ireland from winning her ultimate freedom. If we reject that Treaty England will not make war on us; if she does we will be able to defend ourselves as we have always done.

According to the *Cork Examiner*, the chilling final sentence was uttered 'in so low a voice that he was not distinctly heard', yet it was greeted with 'loud cheers'.[26] In a characteristic switch of register, Harry instantly relapsed into banter with Joseph McGrath, who prefaced his defence of the Treaty by describing himself as 'an out and outer':

> MR BOLAND: You mean a down and outer.
> MR MACGRATH: I am not a Republican of a latter day, neither am I a Republican since I was four years old; but I am one for the past fifteen years, when Republicanism was very low in Ireland.

It was not until the evening sitting that Harry re-entered the debate to assert his consistency in principle when preparing Americans for 'external association', and his independence of judgement in rejecting the terms of the agreement once published. An hour or so later, 'Enrí Ó Beoláin' was among the minority voting against approval: 'Speak and vote against Treaty. Result: for 64, against 57.'[27]

There remained one further opportunity to abort the agreement, as de Valera once again courted the sentimental element in the Dáil by resigning and then allowing himself to be nominated for re-election as President. Harry chose to interpret this motion as a symptom of reviving brotherhood: 'I am very happy to see we all enjoyed our dinner (laughter) and that a better spirit is developing in Dáil Éireann.' He challenged his opponents, who had so far 'fought for the Treaty with the same courage and the same dash as they fought in the fight for the Republic', to put up a rival candidate and so make the election a renewed test of principle. Insisting that de Valera's 'personality has never been intruded in this fight', he forthwith lauded his leader for having refused ever to 'waver in the tightest place' during his 'very difficult time in America'. His prediction of the future conduct of a defeated opposition was strikingly inaccurate:

> If you throw out the man on this side by the vote, we are in honour bound to see to it that you receive from us all the resources that have been at the command of Dáil Éireann. ... All we ask is that we be allowed to hold to our opinions. ... I say to our friends to join issue and have a straight vote, for or against. And then we will, on the first opportunity, go before the Irish people and seek a further mandate for the Irish Republic, and if they in their wisdom decide against us we will be only too happy to obey.[28]

In the event, the Treaty's opponents were to withhold the military resources of the Dáil from the Provisional Government, attempt to avoid a free election through a 'Pact', and refuse to obey the popular mandate for a Free State which emerged in defiance of that Pact. However disingenuous, the promise of adherence to democracy probably contributed to the bizarre outcome of the vote. Despite Griffith's protestation that de Valera's nomination was 'a political manoeuvre to get round the Treaty', two supporters of the Treaty voted for de Valera while the candidate himself and another deputy abstained. Chaos was averted by a majority of two votes, which cleared the way for Griffith's election as President of the Dáil, followed by formal ratification of the agreement five days later at the only meeting of the House of Commons of Southern Ireland.[29] Harry and his allies absented themselves from these proceedings.

Despite the bitter personal invective which enlivened the debates, the collapse of political unity did not rapidly lead to the disintegration of the networks of friendship and brotherhood that were so crucial to Harry's well-being. Indeed, so long as the rift seemed reversible, the incentive to maintain and mobilise these networks was stronger than ever. With one exception, all of Harry's fellow-deputies with experience of the American mission (Liam Mellows, Mary McSwiney, and Donal O'Callaghan) had opposed the Treaty. Patrick McCartan alone voted in its favour, while trying to maintain his intimacy with brethren of all views and to act as a peace-broker. Though sometimes feeling 'creepy' about Collins's occasional 'lapses' into pettiness, McCartan considered him 'the only *big* man of the lot'. His judgement of Harry was coloured by growing contempt for the casuistry of his assumed master, de Valera: 'I later heard Harry re-echo the benefits of Association with England and at the same time belly-aching about the "difficult task" he had before him in America – preparing the people for a compromise.'[30] Yet they remained on close enough terms to sign the same St. Patrick's Day card to Dr. Maloney, depicting a leprechaun in green hat and overalls, carrying an umbrella: 'We drink your health in the Wicklow Bar.'[31] There was no unity of opinion across the broader circle of Harry's trans-Atlantic collaborators outside the Dáil. Liam Pedlar, though acknowledging in late January that 'if the thing went to the country now it would be accepted by a large majority', remained staunchly beside de Valera and Harry. He told McGarrity that 'Harry felt rotten for a while but I think he is over that'.[32] Seán Nunan, though supporting the Treaty, remained 'ever your younger brother' three months later, assuring 'Bo' that 'I'll see you often as of old, as your friendship is one of the greatest treasures I have got from the movement'.[33] The personal rupture caused by the split was therefore less rending than Kathleen Boland had intimated on 9 January: 'Isn't it terrible! I suppose you're heart-broken. This is my first experience of real sorrow.'[34]

Within a fortnight of the split in the Dáil, Harry was in Paris for the Irish Race Congress, a now superfluous extravaganza which had been designed to display Irish revolutionary solidarity in face of the Saxon former foe. While in Washington, Harry had been fertile with proposals for American representation, lining up 'Mr. John McCormack, of musical fame' and 'a group of men who were gathered together to relieve distress; and whilst very few of them have been enthusiastic Republicans, yet I feel sure that their attendance at an Irish Race meeting would strengthen them politically'. Though the response to his own appeals was 'very poor', he urged the organiser in Paris to invite men who would be 'of more service to Ireland by their not taking an active part with us in our more belligerent work'.[35] In the event, the few trans-Atlantic delegates who attended were neither influential nor representative of organised Irish-America.

In a futile attempt to present a united front, the Dáil Ministry had agreed that an equal number of delegates representing the home country should be nominated by itself and by de Valera.[36] Along with the latter, Harry's colleagues were Donal O'Callaghan, Mary McSwiney, and Constance de Markievicz. Far from securing unity, this equitable division merely had the effect of transplanting the split from Dublin to Paris. Four of the Ministry's delegates reported sadly that 'from the beginning there was no communication between the two sections of the Delegation', even though Harry and his ally Fr. Timothy Shanley had travelled on the same train as themselves. The expected welcome at the Grand Hotel by the Irish envoy in Paris (Seán T. O'Kelly) was not forthcoming, and O'Kelly 'left the hotel accompanied by Mr. Harry Boland soon after we had entered it'. The office assigned to O'Kelly as Irish envoy in Paris was 'used as Headquarters' by Harry and the anti-Treatyists, leaving their disorientated opponents dependent for 'assistance' on Michael MacWhite, the envoy to Geneva.[37]

These social and administrative tensions within the Irish delegation were reflected in the fractious proceedings of the Congress, in which de Valera and his associates eventually gained the upper hand. Harry was elected to two of the Congress's five sub-committees, those on 'economic questions' and on 'general arrangements and publicity'. He wasted little time with the former, having 'rather scoffed at cultural and economic discussions, stating that we might as well face the facts in Ireland'.[38] In this he was at one with the implacably secular Fr. Shanley, who considered that 'cultural development' was 'only secondary' to making Ireland 'absolutely independent', an aim which he proposed to pursue in America by appealing for money 'for guns and munitions to send to the men in Ireland who are prepared to carry out that fight'.[39] Though omitted from the crucial sub-committee on credentials, Harry was vigilant as ever in scrutinising the claims of late arrivals. On Monday, 23 January, he announced on behalf of a self-appointed 'committee of the delegates' that 'they would not tolerate' any 'interference' in the Congress from Desmond FitzGerald, the Dáil's newly appointed Director of Publicity.[40] Four days later, Harry defended the entitlement to vote of an O'Dwyer from Ohio who had been delayed at sea, arguing that 'if you are going to suggest now that none but those of Irish birth be admitted you are immediately interfering with other organisations, which you [the Treatyists] promised not to do'.[41]

Harry's most sustained intervention occurred on the final Friday, when many supporters of the Treaty had departed in the deluded belief that their opponents had been routed. His purpose was to ensure de Valera's dominance in the new organisation which was intended to carry through the objectives of the Congress, Fine Ghaedheal (Family of the Gael). Envisaging this body as a publicity machine which would require 'a great deal of money' to organise the promised newspaper and lectures, he and Shanley unsuccessfully urged an immediate financial commitment. However, his advocacy ensured that its Honorary Treasurer would be Dr. J. A. H. Irwin, a Presbyterian minister from Killead, County Antrim, who had served the Protestant Friends of Ireland energetically in America.[42] Outmanoeuvring an attempt to place the election of officers in the hands of the proposed Executive Committee, Harry enabled the anti-Treatyists to make immediate use of their newly acquired supremacy to elect de Valera (unopposed) as the organisation's President, and to outnumber their opponents by four to three on the governing body.[43] In pushing through his proposal by 34 votes to 18, Harry protested his political innocence:

> I offered an amendment to expedite business. I have never met an organisation yet that was afraid or did not wish to nominate its own officers. I realise that we cannot get an agreement on this question of officers, and I am prepared to join issue. I am not a politician, never will be, nor ever have been.[44]

As with all such affirmations, his ringing finale conveyed the precise opposite of its literal meaning.

The largely futile Congress was not entirely without compensations, with a banquet on the Saturday night, a concert on the Tuesday, and visits to an art exhibition, Maxim's, the Café de Paris, and a revue on the following Saturday. Otherwise, Harry's diary conveyed weariness at 'working all day on committee' before the formal opening (where 'chaos' prevailed), and watching as the 'conference drags on' pending a possibly more productive 'secret session'. Despite his impatience with the cultural programme, Harry clearly relished a lecture entitled 'Plays and Lyrics of Modern Ireland' by William Butler Yeats, who had yet to become a smiling public apologist for the Irish Free State. In his diary for Monday, 23 January, Harry jotted his reaction: 'W. B. Yeats lecture. Men may vote for falsehood but they truly die for truth: Yeats.'[45] He left Paris for Dublin at noon on Sunday, so missing de Valera's visit to the Arc de Triomphe to lay a wreath in oblique recognition of those Irishmen who had 'truly' died in the Great War: 'Tribut au soldat inconnu de la France, de la part des délégués au Congrès Mondial Irlandais . . ., parmi les compatriotes desquels l'inconnu a trouvé tant de camarades dans la grande guerre 1914–1918.'[46]

The Congress left no significant legacy except the name Fine Ghaedheal, which in simplified form was appropriated by the Treatyists in 1933. In early March, de Valera asked the Dáil to lend £5,000 to the dormant Executive Committee 'for the expenses of founding and organisation', only to provoke an acrimonious debate on the conduct of republican delegates at the Congress, leading to withdrawal of the motion. When Harry challenged the account of the Congress in George Gavan Duffy's report on Foreign Affairs, Collins suggested that reports from both sides should be published and referred to a committee. Having exclaimed 'I quite agree to that', Harry proceeded to claim that 'we, on this side, were not aware that the deputation going to Paris were representing different sides'. It was characteristic of the post-Treaty Dáil that sniping immediately resumed, as Harry sarcastically invited the argumentative Collins to take the chair, and snarled at Joseph McGrath that 'I was not out with a muck-rake like you anyway' and had 'never abused personal confidence' like his travelling companion to Gairloch.[47] When the committee's report on Fine Ghaedheal was finally presented to the Dáil three months later, it revived the controversial proposal for a loan and aroused protest from both sides of the House. After Collins had proposed adopting the report yet shelving the loan, he received unexpected support from Harry despite murmurs of 'sharp practice' from Constance de Markievicz. Harry explained that 'this report originated out of the charges and counter-charges, when this House was in bad temper. Charges were made about my action in Paris. I made an appointment with the Minister for Finance last night and in discussing this affair I thought this report might very well be left aside. My opinion is that this Association is able to finance itself.' When Collins revealed his alliance with Harry, de Valera was nonplussed: 'I did not know that. If I did I would not have pressed the matter.' Harry snapped back that 'I distinctly stated that the report be put, quite apart from the loan'.[48] Though nothing tangible emerged from this compromise, it confirmed Harry's extraordinary faith in the power of his bond with Collins to transcend fits of temper and even heal the rupture over the Treaty.

A curious result of the uneasy division of authority between the Provisional Government and the Dáil Ministry, notwithstanding Griffith's election as its President, was the temporary retention of republican envoys such as Seán T. O'Kelly and Harry. Gavan Duffy continued to be torn between his republican inclinations and his acceptance of collective responsibility, which had led him to deplore yet sign the Treaty. In a report to Gavan Duffy on 17 January, Harry pointed out that no senior representative remained in America except Joseph Begley, declined to 'interpret the feelings' towards the Treaty of the American Association, with its 750,000 paid-up members, and solemnly warned the new government against floating loans on the American market which might cause Ireland, like Haiti and San Domingo, to be taken over by an American army of occupation at the behest of the National City Bank of New York.[49] A month was to pass before Gavan Duffy formally terminated Harry's 'appointment under the diplomatic service of the Government', while regretting 'that you did not see your way to sending in your resignation'.[50] The ostensible occasion for his dismissal was a circular issued by Harry and O'Kelly on 21 January, calling for republicans to secure control of Sinn Féin at local level in order to pack the forthcoming Ard Fheis.[51] When asked for his 'disclaimer of responsibility', Harry responded that the circular was perfectly 'compatible with my position as Representative of the Government of the Republic'. Following a meeting at the 'Mansion House, with Gavan Duffy, re my politics', he was asked to resign from the service of 'the Government you are engaged in assailing'.[52] This was followed by several strangely placatory messages from Gavan Duffy, enabling Harry to again 'refuse to resign on an unsupported allegation which evidently originated in the minds of a Minister and Cabinet suffering the agonies of guilty consciences'.[53] Harry took his dismissal lightly, as he indicated to Stephen O'Mara after his final interview with Gavan Duffy: 'So I am no longer a "Wandering Statesman".'[54]

Though divested of his title and salary, Harry remained in active contact with his American associates, doing his best to counteract the influence of Treatyist emissaries and to maintain support for his version of the Republic. His efforts were frustrated by the understandable impatience of American sympathisers with the multitude of competing emissaries despatched by each faction in the hope of grabbing control of American funds, arms, and organisations. These included James O'Mara, acting for the Provisional Government, and soon afterwards his estranged brother Stephen, representing the anti-Treatyists in the name of the Dáil. Having announced his dismissal to Frank Walsh, Harry stressed that 'we will require the support of all friends of the Republic in America now more than ever, as we intend to place this question before the Irish people in a few months and will need a great deal of money'.[55] Walsh responded that 'things seem to be at a standstill here', later telling Stephen O'Mara that 'the A.A.R.I.R. is absolutely shot to pieces, Mr. [John J.] Hearn informs me, and it is very doubtful whether contributions from that source will be very large'. In a bizarre attempt to subsidise reconciliation, the Association had decided to risk the opposite consequence by offering equal amounts to both parties, on condition that all emissaries were withdrawn.[56] Both parties rejected the proposal and pressed ahead with fund-raising, further alienating their American former allies.

Walsh's pessimism was echoed by other correspondents in America, including visitors such as Austin Stack. The refusal of the republicans to withdraw their envoys in return for $50,000 irritated the American Association and the Clan Reorganized, as Stack reported while on a fund-raising mission: 'I hope Joe [McGarrity] and Luke [Dillon] come out of their shell. So far they have done *nothing* for us. Joe still seems to think we ought to have jumped at that offer.' Stack moaned that 'we have little or no help. A pity Seán Nunan did not see his way to come along. Poor Pedlar is unwell these days.'[57] Harry, like de Valera, insisted that the republican envoys should not be bought off so cheaply, rejecting strong contrary advice from close friends in Ireland such as Donal O'Callaghan, and key allies in the United States such as McGarrity, Maloney, Walsh, Kinkead, and Doheny.[58] James K. McGuire, while listening to the pleas of both delegations, clearly deplored the republican mission and warned Harry of the 'growing indifference in America as to the fate of Ireland':

The American public and most of the people generally interested in Ireland … view with mingled feelings of perplexity, disgust, amazement and mostly misunderstanding, what is going on in Ireland. … The feeling here among many of your friends is in effect that whatever the majority of the people of Ireland should determine, is the best settlement to accept.[59]

This was a principle with which Harry and his remaining colleagues found it increasingly awkward to comply.

While Irish politicians of all factions shamelessly exported their battles to America, their Irish-American counterparts had been striving to restore harmony in Ireland. Joseph McGarrity, though critical of the terms of the agreement, urged his followers after its approval by the Dáil to press for peace rather than insurrection: 'Any advice offered should be a demand for united action, and a warning against any move on the part of any man or woman that might precipitate civil strife.'[60] The Clan Reorganized was informed that 'we have no feeling against the men who signed the treaty. We do not believe men who fought so bravely would have signed such a document without reservations.'[61] It was these 'reservations', so eloquently deplored by Harry in his address to the Dáil, which offered the prospect of reclaiming the Treatyists for the Republic and inducing republicans to exploit the *fait accompli* of the Treaty. Harry spent numerous afternoons in the Wicklow Hotel trying to persuade his old comrades on the Supreme Council to discard the Oath of Allegiance from the new Constitution, allegedly declaring that 'there's nothing else, nothing but the Oath' dividing the parties.[62] But his attempts to devise a mutually satisfactory formula were frustrated, more by de Valera than by Collins, and Harry's hopes became pinned on external mediation. By late January, he was urging McGarrity to intervene in person: 'I expected to see you in Ireland before now, and it might be well for you to come at your earliest convenience.'[63] Similar advice came from the Irish Consul in New York, Joseph Connolly, who 'had some difficulty at first in persuading him, but eventually he agreed'. Though 'not very optimistic', Connolly hoped that McGarrity's wide-ranging influence would promote reconciliation, and that his first-hand experience would enable the American Association to adopt a more practical policy.[64]

When McGarrity set forth with Peter McSwiney in early February, the Provisional Government welcomed his visit as an opportunity to defend its own credentials while inviting mediation. The volatile J. J. Walsh was deputed to meet him on arrival, and Collins and Griffith were authorised to interview the emissary.[65] The first visitor to McGarrity's Dublin hotel, on 12 February, was another would-be mediator, Patrick McCartan. He was followed by Collins, who 'gave us a very warm shake hands' and left a favourable impression: 'He is full of dash, and ceremony is the last thing he thinks of. He is clean shaven, and wears his hair long, is of athletic build, but does not assume a military bearing.' Collins then despatched the visitors in the direction of his opponents:

He put his car at our disposal to motor to the home of Harry Boland, where we were made very welcome by Harry's mother and sister, who aroused him from his bed, where he had only gone an hour before. He had been on the lookout for us all night.

Their next host was de Valera, who was 'just dressing' on their arrival, 'appeared a bit care-worn, and was most anxious to learn about old friends in the United States'.[66] McGarrity's visit became the focus for a concerted attempt to reconcile Collins with de Valera, in which Harry played the leading rôle.

He also re-introduced the Philadelphian from Tyrone to the country he had left thirty years earlier: 'In company with Harry Boland I went over the battle field of 1916. We walked along the Mount Street Bridge and Boland's Mills where de Valera was in command in that eventful week.'[67] Harry's Easter Week tour was becoming a set piece for Irish-American visitors, as indicated by the recollections of Joseph Cyrillus Walsh, another mediator whose visit coincided with McGarrity's:

Harry Boland took me, one day, over much of the ground of the fighting of Easter Week. At one spot, behind the Post Office, he said 'Up on that roof I first saw Mick Collins. You'd better get him to tell you about it.' As we were walking on Brunswick Street a lorry passed, full of soldiers. The officer in charge saluted Boland. 'Well, there's one man who hasn't forgotten me. And a good man, too [possibly Vinny Byrne]. He's not much over five feet, but he accounted for seven of the best of the British intelligence service on Bloody Sunday.' At the open ground in front of the Rotunda he told me of the savaging of the English soldiers during the night after the surrender, when the f[ront] lawn was filled with prisoners. He blamed one man especially. 'He paid for it though. He was caught with the Black and Tans one day, and didn't come out alive.'[68]

By wallowing in nostalgia for Easter Week and the 'Tan War', Harry and his visitors sought temporary distraction from the discord and mutual resentment of 1922.

The mediation arising from McGarrity's visit was fuelled by numerous luncheons and dinners in which the main protagonists were obliged to treat each other with some civility. Walsh remembered 'a luncheon party at which it was hoped the basis of an understanding between the rival elements might be reached. Or rather after it, as otherwise I would not have been present. All those expected came – except de Valera. Boland persuaded Collins to go to see de Valera at his office after the luncheon. Collins, with his disarming grin, protesting that no good would come of it, agreed to go, I think with McGarrity.'[69] Another account, possibly of the same fruitless meeting, indicates that 'Joe McGarrity had to frequently get between the door and one or the other of them, as they would alternatively [sic.] get up in anger to walk out.'[70] On 16 February, the wife of a prominent obstetrician arranged a 'little dinner party' for the leaders of both factions and the three mediators (Walsh, McCartan, and McGarrity). Harry and the mediators shared Madge MacLaverty's table with Collins, Griffith, and Seán Ó Murthuile.[71] Her hospitality soon took effect: 'At midnight Collins was asking Boland to sing "The West's Awake", and Boland said he would if Collins would recite "Kelly and Burke and Shea" and be sure to pronounce "lent" as "lint". Neither responded immediately but both did in time.' As Walsh recalled: 'I left Dr. MacLaverty's at 2 o'clock. Collins and Boland, I heard afterwards, went at 4, both going to the home of one of them (which, I forget) and they were up again at 6, taking up again the political conflict.'[72] It was during this period of uneasy fraternisation that de Valera allowed himself to be aligned with Harry and Collins in a series of photographs, one of which (plate 21) was emblazoned on the cover of *Irish Life* as 'a picture of good omen'.[73]

McGarrity came not merely as a peace-maker but as an advocate of the Clan Reorganized, which had yet to secure its long-awaited 'credentials' from the IRB. Before departure, he was charged with a catalogue of agitated queries and instructions by the Clan's secretary, Luke Dillon:

> Why did Boland fail to get recognition from the I.R.B. for our body as promised? Is the I.R.B. Supreme Council functioning? If not, why, and what chance there is [*sic.*] to bring them together? Discourage faction. Find out what Harry done with money and why he did not send a receipt.

For Dillon, unity in Ireland was not only desirable in itself but essential for the future of the Clan:

> Bring both sections together if possible regardless of their present cause of division. If they believe in a future Republic see if it would not be advisable to arm our people in the North. . . . Tell the interested parties our strength is about 18,000 in good standing but with proper understanding we could double our members.[74]

During his visit, McGarrity had several meetings with members of the Supreme Council at which he 'endeavoured to lay foundations for peace between Collins and Boland, dealing with the question from an I.R.B. standpoint as a preliminary to general peace'. Shortly after McGarrity's post-prandial mediation at Dr. MacLaverty's, Harry defended his own conduct in America against strong criticism from Collins, who 'told him how he (Collins) had stood over all of his (Boland's) actions in America even when he knew them to be unauthorised and autocratic'. Harry was 'affected considerably' by the 'unfriendliness' of his old comrade, who again jeered that he had changed his stance on the Treaty in deference to de Valera, 'giving as his reason that he "could not let the Long Fellow down"'. Despite this confrontation, Collins and Harry pursued their search for an agreed resolution of 'the ludicrous position of the Clan na Gael', resuming their nocturnal confabulations at Collins's long-standing hideaway on Mountjoy Street.[75]

At 8 o'clock on Wednesday, 22 February, Harry reported to the Dolphin Hotel and Restaurant in East Essex Street, for the IRB's calorific farewell to McGarrity. Along with key brethren such as Ó Murthuile, the O'Hegartys, Emmet Dalton, and the gun-runner 'Major James J. Dineen alias Jim Kelly', Harry was offered oysters, clear 'paysanne purée' of hare, boiled salmon in parsley sauce with braised sweetbreads and peas, boiled chicken and ham with stewed celery and baked potatoes, trifle Chantilly, coffee, and unspecified accompaniments. Collins was not among the guests.[76] Though McGarrity returned to Philadelphia without his credentials, he was pursued by a letter from Ó Murthuile confirming that recognition of the Clan Reorganized had already been granted by the Supreme Council in autumn 1921:

> You may take it then that the recognition asked for is agreed to here, with perhaps some slight reservation regarding the unity amongst your people in the States that we desire to see brought about. This recognition by the parent Organisation at home is purely and simply to be confined to the inner Organisation, and it is not to be extended to the purely political movement.[77]

Collins and Ó Murthuile had thus adopted the curious course of endorsing the faction led by a declared opponent of the Treaty, while spurning the overtures of John Devoy, whose unrepentant republicanism coexisted with emphatic support for the Free State and the opinion 'that the defeat of de Valera's selfish campaign is absolutely necessary in Ireland's interests'.[78]

The brethren of both factions believed that their clandestine solidarity had indeed been restored, as Ó Murthuile revealed: 'You will know, from your own personal experience, that we only differ here on the means by which complete freedom may be achieved, and now that we have secured unity between both political parties, for the time being at any rate, we hope that the example of this may lead to the unification of all forces standing with us in the States for ultimate freedom.'[79] The political expression of this fraternal unity, oblique as always, was an agreement next day to adjourn Sinn Féin's Ard Fheis, a gesture which Kitty Kiernan expected to provoke 'great joy in Dublin' and to gladden the heart of Collins.[80] His instinct, like Harry's, was to rely upon fraternal goodwill to transcend divisions which, in public politics, seemed to signify irreconcilable differences in principle. For the *cognoscenti*, as Ó Murthuile explained to McGarrity, 'the question of the "abandonment of the Republican policy" here is simply an election cry'.[81]

Though the goodwill manufactured for McGarrity's visit was soon exhausted, all parties craved its renewal. By late March, when Collins complained to McGarrity of the 'veritable campaign facing us', he was nonetheless 'hopeful as always, and while hope remains there is really nothing to be feared'.[82] McGarrity and Dillon continued to press for unity, sending an imperious cable to the 'Hon. Harry Boland' in his capacity as chief broker: 'Bring de Valera and Collins together. They can find a basis of agreement which will unite the people if they have but the will to do so. Responsibility for failure will be theirs and yours.'[83] De Valera, in response to a similar appeal, had sent a stark reply: 'Fear suggestion now hopeless.'[84] Harry, though more optimistic, was intent on preparing for war while manoeuvring for peace. His intention by 20 April was to divert 'the full force of the Clan to the Army Executive who now remain the sole hope of saving the situation', to achieve an anti-Treatyist takeover of the IRB, and so to avert civil war.[85] In writing on that day to James K. McGuire, for so long the Clan's most impassioned conciliator, he claimed that 'all here agree that the Irish people are the final judges in this controversy and we are insisting that the Irish people have free choice as between the "Free State" and the Republic'. With the crucial caveats that England remove her threat of 'immediate and terrible war', and that universal adult suffrage be applied, he had 'no hesitation' in predicting 'that the Republic proclaimed in '16 and maintained ever since will be again ratified by the Irish people'. The only snide aside concerned his successor as the Dáil's American envoy, a rather fussy economist from University College, Cork: 'I have no doubt Professor [Timothy A.] Smiddy will fill the post in Washington satisfactorily. I have never met him but I understand that his connection with our movement began last November.'[86]

Harry's interest in the Clan and Irish-America was sustained, above all, by his desire to obtain money and arms for the republican opposition. Within two days of the Dáil's approval of the Treaty, Harry had secured the $60,000 of Clan subscriptions which he had placed in safe hands just before his departure from the United States.[87] Disregarding the fact that this sum had been raised for the Supreme Council, still firmly under Collins's control, Harry transferred it to the anti-Treatyist IRA on the dubious excuse that it was now responsible for defending the Republic. Having robbed the Supreme Council of most of its anticipated revenue, he spent much of the next day carousing with its President and former Treasurer:

8 Feb. Thurs. Mansion House. Oscar Traynor. Arrange money transfer, auth[orise] receipts.

9 Feb. Fri. Dublin. National Bank. Stack, Traynor, Mellows.

10 Feb. Sat. 15 Dame St., Gresham, Vaughan's, 44 [Mountjoy Street] with Mick Collins.[88]

The Clan, which continued to send money to Collins for the Supreme Council,[89] was understandably affronted by this misdirection of its donation and, in late March, demanded its return. Harry's response, conveyed to McGarrity and Dillon on the eve of the newly formed Executive's seizure of the Four Courts as its headquarters, was to affirm that he had 'not the slightest hesitation in placing the money at their [the Executive's] disposal'. In telling Luke Dillon that his request for reimbursement 'cannot be complied with', he defended his application of 'discretionary power' in funding the Executive's attempt to 'preserve the Republic'.[90]

In late May, following the uneasy Pact[91] between Collins and de Valera, he tried to placate his Irish-American allies by promising to transfer their donation to the anti-Treatyist minority of the Supreme Council:

> As a result of the union I will be in a position to secure the return of the money given to the I.R.A. I will have it lodged in the names of the two members of the S. C. pending a Convention, after which I will hand it over to the new S. C. I am very proud of the fact that the Clan money saved the situation and am sorry that there should have been any uneasiness amongst the members of the [Clan] Executive as to my disposal of the money.[92]

Since the two brethren who were to share custody of the money with himself were Liam Lynch and Joseph McKelvey, both key members of the IRA's Executive, the proposed transfer was an empty gesture. However, as Harry explained to Lynch: 'I have had so many sad experiences of the low tactics and dirty suggestions during the past six months that I am very anxious to secure that my action in regard to the monies shall not be "twisted by knaves to make a trap for fools".'[93] Such insinuations had doubtless multiplied as Harry manoeuvred to regain control over another clandestine enterprise, the 'Refugee Fund' raised by the Clan to reimburse the Dáil for his massive purchase of Thompson guns. Though already transferred to the Dáil's American 'Defence Reserve', this fund (amounting to almost $120,000) remained vulnerable to recovery by Harry's allies in New York. As Gilbert Ward informed 'Bo' on 10 March: 'Liam [Pedlar] spoke to me about the matter and thanks to the far sight [sic.] of a particular friend of yours, I think there will be some salvage immediately.'[94] After discussions with Stephen O'Mara, the Dáil's new anti-Treatyist 'Fiscal Agent' in America, Harry was soon confident enough to ask the Dáil's Trustees that the entire fund 'be now placed at the disposal of the Executive of the Irish Republican Army'.[95] No reference was made to the competing claim of Mulcahy's nascent National army to monies raised in support of the pre-Treaty IRA. Such were the stratagems by which the Treaty's opponents prepared their forces for the possible resumption of war.

Throughout the six tense months preceding the Civil War, the anti-Treatyist IRA continued to import American arms in the vain hope of outgunning the National army, which rapidly expanded its arsenal with purchases on account from its former British adversary in addition to imports from America. Harry remained a key link in the chain of supply whereby weapons were acquired with the help of Clan sympathisers, smuggled from America to Ireland, and distributed to 'Executive' units. On the day of the Dáil's vote in favour of the Treaty, an agent sent him a coded warning about divisions among Clansmen, stating that 'they are momentarily expecting word from their mother [McGarrity?] and then I think we can do something, about a few sets of hurleys for the boys or jerseys'. Using the GAA as a metaphor for Irish politics, he promised that he would 'of course do nothing without your approval. Since the championships have been decided there is very little I *can* do. I would like to discuss with you the broader aspect of the G.A.A. and think we could agree on the means of giving it a more than merely national status. Some five or six clubs are playing here now but they have no dash to them.'[96]

The IRA's chief arms agents in America remained Harry's comrades Liam Pedlar and Joseph Begley, who were still receiving salaries from the Dáil in May 1922. As Professor Smiddy informed Gavan Duffy, Pedlar was busy 'purchasing guns for the anti-Treaty party' under instructions from Liam Mellows; while Begley had recently reached New York with a carload of guns and 'some thousands of rounds of ammunition', originally acquired by Harry in Washington.[97] The two agents were attempting to recover '200,000 rounds of ammunition lying here in Washington' and the impounded 'Hoboken guns', whose release was being pursued by a 'secret agent' known as 'Senator King'. Pedlar had managed to persuade the credulous professor not merely that 'he was unaware that any change had been made in the purchasing authority', but even that his salary should be continued for a further month.[98] Smiddy's confidence in Pedlar was misplaced. On 30 May, Harry informed Pedlar that 'I am taking up the matter of the McThomas [Thompson] affair with G.H.Q. and hope to have the matter cleared up at the earliest moment.'[99] Belatedly, on 10 June, Collins severed the official connection with Harry's agents by refusing sanction for Pedlar's salary and stating that Begley had been 'recalled'.[100] For five months, Harry and his comrades had outmanoeuvred their Treatyist adversaries in the American arms market, using agents mysteriously retained on the payroll of the Dáil.

Since the Rebellion, Harry's involvement with the Irish Volunteers and IRA had been informal and unmarked by any staff office or by active affiliation with any unit. On 10 March, however, as the anti-Treatyist forces regrouped and prepared for their first convention, Harry was 'elected to represent F Coy, 2nd Batt. at Brigade Convention'. He had conferred with Oscar Traynor, Liam Lynch, Seamus Robinson, and Tom Barry on the previous day, in connection with Stephen O'Mara's successful attempt to avert an armed confrontation in Limerick. On 15 March, he attended the Dublin Brigade's Convention at Rutland (Parnell) Square, being among the 5 per cent of company delegates selected for the general convention.[101] When the postponed and proclaimed convention gathered at the Mansion House on 26 March, Harry's name was fourth in the list of delegates, ahead of Rory O'Connor, Liam Mellows, Frank Henderson, and also Gerald Boland (then Commandant of the 3rd Battalion, South Dublin Brigade). He was not, however, a candidate for the Executive.[102] Tom Barry, bellicose as always, proposed 'the declaration of a dictatorship' to order 'the dissolution of all pretended Governments in Ireland, including the British Government, Northern Government, Provisional Government and Dáil Éireann', and to prohibit 'parliamentary elections until such time as an election without threat of war from Britain can be held on Adult Suffrage'. This proposal was but the negative corollary of Harry's oft-declared enthusiasm for an election on that basis. After an amendment put forward by Mellows and Liam Deasy, Barry's demand was referred as a mere 'suggestion' to the Executive, which would 'submit their recommendations to the subsequent Convention'.[103] This compromise, according to McCartan, led 'sincere men' to 'say the convention "was entirely in the hands of the politicians". One who was in command of his own county told his brother he would "never again have any respect for Burgess [Brugha], Mellows or Boland".'[104] The declaration of a dictatorship would have terminated Harry's hope of uniting all factions in a continuing but covert struggle for the Republic.

When the adjourned convention reconvened on 9 April, Harry accompanied Liam Lynch, Rory O'Connor, and Seán Moylan in a nocturnal expedition to de Valera's house in Greystones.[105] Soon afterwards, he informed Lynch that 'we have decided to make a fight in Dáil Éireann on the Army question. ... We are satisfied that we can win two or three supporters in the Dáil from the other side on the Army question. If we can secure this, control will pass into our hands and the situation is saved.' He wished all IRA officers to attend the Dáil and a preliminary briefing, and asked Lynch to 'co-operate' by supplying information to himself or Mellows on the extent of the IRA's unpaid debts, the cost of maintaining barracks, and the employment of 'ex-British soldiers or Black and Tans' in Mulcahy's forces. Lynch responded stiffly that the Executive had decided that all data 'which we deemed advisable to have brought forward' would be raised by its representatives in the Dáil.[106] This frisson may have resulted from the fact that Lynch, unlike Harry, was currently participating in a fruitless search for 'army re-unification' through a committee appointed by the IRB's Supreme Council.[107] Harry's rôle in the IRA was that of an intercessor in 'external association' with the Executive, seemingly conciliatory towards its opponents yet energetically partisan in practice. During the protracted negotiations preceding the Pact between Collins and de Valera, in which he was the key mediator, he remained active in encouraging local units to affiliate with the Executive based in the Four Courts.[108] Yet he was also a keen supporter of the temporary truce whereby both factions undertook to abandon 'all operations except training and ordinary army routine' and to suspend 'all penetrative re-organisation'.[109]

Harry's anxiety to avoid irrevocable collision was again displayed just after the General Election in June, when the Executive held yet another banned convention in the Four Courts. Oscar Traynor recalled that 'Harry as well as Liam [Mellows] strongly opposed Tom Barry's motion declaring war on England and giving 72 hours' notice of same.' After the narrow defeat of this motion, the minority left the meeting, banned Liam Lynch and his faction from the building, and so provoked a further split within the anti-Treatyist forces. Barry's intervention had forced suspension of a debate on reunification, based on an agreement recently reached between Mulcahy and Lynch but repudiated by Rory O'Connor, Ernie O'Malley, and the diehards in the Four Courts.[110] Presumably without Lynch's faction but including the irrepressible Harry, the convention resumed a week later, only three days before the shelling of the Four Courts. Harry's diary briefly recorded this chaotic meeting:

> 25 June. Sun. Volunteer Convention Four Courts. Executive split on War policy.
>
> 26 Jun. Mon. Dublin. Attend meeting at Four Courts. Cathal Brugha takes Executive to task of [sic.] insubordination.

Brugha, another opponent of the 'War policy', was dissuaded from walking out by Traynor and other relatively moderate participants.[111] The Executive, while rejecting Barry's latest demand, reportedly 'decided to return to the old way – the Army Executive in control or something like that'. According to Harry's American ally Mrs Mary McWhorter, who dined with him on the Monday evening at Seán T. O'Kelly's home in Ranelagh: 'Harry walked back to the hotel with me that evening in a very much disturbed frame of mind and said he was certain that trouble was brewing.'[112] Though scarcely a blinding insight, this expression of disquiet suggests that even Harry's faith in the power of fraternity was beginning to fray.

Ever since the 'split' in the New Year, both factions in 'the Organisation' had viewed it as the only engine capable of restoring political unity. Even before McGarrity's mission the leading brethren had remained in close contact, as indicated by a characteristic summons to 'dear Harry' from the Supreme Council's secretary in mid January: 'Drawing room, Vaughan's Hotel at eleven o'clock tonight. Eggs. Ó Murthuile.'[113] About a week later, Harry had yet to decide how to respond to the fact that 'a big majority' of the Supreme Council had favoured the Treaty:

> I have not yet decided whether I will sever my connection with the Organisation, or whether I shall, which is most likely, put the issue up to the men. I have no doubt that the rank and file of the organisation detest and abhor this Treaty, and an opportunity will be given to them to decide the question.[114]

While maintaining, on the contrary, that 'the big majority of the members ... accepted the Treaty as a means towards complete independence', Ó Murthuile soon concluded that the 'efforts to restore union within the organisation were useless' after 30 January, when Liam Lynch and other 'Centres' in the South had effectively repudiated the Supreme Council's authority. He added, however, that 'the remnants' of the IRB endeavoured to 'bring about unity right through the spring of 1922 as long as there was a hope left, and even on the eve of the outbreak of Civil War further efforts were made to avoid physical conflict'.[115] Despite Ó Murthuile's claim that the Supreme Council never met after January, Harry's diary refers to such meetings on 25 February ('to frame policy') and 11 March, in addition to two IRB Conventions on 18–19 March and 19 April. These meetings were normally held at no. '41', Harry's old haunt behind Foresters' Hall in Rutland Square.[116] No longer 'supreme', the Council had yet to admit its obsolescence.

The Council convened an 'extraordinary conference' including county Centres just after St. Patrick's Day, a week before the banned Army convention. Harry assessed the meeting in a letter to Austin Stack, then representing the opposition in America:

So far as we could gather from the tone of the gathering, the opinion seemed equally divided on the order issued by the Supreme Council and as we were not anxious to force a division until such time as we were satisfied of securing a majority vote we agreed to postpone the Convention. Meantime, the proposed Constitution of the Free State is to be submitted to the Convention.[117]

As with the final draft of the Treaty, Collins deemed it essential to secure sanction from the Brotherhood before recommending any draft Constitution for public debate. Since his main strategy for restoring 'army unity' was to collaborate in a campaign to destabilise the northern state, it was in Collins's interest to avoid any lasting *modus vivendi* with Craig's government. This may have been the unresolved issue to which cryptic allusion is made in Harry's diary: 'Defeat for M. C.: satisfactory Partition? Win: unsatisfactory.'[118] Over the next month, 'the Organisation' seethed with debate about its future political rôle and its relationship with the IRA and the Civic Guard. Harry's old Circle, the Holts, proposed 'that a meeting of all Dublin Centres be called to discuss the circumstances of the present crisis and that a member of S. C. be deputed to attend and explain the position'. Meanwhile, the Supreme Council, accused by one Dublin Circle of treating the brethren 'as Kindergarten Kids', immersed itself in attempts to restore unity in the Army through negotiations conducted 'from an IRB point of view'.[119] Harry, who was not initially involved in these discussions, concentrated his energy on gaining control over the Supreme Council:

The organisation holds a Convention next week, at which I am certain the proposed Free State will be condemned and all those favouring it will be asked to resign. The new S. C. will, I hope, throw all its strength behind the Army.[120]

Once again, Harry's optimism proved groundless, for the convention was 'postponed' indefinitely after reconvening on 19 April.[121] Collins, as chairman, had done his best to quell various 'personal arguments' and to reassure the twenty-seven delegates that the Supreme Council would be presented with the long-awaited Constitution within a few weeks. Harry, initially nominated for the ultimately fruitless bipartisan committee to discuss the 'army position', was displaced by Martin Conlon.[122] His report to Stack indicated that the Convention was 'a total disappointment for Boland', with no condemnation of the 'proposed Free State', no call for the resignation of Treatyist members of the Supreme Council, and successful procrastination by Collins over the Constitution.[123] Yet Collins was perhaps equally disappointed, noting that O'Duffy was 'without hope of unity' though 'H. B.' still pursued his elusive quarry – 'Goodwill Dáil Éireann'.[124]

After apparently securing that goodwill through approval of the Pact between Collins and de Valera, Harry abandoned his attempt to take over the Supreme Council. Instead, as he indicated to McGarrity in early June, he now hoped to use that body as a forum for selecting the proposed Coalition Government:

The H. O. [Home Organisation] Convention has been held up pending National Unity. We can now reconvene the gathering and work out a 'Coalition'. Meantime, I simply advise you on your side to postpone the holding of your Convention for at least two months, say August 15th. By that time we shall have cleared up matters here and will be able to send a representative of the H. O. to your gathering. If we can work out a successful Constitution for the Nation all may yet be well. If not I begin to despair. Collins is more amenable and favourably disposed for our co-operation than is Griffith; and a very interesting six months will open out for Ireland on July 1st next.[125]

Despite the failure of innumerable attempts to restore unity through the Brotherhood or the IRA, Harry's optimism seemed unconquerable. Frustrated by factionalism within those organisations, he turned increasingly to the Dáil as a forum for achieving a broader political compromise.

Remission

HARRY Boland's open activity as an elected deputy and political organiser mirrored his duality as a conspirator, as the mediator alternated with the faction-fighter. Without efficient mobilisation of his own allies, he could not hope to achieve supremacy in the representative bodies which might eventually reassert the nation's unity. Having failed to win over the Dáil in January, de Valera's faction focused on Sinn Féin, the organisation through which all deputies had hitherto been selected. Since Sinn Féin had become dormant, a tightly organised party within that party stood a good chance of taking over its governing bodies and appropriating its hallowed name for the opposition. Within a day of the Dáil's approval of the Treaty, the organisation of a new party was discussed by Harry and other republican leaders at de Valera's hide-away in Rathmines, while the ever-attentive Kathleen O'Connell 'served tea'.[1] On 16 January, Harry's diary noted the appointment of 'Seán T. [O'Kelly] and H. Boland' as 'Sec. Republican Party'. This was not the only meeting of the new body to be summoned on the same day as Sinn Féin's Standing Committee, reflecting its rôle as a factional lobby.[2] In addition to his secretarial office, Harry joined a 'policy committee' comprising Brugha, Childers, Mellows, Constance de Markievicz, and Mary McSwiney.[3] Five days later, Harry signed the appeal which was to prompt his dismissal as American envoy:

> The help of every Sinn Féin Cumann [club] and Comhairle Ceanntair [constituency council] should be secured for the Republic as far as possible. Where the Republicans form a majority in Cumann and Comhairle Ceanntair they should select delegates to the Ard Fheis who can be relied upon to support the existing Republic by every possible means. If the majority of any Cumann or Comhairle Ceanntair should prove to be on the side which seeks to subvert the Republic the names of the Republican members of those bodies should be noted, the meetings held and the names of such members forwarded at once to Messrs. Seán T. O'Kelly and H. Boland, *Republic of Ireland* offices, 58 Dame Street, Dublin.[4]

The machinery for taking over Sinn Féin was rapidly constructed by Harry and other experienced organisers, including veterans of the American mission such as Mellows and Kathleen O'Connell. It was she who typed up 'any confidential work' required by Harry, working mainly from the party's later headquarters in Suffolk Street.[5] While plotting its takeover of Sinn Féin's central apparatus, the new party (also known as Cumann na Poblachta) created its own separate electoral machinery at local level, as directed in a rather misleading circular issued by Harry and O'Kelly in mid February:

A General Election is about to be sprung upon the Irish people immediately. It is now the duty of all Republicans to get to work to prepare and perfect the election machinery in each district with the least possible delay, to ensure the return of candidates pledged to uphold the existing government of the Republic.

In every district covered by a Sinn Féin club or council, election committees were to be assembled from local republicans, whether or not Sinn Féiners.[6] The party's electoral campaign had recently been launched from three platforms in Sackville (O'Connell) Street, with the help of the Foresters' band and several detachments of the Dublin Brigade. Harry accompanied de Valera to this 'terrific demonstration', but evidently remained silent.[7] The campaign was suspended only ten days later, when both factions in Sinn Féin agreed to postpone the election for at least three months in the hope of negotiating a common policy.

Despite Harry's best efforts, republican unity proved to be elusive and, when seemingly secured, illusory. On 12 January, as Harry noted, the Ard Chomhairle (high council) elected twelve Treatyists and only three republicans to the new Standing Committee.[8] Yet the current officers, most of whom had opposed the Treaty, retained their posts unchallenged throughout the turmoil of the next six months. De Valera remained as President, while Harry still shared the duties of Honorary Secretary with Austin Stack. He made no recorded contribution to the debate, acting as whip to the anti-Treatyists and radiating optimism. Whereas Collins looked 'tired, worried and preoccupied', Harry 'alone seemed blooming'.[9] Jennie Wyse Power, a 'stalwart' against the Treaty, portrayed the leading personalities when writing to her daughter a few days later: 'Austin is looking dreadfully bad, the worst of them all. Harry as fresh as a rose, quite a contrast to A. S. Both sat together as Secs. last night at our Standing Cttee. We spent 2 hours there and of that time Biggar [de Valera] occupied at least half of it talking.'[10] Harry enthusiastically pursued the Standing Committee's decision to summon an extraordinary Ard Fheis for 7 February.[11] In calling for the names of delegates and resolutions from local clubs, he and Stack declared that the aim of the Ard Fheis was 'to authoritatively and decisively interpret the Constitution of the Organisation with special reference to the situation created by the Articles of Agreement for a Treaty ... so as to decide the policy of the Organisation in view of possible forthcoming elections'.[12] During Harry's absence in Paris, Collins managed to exclude members enrolled since 1921 from electing delegates to the Ard Fheis, so subverting the most obvious republican stratagem for packing the meeting. On his return, however, Harry gained effective control over preparations for the assembly through his appointment to the credentials committee and his joint responsibility for conducting the poll.[13]

His work was interrupted by a railway strike which necessitated postponement until 21 February. Though Harry retained his place on the new credentials committee, he played no recorded part in its apparently tempestuous sittings.[14] When the Ard Fheis finally assembled in the presence of the mediator McGarrity, the two factions were evenly poised and primed for confrontation. After some rough exchanges, this was averted by an agreement between Collins, Griffith, Stack, and de Valera to adjourn the meeting for three months and postpone the general election until the new Constitution could be presented to voters along with the Treaty. They also agreed to replace the Treatyist Standing Committee with the mainly republican officer board. Harry had again remained silent in public but 'beaming as usual', while 'Austin was as cool as if he were simply playing a game of draughts'.[15] Unlike Harry, de Valera's secretary was frustrated by the outcome:

> The vast majority were Republicans. What a pity a division wasn't taken. We could start a new Republican party clean. Delays are dangerous. Many may change before the Ard Fheis meets again.[16]

At its last meeting, the old Standing Committee agreed that a quorum of three officers would be sufficient to conduct future business, so making it easier than ever for an expert manipulator such as Harry to control what remained of the organisation. Within a few weeks, however, even the central Executive had fallen into abeyance, pending negotiation of an electoral compromise.[17] It was the Dáil, not Sinn Féin, which provided the focus for consequent discussions. Nonetheless, when the adjourned Ard Fheis reconvened on 23 May, it was able to make the long desired display of unity by ratifying the electoral Pact which de Valera and Collins had signed on the previous day. Harry was present to rejoice in the fruit of his labour.[18]

While manoeuvring for unity and therefore compromise in private, Harry was careful to avoid any qualification of his republicanism when addressing public meetings. Like all those who had accepted de Valera's proposal for 'external association' with the British Empire, he was vulnerable to the taunt that his objection to the Treaty was a mere quibble. In Limerick as in America, he presented himself in late February as an uncomplicated, doctrinaire republican, yet also as a democrat:

> There was only one power that they had a right to swear allegiance to and that was to the Irish people – the sovereign power in Ireland. They were

all anxious to have a settlement of the Irish question, and if the Irish people were going to to turn down the Republic they should get something worth having in return. ... In any fight that was to be waged, they were not going to lower the flag of the Republic.[19]

On 2 April, when addressing a meeting in Glenamaddy, County Galway, he elaborated the republican programme. His auditors included five companies of the IRA and two bands:

'Will you get the Republic without another war?' interjected a voice. 'That,' said Mr. Boland, 'is the voice of those for the Treaty. It is the fear of war and the external threat that England holds over our people.' What right had England to threaten them with war? If the people rejected the Treaty and maintained the Republic, England dare not, in the face of the world, fire one shot in Ireland. Asked how he would manage the Northern difficulty, Mr. Boland said he would fight till the British evacuated, and then would give Ulster a Parliament, and perhaps Munster, too.[20]

A fortnight later, the gulf between the mediator and the orator was displayed in Maryborough (Portlaoise), when Harry primly dismissed the doctrine under-pinning all practical attempts to restore unity among former republicans:

Whatever might be said for Griffith's policy that Ireland's luck was inevitably bound up with the British Empire, there was nothing to be said for the men who preached that this Treaty gave them freedom to achieve freedom. ... If this Treaty was signed and the Irish people ratify it, no body of Irishmen dare go out to assert the Republic again. Why? Because there were brethren, one brother in the Four Courts in the I.R.A. Headquarters and another brother in command of the Free State troops to see that the Republic is disestablished. ... If the election came off, it would be an eye-opener for those who were on the side of the Treaty, for he was satisfied that the Irish people would reject the Treaty (cheers).[21]

Once again, Harry had expressed confidence in electoral victory while proclaiming republican subservience to the popular will, a dangerous principle in case of electoral defeat.

Doubtless encouraged by the growing hope of a Pact which would avert a direct electoral test of the Treaty, he reiterated his democratic convictions throughout late April:

He believed the Irish democracy was about the most intelligent in Europe and he was ready any minute to put the question to them. ... He was prepared to let the people of Roscommon, who elected him, decide, and if they decided to go into the British Empire that was their business, but he would not intrude his opinion on them.[22]

On the sixth anniversary of the Rebellion, he spoke alongside de Valera on Grand Canal Street, opposite Boland's Mills:

They met at a time when that independence, proclaimed in 1916 and won the 12th [*sic.*] of last July, was in danger. It was not likely that the men and women who voted for the Republic would vote to stifle it now. They were not afraid of the will of the people. They respected it, and they admitted that the people had the sole and final voice in the matter. The men who drove the British out of the country were strong enough and determined enough to hold on to their independence and were ready to put this question to the people when they [were] guaranteed that they would have a free choice, [but not?] until adult suffrage were passed, and until the threat of war was withdrawn.[23]

By reiterating these preconditions for an acceptable election, Harry kept alive Tom Barry's alternative option of declaring a 'dictatorship', should these demands not be satisfied.

Despite the election of a hostile Ministry under Arthur Griffith, the minority continued to treat Dáil Éireann as the parliament of the Republic and as its main public platform. The republican deputies held frequent meetings to discuss strategy when the Dáil was in session, forming a parliamentary party (distinct from Cumann na Poblachta) in which Harry was a key organiser. He attended every sitting but one between his return in January and the election in June, playing an active and often combative part in the Dáil's debates.[24] He took a predictable interest in the handling of the Bond money raised in America, asking Collins in mock innocence if the new Provisional Government would 'assume the obligations contracted in the name of the Republic, and honour the pledges given in the Republic's name' – to repay the subscribers once independence had been attained. After an intervention from de Valera, Collins proposed without opposition that 'those funds should remain on in trust' pending negotiations.[25] In late February, Harry and Collins united in deploring the insinuation that de Valera had clandestinely withdrawn $120,000 from New York banks at the end of 1921, though Collins was less eager to adopt Harry's suggestion that he refute such 'vicious propaganda' by publishing the American accounts forthwith. In his desire to display a placatory spirit, Harry even voted with the Government against an opposition motion to reduce the estimates.[26] On the following day, he seconded the nomination of an acting Speaker by Kevin O'Higgins, and engaged in boyish banter with Collins over a proposal to advance the national language:

MR. MICHAEL COLLINS: ... Now, the proposal that births, marriages and deaths, if any, after the first July, 1923, be registered in Irish, reminds me

of the old G.A.A. rule that Irish be spoken as much as possible, and that after 1912 nothing but Irish be used in the playing field –
MR. HARRY BOLAND: The reason for that was that the language used on the playing field was so bad that it was decided to put it in Irish.[27]

For an instant, the parties bickering in the Dáil were whisked back to the charmed world of the hurling pitch, where no defeat was ever fatal or final.

Even in moments of confrontation, Harry embellished his thrusts with sometimes scathing repartee. When Griffith denounced the opposition's 'sudden enthusiasm' for female suffrage as an attempt 'to torpedo the Treaty', adding that 'one of the biggest humbugs which has been attempted to be played on the Irish people is this motion', Harry responded tartly that 'we have been humbugging the Irish people a long time then'. He took particular pleasure in wrong-footing the obtuse Joseph McGrath, advising him to 'take the gloves off' when he deplored 'too much winking at things here in the Dáil', and to 'put the gloves on again' when he accused de Valera of consorting with recent converts to the cause. Harry's brief alignment with O'Higgins was disturbed after the Minister for Local Government's haughty response to a question about the closure of the Hawbouline Royal Dockyard off Queenstown (Cobh):

> MR. KEVIN O'HIGGINS: ... I have only to say that I will deny him no information that he asks for in the proper spirit.
> SEUMAS MACGEARAILT: What spirit?
> MR. K. O'HIGGINS: In a helpful spirit.
> MR. HARRY BOLAND: Do you want him to sing 'God Save the King' outside the door?[28]

His tongue was again unleashed on 26 April, when provoked by Griffith's linkage of the accidental death of an old associate with that of Commandant-General George Adamson,[29] 'foully murdered yesterday':

> I am sure this side of the House would very much like to be associated with the remarks of the President on the death of Mr. Frank Lawless[30] and on the unfortunate business in Athlone. I am sure that sympathy will also be extended to the relatives of Michael Sweeney[31] who was foully murdered by troops under the command of Dáil Éireann.

For once, Harry had allowed venom to lace his wit. He was obliged to plead that he 'did not mean to suggest that murder is a business', and to redescribe the demise of both Adamson and Sweeney as two cases of 'unfortunate death'. His verbal retreat allowed the motion of sympathy to pass without further sniping.[32]

A more characteristic intervention occurred on the following day, when

Griffith resumed his acrimonious dialogue with de Valera by charging him with betraying the Republic through his 'Document No. 2':

MR. DE VALERA: ... My statement is on record.

PRESIDENT GRIFFITH: So is your Cuban statement.

MR. DE VALERA: Oh! you are mean! You are vilely mean! You know you said those who attacked me on that occasion were mainly responsible for the record of terror in Ireland.

AN CEANN COMHAIRLE [Eoin MacNeill]: I think this has gone far enough.

MR. DE VALERA: I think it has.

MR. BOLAND: I want to make a suggestion. The honour of this assembly, the honour of the nation and the honour of the men in this assembly should be of grave concern to us all. And I suggest, in view of the regrettable incident that has just passed, that a Judicial Committee of Inquiry be set up by this House to investigate the charges made by the President of the Republic against Mr. de Valera.[33]

Though his suggestion was not adopted, Harry's belated infusion of parliamentary gravity into an ugly cat-fight had a calming effect, confirming his skill in switching the tone of an unwelcome debate. Wit, humour, sarcasm, and high seriousness all belonged to Harry's rhetorical armoury.

His sustained attempt to avert civil war and restore mutual toleration touched every instrument of power, ranging from the IRB and the IRA to Sinn Féin and the Dáil. In the short term, his extraordinary powers of persuasion and wide circle of influential friends often achieved the desired compromise. His collaboration with Stephen O'Mara, the Mayor of Limerick, helped to preserve the uneasy political truce in late February and to prevent collision between contending armies as the British forces evacuated their Limerick barracks. Shortly before the Ard Fheis, O'Mara had sent him detailed suggestions for a public meeting to be held in Limerick on Sunday, 26 February. The republicans should prepare 'a policy and plan of campaign to be announced on that date' or beforehand, being sure to 'bring no women with you as speakers'. With reference to Sinn Féin's constitutional undertaking to 'adopt every means in our power to obtain our independence',[34] he asked Harry to consider 'whether the present "means" ought not to be that of a watching attitude towards the Free Staters rather than one of active opposition'. O'Mara's shrewdness was apparent in his insistence that a rhetorical attack on Northern Ireland was essential if republican forces were also to be dissuaded from murdering their former British adversaries as they withdrew. Without a strong threat to expel the forces in Ulster, 'by force if necessary', Harry would know 'what the alternative will be. I think you can put it into one word – "chausse" [hunt].' Though claiming that all of O'Mara's suggestions, 'with the possible exception of the evacuation', had already been publicly adopted by Cumann na Poblachta,

Harry promised to 'see that your ideas are carried out'.[35] When addressing the meeting in Limerick's pig-market yard, he mollified his staunch defence of the Republic with a conciliatory message: 'He for one had not abandoned the hope that before the Treaty was totally determined, ... the men who signed it would come back to them for their assistance and whenever they were threatened by an outside enemy every one of them would back them up in the fight.'[36] When rival factions of the IRA subsequently jostled for possession of the evacuated barracks, O'Mara's strategy contributed to the unexpectedly bloodless outcome recorded in Harry's diary for 9 March: 'Meet Oscar Traynor, Liam Lynch, Seamus Robinson, Tom Barry, Stephen M. O'Mara. "Siege of Limerick" lifted.'[37]

Throughout March and April, as civil strife intensified and de Valera's rhetoric became more inflammatory, Harry persisted with his strategy of personal mediation. After de Valera's notorious prediction on St. Patrick's Day that the soldiers of the Republic would have to 'wade through Irish blood',[38] Harry received an outraged summons from Patrick McCartan. As McCartan informed Joseph McGarrity in New York:

I suppose like myself you have been disappointed over the result of the 'Agreement'. It looks now as if it were a political trick in order to secure time to more effectively corrupt the army. I called up Harry and asked him to dinner ... and he thought I had some offer from Mick. I said I had no offer and if he had one I'd be very slow to ask Mick again to consider it. He insists that De V. wants a copy of Constitution – which has not been codified yet by the Provisional Gov. He De V. is against the Treaty, wants it smashed but also wants a copy of the Constitution to see if he can work constitutionally under it.[39]

Though himself a tireless mediator, McCartan relied on the more approachable Harry to represent his capricious leader. As he told Dr. Maloney in New York:

Harry spoke to me of the Constitution as a way out but personally I would not trust De V. round the corner. ... The only hope I see is in Collins. Griffith is immutable as you say but Mick is always reasonable and one can always speak and argue with him unlike the high and mighty "Chief" that you met and diagnosed so accurately.[40]

During the last week of March, in between the adjourned conventions of the IRB and the IRA, Harry approached Collins, Griffith, and Mulcahy with a proposal to avoid a contested election by suspending public meetings (apart from joint rallies arising from 'the Ulster situation'), and seeking agreement as to 'the general lines' of a draft Constitution. Mulcahy also detected 'the elements of a further suggestion in his mind ... that a certain percentage of seats be allotted to them. He mentioned 20% but he ran away from discussion of the point.' When chatting to Mulcahy's wife, whose sister was married to Seán T. O'Kelly, Harry had 'kind of pledged his solemn word of honour that if I could get my party to agree on these terms he could get his party, and he mentioned explicitly Dev and Cathal [Brugha]'.[41] After trying 'to reason' with de Valera on 25 March, Tim Healy interpreted this proposal as a plan 'to stop the elections' which would 'be defeated, except in a few districts'. He believed that Harry shared his sense of foreboding: 'Then they will become like the Parnellite faction thirty years ago, only worse. Harry Boland kept the door of de Valera's room, and left sensing tragedy.'[42] On 6 April, McCartan told McGarrity that 'Harry is reported to-day to have said that this is not time for shooting, but the shooting has begun and no doubt De V. is preparing for the Pilate-like ablution.'[43] Another of Collins's intimates, Batt O'Connor, was no less bleak when writing to Harry on the following day: 'I will do what I can with [Eamon] Duggan and carry out your instructions, and let you know result. The Irish situation to me seems hopeless. We are "in the cart" any way I look at it. Civil war is only a step away and I hope the Provisional Government will resign sooner than all the country come to that.'[44] By the end of April, even Harry seemed to have lost his buoyancy, at least in the opinion of Mary McSwiney: 'Poor Harry! For a long time he believed in Mick; believed that Mick and Dev could be brought together. Personally I am inclined to think that Harry did something to infect you [McGarrity] with that belief. He says now it is hopeless because Mick is determined to put the Treaty through and won't acknowledge he has made a mistake.'[45]

Within four days of this pronouncement, Harry was again scurrying along the corridors of impotence as a member of the Dáil's new 'Peace Committee', appointed to respond to proposals from a panel of ten military leaders, matching Collins and his staff with five relatively conciliatory republican officers from Munster. Calling for 'acceptance of the fact – admitted by all sides – that the majority of the people of Ireland are willing to accept the Treaty', these officers had urged 'an agreed election with a view to forming a government which will have the confidence of the whole country', and 'army unification on above basis'.[46] Harry's republican colleagues on the Peace Committee were Mellows, Seán Moylan, P. J. Ruttledge, and Kathleen Clarke, constituting a decidedly stronger team than their Treatyist counterparts (save Seán McKeown). Having quickly dismissed the officers' proposals as the starting-point for discussion, the Peace Committee spent eleven sessions searching for an alternative 'basis for agreement' before reporting its failure on 10 May.[47] The republican version of the Committee's proceedings emphasised the unwillingness of their opponents 'to get down to the details of the settlement', but revealed the acceptance by both factions of 'an agreed election', preserving the current Treatyist majority but giving rise to 'a Coalition Government'. Other republican demands for the temporary transfer of executive power from the

Provisional Government to the President along with a 'Council of State', and for an Army Council and Minister for Defence elected by the IRA, were never discussed. The negotiations were complicated by presentation of an independent report by the five republican officers from Cork, defending their attempt at compromise and highlighting the tenuous influence of their political leaders.[48] Kathleen O'Connell noted the Dáil's 'astonishment when the Army Deputation read a report. Both sides disclaimed all knowledge of it. H. B. entered a strong protest. Chief very annoyed.'[49]

Harry was not only the most active negotiator, but also the republican spokesman. Kathleen Clarke, who chaired its meetings, preferred to lie low:

> Harry Boland, as a rule, reported what progress, if any, we were making, and he asked me to go with him to report. I refused, saying, 'Harry, I want to keep my mind clear. If I go near that man [de Valera] he will get me confused. I'll get lost in the labyrinth of lanes and byways he will take me up and down.'[50]

Over the following week, the Peace Committee had five further meetings, focused upon the number of seats to be pre-assigned to each faction in the new parliament. Though accusing his opponents of 'a mean spirit of haggling for a few seats', Harry eventually 'asked his colleagues of the Republican group to let the Treaty Party have their "scalps"'. According to his second report to the Dáil, an adjournment was then requested by Mellows, after which the opposition faction decided that they could accept no departure from the current proportions, whereupon 'the Conference again broke down'. After various expressions of indignation over the reference to 'scalps', Harry regretted having given offence, explained that 'it required great effort to bring men to see even the necessity for an election', reiterated that he 'would not take responsibility for breaking' on an issue of electoral arithmetic, and asked deputies 'to remember that Tammany Hall in America is considered a very honourable institution'. Having reiterated that 'I am not a politician', he revealed the essence of his strategy of mediation: 'I can imagine it quite compatible with our position to work in Coalition with the men who claim that they are Republicans but who have a different policy to achieve that end.'[51] He could, after all, collaborate with those practising 'mental reservation' in order to subvert the Treaty settlement from within.

His obvious disappointment at the breakdown reflected, according to Kathleen Clarke, de Valera's failure to supply consistent support. When Harry's colleagues objected to his willingness to allow the Treatyists a majority of 80 seats to 48, as demanded by Seán McKeown, he had whispered to her that 'the Chief says we can agree'. Again, when the entire opposition in the Dáil met to consider the proposal, 'Harry Boland maintained that de Valera had told him we could agree to give the majority. This de Valera hotly denied, and said Harry had misunderstood him.' As Kathleen Clarke waited for a lift in Harry's taxi, she 'heard Harry and de Valera shouting at each other. ... I heard Harry say, "It's all right, Chief, you let me down, but I won't give you away."'[52] For all his insight into de Valera's personality and politics, Harry had once again misinterpreted the enigmatic signals by which de Valera broadcast his intentions.

Aware, however, that de Valera remained in two minds and might vacillate again, Harry pressed on with his campaign for an electoral Pact at further meetings of the Peace Committee and otherwise. The stalemate generated increasingly bitter debate in the Dáil, exacerbated by Griffith's decision to propose an election for 16 June in advance of any Pact:

18 May. Thurs. Dáil. Long discussion on reports, very bad temper.

19 May. Fri. Dáil. Griffith moves for election. Cathal [Brugha] answers in great speech. Mulcahy intervenes.[53]

Harry struggled unavailingly to postpone discussion of the election until the various reports of the Peace Committee had been debated, claiming that an open election in twenty-six counties, as proposed, would be 'a violation of the Treaty' which had admitted 'the unity of Ireland in principle at least'. He advocated 'a constitutional method of winning the Republic', warning that the alternative was 'the way of revolution'. The Treatyists should draft 'a Constitution that will give the Republican ideal in Parliament', put it before the people for approval, risk a break with Britain, and 'force England to accept a Constitution satisfactory to all' through a display of national unity. In a fraternal gesture, he seconded Collins's motion for an overnight adjournment, as the Dáil awaited separate reports in which Collins and de Valera would set out their remaining points of difference.[54]

On the following morning, Seán T. O'Kelly initiated a frenzied attempt to resolve those differences before the Dáil reconvened. After deploying his wife to secure Mulcahy's endorsement of his own peace plan, O'Kelly proposed that Mulcahy and he should attend the forthcoming meeting between de Valera and Collins, along with Harry, 'as he and Mick were still such good friends'. The three peace-makers found the leaders locked in stalemate, having failed (in Collins's words) to get 'past the first b—— line'. Allegedly by the device of reversing the agenda to be followed by the Peace Committee, O'Kelly induced them to sign a Pact after three hours of 'heated argument' and 'abuse, which sometimes almost led to violence'. After the opposition had unanimously approved the Pact, Harry again acted as a messenger, enabling O'Kelly to galvanise Collins in his attempt to win support from recalcitrants such as Griffith, Seán Milroy, and Seán McGarry. After O'Kelly had persuaded even Griffith to concur, de Valera and Collins were ready to present their Pact to the Dáil.[55] Ignoring the vexed issues of the Constitution, the Provisional Government, the Army Executive, the restriction of the election to twenty-six counties, and adult suffrage, it proposed that 'a National Coalition Panel for this Third Dáil' should be put forward in the name of 'the Sinn Féin Organisation'. The semblance of democracy was maintained by the significant provision 'that every and any interest is free to go up and contest the election equally with the National Sinn Féin Panel'. The current division of parties in the Second Dáil would be replicated in the Panel, the candidates being 'nominated through each of the existing Party Executives', and after the election a 'Coalition Government' would be formed with a bare Treatyist majority.[56] The agreement to maintain the current factional balance, rather than adopting McKeown's proposal for a substantial Treatyist majority, entailed a return to Harry's initial draft for the Peace Committee. It was this element of the Pact that caused Churchill and his advisers to regard Harry as 'the real architect of the agreement'.[57] The Pact was indirectly endorsed, without dissent, through Griffith's amendment of his original motion so as to render the election 'subject to the agreement arrived at between the Minister of Finance and Deputy de Valera and approved by Dáil Éireann'.[58] This was Harry's moment of muted triumph, signalled by his cable to McGarrity: 'Agreement reached, Boland.'[59]

As the presumed progenitor of the Pact, Harry received congratulations from old allies such as James K. McGuire, who gathered that he was 'responsible for much of the beneficial results and that the Pact or agreement, arrived at, was largely along the lines of your ideas and resolution'. On 8 June, Harry replied cautiously that 'it is a little early yet to prophesy as to whether the Coalition will be successful'.[60] His caution was justified, for by that date the British Government had rejected the draft Constitution, so ingeniously devised to accommodate republican principles while technically implementing the Treaty. Nevertheless, the Provisional Government had since agreed to issue a joint elec-toral manifesto, incorporating 'certain modifications' to de Valera's draft.[61] On 27 May, Harry and O'Kelly had confirmed their promise 'to use all our influ-ence to secure that members of our Party "shall not make use of snatch divisions or take any mean advantage" which would imperil the life or effec-tiveness of the Coalition Government'.[62] A few days later, Harry joined Austin Stack and Paudeen O'Keeffe in sending instructions from Sinn Féin's secretariat to each constituency council: 'Joint canvassing and public meetings should be arranged in each Constituency, and every possible step taken to ensure the return of the National Panel (Sinn Féin) Candidates in accordance with the spirit of the Collins–de Valera Pact.'[63] Though Panel candidates were duly put forward in each constituency on 6 June, the problem remained that the will of Sinn Féin had been flouted by the nomination of numerous 'Independents' (organised as a group by 'Figgis and Co.') along with representatives of Labour and farming.[64] As Collins had observed on 17 May, 'we know that the commer-cial man, the farmer, and the labourer would be more [pro-]Treaty than anything else. But if we enter into that treaty [the Pact] we would make an appeal to the country to avoid recriminatory contests in the full spirit of the agreement, and we would not go round quietly suggesting that so and so should be put up. We would stick to the letter and spirit of the agreement, because if that is not done, no agreement is worth the paper it is written on.'[65] Within a month, to Harry's dismay, Collins would take a different course.

On 6 June, Harry was in Roscommon: 'Nomination day, no contest in Mayo–Roscommon.'[66] He told his constituents that 'he was very glad to be able to come to them with a message of peace and the announcement of a common platform. ... There had been many failures, but he for one had never lost heart, because he had refused to believe that men who fought together and worked together for Ireland would fail to see a better remedy than pulling guns on one another and letting the Irish people drift into civil war.' He condemned Labour (by implication) for contesting other constituencies on the spurious assumption 'that the Sinn Féin panel did not represent all classes in the country', expressing his personal concern about 'land settlement, housing and the unemployment problem'. He promised that the republican deputies would 'help the pro-Treaty Party every way they could' so that they could 'make every ounce they could out of the Treaty position'. The issue of the Treaty should be postponed until a winter election, when the new state, complete with Constitution, financial agreement, and boundary settlement, could be 'presented in full working order for the judgement of the Irish people'.[67] Still better, the Third Dáil might devise 'an acceptable solution, whereby there would be no necessity for any Irishman to accept the position of a British subject', in which case the next election 'would be on internal and local questions'.[68]

Over the ten days remaining before the poll, Harry was an unusually energetic protagonist of the Pact, sharing a platform with Collins, Mulcahy, Stack, and de Valera at the Mansion House on 9 June. While Collins called for the restoration of administrative order and de Valera (as chairman) had 'very little to say', Harry affirmed that 'he had never lost faith in unity. The policy of Sinn Féin was to press ahead for the full national demand.'[69] He then embarked with de Valera and Stack on a strenuous campaign covering contested constituencies throughout Munster and Leinster.[70] In Macroom, within Collins's Cork constituency, he pronounced that 'the leaders on each side had agreed that in the best interests of the nation the men who had been years in the struggle should be returned to the Third Dáil'. In Ballingarry, he 'said the Treaty had not yet been accomplished, and until England had delivered it the forces of Ireland should remain united'. In Clonmel, he warned that 'there were candidates coming along now who were conspicuous by their absence when there was danger'. In Kilkenny, he asserted that 'if the Third Dáil was allowed to work out its propositions they would come before the people next time not with a dismembered Ireland or an Ireland owing allegiance to any power, but with a free and united Ireland'. If the country were 'to be saved, the forces that had led it for the past five years should be returned to the Third Dáil'. When asked, 'at what cost?', he retorted that 'the people or the man who would give up liberty to purchase a little safety deserves neither'.[71]

On the eve of the poll (after a detour to Eoin O'Duffy's Monaghan) he reached Granard, returning to Dublin in time for depressing news: 'Early results bad for Republicans'; 'Treatyists winning'; 'Labor and Treaty sweep country.'[72] Harry spent that evening at Jammet's restaurant with de Valera and Stephen O'Mara, discussing the election and the prospects for a Coalition.[73] As a result of unexpectedly strong support for non-Panel candidates, perhaps bolstered by Collins's last-minute reminder that electors should feel free to follow conscience,[74] the new Parliament included only 35 republicans, an equal number of unaligned deputies with varying degrees of support for the Treaty, and 58 empanelled supporters of the Provisional Government. The undeniable popular rejection of republicanism, in constituencies where candidates had dared to challenge the Panel, undermined the opposition's claim to almost half of the posts in the proposed Coalition Government. Yet, by accepting a British revision of the draft Constitution which made few concessions to republican rhetoric, and reached the press only on the morning of the poll, the Provisional Government had exposed itself to the charge of deception and betrayal. This encouraged the opposition to reject the claim that the election had given a mandate for the Treaty, and to dream that in a fair contest they might yet prevail.

During the campaign, Harry's guarded optimism was not confined to his oratory. As he told McGarrity on 9 June: 'We hammered out an agreement after very hard and strenuous work and for the moment everything is harmonious!!! – how long it will last I know not. I never despaired and bent all my energies towards a settlement.'[75] After the electoral rout, however, he wrote bitterly to McGarrity that the Constitution which the British Government had forced upon Collins was 'worse than the Treaty', belying Collins's 'specious plea that the Treaty clauses could be interpreted in a Constitution, which would (in effect) secure the National position, eliminate the Oath of Allegiance, the Governor-General, and the British Privy Council'. In retrospect, Harry distanced himself from this strategy: 'You know the dope that was handed out whilst you were in Ireland by Collins and McCartan and you will also remember that I was very sceptical as to the ability or desire of the Treatyists to write such a Constitution.' Scepticism, however, had not prevented Harry from pursuing a united front on precisely that assumption. He told McGarrity that the Pact had displeased 'Griffith and his followers' and provoked a 'howl of rage' in London. Griffith had further undermined the agreement by informing the British Government that the draft Constitution 'was evidently all that Mick wished it to be, namely: an instrument that could be accepted by Republicans without dishonour to their principles'. Faced with the alternative of reoccupation, Collins had accepted the British revision and returned to commit 'treachery' in Cork, by repudiating the Coalition and breaking the Pact. Yet, even now, hope remained: 'We shall see in a few days if the Coalition will develop any further.'[76] As Seán T. O'Kelly recalled, Harry pressed on with his ever more elusive quest:

We frequently sent Harry Boland to Government Buildings to see his pal Mick Collins and to enquire if any progress had been made as to the setting up of the promised Coalition Government. Sometimes Boland would return and say Collins was too busy to see him. Sometimes, he would meet Collins and report afterwards that Collins said he was faced with great difficulties and asked us to be patient.[77]

Despite his indignation at Collins's 'treachery', Harry could not decide between the two strategies then under discussion among republicans for averting civil war, on the assumption that no Coalition would be formed:

There are many in Ireland who believe that we must continue the fight at once, against England. Others, there are who think that we must face the fact, i.e. that the people have repudiated our policy and consequently we should quit and give a free chance to the others to work out the Treaty. I am rent and torn between these two ideas and have not made up my mind as to which is best for Ireland, although I am inclined towards the War Policy and will, please God, be alongside any group who may take the bold and manly way.[78]

Yet, when the issue recurred a few days later at the IRA's convention, Harry was among those who resisted Barry's demand for a 'declaration of war' on the British forces.[79] As it became evident that such a declaration would result not in a renewed Anglo-Irish conflict but in civil war, forcing the Treatyist forces into alliance with the British army, Harry's reluctance to follow 'the bold and manly way' intensified. According to his republican ally Robert Brennan, he had personified the issue:

All this time Harry was very busy. Owing to his continued friendship with Collins and his undoubted loyalty to Dev, he was particularly suited to act as a go-between in the negotiations being carried on in the Mansion House in a desperate effort to avoid civil war. One day Harry came into my office and threw his revolver on the mantelpiece. 'It's going to be war,' he said, 'and I'm not going to fire on Mick. So I can't fire on any of Mick's men.' He meant it at the time, but no sooner were the Republican positions attacked than he joined them at once.[80]

As in his response to the Treaty, Harry preferred confrontations between brothers to be initiated by others.

His state of mind immediately before the Civil War was observed and colourfully reported by an emissary of the Clan na Gael, who visited 'headquarters' on Tuesday, 27 June, and met Harry with Austin Stack and Seán T. O'Kelly:

I asked them what they were going to do about this mix-up they were in? Harry said 'mix it up some more'. Austin said 'make it worse'. Then Harry took me upstairs where Gilbert [Ward] and [Joseph] Begley were awaiting the Chief. Liam [Pedlar] came in shortly, and after a while Harry asked all out to lunch. Went to the Wicklow where an hour was spent in the bar, then we went to lunch. The Chief had been in the dining room looking for the lunch, so he came to the table where Harry, Seán McSwiney, Gilbert, Begley and myself were.

After lunch, de Valera informed the Clansman that 'we are hopelessly beaten, and if it weren't for the Pact it would have been much worse. Someone interjected that if it were a free election and that they all had to go before the country they would be beaten all around. De V.: "Yes that is true."' Dwelling as usual on his disappointed hopes,

Harry said that he was mainly responsible for the 'Pact', that he thought they could *win Mick over*, but he was mistaken, that Mick evidently got a spanking in London when he went there in answer to Churchill's summons, that he came back prepared to carry out his orders and use the Pact to beat the Republicans, which they did by giving their support to the independent candidates. He seen [sic.] no prospect of getting together.

Yet, optimistic as ever, Harry assured his guests that half of the National army was 'disaffected and that if anything did occur, that [sic.] they would not fight against the Republicans. Well actual hostilities knocked that belief into a cocked hat.'[81]

Throughout the six months preceding the Civil War, Harry's valiant but ultimately futile pursuit of political unity had been inseparable from his personal struggle to maintain all of his most intimate friendships. If he could only reconcile Collins, the arch-manipulator, with de Valera, the oddly charismatic word-spinner, then de Valera could square the circle with which Collins encompassed the brethren. National unity was unattainable without a working alliance between the most effective organisers and propagandists in the movement, granted that Harry himself was outstanding in both sectors. The flaw in Harry's strategy was his dubious assumption that the British Government could eventually be induced to accept a Constitution allowing republicans to uphold their honour, in preference to undertaking the formidable risk and expense of reoccupying Ireland and governing her as a Crown Colony. His determination to remain intimate with both leaders had overcome many insults, rebuffs and betrayals. Despite occasional frissons, Harry's friendship with de Valera flourished after his return to Ireland, his frequent and often nocturnal visits to Greystones and Kenilworth Square being chronicled in Kathleen O'Connell's diary. While dignatories such as W. B. Yeats sought in vain to make appointments with the haughty 'Chief', 'H. B. etc.' swooped in and out of his life without ceremony.[82] Harry faced a greater challenge to retain the confidence of his former idol and closest comrade. Collins had allegedly not hesitated to appeal to Harry's mother to induce him 'to come with us', promising him 'two jobs'.[83] Harry had likewise used his family as an inducement to win Collins back to republicanism, as he informed Mary McWhorter during her visit just after the election:

> He also told me how hard Collins worked to try and get him to side with the pro-Treaty crowd and how hard he – Harry – tried to get Mick to come back to his first principles. Night after night Mick walked out to Clontarf with him but Harry would not let him enter the house – saying to him that his mother and sister did not want to see him because they thought he had betrayed his country.[84]

The culmination of the Pact should have been tea with Collins at Marino Crescent; instead, the family celebration occurred in Greystones, perhaps with the de Valeras: 'Greystones. Mother, Kit, Ned, Aunt.'[85]

The toughest test of this fractious friendship was the protracted engagement between Collins and Kitty Kiernan. Once again, Harry's political and private lives followed parallel paths, as Collins asserted his power in both sectors while Harry gamely struggled to regain his own influence over the future of Kitty, as of Ireland. As ever, he refused to admit defeat, imagining that the old 'Triangle' could be reconstituted. Only six days after stiffly acknowledging Kitty's engagement to Collins on 10 January, his persuasive pen was back at work:

> Kitty Dear – Thank you for your letter; I intended to visit you over the week end and 'hied me' to the seven thirty Sat. evening last, only to learn that my fortunate rival had preceded me some hours earlier. I there and then decided to await a more favourable chance to talk things over with you. The only comment I make on your letter is, that you are most unfair in your suggestion that my attitude on the 'Peace' is to be condemned, because men on my side may not be all you or I wd. desire!!! You know from my American letters that I had made up my mind without the aid of [erased: any] outside influence, and I hope you will respect my views in this matter. Any time this week will suit me to meet you. I am anxious to meet you so that you may be easy in your mind! I have no desire to cause you pain or trouble and sincerely wish you all joy and happiness. Love to Larry and Mops – Harry.[86]

Two days later, he blithely informed his 'dear Kitty' that 'I'm off to Paris on to-morrow night to attend the Race Convention. I hope to return within ten days and I will then, D.V., come to Granard and renew old "friendships". Tell

Larry I will be delighted to join him in a hunt and, for your own information, I don't care if I never return from the hunt.'[87] His last surviving letter to Kitty was written almost twelve weeks later, using the letterhead of Cumann na Poblachta, when he had finally taken up Larry's invitation:

> Dear Kitty – I'm recovering slowly from the effects of the hunt. The things I walk with are still very stiff. I write to say that I am not as 'bitter' as you may have imagined from the remarks I made during the very enjoyable holiday of last week. No one would be more happy than I, if old comrades were re-united. Maybe this week may see an effort to procure harmony! Knowing how stubborn I am, maybe you will forgive me if I said anything to offend you during the many bombardments I suffered at the 'tongues' of Kitty, Peggy and Mops, last week. My love to all. Tell Larry I will write soon – the same Harry.[88]

However many setbacks he encountered in politics or love, and however much others might change, he would aways bounce back – 'the same Harry'.

His hovering presence often intruded into Kitty's letters to Collins:

1 Feb. Has Harry got back yet? Wire what night you are coming.

14 Feb. I want to talk to you again. One of the things, about drinking with H. B. If he is *not* to be trusted in other things, I wouldn't take much of that particular thing with him. Enough said!

17 Feb. Larry met Harry in town. Harry said he was coming, but Larry doesn't know the day, I think. However, I didn't ask Larry. I forgot.

23 Feb. Tell Harry that I said he needn't be afraid to come now, and that I am writing to him and that we are expecting him here every day.

15 Mar. I may see Harry too, but trust me. By Saturday evening when you come back I'll be tired of everybody, and then will have *you* to amuse me.

27 Mar. What day can you come? Larry expects Harry here for the point-to-point on Thursday.

5 Apr. Harry wrote to Larry saying he is coming tomorrow for a hunt!

10 Apr. I'll tell you all about H. when I see you. He went off on the 6 o'c. on Saturday. He had a great hunt on Friday.

13 Apr. I had a note from Harry a few days ago. Larry expects him next week, I hear!

17 Apr. I believe H. is coming to-night for a hunt tomorrow!

25 Apr. Harry didn't come last week. I think it was Larry's fault tho'. He wrote to Larry saying he'd like to come to another hunt, and for Larry to wire him. Larry did, but very late, but was with him since in town. He wrote me but I didn't reply yet.

6 June. There were a few men there [at Omard, County Cavan], but don't think that I even bothered looking at them, and you misunderstood about Harry. I was only 'trying' to tease you. Don't be vexed with me.[89]

Kitty's allusions to Harry were indeed designed primarily to 'tease' the elusive Collins, hinting that if he could not find time to meet her, or the will to marry her, an alternative suitor was at hand. Harry's quite frequent visits to Granard could be excused by his old friendship with Kitty's brother Larry, and by the enthusiasm for hunting which he had developed in the United States.[90] Kitty's most welcoming reference to Harry was that of 23 February, at the climax of McGarrity's mission of reconciliation. Her tone was coolest in periods of conflict, as in a letter written on the day of the election:

I was coming from the pictures last night about 11 o'c. and I saw a big car same as yours in the dark at our door. I knew it couldn't be you, so I asked the driver who he had and he said 'Mr Boland is inside'. And there was Harry and a Mr O'Donovan, T.D. from Kerry [Thomas O'Donoghue]. O'Donovan left later for Dublin, but Harry stayed and is here to-day. He got a very cold reception and no invitation to stay. I didn't see him only once to-day, but I just 'killed' him. O'Donovan isn't bad. We gave him a bit about Harry too. I felt like saying to H. – well you knew 'he' wouldn't be here this time anyway. The voting is going on all right here. Great excitement but no news. ... H. is 'killing' in to-day's paper on the Constitution.[91]

Yet at the outset of the campaign, less than a fortnight earlier, Harry's diary had recorded a very different visit: 'Motor to Granard, Roscommon and Dublin with Collins.'[92]

Harry himself was fascinated by the forces of affection and antipathy with which political factions were constructed. In late April, Kitty informed Collins that 'last time H. was here he told me (in a burst of confidence) of Dev's dislike for you, because you were too anxious for power, that Dev liked Griffith, but Harry dislikes Griffith, and (of course) likes you, etc.' Collins responded rather impatiently to Harry's parlour game: 'I knew that about de V. well. I have known it all along. That's what he says of everyone who opposes him. He has done it in America similiarly. It's just typical of him. I wish to God I was rid of it all and was just with you and free from their scurrilities and their accusations and counter accusations.'[93] Otherwise, Collins seldom mentioned Harry in his surviving letters to Kitty, apart from a neutral reference in late March: 'Saw Harry today, he'll be with you I think on Thursday.'[94] He did, however, rise to her rather prim suggestion that he should stop drinking with his rival, a decision which would surely have been fatal to the peace process: 'That was rather severe, what you said about H. this morning but I'm not so sure that your keen womanly "horse sense" is not right.'[95]

For all his buoyancy and optimism, the 'split' had cost Harry much of his lightness of heart as he struggled to reconcile the irreconcilable in every sphere of his life. Political dinners in Jammet's and liquid negotiations in the Gresham or Vaughan's could not compensate for the lost romance and easy camaraderie of his earlier revolutionary life. He was too busy to bother even with the GAA, ignoring its annual congress while on tour with de Valera, and evidently missing the hurling final for 1920 when it was finally held at the most gruelling phase of the negotiations preceding the Pact of 20 May.[96] In late March, he was reminded of happier times by a letter from his golfing companion Kitty (alias Kate) O'Brien, who had decided to seek employment in London ('the Saxons' wonderful town') after failing to find 'suitable work' in Ireland. She thanked Harry for his 'kind efforts' in recommending her skills to his former colleagues in the Foreign Ministry, but reflected that 'anyhow, I am not keen enough on the new government to wish my hand to become its servant'. She hoped he would 'be friendly and write occasionally, though lately I have been wondering if I ever knew one Harry Boland T.D.! ... Give my love to Stephen's Green. I always loved it crazily in April. Thanking you for hundreds of things, Harry – here's to our next merry meeting, and may it be soon.'[97]

XIV

Ruin

HARRY Boland's Civil War began one day early, when he was held up by an armoured car on the eve of the attack on Rory O'Connor's garrison in the Four Courts. Harry and four other veterans of the American mission (Joseph Begley, Gilbert Ward, Liam Pedlar, and Peter McSwiney) were 'ordered to put up our hands which we did not do'.[1] The events which followed on 28 June 1922 were recorded in Harry's diary: 'Beggars' Bush open attack on 4 Courts, with artillery, machine and rifle. Join up at Plaza Hotel and am sent south for reinforcements.'[2] Before departing, he is said to have called at Vaughan's Hotel for his laundry, only to meet an old friend on the same mission: 'Collins, as usual, was in tears.'[3] The long-delayed assault on the occupied law courts, following an ultimatum issued under British pressure by the Provisional Government, shattered the dream of a Coalition ministry backed by a unified Army and Brotherhood. Harry had no recorded hesitation in switching from mediation to combat, telling a future obituarist that 'I hoped it could be settled without pulling guns on one another, but the line is well defined again, and our duty and consciences in this issue are clear.'[4] He had shown the same adaptability in America, when excommunicating Devoy's faction after a year's painstaking struggle to reunify the Clan na Gael. The eruption of Civil War brought much-needed moral relief to opponents of the Treaty, like Harry, whose republican principles had been compromised through the search for a settlement. It enabled them to reclaim membership of a virtuous minority pitting its purity of principle, as in 1916, against the superior force of the Republic's internal and external enemies.

Echoes of Easter Week abounded in Harry's last known letter to Kate Boland:

Dear Mother – The fight is up and I must take my place beside the men who are making a last stand for the Republic. It may be that I shall not return. I have a sum of £500 on deposit in the Provincial Bank and a small balance on current a/c in the same institution. You will find the receipt in my bank book which is in the suitcase marked D. L., the key of which I enclose. May God give you strength to stand whatsoever may come. Maybe I shall come through it safely. If not, I hope to pass out to my God like a man. My love to Kathleen, Ned and Ger, Aunt, and all at home. Your loving son, Harry.[5]

The same ominous yet ecstatic tone coloured his correspondence with Joseph McGarrity, whose response to the outbreak of Civil War was to promise that 'our entire energy public and private will be mobilized behind the Republican Army'.[6] On 13 July, Harry despatched a detailed political testament from somewhere 'on the Dublin Mountains', calling to mind Parnell's appeal to the 'men of the hillsides' three decades earlier, and doubtless anticipating that McGarrity would exploit its propagandist potential in Irish-America. This suspicion is confirmed by the fact that Harry, according to his diary, was based in the city throughout the week. On that afternoon he had ventured as far as the Rathfarnham foothills, meeting his sister and Mary McWhorter for tea with Mrs Pearse at St. Enda's school, having previously told the American visitor that 'I am pinned up here like a rat in a trap when I'd a million times rather be out in the hills fighting with De V.'[7]

From his moderately hilly vantage-point, he told McGarrity that 'as I may not be in position to write to you again for some time, and it may very well be that I shall fall in this awful conflict, I want to place on record the events that have led up to this British manufactured war on the Republic'. Lloyd George had 'raised hell' with Griffith and Collins in London, inducing them to accept 'a Constitution which made Ireland safe for the Empire'; Collins had allegedly broken the Pact on the eve of the poll, declaring in Cork that 'he could now speak unhindered by the Coalition'; yet Harry had never abandoned his quest for unity:

> The elections showed that the people favoured the Treaty and our party lost many seats. Nevertheless, we were prepared to work with them in order to stabilise conditions in the country. As you know I was the liaison or medium between our party and Collins. I expected a call from Mick as to the men on our side who would be required to fill the posts in the Cabinet, in accordance with the agreement. No word came. Instead, in the early hours of Wednesday morning June 28th the Free State Army opened the attack on the Four Courts with 4 pieces of British Artillery. As a result of this attack the country is at war again, and all Ireland is ablaze. O'Connell St. is again in ruins and every county in Ireland is up.[8]

This classic republican analysis placed the primary blame for breakdown on the British Government, acting through its Irish agents, and portrayed the opposition as innocent victims whose commitment to co-operative democracy had survived even electoral defeat. Harry did not speculate about the likely outcome if the Provisional Government had defied British objections to the draft Constitution and the proposal for a Coalition, a response which would scarcely have tended to 'stabilise conditions in the country'. His apologia was concerned not with practicalities but with morality, allowing him to portray the Civil War as an unqualified conflict between good faith and base treachery. Collins, through his apostasy, had become more despicable than the hereditary enemy:

> The Government of the Free State shall not function, as they and their army and officials shall be treated exactly as the Black and Tans were treated by the I.R.A. Mick has outdone Greenwood. His Green and Tans raided St. Enda's at 11.30 p.m. last night and caused Mrs Pearse to break down. . . . The drunken results of a drunken 'Treaty' drunkenly arrived at.

As if himself braced by alcohol, Harry could not 'help feeling that everything will yet work out right for Ireland'. Even 'if it is so ordained that our cause goes down in defeat, then the world will say (when all the evidence has been weighed) that Ireland's latest act of protest against those who would carry her into the British Empire was the most glorious of all her glorious history'.[9] As he wrote to another American admirer on the same day: 'Even tho' "this" be left a smouldering heap of ruins the world shall know that there is one land that preferred death to dishonor.'[10] The moral integrity of Harry and his companions would thus be vindicated. Patrick McCartan took a different view, as he revealed when reproaching McGarrity for ignoring his own letters: 'Still you had time to write to Harry, but Harry is a Republican who would have taken office in a Free State Gov. and I'm only a Free Stater who would not take any kind of a job.'[11] The Civil War was not merely a military conflict, but a relentless tussle for moral supremacy in which all of the combatants taunted their opponents over their recent compromises and collusions.

Harry's part in the military conflict was brief and unproductive, as the remnants of Oscar Traynor's 1st Dublin Brigade struggled unsuccessfully to challenge the Provisional Government's supremacy in and around the capital. Traynor, impatient with O'Connor and Mellows for lingering in the Four Courts in search of vainglory, made an early exit in the hope of securing external support for his inadequate forces. He required no less than 5,000 Munstermen, one-sixth of the 30,000 Volunteers in the Southern Divisions patrolling the 'Republic of Munster', impervious to the edicts of the Provisional Government:

> I sent Harry Boland to Liam Lynch's command, believing that Harry could make the case to Liam as no one else could. However, when Harry arrived in Limerick, where Liam was, he found that a Truce had been arranged between the opposing sides. Harry could make no headway in his appeal to Liam, who informed him that he was 'more concerned now in arranging for peace than in arranging for a war'.[12] The only other response from the Divisions was one from the Second Southern which sent fifty men, all well armed.[13]

Along with Seán Lehane and Mossy Donegan, a teacher from Bandon, Harry began his journey to Munster from Sinn Féin's office at 6, Harcourt Street. As Donegan recalled:

The Countess [Markievicz] was there filling a revolver which was broken open on her lap. I don't know what happened when Boland, Lehane and I decided to go or why, or I don't know where we got the car from, but we drove on out. We were stopped about 50 times, but we got there. We stayed in Tipp. in a place which Harry Boland knew, a farm house, and we came as far as Clonmel.[14]

It was from the 3rd Tipperary Brigade based in Clonmel that Traynor received his only significant reinforcements, when Michael Sheehan led a column towards Dublin which joined other republican units at Blessington.[15] This lakeside village in Wicklow, nearly twenty miles south-west of Dublin, briefly became the headquarters for opposition forces in Leinster. From this base, it was intended to intercept Treatyist reinforcements and eventually to launch a counter-attack on the capital. Meanwhile, Harry had evidently continued by train from Thurles to Limerick,[16] before returning to 'work all night in Wexford and Dublin' during the last hours of republican resistance in the Four Courts. By Friday night, 30 June, he had arrived 'in Blessington to await reinforcements promised'. Two days later, Kathleen Boland was sent a reassuring message from 'G.H.Q.', reporting that Harry was 'in fine form doing most excellently, has returned from Cork and is outside Dublin just at present'.[17]

All three Boland brothers foregathered around Blessington, where the senior officers included Brigadier Andrew McDonnell of the 2nd (South) Dublin Brigade, and Gerald Boland, Commandant of its 7th Battalion. McDonnell, 'a wee, small fighting fellow with a rosy baby face that concealed his guile', proved singularly inept as the commanding officer.[18] As Gerald recalled in a candid letter to Traynor, the republican performance was unimpressive:

My action during the Civil War was just to hold up reinforcements going into Dublin, which meant the Naas Road and the Blessington Road. Andy McDonnell should have done the same but took every man he had from Bray to Arklow and left the road wide open. He brought the whole mob out to Blessington in Furey's Charabancs and not even one loaf of bread; although I told Harry (who had arrived from Clonmel with the news that a column was on the way to relieve Dublin) to go to Bray and tell Andy to send me a lorry load of food and boots and waterproofs, as I had nothing to feed the expected column or my own fellows. Part of his mob sat down, or lay in bed, in Col. [Maurice] Moore's home in Kilbride, and I was told later when in Mountjoy that they robbed the two Blessington banks. Billy Walsh was responsible, he later became a bookmaker. I was overwhelmed with refugees including Ernie O'Malley and Seán Lemass who had escaped from the Four Courts and came out to pester me.[19]

The absence of provisions and equipment had removed all normal inhibitions against pillage, and Gerald had no hesitation in commandeering Kathleen

Clarke's car as she attempted to drive through Blessington from Cork.[20] Sheehan's Clonmel column joined in the fun, shouting 'Up Tipp.' as they robbed 'a, few houses'.[21] The rampaging forces desperately required an efficient Quartermaster to secure the required supplies without dangerously alienating the inhabitants, an objective which was only partially accomplished.[22]

On 1 July, Ernie O'Malley and his fellow 'refugees' from incarceration in Jameson's Distillery reached Blessington, soon establishing a makeshift 'South-Eastern Command' in order 'to relieve Dublin and keep the lines of communication open to the South and West'.[23] The ever resourceful O'Malley, as Assistant Chief of Staff, was responsible for pulling together what remained of the Northern and Eastern commands of the IRA, while Liam Lynch dreamily superintended the much stronger forces in Munster from his peripatetic 'Field General Headquarters':

> A defence scheme was hastily drawn up. Seán Lemass, I appointed Director of Operations, Harry Boland, Quartermaster. Harry's gay face lighted up when he had work to do. The bank was taken over as head-quarters; engineers were sent out on the roads with an engineer from Trinity College to dig up the metalled surface and lay mines to prevent the approach of armoured cars. Movable barricades were placed near the village.[24]

According to a contemporary list of 'Executive Officers operating in Blessington area', however, Harry had initially acted as 'O/C Communications'. O'Malley reminded the senior officers under McDonnell's command that 'thoro' destruction of communications, the establishment of our own communications, and the perfecting of an efficient Intelligence system are of *paramount importance*. Your unarmed men can be as useful as your armed men, and your work in maintaining the line of communications through to Dublin is perhaps more important than that of any unit in Ireland.'[25]

In keeping with his assignment, Harry roved about the countryside, trying to initiate attacks on hostile army posts. On 3 July, he accompanied a party with instructions to attack Ballymore Eustace, four miles to the south-west, noting the outcome in his diary: 'Ballymore Eustace. Mob, chaos, confusion.'[26] Next day, Harry left Blessington on a brief visit to Naas, County Kildare, where the anti-Treatyist troops were led by Con O'Donovan. As Harry's old comrade from Lewes and the hurling pitch reported to his Commandant:

> Harry has just arrived here. It has been decided to attack Naas to-night; plans drawn up by Captain Dowd, who will be in command of operation. It will be necessary to place a mine against the barrack wall. ... Harry is waiting here for you, and must parade in Blessington at 10.0 to-night; in fact he has dictated this dispatch.

The attack was abandoned as the Provisional Government's troops converged towards Blessington, forcing the republicans on the defensive.[27] Over the next two days, Harry's diary recorded further visits to Brittas, five miles up the Dublin road from Blessington, and to several outposts in the nearby hills.[28]

When Oscar Traynor learned that 'a pincer movement was closing in on Blessington', he left Dublin for the village and soon formed an unfavourable impression of its defences. Upon answering 'Friend' when challenged by a sentry near Hillsborough Hall, a mile and a half before Blessington, he was appalled to be let through without further enquiry. At 2 a.m. on 6 July, he found 'everybody asleep in Blessington' and 'shook them up, Gerry and Andy'.[29] As he reported later that day:

> Our posts have been beaten in after desperate resistance by our troops. I have succeeded in escaping through their cordon to Blessington. Here I find things rather mixed up. [Gerald] Boland is working like a hero, but Brig. A. McDonnell has retreated from the whole eastern portion of his area, leaving it in the hands of the enemy. This embarrasses Comdt. Boland somewhat on account of the concentration of troops both friendly and enemy. I have requested Brig. McDonnell to split his Brigade into columns and penetrate back into his old area. Unless some officer of superior command is sent immediately to Dublin or district, things may get into a state of chaos.[30]

Demanding an immediate evacuation of the post, Traynor 'broke them up into small parties and told them not to hold towns, told them to hit and go away'.[31] At this point, the Boland brothers parted, never again to meet. For Gerald, their farewell in Blessington was a moment of sacred communion, as he recounted to his mother in November 1923, after forty days on hunger-strike:

> I lie here thinking of many happy things, no sad ones. I remember the loving embrace we had on the Saturday night I left with the abortive advanced party attack on Dublin, and it consoles me for not being near to see his white soul take its flight to benigner regions.[32]

In response to a false report, Traynor sent out a relief force to Cobb's lodge at Glenasmole, two miles on from Ballinascorney. Harry led an advance guard travelling a mile ahead of Gerald's main party, but failed to discover any troops from either side, leaving Gerald and Traynor (in the rearguard) at a loss. Harry's unit remained in the hills, while Gerald withdrew towards Blessington. After reassembling his bedraggled party at Ballinascorney, Traynor decided to return to the city 'with Ned Boland, a really reckless man', who suggested that they follow Kathleen Clarke's example by getting a lift home from a friendly ambulance driver at Crooksling Sanatorium just north of Brittas.[33] Meanwhile, chaos had duly prevailed in Blessington, which was entered by troops from the Curragh on the night of Friday, 7 July. They found that 'the houses occupied by the Irregulars' had been 'wantonly looted, and all kind of senseless destruction is seen. Roughly twenty prisoners were taken including Gerry Boland and Andy MacDonald [sic.]. Several of the enemy were seen to fall.'[34]

Republican reports confirmed that the rout had been ignominous. Traynor was informed that McDonnell and Gerald Boland had 'surrendered, without firing or attempting to fire a shot, to Hugo MacNeill and seven of his men at barricade about one and a half miles from Blessington. All fully armed.' MacNeill's party had previously captured the sentry whose negligence had so alarmed Traynor, and 'then manned the barricade with one of their men garbed to look like our own men'. About twenty troops had been left behind in the village, without 'orders as to whether to surrender or get away', reflecting 'absolute and complete want of organisation of whole Brigade Staff'.[35] One of the last defenders reported that 'I think it is useless in holding out in position any longer. Blessington is taken and our organisation broken in area. Reports are reaching here of a big encircling movement from Naas to Curragh, and it is only nonsense to let them get our arms. I would recommend to dump all arms in safety, give all men some rations, and let every man mind himself. If possible try and stick to some of the cars.' The arms were duly dumped, the defenders scattered, and all hope of relieving Dublin dissipated.[36] These events demoralised the residue of the Dublin Brigades, which remained ineffectual throughout the Civil War. As one Volunteer recalled: 'There was practically no one left in our Battalion. There was a terrible spirit of defeat after Blessington.'[37]

While resistance faded at Blessington, Harry was preparing to abandon his own hide-out in the nearby hills. By the evening of Friday, 7 July, he was ready to decamp to Rathfarnham with the twenty-one Tipperarymen who had accompanied him from Blessington to Ballinascorney.[38] According to Mick Burke from Clonmel, he was disenchanted with his colleagues' performance:

> Harry Boland stuck on to me for Harry wanted to come down to Tipperary, as he was fed up with that other crowd. No one had informed him about anything nor did anyone know what to do. He decided to go up on the hills, and when we were 3 miles up, we saw 2 columns of F.S. [Free State] troops coming up from Wicklow direction. Harry Boland had a brain wave and he decided to get back to the city and dump the lads there for a few days. We headed across the hills and some of the F.S. columns were only a few hundred yards from us. We went to Mrs Pearse's at St. Enda's, where we dumped our stuff.[39]

An emissary from the Clan (Kitty O'Doherty) heard that Harry had arrived there with no less than 120 companions, 'including doctors and nurses. Mrs.

Pearse told me they were all wet to the skin after a week out on the Dublin Mountains. Harry said that night that Mick would get him done in, because he knew too much about him.'⁴⁰ Having moved their 'stuff' into the city and despatched the troops by train to Tipperary, Harry and Burke had completed their contribution to the defence and relief of Dublin. At least Harry, unlike Gerald, was still at large.⁴¹

After the fiasco at Blessington and the arrest of many senior officers, the Dublin Brigade was left virtually 'without organized leadership, and it was up to Harry to try and re-organize Dublin'.⁴² Just before his return, Cathal Brugha had died from wounds received as he belatedly evacuated Hammam's Family Hotel and Turkish Baths in Upper Sackville (O'Connell) Street. Despite their conflict over Harry's purchase of Thompsons in the previous year, Harry was quick to accept his claim to martyrdom:

> Cathal Brugha is dead! No man is here to replace him. He was easily the greatest man of his day; what a wonderful fight he made, with his 15 men against an army. May God rest his soul and give his comrades the courage of Cathal to fight till the fight is won.⁴³

Brugha's funeral on 10 July gave him an opportunity to meet Stack, Traynor, and Joseph Griffin, the Director of Intelligence. With de Valera departing for Mallow and the 'Republic of Munster' on the following day, Harry was freed from the sometimes irritating supervision of his pernickety Chief. As he set out to 'arrange re-organisation', he remarked sardonically upon the transfer of executive power to a Council of War consisting of his erstwhile brethren Collins, Mulcahy, and O'Duffy: 'Mick, Dick and Eoin "the Big Three": what a change!' The appointment of other members of the Supreme Council to govern the prisons, now overflowing with republicans, prompted the further observation that 'S. C. has evidently taken over gaols and gaolers'.⁴⁴ The Brotherhood was out of Harry's grasp, and his influence had to be exercised through other means.

Harry's organisational work proved no less taxing than his week as a soldier, with results noted in a letter sent to America on 15 July: 'As I am writing this he is sleeping the first time in six days.'⁴⁵ In his attempt to challenge the Treatyist supremacy in the capital, Harry enlisted Mary McWhorter to arrange a dinner for twenty-five guests at the Clarence Hotel on Wellington Quay, ostensibly to mark her return to the United States. Kathleen Clarke and Kathleen Boland were summoned to bolster the group of ladies entertaining each other at the piano, while the gentlemen of the IRA remained in the drawing room to 'transact their business'. The 'delicious fish dinner' had been wasted, but after twenty minutes' discussion Harry emerged alone with his military rôle apparently agreed. Though the American visitor believed that Harry had been 'made C.O. at that meeting', noting that 'for the next week … raids and ambushes became a nightly occurrence', his formal office in fact remained that of acting Quartermaster (to the 'Eastern' or 'Northern and Eastern' Command).[46] On the Monday after Mrs McWhorter's dismal dinner party, Harry's diary indicated that his appointment had been confirmed at a meeting with O'Malley: 'Meet A.C.S., agree to serve. Get busy, meet survivors.'[47] Along with Austin Stack, Seán Lemass, and Thomas Derrig, he attended O'Malley's staff meetings in 'a prim Georgian house' near Mount Street Bridge, trusting in the anonymity of the urban cyclist or pedestrian to avoid arrest by those whom he was plotting to destroy. In O'Malley's view, he was ill suited to his military rôle: 'He had been a general favourite, his gay cheery face always brightened up our meetings, but it was impossible to make him take proper precautions: he could not adjust to the new conditions.'[48] His social life seemed unaffected, as McCartan noted on 21 July: 'Harry is now round town and had lunch the other day at Jammet's.'[49]

The final week's entries in Harry's diary confirm that he found it difficult to take the Civil War seriously:

18 July. Tues. Dublin. As war is forced upon us we must bear it.

19 July. Wed. Dublin. Poor McKeown and his armoured car.[50] Guess Seán would rather lose his wife.[51]

21 July. Fri. Dublin. Funny (??) to be on the run from my old friends.

22 July. Sat. Dublin and wee slip of paper at Foley's compels me to take every precaution.[52]

This belated surge of prudence was provoked by a message sent to Marino Crescent, indicating that an order for two typewriters, signed by Harry as a staff officer, had been seized during a raid on a printer's shop. According to Mary McWhorter, with whom he was relaxing after 'dinner' (lunch): 'Harry was terribly upset by the news and said that the quicker he got away to the hills where De V. was, the happier he would be.' There was 'no turning back' for Collins as an adversary: 'My life to him now does not mean the snap of his finger – then too I am not considered a safe man to be allowed to live – I know too much.'[53] Though doubtless reshaped by hindsight and the fables generated by Harry's death, such anecdotes may point to authentic fear in one who had until recently seemed untouchable.

As ever, Harry's enterprises ranged well beyond his official functions as a 'Quartermaster'. The army for which Harry catered, though impressively embracing the two Dublin Brigades, the 1st Eastern Division, all Northern units, and from 25 July the 1st Midland Division, really consisted of a few hundred men in scattered units, virtually devoid of equipment, communications, or experienced officers. The anti-Treatyist remnant of the 1st Eastern Division, for example, had been reduced to no more than 250 men, with only

10 left in the entire 2nd Brigade.[54] In so forlorn a force, Harry's energy and versatility were indispensable. He acted as a conduit for Intelligence, warning Lynch of the imminent 'invasion of Munster' when he reported the expected departure from Dublin, on 21 July, of three shiploads of troops and provisions.[55] He was also alleged (anonymously) to have 'secured' letters from Lady Lavery to Collins, demonstrating her 'complete control' over him in advocating a 'policy which was dictated by Churchill'.[56]

Harry continued to seek funds and munitions for the IRA from McGarrity's Clan, using his well-tested network of American agents. Since 'the Organisation' still had to be 'righted', the County Centres of the IRB being equally divided, he insisted that the Clan's 'sympathy and support, moral and financial', should be directed to the Army Executive rather than the IRB.[57] The first proof of this sympathy, in the form of $19,000 in American bills, left New York with Kitty O'Doherty on 27 July, showing (in McGarrity's words) that the Clan was 'behind them with sleeves rolled up'.[58] Harry's hunger for American support was confirmed by his letter of the same date, urging Seán T. O'Kelly to leave forthwith to attend the Clan's convention in Philadelphia:

This fight is likely to be long drawn out, and we shall require money, and material. Joe [McGarrity] promises full support of Clan. You could bring back with you all available money and arrange with the Clan to supply Thompsons, revolvers, .303, .450, etc. You could also organise a campaign in U.S.A.[59]

The discovery of this and other letters, when O'Kelly was arrested on the following day, may have contributed to the subsequent raid leading to Harry's death, which in turn left several of his American transactions in doubt. These included a contract for 500,000 rounds of .45 ammunition, for which Harry's agent in buying Thompsons, Gordon Rorke, had already been paid about $13,500. As Pedlar warned McGarrity in early August: 'Rorke may try to get out of the business on a/c of Harry's death. You will see that he comes across either with the goods or the money.'[60] The issue remained unresolved fifteen months later, when Kathleen Boland reasserted the claim of Harry's estate against Rorke for breach of contract.[61] Without Harry at its hub, the intricate web of friendship and influence that he had woven in support of the Republic soon unravelled.

During his last week alive, Harry maintained his extraordinary buoyancy of outlook when writing to comrades in the Clan. On 25 July, he asked McGarrity whether he could 'imagine me on the run from Mick Collins? Well I am!' He reminded McGarrity that 'there was not a happier man in all Ireland than I on the day on which Collins and de Valera made the Pact. Therefore, any statement I make in this letter to you is gospel truth and as far as I can, without malice or bitterness.' Collins had defied the 'mandate from the people' for a Coalition

Government backed by a united army, instead establishing 'a Military Dictatorship' designed 'to wipe out the Republicans'. Yet, after a month of conflict, they were 'stronger than ever':

> Most of Munster is still held by the Republicans, but towns cannot be held against artillery, so that the I.R.A. are again working in columns and will treat the Free State Govt. exactly as they treated the British. ... It is heartbreaking to write of Ireland just now, yet we must fight on until the enemy is defeated. Love to all.

In an addendum written two days later, referring to a request from de Valera that Harry himself should 'go out' once more to America, he explained that 'as I am working the post held by Liam Mellows before the fall of the Four Courts and his arrest, it is impossible for me to attend the Convention'. Echoing the truism that victory for a guerrilla force is achieved through its mere survival, he added that 'we cannot lose the fight altho' the odds be heavy against us'.[62] In elaborating this theme for Luke Dillon, he reiterated that 'victory is impossible for them. It would require at least one hundred thousand men, and countless millions of money to maintain a force sufficient to govern the country against the Republicans. In other words the Free State cannot come into being unless the Republicans accept it explicitly or implicitly.' He still hoped that Collins would cease to be 'blinded by the glamour of his uniform and the possession of British heavy artillery', and that he would resign.[63]

Harry remained a politician to the end. Robert Briscoe, the Jewish gunrunner from Ranelagh, recalled that 'during the dreadful first [sic.] week of civil war he was constantly moving between de Valera and Collins trying to patch up a truce'.[64] Harry's diary twice made reference to a 'party meeting' after his return from Blessington, without indicating whether attempts were being made to negotiate a cease-fire.[65] This hope had not yet been abandoned, for another emissary from the Clan heard in mid July that 'the Pr[esident] met Mick the other day and told him he ought to release all the prisoners; he said "I'll think it over".'[66] Nevertheless, after consulting 'the few Republican members of the Dáil available in the city', Harry and O'Kelly declined the Labour Party's invitation to attend a peace conference in the Mansion House on 20 July. They believed 'that for the moment, your Conference can more efficiently pursue the object in view uninfluenced by our presence'.[67] Harry continued to view Sinn Féin as a potential forum for negotiation, as indicated by his sharp protest to Jennie Wyse Power, a fellow-republican, over her peremptory closure of Sinn Féin's office in Harcourt Street. As he wrote on 27 July: 'Although dictatorships is now the rule I hope you will not attempt to imitate "Mick", "Dick" and "Oweny" by arrogating to yourself the functions of the Ard Fheis as they have attempted to usurp the functions of Parliament.' Practical as ever, he suggested keeping a caretaker, typist, and messenger 'until we meet again', adding sardonically that 'the General Secretary is now acting Gaoler to the Assistant Secretary – this disposes of two of the staff'.[68]

The Provisional Government had likewise not abandoned hope of a negotiated settlement. Instead of driving the political opposition irreversibly underground, it allowed several republican offices to remain open. On 5 July, Mary McWhorter had been able to secure news of republican setbacks at Blessington by visiting Cumann na Poblachta's 'strangely overlooked' headquarters in Suffolk Street.[69] Three weeks later, Harry and O'Kelly still felt confident enough to summon a meeting of Cumann na Poblachta at the office of *Poblacht na h-Éireann* in Dame Street.[70] The policy of moderation had been reinforced on 17 July by the Provisional Government's unanimous decision, on advice from Collins, 'that Members of Parliament, persons engaged in political propaganda for the Irregulars, or mere political suspects, should not be arrested, except of course, those actually captured in arms'. The Government, determined to maintain its façade of implacability, added that 'it was not considered advisable however that any public announcement regarding this decision should be made'.[71] Harry's apparent indifference to the risk of arrest, far from being a sign of unmilitary recklessness, was probably based on the plausible assumption that his opponents deemed him more useful when at liberty. Kate Boland, however, did not share his confidence, which may in any case have been skin-deep. On 23 July, Mary McWhorter found Harry at home, as so often, in Marino Crescent: 'His mother was in great trouble about a dream she had the previous night in which she saw Harry lying on the couch lifeless. Harry of course joked her about it, but he said in confidence to me that he had a foreboding himself that he was not long for life.'[72]

On Friday afternoon, 28 July, the seizure of his letter to Seán T. O'Kelly strengthened the case for Harry's arrest. By asking O'Kelly to attend the Clan's convention in quest of arms and ammunition, he had laid both of them open to being treated as gunmen rather than politicians, despite the Provisional Government's interdict against the arrest of unarmed deputies. Liam Pedlar reported the outcome to McGarrity a few days later:

Perhaps I should explain to you now how his letter [to O'Kelly] fell into F.S. hands. He was just after writing it, and also note to Seán T. to come over to see him. He was in Mrs Clarke's at the time. The message went off to S. T. at Republican offices, 23 Suffolk St., and apparently soon after it was raided and Harry's letter got on Seán T.'s desk, whereupon they straight away raided Mrs Clarke's home, but Harry seeing them coming made his get-away.[73]

Kathleen Clarke was present during the raid in Suffolk Street, when O'Kelly was arrested, and 'hurried home to tell Harry Boland; I had a feeling they would come there for him'. Harry, without asking leave, had made her home in

Fairview 'his headquarters' during her temporary absence from town. Seeing troops turning into Richmond Avenue, she advised him to 'Run!' and hid his papers under her son's pullover during the fruitless search which followed.[74] Pedlar, who was also enjoying her involuntary hospitality, remained for the raid and wittily passed himself off 'as a Mr. Thompson from New York'.[75] Meanwhile, Mary McWhorter had been dealing with O'Kelly's 'hysterical' wife, Nan, and Nan's brother, Dr. James Ryan. Ryan had 'slipped in and asked me to get word to Harry Boland that the matter about which Harry and Seán T. were to confer on, later in the day, was known to him and to have Harry connect with him as soon as possible'. Having been advised by Kathleen Boland to arrange this through the publican Phil Shanahan,[76] she called on Nan O'Kelly in Ranelagh, only to find yet another raid under way there.[77]

The incriminating letters found with O'Kelly were immediately exploited by the Provisional Government. Collins himself advised that 'they ought to be given to the Press exactly as they are':

It would be well to make a comment on Boland's letter: say he is using the Clan which he severed from the old body to maintain and support Civil War in Ireland. Good use can be made of these papers if they are written up in the proper way. The other day *Poblacht na h-Éireann* accused prominent Army men of belonging to the I.R.B.; they lauded de Valera and Boland for not having anything to do with Secret Societies.[78] Now we see de Valera in his true light as being not only a Secret Society man but the maker of a Secret Society specially for his own purposes.[79]

These 'remarkable letters' were issued by the Government Publicity Department on 31 July, and widely reproduced on the Tuesday.[80] The pursuit of Harry, the quintessential 'Secret Society man', was under way. Yet, if one 'private source' is to be believed, Collins had promised not to arrest his former comrade in a boozily histrionic letter sent on 28 July: 'Harry – It has come to this! Of all things it has come to this. It is in my power to arrest you and destroy you. This I cannot do.' Reversing Harry's hope that Collins would rediscover his true loyalty, he added that 'if you will think over the influence which has dominated you it should change your ideal. You are walking under false colours. If no words of mine will change your attitude then you are beyond all hope – my hope.'[81] The last sentence carried the innuendo that some of Collins's colleagues might not share his hopes and his qualms.

Following his escape from Kathleen Clarke's house on the Friday afternoon, Harry sensibly avoided Marino Crescent. As Kitty O'Doherty reported to the Clan, the house was raided that night:

Harry's mother cried bitterly in describing to me a raid on her home on the Friday night before they shot Harry. She said the English soldiers who raided her often were gentlemen in comparison to the Free Staters. They asked jeeringly where Harry was when the war was on against England – then they added that he was hiding in America – and they threatened they would get him yet. They arrested Seán [O']Donovan, her daughter's fiancé, who was in her house.[82]

On that night, Harry and Pedlar 'slept together at the stout man's house', a reference to the Irish-American Edward J. Hearty whose return to Ireland had provided such ingenious cover for the importation of arms. Pedlar 'left him to another place on Sat. night about 11.30 p.m. and that was the last I saw of him alive'. During this period, 'poor Harry' reassured Pedlar 'that they would never put the Free State over even with Churchill's Big Guns'.[83]

On Sunday, 30 July, he again dined at Jammet's celebrated restaurant in Nassau Street with Anna Fitzsimons, one of the adoring secretaries with whom he had worked and cavorted in the Sinn Féin office. As if conducting the Last Supper, he urged her to 'eat well' as it might be 'your last meal with me'.[84] In a more prosaic version, she remembered 'a killing hot day in the last week of July with a war on outside the restaurant. I didn't want to eat, but he pressed me and gave me a lecture on the importance of having a good meal no matter what was going to happen next.'[85] Later that day, he called on several of his senior comrades in the IRA:

Joe Griffin with Austin Stack and Oscar Traynor were staying at Upper Mount Street, probably no. 11.[86] Harry Boland drew up in a taxi and urged Stack and Oscar to go for a breath of fresh air with him. They refused: he then turned to Joe Griffin and asked him would he come.[87]

Traynor had in fact been arrested three days earlier,[88] and it was his wife who farewelled Harry on this occasion. As Annie Traynor recalled: 'I was speaking to him on Sunday evening last, and shook hands with him just before he started on that fatal journey. I am proud to have done so, now. His parting words were a jest.'[89] The Quartermaster and the Director of Intelligence then left for Skerries, nineteen miles north of Dublin, meandering through Fairview towards Malahide and diverting inland to Swords, before striking eastwards to the seaside village.[90] At Coolock, on the Malahide Road, they stopped for a drink. According to information received by Ernie O'Malley, this proved to be a costly indulgence. After shaking hands, the publican left Harry in the shop and withdrew to the parlour, where he identified his visitor to a Frongoch veteran from Artane who had once served in Harry's 2nd Battalion, Dublin Brigade. The patriot in the parlour thereupon 'went out to telephone for troops'.[91]

Why did two senior staff officers drive to Skerries at a period when the republican forces in the district were negligible, whereas substantial 'enemy stations' with 100 troops existed in Swords, Balbriggan, and Julianstown? On

5 August, the 8th (Fingal) Brigade contained only 24 Volunteers (including 8 in Skerries), having lost 16 men since the outbreak of 'hostilities'. The acting Commandant was 'trying to get some more arms into this area and the remnants here can form a column to watch the important roads running through this area. There are no explosives at present here and no engineer available.'[92] It is possible that Harry and Griffin were preparing for this reorganisation; though, according to another speculation, they may have been arranging transport to Liverpool in order to facilitate a mission to America.[93] Whatever Harry's business, it evidently required repeated visits, for one journalist heard that 'Boland had been hiding in Skerries off and on for some time'.[94] The secret of his mission may have been contained in a document which caused Collins to protest to his Director of Intelligence that 'you have not sent me any copies of the letter which was found in the late Harry Boland's note book. Please send me one or two.' If he did so, the letter has eluded detection.[95]

After reaching Skerries, Harry and Griffin booked a room in the Grand Hotel in Great Strand Street. Griffin recalled that 'they retired to the bar and had a few drinks and chatted with the bar-maid, whom Harry seemed to know. Joe ended the session by saying he was going to bed and he was followed by Harry. Both slept in the same room.'[96] Harry retired between 1 and 2 a.m., and remained awake when soldiers from Balbriggan coastguard station burst into the room shortly afterwards.[97] What happened next immediately became a matter of contention between official and republican propagandists, with numerous conflicting reports appearing in the press and circulating in private. By Griffin's own account, he 'didn't want to make it appear that he knew Harry at all', hoping to 'slip away unknown as he had slipped out of the Four Courts with Seán Lemass'. Awakened by the sound of footsteps and a knock, he signalled a warning to Harry, who was 'already up' and made for the door. Griffin heard a scuffle and a shot before asking the troops to summon priest and doctor.[98]

The Dublin newspapers, subject to rather capricious censorship by Piaras Béaslaí, reported that Harry was 'alleged to have resisted' the 'small detachment' endeavouring to arrest him in the bedroom: 'In this struggle a shot was discharged, and Mr. Boland collapsed on the bedroom floor, bleeding profusely.' According to 'another account', he had tried 'to seize a gun from one of the soldiers'. He was attended by Dr. Bernard Healy, jun., and Fr. Michael Ellis, before being conveyed by 'army ambulance' to St. Vincent's Hospital.[99] A source deemed 'reliable' by the *Freeman's Journal* offered a more detailed chronicle:

Mr. Boland was wanted. We went to the hotel, and two or three of us entered his room. He was in bed. We wakened him, and he got out of bed and partly dressed himself. He had no gun. Suddenly he rushed to tackle one of our fellows for his gun. A shot was fired over Boland's head to warn him to desist, but he determined to struggle, and practically had the gun when another shot was fired and Mr. Boland was wounded. The bullet entered the right side about the ribs.[100]

This version of Harry's attempt to resist arrest accords closely with the available official accounts. The first telephoned report of the raid, passed on from Wellington (later Griffith) Barracks, confirmed that the arrest occurred between 1 and 2 a.m. and that 'in attempting to seize a gun from one of our men, Boland was seriously wounded'. The reporting officer asked for an ambulance to be sent 'immediately to Wellington', adding that 'another fellow (unknown)' had also been arrested.[101] A fortnight later, the National army's journal published a detailed refutation of republican claims that the 'murder raid' had required sixty men backed up by an armoured car at the hotel entrance.[102] It also pointed out that 'persons in revolt against the Government, when once made prisoners by the military authorities, are liable to certain well-defined risks, where any effort is made to escape'. According to the anonymous officer in charge of the raiding party:

At 1 a.m. on the morning of the 31st ult., I got information that Mr. H. Boland and a friend were at the Villa, attached to the Grand Hotel, Skerries. I took twelve men (Lancia and Ford) which I left outside the town. I surrounded the place and searched the Villa, but the men were not there. We then went to the Hotel. I went there with another officer, and found Mr. Boland and his friend occupying two different beds in a room. We told them they were under arrest, and that the house was surrounded. I asked them to dress and come along. Mr. Boland asked to be let have his sleep, and said he was willing to report at any place and time he was wanted. We told him we could not agree to that. Mr. Boland and his friend then got up and dressed very slowly. At this time only the other officer and myself were in the room; the other men were outside the Hotel and around it back and front. The second officer was going through some papers which he had taken from the pockets of Mr. Griffin's clothes, when Mr. Boland sprang upon him and tried to wrest the revolver from his hand. I fired two shots over Mr. Boland's head in the hope of inducing him to desist. He did not do so, but, shoving the second officer to one side, dashed out on the corridor. Fire was opened down the corridor. Mr. Boland was five or six yards gone at the time. One bullet took effect and he fell. The only other officer, in the Hotel, who was stationed on the landing, came to Mr. Boland's assistance.[103]

Republican accounts varied as to the scale and circumstances of the raid. A contemporary handbill claimed that 'one unarmed man was surrounded by 16 armed men. The town was filled with armed Free Staters, yet Harry Boland, unarmed, surprised in bed, could not be arrested without being shot.'[104] His sister Kathleen told McGarrity that 'six armed men came into the Hotel and shot him down like a dog. There was a crowd round the hotel, 28 or 30 of the Free Staters in armoured cars. ... He was left in the bed and not brought into the hospital until eight o'clock that morning.'[105] Fr. Ellis, the curate in Skerries who attended him, told Kathleen and Mary McWhorter that he had found Harry 'lying in bed uncovered', with six soldiers in the room, two of whom remained indecently near to the bed while he heard confession, after Griffin's removal to another room. Asked if anything troubled him, Harry had replied 'No, Father, thank you – I am very happy.'[106]

A report in the *Cork Examiner*, as 'passed by Censor' while under republican control, indicated that only two soldiers had entered Harry's room, having previously 'rushed' into a bedroom occupied by two unnamed men who had 'accompanied' Harry and Griffin to the hotel:

One of the Free State soldiers, who had his cap pulled over his eyes, flashed a lamp into ——'s face and roughly enquired, 'What is your name?' The other soldier who stood at the door said 'That is not the man.' They then went into the room where Harry Boland and Joe Griffin were in bed. Joe Griffin was taken out into another room. Immediately shots were fired. An attempt may have been made to kill Harry at once for there is a bullet mark on the ceiling, and he may have tried to save himself by knocking the revolver in the soldier's hand. As there are two marks in the corridor it is assumed he darted out trying to escape. He was shot through the back and stomach. A priest who visited the hotel believes he was shot in bed, as the bed is stained with blood and there are no stains anywhere else. Miss Boland, who saw him in hospital on Monday just before he was operated on, states that Harry said he was shot by a man who was with him in Lewes Gaol.[107]

Despite its outraged tone, this account differed little in substance from that later published in the official Army journal.

In retrospect, Harry's closest comrades rejected the propagandist accusation that Collins and his colleagues had conspired to murder Harry.[108] In 1962, de Valera dictated his verdict to Marie O'Kelly, who had succeeded her aunt (Kathleen O'Connell) as his secretary:

I do not think that Mick Collins willed the death of Harry Boland or that his killing was in any way premeditated or deliberate. The impression which I gained from talking to people such as Joe Griffin ... was that Harry behaved impetuously and that the raiders were men who had not been accustomed to having guns in their hands and that they got excited and fired.[109]

Patrick McCartan, who was still privy to information from both sides, told McGarrity on 3 August that, prior to the raid, 'there was no serious look-out for him and no anxiety to arrest him. It must have been the letters found on Seán T. O'Kelly that caused the change. I also know that his best friends and those he liked best were in this case his enemies. He would not tell his sister the name of the man who shot him.' Two days later, he passed on 'fairly reliable information' that two men had entered Harry's room: 'They talked to him and reasoned with him for a while and he said he would resist arrest. One went off to get assistance and Harry jumped for the man who remained and tried to secure his revolver. In the scuffle Harry was shot.' Though not accusing the raiders of murder, McCartan pronounced that they 'should have had special instructions. They could and should have had enough men to overpower him without guns. Their vicious propaganda made it impossible for men like Harry to surrender without a fight. When they surrendered easily they were sneered at. Propaganda on both sides is rotten and contemptible.'[110]

The Provisional Government was embarrassed by the fact of Harry's arrest, despite its public defence of the shooting of those resisting capture. On 31 July, ministers had reviewed their previous injunction against the arrest of unarmed deputies and propagandists: 'Reference was made to the arrest of Mr. Harry Boland, T.D., and Mr. Seán T. O'Kelly, T.D., and it was decided that the decision of the Government at their meeting of 17th July, 1922, ... should be adhered to.' It took another month of Civil War to persuade the Government that 'any member' of the new Dáil 'who has taken up arms against the Government should be arrested'.[111] Since the decision of 17 July had never been made public, the Government was spared the indignity of having to admit that its instructions had been ignored. The incriminating letter to O'Kelly supplied a justification, but not necessarily the motive, for the raid and its fatal outcome. It is even credible that the operation was carried out on the initiative of a local Army officer, without central instructions or authorisation, acting on a tip-off.

Nearly a month later, Liam Lynch asked O'Malley if it were 'known definitely who shot Harry Boland and exact circumstances of the shooting? The late D/I [Griffin] should be able to throw some light on this fact.' O'Malley replied that 'it is not definitely known who shot him; the late D/I forwarded some information but evidently he did not recognise any of the men there'.[112] In November 1923, however, Joseph McGarrity received a list of four names, purporting to identify 'those who murdered brave Harry Boland'.[113] All four names correspond to officers based in November 1922 at Balbriggan. These were an Intelligence Officer in the 5th Battalion, 2nd Eastern Division (with the temporary rank of Captain) from Lusk, aged 28; a Commandant from Malahide, aged 29; a Vice-Commandant from Balbriggan, aged 24; and a Captain from Donabate, aged 27. All four had been attested in the reorganised Army during the first week of May 1922. All were Catholics, and all but one unmarried.[114] Various records indicate that each had served in the pre-Truce

Dublin or Fingal Brigades and had, with one possible exception, participated in the Easter Rebellion. They included a land steward who had been court-martialled in 1916; an asylum attendant interned at Frongoch; a clerk imprisoned for illegal drilling in 1918; and the son of a prosperous farmer and grocer, notable among the Gaelic footballers at Frongoch and a District Centre in the IRB. None of those named appear in Harry's surviving correspondence or diaries, but the Intelligence Officer had shared his experience of being sentenced to death in 1916 (after fighting in the Mendicity Institution), before undergoing penal servitude in Portland and Lewes. He had joined the IRB in 1915 and become Adjutant of the 8th (Fingal) Brigade before switching to Intelligence. His experience and local knowledge had enabled him to turn in an entire 'Irregular' column at the outset of the Civil War, and he was amply qualified to identify Harry in his bedroom at the Grand Hotel. If such officers as these were indeed members of the raiding party, their revolutionary and military credentials were impeccable. They were no 'murder gang' of inexperienced 'Truciliers' or unprincipled mercenaries. Harry had been struck down by his own kind.

Harry's agony was prolonged and ugly. In any case, he could scarcely have survived the shot which had passed through his abdomen and diaphragm, causing considerable haemorrhage and tearing his spleen, solar plexus, and liver. His condition was worsened by the interval of at least six hours between the shooting and his delivery by ambulance to St. Vincent's Hospital in St. Stephen's Green.[115] When examining him at 8.15 a.m., the House Surgeon noted that 'he was then conscious but collapsed and vomiting'. Harry rejected the surgeon's advice for an immediate operation to remove the bullet, 'which was palpable beneath the skin of the chest wall' on his right side.[116] Before facing the knife, he wished to see Fr. Walter Thornton (the Chaplain) and his sister Kathleen. After the Chaplain had fetched her from Marino Crescent in an outside jaunting-car, Harry spoke about his killer to Kathleen and then prepared for his operation just after midday. A visiting surgeon to the hospital, Dr. Denis Kennedy, proceeded to extract the bullet in a futile operation which left Harry unconscious overnight.[117]

After regaining consciousness next morning, Harry told his mother and sister that he also wished to see Gerald, who had been incarcerated in Mountjoy since his surrender outside Blessington. Kathleen, accompanied by Mary McWhorter, then went to Mountjoy to request Gerald's release on parole.[118] As she left St. Vincent's, the Commandant of the military guard warned her that he had orders to shoot Harry, should he attempt to escape.[119] This was presumably an interpretation of a message to the Director of Intelligence from Collins, who had reason to respect Harry's ingenuity as an organiser of escapes:

Will you please send some good officer to Vincent's Hospital and make a report on the exact condition of Mr. Harry Boland. It is necessary to find out whether he has been operated on and what the doctors think of his condition. There will not be a Guard placed over him but we want to take some precautions to prevent escape.[120]

Kathleen carried a letter for the Governor of Mountjoy (Colm Ó Murchadha), signed by her mother: 'My son Harry is dangerously ill, his life may be only the matter of a few hours or less. He is calling constantly for his brother Gerald. I would be grateful if you will parole my son Gerald in order that he may see his brother before he dies.' The Governor allegedly 'came to the gate himself and told Miss Boland that he had no power to grant paroles', sending her to Portobello (now Cathal Brugha) Barracks to make her appeal to the Adjutant-General, Harry's old comrade Gearóid O'Sullivan. He referred her to his recently enrolled assistant, Kevin O'Higgins, who declared that 'no paroles were to be given and paroles had been refused in just as distressing cases'. Gerald could only be allowed out if he 'signed an undertaking tantamount to treason to the Republic'.[121] Mary McWhorter found O'Higgins 'pompous'; Kathleen felt that 'his attitude was hostile and very hard'.[122] Harry still yearned to see his brother: 'A couple of hours before he died he asked again – and Mrs. Clarke wrote a personal letter to Collins who was known to be in Portobello at the time. Father Albert[123] carried this letter – and the reply was that General Collins could only be seen during office hours.'[124]

Still conscious and besieged by visitors, clerical and lay, Harry responded with characteristic bounce when Patrick McCartan called: 'I am just after visiting him in hospital and I fear it is all up with him. He recognised me though a bit delirious and wanted to get out of bed. Poor Harry.'[125] The end did not come until 9.10 on Tuesday evening, 1 August, after forty-three hours of struggle. Kathleen Clarke recalled that Harry died 'in the most terrible agony. I was present with his mother and sister when he died, and I shall never forget it. His poor mother fainted at the sight of his terrible suffering.'[126] He was 'still bleeding internally' long after death, making it tricky to dress him for burial in the military uniform which Mary McWhorter, unlike other mourners, deemed appropriate for a republican whose normal uniform was a well-cut suit. In the mortuary chapel next morning, blood was still pumping from his mouth, but by evening his body was 'as black as ink'.[127] As his blackened body ceased to wrestle, Harry Boland's 'white soul' took flight into Ireland's history.

Epilogue

MANY models or morals might be drawn from the life and death of Harry Boland. His disposition and values were those of an old-fashioned republican, for whom the use of terror and violence to overthrow 'English' rule in Ireland was a noble aspiration, perfectly compatible with the pursuit of personal honour and Christian salvation. It was for this combination of attitudes, expressed in the manner of his dying, that he has ever since been venerated by revolutionary republicans as a pure-souled martyr. Yet, in his actual conduct as a revolutionary in both Ireland and America, he epitomised the subtleties and ambiguities associated with Sinn Féin since the 'cease-fires' in Northern Ireland. Doctrine was subordinated to the twin quests for republican unity and political supremacy, which entailed reiterated compromise, systematic duplicity, and mastery of the techniques of propaganda and persuasion. He therefore spoke in discordant voices to the brethren, the nation at large, and the American politicians on whom he relied to deliver Irish freedom. If his outlook seems archaic, his practice was astonishingly modern. More than de Valera, more even than Collins, Harry Boland was a forerunner for Adams and McGuinness.

His influence within the revolutionary movement, all pervasive, was not always positive. Though he was famously energetic and persuasive as an organiser and intermediary, his schemes were often too artful to be lastingly effective. When frustrated in the quest for unity between vying factions, in Ireland as in America, he turned from conciliation to dictation with disconcerting ease. Yet, as a dictator, he almost invariably acted on behalf of someone else, usually Collins or de Valera. Far from seeking personal ascendancy, he used his influence to bolster whichever leader or policy seemed most likely to maximise republican solidarity. He was truly a 'secret-society man', for whom the Irish Republic was embodied in the select circle of past and present brethren sharing his convictions. 'Popular sovereignty' signified the will of the illuminati, regardless of the often ill-conceived preferences of the majority. The men of 1916 had been reared in the belief that rebellion was justifiable even when unpopular, a principle to which the minority reverted during 1922. In this respect, his views were indistinguishable from those of de Valera and indeed Collins, for both of whom democracy was a practical tool rather than a guiding principle.

Yet Harry Boland cannot be dismissed as a cynical élitist, contemptuous of the public opinion which he manipulated with such brilliance. The popular triumph of republicanism between 1917 and 1921 seemed to vindicate his view that the people, hitherto 'fooled' by the specious promise of Home Rule, had at last discovered their deeper desires and loyalties. Like Collins, he believed himself to be a man of the people who was entitled by birthright to speak on their behalf, even when they were temporarily misled. Without internal unity, the inner circle could not hope to rescue the nation from its endemic folly. The proper function of the brethren was not to subjugate the people, but to organise and educate them until they qualified for full citizenship of the Republic. Harry Boland was at once a dictator, an élitist, a populist, and a democrat.

More than that, for better or for worse, he was a true revolutionary. Whether we consider that he was driven by a laudable conviction in the inalienable rights of nations, or gripped by a grotesque delusion, the sincerity of his struggle cannot be impugned. He lived the Irish revolution more fully than most, especially in America, discovering unsuspected powers of eloquence, shrewd judgement, and political finesse. He learned to exploit his charm and mother wit for political ends, without corrupting his humanity in the process. Despite innumerable inconsistencies, deceits, and miscalculations, he never surrendered his integrity as a servant of the brethren. Even the rupture of 1922 failed to puncture his buoyancy. While arrogance or envy twisted the minds and motives of his closest comrades, he remained what he had always been. Harry Boland deserves to be remembered as a man of goodwill, who enhanced the lives of all that knew him.

Abbreviations

AARIR	American Association for the Recognition of the Irish Republic
AIHS	American Irish Historical Society (New York)
AOH	Ancient Order of Hibernians
BL	British Library (London)
BP	Boland Papers (in possession of Harry Boland, jun.)
CBS	Crime Branch Special (RIC)
DMP	Dublin Metropolitan Police
EdeV(P)	Eamon de Valera (Papers, UCDA)
FOIF	Friends of Irish Freedom
GAA	Gaelic Athletic Association
GHQ	General Headquarters
GPO	General Post Office
HB(D)	Harry Boland (Diaries, UCDA)
INB	Irish National Brotherhood
IRA	Irish Republican Army
IRB	Irish Republican Brotherhood
KK	Kitty Kiernan
MAD	Military Archives, Dublin
MC	Michael Collins
McG(P)	(Joseph) McGarrity (Papers, NLI)
MP	Member of Parliament (House of Commons)
NAD	National Archives, Dublin
NAW	National Archives, Washington
NLI	National Library of Ireland (Dublin)
NYPL	New York Public Library
PRO	Public Record Office (London)
RIC	Royal Irish Constabulary
TD	Teachta Dála (Deputy of Dáil Éireann)
UCD(A)	University College, Dublin (Archives)

Notes

CHAPTER I. APOTHEOSIS

1   *An t-Óglách*, 12 Aug. 1922: cutting in PRO, WO 35/206/10, f. 13.
2   MC to Director of Intelligence, 3 Aug. 1922, with reply, 4 Aug.: Mulcahy Papers, UCDA, P7/B/4, ff. 73–4.
3   John R. Murphy (editor) to Commandant-Gen. Piaras Béaslaí, 8, 9 Aug. 1922, enclosing *Dublin Evening Mail* ('Final Buff' edn.), 3 Aug.: Béaslaí Papers, NLI, MS 33915/11; *Irish Times*, 4 Aug.: cutting in Childers Papers, NLI, MS 15441/2.
4   *Poblacht na h-Éireann*, War News no. 29 (2 Aug. 1922): BP.
5   Ibid., no. 31 (4 Aug. 1922): BP.
6   *The Torch*, 2 Aug. 1922: O'Malley Papers, UCDA, P17a/251.
7   *New York Times*, 22 Aug. 1922, p. 19.
8   Patrick McCartan to McG, 5 Aug. 1922: McGP, NLI, MS 17457/13; *New York Times*, 22 Aug. 1922, p. 19.
9   Kitty O'Doherty, Report to Clan na Gael (undated, *circa* Aug. 1922), f. 6: McGP, MS 17471.
10   After discussion of a letter from the Commander in Chief on 18 Aug. 1922, the Provisional Government decided to draft remonstrances to Bishop William Codd of Ferns and the Franciscan Provincial, Fr. Dominic Enright. Cosgrave, as acting President, wrote accordingly on 21 Aug., eliciting their diplomatic responses two days later: NAD, Executive Council Papers, S 1622 (referring to P.G. 93, 99). If Fr. Mathew created 'further trouble', his utterances escaped the vigilance of Patrick Murray, whose invaluable catalogue of politically active priests in *Oracles of God: The Roman Catholic Church and Irish Politics, 1922–37* (Dublin, 2000) lists several other Franciscans (pp 460–1).
11   Childers Papers, NLI, MS 15441/7; Barton Papers, NLI, MS 5638; Scrapbook in NLI, ILB 300p13, items 7, 37, 57.
12   Undated list for the IRA's 'National Roll of Honour', *circa* 1924: Twomey Papers, UCDA, P69/166, f. 13. A variant copy with 68 names, attributed to Count Plunkett, was circulated on 27 Mar. 1938 within the committee of the 'Irish Republican Memorial Society', which had been attempting to produce an ornate memorial volume since its formation on 5 Mar. 1924: NLI, MS 13343 (reference kindly supplied by Jane Leonard); Plunkett Papers, NLI, MS 22546.
13   *New York Times*, 3 Aug. 1922, p. 3. The same words were reported in the *Dublin Evening Mail*, 2 Aug., p. 3, with the observation that 'his expression of forgiveness came at midday. Subsequently he became delirious, and remained so until the end.'
14   Kate Boland to Sr. Bartholomew, 26 Oct. 1922. She recounted similar remarks in a letter to de Valera on 16 June 1923, though in this case 'his last words to me on his dying bed' seem to have referred to the Russian Crown Jewels: EdeVP, P 150/1173.
15   Kathleen Boland (Mrs Seán O'Donovan), Statement for the Bureau of Military History (undated typescript), f. 21: BP.

16   *Cork Examiner*, 5 Aug. 1922, p. 5; Kitty O'Doherty, Report, f. 18: McGP, MS 17471.

17   McG to 'A' [Austin Stack], 5 Sept. 1922: McGP, MS 17525/2.

18   Ernie O'Malley, *The Singing Flame* (Dublin, 1978), p. 143. Stack was Harry's successor as Quartermaster.

19   Memorandum in Stack's hand, 2 Aug. 1922: BP.

20   Michael Comyn and Malachi Muldoon, BL, acted for next of kin; James Comyn, BL, for the 'associates of the deceased' (otherwise the 'IRA'); Tim Sullivan, KC, and Kevin O'Shiel, BL, for the Provisional Government.

21   *Weekly Irish Times*, 15 July 1922, p. 5. Comyn also sought to demonstrate that Brugha was shot by a British service rifle. See Official Inquest Report, Cathal Brugha, 8 July: NLI, MS 13661.

22   This account of the Inquest by an anonymous republican observer, marked 'D.P.' (presumably for the Director of Publicity), is in the O'Farrelly Papers, NLI, microform P 7655.

23   *Dublin Evening Mail* ('Final Buff' edn.), 3 Aug. 1922: cutting in Béaslaí Papers, NLI, MS 33915/11. This account differs only in minor detail from the republican report.

24   Report in O'Farrelly Papers, NLI, microform P 7655.

25   Cutting in Béaslaí Papers, NLI, MS 33915/11. The republican observer was unable to follow the medical evidence, 'as it was read rapidly in a low voice and there was some little commotion in the room', but did catch a sharp exchange between a juror and the Coroner.

26   *New York Times*, 3 Aug. 1922, p. 3; unsigned memorandum on funeral arrangements, 3 Aug.: BP. The hospital's Rectress was Mother M. Thecla Maunsell, Irish Sisters of Charity.

27   Austin Stack to Seumas Ryan, 2 Aug. 1922: BP.

28   Harry's uncle, Jack Boland, had however been accorded a special service at the same church before his burial at Glasnevin: *Irish Daily Independent*, 2 Dec. 1895, p. 6.

29   [Pedlar] to McG, 3 Aug. 1922: McGP, MS 17478.

30   Memorandum on funeral arrangements, 3 Aug. 1922: BP.

31   *Freeman's Journal*, 4 Aug. 1922, p. 6; *Dublin Evening Mail*, 4 Aug., p. 3. Magennis had moved to Rome on becoming General of the Order of (Calced) Carmelites in 1919.

32   Luke i: 79 (Douai Version); Thomas MacGreevy, 'Three Historical Paintings by Jack B. Yeats', p. 397, in *Capuchin Annual*, xxxiii (1966; reprinted from 1942 edn.), pp 385–98.

33   *The Fenian*, War Issue no. 19 (5 Aug. 1922): BP.

34   'A Touching Incident', in *Freeman's Journal*, 5 Aug. 1922, p. 6.

35   *Dublin Evening Mail*, 4 Aug. 1922, p. 3.

36   *Roscommon Herald*, 12 Aug. 1922 (copy kindly supplied by Dr. Patrick Murray); *Dublin Evening Mail*, 4 Aug., p. 3; *Freeman's Journal*, 5 Aug., p. 6.

37   Frank Henderson to Kate Boland, 4 Aug. 1922: BP.

38   The stone (modelled on that commemorating the deaths of Jim and Jack Boland in 1895) disappeared in 1997, but was returned after an appeal through the press. A later memorial tablet marks the deaths of Harry, his brother Gerald (5 Jan. 1973), and Gerald's wife Annie (5 Apr. 1970).

39   *A Funeral* (later named *The Funeral of a Republican* and then *The Funeral of Harry Boland*), was painted in 1922, first exhibited at the Royal Hibernian Academy in 1923, purchased by Fr. John Senan Moynihan, editor of the *Capuchin Annual*, in 1941, and acquired for the Sligo County Library and Museum in 1962. See *Jack B. Yeats and the Niland Gallery, Sligo*, ed. Donal Tinney (Sligo, 1998), pp 26–7 (reference kindly supplied by Jane Leonard); MacGreevy, 'Three Historical

Paintings', pp 397–8. Not all cameras were confiscated, as the Boland family's photographic collection demonstrates (see plate 25).

40 Ann FitzGibbon to HB, jun., 4 Feb. 1998: BP.
41 A Lament was painted in 1930, first exhibited in the following year, acquired by Helen (Mrs Ernie) O'Malley in 1944, donated to the Irish American Cultural Institute in 1979, placed on loan in the Irish Museum of Modern Art in 1990, and sold in 2002: De Veres Art Auctions, Sale of Art to be Sold by Auction on Tuesday the 16th April 2002 (Dublin, 2002), lot 140.
42 Resolutions and correspondence: BP; Marie O'Neill, From Parnell to de Valera: A Biography of Jennie Wyse Power, 1858–1941 (Dublin, 1991), p. 144.
43 S. P. Seoldius to Kate Boland, 4 Sept. 1922: BP. Jack Shouldice had been Boland's close friend in the GAA.
44 Joseph Connolly (Dún Laoghaire) to Kate Boland, 3 Aug. 1922: BP.
45 James O'Mara (Galway) to Kate Boland, 2 Aug. 1922: BP. O'Mara's estranged brother Stephen, who as Mayor of Limerick had taken the republican stance, took Holy Communion 'for him', requested a personal memento, and remarked that 'life had no charm for him since last December. Death was well come!': S. M. O'Mara (Limerick) to Kate Boland, 3 Aug.: BP.
46 Patrick McCartan to McG, 1 Aug. 1922: McGP, MS 17457/13; Seán Nunan ('Harry's broken hearted friend') to Kate Boland, 2 Aug.: BP.
47 Maurice [Collins] to Kate and Kathleen Boland, 2 Aug. 1922: BP.
48 McCartan to McG, 1, 2, 5 Aug. 1922: McGP, MS 17457/13.
49 The Separatist, i, no. 24 (5 Aug. 1922), p. 1.
50 The Fenian, War Issue no. 15 (1 Aug. 1922): Childers Papers, NLI, MS 15441/7.
51 Jim Maher, Harry Boland: A Biography (Cork, 1998), p. 244; quoting and citing Tim Pat Coogan, Michael Collins: A Biography (London, 1991 edn.), p. 388 ('weeping uncontrollably'); citing Margery Forester, Michael Collins: The Lost Leader (London, 1972), p. 329 ('in a paroxysm of uncontrolled grief'); citing no source but probably paraphrasing Frank O'Connor, The Big Fellow: Michael Collins and the Irish Revolution (London, 1969; 1st edn. 1937), p. 209 ('crying helplessly'); evidently based on interview with Fionán Lynch. See also Andrew Brasier and John Kelly, Harry Boland: A Man Divided (Dublin, 2000), p. 140 ('wept like a baby'); In Great Haste: The Letters of Michael Collins and Kitty Kiernan, ed. Leon Ó Broin (Dublin, 1996; 1st edn. 1983) [hereafter, IGH], p. 218 ('came crying'); Leon Ó Broin, Michael Collins (Dublin, 1980), p. 136 ('burst into tears'); Meda Ryan, Michael Collins and the Women in His Life (Dublin, 1989), p. 175 ('a fit of uncontrolled grief').
52 Cutting from New York World, 3 Aug. 1922: BP.
53 MC to KK, circa 2 Aug. 1922: IGH, p. 219.
54 Patrick [McCartan] to McG, 5 Aug. 1922: McGP, MS 17457/13.
55 KK to MC, 2 Aug. 1922: IGH, p. 218.
56 KK to MC, 3 Aug. 1922: IGH, pp 219–20.
57 Cork Examiner, 8 Aug. 1922, p. 4.
58 Letters to Kate Boland from T. Burke (Louth County Committee, GAA), 14 Aug. 1922; Seán T. O'Kelly (Kilmainham Prison), 2 Aug.; Frank Henderson (Dublin Brigade), 4 Aug.; Ernie O'Malley (Assistant Chief of Staff, IRA), 2 Aug.; Seán MacCarthy (Cork County Board, GAA), 9 Aug.: BP.
59 Liam Lynch (Fermoy) to Kate and Kathleen Boland, 4 Aug. 1922; Leo Henderson (Mountjoy Prison) to 'Kitty' [Boland], 1 Aug.: BP. Leo's brother Frank, in his letter of 4 Aug., likewise hoped Harry's name would 'be an inspiration along with Cathal Brugha's to the boys who are growing up'.
60 Speeches from the Dock, or, Protests of Irish Patriotism, ed. T. D., A. M., and D. B. Sullivan (Dublin, 52nd edn. 1907; 1st edn. 1867).

[61] Liam MacCrainn (Roscommon) to Kate Boland, 2 Aug. 1922: BP.
[62] John T. Ryan ['Your Cousin'] to McG ['Phil'], 20 Aug. [1922]: McGP, MS 17486/1.
[63] *Gaelic American*, 12 Aug. 1922, p. 2.
[64] Peter Golden, 'An Appreciation of Mr. Harry Boland', in *Cork Examiner*, 5 Aug. 1922, p. 5.
[65] *Catholic Bulletin*, xii, no. 9 (Sept. 1922), pp. 566–9.
[66] Fr. Timothy Shanley to Kate Boland, 3 Aug. 1922: BP.
[67] Maloney to McG, 2 Aug. 1922: McGP, MS 17621.
[68] Luke Dillon to McG, marked 'July' 1922, quoting his telegram to Stephen O'Mara. Dillon added: 'would have used your name but feared you might not like my style': McGP, MS 17444.
[69] McG to Kate Boland, 3 Aug. 1922: BP.
[70] McG to Patrick McCartan, 15 Aug. 1922: McGP, MS 17621.
[71] Mary McSwiney to [Kate and Kathleen Boland], 12 Oct. 1922: BP. Having thanked them for 'the two cards of dear Harry', she requested 'a larger photo' for her collection.
[72] James J. Reilly to McG, 3 Aug. 1922: McGP, MS 17525/1.
[73] McG, circular to clergy, 4 Aug. 1922: McGP, MS 17525/2.
[74] Supt. William B. Mills to McG, 4 Aug. 1922: McGP, MS 17654/2. The American and Irish flags were both displayed.
[75] McG, undated notes: McGP, MS 17424/3.
[76] McG to EdeV, 27 Sept. 1922: McGP, MS 17440.
[77] Cutting from unidentified newspaper. In a letter dated 13 July 1922, from which extracts were widely circulated in both America and Ireland, Harry told McGarrity that 'I cannot help feeling that everything will yet work out right for Ireland': McGP, MS 17424/3, 2.
[78] McG, duplicated report of convention (7–9 Aug. 1922): McGP, MS 17657.
[79] F. H. Lowe in *New York Times*, 9 Aug. 1922, p. 4.
[80] J. I. C. Clarke in *New York Times*, 13 Aug. 1922, secn. vii, p. 8.
[81] *New York Times*, 14 Aug. 1922, p. 15. The speakers included McGarrity and Fr. Shanley.
[82] Extract from 'Harry Boland' (typescript, 20 Nov. 1925): McGP, MS 17558/7. This file includes another verse of the same title (typescript, May 1925): 'As kind as a mother – / Ah! true hearted brother, / There ne'er was another / More loyal and brave.'
[83] Pádraig de Brún, 'Harry Boland': handwritten copy in BP.
[84] 'In Memoriam', in Peter Golden, *Poems of the Irish Republic* (no detail of publication): Villanova University, Philadelphia, McGP, Box 9. Golden (1877–1926), who had left Cork in 1901 and become an American citizen five years later, played no personal part in Easter Week beyond working for Devoy's *Gaelic American*: see Jim Herlihy, *Peter Golden, the Voice of Ireland: A Biography* (Ballincollig, Co. Cork, 1994).
[85] 'In Memoriam, Harry Boland, T.D., shot at Skerries, July 31st, 1922' (copyright A. J. B., Dublin). A handwritten draft annotated 'Mountjoy 1922–23' also survives: BP.
[86] 'For their names are treasured apart, / And their memories green and sweet, / On every hillside and every mart, / In every cabin, in every street, / Of a land, where to fail is more than to triumph, / And victory less than defeat.' See handbill: NLI, LOP 117, f. 80.
[87] *Harry Boland Commemoration Concert: Souvenir Programme* (Dublin, [1924]): BP.
[88] On 17 Nov. 1923, *Eire: The Irish Nation* carried advertisements for picture postcards at 1d., portraits of Harry and other dead republicans on art-boards at 2d., and 'real photographs' at 1s. 2d., published by the Irish Nation Committee and (in

the third case) by the Misses O'Hanrahan, stationers at 384, North Circular Rd. (abstract kindly supplied by Jane Leonard).

89 Letters to Kate Boland from Liam MacCrainn (Roscommon), 2 Aug. 1922; Alice Ginnell (Dublin), 2 Aug.; Frank Henderson, 4 Aug.: BP.

90 Leo Henderson to 'Kitty' [Boland], 1 Aug. 1922: BP.

91 Kathleen O'Connell, Desk Diary, 4 Aug. 1922: UCDA, O'Connell Papers, P 155/140 (reference kindly supplied by Dr. Patrick Murray).

92 Kathleen O'Connell, Pocket Diary, 4 Aug. 1922: UCDA, O'Connell Papers, P 155/139.

93 EdeV to Kate Boland, 10 a.m., 4 Aug. 1922: typed copy, BP.

94 Sinéad de Valera (Greystones) to Kathleen Boland, 14 Aug. 1922: BP. Her own more conventional response was to urge Kathleen to 'keep saying the aspiration "Sacred Heart of Jesus I trust in Thee that all may go well with Ireland". I know you will offer your bitter sorrow for Ireland's good.'

95 EdeV (Dublin) to McG (Philadelphia), 10 Sept. 1922: McGP, MS 17440. Thomas Moore's 'Oft in the Stilly Night' continues: 'Whose lights are fled, / Whose garlands dead, / And all but he departed!'

96 EdeV to Frank P. Walsh (New York), 12 Oct. 1922: NYPL, Maloney Papers, 7/116.

97 EdeV to McG, 12 Oct. 1922: McGP, MS 17440.

98 EdeV to Kate Boland, 12 June 1923: EdeVP, P 150/1173.

99 EdeV to Kate Boland, 21 June 1923, paraphrasing Rudyard Kipling's 'If': BP.

100 *Souvenir Programme.*

101 Kate Boland to EdeV, 16 June 1923: EdeVP, P 150/1173.

102 Administration Papers, registered at Principal Probate Registry, 4 Sept. 1922: Probate Office, Four Courts, Dublin.

103 Mary F. McWhorter, 'Harry Boland R.I.P.' (undated typescript), ff. 13–14: EdeVP, P 150/1173.

104 EdeV to Kate Boland, 21 June 1923. In the event, the *Irish Press* took precedence.

105 Kate Boland to McG, 16 May, 17 July 1923: McGP, MS 17424/4.

106 Kate Boland to McG, 28 Jan. 1924, and his reply, 15 Feb.: McGP, MS 17424/4; Kate Boland to Luke Dillon and McG, 21 May: McGP, MS 17578.

107 Kathleen Boland O'Donovan to McG, 12 Jan. 1925: McGP, MS 17424/5.

108 Kathleen Boland, Statement, f. 23. Within three months, over $42,000 had been raised in the campaign. See Irish Republican Soldiers' and Prisoners' Dependents' Fund, Minutes, 3 Dec. 1922: F. P. Walsh Papers, NYPL, Box 26.

109 Handbills for meetings in Arcadia, 21 Jan. 1923; Minneapolis, 12 Feb.; Buffalo, 9 Sept.: BP.

110 Kathleen Boland, Diary, 31 Oct. 1922 to 17 May 1923: BP; Joanne Mooney Eichacker, *Irish Republican Women in America: Lecture Tours, 1916–1925* (Dublin, 2003), ch. 9 (esp. pp 174–7).

111 Unidentified report of speech at Rochester, New York, 11 Sept. 1923: cutting in BP.

112 Luke Dillon to McG, 23 May 1925: McGP, MS 17610/1.

113 Provisional Government, Minutes, 11 Aug. 1922: NAD, G1/3, f. 231.

114 Kathleen Boland, Statement, f. 23. They were married in Manchester in Dec. 1923. See Seán O'Donovan, 'An Autobiographical Note' (typescript, 1973): BP.

115 Kathleen Boland to McG, 17 Aug. 1922: McGP, MS 17578; *Dublin Evening Mail*, 4 Aug., p. 3. Ned Boland moved to New York after the Civil War, working for a construction company and running a shebeen, before dying of malaria aggravated by pneumonia on Good Friday, 6 Apr. 1928: see especially Caoimhghin Ó Beoláin [Kevin Boland], 'James Boland, 1857–1895: By His Grandson' (typescript, 1993), f. 18: BP.

116 Annie Traynor to Kate Boland, 2 Aug. 1922: BP.

[117] Gerald to Kate Boland, 26 Aug., 7 Sept. 1922: BP.
[118] After his release from internment in July 1924, Gerald Boland became a key organiser for Sinn Féin and Fianna Fáil, as its first Honorary Secretary. He represented Harry's Roscommon constituency continuously between Aug. 1923 and Oct. 1961, when supplanted as Fianna Fáil's only successful candidate by Brian Lenihan, and died in his 88th year on 5 Jan. 1973. His most noteworthy achievement, as Minister for Justice (1939–48, 1951–4), was to induce de Valera to repress the IRA, to the point of executing nine of its members and allowing others to die on hunger-strike. See Michael McInerney, 'Gerry Boland's Story', in *Irish Times*, 11 pts., 8–19 Oct. 1968.
[119] Though perceptible in Michael McInerney, 'Gerry Boland's Story', Gerald's growing disillusionment with Fianna Fáil and idealisation of Harry is overt in his unpublished recollections, being replicated from a different perspective by his son Kevin in 'James Boland'.
[120] Maher, *Harry Boland*; Brasier and Kelly, *Harry Boland*.

CHAPTER II. PREPARATION

[1] Harry's registered (and baptismal) name was simply Henry, James being a later addition. He was baptised a week later, with Joseph Seymour and Honoria Strich as sponsors, presumably in St Peter's Church in Phibsborough (then administered by Franciscans) which lay within the parish of St Paul, Arran Quay: baptismal certificate (kindly supplied by Fr Seán Donohue, PP).
[2] The family of James Boland (1856–95) and Catherine Woods (*circa* 1860–1932) comprised Nellie (1884–98), Gerald (1885–1973), Harry (1887–1922), Kathleen (1889–1954), and Edmund, otherwise 'Ned' (1893–1928).
[3] The address on his birth certificate, 6, Dalymount Terrace, was listed under Phibsborough Rd. in *Thom's Official Directory of the United Kingdom of Great Britain and Ireland* (Dublin, 1891 edn.), which returned James Boland as occupier of no. 76, valued at £9 per annum. The site is now engulfed by the Phibsborough Shopping Centre.
[4] Caoimhghin Ó Beoláin [Kevin Boland], 'James Boland, 1857–1895: By His Grandson' (typescript, 1993), f. 2: BP. This is based largely on documents in the possession of Mr Harry Boland, Dublin, supplemented by family recollections.
[5] John Mallon (Assistant Commissioner, DMP; Chief Supt., G Division, until 1893) to David Harrel (Chief Commissioner), 14 Nov. 1894: CBS Papers, NAD, 9180/S. 'The Hut' still purveys Irish stew daily at 159, Phibsborough Rd.: *Thom's Official Directory* (1891 edn.).
[6] When Catherine Woods died in Glasnevin on 21 Jan. 1932, her age was given as 80 years. Her census schedules, however, recorded her age as 40 in 1901 and 50 in 1911, implying birth in 1860–1. Her father's birthplace was Piedmont, parish of Ballymascanlan.
[7] Gerald Boland, Family Reminiscences (undated typescript): BP.
[8] Woods died in about 1820: J. O'Hanlon, 'James Woods: A County Louth Hero of '98' (typed copy of unlocated article): BP.
[9] Michael McInerney, 'Gerry Boland's Story', pt. 2, in *Irish Times*, 9 Oct. 1968, p. 12.
[10] According to his son Harry, Gerald's passport, now lost, was in the name James Woods.
[11] His birth certificate gives James Boland's birthplace as 56, Thompson St. (Registration Sub-District of St. George); his mother was unable to sign her name

as informant of his birth. Other certificates indicate that his full name was James Henry.

[12] For an informative if quirky account of his career, see Kevin Boland's 'James Boland'.

[13] Robert and Samuel E. Worthington, Contractors, had offices at 41, Dame St.: *Thom's Official Directory* (1883 edn.). After Robert's death aged 80 in July 1922, at Salmon Pool, Islandbridge, the bald patriarch with his white handle-bar moustache was remembered as a 'well known Irish contractor': *Freeman's Journal*, 1 Aug. 1922, p. 2.

[14] Notice of First Assessment for 1882–3, 13 Nov. 1882: BP.

[15] The murder outside the Vice-Regal Lodge of the newly appointed Liberal Chief Secretary, Lord Frederick Charles Cavendish (second son of the 7th Duke of Devonshire), and his Under-Secretary, Thomas Henry Burke, led to a sustained but ultimately unavailing campaign to incriminate Parnell and his Irish Parliamentary Party in this and other conspiracies.

[16] Brady, the first suspect tried in Apr. 1883, was hanged for murder. On the basis of the trial reports, Kevin Boland regretfully echoed his father Gerald's opinion that Jim was not demonstrably an Invincible: 'James Boland', ff. 45, 52–8.

[17] Evidence of Robert Farrell and William Lamie, 10 May 1883, in the trial of Joseph Mullett for the attempted murder of Denis J. Field: W. C. Johnston (reporter), *Report of the Trials at the Dublin Commission Court* (Dublin, 1883), pp 631, 639; also abstracted in Kevin Boland, 'James Boland', ff. 57–8. Jim Boland was said to have attended a meeting of Dublin Centres on 25 Nov. 1882, and to have witnessed the payment of IRB subscriptions by Lamie.

[18] Evidence of Patrick Delaney (Maryborough Prison), 16 Jan. 1889, to the Commission investigating allegations by *The Times* against Parnell: *Special Commission Act, 1888: Report of the Shorthand Notes of the Speeches, Proceedings, and Evidence taken before the Commissioners appointed under the Above Named Act* (12 vols., London, HMSO, 1890), iii, pp 530–1. Jim Boland and Patrick Molloy were said to have been 'watching Mr. Anderson, the Crown Solicitor, the two of them, for weeks'; but Delaney did not implicate Jim in the Phoenix Park murders of the same year. Samuel Lee Anderson, a barrister and Crown Solicitor for Waterford and Kilkenny, handled political Intelligence at Dublin Castle: *Thom's Official Directory* (1883 edn.); Leon Ó Broin, *Revolutionary Underground: The Story of the Irish Republican Brotherhood, 1858–1924* (Dublin, 1976), pp 16, 29.

[19] Evidence of Patrick Molloy (43, York St.), 7 Dec. 1888: *Special Commission Report*, iii, pp 171, 175.

[20] Evidence of James Edward Kennedy (Worthingtons' clerk), 13 Apr. 1883, in the trial of Joseph Brady for the murder of 'one Thomas Henry Burke': Johnston, *Report of the Trials*, p. 87.

[21] William Reddy (Supt., G Division) to Harrel, 2 Jan. 1889, with associated correspondence: NAD, DMP Papers, Box 5, 1326; entries for James Boland in Irish Crime Records, Register of Suspects (Home), f. 55: PRO, CO 904/17; and for Frank Byrne in Register of Suspects (American): CO 904/19. The Law Officer advised that, owing to the murder in July 1883 of the foremost informer, James Carey, there was no legal basis for laying charges after Boland's return from America.

[22] Kevin Boland, 'James Boland', ff. 1–2, citing documents in BP.

[23] *Gaelic American*, 12 Aug. 1922, p. 2. Devoy asserted, contrary to the family's belief, that 'he was not old enough to be in the Rising of 1867'.

[24] Thomas Markham, 'It was Kindled from the Fenian Fire', in *G.A.A. Golden Jubilee: Irish Press Supplement*, 14 Apr. 1934, p. 56; W. F. Mandle, *The Gaelic Athletic Association and Irish Nationalist Politics, 1884–1924* (London, 1987), p. 9. It is also notable that Gerald was born on 25 May 1885, at Chorlton-upon-Metlock (six miles

south-west of Manchester), over three months before Jim reportedly finished work in Brooklyn. The prospect of support from her family in Manchester may have induced Kate Boland to return alone to bear her second child.

25 Henry Thynne (Deputy Insp.-Gen., RIC), Memoranda on Movement of Suspects, March–April 1887; Harrel to Sir Andrew Reed (Insp.-Gen., RIC), 8 Mar., with description of John Boland, otherwise P. J. Boland: DMP Papers, Box 2.

26 Reddy to Sir Redvers Henry Buller (Under-Secretary), 15 Mar. 1887, with associated reports: DMP Papers, Box 2.

27 The National Club occupied 11, Rutland Sq. East, next door to the offices and hall of the Grand Orange Lodge of Ireland at no. 10. The Ship Hotel and Tavern and James Ferguson, hairdresser and perfumer, were located at 5 and 38–9, Lower Abbey St.: *Thom's Official Directory* (1891 edn.).

28 Thomas Dunphy, family grocer, wine and spirit merchant, held premises at 160–1, Phibsborough Rd. (next to 'the Hut': cf. note 5, above); Michael McCarthy, grocer and wine merchant, occupied 69, Pill Lane (now Chancery St.), behind the Four Courts: *Thom's Official Directory* (1883, 1891 edns.).

29 Reports by Detective Insp. Cooper and two constables, 18 Feb. 1888, with leaves from notebook: DMP Papers, Box 3. Jack, though indeed intermittently a journalist, gave his name to the police as John P. Newton of 5, Alfred Pl. West, South Kensington. His companion Joseph Bolger was either better endowed or meaner than Jack, still having £2 6s. 10d. at the time of his arrest.

30 Reddy to Harrel, 15 Mar. 1888; Sgt. Thomas Simons to Reddy, 9 Apr.: DMP Papers, Box 3.

31 J. M. Goldsmith (G Division) to Monro (CBS, Home Office), 18 June 1888: DMP Papers, Box 3; *Gaelic American*, 12 Aug. 1922, p. 2.

32 Reddy to Harrel, 5 Sept. 1889: DMP Papers, Box 5, 1516.

33 Detective Insp. Thomas Lynam to J. J. Jones (Chief Commissioner, DMP), 23 Mar. 1899, citing a conversation with the unusually reliable 'Richmond' on a posthumous investigation of 'Dynamiters' in the British service: CBS Papers, 18945/S; also abstracted in Ó Broin, *Revolutionary Underground*, p. 102.

34 T. M. Healy, *Letters and Leaders of My Day* (2 vols., New York edn., 1929), ii, p. 370. E. G. Jenkinson was Assistant Under-Secretary to the Lord Lieutenant. Michael Davitt is also said to have denounced Jack Boland as a spy: Mallon to Jones, 30 Oct. 1894, in CBS Papers, 9180/S; also cited in Ó Broin, *Revolutionary Underground*, p. 59.

35 'Report of Meeting in Annex[e] Hotel, New York City. Sunday, March 20, 1921', f. 10 (copy of typescript, from unlocated source): BP.

36 His employer by 1894 was Cassel, Petter, and Gilpin of London, Paris, and New York: Mallon to Harrel, 11 Nov. 1894, in CBS Papers, 9212/S. In 1887, he had boasted at a nationalist meeting of being employed by a Tory newspaper, the *St. James's Gazette*: Harrel to Sir Andrew Reed, Insp.-Gen. (RIC), 8 Mar. 1887, in DMP Papers, Box 2.

37 L. J. Lawless (Deputy Surveyor) to Spencer Harty (Borough Surveyor), with Harty's recommendation to Dublin Corporation, 9, 10 Mar. 1891: *Report of the Paving and Lighting Committee*, 1 Apr., in *Dublin Corporation Reports* (Dublin, 1891), no. 48: BP. The elderly incumbent overseer was to be replaced by Jim and his assistant foreman, while the Fenian James Stritch was to be promoted from overseer of concrete-laying to one of two general inspectors of works and materials.

38 Mallon to Harrel, enclosing cutting from *National Press*, 25 June 1891: DMP Papers, Box 12.

39 Note by Gerald Boland, 22 Nov. 1949, with inscribed copy of Rossa's *Irish Rebels in English Prisons: A Record of Prison Life* (New York, 1891), presented to James

Boland, 28 June 1894: BP; John A. Walker to Harrel, 28 Dec. 1892, with note by Mallon: DMP Papers, Box 12, 2420.

40 Information from various police reports and *Thom's Official Directory* shows that the Bolands lived at 15, Peter St. (in a tenement valued at £20 per annum which also housed Boland's fellow-suspect and Corporation pavior, Pat Molloy) before Sept. 1886; 71, Inishfallen Pde. (unvalued) in 1886–7; 76, Phibsborough Rd. (£9 per annum) in 1888–91; 12, Royal Canal Tce. (value unknown) in 1891; and 9, Phibsborough Ave. (£9 per annum) in 1893–5. Until 1890, the occupier was invariably returned in *Thom's* as Mrs Boland (presumably Jim's mother), but subsequently as Mr James Boland. Two of these homes recognisably survive today: the single-storied red-bricked terrace-cottage in Innisfallen Pde.; and the double-storied brown-bricked terrace in Phibsborough Ave., convenient to St. Peter's Catholic Church.

41 Mallon to Harrel, 22 Apr. 1892: DMP Papers, Box 12, 2327.

42 Reddy to Harrel, 22 Nov. 1886: DMP Papers, Box 2, 2055/H. This group included the father of Joe Brady, Boland's colleague in Worthingtons who had been executed for his part in the Phoenix Park murders.

43 Frank Callanan, 'The "Appeal to the Hillsides": Parnell and the Fenians, 1890–91', in *Parnell: The Politics of Power*, ed. Donal McCartney (Dublin, 1991), pp 148–69. It is noteworthy that the 'definitive articulation' of this appeal referred not to 'hillsides', but to 'the illimitable power of our race which has shown itself on these streets of Dublin tonight' (16 Dec. 1890): ibid., p. 149.

44 Thomas F. O'Sullivan, *Story of the G.A.A.: First History of Great Organisation* (Dublin, 1916), p. 93.

45 Ibid., pp 101–3, 112; Marcus de Búrca, *One Hundred Years of Faughs Hurling* (Dublin, *circa* 1985), p. 47; circular denouncing dissidents, 22 Aug. 1893, signed by 12 members of the Central Council including Boland: BP.

46 O'Sullivan, *Story of the G.A.A.*, p. 95.

47 Ibid., pp 96–7; Ó Broin, *Revolutionary Underground*, pp 50–1; Kevin Boland, 'James Boland', f. 9. Nally was convicted of conspiring to murder 8 officials and others involved in evictions and land-grabbing in Co. Mayo, after evidence from his former business partner in Manchester that he had consigned revolvers to Ireland. See Lewis & Lewis, Solicitors, 'Special Commission Act, 1888: The Crossmolina Conspiracy Case' (handwritten memorandum for Defence): bound volume in NLI, ILB 343p21.

48 *Gaelic American*, 12 Aug. 1922, p. 2.

49 Kevin Boland, 'James Boland', f. 70; Kathleen Boland (Mrs Seán O'Donovan), Statement for the Bureau of Military History (undated typescript), f. 2: BP; Statement of Meyrick Shaw Copeland Jones, 14 Oct. 1896 (in papers of G. Gloucester [*recte*, H. Gloster] Armstrong, later British Consul-General, New York): PRO, HO 144/98/A16380C.

50 *Irish Daily Independent*, 6 Feb. 1892: cutting in DMP Papers, Box 12, 2305/S. In his explanatory memorandum to Harrel, Mallon admitted that he had heard of no 'secret business' at the club, but found it 'rather suspicious' that Jim Boland and eight other suspects should have congregated in 'what is known as "the Progressive Club"'.

51 Mallon to Harrel, 22 Apr. 1892: DMP Papers, Box 12, 2327.

52 Mallon to Jones, 8 Feb. 1895: DMP Papers, Box 13.

53 Mallon to Jones, 12, 26 June 1894, with accompanying circular, 6 June; copy of letter from Patrick Casey (Cork) to 'P', 8 June; cutting from *Independent*, 27 June: DMP Papers, Box 13.

54 Chief Insp. Nicholas Cooper to Harrel, 17 Dec. 1892: DMP Papers, Box 12, 2415.

55 *Independent*, 16 Feb. 1893: cutting in DMP Papers, Box 12, 2458; Mallon to Jones, 8 Oct. 1894: DMP Papers, Box 13.

56 *Independent*, 26 Nov. 1894: cutting in CBS Papers, 9291/S.

57 Undated list of suspects abstracted in Ó Broin, *Revolutionary Underground*, p. 43.

58 Gerald Boland, Family Reminiscences, f. 3.

59 Undated fragment in notebook: BP. 'Nero' became the highest paid informer for the RIC, receiving £205 in 1889: Ó Broin, *Revolutionary Underground*, p. 33.

60 Reddy to Harrel, 23 Sept. 1886, 12 Jan. 1888: DMP Papers, Box 2.

61 Harrel to J. W. Redington (Under-Secretary), 22 Oct. 1892: CBS Papers, 5757/S.

62 'Report of Meeting in Annex[e] Hotel', f. 10.

63 Irish Crime Records, Register of Suspects (Home), f. 55.

64 Lynam to Jones, 23 Mar. 1899, summarising 'a long conversation' concerning Jim and Jack Boland with the agent 'Richmond': CBS Papers, 18945/S. See also Ó Broin, *Revolutionary Underground*, pp 52–4; Mandle, *Gaelic Athletic Association*, pp 78, 100.

65 James McDermott, a veteran of the Irish Papal Brigade from Dublin, was a police informer who helped to split the Fenian Brotherhood in 1865–6 and to undermine the Irish dynamiting campaign in the 1880s. He was denounced by Davitt after his arrest in Dublin in 1884: D. J. Hickey and J. E. Doherty, *Dictionary of Irish History, 1800–1980* (Dublin, 1987; 1st edn. 1980), p. 331.

66 Healy had previously been threatened in the office by Boland and P. N. Fitzgerald, carrying revolvers, after a meeting in the Phoenix Park addressed by Parnell. The *Freeman's Journal*, still a Parnellite newspaper, had flippantly attributed the explosion to 'an escape of gas', but Healy and the police viewed it as a serious threat: Healy, *Letters and Leaders*, ii, pp 367–70. In his 'James Boland', ff. 46–51, Kevin Boland asserts that Healy fabricated his evidence.

67 Confidential printed reports by Her Majesty's Inspectors of Explosives, 28 Dec. 1892, 10 May 1893, with associated documents: HO 144/247/A54529; HO 144/248/A54847.

68 Cutting of James Boland's letter to the editor, *Independent*, 11 Dec. 1893, with Mallon to Harrel, 20 Dec.: CBS Papers, 7830/S.

69 John Lowe (Sgt., G Division) to Jones, 30 July 1894: CBS Papers, 8806/S; Mallon to Jones, 21 Oct. 1894: CBS Papers, 9138/S (with 9246/S).

70 P. O'Shea (Secretary, 10, Upper Abbey St.) to Boland, 2 Oct. 1894: BP.

71 Mallon to Jones, 7 Nov. 1894: CBS Papers, 9255/S; Ó Broin, *Revolutionary Underground*, p. 58. H. H. Asquith and John Morley were the reputed targets.

72 Kevin Boland, 'James Boland', f. 51; Kathleen Boland, Statement, ff. 1–2; Kathleen Boland, Recollections (undated MSS): BP. Harry believed a baton to be responsible; whereas Kathleen favoured a chair leg (alternatively a stone).

73 Nolan, an unemployed fitter living with his mother (a dealer in second-hand boots), was unkindly described as having 'the facial expression of a monkey', an impression somewhat confirmed by the photograph in this file: Mallon to Jones, 15, 23 Feb. 1895; Major Nicholas Gosselin (Home Office) to Head Const. Humphreys (Liverpool): DMP, Box 13.

74 Allan to Boland, 20 Oct. 1894: BP.

75 Lynam to Jones, 23 Mar. 1899: CBS Papers, 18945/S; cf. Ó Broin, *Revolutionary Underground*, pp 58–9, 102. The reference to attempted suicide was marked 'quite correct' by a nameless annotator.

76 Mallon to Jones, 6, 14 Nov. 1894: CBS Papers, 9211/S.

77 *Independent*, 2, 6 Mar. 1895: cuttings in CBS Papers, 9692/S.

78 Mallon to Jones, 12 Mar. 1895: CBS Papers, 9692/S. This report was noteworthy enough to be forwarded to the Lord Lieutenant.

79 Cutting from *Independent*, 12 Mar. 1895, with Mallon to Jones, 12 Mar.: CBS Papers, 9692/S.
80 *Independent*, 13 Mar. 1895: cutting in CBS Papers, 9697/S; obituary in *Roscommon Messenger*, 21 June 1917, p. 4. Patrick O'Brien, MP for North Monaghan from 1886 to 1892 and a leading participant in the Plan of Campaign, was regarded as one of the 'moderates' in the Irish Parliamentary Party before the Split, and remained on close enough terms with the 'Stephenites' in the IRB to introduce James Stephens himself to Parnell in October 1891. Following his defeat as Parnellite candidate for Limerick City in 1892, and a narrow victory in Kilkenny City in July 1895, he held the seat unopposed until his death, the consequent by-election being won for Sinn Féin by W. T. Cosgrave in July 1917. See F. S. L. Lyons, *Charles Stewart Parnell* (London, 1977), p. 597; Callanan, 'Appeal to the Hillsides', pp 162–3.
81 Kathleen Boland, Statement, f. 2; Kevin Boland, 'James Boland', f. 3.
82 *Independent*, 15 Mar. 1895, p. 6.
83 Gosselin, Memorandum, 28 Jan. 1887: CBS Papers, 533/S; Ó Broin, *Revolutionary Underground*, pp 61–2, 94; documents on 'trials' of Michael Boland and others in Devoy Papers, NLI, MSS 18018, 18019, 18147. I am unaware of any affinity between Michael and Jack Boland.
84 Kathleen Boland, Recollections.
85 (Sir Harry) Gloster Armstrong (1861–1938), a keen amateur actor and former army officer from Belturbet, Co. Cavan, author of military manuals and member of Dublin's Kildare Street Club, became Consul-General in New York (1920–31). After Major Gosselin took control of Irish Intelligence at the Home Office in 1890, he sent Armstrong to New York (ostensibly on behalf of the Mexican Land Company of London) to infiltrate Irish-American secret societies, which he did with marked success using at least 7 well-placed informers: Leon Ó Broin, *Revolutionary Underground*, p. 75; Nicholas Gosselin, 'Secret and Confidential Report to Sir Matthew White Ridley [Home Secretary], 7th October 1896': Kenneth Young, *Arthur James Balfour* (London, 1963), app. ii (pp 469–73).
86 Statement of Meyrick Jones, 14 Oct. 1896; Lowe to Mallon, 12 Oct. 1894: DMP Papers, Box 13.
87 Kevin Boland, 'James Boland', ff. 58–9 (enteric fever); Kathleen Boland, Statement, f. 2, and *Independent*, 2 Dec. 1895, p. 6 (typhoid fever); Lynam to Jones, 23 Mar. 1899: CBS Papers, 18945/S (poison).
88 Mallon to Jones, 2 Dec. 1895: DMP Papers, Box 13. Allan had broken with the Irish National Brotherhood shortly after its extension to Dublin, becoming President of the IRB's Supreme Council.
89 *Independent*, 2 Dec. 1895, p. 6.
90 Bébé [Nally] to Kate Boland, 29 Nov. 1895: BP; *Independent*, 2 Dec., p. 6. Bébé's wreath for Jim Boland had been scarcely less warmly inscribed: 'Green be the grass above thee, / Friend of our better days; / None knew thee but to love thee, / None shall name thee but to praise.' See *Independent*, 15 Mar., p. 6.
91 Mallon to Jones, 12 Mar. 1895: CBS Papers, 9692/S.
92 Kevin Boland, 'James Boland', ff. 13–15, 28–30, based largely on reports in the *Freeman's Journal* and *Weekly Freeman*; cuttings from several unidentified Dublin newspapers: BP.
93 J. P. O'Brien (Secretary, Old Guard Benevolent 'Union') to Kate Boland, 26 Mar. 1895: BP.
94 Kevin Boland, 'James Boland', ff. 30, 73–6; *Freeman's Journal*, 10 June 1895, p. 7.
95 The district was so named in recognition of its human contribution to the Gallipoli campaign in 1915, and also of the ease with which snipers could pick off patrols in its narrow streets.

[96] M. J. Merrick to Kate Boland, 16 Apr. 1895: BP. Joseph Merrick from Manchester, who spent nine months of each year in Ireland as a traveller in the tobacco trade, was 'intimately acquainted with all the leading IRB Suspects both in England and Ireland including James Boland ... and although he is not a member of IRB he is a trusted man among them': Sgt. William Hughes (Manchester) to Gosselin, 30 Mar. 1892, in DMP Papers, Box 12, 2318.

[97] Undated cutting in album: BP. 'Seanbhean Bhocht' (the poor old woman) personified Ireland.

[98] Michael McInerney, 'Gerry Boland's Story', pt. 2, in *Irish Times*, 9 Oct. 1968, p. 12.

[99] Family Return, 31 Mar. 1901: NAD, Census Schedules, 1901, Dublin 73/40. The house was valued at £23 per annum: *Thom's Official Directory* (1896–1907 edns.). The Roma II Restaurant Takeaway now occupies this four-storied but single-fronted building.

[100] He 'could not stick it': Gerald Boland, Family Reminiscences, f. 7: BP.

[101] Family Return, 2 Apr. 1911: Census Schedules, 1911, Dublin 70/47. The house was valued at £20 per annum: *Thom's Official Directory* (1908–14 edns.). The solid red-brick house at 26, Lennox St., is one of a terrace of six houses with two stories over a basement.

[102] House valued at £22 per annum: *Thom's Official Directory* (1915–32 edns.); Elgy Gillespie, 'The Dracula of Marino Crescent', in *Irish Times*, 30 May 1973, p. 14: cutting in BP.

[103] Kathleen Boland, Statement, ff. 10–11. Samuel J. Jennings, the landlord of much of the Crescent, lived at no. 17: *Thom's Official Directory* (1919 edn.).

[104] Nellie died of tuberculosis in Sept. 1898, while in the care of relatives in Manchester.

[105] Gerald Boland, Family Reminiscences, f. 7. This charitable institution, conducted by the Christian Brothers, was adjacent to the Casino at Marino, near the Bolands' future home.

[106] Harry made three quarterly payments of half a crown (2s. 6d.) in 1915, in return for insurance 'against certain accidents' and, perhaps, improved access to a valuable network of old boys. The Union's office was at 12, Rutland Sq., East, next to the National Club. See Membership Card, 1915: BP.

[107] Kevin Boland, 'James Boland', f. 42; Jim Maher, *Harry Boland: A Biography* (Cork, 1998), pp 12–13.

[108] *The Irish Catholic Directory, Almanac and Registry* (Dublin, 1884 edn.), advertisements, p. 40.

[109] This curriculum applied in 1883, shortly after the opening of the Irish Novitiate at Castletown: John Towey, *Irish de la Salle Brothers in Christian Education* (Dublin, 1980), p. 252.

[110] College and Boarding School Return, and Family Return, Elderfield, Castletown: Census Schedules, 1901, Queen's County 15/25/1. The list of boarders, whose ages ranged from 13 to 28 years, included Michael Tynan from Kilkenny (possibly a son of Harry's sponsors), along with a single Dubliner. Nor was Harry at home with his family on census night.

[111] Gerald Boland, Family Reminiscences, ff. 7–8; Liam C. Skinner, *Politicians by Accident* (Dublin, 1946), pp 214–15.

[112] Maher, *Harry Boland*, p. 14.

[113] *Thom's Official Directory* (1891 edn.), p. 1851.

[114] Ibid. (1901 edn.), p. 1944. The Dunlop Rubber Co. occupied Oriel House, later the headquarters of the CID: ibid. (1915 edn.), p. 1596.

[115] Dermot Keogh, *The Rise of the Irish Working Class: The Dublin Trade Union Movement and Labour Leadership, 1890–1914* (Dublin, 1982), p. 32 (extract from *Dublin Evening Mail*, 21 Aug. 1906). These defamatory allegations provoked

outrage from the Amalgamated Society of Tailors, which had two Dublin branches with about 700 members, paying £6,000 per annum in benefit contributions: ibid., pp 54-5.

116 In the Family Return for 1911, Edmund was returned as a tailor, aged 18 years, and Kathleen as a 21-year-old without occupation. Their letters to Harry in 1917 include numerous references to the staff at Todd, Burns & Co., indicating that both had worked there.

117 *Songs and Ballads of '98*, ed. Denis Devereux (Dublin, 1898), poorly printed on 32 pages of Irish-made paper, provided no music and only a few Irish versions, including William McWilliam's translation of John Keegan Casey's 'The Rising of the Moon'. The editor, or 'conductor', aimed 'to do something practical in bringing our literature into the humblest circles' and so advancing 'National intellectual progress': p. 2. Robert Brennan's performance of an Irish translation of John Kells Ingram's 'Who Fears to Speak of '98?', learned from Devereux's 'penny book of '98 ballads', so puzzled a Wexford audience in 1899 that it was found necessary to establish the Gaelic League in that county: Robert Brennan, *Allegiance* (Dublin, 1950), pp 4-5.

118 Gerald Boland, Family Reminiscences, ff. 7-8.

119 Gearóid Ua Beolláin, 'The United Irishmen' (undated essay, 40 ff., in a schoolboy hand): BP.

120 Kathleen Boland, Statement, f. 3. Their teacher at 24, Upper Sackville St., was probably Nellie (Ellen Lucy) O'Brien, grand-daughter of William Smith O'Brien and a close associate of Douglas Hyde.

121 Crowe, from Limerick, was Divisional Centre for Munster until 1911: Diarmuid Lynch, *The I.R.B. and the 1916 Insurrection*, ed. Florence O'Donoghue (Cork, 1957), p. 22.

122 Gerald Boland, Family Reminiscences, f. 9; Gerald Boland, response to talk by Seán MacEoin (typescript, *circa* 1964), ff. 1-2: BP; Kathleen Boland, Recollections; *Thom's Official Directory* (1901 edn.). Gerald recalled 'a couple' of occasions when the Circle reached its permitted membership of 100, whereupon it split in two like an amoeba.

123 *The Constitution of Wolfe Tone Clubs* (undated); *Directions for Organising and Working Wolfe Tone Clubs* (undated); *Wolfe Tone and United Irishmen Memorial Committee: Report of Honorary Secretaries* (29 Oct. 1910): McGP, NLI, MS 17641.

124 Gerald Boland, Family Reminiscences, f. 9; response to MacEoin, f. 3.

125 J. Anthony Gaughan, *Thomas Johnson, 1872-1963* (Dublin, 1980), p. 30; information on the 'Bolshevik Club' kindly supplied by Jane Leonard.

126 See Maher, *Harry Boland*, pp 15-16, for a more detailed account of Harry's hurling career.

127 Pádraig Puirséal, *The GAA in Its Time* (Swords, Co. Dublin, 1984 edn.), p. 155.

128 De Búrca, *Faughs*, pp 39, 95-9.

129 *Evening Telegraph*, 20 Mar. 1916, p. 4. Harry had played at full back in the semi-final against Kilkenny on 15 Feb.: Maher, *Harry Boland*, p. 23. No Dublin monument to Wolfe Tone was erected until 1967, Edward Delaney's statue being decapitated by a bomb four years later: Judith Hill, *Irish Public Sculpture: A History* (Dublin, 1998), p. 202.

130 *An Camán*, 15 Apr. 1933: cutting in BP.

131 Maher, *Harry Boland*, pp 15, 17; Phil O'Neill, *History of the G.A.A., 1910-1930: A History and Book of Reference for Gaels* (Kilkenny, 1931), pp 42, 63, 79; de Búrca, *Faughs*, pp 39, 117. Harry assumed the presidency in 1920, when his fellow-Faugh Andy Harty became Chairman.

132 Maher, *Harry Boland*, p. 17; Puirséal, *G.A.A.*, p. 162.

133 Maher, *Harry Boland*, p. 18; O'Neill, *G.A.A.*, p. 71.
134 J. J. Walsh, *Recollections of a Rebel* (Tralee, *circa* 1945), pp 18–19.
135 Reddy to Harrel, 19 Nov. 1886: DMP Papers, Box 2.
136 Tim Pat Coogan, *Michael Collins: A Biography* (London, 1990), p. 16; Puirséal, *G.A.A.*, p. 147. Though Collins was initiated by Samuel Maguire, his colleague in the Post Office and an English delegate to the GAA's Central Council, it is believed by Mr Harry Boland, jun., that his uncle set up this fateful event.
137 *Freeman's Journal*, 6 May 1909: quoted by Maher, *Harry Boland*, p. 16.
138 Drill was administered by officers of Na Fianna Éireann, the Irish Boy Scouts: Gerald Boland, response to MacEoin, f. 2; *The Irish Volunteers, 1913–1915*, ed. F. X. Martin (Dublin, 1963), p. 17.
139 Gerald Boland to Michael Hayes (undated draft, *circa* 1966): BP.
140 Kathleen Boland, Statement, f. 4; Kevin Boland, 'James Boland', ff. 65–6.
141 Harry's place was taken by Robert Page, one of the first three subscribers to the Volunteers along with Bulmer Hobson and Eoin MacNeill. Page subsequently joined the British army and addressed recruiting meetings in 1918: Gerald Boland, reponse to MacEoin, ff. 2–3; Martin, *Irish Volunteers*, pp 17–22, 26, 96–7.
142 Handbill headed 'Join the Irish Volunteers', in Mason Photographs, 'Irish Rebellion, 1916': BL.
143 Roll book, 'Irish Volunteers Dublin, Unit F1': BP.
144 Shields, who was to have acted at the opening of a double bill in the Abbey on Easter Tuesday, fought in the GPO and was interned at Frongoch, where he served on the Amusements Sub-Committee of the internees' General Council: Seán O Mahony, *Frongoch: University of Revolution* (Dublin, 1987), pp 46, 48, 54.
145 Oscar Traynor, 'Account written … at request of President de Valera shortly before his death' (typescript, 1963), f. 2: EdeVP, P 150/3297.
146 Kathleen Boland, Statement, f. 4.
147 Kathleen Boland to HB, 23 Jan. 1917; Kate Boland to HB, 14 Oct. 1916, 26 Mar. 1917: BP. Since two of these references are associated with family news, it seems likely that Michael [Hartnett?] and the doctor (husband of 'Gerty') belonged to the extended family, possibly in Manchester.
148 'Michael' [Hartnett?] to HB (undated fragment): BP.
149 Traynor, Account, f. 2. Other members of F Company, however, maintained that the number opposing Redmond in the 'split' was 60 or, by a more sober account, 7. See Charles Saurin, Statement (undated duplicate typescript), ff. 1–2; Harry Colley, idem, f. 2: MAD, Bureau of Military History Papers, WS 288, 1687.
150 Roll book; *Frank Henderson's Easter Rising: Recollections of a Dublin Volunteer*, ed. Michael Hopkinson (Cork, 1998), pp 31–6. The roll book includes an invoice, dated 11 Dec. 1915, for the specified provisions costing £4 3s. 1d.
151 *Evening Herald*, 17 Mar. 1916, p. 1; *Evening Telegraph*, 17 Mar., p. 3.
152 *Evening Telegraph*, 18 Mar. 1916, p. 3.
153 Maurice Collins to HB, 19 Mar. 1917: BP; *Evening Telegraph*, 17 Mar. 1916, p. 3.
154 Copy of circular, 5 June 1915, supplied by Robert Barton to Gerald Boland, 1 Nov. 1943: BP. A rough draft of this circular, predicting that the Government would abandon any proposals for Conscription 'if they find the people do not want them', had been signed by O'Brien, 'Foley', and Boland on 3 June: O'Brien Papers, NLI, MS 13954.
155 William O'Brien, *Forth the Banners Go: Reminscences*, ed. Edward MacLysaght (Dublin, 1969), p. 274.
156 In celebrating the contribution of his father's generation to nationality, he told the Dáil that 'we picked it up in 1916 and we brought the Irish Republic out of the backwoods, away from the dark rooms of secret societies, and preached the gospel

before the Irish people': Dáil Éireann, *Official Report: Debate on the Treaty between Great Britain and Ireland* (Dublin, undated), p. 304 (7 Jan. 1922).

CHAPTER III. REBELLION

1. Gerald Boland, Reminiscences of the Rising (MSS, 1962), ff. 2–3: BP; Oscar Traynor, 'Account written ... at request of President de Valera shortly before his death' (typescript, 1963), f. 2: EdeVP, P 150/3297.
2. *Evening Herald*, 24 Apr. 1916 ('Early Racing Edition'); Pádraig O'Toole, *The Glory and the Anguish* (Galway, 1984), pp 93–5; W. F. Mandle, *The Gaelic Athletic Association and Irish Nationalist Politics, 1884–1924* (London, 1987), pp 31, 104, 156.
3. Gerald Boland, Reminiscences, ff. 2–3. According to *Frank Henderson's Easter Rising: Recollections of a Dublin Volunteer*, ed. Michael Hopkinson (Cork, 1998), pp 40–2, an order to 'stand-to' was received from 2nd Battalion headquarters 'some time after' mid-morning on Easter Sunday.
4. Kathleen Boland (Mrs Seán O'Donovan), Statement for the Bureau of Military History (undated typescript), f. 5; Kathleen Boland, Recollections (undated MSS): BP.
5. *Evening Herald*, 24 Apr. 1916; Kathleen Boland, Statement, f. 7.
6. Michael Joseph ('the') O'Rahilly, who by most accounts had abandoned his opposition to Pearse's mobilisation after hearing of the Proclamation, was joint Treasurer of the Provisional Committee and MacNeill's most emphatic supporter.
7. Traynor, Account, f. 9; *Henderson's Easter Rising*, pp 43–5. Henderson's parents, like Harry's, had both lived in Manchester prior to their marriage. Henderson (a clerk) also lived in Fairview, at 5, Windsor Villas, Philipsburgh Ave.
8. Traynor, Account, f. 9; *Henderson's Easter Rising*, p. 45.
9. Gerald Boland, Reminiscences, ff. 4–5.
10. Traynor, Account, f. 13. Poole (of 11, Russell St.) had three sons and a brother (Capt. Christopher Poole) in the Citizen Army. His 'turbulent nature' (betokened by his 18 summary convictions before 1916 for offences such as assaulting the police) had led to his departure from the Citizen Army by early 1915, until reconciled at the moment of crisis. See Register of American Grants, f. 118, and List of Dependents of Prisoners (undated): Irish National Aid and Volunteer Dependents' Fund [hereafter, INA and VDF] Papers, NLI, MSS 23494, 23499; Frank Robbins, *Under the Starry Plough: Recollections of the Irish Citizen Army* (Dublin, 1977), pp 40–2, 68; 'List of Irish Prisoners in English Convict Prisons', submitted 12 July 1916: PRO, Home Office Registered Papers (Supplementary), HO 144/1453/311980/21.
11. Kathleen Boland, Recollections; Kevin Boland, 'James Boland, 1857–1895: By His Grandson' (typescript, 1993), f. 24: BP.
12. *Henderson's Easter Rising*, pp 48–9; Harry Colley, Statement (undated duplicate typescript), ff. 12–13: MAD, Bureau of Military History Papers, WS 1687. Henderson indicates that Poole was subordinate to Capt. Craven in this unit.
13. *Henderson's Easter Rising*, pp 48–50.
14. Kathleen Boland, Statement, f. 5; Jim Maher, *Harry Boland: A Biography* (Dublin, 1998), pp 26–7.
15. Easter Week Memorial Committee, Report no. 4, *circa* 1936 (Thomas Devine, Kimmage): Diarmuid Lynch Papers, NLI, MS 11131. Henry, formerly of the RIC, was one of 16 prisoners who, under O'Rahilly's direction, endured 4 days of humiliation and discomfort in the GPO: *Weekly Irish Times, Sinn Féin Rebellion Handbook* (Dublin, 1916), pp 13–15.

[16] Kathleen Boland, Recollections; Traynor, Account, f. 11. The Imperial Hotel was above Clery's department store on the east side of Sackville St., opposite the GPO.

[17] Traynor, Account, ff. 11–12; *Henderson's Easter Rising*, pp 51–2. Henderson states that some of his men returned the fire from the Imperial.

[18] Traynor, Account, ff. 12–13; Max Caulfield, *The Easter Rebellion* (Dublin, 1995; 1st edn. 1963), pp 215–16; Michael Foy and Brian Barton, *The Easter Rising* (Stroud, Gloucs., 1999), pp 134–5, 139.

[19] Easter Week Memorial Committee, Report no. 13, 17 May 1937 (Daniel Canny, Capel St.): Lynch Papers, NLI, MS 11131.

[20] Kathleen Boland, Statement, f. 6. Paddy Sheehan, the visitor, was later said to be 'going in for journalism', an appropriate vocation. He became Sinn Féin's acting General Secretary in late 1918. See Robert Brennan, *Allegiance* (Dublin, 1950), p. 176; Kate Boland to HB, 23 Jan. 1917. Unless otherwise stated, all family correspondence cited in this chapter is preserved in BP.

[21] Traynor, Account, ff. 17–18. Had Harry proceeded into the sewers, as proposed, he might have suffered the undignified fate imaginatively assigned to him in Neil Jordan's film, *Michael Collins* (1996).

[22] Traynor, Account, ff. 18–19; *Henderson's Easter Rising*, pp 61–2; Diarmuid Lynch, *The I.R.B. and the 1916 Insurrection*, ed. Florence O'Donoghue (Cork, 1957), pp 107, 179.

[23] Easter Week Commemoration Committee, Report no. 8, 17 May 1937 (Tom Leahy, Partick, Scotland): Lynch Papers, NLI, MS 11131. Leahy remarked that both Traynor and Harry envied him his boilermaker's handiness with heavy tools.

[24] *Henderson's Easter Rising*, p. 64.

[25] Another account credits Pearse with ordering the tunnel down Moore St., which is said to have begun at Cogan's greengrocery and ended at Hanlon's fishmongers: Caulfield, *Easter Rebellion*, pp 262, 272–3. This implies a tunnel from nos. 10 to 20, accounting for one-third of the street's length and falling far short of Parnell St. Among the smashed premises were two stocking china and glass: *Thom's Official Directory* (1915 edn.).

[26] Jam manufacturers at 204–6, Parnell St., to the west beyond King's Inns St.: *Thom's Official Directory* (1915 edn.).

[27] Traynor, Account, f. 22.

[28] Alex Findlater, *Findlaters: The Story of a Dublin Merchant Family* (Dublin, 2001), p. 279 (reference kindly supplied by Jane Leonard).

[29] Gerald 'never had a uniform, neither had Harry': Kathleen Boland, Statement, f. 4.

[30] Gerald Boland, Reminiscences; Michael McInerney, 'Gerry Boland's Story', pt. 2, *Irish Times*, 9 Oct. 1968, p. 12.

[31] *Weekly Irish Times, Handbook*, p. 65.

[32] Gerald Boland, Reminiscences, f. 9.

[33] Gerald to Kate Boland, 22 May 1916. Harry's sentence had been announced in the press on 12 May.

[34] Gerald to Kate and Kathleen Boland, 11 June 1916.

[35] Gerald to Kate Boland, 19 Aug. 1916.

[36] Gerald to Kate Boland, 15 Sept. 1916.

[37] *Weekly Irish Times, Handbook*, p. 15. During its brief existence, the Coliseum Theatre at 24, Henry St., had featured gymnastics, juggling, ju-jitsu, bioscopes, music, and the Trombettes ('a continental comedy duo'): *Evening Telegraph*, 21 Mar. 1916, p. 2; *Evening Herald*, 22 Apr., p. 4. Bewley's offices were a few doors from the theatre at nos. 18–20: *Thom's Official Directory* (1916 edn.).

[38] Kathleen Boland, Statement, f. 6.

39 *The Memoirs of Senator Joseph Connolly*, ed. J. Anthony Gaughan (Dublin, 1996), p. 109. 'L 5' also housed the Labour leader Cathal Shannon, Sinn Féin's future Secretary Paudeen O'Keeffe, Seán Milroy, and Joseph Connolly, the Belfast businessman who succeeded Harry as room 'Commandant'.

40 Gerald Boland to HB, 26 Mar. 1917.

41 'List of Irish Prisoners'; Pádraig Puirséal, *The GAA in Its Time* (Dublin, 1984 edn.), pp 168–9.

42 The official record of Harry's Court Martial is not among the 'sample' preserved in PRO, WO 71/344–359.

43 Corrigan & Corrigan (3, St. Andrew's St.), 'List of Men Undergoing Penal Servitude' (undated, *circa* 1916): INA & VDF Papers, NLI, MS 24363. Michael A. Corrigan acted as solicitor to the Irish Volunteers, while his partner and younger brother (William P.) himself underwent penal servitude in Portland and Lewes Prisons: León Ó Broin, *W. E. Wylie and the Irish Revolution, 1916–1921* (Dublin, 1989), pp 38–41.

44 Kathleen Boland, Statement, f. 7.

45 HB, speech at Academy of Music, Philadelphia, 5 Jan. 1921: *Irish Press* (Philadelphia), 15 Jan. 1921, p. 5; John F. Shouldice, Statement (duplicate typescript, 1952), f. 1: WS 679.

46 *Pádraig Ó Fathaigh's War of Independence: Recollections of a Galway Gaelic Leaguer*, ed. Timothy G. McMahon (Cork, 2000), pp 42–3.

47 Kathleen Boland, Statement, f. 7; HB to Kate Boland, 15 Jan. 1917.

48 Brennan, *Allegiance*, pp 99–101.

49 *Ó Fathaigh's War*, p. 43. Stone also succumbed to the personalities of Gerald Crofts and Michael de Lacy.

50 Report to Home Office, 27 June 1916: HO 144/1453/311980/18. Wilmot's account of Eoin MacNeill's reception differs strikingly from the familiar claim that 'from the time he stepped forward at Dartmoor to order the salute for MacNeill, de Valera had been accepted as the leader of the prisoners': Earl of Longford and Thomas P. O'Neill, *Eamon de Valera* (London, 1970), pp 53, 55.

51 Petitions by de Valera and Ashe, 14 and 20 June 1916: HO 144/10309/315944/1 and HO 144/1459/316398; E. Ruggles Brise (Prison Commission) to Home Office, 22 June: HO 144/1453/311980/13. Though de Valera alone was deemed to have made a sound case for carrying on his 'trade', he was 'informed that he is not yet eligible for the privilege for which he asks'.

52 HB to Kate Boland, 15 Sept. 1916: extract transcribed in Andrew Brasier and John Kelly, *Harry Boland: A Man Divided* (Dublin, 2000), p. 47; Kate Boland to HB, 14 Oct. 1916.

53 HB to Kate Boland, 14 Dec. 1916; Gerald to Kate Boland, 15 Sept. 1916.

54 32 of the 65 Irish convicts made 63 applications, of which only 26 were successful; whereas 32 of the 403 ordinary prisoners made 50 applications, of which 36 were successful. See Dr. E. Battiscombe to E. R. Reade (Governor), 20 Oct. 1916: HO 144/10309 (Prison Commission, 50833/12).

55 E. R. Reade to Kate Boland, 13 July 1916; Reade to Tim O'Mahony (?), 3 Aug., with reference to an earlier message dated 1 June: BP.

56 HB to Kate and Kathleen Boland, 15 Sept. 1916: extract transcribed in Brasier and Kelly, *Harry Boland*, pp 47–50.

57 Kate Boland to HB, 14 Oct. 1916.

58 Mick Treacy to HB, 14 Oct. 1916 (paragraph in family letter). Treacy claimed to be 'in great form at "Drumcollogher"'.

59 Kathleen Boland, Statement, f. 6.

60 Ned Boland to HB, 14 Oct. 1916.

61 HB to Ned Boland, 14 Dec. 1916.
62 Reports and correspondence of Governor Reade, 16–27 Oct. 1916: HO 144/10309 (Prison Commission, 50833/11).
63 Draft regulations, memoranda and minutes, 3–29 Nov. 1916: HO 144/1453/311980/34, 29a. The 18 Irish prisoners serving lighter sentences of imprisonment (rather than penal servitude) at Wormwood Scrubs, though subject to the same relaxation, were not to be united with their convict brethren.
64 Kate Boland to HB, 23 Jan. 1917.
65 HB to Ned Boland, 14 Dec. 1916.
66 Maurice Collins to HB, 5 Mar. 1917.
67 Ó Fathaigh's War, p. 43.
68 HB to Tim O'Mahony, 14 Mar. 1917. His sister claimed that the chained prisoners had 'started to whistle a jig and they danced on the platform, to the amazement of the onlookers', the dancer being identified by Jack Shouldice as Dick King from Wexford: Kathleen Boland, Statement, f. 8; Shouldice, Statement, f. 7.
69 Gaelic American, 12 Aug. 1922, p. 2. In response to a petition from de Valera on 9 Nov. 1916, complaining that on his trip to Maidstone 'three of us were chained together so that when one of us had to perform the natural functions he had to drag his two companions with him and violate every law of common decency', the Home Office had directed that 'this petition will be answered by the removal of this class of convict to Lewes and the dispensing with chaining on the journey there'. See minute for Home Secretary, 27 Nov. 1916: HO 144/10309/315944/4.
70 Longford and O'Neill, Eamon de Valera, p. 54.
71 Ó Fathaigh's War, p. 44.
72 Brennan, Allegiance, pp 120–1.
73 Ó Fathaigh's War, p. 46.
74 This volume of 100 pages (BP), marked 'C 3–16, q 90, H. J. Boland, Lewes Prison, issued 23 Dec. 1916' [hereafter, Lewes Notebook], was eventually posted from Lewes to Marino Crescent. Some entries were added after its return.
75 Marriott to Prison Commissioners, 6 Mar. 1917: HO 144/1453/311980/78. Kelly's punishment resulted from Peppard's attempt to send 'a message for my people' through a prisoner then awaiting release. See Thomas Peppard, Statement (undated duplicate typescript), f. 7: WS 1399.
76 E. Ruggles Brise to Home Secretary, 7 Mar. 1917: HO 144/1453/311980/78.
77 Report by J. R. Farewell (Inspector) to Prison Commissioners, 24 Mar. 1917: HO 144/1453/311980/86.
78 Brennan, Allegiance, pp 124–6.
79 HB to Kate Boland, 2 May 1917.
80 Boland family to HB, 7 May 1917.
81 Kate Boland to HB, after 9 May 1917.
82 HB to Ned Boland, 14 Dec. 1916.
83 Maurice Collins to HB, 5, 19 Mar. 1917.
84 HB to Tim O'Mahony, 14 Mar. 1917. 'Scye' denotes a sleeve-opening; 'basting' is a term for stitching; and 'X order' probably refers to solitary confinement for misconduct.
85 HB to Paddy [Hogan], undated draft in Lewes Notebook, circa May 1917.
86 HB to Kate Boland, 2 May 1917.
87 Kate Boland to HB, after 9 May 1917.
88 Kate Boland to HB, received 26 Mar. 1917. On 7 May, she reiterated her disgust at Harry's unseemly appearance, 'with your ugly brown and white costume and nos. and Broad Arrows'.
89 Kate Boland to HB, 7 May 1917.

90 HB to Kate Boland, 2 May 1917. George Gavan Duffy had prepared Sir Roger Casement's unavailing Defence in 1916.
91 Longford and O'Neill, *Eamon de Valera*, pp 57–8.
92 Cabinet Conclusions, 31 May 1917: PRO, CAB 23/2/153(3). On 14 June, Cabinet agreed to grant an amnesty, preparation for the Irish Convention being the 'only ground' considered: CAB 23/3/163 (19). The Convention did not, in fact, meet until 25 July.
93 Reports by Lt.-Col. J. Winn, 5, 6 June 1917: HO 144/1453/311980/122.
94 John McGarry, a 30-year-old electrician and assistant manager whose death sentence had been commuted to 8 years' penal servitude, became President of the IRB's Supreme Council after the death of Thomas Ashe in Sept. 1917, remaining so until his own arrest in May 1918. For 'Poole's methods', such as a rendition of 'The Green Flag' in the workshop leading to a hunger-strike, and his beating of warders who tried to place him in a strait-jacket, see Brennan, *Allegiance*, pp 118–19.
95 Reports by Winn, 6, 7 June 1917. Brennan recalled that Harry had been cheered after urging the remaining inmates to 'keep the flag flying', and had put up 'a terrific struggle' before being chained and handcuffed: Brennan, *Allegiance*, pp 132–3.
96 HB to Kate Boland, [6 June 1917]; Brennan, *Allegiance*, p. 133; Katherine Boland, Statement, f. 8.
97 Kathleen Boland, Statement, f. 9.
98 Gerald Boland, Reminiscences, ff. 9–10. Gerald (with support from Traynor) refused to sign a 'lying statement' fabricated by Collins for domestic consumption, and was summoned to justify himself before the Camp Council. Gerald's antipathy for Collins seems genuinely to have antedated the conflict of 1922, though no hint of it may be found in his surviving letters from Frongoch.
99 Warre B. Wells and N. Marlowe, *The Irish Convention and Sinn Féin* (London, 1918), pp 44–5. Harry's letter was distributed throughout the country as a handbill: Brennan, *Allegiance*, p. 133. Inspector John Mills, DMP 9,300 (1866–12 June 1917), a native of Westmeath, was the first Crown fatality since the Rebellion: Jim Herlihy, *The Dublin Metropolitan Police: A Short History and Genealogical Guide* (Dublin, 2001), p. 178.
100 Reports and copy of remission (which did not constitute a 'free pardon'), 16 June 1917: HO 144/1453/311980/121.
101 *Ó Fathaigh's War*, p. 48.

CHAPTER IV. INTERMISSION

1 HB to 'Bill' [Duggan], undated draft, *circa* Apr.1917, in volume marked 'C 3–16, q 90, H. J. Boland, Lewes Prison, issued 23 Dec. 1916': BP [hereafter, Lewes Notebook].
2 The first of these maxims, scattered over a single folio of the Lewes Notebook, is from Arthur Hugh Clough's 'Peschiera'.
3 HB to 'Paddy' [Hogan], undated draft in Lewes Notebook, *circa* May 1917.
4 Letters from home refer to 3 prisoners who were released early because of illness: John Cullen ('suffering from consumption of the throat'); Councillor William Partridge ('a dying man, though he is very hopeful of recovering'); and Gerald Crofts (who was 'being released a wreck also'): Kate Boland to HB, 7 May, after 9 May 1917. Unless otherwise stated, all letters cited in this chapter are preserved in BP.
5 HB to Ned Boland, 14 Dec. 1916; British Passport no. LO 14649, issued 29 Sept. 1921: BP. Eamon de Valera ('a man of 6 ft. ¼ in. in height, of good general health, but of spare physique') likewise put on weight in Dartmoor, gaining 8 lbs to reach 12 stone 3 lbs. See Dr. E. Battiscombe to Major E. R. Reade (Governor), 20 Oct.

1916: PRO, Home Office Registered Papers (Supplementary), HO 144/10309 (Prison Commission, 50833/12).

6   HB to Kate Boland, 15 Jan. 1917.
7   HB to 'C.' [Cait Fraher], undated draft in Lewes Notebook, *circa* May 1917.
8   HB to Hogan, *circa* May 1917.
9   HB to Kate Boland, 15 Jan. 1917.
10 HB to Kate Boland, 14 Dec. 1916.
11 HB to Tim O'Mahony, 14 Mar. 1917. Timothy L. O'Mahony lived at 25, Richmond Ave., Fairview, three doors from the republican historian, P. S. O'Hegarty: *Thom's Official Directory of the United Kingdom of Great Britain and Ireland* (Dublin, 1919 edn.).
12 HB to Kate Boland, 2 May 1917.
13 HB to Kate Boland, 15 Jan. 1917.
14 Lewes Notebook.
15 HB to O'Mahony, 14 Mar. 1917.
16 Kate Boland to HB, received 26 Mar. 1917.
17 Poem, marked 'January 6th 1917, Lewes Gaol', in Lewes Notebook.
18 Lewes Notebook.
19 List, giving abbreviated titles and catalogue numbers, in Lewes Notebook.
20 Gerald Boland to Kate Boland, 22 May 1916. Gerald's spiritual experiments incurred the disapproval of a missionary priest of the Holy Cross named Clark (Bro. Albens, CSC): 'I hope he dosen't [*sic.*] believe that trash any more about Yogeism or whatever it was. The Catholic religion is the only religion, because God himself taught it.' See Bro. Albens to Kate Boland, 18 July 1918: BP.
21 Kathleen Boland to HB, after 9 May 1917. Bro. Albens's letter applauded Kathleen's influence: 'Glad Harry is assisted by Kathleen, she is a good young Irishwoman, God bless her!'
22 Kate Boland to HB, 23 Jan. 1917, referring to Thomas F. O'Sullivan, *Story of the G.A.A.: First History of Great Organisation* (Dublin, 1916).
23 The American athlete, adventurer, yarn-spinner, and film-inspirer Rex Ellington Beach (1877–1949) wrote manly tales about miners in Alaska and the like.
24 Ned Boland to HB, after 9 May 1917. 'The Man from Snowy River' was written by the Australian poet Andrew Barton ('Banjo') Paterson (1864–1941), not Adam Lindsay Gordon (1833–70).
25 Harry misremembered the second line as 'Bequeathed thence from Bleeding Sire to Son'.
26 Michael McInerney, 'Gerry Boland's Story', pt. 2, in *Irish Times*, 9 Oct. 1968, p. 12. 'To Mr. Boland there was no-one like Harry and records seem to bear him out. ... He was a great athlete and footballer [*sic.*], but he would scarcely ever read a book. Yet he remembered almost everything he heard and spoke with a most cultured accent.'
27 HB to O'Mahony, 14 Mar. 1917. There were 2 professors and 3 school teachers at Lewes (including Thomas Ashe), in addition to a 'Gaelic teacher' (Patrick Fahy) and an 'organiser Gaelic League' (Colm O'Geary). See 'List of Irish Prisoners in English Convict Prisons', submitted 12 July 1916: HO 144/1453/311980/21.
28 HB to Kate Boland, 15 Sept. 1916: extract in Andrew Brasier and John Kelly, *Harry Boland: A Man Divided* (Dublin, 2000), p. 47. Pts. iv and v of Fr. Eugene O'Growney's *Simple Lessons in Irish* (Gaelic League Series, 5 pts., Dublin, 1894–) were completed by John [Eoin] MacNeill, Harry's fellow-prisoner.
29 Lewes Notebook.
30 HB to Hogan, *circa* May 1917.
31 HB to Kate Boland, 2 May 1917.

32 HB to Cait Fraher, *circa* May 1917.

33 HB to Kate Boland, 15 Jan. 1917.

34 HB to O'Mahony, 14 Mar. 1917. The visitor was probably Robert Morrison, the Bolands' neighbour at 20, Marino Crescent. On his return to Dublin, Morrison made Maurice Collins 'laugh over some of your remarks': Maurice Collins to HB, 5 Mar.

35 HB to Kate Boland, 15 Jan. 1917.

36 Gerald Boland to HB, received 26 Mar. 1917; Kathleen Boland to HB, 7 May. The photograph of the separatist convention chaired by George Noble, Count Plunkett, held at Dublin's Mansion House on 19 Apr., was among various Easter cards which Harry failed to receive.

37 Kate Boland to HB, 23 Jan. 1917.

38 Gerald to Kathleen Boland, 11 June 1916.

39 Kathleen Boland to HB, received 26 Mar. 1917. Harry had indeed received 'several Easter Cards but none from home, Paddy Cards and Shamrock': HB to Kate Boland, 2 May.

40 Kate Boland to HB, 7 May 1917.

41 HB to Cait Fraher, *circa* May 1917.

42 Collins to HB, 5 Mar. 1917.

43 Collins to HB, 19 Mar. 1917. Peter Leech, grocer, wine and spirit merchant, held court at 57–8, Lower Dorset St., and 1–2, Portland Place: *Thom's Official Directory* (1915 edn.).

44 Collins to HB, 19 Mar. 1917.

45 His business flourished, having replaced 68, Upper Sackville St. as the meeting place for the GAA's Dublin County Board: Kate Boland to HB, 23 Jan. 1917. Maurice Collins's address when interned was 230, Clonliffe Rd: Seán O Mahony, *Frongoch: University of Revolution* (Dublin, 1987), p. 177.

46 O Mahony, *Frongoch*, p. 64; report by District Insp. Kirwan, RIC, 31 July 1917: PRO, CO 904/196/65. Hobson, Eoin MacNeill's close ally and Secretary to the Supreme Council, was released on 26 April after an order conveyed to Collins by Seán T. O'Kelly. His kidnap had prompted the O'Rahilly to induce MacNeill to countermand the mobilisation ordered for Easter Sunday. See Max Caulfield, *The Easter Rebellion* (Dublin, 1995; 1st edn. 1963), pp 40–1; Maurice Collins, Statement (undated duplicate typescript), f. 3: MAD, Bureau of Military History Papers, WS 550.

47 HB to Cait Fraher, *circa* May 1917. Collins had left Co. Limerick for Dublin in 1901, joining the IRB in London towards the end of his posting there and playing Gaelic football in both cities. He joined F Company, 1st Dublin Battalion, on the formation of the Irish Volunteers in Nov. 1913: Collins, Statement, f. 1.

48 HB to Ned Boland, *circa* Mar. 1917: extract in Brasier and Kelly, *Harry Boland*, p. 50.

49 O'Mahony to HB, 5 Sept. 1916; Major E. R. Reade, formal message to O'Mahony (?), 3 Aug.; HB to O'Mahony, 14 Mar. 1917. 'Mahogany' was presumably a playful corruption of the name O'Mahony.

50 HB to Ned Boland, 15 Sept. 1916: extract in Brasier and Kelly, *Harry Boland*, p. 47.

51 HB to O'Mahony, 14 Mar. 1917. 'The one bright spot', Sir Edward Grey's inapposite metaphor for Ireland on 3 Aug. 1914, was a pet phrase for Harry and his circle.

52 According to Roman legend, Gaius Mucius Scaevola, having failed to kill the Etruscan invader Porsenna, mortified himself by placing his right hand in a fire.

53 See ch. III, p. 55.

54 O'Mahony's counterpart in Oliver Goldsmith's 'The Deserted Village', ll. 211–16, is the 'village master': 'In arguing too, the parson own'd his skill, / For e'en though

vanquish'd, he could argue still; / While words of learned length, and thund'ring sound / Amazed the gazing rustics rang'd around, / And still they gaz'd, and still the wonder grew, / That one small head could carry all he knew.'

55 HB to O'Mahony, 14 Mar. 1917. 'The Monto' was the red-light district around Montgomery St., just west of Amiens St. Station.

56 This may refer to the request that prisoners undertake not to attempt escape during their transfer from Dartmoor to Lewes, in return for which they would have been allowed civilian clothing and exempted from chains: *Pádraig Ó Fathaigh's War of Independence: Recollections of a Galway Gaelic Leaguer*, ed. Timothy G. McMahon (Cork, 2000), p. 43.

57 'But yesterday the word of Caesar might / Have stood against the world; now lies he there, / And none so poor to do him reverence': *Julius Caesar*, III. ii. 124–6.

58 HB to O'Mahony, 14 Mar. 1917. 'M. O. L. T.' represents T. L. O'M. in reverse.

59 HB to Kate Boland, 15 Jan. 1917.

60 Kate Boland to HB, 23 Jan. 1917.

61 HB to O'Mahony, 14 Mar. 1917.

62 Kathleen Boland to HB, after 9 May 1917; Kate Boland to HB, 23 Jan.; HB to Hogan, *circa* May; 'Andy' [Harty] to HB, 17 Apr.

63 HB to Kate Boland, 15 Jan. 1917.

64 Kate Boland's 58 weekly payments (5 Aug. 1916 to 15 Sept. 1917) varied between £1 and £1 15s. (with £2 12s. 6d. at Christmas), perhaps reflecting changes in Ned's or Kathleen's earnings. See 'Ladies' Committee: Particulars of Weekly Grants' (4 ledgers): Irish National Aid and Volunteer Dependents' Fund [hereafter, INA & VDF] Papers, NLI, MSS 23487–90 (reference kindly supplied by Dr. Peter Hart).

65 Kate Boland to HB, after 9 May 1917.

66 HB to Kate Boland, 14 Dec. 1916.

67 Gerald to Kate Boland, 22 May, 11 June 1916.

68 Gerald to Kate Boland, 26 Sept. 1916.

69 Kate and Ned Boland to HB, received 26 Mar. 1917.

70 HB to Kate Boland, 2 May 1917.

71 Kathleen and Kate Boland to HB, 7 May 1917; family to HB, after 9 May.

72 His 'pro tem. successor' was Andy Harty, 'and a d—— good one he is. His mild innocent appearance administering justice wd do good to an R.M.': Collins to HB, 5 Mar. 1917.

73 HB to O'Mahony, 14 Mar. 1917.

74 Collins to HB, 19 Mar. 1917. David Lloyd George's nickname was 'the Goat'; 'moriah' signifies 'forsooth'.

75 Harty to HB, 17 Apr. 1917.

76 Collins to HB, 5 Mar. 1917; Harty to HB, 17 Apr.

77 The secession, initiated by the Dublin Kickham Club in 1914, engendered the National Association of Gaelic and Athletic Clubs: W. F. Mandle, *The Gaelic Athletic Association and Irish Nationalist Politics, 1884–1924* (London, 1987), pp 173–4; Marcus de Búrca, *The G.A.A.: A History* (Dublin, 1980), p. 146.

78 This club was founded in 1906 by a group of grocers' and vintners' assistants, and collapsed after the Rebellion: Pádraig O'Toole, *The Glory and the Anguish* (Galway, 1984), p. 19.

79 'Frank' [Shouldice] to HB, 23 Jan. 1917; Harty to HB, 17 Apr.; Collins to HB, 5, 19 Mar.

80 Collins to HB, 19 Mar. 1917. John J. Hogan, of 32, Dufferin Ave., should not be confused with Harry's chums in the Faughs, Tom and Paddy Hogan.

81 Ned Boland to HB, after 9 May 1917. No previous congress had been held entirely in camera: Pádraig Puirséal, *The GAA in its Times* (Dublin, 1984 edn.), p. 172.

Michael P. Crowe, of 58, Cabra Park, Dublin, shared the position of Treasurer of the GAA with Daniel Fraher of Dungarvan: Gaelic Athletic Association (Limited), *Official Guide, 1914–15* (Wexford, undated), pp 3–5.

82 Ned Boland to HB, after 9 May 1917.

83 HB to Hogan, *circa* May 1917.

84 Collins to HB, 5 Mar. 1917.

85 HB to Hogan, *circa* May 1917. Ned had reported, in his letter of 7 May, that 'there was a splendid Hurling match yesterday between Faughs and Collegians, each side scoring 2 gls. – 4 pts. It was easily the best for a long time, both sides being splendidly trained and fit.' Tim Gleeson was President of the club for most of the period 1908–26: Marcus de Búrca, *One Hundred Years of Faughs Hurling* (Dublin, *circa* 1985), p. 39.

86 HB to O'Mahony, 14 Mar. 1917. The 'marker' in billiards is the scorer.

87 Ned Boland to HB, 7 May 1917.

88 Collins to HB, 19 Mar. 1917. The newsagent Luke J. O'Toole, the GAA's Secretary (1901–29), is the centrepiece of his grandson's *The Glory and the Anguish*. The Association's first office was in O'Toole's house at 29, Mountpleasant Sq., Ranelagh.

89 Collins to HB, 19 Mar. 1917.

90 HB to Ned Boland, 14 Dec. 1916; HB to O'Mahony, 14 Mar. 1917.

91 Collins to HB, 5, 19 Mar. 1917; Ned Boland to HB, after 9 May.

92 Collins to HB, 19 Mar. 1917; Harty to HB, 17 Apr.

93 Kathleen Boland to HB, 23 Jan. 1917; Collins to HB, 5 Mar. Shouldice recalled communicating with Harry in Lewes by singing 'Galway Bay' – 'and sure enough I heard Harry's well-known voice from his cell rendering "Twenty Men from Dublin Town", one of his favourite ballads'. See John F. Shouldice, Statement (duplicate typescript, 1952), f. 13: WS 679.

94 Kate Boland to HB, 23 Jan. 1917; Ned Boland to HB, after 9 May. The quotation is from the final stanza of Arthur M. Forester's ballad.

95 His name appeared immediately below Harry's in the official 'List of Irish Prisoners' at Dartmoor. Brennan recalled that 'Crofts had the cell immediately beneath mine [at Lewes] and every night he would give us a few songs from his vast repertoire. His voice was never very powerful but he was a real artist and he could make any and every old song sound beautiful': Robert Brennan, *Allegiance* (Dublin, 1950), p. 122.

96 Summary of Defence at his Court Martial, in Corrigan & Corrigan, 'List of Men Undergoing Penal Servitude' (undated, *circa* 1916): INA & VDF Papers, NLI, MS 24363.

97 Lewes Notebook.

98 HB to O'Mahony, 14 Mar. 1917.

99 Kathleen Boland to HB, after 9 May 1917.

100 HB to Cait Fraher, *circa* May 1917.

101 Collins to HB, 5 Mar. 1917.

102 Ned Boland to HB, received 26 Mar. 1917.

103 HB to Hogan, *circa* May 1917. Andy Harty had confirmed the creation of a camogie team in his letter of 17 Apr.

104 HB to O'Mahony, 14 Mar. 1917; Harty to HB, 17 Apr.

105 Collins to HB, 5 Mar. 1917. On 14 Dec. 1916, Harry had asked Ned to convey 'my heartiest congrats', expressing delight 'that Maurice rose supreme above misfortune'.

106 HB to Cait Fraher, *circa* May 1917.

107 'To Gerald Crofts': Lewes Notebook.

[108] HB to Kate Boland, 15 Jan. 1917; HB to O'Mahony, 14 Mar. These ministering angels of uncertain affiliation were Mary O'Keefe and Kitty Kevans.

[109] HB to Ned Boland, 14 Dec. 1916.

[110] Kathleen Boland to HB, 23 Jan. 1917.

[111] Reports by Head Const. John O'Toole, 29 Apr., 3 May, 8 May, 27 Dec. 1916; Memorandum, Directorate of Special Intelligence (M.I.9.C(3) to M.I.5.G), June 1917: CO 904/214/405. Sgt. Henry Shouldice (no. 11,918), pensioned from the RIC in 1879, was reputedly the son of a German employed on the King-Harman estate. F. J. Shouldice was an assistant clerk in the National Health Insurance Commission; J. F. Shouldice was a second-division clerk in the Statistics and Intelligence section of the Department of Agriculture: *Thom's Official Directory* (1915 edn.), pp 835a, 872.

[112] HB to Kate Boland, 15 Jan. 1917. Ena's letter has not been traced.

[113] Kathleen Boland to HB, after 26 Mar. 1917; Kate and Ned Boland to HB, 7 May; HB to Ned Boland, 14 Dec. 1916.

[114] HB to Kate Boland, 2 May 1917.

[115] Kathleen Boland to HB, 7 May 1917. Three Rock Mountain is near Stepaside, 7 miles south of Dublin.

[116] When reporting the unexpected absence from the annual congress of Harry's 'Father in Law', Andy Harty was presumably referring to his Godfather Fraher: letter to HB, 17 Apr. 1917.

[117] Kate and Kathleen Boland to HB, 7 May 1917.

[118] HB to Cait Fraher, *circa* May 1917. His mother was sent a more prosaic version on 2 May: 'This is a glorious climate just now, sun up at 5.30 and sets about 9 p.m. I watch it setting every evening thro' my bars. It is tough enough to be locked up for the night at 4.30, this is the worse part of it. One does not mind on the winter days study and reading comes easy then, but when the sun shines and the birds sing and from my window I can see the people walking on the downs I often long for home and then again I think of our gallant friends who gave their life for Ireland and take heart and glory in my lot.'

[119] HB to Cait Fraher, *circa* May 1917. For an account of their reputed engagement, as recalled by Kevin Boland, see Brasier and Kelly, *Harry Boland*, pp 3–4.

[120] Undated verse, signed 'An Beolanach', in Lewes Notebook.

[121] HB to O'Mahony, 14 Mar. 1917.

[122] This analysis compares Harry and his 37 acquaintances with the remaining 84 convicts from Dartmoor and Portland in the 'List of Irish Prisoners'. One convict at Lewes was omitted from the tabular returns. For Harry's circle, mean age was 33.3 years; 71 per cent had been initially sentenced to death; 44 per cent had been sent to Dartmoor; and 63 per cent were in professional, clerical, or managerial occupations. The corresponding figures for the residue were 28.7 years, 57 per cent, 57 per cent, and 24 per cent.

[123] Memorandum by A. J. (Home Office), 18 May 1916: HO 144/1453/311980/4. Hall's copy of *Security Intelligence Service: Seniority List and Register of Past and Present Members, December, 1919* (confidential print), showing that Hall (born 1876 and alive in 1958) joined M.I.5 on 7 Dec. 1914 (becoming Assistant Director by 1919), is preserved in PRO, KV 4/127/16.

[124] Several passages were inked over in the first family letter to Dartmoor (14 Oct. 1916), and a few lines were overwritten, possibly by the censor, in the letter to O'Mahony (14 Mar. 1917).

[125] HB to Duggan, *circa* Apr. 1917.

[126] HB to Kate Boland, 15 Jan. 1917.

[127] HB to O'Mahony, 14 Mar. 1917. The Volunteers, or 'Gorgeous Wrecks', carried the

insignia 'Georgius Rex' on their red brassards. They carried no bayonets or ammunition with their rifles, most of which were obsolete Italian weapons: *Weekly Irish Times, Sinn Féin Rebellion Handbook* (Dublin, 1916), pp 19–20, 51.

128 HB to O'Mahony, 14 Mar. 1917. In the first stanza of 'Nationality', Thomas Osborne Davis likened 'a nation's voice' to 'the light of many stars, / The sound of many waves; / Which brightly look through prison bars / And sweetly sound in caves'.

129 HB to Kate Boland, 15 Jan. 1917.

130 HB to Cait Fraher, *circa* May 1917.

131 HB to O'Mahony, 14 Mar. 1917.

132 HB to Kate Boland, 2 May 1917.

133 Kate and Kathleen Boland to HB, 23 Jan. 1917; Kathleen Boland to HB, 7 May; Kate Boland to HB, after 9 May.

134 Kathleen Boland to HB, 7 May 1917.

135 Kate Boland to HB, received 26 Mar. 1917.

136 Undated poem in Lewes Notebook. Though later circulated as 'Lines written by Harry Boland on boat coming into Dublin Bay on his return from Penal Servitude' (BP), the poem could not have been inscribed in transit since the notebook was temporarily retained.

137 Shouldice to HB, 23 Jan. 1917; Harty to HB, 17 Apr. Harty remarked that 'Crowe is staying in Dalkey at present. He expects to get settled in Limk on 1st. May. You know he was appointed to that Centre.'

138 Seán Ó Murthuile, Memoir (typescript, *circa* 1928–31), ff. 48–59: Mulcahy Papers, UCDA, P 7a/209; Gerald Boland to Michael Hayes, 4 Apr. 1966: BP.

139 Oscar Traynor, 'Account written ... at request of President de Valera shortly before his death' (typescript, 1963), f. 32: EdeVP, P 150/3297. Sweeney's name does not appear in Harry's correspondence.

140 The first of 4 stanzas in Lewes Notebook, signed 'q 90, Sunday June 3rd, Lewes Gaol'. On 21 May, Lloyd George had announced the formation of a nominated Irish Convention, which sat between July 1917 and Apr. 1918. Sinn Féin's unofficial spokemen were two literary fellow-travellers, Edward (Mac)Lysaght and George Russell ('AE').

141 HB to Kate Boland, 15 Jan. 1917, referring to an untraced letter from Frank Shouldice.

142 Shouldice to HB, 23 Jan. 1917.

143 Kate Boland to HB, 7 May 1917.

144 Gerald Boland to HB, after 9 May 1917.

145 Kate Boland to HB, received 26 Mar. 1917. Charles O'Neill, aged 19, had been sentenced to one year's hard labour on 8 May 1916.

146 Ned Boland to HB, received 26 Mar. 1917.

147 Kate Boland to HB, after 9 May 1917.

148 House of Commons, *Parliamentary Debates*, 5th series, xci, cols. 425–527 (7 Mar. 1917). T. P. O'Connor's resolution (col. 425) prompted an amendment from Lloyd George precluding the impositon 'by force on any section or part of Ireland [of] a form of government which has not their consent' (col. 466). John Redmond subsequently withdrew his supporters from the chamber, so ending 'a useless, futile, and humiliating Debate' (col. 481).

149 Collins to HB, 5 Mar. 1917.

150 Collins to HB, 19 Mar. 1917.

151 HB to O'Mahony, 14 Mar. 1917.

152 Draft in Lewes Notebook, possibly of the 'wild article' written by Harry for the second issue of the prisoners' newspaper, which the editor (Patrick Fahy) destroyed during the final confrontation at Lewes: *Ó Fathaigh's War* , pp 46–7.

[153] In quoting Longfellow's 'Retribution: From the *Sinngedichte* of Friedrich von Logau' (1605–55), Harry carefully over-wrote 'though' with the correct 'yet'.

[154] Following the rejection of compulsory overseas service in the first Australian referendum (28 Oct. 1916), the Conscriptionist Prime Minister (W. M. Hughes) was expelled from the Australian Labor Party and formed a National Coalition Government, which triumphed at the general election of 5 May 1917. Since the election campaign coincided with the Imperial War Conference held in London between 21 Mar. and 27 Apr., Australian ministers were unable to attend.

[155] HB to Kate Boland, 2 May 1917. The identity of the New Zealander is unknown.

[156] Katherine O'Doherty, *Assignment: America: De Valera's Mission to the United States* (New York, 1957), pp 4–6.

[157] Lewes Notebook.

[158] Ned Boland to HB, received 26 Mar; 7 May; after 9 May 1917. The Ancient Order of Hibernians and the United Irish League were the principal organisations of the Home Rule movement.

[159] HB to Duggan, *circa* Apr. 1917.

[160] Gerald Boland to HB, after 9 May 1917.

[161] Diarmuid Lynch, *The I.R.B. and the 1916 Insurrection*, ed. Florence O'Donoghue (Cork, 1957), pp 11–12.

[162] Michael Laffan, *The Resurrection of Ireland: The Sinn Féin Party, 1916–1923* (Cambridge, 1999), pp 96–103; Seán Ó Luing, *I Die in a Good Cause: A Study of Thomas Ashe, Idealist and Revolutionary* (Tralee, 1970), p. 120.

[163] Harty to HB, 17 Apr. 1917. McCarthy had campaigned for Count Plunkett in the by-election for North Roscommon (3 Feb.).

[164] Kate Boland to HB, 7 May 1917.

[165] Kathleen Boland to HB, 7 May 1917. Countess Plunkett was wife to George Noble Plunkett and mother of two convicts at Lewes; Tom Clarke's widow, Kathleen, had founded the Irish Volunteer Dependents' Fund, which merged with the Irish National Aid Association on 19 Aug. 1916. During the campaign, Joe's brother Frank McGuinness, JP, declined to stand down from cases arising from such attacks, declaring that 'this objection is raised by a pack of scoundrels': *Longford Independent*, 19 May 1917, p. 3.

[166] Ned Boland to HB, 7 May 1917. The 'Hibs' were members of the Ancient Order of Hibernians, whose Secretary and President were Nugent and Devlin; 'separation allowances' were paid to dependents of servicemen; and the emblem of the Union imposed on a harp with green background is indeed found in wartime flags.

[167] Gerald Boland to HB, after 9 May 1917.

[168] Kathleen and Ned Boland to HB, after 9 May 1917.

[169] HB to Cait Fraher, *circa* May 1917.

[170] Incomplete letter to HB sent from Dingle, Liverpool, 10 Sept. 1916, referring to 'the old firm'. The Irish International Exhibition was opened in Herbert Park, Ballsbridge, on 4 May 1907, and visited by the Royal family two months later: *Thom's Official Directory* (1929 edn.), p. 1259.

[171] Shouldice to HB, 23 Jan. 1917.

[172] HB to Kate Boland, 15 Jan., 2 May 1917.

[173] Collins to HB, 5 Mar.; Kate Boland to HB, received 26 Mar.

[174] HB to O'Mahony, 14 Mar. 1917. Fairview Park has since been built on the 'sloblands' reclaimed from the sea to the south-east of Fairview Strand.

[175] Fr. Walter McDonald (not the Maynooth controversialist), who offered confession and his blessing to the 2nd Battalion at Fr. Mathew Park on Easter Monday, 1916, was transferred during Harry's absence from Fairview to Arran Quay (parish of St. Paul's): Kate Boland to HB, received 26 Mar. 1917; *Frank*

Henderson's Easter Rising: Recollections of a Dublin Volunteer, ed. Michael Hopkinson (Cork, 1998), p. 44. He was one of only three priests named in Harry's prison correspondence.

176 HB to Kathleen Boland, 15 Sept. 1916: extract in Brasier and Kelly, *Harry Boland*, pp 49–50. The Thompson Motor Co., Ltd., of 19–20, Great Brunswick St., offered vehicles for hire: *Thom's Official Directory* (1915 edn.).

177 Kathleen Boland to HB, 25 Oct. 1916.

178 Kathleen Boland to HB, after 9 May 1917.

179 Gerald Boland to HB, received 26 Mar. 1917.

180 Collins to HB, 5, 19 Mar. 1917.

181 HB to Duggan, Hogan, and Cait Fraher, *circa* Apr.–May 1917. 'Maurice' probably refers to Cait's brother rather than Mossy Collins.

CHAPTER V. CELEBRITY

1 Kathleen Boland (Mrs Seán O'Donovan), Statement for the Bureau of Military History (typescript, undated), f. 9: BP; Ena [Christina Shouldice] to Jim B. Shouldice, 10 July 1917: PRO, CO 904/214/405. This letter, among others cited below, was forwarded by M.I.9.C(3) to M.I.5.G for examination and extraction.

2 Kathleen Boland to HB, 23 Jan. 1917: BP.

3 Kathleen Boland, Statement, f. 9. The only such hotel listed in *Thom's Official Directory of the United Kingdom of Great Britain and Ireland* (Dublin, 1919 edn.) is the Norfolk Hotel at 3, Gardiner's Row.

4 Ena to Jim Shouldice, 10 July 1917. On the same day, de Valera defeated Patrick Lynch, in the East Clare by-election, by 5,010 votes to 2,035.

5 Mrs Condon to HB, 12 July 1917: BP.

6 Ena to Jim Shouldice, 3 Aug. 1917. George Noble Plunkett belonged to a Papal order; the absentee husband of Constance de Markievicz (née Gore-Booth) was widely but wrongly credited with a Polish title.

7 Ena to Jim Shouldice, 9 June, 3 Aug. 1917.

8 Ibid., 3 Aug. 1917.

9 Extracts from Ena to Frank Shouldice (Usk Prison), 5 Dec. 1918; Jack to Frank Shouldice, 21 Dec.; Frank to Jim Shouldice (New York), [23?] Dec.; in Postal Censor, 5th Report, f. 46: PRO, Home Office Registered Papers (Supplementary), HO 144/1496/362269/135. 'Miss Shouldice' was paid £2 per week for her work in the General Secretariat: Minutes of Standing Committee, Sinn Féin, 3 Oct.: NLI microfilm, P 3269 [hereafter, SC Minutes].

10 Handwritten address in Irish, 4 Oct. 1917: Béaslaí Papers, NLI, MS 33916/11; English translation in BP.

11 See Andrew Brasier and John Kelly, *Harry Boland: A Man Divided* (Dublin, 2000), pp 3–4.

12 *In Great Haste: The Letters of Michael Collins and Kitty Kiernan*, ed. Leon Ó Broin (Dublin, 1996; 1st edn. 1983), includes some correspondence between Kitty and Harry.

13 KK to HB, 3 Feb. 1919: BP.

14 Robert Brennan, *Allegiance* (Dublin, 1950), p. 153.

15 Piaras Béaslaí, *Michael Collins: Soldier and Statesman* (Dublin, 1937), p. 52.

16 Batt O'Connor, *With Michael Collins in the Fight for Irish Independence* (London, 1929), p. 111.

17 Descriptions of Collins by Detective P. Murphy (G Division, DMP), 13 Aug. 1917, and from *Hue and Cry*, copied 14 Apr. 1919: CO 904/196/65; 'latest description',

4 June 1921: PRO, WO 35/206/35. Since Collins was born on 16 Oct. 1890, the police consistently overstated his age.

18 Seán Ó Murthuile, Memoir (typescript, circa 1928–31), ff. 68, 77: Mulcahy Papers, UCDA, P 7a/209.

19 Béaslaí, Michael Collins, pp 101–2. This discussion reportedly occurred just before Harry's departure for America.

20 Ned to Kate and to Gerald Boland, undated: BP. The chronology of Ned's migration is unclear, but the second extract clearly refers to 1918.

21 Undated extract from Kathleen Boland to 'Considine' O'Donovan, in Postal Censor, 1st Report, Usk Prison, f. 18. O'Donovan, like Gerald, had formerly acted as land steward at Crooksling Sanatorium. His brother Seán married Kathleen in 1923.

22 Membership Certificate no. 262, 1917: BP.

23 Vulgate Bible (Dublin, undated: Duffy edn.): BP; report of Circuit Court Martial, Ship St. Barracks, Dublin, 4 June 1918: WO 35/132. Gerald was sentenced to six months' hard labour under the Defence of the Realm Regulations (9E).

24 Liam C. Skinner, Politicians by Accident (Dublin, 1946), pp 213–15.

25 Gerald Boland, Account (undated MS) for Belfast Jail Inquiry under Mr Justice [William Huston] Dodd, 19 Dec. 1918: BP.

26 Gerald to Kate Boland, 1 Aug. 1918: BP.

27 HB to Secretary, Irish National Aid and Volunteer Dependents' Fund [hereafter, INA & VDF], 2 Aug. 1917: INA & VDF Papers, NLI, MS 24357/2 (reference kindly supplied by Dr. Peter Hart).

28 Undated draft in Lewes Notebook, replying to letter from INA & VDF, '1st inst.' [Aug. 1917]: BP.

29 HB to Secretary, 9, 15 Sept. 1917: INA & VDF Papers, MS 24357/2.

30 Register of American Grants, f. 137 (19 Sept. 1917); HB to Secretary, 9 Oct.: INA & VDF Papers, MSS 23494, 24357/2. Harry had previously been granted £10 from the American Relief Fund as well as the customary £20 (approved on 20 June) for a 'holiday' after his release.

31 Kate Boland to Luke Dillon, 18 Mar. 1924: McGP, NLI, MS 17447; Kathleen Boland, Statement, f. 11. The tenancy agreement was dated 9 Sept. 1917: see below, ch. x, n. 4.

32 In Thom's Official Directory (1919 edn.), he is listed as a 'merchant tailor', sharing a building valued at £38 10s. per annum with four other tenants. Nos. 62, 66, 69–71, 73–6, and 81–96 were all returned as 'destroyed in Rebellion, 1916', while no. 78 was marked 'rebuilding'.

33 This letterhead was still in use in July 1919: BP.

34 Joseph Cyrillus Walsh, 'Reminiscences of the Irish Movement for Independence, 1914–' (MSS, circa 1947), f. 281: NYPL, J. C. Walsh Papers, in slipcase. Walsh's informant was James O'Mara.

35 HB to Secretary, 25 Feb. 1918; Register of American Grants, f. 137 (26 Feb.): INA & VDF Papers, MSS 24357/3, 23494.

36 Early disbursements from the fund included several substantial payments for clothes from Todd, Burns & Co., some marked 'a/c H. Boland'; while Harry himself supplied clothes for Michael Brennan and other ragged rebels between Nov. 1917 and June 1918. See Cash Book, 26 June, 28 July, 27 Nov. 1917, 4 Jan., 18 June 1918: INA & VDF Papers, MS 23477.

37 Register of American Grants, ff. 134, 116, 199, 83: INA & VDF Papers, MS 23494. Shouldice received £295 in total; McGarry, £320; Peppard, £55; and de Valera, £740.

38 Special Grants Committee, Minutes, 21 Nov. 1916: INA & VDF Papers, MS 23473. On 17 Apr. 1917, possibly for this purpose, Mrs de Valera was awarded a grant of £50.

39 Phil O'Neill, *History of the G.A.A., 1910–1930* (Kilkenny, 1931), p. 148; Jim Maher, *Harry Boland: A Biography* (Cork, 1998), p. 54.

40 HB to Secretary, 25 Feb. 1918: INA & VDF Papers, MS 24357/3.

41 Report for Dublin County Board, 1 Oct. 1917 (unsigned MS): BP. The Christian Brothers' Schools agreed to enter teams in both sections of the nascent Colleges' and Schools' League, but the Jesuit Rector of Belvedere 'did not expect they could enter the competitions and also run their Rugby teams'. Harry seconded a Cork motion to introduce interprovincial competitions for this League at the annual congress, 20 Apr. 1919: Maher, *Harry Boland*, p. 82.

42 Report of annual congress, GAA, in *Weekly Freeman*, 26 Apr. 1919.

43 W. F. Mandle, *The Gaelic Athletic Association and Irish Nationalist Politics, 1884–1924* (London, 1987), p. 183; Marcus de Búrca, *The GAA: A History* (Dublin, 1980), pp 141–2; *Weekly Freeman*, 10 Aug. 1918, p. 4.

44 *Irish Weekly Independent*, 12 Apr. 1919, p. 6. This match, in support of the Irish Republican Prisoners' Dependents' Fund, was attended by 20,000 spectators including de Valera, Michael Collins, and the Lord Mayor, Laurence O'Neill.

45 *Weekly Freeman*, 26 Apr. 1919, p. 2; *Irish Weekly Independent*, 26 Apr., p. 4; Mandle, *Gaelic Athletic Association*, pp 185–8. Shouldice, a former civil servant, argued that the oath had been 'taken under duress' when imposed on civil servants already employed in Oct. 1918, but accepted the exclusion of those who had subsequently agreed to take the oath. The same congress excluded ex-servicemen from the GAA for two years after discharge, and for life in the case of those accepting pensions.

46 The resolution was defeated by 45 votes to 32: *Weekly Freeman*, 26 Apr. 1919, p. 2.

47 Leon Ó Broin, *Revolutionary Underground: The Story of the Irish Republican Brotherhood, 1858–1924* (Dublin, 1976), pp 176–8; Ó Murthuile, Memoir, f. 64; Diarmuid Lynch, *The I.R.B. and the 1916 Insurrection*, ed. Florence O'Donoghue (Cork, 1957), p. 32.

48 O'Connor, *With Michael Collins*, p. 103.

49 Ó Murthuile, Memoir, f. 69; Richard Mulcahy, notes of conversation with Seán MacEoin, 15 June 1967: Mulcahy Papers, UCDA, P 7/D/16.

50 The sole source for Moylett's appointment is Maurice Twomey (Chief of Staff, IRA, 1926–36), as reported by Ó Broin, *Revolutionary Underground*, p. 184. Moylett, an importer from Ballyhaunis, with offices in Galway and Dublin, acted as a rather ineffectual intermediary between Griffith and Lloyd George in 1920: Tim Pat Coogan, *Michael Collins: A Biography* (London, 1991; 1st edn. 1990), pp 186–7; [Patrick Moylett], Statement for the Bureau of Military History (undated typescript): EdeVP, P 150/3650.

51 Collins informed Harry in late 1920 that 'the Chairman met with a very bad accident recently which has kept him laid up for a couple of months', implying that he himself remained Treasurer six months later: MC ['Field'] to HB ['Woods'], 27 Sept. 1920, 7 Mar. 1921: EdeVP, P 150/1125. John Devoy later learned from an envoy that 'B. is no longer Chairman', having been replaced not by Collins but by 'a great friend of mine'. See Devoy to Cohalan, 3 Aug. 1921: Devoy Papers, NLI, MS 15416/5. In autumn 1921, however, Collins presided as Chairman of the Supreme Council over the biennial election for the Divisional Centre for South Munster: Florence O'Donoghue, *No Other Law: The Story of Liam Lynch and the Irish Republican Army, 1916–1923* (Dublin, 1954), pp 191–2.

52 Richard Mulcahy, notes of conversation with Denis McCullough, 1961: Mulcahy Papers, UCDA, P 7/D/15.

53 Ó Murthuile, Memoir, f. 64; rough notebook giving officers and monthly attendance of various Dublin Circles, 1918–22: Conlon Papers, UCDA, P 97/15/1. The

McDermott Cumann's officers in about 1921 were 'M.' Collins (Centre), Joe Furlong, P. Caldwell, and F. Thornton. Contrary to McCullough's speculation, there appear to have been at least 5 monthly meetings of this Circle in 1918, 6 in 1919, 5 in 1921, and 3 in 1922.

54 Richard Mulcahy, 'The Irish Volunteer Convention: 27th October, 1917', pp 404–8, in *Capuchin Annual*, xxxiv (1967), pp 400–10.

55 In his account of promotions in 1917–18, Oscar Traynor makes no reference to Harry. See 'Account written ... at request of President de Valera shortly before his death' (typescript, 1963), f. 2: EdeVP, P 150/3297.

56 In the poll held on 2 Feb. 1918, Donnelly, a Newry solicitor (Nationalist, 2,324 votes) defeated McCartan, absent in the United States (Sinn Féin, 1,305), and T. Wakefield Richardson (Independent Unionist, 40). Richardson, whose potential vote probably fell short of 300, had withdrawn from the contest after pressure from 'a certain section of the Unionists': *Weekly Freeman*, 2 Feb. 1918, p. 1; 9 Feb., p. 5.

57 *Longford Leader*, 2 Feb. 1918, p. 3.

58 Ó Murthuile, Memoir, ff. 66–8; Maher, *Harry Boland*, p. 56. 'Walter House' belonged to a Fenian's widow whose son, Michael Lynch, was a musician and veteran of the Rebellion.

59 Kathleen Boland, Statement, ff. 10–11; *Thom's Official Directory* (1919 edn.). Samuel J. Jennings occupied 17, Marino Crescent, a slightly smaller property than no. 15. According to Shouldice, the fugitives (though 'bootless' and 'dishevelled') donned shirts and trousers before their escape, bolting the skylight from outside. See John F. Shouldice, Statement (duplicate typescript, 1952), ff. 20–1: MAD, Bureau of Military History Papers, WS 679.

60 Extract from Seán McEntee to Nancy [Wyse] Power, 24 Nov. 1918, in Postal Censor, 3rd Report, f. 26.

61 Béaslaí, *Michael Collins: Soldier and Statesman*, p. 66.

62 'Harry Boland: Some Random Recollections', in *Waterford News*, 9 May 1924: cutting in EdeVP, P 150/1173.

63 *Gaelic American*, 21 June 1919, p. 1. Viscount French of Ypres was 'Viceroy' of Ireland from May 1918 to Apr. 1921.

64 MC to Austin Stack, 28 Nov. 1918: Stack Papers, NLI, MS 5848.

65 Précis of RIC reports on 'The Sinn Féin Movement', f. 11 (Strokestown, 1 July 1917); f. 52 (Driney, 31 July); f. 53 (Drumlish, Co. Longford, 4 Aug.): CO 904/23/3.

66 'The Sinn Féin Movement', ff. 54, 62 (Lanesborough, 15 Aug. 1917; Frankford, King's Co. (Offaly), 19 Aug.). For Harry's reported assertion that he went out on Easter Monday to 'beat the bloody British Empire', ch. III, p. 46.

67 Report from Mohill, Co. Leitrim, 18 Nov. 1917, in *Longford Independent*, 24 Nov., p. 3.

68 Note on reverse of 'very urgent' request that Harry speak in Maryborough (Portlaoise) from Páidraig Ó Caoimh (Paudeen O'Keeffe, Secretary to Sinn Féin), 14 Sept. 1917: BP.

69 Pencilled text on Irish-made jotter of an undated 'lecture', composed after John Redmond's death (Mar. 1918): BP.

70 SC Minutes, 31 Dec. 1918.

71 Brennan, *Allegiance*, pp 154–5; Lynch, *The I.R.B.*, pp 33–4; Michael Laffan, *The Resurrection of Ireland: The Sinn Féin Party, 1916–1923* (Cambridge, 1999), p. 120. A rival slate organised by Darrell Figgis was also widely ignored.

72 Nancy Wyse Power, Statement for Bureau of Military History, pt. 2, ff. 9–11: paraphrased in Marie O'Neill, *From Parnell to de Valera: A Biography of Jennie Wyse Power, 1858–1941* (Dublin, 1991), p. 106.

73 Brian P. Murphy, *Patrick Pearse and the Lost Republican Ideal* (Dublin, 1991), pp 93–4. These figures exclude the 7 officers, whose votes invariably exceeded Harry's.
74 Report from Mohill, 18 Nov. 1917, in *Longford Independent*, 24 Nov., p. 3.
75 *American Commission on Irish Independence, 1919: The Diary, Correspondence and Report*, ed. F. M. Carroll (Dublin, 1993), pp 80–1; Laffan, *Resurrection*, pp 143–4 (citing SC Minutes, 1 Mar., 17 May 1918). In preparation, Harry had already attended 2 meetings as a member of the Ard Chomhairle: SC Minutes, 10, 18 Apr.
76 J. Anthony Gaughan *Austin Stack: Portrait of a Separatist* (Dublin, 1977), p. 86; SC Minutes, 17 May 1918; Laffan, *Resurrection*, p. 145. Stack was arrested in Tralee on 3 May and imprisoned in Belfast.
77 Brennan, *Allegiance*, p. 172. One of Collins's better biographers suggests that 'the whole organization on the political side would have faltered and failed had it not been for his [Harry's] matchless energy': Rex Taylor, *Michael Collins* (London, 1961; 1st edn. 1958), p. 72.
78 SC Minutes, *passim*; MC to Austin Stack, *passim* (27 July 1918 to 11 Aug. 1919): Stack Papers, NLI, MS 5848. Harry attended 41 of the 69 meetings between 10 May 1918 and 23 Apr. 1919, and 20 of the 22 meetings between 1 Aug. and 19 Nov. 1918. Collins attended only 16 meetings, including 4 in the latter period.
79 Darrell Figgis, *Recollections of the Irish War* (London, 1927), pp 218–19.
80 SC Minutes, 13 June 1918. Though these minutes were normally kept by the paid Secretary (initially Paudeen O'Keeffe), Harry's meticulous hand was at work on 29 Aug. and 6 Sept.
81 Eamon Duggan to Piaras Béaslaí, 16 May 1918: Béaslaí Papers, NLI, MS 33917/8; undated extract from HB to Seán McGarry (July–Oct.), in Postal Censor, 1st Report, Lincoln Prison, f. 13.
82 Handbill signed by O'Flanagan, HB, and Tom Kelly: Barton Papers, NLI, MS 8786/1.
83 Having led an 'Irish Brigade' against the British army in South Africa, the eccentric Australian-born MP for West Clare had been commissioned in 1918 to raise a second 'Irish Brigade' in support of the Allies.
84 'David Hogan' [Frank Gallagher], *The Four Glorious Years* (Dublin, 1953), pp 36–8; Ó Murthuile, Memoir, f. 17.
85 Report of acting Secretaries to Ard Chomhairle, 20 Aug. 1918 (copy of captured document): CO 904/203/172.
86 MC to Stack, 22 Aug. 1918: Stack Papers, NLI, MS 5848.
87 *Irish Weekly Independent*, 2 Nov. 1918, p. 3; *Weekly Freeman*, 2 Nov., p. 1. Collins, with 361 votes, took eleventh place among the 23 members elected.
88 Maher, *Harry Boland*, pp 63–5; MC to Stack, 4 Nov. 1918: Stack Papers, NLI, MS 5848. This 'old idea' probably refers to a rescue plan, rendered superfluous by the transfer of the Belfast inmates to Dundalk on 8 Nov. and their temporary release 9 days later: Gaughan, *Austin Stack*, pp 76–8.
89 Extracts from T. M. Healy to William O'Brien, 3, 4 Nov. 1918: Frank Callanan, *T. M. Healy* (Cork, 1996), pp 546–7; extracts from T. M. Healy to Maurice Healy, 7 Nov.: T. M. Healy, *Letters and Leaders of My Day* (2 vols., New York, 1929), ii, p. 608.
90 Healy, *Letters and Leaders*, ii, p. 651.
91 HB to O'Neill, 12 Nov. 1918: O'Neill Papers, NLI, MS 35294/4.
92 Extract from Kathleen Boland to Con O'Donovan (Usk Prison), Nov. 1918, in Postal Censor, 2nd Report, f. 48. She remarked of the Women's Auxiliary Army Corps that 'I surely won't call the things that were with them [the soldiers] women, W.A.A.C. they call them, they were all drunk too.'
93 *Weekly Freeman*, 16 Nov. 1918, p. 2. When alluding in the Round Room of the

Mansion House to that afternoon's incident, Harry 'said he could admire a soldier who fought for his Union Jack waving it, but could not admire a slacker from Trinity College or any other College who saved his miserable carcase from conscription beneath the flag of the Irish Republic': *Irish Weekly Independent*, 16 Nov., p. 3.

94   J. C. Walsh, 'Reminiscences', f. 283. Walsh, who heard this anecdote from Seán Nunan, thought that it referred to 'Armistice night, when the soldiers in Dublin gathered near the Sinn Féin offices, bent on making trouble'.

95   MC to Austin Stack, 28 Nov. 1918: Stack Papers, NLI, MS 5848. According to some accounts, these alleged casualties (unreported in the press) occurred not on Armistice afternoon or night but on Wednesday, 13 Nov.: Piaras Béaslaí, *Michael Collins and the Making of a New Ireland* (2 vols., Dublin, 1926), i, pp 240–1; *An t-Óglách*, 30 Nov., pp 3–4: cited and sceptically assessed in Ben Novick, *Conceiving Revolution: Irish Nationalist Propaganda during the First World War* (Dublin, 2001), pp 243–4.

96   P. O'Sheehan [Patrick Sheehan] to EdeV, 3 Aug. 1918 (annotated copy), in Security Service [M.I.5], Personal Files, Eamon de Valera: PRO, KV 2/515, f. 12.

97   HB and T. Kelly to Archbishop William Walsh, 14 Nov. 1918; Kelly to Walsh, 17 Dec.: Dublin Diocesan Archives, Walsh Papers, Box 390/I, File 386/2 (copies kindly supplied by Rory Sweetman).

98   SC Minutes, 14, 16, 22 Aug., 12 Sept. 1918; Brian Farrell, *The Founding of Dáil Éireann* (Dublin, 1971), pp 36–7.

99   SC Minutes, 19, 23 Sept. 1918; William O'Brien, Diary, 22 Sept.: O'Brien Papers, NLI, MS 15705/11. Harry, Robert Brennan, and perhaps Tom Kelly (selected but not listed by O'Brien), met O'Brien, Thomas Farren, and Cathal O'Shannon.

100 SC Minutes, 7 Oct. 1918. The withdrawn candidate was James V. Lawless, Assistant Secretary to the Dublin County Council and Harry's fellow-inmate at Lewes.

101 SC Minutes, 7 Oct., 7 Nov. 1918; HB to Ard Fheis, 30 Oct., in *Weekly Freeman*, 2 Nov., p. 1; Laffan, *Resurrection*, pp 158–9; J. Anthony Gaughan, *Thomas Johnson 1872–1963* (Dublin, 1980), pp 117–20. A further fruitless meeting had been held between Labour leaders and Sinn Féin (represented by Harry, Brennan, and Tom Kelly): O'Brien, Diary, 14 Oct.

102 O'Brien, Diary, 11 Nov. 1918.

103 C. Desmond Greaves, *Liam Mellows and the Irish Revolution* (London, 1971), p. 147.

104 'C.' [Brugha] to HB, *circa* Oct. 1918: BP. Brugha, who had never attended the Standing Committee, resigned in protest against the participation of de Valera and Griffith in the Mansion House Conference. He evidently returned to the Standing Committee after the next Ard Fheis in Oct.: SC Minues, 10 Apr., 21 Nov.; Laffan, *Resurrection*, p. 138.

105 HB to [Brugha], 28 Oct. 1918; 'C. B.' [Brugha] to HB, 2 Nov.: BP.

106 Ó Broin, *Revolutionary Underground*, p. 181.

107 SC Minutes, 21 Nov. 1918; Seumas MacTiona (Dundalk) to HB, 26 Sept.: BP. John Joseph O'Kelly ('Sceilg'), the muck-raking editor of the *Catholic Bulletin* and President of the Gaelic League, defeated the Irish Party's Richard Hazleton by 155 votes. The writer had 'acted very cautiously, so that nobody but trustworthy men are aware of Sceilg's drawbacks'; the nature of O'Kelly's 'weakness' is not revealed.

108 Austin Stack to HB, undated, 18 Oct., 9 Nov. 1918: BP; SC Minutes, 10 Oct.; précis of HB to EdeV, 25 Oct.: EdeVP, P 150/71 (former number).

109 Kathleen Clarke, *Revolutionary Woman: Kathleen Clarke, 1878–1972, an Autobiography*, ed. Helen Litton (Dublin, 1991), p. 164. Michael Colivet was returned unopposed for Limerick City.

110 *Irish Weekly Independent*, 16 Nov. 1918, p. 2.
111 SC Minutes, 30 Sept. 1918; Laffan, *Resurrection*, p. 155. The sub-committee comprised the acting President, the two Honorary Secretaries, and the Director of Elections.
112 Both Brennan and Seán T. O'Kelly (who was not originally on the sub-committee) claimed primary responsibility for the outcome, though O'Kelly acknowledged the revision carried out by O'Flanagan and the ubiquitous 'Sceilg': Brennan, *Allegiance*, p. 239; Seán T. O'Kelly, 'Memoirs of Seán T.', in *Irish Press*, 25 July 1961, p. 9 (from typescript in Ó Ceallaigh Papers, NLI, MS 27707). The Manifesto, published in *Nationality*, 19 Oct. 1918, appears in *Irish Historical Documents, 1916–1949*, ed. Arthur Mitchell and Pádraig Ó Snodaigh (Dublin, 1985), pp 48–50.
113 Corrected typescript, signed 'H. Boland, October 10th, 1918': BP.
114 Harry's references to whining and war chariots were retained, but those to manacles and heroic sacrifice were omitted, along with most of his potted history.
115 SC Minutes, 12 Sept. 1918; *Irish Weekly Independent*, 14 Sept., p. 1; *Longford Independent*, 14 Sept., p. 3.
116 Seán Ó Doghair [Dore?] to HB, 14 Sept. 1918, with draft reply: BP. Brugha defeated James John O'Shee, MP for West Waterford since 1895, by 12,890 votes to 4,217. The language requirement applied to constituencies 'in which there are Irish-speaking districts' (such as 'the Ring' in Waterford): *Irish Weekly Independent*, 14 Sept., p. 1.
117 SC Minutes, 30 Sept., 14 Nov. 1918. Mulcahy defeated the Irish Party's Sir Patrick Shortall by 5,974 votes to 3,228.
118 *Roscommon Herald*, 30 Nov. 1918: cutting in album, BP. Harry was supported by his 'personal friend', Frank Shouldice, who demanded a 'sweeping majority' for Sinn Féin and retiterated that 'we won't have Partition'.
119 HB to EdeV, 4 June 1919: EdeVP, P 150/1132; *Roscommon Herald*, 21 Dec. 1918: cutting in album, BP.
120 *Roscommon Messenger*, 7 Dec. 1918; *Roscommon Herald*, [28?] Dec. 1918: cutting in album, BP, reporting a speech in Athleague by Canon Cummins, Harry's nominator. The discrepancy may partly be explained by the greater propensity of curates than of parish priests to support Sinn Féin.
121 *Roscommon Messenger*, 21 Sept. 1918, p. 3; 23 Nov., p. 1; 19 Oct., p. 3.
122 *Longford Independent*, 16 Nov. 1918, p. 3.
123 *Roscommon Messenger*, 7 Dec. 1918, Supplement, p. 2.
124 *Roscommon Herald*, 21 Dec. 1918: cutting in album, BP. An eighteenth-century depiction of the 'journeyman-taylor' as 'this whey-faced ninny, who is but the ninth part of a man', draws upon the earlier proverb that 'nine [or two, or three] tailors make a man': Eric Partridge, *The Routledge Dictionary of Historical Slang* (London, 1973; 1st edn. 1937), p. 623.
125 Ballot paper: BP.
126 *Roscommon Herald*, [28?] Dec. 1918: cutting in album, BP. The presiding officer, having marked her vote in keeping with her husband's, was obliged to procure a second ballot paper.
127 *Longford Independent*, 21 Dec. 1918, p. 3.
128 *Roscommon Messenger*, 21 Dec. 1918, p. 3. The High Sheriff was Owen Phelim O'Conor of Clonalis, Castlerea ('the Don O'Conor').
129 Gerald Boland, Reminiscences (typescript, 1962), f. 2: BP.
130 Sinn Féin, Printed Instructions, *circa* Dec. 1918 (original emphasis): Barton Papers, NLI, MS 8786/1.
131 On 3 Jan. 1919, Harry renewed his appeal for nationalist unity behind Sinn Féin,

'as their difference was only in methods, not in principles': *Roscommon Messenger*, 4 Jan., p. 3.

¹³² *Roscommon Messenger*, 4 Jan. 1919, p. 3; *Irish Weekly Independent*, 4 Jan., p. 2.

¹³³ Billy Farrell to unknown recipient, 18 Dec. 1918: extract in KV 2/515, f. 29.

¹³⁴ HB to Hanna Sheehy-Skeffington, 23 Dec. 1918: Sheehy-Skeffington Papers, NLI, MS 24107.

¹³⁵ The names listed in *Parliamentary Election Results in Ireland, 1801–1922*, ed. B. M. Walker (Dublin, 1978) were collated with those in 'List of Irish Prisoners in English Convict Prisons', submitted 12 July 1916: HO 144/1453/311980/21; and Seán O Mahony, *Frongoch: University of Revolution* (Dublin, 1987). The inmates included 21 from Lewes, 18 internees from Frongoch, and one each from Aylesbury, Reading, and Wormwood Scrubs. Several of the remaining 27 TDs were imprisoned at other periods. Laffan, in *Resurrection*, p. 194, states that 46 TDs 'had been arrested in the aftermath of the rising' and that 'only three had never been jailed or interned'.

¹³⁶ Report of interview by 'E. W.', reproduced in *Evening Telegraph*, 2 Jan. 1919, p. 1.

¹³⁷ *Roscommon Herald*, 11 Jan. 1919: cutting in album, BP.

¹³⁸ SC Minutes, 19 Dec. 1918; O'Kelly, 'Memoirs', in *Irish Press*, 26 July 1961, p. 9.

¹³⁹ Collins and he 'failed to turn up' to a meeting with O'Brien and others on 3 Jan. 1919, but participated in a discussion of plans for the Congress 8 days later: O'Brien, Diary, 3, 11 Jan.: O'Brien Papers, NLI, MS 15705/12.

¹⁴⁰ O'Kelly, 'Memoirs', in *Irish Press*, 27 July 1961, p. 9; Gaughan, *Thomas Johnson*, p. 160; O'Brien, Diary, 11, 14, 18 Jan. 1919; Farrell, *Founding of Dáil*, pp 57–61; 'The Sovereign People' (31 Mar. 1916), in P. H. Pearse, *Political Writings and Speeches* (Dublin, undated edn.), pp 335–72.

¹⁴¹ O'Brien, Diary, 21 Jan. 1919. The reception and dinner were held in the Oak Room of the Mansion House after the inaugural meeting in the Round Room, the shivering guests being treated to songs from Seán Ó Murthuile and Gerald Crofts: Arthur H. Mitchell, *Revolutionary Government in Ireland, 1919–22* (Dublin, 1995), p. 17; *Irish Weekly Independent*, 25 Jan., p. 1.

¹⁴² Dáil Éireann, *Minutes of Proceedings*, 21 Jan. 1919, p. 12; Béaslaí, *Michael Collins: Soldier and Statesman*, p. 81; *Weekly Freeman*, 25 Jan., p. 5; *Irish Weekly Independent*, 25 Jan., p. 1 (naming Harry and Collins as present). By another account, both men left 'shortly afterwards': Kathleen Boland, Statement, f. 12.

¹⁴³ Interview with Seán T. O'Kelly (Press Association, 28 Feb. 1919), in *Irish Weekly Independent*, 8 Mar., p. 6; 'official report' of second meeting of republican MPs, in *Weekly Freeman*, 18 Jan., p. 5. Both Harry and Collins were returned as present.

¹⁴⁴ Earl of Longford and Thomas P. O'Neill, *Eamon de Valera* (London, 1970), pp 81–5; précis of reports on preparations for escape: EdeVP, P 150/615; Maher, *Harry Boland*, pp 74–5; Kathleen Boland, Statement, f. 13. There are many inconsistencies of detail in the available accounts, the most meticulous synthesis being that by Longford and O'Neill.

¹⁴⁵ Précis of letter in Irish, EdeV ['Seán'] to HB ['Mícheál'], *circa* 31 Jan. 1919: EdeVP, P 150/615; extract from Miss R. Green (Ashton-under-Lyne) to Seán Milroy (Lincoln Prison), '21' Jan. 1919, in Postal Censor, 7th Report, f. 27. 'Seán' reported that 'the things came. We are sure that they will do fine. We'll be ready on the arranged day at 6.45. Two letters came (through the censor) from M. and L. [Manchester and Liverpool], saying that Kamerad was in M.' A pencil annotation identifies 'Kamerad' as Harry Boland, and 'the things' as the 'final key'.

¹⁴⁶ Longford and O'Neill, *Eamon de Valera*, pp 84–5.

¹⁴⁷ HB to EdeV, 26 Jan. 1919: EdeVP, P 150/615 (copy kindly supplied by Dr. Patrick Murray). Harry's letter enclosed a lost note from 'M. Field' [Collins].

¹⁴⁸ The final cake was baked and delivered by Kathleen Talty, a Clarewoman teaching

in Fallowfield near Manchester, for whom Harry inscribed a tribute on 19 Mar. 1919: 'Brave brave Irish girl, well may we call ye brave. H. Boland, q 90.' See Padraig de Bhaldraithe, 'Brave Brave Irish Girls', p. 35, in *The Other Clare*, xii (1988), pp 35–7.

149 Longford and O'Neill, *Eamon de Valera*, pp 84–6; 'Pierse Beasley' [Piaras Béaslaí] in *Cork Examiner*, copied in *Waterford News*, 23 July 1926: cutting in MAD, A 0392. These accounts attribute the breakage of the key to Harry and Collins respectively.

150 J. C. Walsh, Reminiscences, f. 275 (recalling a conversation between Harry and James O'Mara).

151 Longford and O'Neill, *Eamon de Valera*, p. 86 (asserting, however, that Harry accompanied Collins to London).

152 James Fitzgerald, a Volunteer driver, allegedly received 2 files and at least 6 keys from Harry in Manchester, one of which he later returned to Harry at 6, Harcourt St. The residue included a broken key and 3 blanks. Seán McGarry, when claiming ownership of 4 of these keys and responsibility for breaking one of them, stated that he had surrendered them in Manchester after assurances from Harry that they would be given to his wife in Dublin. Custody of the successful key made by de Loughry and returned by Fitzgerald was long disputed, as it passed from Kathleen and Kate Boland through de Valera to the de Loughrys, before reaching the National Museum. See Fitzgerald to editor, *Irish Independent*, 29 Nov. 1938: cutting in BP; interview with Fitzgerald (4, Leeson Park Ave.), with photograph of keys, 13 Jan. 1936; McGarry to editor, 14 Jan. 1936; article by 'T. M.', 5 Nov. 1938: cuttings from *Irish Independent* in MAD, A 0392; Mrs L. Mangan (de Loughry's sister) to editor, 1 Dec. 1938: cutting from *Irish Press* in MAD, A 0392.

153 Longford and O'Neill, *Eamon de Valera*, pp 86–7, 84.

154 Report of Enquiry by J. Winn and J. R. Farewell (Inspectors), 7–8 Feb. 1919: HO 144/1496/362269/163a.

155 Report from *Daily Chronicle* summarised in *Irish Independent*, 7 Feb. 1919: cutting in KV 2/515, f. 31.

156 *The Shamrock*, i (n.s.), nos. 4, p. 15; 5, p. 15; 8, p. 13 (1, 8, 29 Mar. 1919).

157 Report of Harry's speech from the roof of a taxi-cab (17 Feb. 1919), during a dinner at the Gresham Hotel to welcome Kathleen Clarke home from prison: *Irish Weekly Independent*, 22 Feb., p. 2.

158 Extract from Paul Dawson Cusack to Miss Violet Davies, 15 Feb. 1919, in Postal Censor, 8th Report, f. 31.

159 *Weekly Freeman*, 8 Mar. 1919, p. 6. O'Kelly imagined the sirens as 'two handsome young women both highly cultivated University graduates, who dressed themselves as shopgirls and crossed the Channel', a suggestion which drew mock indignation from 'A Western Shopgirl' in the same issue. Though the flamboyant O'Kelly was quite capable of spinning such a tale, Harry asserted that the 'interview' with O'Kelly was a British fabrication, the rescue being 'a man's work and it was done by men': *Irish Weekly Independent*, 8 Mar., p. 1.

160 Extract from Paul Cusack to Mr and Mrs P. McEvoy (Ballyjamesduff, Co. Cavan), 3 Mar. 1919, in Postal Censor, 9th Report, f. 21 (with two letters of the same date from Philip Monahan reporting the 'huge merriment here' following publication of O'Kelly's interview).

161 Extracts from Frank Thornton to Stasia Toomey, 9 Feb. 1919; Peter O'Hourihane to Miss Brigid O'Mahoney, 27 Feb.; in Postal Censor, 8th Report, f. 32; 9th Report, f. 9. 'Cahill' was a *nom de guerre* for de Valera.

162 Brennan, *Allegiance*, pp 234–6. The body of the TD for East Tipperary was carried from the hearse to the mortuary van by Michael and Con Collins, Seán Ó Murthuile, and Harry: Newspaper Album, NLI, MS 25588.

163 *Irish Weekly Independent*, 5 Apr. 1919; [Piaras Béaslaí?] to 'Harry Old Sport', 12 Mar.: BP.
164 Corrected draft: BP; Longford and O'Neill, *Eamon de Valera*, p. 88.
165 Ibid., p. 89.
166 *Freeman's Journal*, 15 Mar. 1919, p. 5. Having published extracts from two versions of the interview on the two previous days, the paper juxtaposed Harry's letter with the complete text as supplied by the Exchange Telegraph News Agency, which differed sharply from 'the official copy of the interview issued for publication' subsequently by Sinn Féin: ibid., 13 Mar., p. 3; 14 Mar., p. 4.
167 George Creel, *Rebel at Large: Recollections of Fifty Crowded Years* (New York, 1947), pp 219–21. The draft Covenant was laid before the Peace Conference by Wilson on 14 Feb. 1919 and adopted on 25 Mar. Creel's report was submitted on 1 Mar., receiving a non-committal response from Wilson on 20 Mar.: F. M. Carroll, *American Opinion and the Irish Question, 1910–23* (Dublin, 1978), pp 124, 247–8; *Irish Weekly Independent*, 8 Mar., p. 1.
168 Dáil Éireann, *Minutes of Proceedings*, pp 75–6 (11 Apr. 1919). The rather garbled published account of this debate was taken from the *Irish Independent*, the official minutes having been destroyed. Harry attended meetings on 1, 2, 10, and 11 Apr., no roll-call being recorded on 4 Apr.
169 Dáil, *Minutes*, pp 32–3, 36–8 (1, 2 Apr. 1919).
170 SC Minutes, 13 Feb. to 23 Apr. 1919.
171 SC Minutes, 18 Feb. 1919. A fortnight later, Hugh Barrie (Unionist, 9,933 votes) defeated Patrick McGilligan (Sinn Féin, 4,333).
172 SC Minutes, 27 Feb., 3 Apr. 1919. Harry addressed the inaugural conference of the League at Manchester on 30 Mar., asking 'the audience to propagate all over the world that Ireland is held by force' and boasting that 'they could not keep them in prison': *Irish Weekly Independent*, 5 Apr., p. 2.
173 HB to Diarmuid O'Hegarty (Clerk of the Dáil), 22 Apr. 1919: NAD, DE 2/175; SC Minutes, 23 Apr.
174 Moore ('Assistant Press Censor', c/o Dublin University Philosophical Society) to HB, 16 Apr. 1919: BP. Theodore Conyngham Kingsmill Moore became a Senator for Dublin University (1944–7) and Judge of the Supreme Court (1951–65). He had served in the Dublin University Officers' Training Corps in 1916 (information kindly supplied by Jane Leonard).
175 'Hogan', *Glorious Years*, p. 121. Sgt. John Bruton, DMP 8703, born in Eyrecourt, Co. Galway, in 1870, received the King's Police Medal for an attempted arrest in May 1919; Const. Thomas Wharton, DMP 11050, was shot and wounded in Oct. 1919 and pensioned in June 1920: Jim Herlihy, *The Dublin Metropolitan Police: A Short History and Genealogical Guide* (Dublin, 2001), pp 161, 180.
176 SC Minutes, 18 Feb., 6 Mar. 1919. Harry was assigned to speak in Longford when protest meetings were arranged for every constituency on 6 Jan., and wrote movingly on the plight of the Belfast prisoners, who (unlike Brennan in Gloucester) had 'honourably kept their parole, and every agreement entered into'. See *Irish Independent*, 2 Jan.: cutting in CO 904/196/65; HB to editor (5 Apr.), in *Irish Weekly Independent*, 12 Apr., p. 2.
177 P. S. O'Hegarty to HB, 25 Mar. 1919: extract in Longford and O'Neill, *Eamon de Valera*, p. 90. On 8 Oct. 1843, Daniel O'Connell disappointed his militant followers by cancelling his last 'monster meeting' in response to its proscription.
178 Brennan, *Allegiance*, p. 238. According to Figgis, however, it was Collins who urged defiance and Figgis who challenged his authority to press ahead: Figgis, *Recollections*, pp 242–5; Coogan, *Michael Collins*, pp 102–4.
179 *Weekly Freeman*, 5 Apr. 1919, p. 6.

[180] Ard Fheis, Reports (duplicated, 8-9 Apr. 1919): Barton Papers, NLI, MS 8786/1; Mitchell, *Revolutionary Government*, p. 36; Figgis, *Recollections*, p. 246.

[181] Ó Murthuile, Memoir, f. 69 (claiming that Harry's original nomination had been merely 'a spontaneous effort on the part of the Supreme Council to see that the work of Sinn Féin was carried on pending the release of its elected officers').

[182] SC Minutes, 1, 2, 15 May 1919; MC to Stack, 17 May: Stack Papers, NLI, MS 5848. After Fr. O'Flanagan's ruling that the appointment of regular substitutes for Stack and Harry was up to the Ard Chomhairle, a ballot was held for 2 temporary Secretaries. Kelly (10 votes) and Sheehy-Skeffington (8) prevailed over Con Collins (7) and Milroy (3).

[183] Ó Murthuile, Memoir, ff. 73, 77.

[184] MC ['W. Field'] to [C. J.?] 'Lee' (undated typescript): EdeVP, P 150/1132.

[185] Signed by 'Éamon de Valera, President', 30 Apr. 1919: EdeVP, P 150/1132.

[186] Dáil Ministry, Minutes, 2, 16 May 1919: NAD, DE 1/1, pp 4, 6.

[187] MC to Stack, 17 May 1919: Stack Papers, NLI, MS 5848. The reference to 'five weeks' suggests that Harry was appointed as envoy on about 10 Apr., three weeks before his departure.

[188] E. J. Duggan to HB, 13 Sept. 1921: BP; Kathleen Boland, Statement, ff. 15-18. Eamon Duggan, solicitor and Lewes veteran, was unconnected with Bill Duggan.

[189] Maher, *Harry Boland*, p. 82; SC Minutes, 23 Apr. 1919.

[190] 'Hogan', *Glorious Years*, p. 251; Kathleen Boland, Statement, f. 14.

[191] Seán Nunan to MC, 3 Sept. 1919: NAD, DE 2/292 (also transcribed in *Documents on Irish Foreign Policy*, i (1919-1922), ed. Ronan Fanning et al. (Dublin, 1998), p. 45). Republicans frequently consorted in Mrs Vaughan's Private Hotel at the north-west corner of Rutland Sq. (29 & 32), and 15-16, Granby Row: *Thom's Official Directory* (1915 edn.).

[192] Ó Murthuile, Memoir, f. 73.

[193] HB, Diary, 19 May 1920: EdeVP, P 150/1169a; *The Times*, 6 May 1919, p. 22 (Shipping Intelligence). For conflicting evidence on the identity of the vessel, see ch. VI, n. 1.

CHAPTER VI. CAVALCADE

[1] HB, Diary, 18 May 1920: EdeVP, P 150/1169a [hereafter, HBD]; Seán Ó Murthuile, Memoir (typescript, *circa* 1928-31), f. 73: Mulcahy Papers, UCDA, P 7a/209; *The Times*, 19 May 1919, p. 22 (Shipping Intelligence). According to Béaslaí, Harry's vessel was the *Celtic*, a White Star liner which left Liverpool on 9 May, took the direct route avoiding Halifax, and reached New York on Saturday, 17 May: Piaras Béaslaí, *Michael Collins and the Making of a New Ireland* (2 vols., Dublin, 1926), i, p. 308; *The Times*, 9 May, p. 17; 19 May, p. 22 (Shipping Intelligence). This later date of arrival is incompatible with the chronology implied in the *Gaelic American*, 12 Aug. 1922, p. 2 (see n. 5 below).

[2] Seán Nunan to MC, 27 June, 17 Sept. 1919: NAD, DE 2/292. In EdeVP, P150/1165, there is a transcribed 'Memorandum' from the 'Pursar' [*sic*.] of the S.S. *Celtic*, to 'E. Boland', purporting to be 'Extract of Official Log Book Dated 10th May 19. E. Boland 112, Fireman, disrated to Trimmer @ £11 10/- from 8th. inst. owing to incompetency. F. B. Howarth Master, James McGowan Chief Engineer.' Though Harry might have secured a seaman's identity card in his brother's name, this record may in fact concern the peripatetic Edmund.

[3] Kathleen Boland (Mrs Seán O'Donovan), Statement for the Bureau of Military History (undated typescript), f. 14: BP; *Gaelic American*, 12 Aug. 1922, p. 2. Harry's

illicit sailings were handled by Neil Kerr (of the Cunard Line) and Barney Downs in Liverpool, with Jim McGee and Jim Gleeson in New York.

4   Diarmuid Lynch, *The I.R.B. and the 1916 Insurrection*, ed. Florence O'Donoghue (Cork, 1957), p. 209; Patrick McCartan, *With de Valera in America* (New York, 1932), pp 135–9.

5   *Gaelic American*, 12 Aug. 1922, p. 2. For a similar account, see Devoy to Luke Dillon, 15 June 1920: McGP, NLI, MS 17610/2.

6   *Gaelic American*, 21 June 1919, p. 1. The accompanying photograph, despite the tie, suggests a pugilist more than a dandy.

7   P. E. Magennis, 'An American Memory of Harry Boland', p. 568, in *Catholic Bulletin*, xii, no. 9 (Sept. 1922), pp 566–9.

8   *New York Times*, 23 June 1919, p. 4.

9   M. J. Davis, 'Harry J. Boland: Sinn Féin Activities' (typed report, 25 June 1919): NAW, RG 65, Records of [Federal] Bureau of Investigation [hereafter, RBI], 373017 (microform M 1085/810).

10 An Aliens officer in Liverpool later reported that 'Edward de Valera signed on the S.S. *Royal George* in May or June of this year in the name of John Flaherty, British subject born in Galway'. See report to H.M. Inspector of Aliens [W. Haldane Porter], 8 Oct. 1919: PRO, Home Office Registered Papers (Supplementary), HO 144/10309/315944/19. This account evidently conflated the journeys of Harry and de Valera, who travelled on the American Line's *Lapland*. The *Lapland* reached New York after 9 days on 11 June, whereas the *Royal George* was at sea from 7–18 June: Earl of Longford and Thomas P. O'Neill, *Eamon de Valera* (London, 1970), p. 96; *The Times*, 4 June, p. 20; 13 June, p. 22; 9 June, p. 14; 20 June, p. 24 (Shipping Intelligence).

11 HBD, 18 May 1920. In repeating Harry's anecdote, J. C. Walsh remarked that 'he loved to give the verbatim et literatim of the language attributed to his straight faced chief': Joseph Cyrillus Walsh, 'Reminiscences of the Irish Movement for Independence, 1914–' (MSS, *circa* 1947), f. 231: NYPL, J. C. Walsh Papers, in slipcase.

12 Lanier H. Winslow [?] (State Department) to Edward Bell (American Embassy, London), 10 Apr. 1919: NAW, RG 59, Department of State, Records of the Office of the Counselor [hereafter, ROC], 841.D/32. This letter confirmed that, in accordance with a request from the American Embassy in London dated 14 Mar., the State Department had 'caused Edward Valera's name to be placed on the passport refusal list, which I trust will effectively prevent his entering this country'.

13 Barney Downs [?], 'Deverant's Story' (undated typescript of interview), f. 4: McGP, MS 17608. This coded account evidently refers to the *Lapland* as the *Scow*, and also to the *Royal George* (or *Celtic*), in which Harry travelled, as the *Lighter*.

14 Extract from report by 'Q', 9 July 1919, in Security Service [M.I.5], Personal Files, Eamon de Valera: PRO, KV 2/515, f. 95 (reference kindly supplied by Dr. Eunan O'Halpin).

15 EdeV to HB, [11 June 1919], with HB's explanatory note: EdeVP, P 150/1132.

16 'Deverant's Story', f. 4; *Gaelic American*, 12 Aug. 1922, p. 2. When Liam Mellows returned next day to the room that he shared with Harry, he found 'old clothes' and signs that 'a crowd had been there', later learning that the crowd consisted of de Valera, McGarrity, McCartan, and Boland. See Mellows, Diary, 11, 12 June 1919: EdeVP, P 150/956.

17 Mellows, Diary, 12 June 1919; *New York Times*, 22 June, p. 12; 23 June, p. 4; Longford and O'Neill, *Eamon de Valera*, pp 96–7 (variant detail); HB's explanatory note to EdeV's message of 11 June: EdeVP, P 150/1132.

18 EdeV to Griffith, 21 Aug. 1919: *Documents on Irish Foreign Policy*, i (1919–1922), ed. Ronan Fanning et al. (Dublin, 1998) [hereafter, *DIFP*], p. 43 (citing NAD, DE 2/245).

19 HB to Ned Boland, 23 Sept. 1919. All such extracts are taken from family correspondence in BP.

20 McGuire to Cohalan, 22, 31 Aug. 1919: AIHS, Cohalan Papers, 10/6.

21 HBD, 3, 16, 18, 31 Dec. 1919, 7, 26 Jan., 25 Feb., 23, 25 Mar., 8 Apr., 5 May 1920.

22 Cáit Bean Ní Cheallaigh [Mrs Seán T. O'Kelly] to Frank P. Walsh, 11 Feb. 1920: NYPL, F. P. Walsh Papers, Box 28.

23 Circular for Legal Defense Fund, 12 July 1918: McGP, MS 17609/11; P. J. Aherne (Operative in Charge, New York) to W. H. Moran (Chief, Secret Service Division, Washington), 24 Apr. 1919: NAW, ROC, 841.D/12; McCartan, *With de Valera*, chs. 4, 5.

24 Major Frank Hall (Military Intelligence, Waterloo House, London) to Lt.-Col. Stephen Slocum (Military Attaché, American Embassy), 26 Oct. 1917: NAW, RG 165, Records of War Department, General and Special Staffs [hereafter, MID], 9771/37.

25 *Hue and Cry*, circa 15 May 1916: cutting in McGP, MS 17458/3.

26 HBD, 2 May 1920; McCartan, *With de Valera*, pp 135–9.

27 HB to EdeV, 4 June 1919: EdeVP, P 150/1132 (copy in BP). Mellows also postponed his departure, initially because of Harry's breakdown: C. Desmond Greaves, *Liam Mellows and the Irish Revolution* (London, 1971), p. 209.

28 Mellows to 'N.' [Nora Connolly], 14 Sept. 1919: *An Phoblacht*, n.s. vii, no. 35 (8 Oct. 1932), p. 3. Those mentioned were de Valera, McCartan, McGarrity, Harry, and Mellows himself.

29 Seán Nunan, Statement for the Bureau of Military History (undated typescript), *passim*: EdeVP, P 150/3652; J. C. Walsh, 'Reminiscences', f. 298.

30 Nunan to MC, 27 June, 19 Aug., 17 Sept. 1919, with reply, 6 Oct.: NAD, DE 2/292.

31 Nunan, Statement, ff. 10–11. Collins gave him £5 for the journey, which he spent on a ticket to Liverpool and a seaman's outfit for use on the *Aquitania*.

32 Nunan to MC, 27 June 1919: NAD, DE 2/292.

33 Seán Nunan, 'President Éamon de Valera's Mission to the United States of America, 1919–1920', p. 239, in *Capuchin Annual*, xxxvii (1970), pp 236–49; Nunan to Kate Boland, 2 Aug. 1922: BP. For 'the hospitality of these good Carmelites' enjoyed by Mellows, McCartan, Harry, de Valera, and 'every Irish exile', see McCartan, *With de Valera*, p. 40.

34 Gerald Boland's anecdote of a journey during the Bond Drive with 'Seán', recalled by his son Harry.

35 Patricia Lavelle, *James O'Mara: A Staunch Sinn-Féiner: 1873–1948* (Dublin, 1961), *passim*; autobiographical note (circa 1920): O'Mara Papers, NLI, MS 21547; commonplace book, opposite entry dated 22 Dec. 1918: O'Mara Papers, MS 21550/1.

36 J. C. Walsh, 'Reminiscences', ff. 231, 137, 139. For O'Mara's arrival in New York, see HBD, 2, 3 Nov. 1919.

37 Devoy to John McGarry, 26 Nov. [1919]: transcription in McGP, MS 17486/4.

38 HBD, 6, 7, 8 Mar. 1920. On this occasion, Harry's diplomacy prevailed.

39 Fawsitt, later a barrister and Judge of the Circuit Court, had been Secretary to the Irish Industrial Development Association (1902–19): *Memoirs of Senator Joseph Connolly (1885–1961): A Founder of Modern Ireland*, ed. J. Anthony Gaughan (Dublin, 1996), p. 210.

40 HBD, 2 Dec. 1919, 14, 17 Feb. 1920.

41 J. L. Fawsitt to James O'Mara, 14 Mar. 1920, with reply, 25 Mar.: O'Mara Papers, MS 21548/2.

42 HBD, 3, 14 Oct. 1919, 1, 5 Jan. 1920.

43 Katherine Hughes, Secretary of the Irish National Bureau in Washington, resigned

on 8 May 1920 after many personal clashes and returned to Canada. Kathleen O'Connell (1888–1956), born in Caherdaniel, Co. Kerry, emigrated to the United States in 1904, becoming active in the Gaelic League and Cumann na mBan before working for Fawsitt, Harry, and de Valera, whom she followed back to Ireland (acting as his Private Secretary, 1919–54). See FOIF, *Newsletter*, no. 50 (12 June 1920): AIHS, FOIF Papers, 4/8; National Executive, Minutes, 8 May: FOIF Papers, 6/3; information on Kathleen O'Connell kindly supplied by Dr. Patrick Murray.

44 HBD, 18 Feb., 6 Apr. 1920.

45 HB to MC, 30 Jan. 1920: EdeVP, P 150/1125.

46 HB to EdeV, 4 June 1919: EdeVP, P 150/1132 (copy in BP).

47 Katherine O'Doherty, *Assignment: America: De Valera's Mission to the United States* (New York, 1957), *passim*.

48 Devoy to Cohalan, 24 June 1919: Cohalan Papers, 4/4.

49 O'Doherty, *Assignment: America*, p. 46.

50 Typed report of speech, 29 June 1919: EdeVP, P 150/1162.

51 HB to Kate Boland, 8 July 1919: copy in EdeVP, P 150/1165.

52 O'Doherty, *Assignment: America*, p. 82; *Sunday Times* (Scranton), 10 Aug. 1969, concerning meeting on 7 Sept. 1919: cutting in EdeVP, P 150/83/6 (former number: copy in BP).

53 HB to Cohalan and reply, 4, 6 Sept. 1919: Cohalan Papers, 2/5; Charles N. Wheeler to McG, undated [18 June]: Villanova University, Philadelphia, McGP, 3/10.

54 HB to Kate Boland, 30 Sept. 1919.

55 In his 'Leatherstocking Tales' such as *The Last of the Mohicans: Or, a Narrative of 1757* (1826), set in the Lake Champlain region, James Fenimore Cooper (1789–1851) recounted the adventures of the forester-frontiersman Natty Bumppo (otherwise Hawkeye), and his Indian friend Chingachcook.

56 HB to Ned Boland, 23 Sept. 1919.

57 A statue of Commodore John Barry from Co. Wexford (1745–1803), an American naval pioneer, was erected in 1907 by the Friendly Sons of St. Patrick in front of Independence Hall, Philadelphia: John A. Barnes, *Irish-American Landmarks: A Traveler's Guide* (Detroit, 1995), p. 154.

58 John A. Ryan to McG, 12 Aug. 1920 (giving auditor's report on the event, dispute having arisen over 128 unpaid suppers): McGP, MS 17439/1; HBD, 1, 2 Oct. 1919.

59 Bro. Albens, CSC, a Holy Cross missionary from Ireland who lectured for Sinn Féin in America, recalled that 'Harry was glad to see me, for he embraced me before the whole crowd of students, about 2,000'. See Albens to Kate Boland, 25 Oct. 1922: BP.

60 HBD, 3, 5, 6, 7, 15 Oct. 1919.

61 Nunan, 'Mission', p. 242.

62 Mellows to HB, 9 Oct. 1919: EdeVP, P 150/1163. At Notre Dame, where de Valera was to lay a wreath on the statue of Fr. Corby, Chaplain to the Irish Brigade in the Civil War, Mellows spelt out the 'analogy' between his general absolution for that unit at Gettysburg in 1863, and that 'administered to Irish Republican Army, fighting for liberty, Easter Week 1916'.

63 Mellows to HB, 6 Oct. 1919: EdeVP, P 150/1163.

64 HBD, 13 Oct. 1919.

65 HB to McG, 10 Oct. 1919: McGP, MS 17424/1.

66 HB to 'Mac' [James O'Mara], 12 Oct. 1919: O'Mara Papers, MS 21550/1. Harry added that 'Seán [Nunan] and I are on the road with him and we often talk of you and wish we were near you. ... I often talk over the great Election days with Seán.' Confusingly, Harry also adopted the pseudonym 'Mac' in later correspondence with O'Mara.

[67] HB to Kate Boland, 6, 15, 16 Oct. 1919.

[68] HB to Ned Boland, 23 Sept. 1919; Mellows to HB, 14 Oct.: EdeVP, P 150/1163. Mellows promised that 'all the Indians, Catholic and Pagan, will be present, as well as Chiefs of the Sioux and Cree Nations, who will come from Minnesota'.

[69] HB to Kate Boland, 20 Oct. 1919. His diary entry for the 'best day so far' gave de Valera's soubriquet as 'Nay, nay, ong, ga, be' and referred also to 'Medicine man, Tom Tom': HBD, 18 Oct.

[70] HBD, 18–20 Oct. 1919.

[71] HBD, 24 Oct. 1919. Wolfe Tone's refrain, ' 'Tis but in vain for soldiers to complain' (the second element often being replaced by 'etc.') was a favourite republican catch-phrase, also quoted in Ernie O'Malley, *The Singing Flame* (Dublin, 1978), p. 141; Mellows to McCartan, 6 Mar. 1920: McGP, MS 17652/5. Tone learned this line of a song from Thomas Russell: William Thomas Wolfe Tone, *Life of Theobald Wolfe Tone*, ed. Thomas Bartlett (Dublin, 1998; 1st edn. 1826), pp 154–5 (Journal, 23 Sept. 1792).

[72] HBD, 25 Oct. 1919.

[73] HBD, 11, 21 Dec. 1919.

[74] HBD, 1 Mar. 1920.

[75] HBD, 1 Feb., 22 Jan. 1919.

[76] Mary O'Connor Meagher (Dorchester, Mass.) to Anna O'Rahilly, 21 Feb. 1921: Humphreys Papers, UCDA, P 106/1289.

[77] Mellows (Columbia, South Carolina) to HB, 6 Apr. 1920: EdeVP, P 150/1163.

[78] HB to EdeV, 4 June 1919: EdeVP, P 150/1132 (copy in BP). Harry was then unaware of de Valera's departure for America.

[79] *Gaelic American*, 12 Aug. 1922, p. 2.

[80] MC to Austin Stack, 20 July 1919: Stack Papers, NLI, MS 5848.

[81] HB to Patrick McCartan, 7 Oct. 1919: McCartan Papers, NLI, MS 17674/1.

[82] 'Intervention in the affairs of Allied States seems to me a question which the present Peace Conference can in no way consider under any circumstance whatever.' See Georges Clemenceau to Robert Lansing (Secretary of State), 25 June 1919: *The Papers of Woodrow Wilson*, ed. Arthur S. Link (69 vols., Princeton, N.J., 1966–94), lxi (1994), p. 467.

[83] Francis M. Carroll, *American Opinion and the Irish Question, 1910–23* (Dublin, 1978), p. 147.

[84] HB to Arthur Griffith, 9 July 1919: EdeVP, P 150/1127 (also transcribed in *DIFP*, p. 36).

[85] HBD, 16 Oct. 1919.

[86] HBD, 3, 19 Nov. 1919, 22 Mar. 1920. Harry admired Senator Gore at first meeting, on 12 Mar. 1920: 'Gore very remarkable man, tall, straight as a die, blind, promises to do his best.' Thomas Pryor Gore (1870–1949), though blind from childhood, served as Democratic Senator for Oklahoma (1907–20, 1930–6). A Progressive until 1898 and thereafter an increasingly conservative Democrat, he opposed Wilson's wartime policy and pushed through a Senate resolution affirming American neutrality, being defeated at the Democratic Primary in 1920. His most notable legacy was his grandson, the novelist Gore Vidal: *Encyclopedia Americana* (30 vols., Danburg, Conn., 1990 edn.), xiii, p. 89; *American National Biography*, ed. John A. Garraty and Mark C. Carnes (24 vols., New York, 1999), ix, pp 299–300.

[87] Harding to Walsh, 24 Mar. 1920: O'Mara Papers, MS 21548/2. Harding had also shown some inconsistency by voting against the Irish reservation (carried by 38 votes to 36), while supporting the amended Treaty Bill (carried by 49 votes to 35, short of the requisite two-thirds majority): Charles Callan Tansill, *America and the Fight for*

Irish Freedom, 1866–1922: An Old Story Based on New Data (New York, 1957), p. 372.

88 HBD, 3 Apr. 1920. A variant of this slur had been applied to Dr. Maloney by his opponents shortly after Harry's arrival, when he heard 'all the same old things trotted out about the British spy and the "fine Italian hand of the gallant captain"'. See HB, transcript of speech to Clan na Gael Reorganized, 20 Mar. 1921, f. 13: BP (copy from unlocated document).

89 HB to MC, 30 Jan. 1920: EdeVP, P 150/1125.

90 HB to 'Pierce' [Béaslaí], 14 Jan. 1920: Béaslaí Papers, NLI, MS 33912/24.

91 HBD, 30 Dec. 1919.

92 HBD, 15 Dec. 1919, 9 Jan. 1920.

93 The Census of 1920 recorded 1,037,234 American 'natives' of Irish birth and 2,971,688 white natives of America with at least one parent of Irish origin (of whom 1,966,968 had two foreign-born parents): USA, Department of Commerce, Bureau of the Census, *Fourteenth Census of the United States Taken in the Year 1920* (9 vols., Washington, 1922), ii, pp 693, 897.

94 HB to McG, 29 Aug. 1919: McGP, MS 17424/1.

95 HB to MC, 30 Jan. 1920: EdeVP, P 150/1125.

96 Oswald Garrison Villard (1872–1949), who inherited control of the *New York Evening Post* and the *Nation* (its weekly literary supplement) in 1900, sold the *Post* to J. P. Morgan in 1918 after alienating many readers through his opposition to American intervention in the War. He bitterly denounced Wilson and the Versailles settlement, espoused the Irish and Soviet Russian causes, and broke with the *Nation* in 1940 when it abandoned pacifism. He joined the National Advisory Committee of the Protestant Friends of Ireland (1919) and used the *Nation* to promote the American Commission on Conditions in Ireland (1920): *American National Biography*, xxii, pp 362–4; Carroll, *American Opinion*, p. 206.

97 HBD, 15 Jan., 24 Feb. 1920.

98 O'Doherty, *Assignment: America*, p. 84. Boland, along with Malone, Padraic Colum, and John Fitzpatrick (President of the Chicago Federation of Labor) were named by American Military Intelligence as supporters who were 'focusing a large radical Irish element' upon the League. See Memorandum on League of Oppressed Peoples (undated, *circa* June 1920): NAW, MID, 124/397.

99 HBD, 28 Feb. 1920.

100 Ludwig Christian Alexander Karlovich Martens (1874–1948), an engineer, had been exiled to Germany in 1899, before moving to Britain in 1906 and the USA in 1916. He returned to Russia and survived the Purges, editing the *Technical Encyclopedia* (1927–41): *Great Soviet Encyclopedia*, ed. A. M. Prokhorov, English trans. of 3rd edn. (31 vols., New York, 1973–82), xv (1977), p. 502; *Encyclopedia of the American Left*, ed. Mari Jo Buhle, Paul Buhle, and Dan Georgakas (New York, 1998; 1st edn. 1990), pp 692–4, 819.

101 The Comintern supplied American agents (including John Reed) with jewels and precious metals valued at 2,728,000 roubles between July 1919 and Jan. 1920: receipts by 'Krumina', translated in Harvey Klehr, John Earl Haynes, and Fridrikh Igorevich Firsov, *The Secret World of American Communism* (New Haven, Conn., 1995), pp 22–4.

102 Nuorteva, who had worked at the Bureau in New York since Apr. 1918, returned to the Commissariat of Foreign Affairs in Moscow and was imprisoned in 1921 as a suspected 'British agent': McCartan, Memorandum, June 1921: *DIFP*, pp 148–56 (citing NAD, Department of Foreign Affairs, Early Series, 32/228).

103 Edward Bell (American Embassy, London) to L. Lanier Winslow (State Department), 9 June 1919: NAW, ROC, 841.D/82; McCartan to Martens, 8 May: EdeVP, P 150/1320 (copy in BP).

[104] Report by M. J. Davis (New York), 25 June 1919, citing information 'by a former confidential employé of this department': NAW, RBI, 373017 (microform M 1085/810); Buhle, *American Left*, pp 692–4, 819.

[105] HBD, 9, 27 Jan., 3 Mar. 1920.

[106] HB to MC, 9 Apr. 1920: EdeVP, P 150/1125; L. Martens, receipt, 16 Apr.: NAD, Department of Taoiseach, S 14205.

[107] HBD, 11, 14, 15 Apr. 1920.

[108] Department of External Affairs, Memorandum on Sale of Russian Jewels, 9 July 1949, and G. Zaroubin (Soviet Ambassador, London), receipt for jewels, 13 Sept.: NAD, Department of Taoiseach, S 14205. According to a receipt for the 'security' dated 16 Apr. 1920, probably by O'Mara, the value of the four jewels (supposedly containing numerous diamonds ranging from 6 to 16 carats) was $25,500: copy in BP. The jewels were eventually valued by Christie's at £1,600: Jane Leonard, 'Contacts between Ireland and Russia, 1900–1960' (BA Dissertation, Department of Russian, TCD, 1987), f. 32.

[109] The jewels were handed to the Government in 1938, in rough accordance with Harry's reported instruction 'to give them to Dev. when returned to power and Irish Republic re-established. If anything happened Dev. [*sic*.] don't give them to the Free State Crowd.' See Kathleen (Boland) O'Donovan, undated statement: BP.

[110] Greaves, *Mellows*, p. 207.

[111] Alice Paul (1885–1977), suffragist and founder of the militant Congressional Union for Women's Suffrage (1913) and National Woman Party (1917), served several prison terms in England and America. Her lobbying was instrumental in forcing through Congress the 19th Amendment to the Constitution (26 Aug. 1920) which affirmed universal adult suffrage, and in launching the first Congressional campaign for an Equal Rights Amendment in 1923: *Encyclopedia Americana*, xxi, p. 548; xxix, p. 104.

[112] HBD, 15–19 Apr. 1920.

[113] HB to Cohalan, 19 Apr. 1920: Cohalan Papers, 2/5.

[114] John Elmer Milholland (1860–1925), a Presbyterian who made his reputation on the *New York Tribune*, espoused 'the Boers' cause' as well as 'negroes' constitutional rights, prison reform, federal aid to education, cutting down of Southern representation in Congress, etc.' He participated in a World's Race Congress in London (1911), 'helped to inaugurate Saturday half holiday in America', saved Fort Ticonderoga, and also served as supervising Inspector of Immigration at New York: *Who was Who in America*, i, 1897–1942 (Chicago, 1943), p. 838.

[115] Milholland to Cohalan, 27 Apr. 1920: Cohalan Papers, 11/7. Milholland added that 'Harry Bowland [*sic*.], who is working with his coat off, tells me you are coming to Wilmington, Saturday. Good!'

[116] Cohalan to Milholland, 30 Apr. 1920 (unfinished draft): Cohalan Papers, 11/7.

[117] HBD, 12 Apr. 1920.

[118] HB to Charles J. Dolan (St. Louis), 16 Sept. 1919: EdeVP, P 150/875.

[119] Mellows to HB, 29 Sept. 1919: EdeVP, P 150/1163. 'Prohibition' was given legal effect throughout the USA on 17 Jan. 1920, through the 18th Amendment to the Constitution (repealed in 1933).

[120] Mellows to HB, 16 Oct. 1919: EdeVP, P 150/1163.

[121] William Corkey, *Gladly Did I Live: Memoirs of a Long Life* (Belfast, 1963 edn.), ch. 13. For a dismissive account of the mission, tracing its genesis to Beaverbrook's *Sunday Express* (28 Sept. 1919), see Arthur Mitchell, *Revolutionary Government in Ireland: Dáil Éireann, 1919–22* (Dublin, 1995), pp 116–17.

[122] HBD, 7 Dec. 1919.

[123] Corkey, *Gladly*, p. 209.

[124] O'Doherty, *Assignment: America*, pp 114–15.

[125] HB to MC, 30 Jan. 1920: Ede VP, P 150/1125.

[126] Circular from National Executive Secretary [Mythen], Protestant Friends of Ireland, *circa* late 1919: FOIF Papers, 24/9. 'If it be impossible to obtain one active Protestant act as sponsor for the meeting in your vicinity, we will arrange this meeting from National Headquarters, acting on your advices in the manner following: ... List of the Roman-Catholic clergy who, while not taking an active part in this meeting, must be relied on to give their assistance.'

[127] Norman Thomas (1884–1968), ordained at Union Theological College (Presbyterian) in 1911, became a prominent pacifist, campaigner against Conscription, and assistant editor of the *Nation*. He was the Socialist candidate for President in every election between 1928 and 1944 (winning almost 885,000 votes in 1932), but switched his support to the Democratic Party before resuming his radicalism as a campaigner against American intervention in Vietnam: Harry Fleischman, 'Norman Thomas', in Buhle, *American Left*, pp 820–1.

[128] Patrick J. Moynihan (State Secretary, Mass.) to Diarmuid Lynch, 3 Jan. 1920: FOIF Papers, 24/8; Mythen to Cohalan, 22 Nov. 1921 (letterhead): Cohalan Papers, 11/19.

[129] 'Fenian Bonds' to the value of $500,000 were issued in 1866, 'to finance an invasion of Canada': Mitchell, *Revolutionary Government*, p. 115 (citing the *Nation*, 12 July 1919).

[130] Dáil Éireann, *Minutes of Proceedings, 1919–1921: Official Record* (Dublin, undated), pp 41, 139, 150 (4 Apr., 19, 20 Aug. 1919); O'Doherty, *Assignment: America*, pp 64–9.

[131] Wheeler to McG, [18 June 1919]: Villanova University, McGP, 3/10.

[132] National Council, Minutes, 16 Apr. 1920: FOIF Papers, 8/6.

[133] Account of post-prandial discussion in New York with John D. Ryan, Nick Brady, and Joe Grace: W. Bourke Cockran to Cohalan, 14 July 1919: Cohalan Papers, 3/3. Ryan later told Cockran that even 'love of country would not suffice to make men of high standing in business sponsor such a loan'.

[134] Copy of EdeV to Frank P. Walsh, Sept. 1919: Catholic University of America, Washington, National Catholic War Council Papers (Collection 10/2), 46/22.

[135] National Executive, Minutes, 24 Sept. 1919: FOIF Papers, 6/2.

[136] Printed appeal by Walsh, 1 Oct. 1919, reproducing EdeV to Walsh, 28 Sept.: McGP, MS 17522. The form 'Bond Certificates' was chosen in the hope of evading the 'Blue Sky' laws operating against 'Bonds' in about 30 states. See Devoy's account of a conversation with Harry in Devoy to Cohalan, 16 Sept.: Devoy Papers, NLI, MS 15416/3.

[137] HBD, 22–24 Oct. 1919.

[138] 'Statement of Edward F. McSweeney' (undated typescript, responding to an attack by McCartan in the New York *World*, 22 June 1920): Cohalan Papers, 10/13.

[139] HBD, 4, 6, 8 Nov. 1919.

[140] HBD, 30 Nov. 1919.

[141] National Executive, Minutes, 3 Oct. 1919: FOIF Papers, 8/5.

[142] James O'Mara to Diarmuid Lynch, 17 Dec. 1919, enclosing accounts of campaign expenses: Cohalan Papers, 13/8; accounts (14 Oct. to 20 Dec. 1919) of American Commission on Irish Independence, 22 Dec.: EdeVP, P 150/1163. Lynch had previously provided two cheques for $10,000 on 9 July and 25 Sept.

[143] HB to James O'Mara, 9 Jan. 1920: O'Mara Papers, MS 21548/1.

[144] National Council, Minutes, 11 June 1919, 16 Apr. 1920: FOIF Papers, 8/5–6. The initial decision was not to be 'made known to anyone not an officer of the organization', while the retention of the balance of one-quarter of the sum raised

($850,000) was justified by the claim that a larger amount had been contributed, 'directly and indirectly, to or for the account of our friends in Ireland'.

[145] MC to HB, 23 Nov. 1919: EdeVP, P 150/1125. On 12 Sept., the Dáil Ministry had deferred 'discussion of assistance for Loan' after reading letters from de Valera and Harry. See Dáil Ministry, Minutes, f. 47: NAD, DE 1/1.

[146] Memorandum by O. L. M. (Division of Western European Affairs, State Department), circa Feb. 1920, and associated correspondence on Bonds: NAW, ROC, 841.D/51/2 (microform M 580/243).

[147] Unsigned memorandum (possibly by Cohalan), 27 Feb. 1920: Cohalan Papers, 1/9. Fogarty, nominally one of the Dáil's three Trustees, had assigned 'the management and supervision of the Dáil Funds' to his fellow-Trustees then in America (O'Mara and de Valera). See Fogarty to EdeV, 12 Oct. 1919: O'Mara Papers, MS 21547.

[148] MC ['W. F.'] to HB ['J. W.'], 12 May 1920: EdeVP, P 150/1125.

[149] An account of the Dáil Trustees, to Dec. 1920, records loan receipts of only £219,444 (external) compared with £398,882 (internal): EdeVP, P 150/1140 (former number).

CHAPTER VII. CONSPIRACY

[1] Flood, one of four election organisers appointed by Robert Brennan in June 1918, sent reports of election arragements to Seán Milroy in Lincoln Prison. He helped found Sinn Féin in Longford in 1907, becoming its joint Honorary Secretary for North Longford and a District Court Justice (1920). Flood was interned in Frongoch and joined the IRB in 1917, becoming Adjutant and Intelligence Officer of the North Longford Brigade after a visit to Granard by Michael Collins which prompted reorganisation of the Volunteers. See printed reports for Sinn Féin, Ard Fheis, Oct. 1918: Barton Papers, NLI, MS 8786/1; Postal Censor, 1st Report, f. 9: PRO, Home Office Registered Papers (Supplementary), HO 144/1496/362269/135; Marie Coleman, County Longford and the Irish Revolution, 1916–1923 (Dublin, 2003), p. 103; James P. Flood, Statement (duplicate typescript, 1951), ff. 2–5: MAD, Bureau of Military History Papers, WS 606.

[2] Transcripts (with photostats) of three letters from 'Pat' (alias 'Peter' and 'P. F.') to J. P. Flood (his 'cousin' or 'little brother') were forwarded by W. L. Hurley (American Embassy, London) to L. Lanier Wilson (State Department), 27 June 1919: NAW, Department of State, Records of the Office of the Counselor [hereafter, ROC], 841.D/66. At a time when the postal censorship conducted by British Military Intelligence 'was closing down', the original letters had 'with considerable difficulty' been located in the possession of M.I.5, which reluctantly agreed to have them photostated for the American Secret Service (a process which took two days). The writer's obvious familiarity with Granard suggests that he may indeed have been Flood's kinsman.

[3] 'Pat' to J. P. Flood, 11 Apr. 1919.

[4] 'Peter' to Flood, 10 May 1919 (date of postscript), recommending Fr. O'Shea of Philadelphia, an emissary to Ireland who would report on 'Kathleen's affairs' to 'Edward and Harry'.

[5] 'Peter' to Flood, 26 May 1919.

[6] 'Manx cat' may allude to Sinn Féin's most influential advocate in Australia, Dr. Daniel Mannix (1864–1963), the Catholic Archbishop of Melbourne from 1917. No proposal to send Harry to Australia has been located.

[7] Helen was the first of the Kiernan sisters to become involved with Collins, but by spring 1919 he was in correspondence with 'my darling Kitty': In Great Haste: The

Letters of Michael Collins and Kitty Kiernan, ed. León Ó Broin (Dublin, 1996; 1st edn. 1983) [hereafter, *IGH*], pp 5–7.

8   Telegram from London to Military Intelligence Division, Washington, 24 Nov. 1919: NAW, Records of Bureau of Investigation [herefter, RBI], 373017 (microform M 1085/810). This report was based on a 'message' attributed to Harry, 'nominally secretary to Valera'.

9   MC ['Field'] to HB ['Woods'], 23 Nov. '1913' [1919]: extract in Seán Ó Murthuile, Memoir (undated typescript, *circa* 1928–31), f. 91: Mulcahy Papers, UCDA, P 7a/209.

10 EdeV to Cabinet, 6 Mar. 1920; MC to HB, 19 Apr. (warning against any overt involvement by 'Irish American representatives' in the proposed purchase): EdeVP, P 150/1125; Patrick McCartan to Weinstein (Moscow), 31 May 1921: *Documents on Irish Foreign Policy*, i (1919–1922), ed. Ronan Fanning et al. (Dublin, 1998) [hereafter, DIFP], pp 56, 143 (citing NAD, DE 2/245; Department of Foreign Affairs, Early Series, 32/228). Moore & McCormack, Inc., was one of three 'managing operators' for vessels owned by the United States Shipping Board. Through the 'United States Lines' at 45, Broadway, New York, these companies jointly advertised voyages 'direct to Ireland under the American flag' in 'great government ships': *Irish World and American Industrial Liberator*, 31 Dec. 1921, p. 11.

11 MC ['W. F.'] to HB ['J. W.'], 29, 26 Apr. 1920: EdeVP, P 150/1125.

12 HB to EdeV, 24 May, 4 June 1919: EdeVP, P 150/1132 (copies in BP).

13 From the 1830s, the term 'Fardowns' was applied to gangs of Ulster Catholics on the American railroads (rivals of the 'Corkonians'), and more broadly to emigrants from the north of Ireland.

14 HB, Diary, 24, 25 Nov. 1919: EdeVP, P 150/1169a [hereafter, HBD].

15 Ricard O'Sullivan Burke (1838–1922), a veteran of the Cork Militia and the Federal Army in the American Civil War, smuggled arms into Liverpool for Stephens's Fenians, and organised the rescue of Col. Thomas J. Kelly (Harry's kinsman) in Manchester (1867). Released from penal servitude after feigning insanity, he returned to America and joined Clan na Gael. Harry again visited Burke in Chicago two years later: HBD, 24 Oct. 1921.

16 HB to Ned Boland, 23 Sept. 1919. All such extracts are taken from family correspondence in BP.

17 HBD, 7 Nov. 1919.

18 HBD, 27 Dec. 1919. Most of these incidents and individuals are celebrated by Joseph Denieffe (1833–1910), in his *A Personal Narrative of the Irish Revolutionary Brotherhood*, ed. Seán Ó Luing (Shannon, 1969; 1st edn. 1906). Denieffe, a Kilkenny tailor, emigrated to the United States in 1851 and joined the Emmet Monument Association, founded (Mar. 1855) by the Confederate veterans Michael Doheny (1805–63) and John O'Mahony (1816–77). This body was soon locked in competition with the new Irish Emigrant Aid Society, formed in Boston (Aug. 1855). He then returned to Ireland, with instructions to establish a parallel revolutionary body, and secured support from Dr. Robert Cane (1807–58), founder of the Celtic Union and a former Mayor of Kilkenny, and Peter Langan, a Dublin lumber merchant who hosted a meeting in Dec. 1857 between Denieffe and James Stephens (1825–1901), another Confederate rebel who had recently returned from Paris. Stephens sent Denieffe back to New York with a request for three monthly instalments of £100 ($500) to organise a new Irish revolutionary body. When Denieffe read out this letter in Doheny's law office, Capt. Michael Corcoran (69th Regiment, New York) suggested that each participant turn out his pockets, leading to the collection of a miserable £80 ($400) after two months. Denieffe returned with

this pittance to Dublin, and attended the meeting on St. Patrick's Day, 1858, at which an oath-bound Irish Revolutionary (later Republican) Brotherhood was founded. Denieffe and Stephens immediately set about organising 'the South' ('Stephens' walk'). See Denieffe, *Personal Narrative*, pp 3–27; *Irish American Voluntary Organizations*, ed. Michael Funchion (Westport, Conn., 1983), pp 101–5.

19   HBD, 12 Feb. 1920.
20   Daniel Francis Cohalan (1865–1946), Grand Sachem (1908–11), had been chief adviser to Charles F. Murphy, the notorious boss at Tammany Hall: *The Encyclopedia of the Irish in America*, ed. Michael Glazier (Notre Dame, Indiana, 1999), p. 170.
21   The 6th modern Olympiad, held at Antwerp in Aug. 1920, was dominated by American athletes (their British rivals taking third place). The participants represented 29 countries, excluding the former Russian Empire, Central Europe, and Ireland.
22   HBD, 31 Oct. 1919, 11 Feb., 10 Apr. 1920.
23   HB to Cohalan, 23 Dec. 1919: AIHS, Cohalan Papers, 2/5.
24   [Revd. Timothy Shanley], Reminiscences (undated typescript), ff. 3–4: EdeVP, P 150/1309 (copy in BP).
25   Kathleen Boland (Mrs Seán O'Donovan), Statement for the Bureau of Military History (undated typescript), f. 15: BP. Cohalan graduated from Manhattan College in 1885, before studying law and gaining admittance to the New York Bar three years later: Glasier, *Irish in America*, p. 170.
26   See Marie Veronica Tarpey, *The Role of Joseph McGarrity in the Struggle for Irish Independence* (New York, 1976); Seán Cronin, *The McGarrity Papers* (Tralee, 1972); Joseph McGarrity, Memoirs (typescript, 1939): Villanova University, Philadelphia, McGP, 6/1.
27   Return of Income Tax for 1918: Villanova University, McGP, 1/10.
28   McCartan, like McGarrity, came from Carrickmore, Co. Tyrone.
29   American passport, 3 Feb. 1922: McGP, NLI, MS 17525/2; Diary, 20 Jan. 1921: McGP, MS 17551/4. McGarrity weighed in at 190 lb. on a frame of 5 ft. 11 in.
30   De Valera was Godfather to Joe's sixth child, Eamon de Valera McGarrity, born on 16 Dec. 1919. Punctilious as ever, de Valera charged the cost of the gold Christening cup ($274) to the Dáil. See McGarrity, Notebook, 16 Dec. 1919: McGP, NLI, MS 17552; Tarpey, *McGarrity*, p. 115; 'President's Personal Expenses' (undated return, *circa* June 1921): NAD, DE 2/450.
31   HBD, 2 Oct., 1 Nov. 1919; 11 Jan., 27 Mar. 1920.
32   HBD, 9, 29 Apr. 1920.
33   See, for example, Francis M. Carroll, *American Opinion and the Irish Question, 1910–23* (Dublin, 1978), ch. 6; Earl of Longford and T. P. O'Neill, *Eamon de Valera* (London, 1970), ch. 8–9; Charles Callan Tansill, *America and the Fight for Irish Freedom, 1866–1922: An Old Story based on New Data* (New York, 1957), ch. 11, 12 (for a robust defence of Devoy and Cohalan, to whom the book was jointly dedicated).
34   His presence at meetings of the National Executive was recorded on 16 June and 28 July 1919, and 7 Sept. 1920, while he attended the National Council on 11 July and 7 Nov. 1919. See Minutes, *passim*: AIHS, FOIF Papers, 6/2, 8/5.
35   National Council Minutes, 7 Nov. 1919: FOIF Papers, 8/5.
36   Nunan to MC, 3 Sept. 1919: NAI, DE 2/292 (also transcribed in *DIFP*, p. 45).
37   Devoy to John McGarry, 5 Sept. 1919: McGP, MS 17521/1. Devoy adjudged that 'Harry is a great man of action, but is incapable of understanding conditions here.'
38   W. J. A. Maloney, article in *New York Herald*, 1 July 1921: cutting in NYPL, Maloney Papers, 8/133. Maloney's family hailed from Loughinisland near

Ballynahinch, Co. Down. He qualified in Scotland and practised in New York before the Great War (information kindly supplied by Jane Leonard).

39 Devoy to HB, 6 Sept. 1920: EdeVP, P 150/1154; EdeV to MC, 13 Aug. 1919; MC to EdeV, 13 Sept. 1919: EdeVP, P 150/726 (copy in BP).

40 Devoy to Luke Dillon, 15 June 1920: McGP, MS 17610/2.

41 Devoy to Cohalan, 6 Sept. 1919: Devoy Papers, NLI, MS 15416/3.

42 HB to MC, 30 Jan. 1920: EdeVP, P 150/1125.

43 HB ['Woods'] to MC ['Field'], 26 Feb. 1920: EdeVP, P 150/1125.

44 Longford and O'Neill, *Eamon de Valera*, p. 103.

45 HBD, 5, 6 Feb. 1920.

46 HB to Lt.-Col. A. E. Anderson (New York), 10 Mar. 1920: Cohalan Papers, 2/5.

47 EdeV to Cabinet, 10 Mar. 1920: *DIFP*, p. 58 (citing NAD, DE 2/245).

48 Among the labours of Heracles was his purification of the stable of Augeas, King of Elis, whose 3,000 oxen had spent 30 years accumulating uncleansed excrement. This feat was achieved in a single day by diverting the river Alpheus through the stable.

49 HBD, 16–22 Feb. 1920.

50 HB ['Woods'] to MC ['Field'], 20 Apr. 1920: EdeVP, P 150/1125.

51 HB ['Woods'] to MC ['Field'], 26 Feb. 1920: EdeVP, P 150/1125.

52 Devoy to Fr. James A. Geary, 20 Apr. 1921: Catholic University of America (Washington), Geary Papers, 78/2/1.

53 Devoy to Cohalan, 9 Mar. 1920: Devoy Papers, MS 15146/4; 'Wexford' to McG, 8 Mar.: McGP, MS 17523/4; memorandum by McG, 11 Mar.: McGP, MS 17521/2. McGarrity, a practised amateur sleuth, satisfied himself that letters signed by Devoy and Cohalan were typed on the same machine.

54 McG Diary, 12, 14, 15 Mar. 1920: McGP, MS 17551/3. McGarrity's chief 'mole' was John T. Ryan, a shady lawyer from Buffalo, NY, whose cover was blown by Harry's 'spilling the letter' on 19 Mar. As he moaned to McGarrity just before retreating to Mexico, 'it means the destruction of the last bridge behind me' and deprivation of the funds hitherto available to him from 'a certain source' (possibly Cohalan). See Ryan ['Your Cousin'] to McG ['Cousin Phil'], 16 Apr.: McGP, MS 17486/1.

55 HBD, 18, 19 Mar. 1920.

56 McG Diary, 18, 19 Mar. 1920: McGP, MS 17551/3; Report of meeting, 19 Mar. (typescript, 25 Mar.): McGP, MS 17521/2. McGarrity's copy (in the same file) of the letter from Devoy ['Hudson'] to McGarry ['J. Schell'], 20 Feb., reveals that Devoy took the opposite position to that alleged. Though he considered that de Valera was 'mad with egoism and presumption', Devoy proposed 'no drastic action' and deprecated 'an open rupture if it can be avoided'. He also maintained that, had an offensive letter from de Valera to Cohalan been made public, 'the row which we all want to avoid would have come on that "reading out" anyhow and would have resulted in D. V.'s having to go home an utterly defeated and discredited man'.

57 Grace to Andrew J. Ryan (Secretary to Central Council of Irish County Associations, Boston), 28 June 1920: Cohalan Papers, 6/6.

58 *Gaelic American*, 12 Aug. 1922, p. 2.

59 HB to MC, 25 Mar. 1920: EdeVP, P 150/1125.

60 Devoy to HB, 26 Mar. 1920: EdeVP, P 150/1154.

61 Armstrong to Foreign Office, 26 Mar. 1920: PRO, CO 904/185, ff. 510–11. For Armstrong's career, see above, ch. II, n. 85.

62 National Executive, Minutes, 29 Mar. 1920: FOIF Papers, 6/3.

63 For Collins's offices in the Supreme Council, see above, ch. V, n. 51.

64 MC ['W. F.'] to HB ['J. W.'], 5 Mar. 1920: EdeVP, P 150/1125.

65 MC ['W. F.'] to HB ['J. W.'], 20 Mar., 26 Apr. 1920: EdeVP, P 150/1125.

[66] H. W. Quinlisk, alias Quinn, formerly a Corporal in the Royal Irish Regiment who joined Casement's Irish Brigade in Germany, acted as a double agent for Collins and Dublin Castle from 11 Nov. 1919 to 18 Feb. 1920, when he was 'executed' by Volunteers in Cork: Piaras Béaslaí, *Michael Collins and the Making of a New Ireland* (2 vols., Dublin, 1926), i, pp 394–401.

[67] HBD, 1 Nov. 1919, 25, 31 Jan., 20 Feb. 1920.

[68] MC to HB, 7 July 1919: EdeVP, P 150/1125. Like Harry, Collins was inclined to shed his IRB pseudonym in the course of writing, giving his signature as 'Mick' to a 'Memo from W. F.', 20 Mar. 1920: ibid.

[69] MC to HB, 25 Aug. 1919: EdeVP, P 150/1125.

[70] Extract from HB to MC, 26 Aug. 1919: Ó Murthuile, Memoir, f. 91.

[71] MC to HB, 10, 13 Sept., 6 Oct. 1919: EdeVP, P 150/1125. According to Ó Murthuile, Memoir, f. 92, the pressure for Collins's departure came from Brugha and Stack.

[72] Collins requested Patrick J. P. Tynan's *The Irish National Invincibles and their Times* (New York, 1894) and John Mitchel's *1641: Reply to the Falsification of History by James Anthony Froude* (Glasgow and London, circa 1870s; no American edn. located). Harry dutifully asked McGarrity for a copy of the latter work, but displeased Collins by sending him the English rather than American edition of Tynan. See MC to HB, 15 Dec. 1919; MC ['W. F.'] to HB ['J. W.'], 5 Mar. 1920: EdeVP, P 150/1125; HB to McG, 13 Jan. 1920: McGP, MS 17578.

[73] MC to HB, 7 July 1919: EdeVP, P 150/1125; Nunan to MC, 19 Aug. 1919: NAD, DE 2/292.

[74] MC to HB, 25 Aug., 15 Dec. 1919: EdeVP, P 150/1125.

[75] Undated extracts in Ó Murthuile, Memoir, f. 78. The original correspondence is unlocated. When alerting Harry to this production, Collins remarked that 'the Film was produced at a good number of Halls here and had a satisfactory effect. Of course it was really intended for America, where, I think, great use can be made of it.' See MC to HB, 5 Jan. 1920: EdeVP, P 150/1125. The film *Republican Bonds* was shot in 1919 at St. Enda's, Rathfarnham, during the making of *Willie Reilly and his Colleen Bawn* by the Film Co. of Ireland.

[76] MC to HB, 7 July 1919: EdeVP, P 150/1125.

[77] MC to HB, 5 Jan., 12 May 1920: EdeVP, P 150/1125.

[78] Runaidhe na hAireachta [Diarmuid O'Hegarty] to HB, 12 July 1919: EdeVP, P 150/1126. It seems that no such credentials from the Dáil were compiled until 24 Sept. 1921 (copy in BP). O'Hegarty also jested about the election campaign for South Roscommon and the manner of Harry's passage to New York: 'We note your quotation from Mr. Hayden, "I'm only a tramp tailor", but then you have an unfortunate knack of making mistakes about initial letters.'

[79] Fr. M. O'Flanagan to HB, 29 Aug. 1919: BP. O'Flanagan appears to have remained a sworn Fenian: 'You will be glad to know that I returned according to my own programme, without any sacrifice of principle. I am on the same footing as all the brethren.' The Bishop of Elphin, Dr. Bernard Coyne, had moved Fr. P. J. Murray to a curacy in the episcopal parish of Sligo: *Irish Catholic Directory* (Dublin, 1920 edn.), pp 290–2.

[80] Brennan to HB, 13 May 1919: EdeVP, P 150/1124.

[81] Report by Honorary Secretaries, in Annual Ard Chomhairle of Sinn Féin, 21st August, 1919, Résumé of Proceedings (duplicated): Barton Papers, MS 8786/1. At the Ard Fheis on 16 Oct., the Secretaries reiterated their praise for 'our untiring Honorary Secretary', who was 'also doing Trojan work in educating American opinion on the Irish question': Reports of Officers and Directors, idem.

[82] Liam W. McMahon to HB, 2 Sept. 1919: BP. McMahon, an agent for Donnelly's Irish Bacon, participated in the Lincoln Prison escapade: Kathleen Boland, Statement, f. 13.

[83] HBD, 8 Oct., 8 Dec. 1919. *East is West*, a banal comedy by Harold Shipman and John B. Hymer, set in San Francisco's Chinatown, was first performed at the Astor Theatre on 25 Dec. 1918. It was 'one of the greatest hits of the era', receiving 680 performances: Gerald Bordman, *The Oxford Companion to American Theatre* (New York, 1992; 1st edn. 1984), p. 221.

[84] HBD, 24 Jan. 1920.

[85] EdeV to Mrs Harold S. Bradley (née Celia Walsh), 30 Mar. 1955: NYPL, F. P. Walsh Papers, Box 29.

[86] MC to HB, 22 July 1919: EdeVP, P 150/1125.

[87] Nunan to MC, 11 Dec. 1919; MC to Nunan, 5 Jan. 1920: NAD, DE 2/292. Collins added that 'if you don't know this particular story there are several children's books in which you can look it up'.

[88] Phil [McMahon] to HB, 8 Sept. 1919: BP. McMahon's letter was sent from Harry's shop at 64, Middle Abbey St.

[89] HBD, 10 Oct. 1919.

[90] HBD, 31 Oct., 20, 22 Dec. 1919, 4 Jan., 4, 6, 26 Feb., 14 Mar., 3, 10 May 1920. *The Gold Diggers*, a comedy by Avery Hopwood, was first performed at the Lyceum Theatre on 30 Sept. 1919. Though reportedly a 'trivial hodge-podge of chorus girl slang, bedroom suggestiveness and false sentiment', it achieved no less than 720 performances: Bordman, *American Theatre*, pp 298–9.

[91] HBD, 2, 26 Nov. 1919, 1, 9 May 1920.

[92] James K. McGuire to Cohalan, 22 Sept. 1919: Cohalan Papers, 10/6; Katherine O'Doherty, *Assignment: America: De Valera's Mission to the United States* (New York, 1957), p. 50. This party was also entertained by the 'fiddle and songs' of Liam Mellows.

[93] HBD, 29 Dec. 1919. His diary for 27 Nov. 1919 simply stated 'I go to Football', before noting an enjoyable concert after Thanksgiving with F. P. Walsh and his family.

[94] Fan-Tan, from Chinese terms signifying division and spreading out, has two distinct forms – 'a Chinese betting game in which the players lay wagers on the number of counters that remain when a hidden pile of them has been divided by four'; and 'a card game in which sevens and their equivalent are played in sequence and the first player out of cards is the winner': *The American Heritage Dictionary* (Boston, 1985; 1st edn. 1969), p. 489. Since Harry had not yet had his 'first game of cards since left Ireland' (HBD, 21 Mar. 1920), he presumably played the Chinese version.

[95] HBD, 24 Nov. 1919, 2, 19 Jan., 21 Mar. 1920.

[96] Patrick McCartan, *With de Valera in America* (New York, 1932), p. 139.

[97] HBD, 12 May 1920.

[98] Unidentified recent newspaper cutting concerning visit by Harry and de Valera in '1921' and the origins of the Harry Boland Hurling Club, founded in Chicago in '1927'; inscription on plaque: 'To Kevin Boland on the occasion of his visit to Chicago for the Golden Jubilee Banquet of the Harry Boland Hurling Club, named in honor of Harry Boland in 1925; presented March 29, 1975': BP.

[99] HB to Ned Boland, 23 Sept. 1919.

[100] HBD, 20 Apr. 1920.

[101] Devoy to Cohalan, 16 July 1919: Cohalan Papers, 4/4.

[102] HB to McG, 26 July 1919: McGP, MS 17578. This 'breakdown' was also mentioned in Tomás Ua Conchubhair [Tommy O'Connor] to HB, 28 July 1919: BP.

[103] 'If Maloney is as good an agent as he is a doctor, England is to be congratulated on her man': HBD, 21 Nov. 1919.

[104] HBD, 24–28 Nov. 1919; 1 Apr. 1920.

[105] Muhammad Mahmud (1877–1941) soon repudiated his support for the revolutionary Wafd movement, founding a Constitutional Liberal Party in 1922.

According to a British assessment in 1927, 'he does not consider any Egyptian but himself clever enough to run the country without the English, and so wants to keep them there till he has maneuvered himself to the head of affairs': Arthur Goldschmidt, jun., *Historical Dictionary of Egypt* (Metuchen, N. J., 1994), pp 176–7.

106 McGP to HB, 20 Dec. 1919: EdeVP, P 150/1139; HB to McG, 20 Dec.: McGP, MS 17424/1; HBD, 25 Dec. Samuel Johnson's play, *Irene*, was first performed in 1749.

107 Unsigned letter (67, Drumcondra Road) to HB, 8 Jan. 1920: BP. The occupier at this address was a Mrs Margaret Nolan: *Thom's Official Directory of Great Britain and Ireland* (Dublin, 1919, 1927 edns.).

108 A 'personal' letter from 'Miss F.' (possibly Anna Fitzsimons of the Sinn Féin office or Cait Fraher from Dungarvan) was listed with despatches from Collins to be sent on 26 Apr. 1920, but (as Collins noted) was 'not enclosed': EdeVP, P 150/1125.

109 HB to KK, 9 Oct. 1919: *IGH*, p. 8. Those mentioned were Kitty's four siblings, along with their cousin Paul Dawson Cusack, a draper and Sinn Féin organiser in Granard.

110 Dáil Éireann, *Minutes of Proceedings, 1919–1921: Official Record* (Dublin, undated), p. 135 (19 June 1919). According to an illegibly signed letter sent to Kate Boland from the Mansion House on 21 May, 'before Harry went away he arranged that any money I would have to send it to you so I enclose cheque for £100': BP.

111 Kate Boland to HB, 3 July 1919. The Treaty of Versailles was signed on 28 June.

112 Ned Boland to HB, 2 July 1919. Collins was unable 'to fix up Ned', who could find nothing better in Dublin than 'clerking for Jim' [Clarke], a bookmaker. See MC to HB, 7 July: EdeVP, P 150/1125; HB to Ned Boland, 23 Sept.

113 Ned Boland to HB, 16 Aug. 1919; Kate Boland to HB, 28 Aug.; HB to Kate Boland, 30 Sept.; HB to Ned Boland, 23 Sept.

114 HBD, 29 Oct., 1 Nov., 8 Dec. 1919.

115 HB to EdeV, 4 June 1919: EdeVP, P 150/1132.

116 HB to Kate Boland, 8 July 1919: copy in EdeVP, P 150/1165.

117 MC to Nunan, 20 Mar. 1920: EdeVP, P 150/1125. In particular, as Collins explained, he was 'in a very depressed mood owing to the shocking murder of Tomás MacCurtain last night'.

118 HBD, 5 Dec. 1919, 4 Apr. 1920.

119 HBD, 31 Dec. 1919, 29 Feb., 30 Apr., 15 May 1920.

120 HBD, 12, 13 May 1920.

121 Downs collected Harry's wages for both trips: [Shanley], Reminiscences. He travelled on the American Line's *Philadelphia*, reaching Southamton on 24 May 1920: *The Times*, 18 May, p. 15; 26 May, p. 4 (Shipping Intelligence).

122 Neil Kerr, an associate of Collins since 1908 and his chief Liverpool arms agent, used his post in the Cunard Steamship Co. to recruit messengers and smuggle consignments between Liverpool and Dublin, as well as arranging clandestine passages to New York and organising the burning of warehouses in Liverpool (Nov. 1920): Béaslaí, *Michael Collins*, i, pp 217–18; ii, p. 98.

123 HBD, 14–27 May 1920. The entries for 16 May onwards were originally misdated.

CHAPTER VIII. TAKEOVER

1 HB, Diaries, 28 May 1920: EdeVP, P 150/1169a [hereafter, HBD]. Extracts relating to dates after 4 Aug. are taken from the less detailed 'date book' for 1920 (1169b).

2 Kate Boland to HB, 25 May 1920: BP.

[3] Seán Nunan apologised to Kathleen O'Connell for telling her 'a crammer' since he 'was told not to tell a soul' about Harry's departure; and James O'Mara, when given Harry's watch with its radium numerals for safe-keeping, had to tell his wife that he had bought it in Chicago. See Nunan to O'Connell, 3 July 1920: EdeVP, P 150/960; Joseph Cyrillus Walsh, 'Reminiscences of the Irish Movement for Independence, 1914–' (MSS, circa 1947), p. 229: NYPL, J. C. Walsh Papers, in slipcase.

[4] Joe Hyland and his brother Batt, proprietor of the Southern Motor Garage, 17 & 20 Denzille Lane, acted as Collins's 'personal transport officers': Piaras Béaslaí, Michael Collins and the Making of a New Ireland (2 vols., Dublin, 1926), i, p. 221; Thom's Official Directory of the United Kingdom of Great Britain and Ireland (Dublin, 1919 edn.).

[5] HBD, 28 May 1920.

[6] Robert Brennan, Allegiance (Dublin, 1950), p. 265.

[7] This presumably refers to the triumvirate running the IRB (Harry, Collins, and Ó Murthuile), not Sinn Féin's executive body, which had met without Harry's presence on the previous day: Minutes of Standing Committee, Sinn Féin, 1 June 1920: NLI microfilm, P 3269 [hereafter, SC Minutes]. Harry did attend such a meeting on 22 June, without making any recorded contribution.

[8] HBD, 2, 6 June 1920.

[9] Liam Lynch to Tom Lynch, 4 July 1920: Lynch Papers, NLI, MS 36251 (11).

[10] HBD, 5 June 1920.

[11] Seán Ó Murthuile, Memoir (typescript, circa 1928–31), p. 95: UCDA, Mulcahy Papers, P 7a/209. The date of Harry's visit is wrongly given as Sept. 1920, and a vital page presumably dealing with the conflict is missing from the typescript.

[12] Kathleen Clarke, Revolutionary Woman: Kathleen Clarke, 1878–1972, an Autobiography, ed. Helen Litton (Dublin, 1991), p. 174.

[13] Kate Boland to HB, 25 May 1920.

[14] HBD, 4 June 1920.

[15] The weapon was returned in 1993 to Harry Boland, jun., by the niece of Mrs Ellen Goodwin with whom Harry had left it.

[16] MC to Nunan, 12 June 1920: EdeVP, P 150/1125.

[17] HBD, 1, 7 June 1920.

[18] Dáil Ministry, Minutes, 31 May, 5 June, 6, 17 July, 4 Aug. 1920: NAD, DE 1/2, ff. 93, 99, 121, 131, 150. Though twice failed by O'Kelly, Gilbert Ward regularly signed his American letters with an Irish version of his name, as in 'G. Mac an Bhaird' to HB ['Bo'], 10 Mar. 1922: EdeVP, P 150/1171.

[19] Dáil Ministry, Minutes, 5 June 1920, ff. 98–9; Diarmuid O'Hegarty to EdeV, 8 June 1920: NAD, DE 2/245 (transcribed in Documents on Irish Foreign Policy, i (1919–1922), ed. Ronan Fanning et al. (Dublin, 1998) [hereafter, DIFP], p. 74). According to Brennan, it was he, not the Ministry, that rejected Harry's proposal for his transfer to the USA: Brennan, Allegiance, p. 265.

[20] Dáil Ministry, Minutes, 22 June 1920, f. 111.

[21] KK to HB, 31 May 1920: BP.

[22] Meda Ryan, Michael Collins and the Women in His Life (Cork, 1996), p. 57.

[23] HB to KK, 17 June 1920: In Great Haste: The Letters of Michael Collins and Kitty Kiernan, ed. León Ó Broin (Dublin, 1996; 1st edn. 1983) [hereafter, IGH], pp 8–9.

[24] HB to KK, 26 June 1920: extract in IGH, p. 10.

[25] Freeman's Journal, 28 June 1920, cutting in personal file on de Valera, item 84: PRO, CO 904/199. This stanza of Francis Scott Key's anthem was inscribed as follows during his detention on a British vessel bombarding Fort McHenry, Baltimore, in 1814: 'And where is that band who so vauntingly swore, / That the havoc of war and the battle's confusion / A home and a Country should leave us no more? / Their

blood has wash'd out their foul footstep's pollution. / No refuge could save the hireling and slave / From the terror of flight or the gloom of the grave.' See *Encyclopedia Americana* (30 vols., Danburg, Conn., 1990 edn.), xxv, pp 609–10.

26 HBD, 23–27 June 1920.

27 HB to Cathal Brugha, 11 Aug. 1920: EdeVP, P 150/1128. The *Philadelphia* left Southampton on 26 June, reaching New York 9 days later: *The Times*, 28 June, p. 24; 8 July, p. 24 (Shipping Intelligence).

28 HBD, 5 July 1920.

29 HBD, 9 July 1920. The Republicans had rejected de Valera's uncompromising plank in Chicago on 8 June, while in early July the Democratic Party's convention in San Francisco rebuffed an amended undertaking making reference to 'recognition': Charles Callan Tansill, *America and the Fight for Irish Freedom, 1866–1922: An Old Story Based upon New Data* (New York, 1957), pp 374–83.

30 HBD, 7, 12 July 1920.

31 Nunan to MC, 27 May, 10 July 1920: NAD, DE 2/292.

32 HB to KK, 18 Sept. 1920: BP.

33 HB to MC, 5 Nov. 1920: EdeVP, P 150/1125.

34 HBD, 26 July, 1, 2 Aug., 5 Sept. 1920.

35 HB to Kathleen O'Connell, 16 July, 9 Sept. 1920: O'Connell Papers, UCDA, P 155/115/1, 2. When she left New York for London and Dublin on New Year's Day, Kathleen noted in her diary that she was 'seen off by Harry Boland': O'Connell Papers, P 155/138.

36 HB to KK, 18 Sept. 1920: BP. After their arrival, Harry felt that 'we have now a good group to keep things moving'.

37 HBD, 23 July 1920.

38 Patricia Lavelle, *James O'Mara: A Staunch Sinn-Féiner, 1873–1948* (Dublin, 1961), pp 177, 180.

39 An exclamation in his diary ('Dr. Gertrude Kelly – WOW!') suggests that Harry did not reciprocate her aversion: HBD, 5 Sept. 1920. Dr. Gertrude B. Kelly, a veteran of the United Irish League and Cumann na mBan in New York, and a founder of the Irish Progressive League in 1917, supported the republican cause in the Civil War: Francis M. Carroll, *American Opinion and the Irish Question, 1910–23* (Dublin, 1978), pp 48, 67, 239; Joanne Mooney Eichacker, *Irish Republican Women in America: Lecture Tours, 1916–1925* (Dublin, 2003), p. 171.

40 Soon after reaching New York in autumn 1921, James Douglas of the Irish White Cross, a teetotaller, learned 'that the head waiter in Shanley's restaurant would provide me with any liquor I might require'. The waiter later claimed to have 'organised the smuggling of de Valera into the USA': *Memoirs of Senator James G. Douglas (1887–1954): Concerned Citizen*, ed. J. Anthony Gaughan (Dublin, 1998), p. 71.

41 Devoy to Cohalan, 17 Oct. 1920: AIHS, Cohalan Papers, 4/5.

42 HB to KK, 12 Aug. 1920: BP. Harry eventually revisited the Indian Reserve and Fr. Gordon (the Indian priest) in early Oct., but the promised gifts did not arrive. See HBD, 3 Oct. 1920; KK to HB, 15 Apr. 1921: BP.

43 HB to KK, 18 Sept. 1920: BP. 'The Mimber' doubtless alludes to his performance as MP for South Roscommon.

44 The Royal Dublin Society's August show, ostensibly of horses, was above all a social spectacle.

45 HB to KK, 24 Sept. 1920: BP.

46 MC to HB, 17 Nov. 1920 (receipt marked 5 Dec.): EdeVP, P 150/1125; *IGH*, pp 10–11.

47 KK to HB, 15 Apr. 1921: BP.

48 HB to McG, 3 Aug. 1920: McGP, NLI, MS 17424/1.
49 HB to Griffith, 11 Aug. 1920: EdeVP, P 150/727.
50 HBD, 18 July 1920.
51 Mary McSwiney and her brother's widow Muriel reached New York in the *Celtic* on 4 Dec. 1920. They were met by Harry at Pier 60, West 19th St., welcomed by a committee of 500 women, and mobbed by 10,000 supporters: Eichacker, *Irish Republican Women*, p. 95.
52 J. C. Walsh, Reminiscences, f. 195.
53 HBD, 18, 20 Dec. 1920.
54 John T. Ryan ['Your Cousin'] to McG ['Phil'], 21 June 1920: McGP, MS 17486/1. Parley Parker Christensen, candidate of the Farmer-Labor ('Third') Party, secured only 265,411 votes at the presidential election on 2 Nov., less than a third of those supporting the third-placed Socialist, Eugene Victor Debs. The Farmer-Labor Party was launched at the Chicago convention on 13 July: James T. Havel, *U.S. Presidential Candidates and the Elections: A Biographical and Historical Guide* (2 vols., New York, 1996), ii, pp 106, 109, 113.
55 John Fitzpatrick acted as 'Keynoter' for the Third Party's convention, held in Chicago (13–15 July 1920) at Morrison's Hotel and Carmen's Hall. Fitzpatrick (1870–1946), who emigrated as a child from Athlone to Chicago, was a militant but anti-Communist organiser for the American Federation of Labor from 1902, and President of the Chicago Federation of Labor (1899–1901, 1905–46). He promoted 'federated unionism', bypassing conventional labour organisations (1917–22). The short-lived Farmer-Labor Party was a product of his unavailing attempt to launch an American Labor Party (1918–23): *Dictionary of American Biography, Supplement Four: 1946–50*, ed. John A. Garraty and Edward T. James (New York, 1974), pp 279–80.
56 HBD, 10–13 July 1920.
57 Dáil Ministry, Minutes, 9 Oct. 1920: NAD, DE 1/3, f. 13.
58 HBD, 4 Aug. 1920.
59 HB to McG, 3 Aug. 1920: McGP, MS 17424/1. The 'Coercion Bill' was embodied in the Restoration of Order in Ireland Act (assented 9 Aug. 1920) which extended and amplified wartime curtailment of civil liberties.
60 T. M. Reddy (New York) to Chief, Bureau of Investigation (for attention of J. Edgar Hoover), 25 June 1921, giving extracts from 'a letter sent to Agent Scully from a confidential source', 23 Sept. 1920: NAW, Records of Bureau of Investigation, 52-505/88 (microform M 1085/910). Other guests dining in Helen and Peter Golden's apartment, at the corner of Amsterdam Ave. and 121st St., included Mellows, Padraic and Mary Colum, Fawsitt, and Laurence Ginnell. No corresponding entry appears in HBD, which was not regularly filled out at this period.
61 HB to MC, [12 Aug. 1920]: EdeVP, P 150/1125.
62 HBD, 27, 28, 31 July 1920.
63 The Committee's Treasurer was the ubiquitous Larry Rice, the source of 'more trouble': HBD, 31 Aug., 6, 7 Sept. 1920; National Executive, Minutes, 7 Sept.: AIHS, FOIF Papers, 6/3.
64 HBD, 8 Aug. 1920; HB to Cathal Brugha, 11 Aug.: EdeVP, P 150/1128.
65 HBD, 14 July 1920.
66 HBD, 3 Aug. 1920.
67 McG, Diary, 16 May 1920: McGP, MS 17551/3. McGarrity, still confined to his 'sick room', noted after meeting de Valera that 'H. B. is gone to Ireland. Brave boy Dr. is to go to Russian Lake to go on a rest.'
68 HB to McCartan, 9 Aug. 1920: EdeVP, P 150/1137.
69 Receipt, 29 Oct. 1920: NAD, Department of the Taoiseach, S 14205 (copy in BP). The cash was withdrawn from an account in the Hudson Co. Bank, using a cheque

in Harry's favour dated 22 Oct., authorisation for the loan being given to Harry by de Valera on 27 Oct.: documents in EdeVP, P 150/1321 (copy of authorisation in *DIFP*, p. 98).

70 Diarmuid O'Hegarty to HB, 24 Aug. 1920: EdeVP, P 150/1126.

71 Patrick McCartan, *With de Valera in America* (New York, 1932), pp 219–21.

72 McCartan, Memorandum, June 1921: NAD, Department of Foreign Affairs, Early Series, 32/228 (transcribed in *DIFP*, pp 148–56, where Nuorteva is misrendered as 'Nuratova').

73 MC to HB, 15 Oct. 1920: EdeVP, P 150/1125.

74 HBD, 25 Oct., 21, 22 Nov. 1920.

75 HBD, 17 July 1920.

76 He subsequently learned that 'Seán [Nunan]'s captured letters have not done any harm': HBD, 7, 15, 17 July 1920.

77 HBD, 22 July 1920. 'G.' may have been Gordon Rorke, intermediary in Harry's acquisition of Thompson sub-machine-guns.

78 HB to Brugha, 11 Aug. 1920: EdeVP, P 150/1128.

79 [HB] to MC ['Field'], *circa* 12 Aug. 1920: EdeVP, P 150/1125.

80 HB to MC, 27 Aug. 1920: EdeVP, P 150/1125.

81 HB to MC, 22 Sept., and reply, 15 Oct. 1920: EdeVP, P 150/1125.

82 Brugha ['Porter'] to HB ['Cowe'], 17 Nov. 1920; Brugha, letter (in Irish) giving authority to HB, 17 Nov.: EdeVP, P 150/1128.

83 O'Mara to EdeV, 16 Sept., and reply, 1 Oct. 1920: EdeVP, P 150/1204.

84 MC to Nunan, 30 Sept. 1920: NAD, DE 2/292; HB to MC, 4 Nov.: EdeVP, P 150/1125; L. Lanier Wilson (American Embassy, London) to W. L. Hurley (State Department), 9 Dec.: NAW, RG 59, Department of State, Records of the Office of the Counselor [hereafter, ROC], 841.D/141.

85 William Lahey (Chief Insp., Police Department, New York) to W. L. Hurley, 11 Jan. 1921: NAW, ROC, 841.D/177.

86 Dáil Ministry, Minutes, 23 Oct., 6 Nov. 1920: DE 1/3, ff. 29, 35. The second decision was phrased with appropriate care: 'Defence (b) England. C. B.'s scheme approved as far as industrial part is concerned. President to be consulted about remainder.' It appears from Brugha's correspondence that he had previously discussed industrial sabotage with Harry, and assassinations with de Valera. Harry's reference to Brugha's request was enigmatic: 'Crisis; Chief: decision for Cathal.' See Brugha ['Porter'] to EdeV ['Cahan'] and to HB ['Cowe'], 17 Nov.: EdeVP, P 150/1128; HBD, 5 Dec.

87 HB to McG, 6 Nov. 1920: McGP, MS 17641. The American fund of 'the Wolfe Tone and United Irishmen Memorial Association' was among the IRB's major assets.

88 HB to O'Mara, *circa* 30 Oct. 1920: O'Mara Papers, NLI, MS 21548/4.

89 HB to MC, 4 Nov. 1920: EdeVP, P 150/1125.

90 HBD, 29 Dec. 1920; Carroll, *American Opinion*, p. 32. The Committee for Relief, which raised $5,250,000, was a product of the American Commission on Conditions in Ireland (sitting between 18 Nov. 1920 and 21 Jan. 1921), itself the outcome of a 'Committee of 150' American fellow-travellers, established on 9 Oct. 1920 to investigate charges of British atrocities in Ireland: Eichacker, *Irish Republican Women*, pp 92–4.

91 Circular from Lynch to FOIF, 10 Nov. 1920: McGP, MS 17658/2. In defending the National Council against charges of 'dilatoriness' following its failure to act on a previous circular of 22 Oct., Lynch cited a succession of broken undertakings by Harry between 30 Oct. and 2 Nov.

92 HBD, 5, 6 Nov. 1920; Arthur Mitchell, *Revolutionary Government in Ireland: Dáil Éireann, 1919–22* (Dublin, 1995), p. 148.

93 Carroll, *American Opinion*, p. 152; receipt, 22 July 1920: BP.
94 MC to HB, 14 Aug. 1920: EdeVP, P 150/1125.
95 HB to MC, 22 Sept., and reply, 15 Oct. 1920: EdeVP P 150/1125.
96 Up to Dec. 1920, the Dáil's Trustees had recorded receipts of £186,447 from the External Loan: EdeVP, P 150/1140 (former number).
97 Bishop Michael Fogarty to EdeV, 14 Nov. 1920; EdeV to O'Mara, with enclosures, 10 Dec.: NLI, O'Mara Papers, MS 21548/3, 4. Harry and McGarrity were among the four co-signatories for all bank deposits, each requiring two signatures for a withdrawal. Together, they also shared nominal custody of all three safe-deposits of Liberty Bonds. In late Nov., the Dáil Ministry had sanctioned a reserve of only $500,000 in Liberty Bonds, and had agreed that 'Irish Govt. must be responsible for expenditure of all relief collected' by 'De Valera's organisation'. See Dáil Ministry, Minutes, 20 Nov.: NAD, DE 1/3, f. 43.
98 O'Mara to EdeV, 1 Dec. 1920: McGP, MS 17522. An estimate of $500,000 was allocated to 'advances for food ships or relief committee (D. Fawsitt)', possibly referring to Fawsitt's grandiose scheme for buying part of a shipping line (Moore & McCormack).
99 Devoy to Cohalan, 15 July 1920: Cohalan Papers, 4/5.
100 McGuire to Devoy, 16 July 1920: Devoy Papers, NLI, MS 15416/4. McGuire had temporarily replaced the peripatetic John T. Ryan as Chairman (equivalent to President of the Supreme Council). The true location of power within the Clan was revealed by Devoy's observation to Cohalan in the same file (17 July): 'We'll have to accept his resignation and put [John Archdeacon] Murphy in his place.'
101 HB to Devoy, 17 July 1920, with acrimonious subsequent exchanges: EdeVP, P 150/1154; HBD, 21 July 1920. McGarrity and Montague represented the districts of Philadelphia and Passaic, New Jersey, on the Clan's Executive. See HB to Supreme Council, undated [*circa* Sept. 1921]: EdeVP, P 150/1155.
102 Devoy to Cohalan, 20 July 1920: Devoy Papers, MS 15416/4; Devoy to Cohalan, 23 July: Cohalan Papers, 4/5.
103 Devoy to Cohalan, 3 Aug. 1920: Devoy Papers, MS 15416/4; Devoy to HB, 5 Aug., and HB to Devoy, 11 Aug.: EdeVP, P 150/1154.
104 A copy of this version of the resolutions, typed by Devoy and annotated with a note ascribed to HB that 'I approve the above resolutions', is appended to Devoy to HB, 17 Aug. 1920: EdeVP, P 150/1154. Count Plunkett's specific denunciations of Irish-American leaders were eventually deleted on de Valera's proposal: Dáil Éireann, *Minutes of Proceedings, 1919–1921: Official Record* (Dublin, undated), p. 250 (25 Jan. 1921).
105 James K. McGuire to Cohalan, 19 Aug. 1920: Cohalan Papers, 10/7.
106 John Archdeacon Murphy (a layman) represented the Buffalo district on the Clan's Executive, and was intended by Devoy to succeed McGuire as its Chairman (see above, ch. VIII, n. 100).
107 Devoy to Cohalan, 16, 18 Aug. 1920: Devoy Papers, MS 15416/4.
108 Lynch to Cohalan, 25 Aug. 1920: Cohalan Papers, 3/1.
109 Devoy to HB, 17 Aug. 1920: EdeVP, P 150/1154. The novelist Charles Joseph Kickham (1828–82) was President of the Supreme Council (*circa* 1874–82).
110 HB to MC, 27 Aug., 22 Sept. 1920: EdeVP, P 150/1125. 'The Chicago business' refers to de Valera's conflict with Cohalan at the Republican Party's convention.
111 'Substance of Agreement' of 15 Aug. 1920: McGP, MS 17521/2.
112 Devoy to Cohalan, 24 Sept. 1920: Cohalan Papers, 4/5.
113 MC ['Field'] to HB ['Woods'], 1 Oct. ('for the Executive C. na G.'), 15 Oct. 1920: EdeVP, P 150/1125. Harry had requested further support from the Supreme Council on 22 Sept.: EdeVP, P 150/1155.

114 Devoy to Cohalan, 19 Oct. 1920: Cohalan Papers, 4/5.

115 EdeV to HB, 21 Oct. 1920: Gallagher Papers, NLI, MS 18375/15; HB to editor, *Gaelic American*, 22 Oct. (typescript): EdeVP, P 150/1154.

116 *Gaelic American*, 30 Oct. 1920, pp 1, 8. Devoy also dismissed the Home Body's claim to revolutionary seniority: 'The I.R.B. is not the parent organization of the Clan-na-Gael. The Fenian Brotherhood in America was the parent of both.'

117 James Quinn (Torrington, Conn.) to HB, '7 Oct.' [*recte*, Nov.] 1920; S. J. Dunleavy (Freeport, NY) to HB, 27 Oct.: EdeVP, P 150/1157.

118 Eamon S. Garrity (Medford, Mass.) to HB, 23 Nov. 1920: EdeVP, P 150/1157.

119 HB to MC, 4 Nov. 1920, and reply, 19 Nov.: EdeVP, P 150/1125.

120 Ó Murthuile, Memoir, f. 96.

121 McG to Clan Officers (District 12) and duplicated resolution by FOIF local council (Philadelphia), 23 June 1920: McGP, MS 17521/2, 3.

122 HB to MC, 4 Nov. 1920: EdeVP, P 150/1125. Harry could not contact the Clansmen personally, 'as Devoy refused to give me the names and addresses'.

123 Draft circular, 11 Nov. 1920: EdeVP, P 150/1155. Reorganisation was seriously impeded by the difficulty of securing the Clan's mailing lists. Those named and expelled were Devoy, Murphy, McGarry, Martin Joseph Liddy (Indianapolis), and Michael B. McGreal (New Haven). The unnamed loyalists were McGuire, McGarrity, and Montague (the Treasurer). See HB to Supreme Council, undated [*circa* Sept. 1921]: EdeVP, P 150/1156.

124 Devoy to Dillon, 12 Nov. 1920: McGP, MS 17610/2.

125 Draft circular, HB to Clan, 12 Nov. 1920: McGP, MS 17578.

126 Circular, Executive to Clan, 15 Nov. 1920: McGP, MS 17521.

127 James [K. McGuire] to HB, 16 Nov. 1920: EdeVP, P 150/1157.

128 HB to MC, 10 Dec. 1920: EdeVP, P 150/1125.

129 Mary F. McWhorter (Chicago; President, Ladies' Auxiliary, AOH of America) to McG, 16 Dec. 1920: McGP, MS 17609/1.

130 Maloney to McGarrity, 1 July 1920: McGP, MS 17621. The Carmelite Fr. O'Connor confided that Cohalan had 'told his henchmen to lie low and stick together', while a Fr. Tierney gathered that Cohalan 'was much maligned, especially by women in my [Maloney's] entourage'.

131 McCartan to McGarrity, 12 July 1920: McGP, MS 17457/13.

132 HBD, 16, 19 July 1920. At the end of July, Harry had a 'smart passage at arms with Judge', while de Valera, showing himself 'determined to have full publicity on recent events, asks for a democratisation of the F.O.I.F. and Race Convention': HBD, 30, 31 July 1920.

133 Copy of Lynch to Cohalan, 25 Aug. 1920: Cohalan Papers, 3/1.

134 National Council, Minutes, 17 Sept. 1920: FOIF Papers, 8/7.

135 Devoy to Cohalan, 18 Sept. 1920: Cohalan Papers, 4/5. Devoy's informant was Harry's old adversary, Larry Rice.

136 John D. Moore to Cohalan, 19 Sept. 1920: Cohalan Papers, 11/11.

137 National Council, Minutes, 8 Nov. 1920: FOIF Papers, 6/3.

138 Constitution, 16 Nov. 1920: NYPL, Maloney Papers, 9/145.

139 Diarmuid Lynch, *The I.R.B. and the 1916 Insurrection*, ed. Florence O'Donoghue (Cork, 1957), p. 214.

140 John F. Buckley (Scranton) to McG, 13 Oct. 1920: Villanova University, Philadelphia, McGP, 1/2; HBD, 27, 28 Nov. 1920, referring to 'F.O.I.F. merger'.

141 J. C. Walsh, Reminiscences, ff. 192–9. According to Walsh, de Valera had aimed merely to match the current membership of the Friends (reportedly, 69,000).

142 HB to EdeV, 29 Oct. 1920: EdeVP, P 150/1132; HB to MC, 4 Nov.: EdeVP, P 150/1125.

[143] HB to KK, 18 Sept. 1920: BP.
[144] Sinéad de Valera to Kathleen O'Connell, 18 Nov. 1920: O'Connell Papers, UCDA, P 155/4 (extract kindly supplied by Dr. Patrick Murray).
[145] [HB] to MC ['Field'], *circa* 12 Aug. 1920: EdeVP, P 150/1125.
[146] HB to MC, 6 Dec. 1920: EdeVP, P 150/1125.
[147] McG, Memorandum, 9–10 Dec. 1920: McGP, MS 17439/2.
[148] Translation in caption to photograph: Andrew Brasier and John Kelly, *Harry Boland: A Man Divided* (Dublin, 2000), after p. 52.
[149] EdeV to HB, [?11] Dec. 1920: EdeVP, P 150/1132 (copy kindly supplied by Dr. Patrick Murray).
[150] EdeV to Nunan, 10 Dec. 1920: EdeVP, P 150/1739 (former number).
[151] Seán Nunan, 'President Éamon de Valera's Mission to the United States of America, 1919–1920', pp 248–9, in *Capuchin Annual*, xxxvii (1970), pp 236–49; *New York Times*, 17 Dec. 1920, p. 19; 19 Dec., p. 3; 20 Dec., p. 15; 28 Dec., p. 4.
[152] Paraphrase of telegram, Gloster Armstrong (New York) to Foreign Office, 20 Dec. 1920; Minute by 'W. M.', 20 Dec.: PRO, Home Office, Registered Papers (Supplementary), HO 144/10309/315944/18, 19. De Valera reached Dublin early on 23 Dec.: Tim Pat Coogan, *De Valera: Long Fellow, Long Shadow* (London, 1993), p. 196.
[153] *New York Times*, 1 Jan. 1921, p. 1. Harry's satisfaction was expressed in his diary: 'Release de Valera's story, secure great press for same.' See HBD, 31 Dec. 1920.
[154] HBD, 25 Dec. 1920.

CHAPTER IX. ANTICLIMAX

[1] *New York Times*, 4 Jan. 1921, p. 17; 6 Jan., p. 6.
[2] McG, Diary, 5, 6 Jan. 1921, with cutting, evidently from *Philadelphia Public Ledger*, 6 Jan.: McGP, NLI, MS 17551/4. Similar views were indeed expressed by EdeV to HB, 1 Jan., in Epitome of Seized Documents (D1), f. 56: PRO, CO 904/23/7.
[3] Corrected typescript (published in *Irish Press* (Philadelphia), 15 Jan. 1921, p. 3): McGP, NLI, MS 17578.
[4] Slightly variant report: *New York Times*, 7 Jan. 1921, p. 2.
[5] *New York Times*, 7 Jan. 1921, p. 2; 8 Jan., p. 10.
[6] J. E. Hoover (Special Assistant to Attorney-General) to W. L. Hurley (State Department), 12 Jan. 1921: NAW, RG 59, Department of State, Records of the Office of the Counselor [hereafter, ROC], 841.D/177.
[7] The Daughters of the American Revolution, founded in Washington (1890) and chartered by Congress (1896), are restricted to lineal descendants of those aiding or serving in the War of Independence: *Encyclopedia Americana* (30 vols., Danburg, Conn., 1990 edn.), viii, p. 522.
[8] 'Chief' [L. J. Baley?] to T. M. Reddy (New York), 12 Jan. 1921, with associated correspondence: NAW, RG 65, Records of [Federal] Bureau of Investigation [hereafter, RBI], 202997-22 (microform M 1085/942); semi-literate denunciation from Bridgeport, Conn., to Assistant Secretary of State (Washington), 18 Jan.: NAW, ROC, 841.D/139.
[9] *New York Times*, 8 Jan. 1921, p. 2; 10 Jan., p. 10.
[10] HB, Diary, 7, 8 Jan. 1921: EdeVP, P 150/1169c [hereafter, HBD]. By 13 Jan., however, Harry's self-righteousness had somewhat recovered: 'Not a single Irish man or woman outside of John Devoy have [sic.] criticised my Madison Garden speech.'
[11] Notes, in HB's hand, for undated address to a 'great gathering of the Race': BP.
[12] HB to O'Mara, 14 Apr. 1921: O'Mara Papers, NLI, MS 21549/4. Nunan was 'doubtful', and O'Mara 'struck out' the passage when asked for his adjudication.

[13] HB to EdeV, 13 Jan. 1921, and reply: extracts in Jim Maher, *Harry Boland: A Biography* (Cork, 1998), pp 136–7 (citing EdeVP, P 150/1132).

[14] HBD, 15 Feb. 1921.

[15] HB to Walsh, 19 Jan. 1921: NYPL, Maloney Papers, 7/115; HB to Walsh, 12 Feb.: NYPL, F. P. Walsh Papers, Box 29.

[16] Walsh to Bainbridge Colby (Secretary of State), 21 Jan. 1921: Maloney Papers, 7/115.

[17] Milholland to Walsh, 26 Feb. 1921: F. P. Walsh Papers, Box 29. Four months later, Harry himself was regaled 'with schemes' by Milholland on the train from Washington to New York: HBD, 17 June.

[18] Undated drawing, *circa* 24 Mar. 1921: F. P. Walsh Papers, Box 29.

[19] Walsh to O'Mara, 11 Apr. 1921: F. P. Walsh Papers, Box 29. Kinkead (1876–1960) became first Vice-President of the Association's National Policy Committee. He was thrice elected as a Democrat to the House of Representatives (New Jersey, 1909–15), but was soundly defeated at his last attempt in Nov. 1916.

[20] Several attempts were made to rescue the imprisoned Seán McKeown, the fabled 'Blacksmith of Ballinalee', whose execution (following his sentence for murder on 14 June) seemed imminent. Republican participation in the subsequent Peace Conference was made conditional on his release, which occurred on 8 Aug.

[21] HBD, 9 Apr., 7 May, 16 June 1921.

[22] HB to EdeV, 20 July 1921: NAD, Department of Foreign Affairs, Early Series [hereafter, DFA, ES], 27/158 (also transcribed in *Documents on Irish Foreign Policy*, i (1919–1922), ed. Ronan Fanning et al. (Dublin, 1998) [hereafter, *DIFP*], p. 174). The passage immediately following this report was cut out in accordance with a departmental instruction ('parts of above to be destroyed'). Joseph Scott and F. P. Walsh had met Harding a week earlier: HBD, 13 July.

[23] HB to Robert Brennan, 20 July 1921: EdeVP, P 150/1124.

[24] *Chicago Herald*, 4, 8 Mar. 1921: cuttings in O'Mara Papers, MS 21549/3; programme in McGP, MS 17641.

[25] Mary McSwiney to O'Mara, 15 Mar. 1921: O'Mara Papers, MS 21549/3; assessment by Joseph Cyrillus Walsh, 'Reminiscences of the Irish Movement for Independence, 1914–' (MSS, *circa* 1947), f. 213: NYPL, J. C. Walsh Papers, in slipcase.

[26] McSwiney to HB, 26 Jan. 1921: EdeVP, P 150/655. Ten weeks later, Catherine Flanagan's devotion was rewarded. 'Meet Mary McSwiney – splendid woman – wonderful tour ended. Take Miss McS. and Catherine to lunch': HBD, 8 Apr.

[27] McSwiney to James O'Mara, 11 Feb. 1921, and to HB, 12 Feb.: O'Mara Papers, MS 21549/2.

[28] Walsh to HB, 2 Apr. 1921: EdeVP, P 150/1140.

[29] McSwiney to EdeV, 25 Apr. 1921, in Epitome of Seized Documents (H4), f. 76: CO 904/23/7.

[30] 'Magna est veritas et praevalet' ('Great is truth and it prevails'): 3 Esdras iv: 41 (Vulgate *Apocrypha*). This proverb is sometimes rendered in the future tense ('praevalebit').

[31] HB to McSwiney, 26 July 1921, and reply, 3 Aug.: McSwiney Papers, UCDA, P48a/115/50, 56.

[32] J. C. Walsh (Chicago) to Frank P. Walsh (Washington), 5 Mar. 1921: F. P. Walsh Papers, Box 29.

[33] HB to O'Mara, 1 Mar. 1921: O'Mara Papers, MS 21549/3.

[34] O'Mara to HB ['Mac'], 18 Mar. 1921: O'Mara Papers, MS 21549/3.

[35] John D. Ryan (1864–1933), from Michigan, headed the Anaconda and Chile Copper Mining Cos., and was a Director of the National City Bank of New York and the Emigrants' Industrial Savings Bank. He became Wilson's Director of Aircraft

Production, and later of the Air Service, in 1918. Nicholas Frederic Brady (1878–1930), from Albany, NY, chaired two Edison Cos. and was also associated with the National City Bank. Edward Laurence Doheny (1856–1935), from Wisconsin, became the world's largest producer of crude oil through his Pan American Petroleum and Transport Co., the holding company for his ventures in Mexico, California, and elsewhere. He contributed heavily to Wilson's election fund in 1912 and was considered as a Democratic vice-presidential candidate in 1920. He escaped conviction for corruption after lending the Secretary of the Interior $100,000 in 1924 while negotiating an oil lease in Elk Hills, California (an element of the 'Teapot Dome' scandal). Morgan Joseph O'Brien (1852–1937), from New York City, a Judge in New York State (1887–1906) and corporate lawyer, actively supported Democratic politicians such as Grover Cleveland and Franklin Delano Roosevelt. See *Who was Who in America*, i (1897–1942) (Chicago, 1943), pp 1070, 129; *American National Biography*, ed. John A. Garraty and Mark C. Carnes (24 vols., New York, 1999), vi, pp 700–1; xvi, pp 592–3.

36 HB to MC, 20 July 1921: EdeVP, P 150/1125.
37 HB ['Mac'] to O'Mara, 25 Mar. 1921, and reply, 29 Mar.: O'Mara Papers, MS 21549/3.
38 HBD, 15 Apr. 1921. 'Young Scotland' may have been an offshoot of the Young Scots Society, founded in 1900 with the purpose of 'educating young men in the fundamental principles of Liberalism and of encouraging them in the study of social science and economics'. Between 1905 and 1914, 30 of its members were elected to the House of Commons, as Liberals seeking 'Home Rule' for Scotland: T. M. Devine, *The Scottish Nation, 1700–2000* (London, 1999), pp 306–7.
39 HBD, 6 June 1921; *New York Times*, 20 June, p. 15; HB to Robert Brennan, 20 July: EdeVP, P 150/1124.
40 HBD, 20 Jan. 1921.
41 Undated instructions in code to HB ['Mr. Cowe'], referring to Martens, McGarry, and Mexico as 'Mr. Northman's manager here', 'Bison', and 'Tirhess': BP. 'Bo' or 'Bó' (meaning 'cow' in Irish) was another of Harry's soubriquets.
42 McCartan ['Henry Anderson'] to HB, 8 Feb. 1921: EdeVP, P 150/1131; McCartan to McG, 10 Feb.: McGP, MS 17457/13.
43 HB to McCartan ['Anderson'], 4 Apr. 1921: EdeVP, P 150/1131; HB to MC, 31 Mar., replying to MC's instruction to send O'Callaghan to Russia, 8 Mar.: EdeVP, P 150/1125. Harry again discussed sending O'Callaghan to Russia over dinner with Charles Recht in mid May: HBD, 14, 16 May.
44 EdeV to HB, 8 Apr. 1921: EdeVP, P 150/1132.
45 Eamonn Martin (Berlin) to HB, 5 Apr. 1921: BP; McCartan, Memorandum, June: *DIFP*, pp 148–56 (citing DFA, ES, 32/228).
46 J. C. Walsh to O'Mara, 17 Jan. 1921: J. C. Walsh Papers, 2/4.
47 EdeV to HB, 30 May 1921: *DIFP*, pp 145–6 (citing DFA, ES, 27/158).
48 EdeV to HB, undated draft: EdeVP, P 150/1132. As the ever-reflective author admitted on 1 Apr. 1963, a 'casual reading' might confirm Cohalan's charge against de Valera of dictation to Irish-America.
49 HBD, 17 Feb., 18 Mar., 6 Apr. 1921.
50 HB to O'Mara, 4 Apr. 1921, and reply, 7 Apr.: O'Mara Papers, MS 21549/4.
51 HB to MC, 14 Apr. 1921: EdeVP, P 150/1125.
52 James O'Mara ['Ben'] to HB, 3 Apr. 1921: O'Mara Papers, MS 21549/4. Edward L. Doheny, the oil magnate, was elected President.
53 J. C. Walsh, Reminiscences, ff. 217–23.
54 Agnes O'Mara, Diary, 16–20 Apr. 1921: extracts in O'Mara Papers, MS 21549/4.
55 HBD, 16–20 Apr. 1921.

56 HB to EdeV, 28 Apr. 1921: 'main points' in EdeVP, P 150/1132.

57 Stephen M. O'Mara to EdeV, 12 Aug. 1921: extract in DFA, ES, 27/170.

58 EdeV to James O'Mara, 1 Mar. 1921; O'Mara to HB, 31 Mar.; EdeV to O'Mara, 24 Mar.: O'Mara Papers, MS 21549/3.

59 Diarmuid Lynch to FOIF, 5 Jan. 1921: McGP, MS 17658/3; Mary F. McWhorter to McG, 5 May: McGP, MS 17653/1.

60 *Irish Press* (Philadelphia), 26 Feb. 1921, p. 3.

61 HB to O'Mara, after 26 Mar. 1921: F. P. Walsh Papers, Box 29.

62 HBD, 14 Jan., 13 Apr. 1921; *Memoirs of Senator James G. Douglas (1887–1954): Concerned Citizen*, ed. J. Anthony Gaughan (Dublin, 1998), esp. pp 64–71.

63 HB to EdeV, 5 Aug. 1921: *DIFP*, p. 178 (citing DFA, ES, 27/158). He urged de Valera to press the Executive of the White Cross to broaden its Irish operations and spend the available funds, so demonstrating the vitality of American support for the Republic, as well as benefiting the Irish economy (p. 179). In the event, the White Cross confined itself to personal relief and avoided outlay on 'reconstruction'.

64 Dáil Ministry, Minutes, 6 Apr. 1921: NAD, DE 1/3, f. 94.

65 EdeV to HB, 8 Apr. 1921, with 'main points' of reply, 28 Apr.: EdeVP, P 150/1132; EdeV to O'Mara, 8 Apr., in Epitome of Seized Documents (D14), f. 60: CO 904/23/7; report by Thomas F. Mullen (Chicago) for Bureau of Investigation, 18 Apr.: NAW, RBI, 202600-448 (microform 1085/928).

66 O'Mara to HB, 25 Apr. 1921: EdeVP, P 150/1138.

67 Agnes O'Mara, Diary, 29 Apr. 1921: extract in O'Mara Papers, MS 21549/4.

68 F. P. Walsh to O'Mara, 4 May 1921: F. P. Walsh Papers, Box 29; draft of HB to O'Mara, 11 May: BP.

69 HB to EdeV, 16 May 1921: abstract in EdeVP, P 150/1132 (copy in BP).

70 J. C. Walsh, Reminiscences, f. 227.

71 Undated note: O'Mara Papers, MS 21549/6.

72 HBD, 9, 12 May 1921; Dáil Ministry, Minutes, 25 May: DE 1/3, f. 105. The conflict with de Valera is amply documented in Patricia Lavelle, *James O'Mara: A Staunch Sinn-Féiner: 1873–1948* (Dublin, 1961), *passim*.

73 HBD, 18 June 1921.

74 EdeV to Stephen O'Mara, 13 'May' [June] 1921: typed copy in EdeVP, P 150/1211. In previous instructions sent on 26 May, which evidently went astray, de Valera had proposed retaining James as 'Financial Agent' to raise the Loan, while assigning the other functions to Stephen – an arrangement which would surely have precipitated a 'war of brothers'. See Epitome of Seized Documents (D21), f. 60: CO 904/23/7.

75 EdeV to HB, 29 Apr. 1921: EdeVP, P 150/1132.

76 Dáil Éireann, *Minutes of Proceedings, 1919–1921: Official Record* (Dublin, undated), p. 290 (10 May 1921). The Dáil confirmed the expenditure reported by Collins, and added $250,000 to the American 'reserve'.

77 Extracts from MC to EdeV, 30 May 1921; EdeV to MC, 1 June; MC to EdeV, 4 June: DE 2/450.

78 MC, Statement of Receipts and Expenditure, 14 Aug. 1921: EdeVP, P 150/1140 (former number). The stated American balance excluded $500,000 designated as 'General Reserve'.

79 HB to National Directorate, 23 May 1921: Hearn Papers, NLI, MS 15991.

80 Only $622,720 was secured, mainly in Illinois: F. M. Carroll, *American Opinion and the Irish Question, 1910–23* (Dublin, 1978), pp 179, 282.

81 Mellows ['Bawn'] to James O'Mara, 6 Feb. 1921: O'Mara Papers, MS 21549/2.

82 Mellows ['Bawn'] to HB ['Cowe'], 16 Apr. 1921: EdeVP, P 150/1130. The 'goold in California' may allude to the long-rumoured arrival in America of Collins (in the persona of 'Gould' or 'Goold').

83 HB ['Bo'] to James O'Mara, 24 Feb. 1921: O'Mara Papers, MS 21549/2.
84 Fawsitt to EdeV, undated: EdeVP, P 150/1673 (former number); Fawsitt to HB, 13 Aug. 1921: EdeVP, P 150/1141.
85 Mary McSwiney to HB, 19 July 1921: EdeVP, P 150/1444 (former number).
86 Walsh to James O'Mara, 16 Apr. 1921: F. P. Walsh Papers, Box 29.
87 EdeV to HB, 7 Mar., 29 Apr. 1921: EdeVP, P 150/1132.
88 Laurence de Lacy, a journalist from Enniscorthy in Wexford and ex-editor of the *Irish Volunteer*, fled to America after the discovery of gelignite in his home in 1915 and worked for Devoy's *Gaelic American* before moving to San Francisco and editing the *Leader*. Imprisoned for 18 months for conspiring to free two interned German officials, he later became one of Harry's key arms smugglers: Ben Novick, *Conceiving Revolution: Irish Nationalist Propaganda during the First World War* (Dublin, 2001), pp 30–1; William J. Helmer, *The Gun that Made the Twenties Roar* (London, 1969), p. 59; Nellie Leahy to Devoy, 25 Sept. 1919, with Devoy's affidavit to prevent de Lacy's deportation, 2 Oct.: Devoy Papers, NLI, MS 18140.
89 Tommy O'Connor, a Dubliner who acted as a courier between the IRB and the Clan both before and after the Rebellion (in which he fought), was imprisoned in late 1918 but released after a few months, enabling him to recuperate in California and resume his conspiratorial activities: Piaras Béaslaí, *Michael Collins and the Making of a New Ireland* (2 vols., Dublin, 1926), i, p. 219.
90 Report by McG to HB, 13 Jan. 1921: McGP, MS 17424/3; Marie Veronica Tarpey, *The Role of Joseph McGarrity in the Struggle for Irish Independence* (New York, 1976), pp 131–2.
91 Executive Report, Clan na Gael (Reorganized) Conference, Mar. 1921: EdeVP, P 150/1668 (former number).
92 McG, Diary, 11 Jan. 1921: McGP, MS 17551/4.
93 Reports by McG to HB, 13 Jan. 1921: McGP, MS 17424/3; HB to 'Ireland', 14 Jan.: EdeVP, P 150/1156. Harry's version of the report was markedly more positive in its tone and statistical detail.
94 Executive Report, Mar. 1921.
95 Printed report of conference by Luke Dillon (Secretary), 1 Apr. 1921: McGP, MS 17657; 'Report of Meeting in Annex[e] Hotel' with typed transcript of speeches, 20 Mar. (copy from unlocated source): BP.
96 HB to James O'Mara, 21 Mar. 1921 (2 letters): O'Mara Papers, MS 21549/3; HBD, 20–22 Mar.
97 Printed copies of Power to HB, 3 Aug. 1921, and reply, 10 Aug.: O'Malley Papers, UCDA, P 17a/147.
98 Printed report of 'Envoy's Address' by Luke Dillon, 21 July 1921: McGP, MS 17657.
99 Undated circular by Dillon (after 13 July 1921): McGP, MS 17445.
100 HB ['Woods'] to MC ['Field'], 19 July 1921: EdeVP, P 150/1125. Harry was 'very glad to know that Field and Woods can still continue to work under the old name', despite the capture of some coded correspondence.
101 Col. Mathew J. Smith (Chief, Negative Branch, General Staff, Washington) to W. L. Hurley (State Department), 31 Jan. 1921; report by agent J. A. Connell to State Department, 11 Feb.: NAW, ROC, 841 D/148.
102 HB ['Woods'] to MC ['Field'], 30 Mar. 1921: EdeVP: P 150/1125. 'Men for active service in Ireland' had evidently been selected by Harry at an earlier meeting with the Clan in Chicago: HBD, 6 Mar.
103 HB ['Cowe'] to Brugha ['Porter'], 30 Mar. 1921; Brugha to HB, 21 June: EdeVP, P 150/1128. Brugha specified 6 tactical instructors, 6 sniping instructors

and expert riflemen, 6 revolver and pistol experts, 4 machine-gun experts, and 3 men familiar with French mortars and the like.

104 HB to Brugha, 15 July 1921: EdeVP, P 150/1128.

105 Arthur H. Mitchell, *Revolutionary Government in Ireland, 1919–22* (Dublin, 1995), p. 313 (citing HB to Mulcahy, 23 Sept. 1921: Mulcahy Papers, UCDA, P7A/37).

106 MC ['Field'] to HB ['Woods'], 7 Feb. 1921: EdeVP, P 150/1125.

107 McGuire ['J. Shell'] to MC ['Field'], 22 Feb. 1921; HB to MC, 25 Feb.: EdeVP, P 150/1125.

108 HB to MC, 29 May 1921; MC to HB, 29 June: EdeV, P 150/1125.

109 *Boston Post*, 7 July 1921: cutting in AIHS, Cohalan Papers, 3/1.

110 Report by Executive on convention, 4–5 July 1921, sent by Gloster Armstrong (Consul-General, New York) to Foreign Office, 25 July: PRO, FO 115/2672, ff. 274–82.

111 Seán Ó Murthuile, Memoir (undated typescript, *circa* 1928–31), ff. 161–2: Mulcahy Papers, P 7a/209.

112 Devoy to Cohalan, 26 July 1921: Cohalan Papers, 4/6.

113 See MC ['Field'] to HB ['Woods'], 7 Mar. 1921, indicating that Collins had been 'responsible' for the IRB's accounts since April 1918; see above, ch. V, n. 51.

114 Devoy to Cohalan, 3, 17 Aug. 1921: Devoy Papers, NLI, MS 15416/5.

115 HB ['Woods'] to MC ['Field'], 4 Aug. 1921: EdeVP, P 150/1125.

116 HB ['Woods'] to MC ['Field'], 13 Jan. 1921: EdeVP, P 150/1125. On 24 June, he complained to 'Gould' that one of his messengers was 'very angry' after being kept waiting for two hours in Liverpool and had threatened to quit if this 'embarrassment' were repeated.

117 EdeV to HB, 28 Feb. 1921: EdeVP, P 150/1132; Brugha to HB, 2 Mar.: EdeVP, P 150/1128.

118 HB ['Cowe'] to Brugha ['Porter'], 30 Mar. 1921: EdeVP, P 150/1128. He later promised Collins to 'deliver "short" [ammunition] in future': HB ['Woods'] to MC ['Field'], 14 Apr.: EdeVP, P 150/1125.

119 Liam Pedlar, Interview with Ernie O'Malley: O'Malley Notebooks, P 17b/94, f. 76.

120 HB to MC, 13 Jan. 1921: EdeVP, P 150/1125. On 18 Jan., he noted that '100 Col. Thompsons' had been 'landed', presumably meaning that the order had been delivered: HBD.

121 HBD, 13, 29 Mar., 30 Nov. 1921; *New York Times*, 27 Sept., p. 1; 2 Oct., p. 5; Patrick Jung, 'The Thompson Sub Machine Gun during and after the Anglo-Irish War: New Evidence', p. 197, in *Irish Sword*, xxi, no. 84 (1998), pp 190–218.

122 MC ['Field'] to HB ['Woods'], 7 Feb. 1921: EdeVP, P 150/1125.

123 HB to MC, 25 Feb. 1921: EdeVP, P 150/1125. This second order may correspond to the purchase on 19 Feb. of 50 guns, by 'John J. Murphy', ostensibly for 'prospecting and mining purposes in Alaska': Jung, 'The Thompson', p. 199. The expected delivery date for the first 150 guns was soon revised to 1 April: HB ['Cowe'] to Brugha ['Porter'], 30 Mar.: EdeVP, P 150/1128.

124 HBD, 29 Mar. 1921. Though miscopied as '$133.30.40' in the diary, the figure as given above corresponds to the stated terms and to that specified in HB ['Cowe'] to Brugha ['Porter'], 14 Apr.: EdeVP, P 150/1128. On 21 July, he told Brugha that the cost was $132,634.40: O'Malley Papers, P 17a/158. An order for 500 guns, with options for as many again, was lodged by Rorke on 4 Apr.: Jung, 'The Thompson', p. 197.

125 J. Bowyer Bell, 'The Thompson Submachine Gun in Ireland, 1921', p. 100, in *Irish Sword*, viii, no. 31 (1967), pp 98–108; Helmer, *The Gun*, p. 59; Peter Hart, 'The Thompson Submachine Gun in Ireland Revisited', p. 163, in *Irish Sword*, xix, no. 77 (1995), pp 161–70. By another account, 'Frank Williams' was in fact the

Kerryman Dan Fitzgerald, de Lacy masquerading as his brother 'Fred': Jung, 'The Thompson', pp 198–9.

126 HB ['Cowe'] to Brugha ['Porter'], 30 Mar. 1921: EdeVP, P 150/1128.

127 Jung, 'The Thompson', pp 191, 202.

128 HB ['Cowe'] to Brugha ['Porter'], 30 Mar. 1921: EdeVP, P 150/1128.

129 HBD, 30 Mar., 7, 21 Apr., 3 May 1921.

130 MC to HB, 28 May: EdeVP, P 150/1125.

131 Oscar Traynor, 'Account written ... at request of President de Valera shortly before his death' (typescript, 1963), ff. 79–80: EdeVP, P 150/3655. A report by O/C Guard, Dublin Brigade, on train ambush, Drumcondra, 27 June 1921, indicated that one gun was inoperative, while the other 'checked when four bursts had been fired. The 50 or 60 rounds that were fired appeared to take good effect.' See Epitome of Seized Documents (G3), f. 71: CO 904/23/7.

132 HB ['Cowe'] to MC ['Gould'], 29 Apr. 1921; MC to HB, 29 June: EdeVP, P 150/1125. This scheme was prompted by failure to maintain a satisfactory arrangement with Moore & McCormack, Inc., and the 'United States Lines': see above, ch. VII, n. 10.

133 HB ['Woods'] to MC ['Field'], 29 Apr. 1921; MC ['Field'] to HB ['Woods'], 30 Apr.: EdeVP, P 150/1125.

134 New York Times, 16 June 1921, p. 1; Hart, 'The Thompson', p. 162.

135 Notes and documents on Pedlar: McGP, MSS 17483, 17651/2.

136 Pedlar, Interview, ff. 74–5.

137 HBD, 11–14 June 1921.

138 MC to HB, 29 June 1921: EdeVP, P 150/1125.

139 Hart, 'The Thompson', pp 162–5.

140 Pedlar, Interview, ff. 76–7; Seán Nunan, Statement for the Bureau of Military History (undated typescript), f. 13: EdeVP, P 150/3652.

141 HB to Brugha, 15 July 1921: EdeVP, P 150/1128. Presumably to this end, Harry proposed to employ 'a whole time man' at $75 weekly, at the expense of the Defence account.

142 Portion of undated letter, HB to Brugha: O'Malley Papers, P 17a/158.

143 Hart, 'The Thompson', pp 165–6. By one account, most of the guns not yet loaded on the East Side were rescued by the Fire Department's (Irish) Salvage Corps from the pier, following sharp exchanges with the (Swedish) Excise Police. See [Patrick Moylett], Statement for the Bureau of Military History (undated typescript), ff. 20–1: EdeVP, P 150/3650.

144 Brugha to HB, 2 Mar. 1921: EdeVP, P 150/1128.

145 HB ['Cowe'] to Brugha ['Porter'], 30 Mar. 1921: EdeVP, P 150/1128. If preferred, he could send the money so collected to Brugha for dispersal.

146 HB ['Mac'] to O'Mara, 4 Apr. 1921, and reply, 7 Apr.: O'Mara Papers, MS 21549/4.

147 HB to MC, 14 Apr. 1921: EdeVP, P 150/1125.

148 HB ['Cowe'] to Brugha ['Porter'], 14 Apr. 1921: EdeVP, P 150/1128.

149 Brugha to HB, 4, 22 Apr. 1921 [as 'Porter' to 'Cowe' in second letter]: EdeVP, P 150/1128.

150 MC to HB, 30 Apr. 1921: EdeVP, P 150/1125.

151 Brugha ['Porter'] to HB ['Cowe'], 4 May 1921: EdeVP, P 150/1128.

152 EdeV to HB, 29 Apr. 1921: EdeV, P 150/1132.

153 Under the heading of 'Communications', Harry had written thus to de Valera: 'Re business you were interested in in Cleveland. We have been fortunate.' See 'main points' of HB to EdeV, 15 Apr. 1921: EdeVP, P 150/1132.

154 Summary of HB to EdeV, 16 May 1921: EdeVP, P 150/1132. The link between

'Cleveland' and the purchase of Thompsons is confirmed by the statement that 'Cleveland affair was vital to urgent, saved postponement for 12 months'.
155 Brugha ['Porter'] to HB ['Cowe'], 29 June 1921: EdeVP, P 150/1128.
156 HB to Brugha, 19 July 1921: EdeVP, P 150/1128.
157 HB to MC, 21 July 1921: EdeVP, P 150/1125; HB to Brugha, 21 July: EdeVP, P 150/1128.
158 Brugha to HB, 9 Aug. 1921: EdeVP, P 150/1128.
159 EdeV to MC, 18 Jan. 1921: DE 2/448 (also in Epitome of Seized Documents (D3), f. 57: CO 904/23/7).
160 MC to HB, 7 Feb. 1921; HB to MC, 25 Feb.: EdeVP, P 150/1125.
161 HB ['Mac'] to O'Mara, 25 Mar. 1921: O'Mara Papers, MS 21549/3.
162 MC ['Field'] to HB ['Woods'], 14 Mar. 1921: EdeVP, P 150/1125.
163 HB to James O'Mara, 28 Mar. 1921: O'Mara Papers, MS 21549/3; HB to MC, 31 Mar.: EdeVP, P 150/1125.
164 HB ['Woods'] to MC ['Field'], 16 May 1921: EdeVP, P 150/1125.
165 MC ['Field'] to HB ['Woods'], 29 June 1921; HB to MC, 20 July: EdeVP, P 150/1125. The papers seized at 'Glenvar', de Valera's hide-out off Mount Merrion Ave., Blackrock, provided a comprehensive record of the Dáil's recent activities, summarised in Epitome of Seized Documents: CO 904/23/7.
166 HB ['Woods'] to MC ['Field'], 16 May 1921, and reply, 29 June: EdeVP, P 150/1125.
167 HB to MC, 20 July: EdeVP, P 150/1125.
168 HB ['Woods'] to MC ['Field'], 11 Feb. 1921; MC to HB, 12, 28 May, 29 June: EdeVP, P 150/1125.
169 HB to Brennan, 24 Mar., 1 Apr. 1921; Brennan to HB, 7 Apr.: EdeVP, P 150/1124.
170 Nunan to HB, 26 Apr. 1921: EdeVP, P 150/1140.
171 HB to Brennan, 27 Apr. 1921, and reply, 26 May: EdeVP, P 150/1124.
172 HBD, 2, 10 Jan. 1921.
173 HBD, 9 Jan., 17 Mar., 30 Apr., 15, 22, 30 May 1921.
174 Frances G. McGuire (New York) to HB, 26 Apr. 1921: BP.
175 HBD, 22 Jan.–6 Feb., 2–4 Mar., 6–9 July 1921. The terms of the draft Truce were revealed by the Irish Command, Parkgate St., in advance of the joint announcement on 9 July: Dorothy Macardle, *The Irish Republic* (Dublin, 1951; 1st edn. 1937), pp 475–6.
176 Kathleen Boland (Mrs Seán O'Donovan), Statement for the Bureau of Military History (undated typescript), f. 17: BP. Daly was Collins's chief gun-runner in Liverpool: Hart, 'The Thompson', p. 165.
177 HB ['Woods'] to MC ['Field'], 11 Feb. 1921; MC to HB, 14 Mar.: EdeVP, P 150/1125.
178 Brennan to HB, 7 Apr. 1921: EdeVP, P 150/1124.
179 KK to MC, 'Monday' [circa May–June 1922]: *In Great Haste: The Letters of Michael Collins and Kitty Kiernan*, ed. León Ó Broin (Dublin, 1996; 1st edn. 1983), p. 173. She feared that 'poor Lionel will never believe in women again after I promising to marry him (always a perhaps tho')'.
180 KK to HB, 15 Apr. 1921: BP.
181 HB, statements of 12, 16 May 1921: MacKenna Papers, NLI, MS 22612; *New York Times*, 13 May, p. 2.
182 Report on Radical Activities, New York City, 2 July 1921, f. 20: NAW, RBI, 202600-1628/99 (microform M 1085/939).
183 MC to HB, 6 July 1921: EdeVP, P 150/1125.
184 HB to EdeV, 20 July 1921: DFA, ES, 27/158.
185 HB to MC, 20 July 1921: EdeVP, P 150/1125.

[186] HBD, 10 Aug. 1921.

[187] Quoted in *Irish Press* (Philadelphia), 20 Aug. 1921, p. 1.

[188] HB to Mary McSwiney (telegram), 11 Aug. 1921: McSwiney Papers, UCDA, P 48a/115/58.

[189] HB to Maloney, 13 Aug. 1921: Maloney Papers, 7/115.

[190] 'Jene' to HB, 13 Aug. 1921: BP.

[191] J. M. Kennedy (General Passenger Agent) to HB, 12 Aug. 1921: BP.

[192] Armstrong to Foreign Office, 19 Aug. 1921: FO 115/2672, f. 293.

[193] HBD, 13 Aug. 1921; F. P. Walsh (Savoy Hotel, London) to HB, 10 Aug.: BP; Mary McSwiney to EdeV, 20 July: McSwiney Papers, P 48a/115/48 (partly transcribed in *DIFP*, pp 175–6). In reiterating her opinion that American recognition was 'only a question of months', she stated that should the matter of compromise be put 'before the country I shall take the first boat home to add my voice to the "No Surrender" side'.

[194] Mary McSwiney to S. MacGraith (Accountant-General), 5 Apr. 1922: Childers Papers, TCD, MS 7835/7.

[195] In the mid-nineteenth-century American West, 'hash slinger' signified a 'short-order cook', kitchen-worker, or waiter in a cheap restaurant: *A New Dictionary of American Slang*, ed. Robert L. Chapman (London, 1987; 1st edn. 1986), p. 196. This suggests that Harry's shipboard tasks had embraced cooking as well as shovelling.

[196] Nunan to HB ['My Dear Bro.'], 18 Aug. 1921: BP.

[197] Pedlar to HB, 19 Aug. 1921: BP.

[198] O'Mara to EdeV, 12 Aug. 1921: extract in DFA, ES, 27/170 (also transcribed in *DIFP*, pp 190–2).

[199] 'Your sincere friend' to 'My dear Gertrude' [probably Brennan to Nunan], 14 June 1921: EdeVP, P 150/1673 (former number).

[200] HBD, title page. 'Owen Meredith' was the pseudonym of Edward Robert Bulwer-Lytton, 1st Earl of Lytton (1831–91). Harry also applied this passage to Dr. William Maloney ('That's You!!'), in HB to Maloney, 3 Sept. 1921: Maloney Papers, 7/115.

[201] Undated typescript ['possibly by Joe McGarrity'] calling upon the Association to pledge its support for de Valera and 'the present envoy of the Irish Republic, the Honorable H. J. Boland': Hearn Papers, NLI, MS 15996.

CHAPTER X. ENLIGHTENMENT

[1] HB, Diary, 20, 21 Aug. 1921: EdeVP, P 150/1169c [hereafter, HBD].

[2] Cutting from *Irish Independent*, 22 Aug. 1921, in personal file on HB, f. 11: PRO, WO 35/206/10.

[3] *New York Times*, 22 Aug. 1921, p. 1.

[4] HB to McG, 1 Sept. 1921: McGP, NLI, MS 17424/1.

[5] Ibid. Harry was held liable for these debts under his original tenancy agreement of 9 Sept. 1917, since no proof could be produced that he had transferred his share of the business to Bill Duggan: E. J. Duggan to HB, enclosures omitted from missing letter, 13 [Sept.] 1921: BP.

[6] Kathleen Boland (Mrs Seán O'Donovan), Statement for the Bureau of Military History (undated typescript), f. 20: BP.

[7] See Louis Whyte, *The Wild Heather Glen: The Kilmichael Story of Grief and Glory* (Kilmichael, 1995), pp 20–1, for this photograph with identification of the entire assembly.

[8] MC to KK, 21 Aug. 1921: *In Great Haste: The Letters of Michael Collins and*

Kitty Kiernan, ed. León Ó Broin (Dublin, 1996; 1st edn. 1983) [hereafter, *IGH*], p. 14.

9 Personal file on James Emmet Dalton: PRO, WO 206/52; Oscar Traynor, 'Account written ... at request of President de Valera shortly before his death' (typescript, 1963), ff. 75–6: EdeVP, P 150/3655; Minutes, Dublin County Board [?], IRB, 6 Oct. 1921: Conlon Papers, UCDA, P 97/16(c). The three 'proposals' at this meeting included 'Emmett D'Alton to be taken in. E. Kelleher Pearse' (a Dublin Circle).

10 HB to KK, 1 Sept. 1921. Except for those transcribed in *IGH*, all such extracts are taken from photocopies of letters in BP.

11 Voucher, stamped 'Irish Republican Prisoner Dependents' Fund', 24 Aug. 1921: BP.

12 MC to KK, 31 Aug. 1921: *IGH*, p. 15. It is also conceivable that Harry's 'claims' concerned the status of his Clan na Gael Reorganized, or else his suitability as a plenipotentiary: *IGH*, p. 16; Jim Maher, *Harry Boland: A Biography* (Dublin, 1998), p. 152.

13 HB to KK, 8 Sept. 1921: *IGH*, p. 18.

14 KK to HB, *circa* 13 Sept. 1921.

15 The show at the Gaiety Theatre was Lady Arthur Lever's decidedly un-Irish *Brown Sugar*, a 'sparkling original comedy ... direct from the Garrick Theatre', featuring the 'Earl of Knightsbridge': *Irish Times*, 19 Sept. 1921, p. 4.

16 HB to KK, 20 Sept. 1921: *IGH*, pp 18–19. The party included Kitty's sisters 'Mopsy' (Maud) and Helen (who was to marry Paul McGovern on 5 Oct.).

17 Kathleen O'Connell, Diary, 21 Aug. 1921: O'Connell Papers, UCDA, P 155/138. On 23 Aug., she 'had lunch with Harry at Wicklow', an event recorded in shorthand but expanded in the accompanying typed transcript.

18 HBD, 22–27 Aug. 1921, mentioning meetings on 22, 23, 24, 26, and 27 Aug. The Dáil's published reports indicate that the third private session was held on 25, not 24 Aug.: *Private Sessions of Second Dáil: Minutes of Proceedings, 18 August 1921 to 14 September 1921, and Report of Debates, 14 December 1921 to 6 January 1922*, ed. T. P. O'Neill (Dublin, undated, *circa* 1976).

19 Dáil Éireann, *Official Report for Periods 16th August, 1921, to 26th August, 1921, and 28th February, 1922, to 8th June, 1922* (Dublin, undated), p. 82; *Private Sessions*, p. 84. He came third among the 7 deputies elected to represent Connacht, being outpolled by Liam Mellows and Frank Fahy.

20 Kathleen O'Connell, Diary, 30 Aug. 1921. Next day, 'P[resident] and Harry went to M. H. [Mansion House] about 3 p.m. Wrote report for H. B. for IRB Executive.'

21 HBD, 30 Aug. 1921.

22 On 9 Sept., on his own casting vote, the Ministry accepted de Valera's plea for exemption and selected Griffith, Collins, Barton, Gavan Duffy, and Duggan as 'plenipotentiaries', their appointment being ratified by the Dáil five days later: Earl of Longford and T. P. O'Neill, *Eamon de Valera* (London, 1970), pp 145–6.

23 HB to KK, 1 Sept. 1921.

24 HB to W. J. Maloney, 3 Sept. 1921: NYPL, Maloney Papers, 7/115.

25 The 15 members of the Supreme Council had elected an executive of 3, including Ó Murthuile and Collins: Seán Ó Murthuile, Memoir (typescript, *circa* 1928–31), f. 161: Mulcahy Papers, UCDA, P 7a/209. The answer to Mulcahy's annotation ('Who was No. 3?') is implicit in Harry's diary-entry.

26 HBD, 1 Sept. 1921. In his letter to Lloyd George of 24 Aug., read to an unprotesting public session of the Dáil two days later, de Valera looked forward to negotiating 'a peace that will be just and honourable to all': Dáil Éireann, *Official Report*, p. 81. The term 'external association' had been coined by de Valera on 27 July, quickly approved by the Ministry, and incorporated periphrastically in EdeV to Lloyd George, 10 Aug.: Longford and O'Neill, *De Valera*, pp 139–40; *Documents on Irish Foreign*

Policy, i (1919–1922), ed. Ronan Fanning et al. (Dublin, 1998) [hereafter, *DIFP*], p. 255.

27 Ó Murthuile, Memoir, f. 160. This account, admittedly based on 'my notes and the record of our decisions about that time', is coloured by Ó Murthuile's suspicion that there was 'something sinister about the suggestion' and that Collins was to be de Valera's 'scapegoat'.

28 HB to McG, 1 Sept. 1921: McGP, MS 17424/1; see also Maher, *Harry Boland*, p. 150.

29 [O'Duffy] to MC, 'Thursday' [1 Sept. 1921]: NAD, DE 2/274. O'Duffy nominated McKeown and 'George' [Gearóid O'Sullivan] as speakers, but not Harry. 'Gudgeon', being a metallic pin or pivot, provides an apt metaphor for brethren seeking to secure and unify disparate interest-groups.

30 HBD, 4, 5 Sept. 1921.

31 In May 1921, Collins was elected for Co. Armagh in the Northern House of Commons as well as for a Cork electorate in the Southern House of Commons. He therefore represented two constituencies in the Second Dáil. The City Council's presentation was supported by 4 Constitutional Nationalists and 4 Sinn Féiners, with opposition from the 2 Unionists at the meeting on 2 Sept. (6 Unionists and 2 other councillors being absent): *Ulster Gazette*, 10 Sept., p. 3.

32 [O'Duffy] to MC, 'Thursday' [1 Sept. 1921]: NAD, DE 2/274; *Armagh Guardian*, 9 Sept., pp 2, 4. Estimates of the attendance varied between 4,000 and 20,000 or more – as in *Irish News* (Belfast), 5 Sept., p. 5.

33 The poorly attended yet faction-ridden Irish Race Congress, held in Paris in Jan. 1922, failed to confirm the might of the Irish empire.

34 *Irish News*, 5 Sept. 1921, p. 6.

35 *Ulster Gazette*, 10 Sept. 1921, p. 3; *Irish News*, 7 Sept., p. 5; *Armagh Guardian*, 9 Sept., p. 2 (reference to Black procession kindly supplied by Jane Leonard); *Belfast Telegraph*, 5 Sept., p. 5.

36 Ó Murthuile, Memoir, f. 153. O'Duffy, Ó Murthuile, and Dan Hogan were also aboard.

37 Frank O'Connor, *The Big Fellow: Michael Collins and the Irish Revolution* (London, 1969; 1st edn. 1937), p. 157. The 'G.S.S.' evidently signifies the Great Statesman's Secretary.

38 *Irish News*, 6 Sept. 1921, p. 5.

39 HBD, 6, 7 Sept. 1921. Fr. J. Finan was a curate in the parish of Kilteevan (diocese of Elphin).

40 *Irish News*, 10 Sept. 1921, p. 5.

41 Richard Mulcahy, notes of conversation with Seán MacEoin, 15 June 1967: Mulcahy Papers, UCDA, P7/D/16.

42 HB to KK, 8 Sept. 1921: *IGH*, p. 18.

43 Kathleen O'Connell, Diary, 8 Sept. 1921.

44 Máire [McSwiney] to HB, 7 Sept. 1921: BP. She warned that if the President, in whom she had 'complete confidence', nevertheless failed to 'stand fast', then 'well it would mean a split of course'.

45 McSwiney to HB, 21 Sept. 1921: BP.

46 'Orders on Publicity *in re* de Valera's Letter to Lloyd George of Sept. 12th carried by Joe McGrath and I to Gairloch Tuesday Sept. 13th '21' (rough notes): BP.

47 Speech by Joseph McGrath, 7 Jan. 1922: Dáil Éireann, *Official Report: Debate on the Treaty between Great Britain and Ireland* (Dublin, undated), p. 307. De Valera intervened to assert that this referred to his proposal for 'external association', which was admittedly 'short of the isolated Republic' (pp 307–8).

48 Sir Edward William Macleay Grigg (1879–1955), later Governor of Kenya (1925–30), was Lloyd George's Private Secretary (1921–2).

49 Under the Treaty of Sèvres (1920), the impotent Sultan accepted the annexation of Smyrna by Greece (an action strongly supported by Lloyd George), subject to a local plebiscite within five years. Lloyd George may have been playfully suggesting an analogous solution of the 'Ulster Problem'. However, following the expulsion of the Greeks by the forces of Gazi Mustafa Kemal Pasha ('Atatürk'), Smyrna was restored to Turkey under the Treaty of Lausanne (1923).

50 HBD, 12–14 Sept. 1921.

51 Michael McInerney, 'Gerry Boland's Story', pt. 5, in *Irish Times*, 12 Oct. 1968, p. 12.

52 EdeV to Lloyd George, 12 Sept. 1921: *DIFP*, p. 266.

53 Joseph McGrath and HB to EdeV, 14 Sept. 1921: *DIFP*, pp 267–8 (citing EdeVP, P 150/1480). The authorship of this jointly signed letter is uncertain.

54 'Lloyd George: Notes on his Remarks, Tuesday Sept. 13th '21' (in HB's hand): BP.

55 Lloyd George to EdeV, 15 Sept. 1921: PRO, CAB 24/128 (Cabinet Memoranda, C.P. 3331).

56 Conclusions of a Conference of Ministers (Flowerdale House, Gairloch), 21 Sept. 1921: CAB 23/27 (Cabinet Conclusions, 74 (21), app. iii). The typed aside referring to Harry was a marginal addition.

57 Robert Brennan, *Allegiance* (Dublin, 1950), pp 314–19.

58 Lloyd George to EdeV, 15 Sept. 1921: CAB 24/128 (Cabinet Memoranda, C.P. 3331).

59 EdeV to Lloyd George, 30 Sept. 1921: *DIFP*, p. 270.

60 Dáil Éireann, *Private Sessions*, pp 96–7 (14 Sept. 1921). Following a challenge by J. J. Walsh to de Valera's nomination of Harry, Erskine Childers, and Kevin O'Higgins (on the principle that at least one of the secretaries should know Irish), the President sought to withdraw his motion and ask the Dáil to leave the selection of secretaries to the Ministry, only to be informed that this request was superfluous. The Ministry subsequently appointed Childers, Fionán Lynch, and John Chartres: Brian P. Murphy, *John Chartres: Mystery Man of the Treaty* (Dublin, 1995), p. 49.

61 Clark[e], appropriately, was a bookmaker. On 16 Aug. 1919, Ned Boland had informed Harry that 'I expect to go with Jim Clarke soon, all the Bookies' clerks seem to be the best off of the lot': BP.

62 HBD, 15, 16 Sept. 1921.

63 HBD, 25 Sept. 1921; *Irish Independent*, 26 Sept., pp 3, 7. Dublin (8–4) defeated Leix (3–1) in a 'splendidly contested' match.

64 HBD, 26 Sept. 1921.

65 Liam Pedlar to HB, 2 Sept. 1921: EdeVP, P 150/1149; O'Mara to HB, 15 Sept.: NAD, Department of Foreign Affairs, Early Series [hereafter, DFA, ES], 27/158.

66 HBD, 25 Aug. 1921.

67 HB to Maloney ['My dear Doc.'], 3 Sept. 1921: Maloney Papers, 7/115.

68 HB to KK, 20 Sept. 1921: *IGH*, p. 19; HB to Robert Brennan, [18 Sept.]: DFA, ES, 27/158.

69 HB to EdeV, 18 Sept. 1921, and reply, 19 Sept.: EdeVP, P 150/1132. In a rather inconsistent postscript, de Valera promised to 'try to have you relieved as soon as possible'.

70 Dáil Ministry, Minutes, 23 Sept. 1921: NAD, DE 1/3, f. 121; Robert Brennan to HB, 23 Sept.: DFA, ES, 27/170. The salary replaced the previous system of reimbursing his 'expenses', the allowance previously paid to his family being terminated. On 10 Mar. 1922, Harry told George Gavan Duffy that he had 'worked solely on expenses during my term in America, from May 1919 until October 1st, 1921, when a definite salary was apportioned to the Washington office. I drew salary from October 1st, 1921, until January 1st of the present year': EdeVP, P 150/1172.

[71] HB to MC, 30 Nov. 1921: EdeVP, P 150/1125; G. McGrath (Accountant-General) to Kate Boland, *circa* 27 Oct., also promising her arrears of £50: BP.

[72] Copies of credentials, 24 Sept. 1921: BP.

[73] Passport no. LO 14649, stamped at Liverpool, 29 Sept. 1921: BP. The American Consul at Queenstown added the required visa for a year in the United States on 1 Oct.

[74] 'Andy' [Sir Alfred William] Cope (1880–1954), a Joint Assistant Under-Secretary at Dublin Castle (1920–2) and Lloyd George's confidential agent, later General Secretary, National Liberal Organisation (1922–4), had long consorted with leading republicans at Vaughan's Hotel and elsewhere.

[75] HBD, 29, 30 Sept., 1 Oct. 1921.

[76] Piaras Béaslaí, *Michael Collins: Soldier and Statesman* (Dublin, 1937), p. 302. If Béaslaí is correct, the party moved on from the Gresham to Vaughan's for supper.

[77] HB to KK, 30 Sept. 1921.

[78] HB to KK, 1 Oct. 1921: *IGH*, pp 20–1.

[79] Jennie Wyse Power ['Sara'] to her daughter Nancy, 11 Oct. 1921: Humphreys Papers, UCDA, P 106/726. The identification of 'Uncle B.' as Harry is uncertain.

[80] Annie to Peter McSwiney, 1 Jan. 1922: Hearn Papers, NLI, MS 15993. With hindsight, she added: 'That was the essence of de Valera's Document No. 2.'

[81] The founding members of the Dublin Blue Terrier Club (precursor of the Irish Kennel Club) included the Rt. Hon. James MacMahon (Under-Secretary for Ireland) and Michael Collins, who entered 'Convict 224' in its first Breed Show (16 Oct. 1920): Justin Comiskey, 'An Irishman's Diary', in *Irish Times*, 12 Nov. 1996 (cutting kindly supplied by Jane Leonard). The name referred to Austin Stack, Minister for Home Affairs, whose number as a convict at Lewes was q 224.

[82] Mason Mitchell (American Consul, Queenstown) to State Department, 3 Oct. 1921, with extracts from *Cork Examiner* and *Irish Independent*, 3 Oct., and reply, 8 Nov.: NAW, RG 65, Records of [Federal] Bureau of Investigation, 373017 (microform M 1085/810).

[83] Extract from Melbourne *Tribune* in *Irish Independent*, 18 Oct. 1922, p. 5. The interview was taken up by several provincial papers, including the *Weekly Observer* (Limerick), 28 Oct. (transcription kindly supplied by Frank Bouchier Hayes). Bishop Phelan had admittedly become a strong partisan of the Free State, excoriating 'the reign of terror which was created by the extremists'.

[84] EdeV, typed transcript of speech, 26 Oct. 1917, f. 51: NLI, MS 21523.

CHAPTER XI. COMPROMISE

[1] Reports to Intelligence Branch by Victor J. Valjavek, 10 Oct., 8 Nov. 1921; Special Agent Hall Kinsey (New York) to R. S. Sharp, 23 Nov.: NAW, RG 59, Department of State, Records of the Office of the Counselor [hereafter, ROC], 841.D/77. The 'so-called passport' consisted of 3 pages in a green cover, and was probably Harry's credentials (preserved in BP). The arrival of 'Harry Bollin' also interested J. Edgar Hoover (at the Bureau of Investigation), who solicited various reports from the Secret Service: Hoover to Grimes, 5 Oct.; telegram from E. J. Brennan (State Department), 10 Oct.: NAW, RG 65, Records of [Federal] Bureau of Investigation, 202997-26 (microform M 1085/1942).

[2] HB, Diary, 10 Oct. 1921: EdeVP, P 150/1169c [hereafter, HBD].

[3] HB to KK, 11 Oct. 1921: *In Great Haste: The Letters of Michael Collins and Kitty Kiernan*, ed. León Ó Broin (Dublin, 1996; 1st edn. 1983) [hereafter, *IGH*], p. 26.

[4] *New York Times*, 11 Oct. 1921, p. 2.

5   *New York Times*, 16 Oct. 1921, p. 19; F. P. Walsh to Hon. Joseph Scott (Los Angeles), 19 Oct.: NYPL, F. P. Walsh Papers, Box 26; HBD, 15, 16 Oct.
6   Photocopy of platform ticket, 15 Oct. 1921: BP; HB to KK, [16 Oct.]: *IGH*, p. 28. The platform ticket indicated that 'America's reception' to the 'Honorable Harry Boland' had been arranged by 'Clan-na-Gael (Reorganized)'.
7   Milholland to Walsh, 17 Oct. 1921: F. P. Walsh Papers, Box 26.
8   *Irish Independent*, 17 Oct. 1921, p. 5; HB to McG, 18 Oct.: McGP, NLI, MS 17424/1.
9   HB to Secretary of State, 17 Oct. 1921: F. P. Walsh Papers, Box 26.
10 EdeV to HB, 5 Nov. 1921: extract in *Documents on Irish Foreign Policy*, i (1919–1922), ed. Ronan Fanning et al. (Dublin, 1998) [hereafter, *DIFP*], p. 301 (citing NAD, Department of Foreign Affairs, Early Series [hereafter, DFA, ES], 27/158).
11 Brennan to HB, 3 Nov. 1921: DFA, ES, 27/158; *Irish Independent*, 17 Oct., p. 5 ('Exchange Cablegram').
12 HB to EdeV, 30 Nov. 1921: DFA, ES, 27/159.
13 HBD, 23 Oct. 1921; HB to KK, '26' [*recte*, 24] Oct.
14 *Memoirs of Senator James G. Douglas (1887–1954): Concerned Citizen*, ed. J. Anthony Gaughan (Dublin, 1998), p. 70.
15 MC to HB, 14 Oct. 1921: EdeVP, P 150/1125.
16 The Irish Convention, held without Sinn Féin's participation from July 1917 to Apr. 1918, failed to agree upon an extended scheme of Home Rule.
17 Kate Boland to HB, 1 Nov. 1921: BP.
18 HB to KK, 14 Oct. 1921: *IGH*, p. 27; 17 Oct.: BP. Unless otherwise stated, copies of all such letters were consulted in BP.
19 McG, Diary, 9 Nov. 1921: McGP, NLI, MS 17551/4; annotated transcript of J. T. Ryan ['Jetter'] to McG, 8 Nov.: McGP, MS 17637/1; HB to Brennan, 9 Nov., with copy of cable from HB ['Toddles'] to Brennan ['Apparatus']: EdeVP, P 150/1124.
20 Dáil Ministry, Minutes, 23 Sept. 1921: NAD, DE 1/3, f. 121.
21 HB ['Henry Hampden'] to 'Dublin', 20 Oct. 1921: DFA, ES, 27/156/3; HB to Brennan ['Tanners'], 21 Oct.: EdeVP, P 150/1124.
22 EdeV to HB, 5 Nov. 1921; transcript of C. de Markievicz to Brennan, [Nov. 1921]: DFA, ES, 27/156/3. Having married an alien, 'Madame' (otherwise, 'the Countess') was deemed to have discarded her British citizenship. She recalled having been 'married in Marylebone P. Church and Registry Office either in 1900 (the year of the Great Exhibition in Paris) or the year previously in the late summer', to Casimir Dunin Markievicz, who 'might possibly be technically an Ukrainian, . . . ranked as a Russian in pre-war days and was a patriotic Pole'. Acceptable travel documents were eventually secured on 10 Dec., a fortnight after the meeting in Chicago for which she was particularly required, allowing her to visit America in 1922.
23 Brennan to Revd. M. O'Flanagan, 19 Oct. 1921, and reply, 20 Oct.; Seán MacEntee to Brennan, 31 Oct.: DFA, ES, 27/156/3; Denis Carroll, *They Have Fooled You Again: Michael Flanagan (1876–1942), Priest, Republican, Social Critic* (Dublin, 1993), pp 136–8.
24 O'Mara to MC, 10 Nov. 1921: EdeVP, P 150/1211.
25 O'Mara to Brennan (cable), 17 Nov. 1921: DFA, ES, 27/156/3.
26 Muriel McSwiney ['Muirgheal'] to Kathleen O'Connell, 20 Oct. 1921: O'Connell Papers, UCDA, P 155/5.
27 Extract from Dáil Ministry, Minutes, 30 Sept. 1921: NAD, DE 2/450.
28 HB to Kathleen O'Connell (for EdeV), 18 Oct. 1921: DFA, ES, 27/158.
29 Just before signature of the Anglo-Irish Treaty, H. W. Nevinson reported from Washington that 'the course of the [Irish] negotiations next week will influence the Prime Minister's decision as to his visit to the Washington Conference. I am told that

it is now doubtful whether he will go to Washington, even if the negotiations succeed. The critical days are passing during which his presence would be important': *Manchester Guardian*, 3 Dec. 1921, p. 8.

30 Drafts of HB to Harding, 19, 25 Oct. 1921: *DIFP*, pp 201–2 (citing DFA, ES, 27/158).

31 HB to Brennan, 27 Oct., 30 Nov. 1921: EdeVP, P 150/1124 (transcribed in *DIFP*, pp 203–4, 207–9).

32 HB to Samuel Gompers, 27 Oct. 1921, with associated documents: DFA, ES, 27/168; HBD, 14 Nov.

33 The Naval Disarmament Conference, sitting between 12 Nov. 1921 and 6 Feb. 1922, was marked by an Anglo-American naval accord markedly favourable to the United States, though most of the resultant treaties proved to be unworkable.

34 Extract from HB to EdeV, 30 Nov. 1921: DFA, ES, 27/156/4.

35 HBD, 27, 28 Nov., 1, 2, 8 Dec. 1921. Peter A. Drury, President of the Merchants' Bank in Washington, repeatedly facilitated the mission's financial arrangements; Thomas Joseph Shahan (1857–1932) was President of the Catholic University of America, Washington (1909–28).

36 Extracts from HB to EdeV, 30 Nov. 1921: EdeVP, P 150/1132.

37 F. M. Carroll, *American Opinion and the Irish Question, 1910–23* (Dublin, 1978), p. 282. The amount raised would have been greater but for the abandonment of the Bond Drives planned for other states after the Treaty of 6 Dec. 1921.

38 HBD, 12, 13 Dec. 1921.

39 Carroll, *American Opinion*, p. 167.

40 C. J. France (American Committee for Relief in Ireland, Dublin) to HB, 30 Sept. 1921: BP.

41 HB to Mme. O'Rahilly, 30 Nov. 1921: EdeVP, P 150/1131.

42 James J. Reilly to McG, 15 Sept. 1921, with enclosures: McGP, MS 17653/1. The three members managing Gaelic Park, who 'were so strong with Boland that no one could touch them', had since been suspended for insubordination; and Harry's arms courier, Captain Dinneen, had been reinstated in the club and asked to reorganise it.

43 HB to McG, 13 Oct. 1921: McGP, MS 17578. A month later, Harry anxiously enquired if de Valera had received two suits, hoping that 'they were both satisfactory in colour and fit'. See HB to EdeV, 14 Nov.: DFA, ES, 27/158.

44 HB ['Woods'] to MC ['Field'], 21 Oct., 15 Nov. 1921: EdeVP, P 150/1125; HB to Hugh Montague, 9 Nov., and replies enclosing cheques, 16, 29 Nov.: EdeVP, P 150/1157.

45 Resolution (no provenance), 21 Dec. 1921: EdeVP, P 150/1171; HBD, 21 Dec. The other signatories, McGarrity and Luke Dillon, handled the account in his absence. This pre-emptive act contrasted with his pre-Treaty query to Collins as to whether money voted 'to me for Home Affairs' should be transmitted to Dublin immediately or deposited in the United States. See HB ['Woods'] to MC ['Field'], 30 Nov.: EdeVP, P 150/1125.

46 HB to Luke Dillon, 26 Dec. 1921: McGP, MS 17447. A note by McGarrity states that this subsidy was subsequently 'sent to the IRA in Ireland' by Luke Dillon and himself.

47 HB ['Toddles'] to Mellows ['Leamy'], 13 Oct. 1921; HB ['Toddles'] to Brugha ['Waters'], 21 Oct.: EdeVP, P 150/1128.

48 Brugha to HB, 4 Nov. 1921; HB ['Toddles'] to Brugha ['Waters'], 30 Nov.: EdeVP, P 150/1128. Of $157,000.89 borrowed for arms purchases by 30 Sept. 1921, $128,853.14 was attributable to the 653 Thompsons (some $5,000 less than the price initially reported), of which $120,000 had been credited to the Finance Department by 30 Nov.

49 Mellows to [Pedlar], 12 Sept. 1921, and associated documents: Twomey Papers, UCDA, P 69/217 (19, 22, 24, 43–5).
50 Mellows to [Pedlar], 2 Nov. 1921, enc. Chief of Staff to O/Cs, 31 Oct.: Twomey Papers, P 69/217 (17, 18). Mulcahy introduced this as an involuntary undertaking: 'As a result of representations made by the British representatives conducting the present negotiations, the following agreement has had to be made by the Irish representatives.'
51 HBD, 19 Nov. 1921. The *Baltic*, a White Star liner, reached the Mersey on 28 Nov.: *Irish Times*, 29 Nov., p. 2. Harry was to spend his second-last night alive at the house of Edward J. Hearty, identified by Liam Pedlar as 'the stout man', a Clansman, and 'a brick to us all': Pedlar to McG, 3 Aug. 1922: McGP, MS 17478. Hearty's subsequent 'message of condolence' to the Boland family was mentioned in the *Cork Examiner*, 7 Aug.
52 Mellows ['Leamy'] to Pedlar ['L.'], 30 Nov. 1921: Twomey Papers, P 69/217 (10–11). The trunks were to be addressed to three recipients named Carson, Bayliss, and Cohen in Belfast, Cumberland, and Liverpool, and marked 'not wanted on voyage'. The *Baltic* was due to arrive on Christmas Eve.
53 Kathleen Boland (Mrs Seán O'Donovan), Statement for the Bureau of Military History (typescript, undated), f. 16: BP. A despatch had been delivered to the shop at 64, Middle Abbey St., 'telling me to inform Mick Collins who would make the necessary arrangements'.
54 HB ['Woods'] to MC ['Field'], 21 Oct., 30 Nov. 1921: EdeVP, P 150/1125.
55 *Irish Press* (Philadelphia), 31 Dec. 1921, p. 8.
56 T. J. McElligott to HB, 21 Sept. 1921; MC to HB, 22 Sept., inviting him to a meeting with McElligott at the Mansion House: BP.
57 Dáil Éireann, *Official Report: Debate on the Treaty between Great Britain and Ireland* (Dublin, undated), p. 303 (7 Jan. 1922).
58 *Private Sessions of Second Dáil: Minutes of Proceedings, 18 August 1921 to 14 September 1921, and Report of Debates, 14 December 1921 to 6 January 1922*, ed. T. P. O'Neill (Dublin, undated, *circa* 1976), pp 10–11, 14 (18 Aug. 1921). During the debate, Walsh himself discerned that his proposal 'would be turned down as it was a bit wide': p. 11.
59 Walsh to HB, 20 Oct. 1921, and reply, 25 Oct.: F. P. Walsh Papers, Box 26.
60 Undated tabulation (handwritten, *circa* Nov. 1921): EdeVP, P 150/1157.
61 HB ['Woods'] to MC ['Field'], 21 Oct., 30 Nov. 1921: EdeVP, P 150/1125.
62 HBD, 5 Nov. 1921. When abandoning his newspaper, *Sinn Féiner*, and the Speakers' Bureau for Irish Independence, O'Leary bitterly denounced Harry, who declined to respond. See O'Leary to HB, 26 Oct., 3 Nov., and reply, 31 Oct.: EdeVP, P 150/1151.
63 Clan circular (corrected proof), 15 Nov. 1921: McGP, MS 17522.
64 HB to KK, 19 Oct. 1921.
65 Begley's engagement was rather stormy: 'I am not married myself yet, but I fear the grappling hooks are deeply in me. The little Christmas affair was settled after the throwing of a few pots and pans and things have gone more or less smoothly since.' See Begley to HB, 30 Mar. 1922: EdeVP, P 150/1171.
66 HBD, 12, 31 Oct., 4, 19, 21, 22, 24 Nov., 2 Dec. 1921.
67 HB to KK, 19 Oct. 1921.
68 HBD, 28–30 Oct. 1921.
69 HB to KK, 11, 14 Oct. 1921: *IGH*, pp 26, 27; 17 Oct.: BP. The shared apartment was in Stoneleigh Court, at Connecticut Ave. and L St.
70 HBD, 10 Dec. 1921. Mary was presumably a daughter of John J. Hearn of Westfield, Mass., Treasurer of the AARIR.

71 *Memoirs of Senator Joseph Connolly (1885–1961): A Founder of Modern Ireland,* ed. J. Anthony Gaughan (Dublin, 1996), p. 223. Connolly had recently replaced Fawsitt as 'Consul-General'.

72 Kitty O'Brien to HB, 'Thursday' [*circa* 22 Dec. 1921]: BP.

73 *Ordinary People Dancing: Essays on Kate O'Brien,* ed. Eibhear Walshe (Cork, 1993), esp. p. 12.

74 KK to HB, 8 Oct. 1921.

75 Kate Boland to KK, 4 Oct. 1921: *IGH,* p. 22.

76 Kate Boland to HB, 1 Nov. 1921: BP.

77 Emmet Dalton (London) to HB, 14 Oct. 1921: BP.

78 HB to KK, 11, 14 Oct. 1921: *IGH,* pp 27, 28; 17 Oct.: BP.

79 HB to KK, 19, 24 Oct. 1921: BP; 30 Oct.: *IGH,* pp 57–8; 19 Nov.: BP.

80 KK to MC, 12 Oct. 1921: *IGH,* p. 32.

81 KK to MC, 'Friday' [14? Oct. 1921]: *IGH,* p. 37.

82 KK to MC, 'Thursday' [10? Nov. 1921]: *IGH,* p. 61.

83 MC to KK, 15 Nov.1921: *IGH,* p. 64.

84 KK to MC, 'Tuesday' [15 Nov. 1921]: *IGH,* pp 30, 66.

85 KK to MC, 'Tuesday' [22? Nov. 1921]: *IGH,* pp 69–70.

86 KK to MC, 'Thursday' [24? Nov. 1921]: *IGH,* p. 72.

87 KK to MC, [1] Dec. 1921: *IGH,* p. 80.

88 HB to KK, 12 Dec. 1921: BP.

89 Maud Kiernan to HB, 6 Dec. 1921: BP. Emmet Dalton married Alice Shannon, of Dublin, on 9 Sept. 1922: personal file in PRO, WO 35/206/52.

90 Their wedding, on 19 Oct. 1922, was to have coincided with that of Collins and Kitty: Gearóid O'Sullivan, 'Gearóid O'Sullivan: Friend and Ally', p. 51, in *Michael Collins and the Making of the Irish State,* ed. Gabriel Doherty and Dermot Keogh (Cork, 1998), pp 45–51.

91 Extract from EdeV to HB, 29 Nov. 1921: *DIFP,* pp 318–19 (citing DFA, ES, 27/158).

92 Harry's reference to the *Manchester Guardian* preceded publication of the relevant report by two days: HBD, 8 Dec. 1921; *Manchester Guardian,* 10 Dec., p. 12.

93 HBD, 6–10 Dec. 1921.

94 Sean O'Casey, *Inishfallen, Fare Thee Well* (1st edn. London, 1949), in *Autobiographies* (2 vols., London, 1963), ii, p. 68.

95 *New York Times,* 7 Dec. 1921, p. 2. Harry was prematurely described as 'representative of the Provisional Irish Government in Washington'.

96 Ibid. A similar stance was adopted by Cohalan's opponent, Judge John W. Goff, Vice-President of the American Association.

97 Statement reproduced in printed broadside by Devoy's faction: McGP, MS 17653/6.

98 HBD, 7 Dec. 1921.

99 *New York Times,* 9 Dec. 1921, p. 4.

100 In retrospect, he misidentified Harry and Stephen as 'John [Pius] Boland, long a Nationalist member in the London Parliament, and James O'Mara, Lord [*sic.*] Mayor of Limerick': Henry W. Nevinson, *Last Changes, Last Chances* (London, 1928), p. 199. Like many journalists, Nevinson was evidently at his sharpest on the morning after.

101 *Manchester Guardian,* 10 Dec. 1921, p. 12.

102 Nevinson, *Last Changes,* p. 199.

103 Earl of Longford and Thomas P. O'Neill, *Eamon de Valera* (London, 1970), p. 169. Kathleen O'Connell's diary indicated de Valera's perturbation on 7 Dec. 1921, two days before publication of his manifesto: 'P[resident] is in an awful state. Oh what a disappointment to our bright hopes – what a fiasco.' See Kathleen O'Connell Papers, UCDA, P 155/138.

[104] *Irish Press*, 10 Dec. 1921. It is probable that the leader on p. 4 was set up before receipt of the report received 'last night' and published on p. 1.

[105] After a last-minute amendment, the oath specified in art. 4 required deputies to 'swear true faith and allegiance to the Constitution of the Irish Free State', but merely to 'be faithful' to the monarch, 'in virtue of the common citizenship of Ireland with Great Britain and her adherence to and membership of the group of nations forming the British Commonwealth of Nations': Dáil Éireann, *Private Sessions*, pp 308, 312. This canny formulation could be construed as conceding the principle of 'external association'.

[106] Unidentified newspaper cutting, 12 Dec. 1921: BP.

[107] National Council, Minutes, 13 Jan. 1922: AIHS, FOIF Papers, 8/8.

[108] HBD, 14 Dec. 1921. The cable, with minor textual variants, was read by MacNeill to the Dáil on 15 Dec.: Dáil Éireann, *Private Sessions*, p. 162.

[109] Quoted in Brennan to EdeV, 12 Dec. 1921: NAD, DE 1/526 (transcribed in *DIFP*, p. 215). It seems improbable, as asserted in the *Gaelic American*, 12 Aug. 1922, p. 2, that Harry 'spoke in favour of the Treaty' to a reunion of the Clan Reorganized in Philadelphia, so raising 'a storm of abuse'. His diary noted that he was 'very tired and weary' after this 'very good' meeting of the Clan: HBD, 11 Dec. 1921.

[110] HB to KK, 12 Dec. 1921.

[111] MC to KK, 18 Dec. 1921: *IGH*, p. 98.

[112] *Irish Press*, 17 Dec. 1921: extract in Marie Veronica Tarpey, *The Role of Joseph McGarrity in the Struggle for Irish Independence* (New York, 1976), p. 150.

[113] Doheny considered 'that the greater number of Americans having sympathies with the aspirations of the Irish people have tried to get them not to be too extreme. The accomplishment of the Irish Free State is what I had hoped for': *New York Times*, 7 Dec. 1921, p. 2.

[114] New York *World* and *New York Times*, 18 Dec. 1921: cuttings in BP.

[115] Dáil Éireann, *Debate on the Treaty*, pp 334–5 (7 Jan. 1922).

[116] 'F. Greene' (c/o 'Irish Women's Purchasing league', 229, Lexington Ave., New York) to McG, 19 Jan. '1921' [*recte*, 1922]: McGP, MS 17524/2. The unidentified writer, otherwise 'your carpenter', had been in the United States since May 1921.

[117] Extract from *New York Sun* in *Roscommon Herald*, 21 Oct. 1922 (copy kindly supplied by Dr. Patrick Murray).

[118] Seán Ó Murthuile, Memoir (typescript, *circa* 1928–31), ff. 167–73: Mulcahy Papers, UCDA, P 7a/209.

[119] On 12 Dec. 1921, he proposed to reach Dublin by 21 Dec. if given an 'immediate' reply; two days later, in the absence of a response, he gave his earliest possible date of arrival as 27 Dec. See cables, quoted in Brennan to EdeV, 12 Dec.: NAD, DE 2/526 (transcribed in *DIFP*, p. 215); HB to Brennan, 14 Dec.: DFA, ES 27/158.

[120] Liam Mellows to HB, 23 Dec. 1921: EdeVP, P 150/1130. On the previous day, Mellows had been among the minority opposing Collins's motion to adjourn until 3 Jan. 1922: Dáil Éireann, *Debate on the Treaty*, pp 170–1.

[121] Peter Golden (1877–1926), born near Macroom in Cork, emigrated to the USA in 1901 and worked as an actor and journalist. He became founding Secretary of the Irish Progressive League in 1917 and the AARIR in 1920. In 1916, he married a wealthy feminist actor from New York, Helen Lyon Merriam, whose dinner parties attracted Harry, his brethren, and an anonymous informer for the Bureau of Investigation: Jim Herlihy, *Peter Golden, the Voice of Ireland: A Biography* (Ballincollig, Co. Cork, 1994); see above, ch. VIII, n. 60.

[122] HBD, 23–27 Dec. 1921.

[123] Gloster Armstrong (Consul-General, New York) to Foreign Secretary, 22 Dec. 1921: PRO, FO 115/2672, f. 361. Though Harry had reportedly 'obtained a

passport, no. 2624', this may have been a permit additional to the two-year passport that he used for his return to New York in September.

[124] Stephen O'Mara returned in early January, upon a summons from Harry; while Walsh, even before the New Year, was considering an offer of $100,000 from the Soviet Mission. See O'Mara to McG, 7 Jan. 1922: McGP, MS 17654/2; memorandum by W. J. Maloney of conversation with F. P. Walsh, 30 Dec. 1921: NYPL, Maloney Papers, General Correspondence, 9/144.

[125] *Irish Press*, 7 Jan. 1922, p. 1. The cup remains in family possession.

[126] *New York Times*, 27 Dec. 1921, p. 3.

[127] Arthur Yencken (British Embassy, Washington) to W. L. Hurley (State Department), 14 June 1922: NAW, ROC, 841.D/172. The purchase had been arranged by John W. Goff, jun. (son of a Vice-President of the AARIR).

[128] *New York Times*, 28 Dec. 1921, p. 3; *Irish Press*, 31 Dec., p. 1.

[129] *New York Times*, 28 Dec. 1921, p. 3. John F. Hylan (1868–1936), a Catholic lawyer and Democrat married to one Marian O'Hara, was Mayor of New York (1918–25).

[130] Admission card, 27 Dec. 1921: Villanova University, McGP, 4/28.

[131] *Irish Press*, 31 Dec. 1921, p. 2.

CHAPTER XII. RUPTURE

[1] *Roscommon Herald*, 7 Jan. 1922 (cutting kindly supplied by Dr. Patrick Murray).

[2] O'Mara to HB, 3 Jan. 1922: BP.

[3] Seán O'Donovan, 'An Autobiographical Note' (typescript, 1973): BP; HB, Diary, 5 Jan. 1922: EdeVP, P 150/1169d [hereafter, HBD].

[4] *Roscommon Herald*, 7 Jan. 1922.

[5] Kathleen O'Connell, Desk Diary, 5 Jan. 1922: O'Connell Papers, UCDA, P 155/140. Mrs Annie Peterson, the occupier of 53, Kenilworth Sq., Rathmines, provided de Valera with a convenient alternative to Greystones: *Thom's Official Directory of the United Kingdom of Great Britain and Ireland* (Dublin, 1923 edn.).

[6] MC to KK, 6 Jan. 1922: p. 10: *In Great Haste: The Letters of Michael Collins and Kitty Kiernan*, ed. León Ó Broin (Dublin, 1996; 1st edn. 1983) [hereafter, *IGH*], p. 2.

[7] Seán Nunan, Statement for the Bureau of Military History (undated typescript), f. 16: EdeVP, P 150/3652; MC to HB, 6 Jan. 1922, acknowledging 'a receipt from the Russian Soviet Republic for a loan from the American Account of $20,000 and jewels being security against another loan of $20,000 with receipt for that amount also': NAD, Taoiseach's Department Papers, S 14205.

[8] Kathleen Boland (Mrs Seán O'Donovan), Statement for the Bureau of Military History (undated typescript), f. 22: BP. The jewels remained until 1938 in 'various hiding places', including 'a little recess with a sliding door in the hot-press, which my husband made'.

[9] HB to KK, 10 Jan. 1922: *IGH*, p. 103.

[10] Revd. Francis McDermott, PP, in *Freeman's Journal*, 3 Jan. 1922 (extract kindly supplied by Dr. Patrick Murray); T. H. Canon Cummins to HB, 5 Jan. (letter), 6 Jan. (telegram): BP; South Roscommon council to HB (telegram), 3 Jan.: BP.

[11] Dáil Éireann, *Official Report: Debate on the Treaty between Great Britain and Ireland* (Dublin, undated), p. 301 (7 Jan. 1922). Harry had been obliged to publicly repudiate this promise, possibly by his principal nominator (Canon Cummins).

[12] *Cork Examiner*, 6 Jan. 1922, p. 5. The official report states merely that Harry's entry 'was heartily applauded': Dáil Éireann, *Debate on the Treaty*, p. 265 (5 Jan.).

13 Report of joint conference, 4, 5 Jan. 1922: Mellows Papers, NLI, MS 18548. Mellows was the only dissentient.

14 *Private Sessions of Second Dáil: Minutes of Proceedings, 18 August 1921 to 14 September 1921, and Report of Debates, 14 December 1921 to 6 January 1922*, ed. T. P. O'Neill (Dublin, undated, *circa* 1976), p. 281 (6 Jan. 1921).

15 Dáil Éireann, *Debate on the Treaty*, pp 277, 279 (6 Jan. 1922).

16 Elizabeth Lazenby, *Ireland: A Catspaw* (London, 1928), p. 65. Lazenby visited the Dáil in May 1922, prior to the 'Pact' signed on 20 May by Collins and de Valera.

17 HBD, 3 Apr. 1920: EdeVP, P 150/1169a.

18 Seán T. O'Kelly, 'Memoirs of Seán T.', in *Irish Press*, 7 Aug. 1961, p. 8.

19 Dáil Éireann, *Debate on the Treaty*, pp 279, 274–5 (6 Jan. 1922).

20 Ibid., p. 281 (6 Jan. 1922).

21 HBD, 6 Jan. 1922.

22 Dáil Éireann, *Debate on the Treaty*, p. 302 (7 Jan. 1922).

23 Ibid., p. 35 (19 Dec. 1921).

24 Ibid., p. 303 (7 Jan. 1922).

25 Ibid., p. 304 (7 Jan. 1922).

26 Ibid., p. 304 (7 Jan. 1922); *Cork Examiner*, 9 Jan., p. 5.

27 HBD, 7 Jan. 1922; Dáil Éireann, *Debate on the Treaty*, pp 305, 334–5, 345 (7 Jan.).

28 Ibid., p. 374 (9 Jan. 1922).

29 Ibid., pp 375, 378–9 (9 Jan. 1922); HBD, 14 Jan.

30 McCartan to W. J. A. Maloney, 31 Jan. 1922: NYPL, Maloney Papers, 6/101.

31 T. St. John Gaffney, et al., to Maloney, 16 Jan. 1922 (so allowing two months for delivery!): Maloney Papers, 7/115.

32 Pedlar to McG, 26 Jan. 1922: McGP, NLI, MS 17635.

33 Nunan to HB, 21 Apr. 1922: EdeVP, P 150/1171.

34 Kathleen Boland to 'Madge' [MacLaverty?], 9 Jan. 1922: BP.

35 HB to Robert Brennan, 31 Oct. 1921; extract from HB to EdeV, 30 Nov.: NAD, Department of Foreign Affairs, Early Series [hereafter, DFA, ES], 27/167.

36 Dáil Ministry, Minutes, 11, 12, 16 Jan. 1922: NAD, DE 1/4, ff. 6, 10, 20–1.

37 Report on the 'Irish Race Conference', Feb. 1922: *Documents on Irish Foreign Policy*, i (1919–1922), ed. Ronan Fanning et al. (Dublin, 1998) [hereafter, *DIFP*], pp 390–7 (citing DFA, ES, 11/77). Three variant drafts of this report appear in the FitzGerald Papers, UCDA, P 80/703–4.

38 Report: *DIFP*, p. 392. Harry was not present at the sub-committee's meeting on the Tuesday. See Minutes, Irish Race Congress (typescript), f. 10: McSwiney Papers, UCDA, P 48a/354 (2).

39 *Proceedings of the Irish Race Congress in Paris, January, 1922* (Dublin, [1922]), p. 92.

40 Report: *DIFP*, p. 393.

41 *Proceedings*, pp 182–3.

42 Irwin received bipartisan support, his nomination by Eoin MacNeill being seconded by Harry: *Proceedings*, p. 185.

43 Minutes, f. 18; Report: *DIFP*, p. 396. The anti-Treatyist majority was achieved by securing Art O'Brien's election to the Executive Committee, with 29 votes to P. J. Kelly's 21: *Proceedings*, p. 98.

44 *Proceedings*, p. 196.

45 HBD, 21–28 Jan. 1922; Minutes, ff. 8, 10. This opinion also appealed to an anti-Treatyist journal: 'Men may vote for a falsehood, but they will never die for it. Mr. W. B. Yeats at the Irish Race Congress.' See *Poblacht na h-Éireann*, i, no. 6 (31 Jan.), p. 1: BP. Harry evidently missed the next evening's lecture by Jack B. Yeats, on 'Ireland and Painting'.

46 The party then moved to Montmartre, where de Valera delivered a speech in Irish by the grave of Myles Byrne: *Proceedings*, pp viii, ix.

47 Dáil Éireann, *Official Report for Periods 16th August, 1921, to 26th August, 1921, and 28th February, 1922, to 8th June, 1922* (Dublin, undated), pp 214, 217–18 (2 Mar. 1922).

48 Ibid., pp 498–9 (8 June 1922).

49 HB to Gavan Duffy, 17 Jan. 1922: extract from report in DE 2/450. The Ministry took 'no action' on Harry's suggestion 'that Mr. Frank P. Walsh should cease to be paid his present enormous salary as Legal Adviser'. See Dáil Ministry, Minutes, 24 Jan.: DE 1/4, f. 34.

50 Gavan Duffy to HB, 16 Feb. 1922: EdeVP, P 150/1172; Dáil Ministry, Minutes, 24 Feb.: DE 1/4, f. 62. See also Jim Maher, *Harry Boland: A Biography* (Cork, 1998), pp 183–5; Brian P. Murphy, *John Chartres: Mystery Man of the Treaty* (Dublin, 1995), pp 103–4.

51 Typed copy, misattributed to *Poblacht na h-Éireann*, i, no. 3 [10 Jan. 1922], in Gavan Duffy to HB, 28 Jan.: EdeVP, P 150/1172.

52 Gavan Duffy to HB, 28 Jan., 2 Feb. 1922, and reply, 30 Jan.: EdeVP, P 150/1172; HBD, 30 Jan. The grounds for Harry's dismissal became public when Gavan Duffy eventually responded to a question from Joseph MacDonagh, TD for North Tipperary: Dáil Éireann, *Official Report*, pp 312–13, 355 (27 Apr., 3 May).

53 Gavan Duffy to HB, 3, 4 Feb. 1922, and reply, 9 Feb.: EdeVP, P 150/1172.

54 HB to Stephen O'Mara, 16 Feb. 1922: EdeVP, P 150/1171.

55 Walsh was promised 'a long love letter soon': HB to Walsh, 28 Feb. 1922: NYPL, F. P. Walsh Papers, Box 26.

56 Walsh to HB, 13 Feb. 1922; Walsh to Stephen O'Mara, 17 Mar.: F. P. Walsh Papers, Boxes 26, 27.

57 Stack to HB, 3 Mar. 1922: BP.

58 O'Callaghan to HB, 8 Mar. 1922, and reply, 10 Mar.: EdeVP, P 150/1171; EdeV to John J. Hearn, 16 Mar., and reply, 23 Mar.: Hearn Papers, NLI, MS 15992–3.

59 McGuire to HB, 7 Apr. 1922: EdeVP, P 150/1171.

60 *Irish Press* (Philadelphia), 14 Jan. 1922, p. 4.

61 Undated circular from 'Headquarters U. B.' [United Brotherhood], *circa* Jan. 1922: McGP, MS 17657.

62 According to P. S. O'Hegarty, Harry responded to news of a conditional promise by Collins to drop the Oath by getting up, 'his whole face shining, his person just a mass of animation. "Cheers, boys," said he, "I'm going to Dev. We'll all be together again in an hour's time." We were not of course.' For his partisan but circumstantial account of these meetings with Ó Murthuile, Diarmuid O'Hegarty, and sometimes Collins himself, see P. S. O'Hegarty, *A History of Ireland under the Union, 1801–1921* (London, 1952), pp 786–7.

63 HB to McG, 26 Jan. 1922: McGP, MS 17424/2.

64 Joseph Connolly, *Memoirs of Senator Joseph Connolly (1885–1961): A Founder of Modern Ireland*, ed. J. Anthony Gaughan (Dublin, 1996), p. 226.

65 Provisional Government, Minutes, 10, 13 Feb. 1922: NAD, G1/1, ff. 67, 71.

66 *Irish Press*, 8 Apr. 1922, pp 1–2; draft article: McGP, MS 17654/5. McGarrity noted 'a very close resemblance between Harry and his mother'.

67 Draft article: McGP, MS 17525/2.

68 Walsh, 'Reminiscences of the Irish Movement for Independence, 1914–' (MSS, *circa* 1949), ff. 277, 279: NYPL, J. C. Walsh Papers, slipcase. In the early hours of 21 Nov. 1920, 14 alleged Intelligence agents were fatally shot, in or about their beds, by members of Collins's 'Squad'.

69 Walsh, Reminiscences, f. 287. Walsh later heard that the point at issue during this meeting was Collins's resentment at de Valera's failure to reciprocate the 'full confidence' that he received from Collins during the Anglo-Irish negotiations, on the pretext that a superior need not confide in his subordinates.

70 Ernie O'Malley, abstract of interview with Patrick McCartan: O'Malley Papers, UCDA, P 17b/89, f. 22 (for another such recollection by McCartan, see P 17b/95, f. 54).

71 Madge MacLaverty to Walsh, 16 Feb. 1922: J. C. Walsh Papers, 2/1; Seán Ó Murthuile, Memoir (typescript, circa 1928–31), f. 224. Dr. Robert A. MacLaverty's practice at 55, Merrion Sq. South was later shared by McCartan (already his lodger in 1922): Thom's Official Directory (1927 edn.). In her letter of condolence to Kathleen Boland, 3 Aug., Madge sighed for 'poor Harry whom we all loved so dearly and shall never forget!': BP.

72 Walsh, Reminiscences, ff. 275, 277.

73 Irish Life, xxxix, no. 2 (3 Mar. 1922). The photograph was taken outside the Mansion House on 21 Feb., during Sinn Féin's Ard Fheis.

74 Dillon to [McG], 2 Feb. 1922: McGP, MS 17610/1.

75 Ó Murthuile, Memoir, f. 224. Collins had 'lived for years' at Miss Myra T. McCarthy's Munster Private Hotel at 44, Mountjoy St.: ibid., f. 224; IGH, p. 137.

76 McGarrity's signed menu card: McGP, MS 17654/6; HBD, 22 Feb. 1922.

77 Ó Murthuile to McG, 23 Feb. 1922: McGP, MS 17525/1.

78 Devoy to MC, [16 Feb. 1922]: Devoy Papers, NLI, MS 15416/6. Devoy's endorsement was admittedly qualified by his justified accusation that 'these infamous actions of de Valera were approved or condoned by all of you'.

79 Ó Murthuile to McG, 23 Feb. 1922: McGP, MS 17525/1.

80 KK to MC, 23 Feb. 1922: IGH, pp 133–4.

81 Ó Murthuile to McG, 23 Feb. 1922.

82 MC to McG, 25 Mar. 1922: McGP, MS 17436.

83 Dillon and McG to HB, [circa 1 Apr. 1922]: McGP, MS 17525/2.

84 EdeV to McG, 31 Mar. 1922: McGP, MS 17608.

85 HB to McG, 20 Apr. 1922: Seán Cronin, Frank Ryan: The Search for the Republic (Dublin, 1980), pp 19–20 (citing McGP).

86 HB to McGuire, 20 Apr. 1922: EdeVP, P 150/1171.

87 Luke Dillon to HB, circa 7 Jan. 1922: BP; Peter A. Drury (Merchants' Bank, Washington) to McG, 24 Jan.: McGP, MS 17525/1.

88 HBD, 8–10 Feb. 1922.

89 Informal receipt for $17,000, signed by MC at 55, Merrion Sq. South, 23 Feb. 1922: McGP, MS 17436.

90 HB to McG, 12 Apr. 1922: McGP, MS 17424/2; HB to Dillon, 12 Apr.: McGP, MS 17447.

91 See ch. XIII, pp 296–7.

92 HB to McG, 30 May 1922: McGP, MS 17424/2.

93 HB to Liam Lynch, 30 May 1922: EdeVP, P 150/1171. See also Maher, Harry Boland, p. 194.

94 Ward to HB, 10 Mar. 1922: EdeVP, P 150/1171.

95 HB to Trustees, 27 Mar. 1922: EdeVP, P 150/1171.

96 'Peadar' [Peter Golden?] to HB, 7 Jan. [1922]: BP.

97 The car, driven by a son of F. P. Walsh, had been held up in Jersey and both men locked up, but they were released along with their booty upon payment of a bribe of $20. See Smiddy to George Gavan Duffy, 15 May 1922: DIFP, pp 457–8 (citing DFA, ES, 30/199).

98 Smiddy to Gavan Duffy, 29 May 1922: DFA, ES, 30/199 (copy kindly supplied by

Jim Kirwan). 'Senator King' may have been Eugene F. Kinkead, a former Congressman.

99 HB to Pedlar, 30 May 1922: EdeVP, P 150/1149. 'McThomas' was one of several playful soubriquets for the Thompson sub-machine-gun.

100 MC to Gavan Duffy, 10 June 1922: DFA, ES, 17/111 (copy kindly supplied by Jim Kirwan).

101 HBD, 9, 10, 15, 26 Mar. 1922; 'Instructions for Selection of Delegates to General Convention to be held in Dublin on 5th February, 1922': MAD, Captured Documents, A/1032 (Lot 43); see also Maher, *Harry Boland*, p. 190.

102 'Óglaigh na h-Éireann, Convention, March 25th [*sic*.] 1922', agenda, forwarded with reports from 'two of my men' to Mulcahy by Col. Commandant Frank Thornton (Oriel House), 26 Mar.: Mulcahy Papers, UCDA, P7/B/191.

103 Divisional Adjutant [Dublin Brigade], report on Convention, Óglaigh na h-Éireann, 29 Mar. 1922: Aiken Papers, UCDA, P 104/1234.

104 Patrick McCartan to McG, 29 Mar. 1922: McGP, MS 17457/13.

105 Kathleen O'Connell, Diary, 9 Apr. 1922; HBD, 9 Apr.

106 HB to Lynch, 20 Apr. 1922, and reply, 24 Apr.: EdeVP, P 150/1171.

107 Florence O'Donoghue, *No Other Law: The Story of Liam Lynch and the Irish Republican Army, 1916–1923* (Dublin, 1954), pp 235–6. The committee first sat on 20 Apr. 1922, immediately after a special convention of the IRB attended by Harry.

108 Maurice Twomey (Commandant, for Chief of Staff, Four Courts) to HB, 5 May 1922, responding to his notification on 3 May that two battalions had been formed in the area of the Longford Brigade which 'wish to come under the Executive': EdeVP, P 150/1141.

109 Circular from Adjutant-General [Gearóid O'Sullivan], 4 May 1922, enclosing terms of truce, signed by 'Owen' O'Duffy and Liam Lynch, to provide 'an immediate opportunity to discover a basis for Army unification': Mulcahy Papers, UCDA, P 7/B/191. The truce resulted from negotiations which did not directly involve Harry, the Supreme Council, or the 'Army Council' in the Four Courts: O'Donoghue, *No Other Law*, pp 238–40.

110 Oscar Traynor, replies to questionnaire (typescript, June 1958): EdeVP, P 150/3297; O'Donoghue, *No Other Law*, pp 244–6. The location of this file suggests that it refers to Barry's earlier motion in March, but its content matches his proposal in June. According to O'Donoghue, this (fourth) convention was held on Sunday, 18 June 1922, the day before the relevant entry in HBD.

111 HBD, 25, 26 June 1922; Traynor, replies to further questionnaire by Florence O'Donoghue (undated typescript): EdeVP, P 150/3297. The suspended sitting is ignored in O'Donoghue's *No Other Law*, yet confirmed (though misdated) by Traynor's response to his questionnaire.

112 Mary F. McWhorter, 'Harry Boland R.I.P.' (undated typescript), f. 2: EdeVP, P 150/1173.

113 Ó Murthuile to HB, 17 Jan. 1922: EdeVP, P 150/1171. Whether 'eggs' signified Mills bombs, money, or an omelette, is unknown.

114 HB to Luke Dillon, 25 Jan. '1921' [*recte*, 1922]: McGP, MS 17424/2.

115 Ó Murthuile, Memoir, ff. 175–7, 188.

116 HBD, 25 Feb., 11, 18, 19 Mar., 19 Apr. 1922. Though the first two entries refer only to the 'S. C.' and no. '41' without specification of the IRB, no meetings of Sinn Féin's Standing Committee were held on these dates.

117 HB to Stack, 14 Apr. 1922: J. Anthony Gaughan, *Austin Stack: Portrait of a Separatist* (Dublin, 1977), p. 202. According to O'Donoghue, a 'small majority' of those present opposed the Treaty, but had no constitutional authority to over-ride the Treatyist majority on the Supreme Council. This conference had been convened

but adjourned on 12 March, as confirmed by Harry's diary entry ('41 – 11.30'): O'Donoghue, *No Other Law*, p. 233; HBD, 12 Mar.
118 HBD, 19 Mar. 1922.
119 Minutes, Dublin County Board [?], 6 Apr. 1922: Conlon Papers, UCDA, P 97/16 (1); Ó Murthuile, Memoir, ff. 190–3.
120 HB to Luke Dillon, 12 Apr. 1922: McGP, MS 17441.
121 HBD, 19 Apr. 1922.
122 Minutes, IRB Convention, 19 Apr. 1922: O'Donoghue Papers, NLI, MS 31250. In O'Donoghue's list of three names from each faction, 'Ha B' was erased in favour of 'Conlon'. See also O'Donoghue, *No Other Law*, pp 233–5.
123 HB to Stack, 21 Apr. 1922: paraphrase in Gaughan, *Austin Stack*, p. 202.
124 MC, Notebook, 19 Apr. 1922: extracts in Rex Taylor, *Michael Collins* (London, 1958), p. 185. Mulcahy, the Minister for Defence, evidently applied his customary perspective to the Convention: 'Dick – Organisation'.
125 HB to McG, 9 June 1922: McGP, MS 17424/2. It is conceivable that the term 'Coalition' referred not to the future Government proposed in the Pact, but to the next Supreme Council.

CHAPTER XIII. REMISSION

1 Kathleen O'Connell, Desk Diary, 8 Jan. 1922: O'Connell Papers, UCDA, P 155/140. The other visitors were Mary McSwiney, Liam Mellows, Erskine Childers, Cathal Brugha, and Austin Stack.
2 HB, Diary, 16, 31 Jan. 1922: EdeVP, P 150/1169d [hereafter, HBD].
3 'Republican Party: Officers and Standing Committee' (undated, with annotations in the hand of its President, de Valera): EdeVP, P 150/1135 (former number).
4 Typed copy, misattributed to *Poblacht na h-Éireann*, i, no. 3 [10 Jan. 1922], in Gavan Duffy to HB, 28 Jan.: EdeVP, P 150/1172.
5 Kathleen O'Connell, transcript of evidence to Military Pensions Committee, 28 June 1945: O'Connell Papers, P 155/190 (copy kindly supplied by Dr. Patrick Murray).
6 S. T. O'Kelly and HB, circular, 14 Feb. 1922: Barton Papers, NLI, MS 8786/3.
7 *Weekly Freeman*, 18 Feb.1922, p. 6; *Irish Independent*, 13 Feb., pp 5–6; Kathleen O'Connell, Diary, 12 Feb. Her exhausting day's work in O'Connell St. and the Mansion House ended happily when 'Harry took me home'.
8 HBD, 12 Jan. 1922.
9 *Weekly Freeman*, 21 Jan. 1922, pp 1–2; *Irish Independent*, 13 Jan., p. 6; Michael Laffan, *The Resurrection of Ireland: The Sinn Féin Party, 1916–1923* (Cambridge, 1999), p. 363; *Irish Press* (Philadelphia), 11 Feb., p. 2.
10 Jennie Wyse Power ['Sara'] to her daughter Nancy, 17 [Jan. 1922]: Humphreys Papers, UCDA, P 106/741. Of Darrell Figgis, she wrote 'D. F. as usual irritating'.
11 Minutes of Standing Committee, Sinn Féin, 16 Jan. 1922: NLI microfilm, P 3269 [hereafter, SC Minutes].
12 Stack and HB, circular to Sinn Féin officers, 17 Jan. 1922: Barton Papers, MS 8786/3.
13 SC Minutes, 23, 31 Jan. 1922. Stack's amendment, negating Collins's resolution, was defeated by 9 votes to 3, and Collins's motion was confirmed at the next meeting. The credentials committee was to vet resolutions and investigate complaints against delegates, while Harry and Paudeen O'Keeffe (the paid Secretary) were 'to make all the necessary arrangements for the poll, provide booths, ballot-boxes, etc.'
14 SC Minutes, 13, 20 Feb. 1922.

15 *Irish Independent*, 23 Feb. 1922, p. 4.
16 Kathleen O'Connell, Diary, 22 Feb. 1922.
17 SC Minutes, 3 Mar. 1922. The Director of Organisation (Hanna Sheehy-Skeffington) reported by letter that her department had 'ceased working' since the end of Jan. At the last minuted meeting, noted in HBD on 24 Mar., the reorganised Executive appointed P. J. Little and Cathal Brugha as proxies for Harry and Stack respectively, drawing Treatyist objections to both appointments which were overruled by de Valera as chairman.
18 Admission card no. 2,359 to Sinn Féin Ard Fheis for Harry Boland, TD, Standing Committee: BP.
19 *Irish Times*, 27 Feb. 1922, p. 6.
20 *Irish Independent*, 4 Apr. 1922: cutting in PRO, WO 35/206/10, f. 9.
21 *Nationalist and Leinster Times*, 22 Apr. 1922 (cutting kindly supplied by Dr. Patrick Murray).
22 *Irish Independent*, 25 Apr. 1922: cutting in WO 35/206/10, f. 9.
23 *Weekly Freeman*, 29 Apr. 1922, p. 5. De Valera's secretary deemed the meeting, on the evening of Labour's protest against militarism, 'a great success': Kathleen O'Connell, Diary, 24 Apr.
24 Between his return on 5 Jan. 1922 and the Dáil's final adjournment on 8 June, Harry's attendance was recorded on 17 of the 20 days of sitting, while his diary indicates his presence on two of the other three days: Dáil Éireann, *Official Report: Debate on the Treaty between Great Britain and Ireland* (Dublin, undated), *passim*; Dáil Éireann, *Official Report for Periods 16th August, 1921, to 26th August, 1921, and 28th February, 1922, to 8th June, 1922* (Dublin, undated), *passim*; HBD, 5 Jan., 28 Apr.
25 Dáil Éireann, *Debate on the Treaty*, pp 381–2 (9 Jan. 1922).
26 Dáil Éireann, *Official Report*, pp 112–14, 127 (28 Feb. 1922). After contributing to the defeat of this motion by 54 votes to 40, Harry supported an alternative amendment by de Valera (who had abstained from the previous vote) which was lost by 55 votes to 44 (pp 128–9).
27 Ibid., pp 132, 164 (1 Mar. 1922). This transaction may refer to the transfer to a Dáil deposit of a similar sum, raised as the 'Refugee Fund', which Harry subsequently tried to recover: see ch. XII, p. 280.
28 Ibid., pp 202–3, 227 (2 Mar. 1922).
29 George Adamson, Commandant of the 6th (Athlone) Brigade, had been shot down in the street on the previous night: *Weekly Freeman*, 29 Apr. 1922, p. 1. A few days later, when asked in Longford to identify Adamson's assailants, Harry responded that 'every true Irishman regretted the death of Brigadier Adamson', adding that 'there would be no civil war in Ireland, because no Irish soldier would fire a shot against a soldier of the Republic'. Whether the converse applied he left his audience to judge. See *Irish Independent*, 1 May: cutting in WO 35/206/10, f. 9.
30 Frank Lawless, an early Gaelic Leaguer and Sinn Féiner who was imprisoned with Harry in Lewes after assisting Thomas Ashe in the 'Battle of Ashbourne' in 1916, died aged 50 on 16 Apr. 1922 after being thrown from a horse-trap near his home at Saucerstown, Swords. The funeral of the Treatyist TD for North Co. Dublin was attended by many deputies from both parties, including Harry: *Irish Independent*, 17 Apr. 1922, p. 6; 19 Apr., p. 7.
31 Michael Sweeney, a Lieutenant in the 4th Battalion, Dublin Brigade, was killed by a military escort in Grafton St. while allegedly trying to escape from a lorry conveying him from a Court Martial at Beggars' Bush, after 8 weeks' incarceration in Mountjoy and 6 days on hunger-strike. The Inquest found that his death was 'accidental', a verdict accepted by Brigade Commandant Oscar Traynor in his grave-side oration at Glasnevin: *Irish Independent*, 11 Apr. 1922, p. 5; 13 Apr., p. 7;

17 Apr., p. 7. Harry was absent in Tullamore and Maryborough (now Portlaoise) on the day of his funeral: HBD, 16 Apr.

32 Dáil Éireann, *Official Report*, pp 235–6 (26 Apr. 1922).

33 Ibid., p. 309 (27 Apr. 1922). The 'statement' mentioned by de Valera accused Griffith of betraying the Republic, and preceded his withdrawal from the Dáil in protest at Griffith's nomination as President: Dáil Éireann, *Debate on the Treaty*, p. 410 (10 Jan.).

34 Clause 3(b) of the Constitution, approved on 26 Oct. 1917, undertook to 'make use of any and every means available to render impotent the power of England to hold Ireland in subjection by military force or otherwise': PRO, CO 904/23/5.

35 Stephen O'Mara to HB, 15 Feb. 1922, and reply, 16 Feb.: EdeVP, P 150/1171.

36 *Irish Independent*, 27 Feb. 1922, p. 5.

37 *Limerick Leader*, 1 Mar. 1922, p. 3; HBD, 9 Mar.

38 In Thurles, de Valera had explained that 'if they accepted the Treaty, and if the Volunteers of the future had tried to complete the work the Volunteers of the last four years had been attempting, . . . they would have to wade through Irish blood, through the blood of the soldiers of the Irish Government, and through, perhaps, the blood of some of the members of the Government in order to get Irish freedom': *Irish Independent*, 18 Mar. 1922, p. 7.

39 McCartan to McG, 29 Mar. 1922: McGP, NLI, MS 17457/13. McCartan added that 'Harry told me once that De V. would lead us all to the brink of the precipice but when he got there he would stop dead and would not go over.'

40 McCartan to Maloney, 31 Mar. 1922: NYPL, Maloney Papers, 6/101.

41 Richard Mulcahy to MC, 25 Mar. 1922: Mulcahy Papers, UCDA, P 7/B/192, pp 64–5. Mary Josephine ('Min') Mulcahy and Mary Kate ('Nan') O'Kelly were among the 12 children of John and Elizabeth Ryan of Tomcoole in Wexford, their sister Agnes being married to Denis McCullough. Sharply divided over the Treaty, the Ryan family provided an essential conduit between the factions: Risteárd Mulcahy, *Richard Mulcahy (1886–1971): A Family Memoir* (Dublin, 1999), pp 275–300.

42 T. M. to Maurice Healy, 25 Mar. 1922: T. M. Healy, *Letters and Leaders of My Day* (2 vols., New York edn., 1929), ii, p. 653.

43 McCartan to McG, 6 Apr. 1922: McGP, MS 17457/13.

44 O'Connor to HB, 7 Apr. 1922: EdeVP, P 150/1171.

45 Mary McSwiney to McG, 29 Apr. 1922: McGP, MS 17654/3.

46 Transcription of statement by 'Army Officers', 1 May 1922: Mulcahy Papers, P7/B/192.

47 Dáil Éireann, *Official Report*, pp 365, 367, 379 (3, 10 May 1922).

48 Ibid., pp 401–4 (11 May 1922).

49 Kathleen O'Connell, Diary, 11 May 1922.

50 Kathleen Clarke, *Revolutionary Woman: Kathleen Clarke, 1878–1972, an Autobiography*, ed. Helen Litton (Dublin, 1991), p. 194. Though imprecise in detail and implicitly misdated as Jan. rather than May 1922, this account clearly refers to the Peace Committee.

51 Dáil Éireann, *Official Report*, pp 412–15, 420–2 (17 May 1922).

52 Clarke, *Revolutionary Woman*, p. 195.

53 HBD, 18, 19 May 1922.

54 Dáil Éireann, *Official Report*, pp 472–3, 478 (19 May 1922).

55 Seán T. O'Kelly, Memoirs (undated typescript), ff. 336–9: Ó Ceallaigh Papers, NLI, MS 27707.

56 The new Executive would consist of a President elected by the Dáil, a Minister for Defence 'representing the Army', five ministers chosen by 'the majority Party', and four by the 'minority'. Adult suffrage would be introduced only at a subsequent

election, should the Coalition Government collapse: Dáil Éireann, *Official Report*, p. 479 (20 May 1922).
57 Brian P. Murphy, 'Nationalism: The Framing of the Constitution of the Irish Free State, 1922', p. 149, in *The Irish Revolution, 1913–1923*, ed. Joost Augusteijn (Houndmills, Hants, 2002), pp 135–50 (citing memorandum by Lionel Curtis, 21 May 1922: PRO, CO 739/5, f. 9); Jim Maher, *Harry Boland: A Biography* (Cork, 1998), p. 208 (citing Cabinet Sub-Committee on Ireland, Minutes, 24 May 1922: PRO, CAB 43/7).
58 Dáil Éireann, *Official Report*, pp 479–80 (20 May 1922).
59 HB to McG, 20 May 1922: McGP, MS 17578.
60 McGuire to HB, 24 May 1922, and reply, 8 June: EdeVP, P 150/1171.
61 Provisional Government, Minutes, 3 June 1922: NAD, G 1/2, f. 74.
62 Seán T. O'Kelly and HB to MC, 27 May 1922: Béaslaí Papers, NLI, MS 33916/11.
63 Circular, 1 June 1922, in cutting from *Freeman's Journal*, 3 June: WO 35/206/10, f. 7.
64 HBD, 31 May 1922. Figgis, a strong Treatyist and chairman of the committee drafting the Constitution, was punished for his independence on 12 June, as Kitty Kiernan observed: 'Poor Darrell Figgis lost his nice red beard. When I read about it I could imagine you laughing and enjoying it very much. But it was a mean thing for some of Harry's cronies to do, wasn't it? ... He was lucky it was only his beard.' See KK to MC, 13 June 1922: *In Great Haste: The Letters of Michael Collins and Kitty Kiernan*, ed. Leon Ó Broin (Dublin, 1996; 1st edn. 1983) [hereafter, *IGH*], p. 189; *Weekly Freeman*, 17 June, p. 5.
65 Dáil Éireann, *Official Report*, p. 439 (17 May 1922).
66 HBD, 6 June 1922. Earlier entries state that he and Tom Maguire had been nominated for the Republican Party on 27 May, and the nomination papers sent to the Dáil on 1 June.
67 *Roscommon Herald*, 10 June 1922 (copy of cutting kindly supplied by Dr. Patrick Murray). Harry's speech suggests that he was 'one of the few Republican candidates who had learned at last the need for a social policy': C. Desmond Greaves, *Liam Mellows and the Irish Revolution* (London, 1971), p. 330.
68 *Irish Times*, 7 June 1922: cutting in WO/35/206/10, f. 7.
69 *Irish Independent*, 10 June 1922, p. 7; J. Anthony Gaughan, *Austin Stack: Portrait of a Separatist* (Dublin, 1977), p. 206.
70 HBD, 10–16 June 1922; Maher, *Harry Boland*, p. 214.
71 *Irish Independent*, 12 June 1922, p. 5; 14 June, p. 5; 15 June, p. 7.
72 HBD, 16, 19, 20, 22 June 1922.
73 Earl of Longford and Thomas P. O'Neill, *Eamon de Valera* (London, 1970), p. 190.
74 In Clonakilty, Collins pointed out that no 'Government that could last, could allow certain actions either in the name of Labour or in the name of the Irish Republic. ... Vote for the candidates you think best of, whom [sic.] you think will carry on best in future the work you want carried on.' He did not, however, explicitly repudiate any element of the Pact: *Irish Independent*, 16 June 1922, p. 7.
75 HB to McG, 9 June 1922: McGP, MS 17424/2.
76 HB to McG, 22 June 1922: transcript in EdeVP, P 150/1171.
77 O'Kelly, Memoirs, f. 343.
78 HB to McG, 22 June 1922.
79 See above, ch. XII, p. 283.
80 Robert Brennan, *Allegiance* (Dublin, 1950), p. 337.
81 'Joe' [O'Doherty?] to [McG?], 19 July 1922: McGP, MS 17525/2. Though the emissary later joined the republican forces, fighting in 'Blessington and away up in the Mountains', he had initially felt aggrieved at his reception from the republicans,

particularly Harry: 'I have seen him several times since, and I may say that he hasn't improved any in my estimation by his manner of receiving, or rather of not receiving me. He could, at least, interduce [*sic*.] me so that one could feel at home.'

82 Kathleen O'Connell, Diary, 15 Apr. 1922.

83 Kathleen Boland (Mrs Seán O'Donovan), Statement for the Bureau of Military History (undated typescript), f. 20: BP. Kate Boland is said to have replied: 'Ah, Mick! We never had much money but we had patriotism, and Harry couldn't sell it. It was born with him.'

84 Mary F. McWhorter, 'Harry Boland R.I.P.' (undated typescript), f. 2: EdeVP, P 150/1173.

85 HBD, 21 May 1922.

86 HB to KK, 10, 16 Jan. 1922: BP.

87 HB to KK, [18 Jan. 1922; misdated 16 Jan. 1921]: *IGH*, p. 12.

88 HB to KK, 10 Apr. 1922: BP.

89 KK to MC, 1, 14, 17, 23 Feb., 15, 27 Mar., 5?, 10, 13?, 17, 25 Apr., 6 June 1922: *IGH*, pp 113, 127, 130, 133, 146, 149, 155, 156, 159, 161, 167, 186. Queried dates refer to letters received on the following day.

90 Harry's diary noted his attendance at a 'Point to Point' on 30 Mar. and a 'hunt' on 7 Apr., along with seven days simply in 'Granard': HBD, 29 Mar., 1 May, 4, 15, 16, 17, 18 June 1922.

91 KK to MC, 'Friday' [16 June 1922]: *IGH*, pp 192–3.

92 HBD, 4 June 1922.

93 KK to MC, 25 Apr. 1922, and reply, 26 Apr.: *IGH*, p. 167, 168.

94 MC to KK, 28 Mar.: *IGH*, p. 149.

95 MC to KK, 16? Feb. 1922: *IGH*, p. 128.

96 The hurling final was held on Sunday, 14 May 1922, in between nocturnal sessions of the Peace Committee on the Saturday and Sunday nights. When the congress convened on 16 April, Harry was in Tullamore and Maryborough; when it resumed on 21 May, he was celebrating the Pact with his family in Greystones: *Irish Independent*, 17 Apr., p. 8; 15 May, p. 5; 22 May, p. 8; HBD, 16 Apr., 14, 21 May.

97 Kitty O'Brien (Fermoy) to HB, 28 Mar. 1922: BP. Her address in London was the Professional Women's Club in Brunswick Sq., Bloomsbury.

CHAPTER XIV. RUIN

1 Pedlar to McG, 27 July [1922]: McGP, NLI, MS 17635; HB, Diary, 27 June: EdeVP, P 150/1169d [hereafter, HBD].

2 HBD, 28 June 1922. The Plaza, at 98–101, Middle Abbey St. (close to Harry's business), offered 'dancing, restaurant, billiards and garage': *Thom's Official Directory of the United Kingdom of Great Britain and Ireland* (Dublin, 1929 edn.).

3 Frank O'Connor, *The Big Fellow: Michael Collins and the Irish Revolution* (London, 1969; 1st edn. 1937), p. 208.

4 *Cork Examiner*, 5 Aug. 1922, p. 5.

5 HB to Kate Boland, undated: BP.

6 McG to HB, 5 July 1922: McGP, MS 17424/3. On 27 July, Harry told Seán T. O'Kelly that 'Joe's letter only reached me last night via Cork': copy in Mulcahy Papers, UCDA, P 7/B/4, f. 33.

7 HBD, 9–15 July 1922; Mary F. McWhorter, 'Harry Boland R.I.P.' (undated typescript), ff. 3–4: EdeVP, P 150/1173. His diary for 13 July confirms the timing of this visit: 'Mrs McW., Katie [Clarke?], Kathleen to St. E.'

8 HB to McG, 13 July 1922 (in Harry's hand): McGP, MS 17424/2.

9 Ibid.
10 HB to 'Sally', 13 July 1922: copy in Hearn Papers, NLI, MS 15991. He was responding to an anxious message 'wondering where you are and if you're safe and if you are near "the Chief" – oh I do hope you are – for no matter what the tales are about you, your adorable loyalty has left an impression that can never be effaced'. See 'Sally' to HB, 1 July: BP.
11 McCartan to McG, 21 July 1922: McGP, MS 17457/13. McCartan blamed the opposition for the breakdown: 'Rory O'Connor killed that Pact very effectively and Bolshevism has taken the place of Document No. 2.'
12 Lynch moved from Mallow to Limerick, where he set up his headquarters, on 29 June 1922. His agreements with Michael Brennan and Donncadha Hannigan (formalised on 4 and 7 July but terminated by Brennan on 11 July) appeared to strengthen the republican position by allowing both sides to occupy barracks, but it also enabled Brennan to secure reinforcements and eventually to drive his opponents out of Limerick by 21 July: Florence O'Donoghue, *No Other Law: The Story of Liam Lynch and the Irish Republican Army, 1916–1923* (Dublin, 1954), pp 260–4; Michael Hopkinson, *Green against Green* (Dublin, 1988), pp 147–50.
13 The Belfast Brigade also sent 50 men, unarmed and 'more of a hindrance than a help': Oscar Traynor, 'Account written ... at request of President de Valera shortly before his death' (typescript, 1963), f. 110: EdeVP, P 150/3297. See also Ernie O'Malley, interview with Traynor: O'Malley Papers, UCDA, P 17b/96, f. 68. The size of the column is given elsewhere as 70, over 100, and 109 (on 2 July): Ernie O'Malley, *The Singing Flame* (Dublin, 1978), p. 129; Hopkinson, *Green against Green*, p. 142; return, 'Strength of Irregulars at Blessington', 2 July 1922: Mulcahy Papers, P 7/B/106, f. 348.
14 Ernie O'Malley, interview with Mossy Donegan (Bandon): O'Malley Papers, P 17b/108, f. 75; see also Jim Maher, *Harry Boland: A Biography* (Cork, 1998), p. 225.
15 Ernie O'Malley, interview with Tom Smyth (Clonmel): O'Malley Papers, P 17b/103, f. 41; John P. Duggan, *A History of the Irish Army* (Dublin, 1991), pp 85–6.
16 It is possible that he proceeded to Mallow in search of Lynch, before following him to Limerick, as O'Donoghue states that Harry 'had gone to Mallow on 29th June to seek reinforcements and munitions': O'Donoghue, *No Other Law*, p. 257.
17 HBD, 30 June 1922; Robert Barton to Kathleen Boland, 2 July 1922: BP.
18 Robert Briscoe (with Alden Hatch), *For the Life of Me* (Boston, 1958), p. 144.
19 Gerald Boland, Recollections (undated MSS, file 'p', addressed to Oscar Traynor): BP.
20 Kathleen Clarke, *Revolutionary Woman: Kathleen Clarke, 1878–1972, an Autobiography*, ed. Helen Litton (Dublin, 1991), pp 197–9. In return, she and her passengers were put up for the night in the Crooksling Sanatorium, and driven back to Dublin by ambulance.
21 Ernie O'Malley, interview with Mick Burke (Clonmel): O'Malley Papers, P 17b/103, f. 58.
22 After the fall of Blessington, it was reported that 'some of the inhabitants were very bitter against the Irregulars, who had helped themselves liberally to food and other articles', whereas one otherwise unsympathetic witness stated 'that they acted with moderation and only took what was necessary for their subsistence', without – 'of course' – paying for commandeered goods: *Weekly Irish Times*, 15 July 1922, p. 1.
23 O'Malley to Liam Lynch, 12 July: Twomey Papers, UCDA, P 69/38, ff. 66–8.
24 O'Malley, *Singing Flame*, p. 129.
25 O'Malley (GHQ, Blessington) to Brigade and Battalion Commandants, 3 July 1922, with undated list of Executive Officers: Mulcahy Papers, P 7/B/106, ff. 350, 356.

26 O'Malley to Liam Lynch, 12 July 1922: Twomey Papers, P 69/38, ff. 66–8; HBD, 3 July. National forces occupied Ballymore Eustace on the following day, taking 13 prisoners: report by P. Cronin (O/C, Curragh), 15 July: Mulcahy Papers, P 7/B/107, f. 46.

27 C. O'Donovan (Vice-Commandant, 3rd Battalion) to O/C, 4 July 1922: Mulcahy Papers, P 7/B/106, f. 347; HBD, 4 July; Maher, *Harry Boland*, p. 230; Duggan, *Irish Army*, p. 86.

28 Based at Ballinascorney House, three miles east of Brittas, he also made detours to nearby Glenasmole and Kilbride: HBD, 5–7 July 1922.

29 Traynor, Account, ff. 116–18; Ernie O'Malley, interview with Traynor: O'Malley Papers, P 17b/96, f. 72.

30 Traynor to Chief of Staff [Lynch], 6 July 1922 (handwritten original): Twomey Papers, P 69/38, ff. 73–4. A copy of this despatch was captured at Blessington and transcribed: Mulcahy Papers, P 7/B/106, f. 340.

31 O'Malley, interview with Traynor, f. 73.

32 Gerald to Kate Boland, 11 Nov. 1923: McGP, MS 17578.

33 HBD, 7 July 1922; Traynor, Account, f. 118.

34 Report by P. Cronin, 15 July 1922, f. 47. Most of Cronin's troops withdrew to the Curragh on the Saturday evening. An operation report, sent at 12.30 a.m. on 8 July, indicated that over 100 of the 200–300 'Irregulars' had already been taken prisoner: Mulcahy Papers, P 7/B/60, f. 225.

35 'F. D.' (Blessington) to Traynor, 8 July 1922: copy in Twomey Papers, P 69/38, f. 79; Traynor, Account, ff. 119–20.

36 R. Harris (Blessington) to O/C, Barracks, 8 July 1922 (enclosed in Adjutant, Eastern Command, to Mulcahy et al., 11 July): copy in Mulcahy Papers, P 7/B/60, f. 219. The unit duly left behind 20 bombs, 14 detonators, 14 fuses, 5 shotguns, and a motorcar.

37 Ernie O'Malley, interview with George Gilmore: Hopkinson, *Green against Green*, p. 143 (citing O'Malley Papers, P 17b/106).

38 'F. D.' to Traynor, 8 July 1922, ff. 79–80.

39 Ernie O'Malley, interview with Mick Burke, f. 59.

40 Kitty O'Doherty, Report to Clan na Gael (undated, *circa* Aug. 1922), f. 17: McGP, MS 17471.

41 Ernie O'Malley, interview with Mick Burke, f. 59.

42 McWhorter, 'Harry Boland', f. 4. This account mistakenly indicates that Traynor had been arrested 'a few days previous' to the visit to St. Enda's on 13 July, a fortnight before the true date of his arrest at Baggot St. Bridge: Niall C. Harrington, *Kerry Landing* (Dublin, 1992), p. 40.

43 HB to McG, 13 July 1922: McGP, MS 17424/2. Brugha was wounded on 5 July and died two days later.

44 HBD, 10, 11, 12, 14 July 1922. The triumviral Council of War was appointed by the Provisional Government on the evening of 12 July: Rex Taylor, *Michael Collins* (London, 1961; 1st edn. 1958), p. 194 (citing MC, Notebook, 12 July).

45 Unattributed letter from 'Your Red Cross Pal', 15 July 1922: copy in Hearn Papers, MS 15993. The writer added that 'he is not well and looks pale and bad'.

46 McWhorter, 'Harry Boland', ff. 4–5; Ernie O'Malley to Kate Boland, 2 Aug. 1922: BP; O'Malley to Liam Lynch, 31 July: Twomey Papers, P 69/38, f. 5. This dinner apparently occurred on Friday, 14 July, long before Mrs McWhorter's actual departure from Dublin on 30 Sept.

47 HBD, 17 July 1922.

48 O'Malley, *Singing Flame*, pp 143, 149.

49 Patrick McCartan to McG, 21 July 1922: McGP, MS 17457/13.

50 The *Ballinalee*, so named in honour of the Blacksmith's greatest triumph as an ambusher in Jan. 1921, was captured on 12 July 1922 outside Markree Castle near Collooney, Co. Sligo, in an ambush from which only one soldier escaped. The 'Irregular' forces were subsequently expelled from Collooney by a party led by McKeown from Athlone, and the *Ballinalee* was recaptured on 29 July. See reports by McKeown and Cooney (summary of telephone call), 15, 29 July: Mulcahy Papers, P 7/B/107, ff. 31, 211.

51 McKeown had been married to Mary Cooney, with a military guard of honour, on 22 June 1922: Duggan, *Irish Army*, p. 80.

52 HBD, 18, 19, 21, 22 July 1922.

53 McWhorter, 'Harry Boland', f. 5; see also Maher, *Harry Boland*, p. 258.

54 Liam Lynch to Ernie O'Malley, 25 July 1922, and reply, 28 July: O'Malley Papers, P 17a/60, 54.

55 HB (GHQ, 'Eastern Command') to Liam Lynch (Field GHQ, Fermoy), 21 July 1922: Twomey Papers, P 69/38, f. 33. The first shipload reached Waterford on 23 July: O'Donoghue, *No Other Law*, p. 266.

56 Anonymous, undated letter to Sir John Lavery: Sinéad McCoole, *Hazel: A Life of Lady Lavery, 1880–1935* (Dublin, 1996), p. 104.

57 HB to Luke Dillon, 27 July 1922: copy in FitzGerald Papers, UCDA, P 80/764.

58 Kitty O'Doherty, Report, ff. 1–3. When she reached Cork with the booty, the man responsible for procuring it was dead. The money intended for Harry was delivered to Seán McSwiney. Kitty O'Doherty, whose husband Joe had acted briefly as President of the IRB's Supreme Council after the Rebellion, later claimed to have transported $60,000 in gold, sewn into a linen bag strapped to her body. See O'Doherty, Statement (undated duplicate typescript), ff. 35, 49–50: MAD, Bureau of Military History Papers, WS 355.

59 HB to O'Kelly, 27 July 1922: copy in Mulcahy Papers, P 7/B/4, f. 33.

60 Pedlar to McG, undated, with sequel, 18 Aug. 1922: McGP, MS 17478. Other recoverable material included 4 Thompsons, held by Hugh Montague, 'a case of spare parts with Culhane', and ammunition in the possession of Eugene F. Kinkead.

61 John T. Ryan to Kathleen Boland, 16 Nov. 1923: McGP, MS 17578. Rorke counter-alleged that $13,500 (half of the original sum contracted) had never been paid.

62 HB to McG, 25–27 July 1922: McGP, MS 17424/2. Mellows had been the Executive's Director of Purchases, a post apparently assimilated into Harry's office of acting Quartermaster. De Valera is here designated as 'acting Chief of Staff' at Field GHQ, not the humble 'private' of republican folklore.

63 HB to Dillon, 27 July 1922: typed copy in FitzGerald Papers, P 80/764.

64 Briscoe, *For the Life of Me*, p. 179. Since Harry did not return to Rathfarnham until 8 July, three days before de Valera's departure for Mallow, these missions presumably occurred during the second week: HBD, 8, 11 July 1922.

65 HBD, 10, 11 July 1922.

66 'Joe' to McG, 19 July 1922: McGP, MS 17525/2. The writer considered that 'the Chief could not bring about peace if he tried'.

67 HB and O'Kelly (Cumann na Poblachta) to Thomas Johnson (Secretary, Irish Labour Party), 19 July 1922: Johnson Papers, NLI, MS 17139. Harry's signature to this letter was faked by O'Kelly.

68 HB to Jennie Wyse Power, forwarded to MC from Sinn Féin Head Office, 29 July: Mulcahy Papers, P 7/B/4, f. 92; extract (dated 27 July) in Marie O'Neill, *From Parnell to de Valera: A Biography of Jennie Wyse Power, 1858–1941* (Dublin, 1991), p. 143. Paudeen O'Keeffe (General Secretary) had become Deputy Governor of Mountjoy Prison; his assistant was perhaps Paddy Sheehan (acting General Secretary in Aug. 1918).

69 McWhorter, 'Harry Boland', f. 4.
70 HB and S. T. O'Kelly to Cumann na Poblachta, 24 July 1922: EdeVP, P 150/409 (former number). The meeting was to be held on Friday afternoon, 27 July.
71 Provisional Government, Minutes, 17 July 1922: NAD, G 1/2, f. 160.
72 McWhorter, 'Harry Boland', f. 6.
73 HB to O'Kelly, 27 July 1922: copy in Mulcahy Papers, P 7/B/4, f. 33; Pedlar to McG, 3 Aug.: McGP, MS 17478. Harry had suggested to O'Kelly that they 'talk matters over' at 31, Richmond Ave., Fairview, the house formerly occupied by P. S. O'Hegarty but currently by Kathleen Clarke: Thom's Official Directory (1919, 1922 edns.).
74 Clarke, Revolutionary Woman, p. 199.
75 Kitty O'Doherty, Report, f. 16.
76 McWhorter, 'Harry Boland', f. 6. Shanahan, a grocer and publican at 134, Foley St. (near Amiens St. Station), had previously looked after the guns and troops of the Tipperary column which left Blessington with Harry: Ernie O'Malley, interview with Mick Burke, f. 59; Thom's Official Directory (1919 edn.).
77 After their marriage in 1918, O'Kelly moved into the house at 19, Ranelagh Rd., already occupied by Mary Kate ('Nan') Ryan: Thom's Official Directory (1919 edn.).
78 Poblacht na h-Éireann, War News no. 23 (25 July 1922), when execrating 'Government by the I.R.B.' through a 'Military Dictatorship' monopolised by members of the Supreme Council, praised de Valera and Brugha, but not Harry, for refusing 'to have anything further to do with the I.R.B., as soon as it became possible for Irishmen to organise openly for independence'.
79 MC to 'Government', 29 July 1922: Mulcahy Papers, P 7/B/29, ff. 159, 162; see also Brian P. Murphy, John Chartres: Mystery Man of the Treaty (Dublin, 1995), p. 129.
80 Irish Independent, 1 Aug. 1922, p. 8 (letters from HB and O'Malley to O'Kelly, with official commentary); Dublin Evening Mail, 1 Aug. ('City Final' edn.), p. 3.
81 MC to HB, 28 July 1922: Taylor, Michael Collins, p. 194 (citing a 'private source').
82 Kitty O'Doherty, Report, f. 17.
83 Liam Pedlar to McG, 3 Aug. 1922: McGP, MS 17478; for Hearty, see above ch. XI, pp 246–7.
84 Meda Ryan, Michael Collins and the Women in His Life (Cork, 1996), p. 175 (citing Anna (Fitzsimons) Kelly, Irish Press, 1 Aug. 1938). This passage does not appear in Anna Kelly's appreciation, 'A Gay and Gallant Spirit', in ibid. ('City' edn), p. 8: NLI.
85 'A. K.', 'The Evening Round': undated cutting from Irish Press in BP.
86 This property, formerly occupied by a Church of Ireland clergyman, was 'let in flats': Thom's Official Directory (1915, 1922, 1929 edns.).
87 EdeV, dictated account of interview with Griffin, 18 Apr. 1963: EdeVP, P 150/1173. Griffin, a Kerryman, had previously helped Harry during his peregrinations through the Dublin mountains, 'as he knows the country better'. See Harrington, Kerry Landing, p. 67; unattributed letter from 'Your Red Cross Pal', 15 July 1922.
88 Harrington, Kerry Landing, p. 40.
89 Annie Traynor (Ballybough) to Kate Boland, 2 Aug. 1922: BP.
90 EdeV, interview with Griffin; Maher, Harry Boland, p. 241 (citing Kevin Boland's recollection that they called on his family home).
91 O/C, Dublin to acting Ass. Chief of Staff [O'Malley], as forwarded to Director of Intelligence, 3 Aug. 1922: Humphreys Papers, UCDA (reference kindly supplied by Dr. Brian Hanley). Though O'Malley asked Griffin's successor to 'please verify' the report, no response survives.
92 Report by J. O'Reilly, acting O/C, 1st Eastern Division, 5 Aug. 1922: MAD,

Captured Documents, A/0989 (Lot 1). The entire Division had but 69 rifles at the onset of the Civil War.

93 Maher, *Harry Boland*, p. 241 (citing Kevin Boland's supposition that Harry wished to contact a Captain Martin, a native of Skerries who sailed boats to Liverpool).

94 *New York World*, 1 Aug. 1922 (cable from P. J. Kelly, 31 July): cutting in BP.

95 MC to Director of Intelligence, 4 Aug. 1922: Mulcahy Papers, P 7/B/4, f. 72.

96 EdeV, interview with Griffin.

97 *Dublin Evening Mail*, 31 July 1922 ('Final Buff' edn.), p. 3; New York *World*, 1 Aug. Balbriggan had been occupied by Government troops since 17 July, when 25 prisoners were taken during the retreat by 100 'Irregulars'. See Report on Military Situation, Eastern Command, 17 July: Mulcahy Papers, P 7/B/60, f. 192.

98 EdeV, interview with Griffin.

99 *Dublin Evening Mail*, 31 July 1922, p. 3. Healy was the Dispensary Doctor and Ellis a curate at Skerries.

100 *Freeman's Journal*, 1 Aug. 1922, p. 5. The House Surgeon, however, reported 'an entry wound between the 8th and 9th ribs on the left side of the chest': Dr. William Robert Cussen, report to Inquest, 3 Aug.: Official Inquest Report, NLI, MS 13661. A report that the bullet entered his left side convinced Mary McWhorter that, contrary to the insinuation of Mulcahy's wife Min, right-handed Harry had not shot himself: McWhorter, 'Harry Boland', f. 10.

101 Notes of telephoned report from Adjutant, 5th Battalion, Dublin Brigade, 31 July 1922: Mulcahy Papers, P 7/B/107, f. 250. Griffin carried a permit (no. 983) issued at Portobello Barracks to J. J. Murphy of 3, Castlewood Ave., Ranelagh (a building contractor). See also report on Military Situation, Eastern Command, 2nd Eastern Division, 31 July: Mulcahy Papers, P 7/B/60, f. 158.

102 In *Poblacht na h-Éireann*, War News no. 31 (4 Aug. 1922), it was claimed that the party, reinforced from Balbriggan, included 60 men, machine guns, and an armoured car, with men guarding every exit as well as patrolling the corridor and staircase.

103 *An t-Óglách*, 12 Aug. 1922, p. 3: cutting in PRO, WO 35/206/10, f. 13.

104 'Harry Boland Shot Trying to Escape' (undated handbill): Barton Papers, NLI, MS 5638.

105 Kathleen Boland to McG, 17 Aug. 1922: McGP, MS 17578.

106 McWhorter, 'Harry Boland', f. 10. She and Kathleen spoke to Ellis after picking up Harry's clothes on the day after his burial.

107 *Cork Examiner*, 5 Aug. 1922, p. 5.

108 See above, ch. 1, pp 1–3.

109 Transcript of statement by EdeV, 7 Dec. 1962: EdeVP, P 150/1173. De Valera reached this conclusion four months before his previously cited interview with Griffin.

110 McCartan to McG, 3, 5 Aug. 1922: McGP, MS 17457/13. His informant was 'a man who should know'.

111 Provisional Government, Minutes, 17, 31 July 1922: G 1/3, ff. 160, 208; NAD, Executive Council Papers, S 1428 (including extract of Minutes, 30 Aug.).

112 Lynch to O'Malley, 27 Aug. 1922, and reply, 3 Sept.: Mulcahy Papers, P 7a/81, ff. 46, 36. Griffin, though living, had relinquished office upon his arrest.

113 Note in McG's hand, 26 Nov. 1923: McGP.

114 Army Census, 12–13 Nov. 1922: MAD.

115 According to Anna Kelly, he was left in Skerries for four hours, 'then taken to Portobello Barracks and from that to the hospital': *Irish Press*, 1 Aug. 1938, p. 8. Another report gave his time of arrival as 6.30 a.m.: *Irish Independent*, 1 Aug. 1922, p. 5.

[116] Cussen, report to Inquest: *Dublin Evening Mail*, 3 Aug. 1922, p. 3; Official Inquest Report.

[117] Kathleen Boland (Mrs Seán O'Donovan), Statement for the Bureau of Military History (undated typescript), f. 21; McWhorter, 'Harry Boland', f. 7; Sgt. P. Manning (DMP, College St., Dublin) to Dr. Louis A. Byrne (Coroner), 2 Aug. 1922 (reporting Harry's death and his treatment by Cussen and later by 'Surgeon Kennedy'): Official Inquest Report. The American claimed that Dr. Kennedy had told her that Harry's 'insides were literally shattered' by 'dum-dum' bullets.

[118] McWhorter, 'Harry Boland', f. 8.

[119] Kathleen Boland, Statement, f. 21.

[120] MC to Director of Intelligence, 31 July 1922: Mulcahy Papers, P 7/B/4, f. 90. The guard on his room remained 'until a few hours before he died': Kate Boland to McG, 17 Aug.: McGP, MS 17578.

[121] Kathleen Boland, Statement, f. 21; *The Fenian*, War Issue no. 17 (3 Aug. 1922): Childers Papers, NLI, MS 15441/7; *Poblacht na h-Éireann*, War News no. 31 (4 Aug.).

[122] McWhorter, 'Harry Boland', f. 8; Kathleen Boland, Statement, f. 21.

[123] Fr. Albert Bibby, along with his fellow-republican activist Fr. Dominic O'Connor, was eventually (in 1924) induced by the Capuchin Provincial to volunteer for the American mission, in response to complaints from the Provincial Government and the Bishop of Cork: Patrick Murray, *Oracles of God: The Roman Catholic Church and Irish Politics, 1922–37* (Dublin, 2000), p. 28.

[124] Kitty O'Doherty, Report, f. 18. It was also claimed that Collins himself had refused a request for Gerald's parole by Fr. Thornton's brother, presumably Frank Thornton of Collins's 'Squad' and the IRB: *The Fenian*, War Issue no. 19 (5 Aug.): BP.

[125] McCartan to McG, 1 Aug. 1922: McGP, MS 17457/13.

[126] Clarke, *Revolutionary Woman*, p. 200. According to Mary McWhorter, however, he died serenely with his eyes upon an effigy of the Sacred Heart at the foot of his bed: McWhorter, 'Harry Boland', f. 8.

[127] McWhorter, 'Harry Boland', f. 9. The uniform prompted 'some little dispute', in which she was allegedly invited to adjudicate by Kathleen Boland.

Chronology

1886

Feb. 1   Gladstone (Liberal) replaced Salisbury (Conservative) as Prime Minister.

June 8   Gladstone's first Government of Ireland Bill defeated, House of Commons, after split in Liberal Party (introduced, 8 Apr.).

July   General Election, following Gladstone's resignation, resulted in Salisbury's return to power (25 July); 84 nationalists (and 19 others) elected in Irish constituencies.

1887

Apr. 27   Harry Boland born, Dublin.

Nov. 9   GAA (founded, 1884) split between 'Fenian' and 'clerical' factions at convention, Thurles, Co. Tipperary.

1888

Aug. 13   Special Commission Act instituted judicial inquiry into charges by *The Times* against Parnell and colleagues.

1889

May 4   Disappearance followed by murder of Dr. Cronin, Chicago, led to further fragmentation of Clan na Gael (split, 1883).

July 19   HB's sister Kathleen born, Dublin.

1890

Feb. 13   Special Commission rejected most charges against Parnell and colleagues.

Nov. 17   O'Shea granted decree nisi for divorce, naming Parnell as co-respondent (suit instigated, 24 Dec. 1889).

Dec. 6   Parnell repudiated as leader of Irish Parliamentary Party by 45 members led by Justin McCarthy, 28 remaining loyal to Parnell.

1891

Oct. 6   Parnell died, Brighton (funeral in Dublin, 11 Oct.).

Oct., late   Explosion at office of *National Press*, Dublin.

Nov. 9   Fenian P. W. Nally died, Mountjoy Prison.

1892

Mar.   HB's father, Jim, elected President, Dublin Co. Committee, GAA.

July   General Election resulted in Gladstone's return to power (15

Aug.); 80 nationalists (including 9 Parnellites, led by Redmond) elected in Irish constituencies.

Dec. 24   Explosion at detective office, Exchange St., Dublin.

1893
HB's brother Ned born, Dublin.

May 6   Explosion at Four Courts, Dublin.

July 31   Gaelic League founded, Dublin.

Sept. 9   Gladstone's second Government of Ireland Bill defeated, House of Lords (introduced in Commons, 13 Feb.).

1894
Mar. 5   Rosebery succeeded Gladstone as Liberal Prime Minister.

Apr. 27–28   First Irish Trades Union Congress.

July   IRB's Supreme Council, including Jim Boland, reorganised under Fred Allan.

1895
Mar. 11   Jim Boland died, Dublin (funeral, 14 Mar.).

May 6   Irish National Brotherhood established in Dublin, in competition with IRB.

June 25   Rosebery replaced as Prime Minister by Salisbury.

July   General Election confirmed Conservative Government under Salisbury; 81 nationalists (including 12 Parnellites) elected in Irish constituencies.

Nov. 29   HB's uncle Jack Boland died, Liverpool (funeral in Dublin, 1 Dec.).

1896
Feb. 18   Dillon elected as leader by anti-Parnellites, following McCarthy's resignation (2 Feb.).

1898
July 1   Union of two factions of AOH in America.

Sept. 11   HB's sister Nellie died, Manchester.

1899
Oct. 11   Outbreak of 'Boer War' (concluded by Treaty of Vereeniging, 31 May 1902).

1900
Jan. 30   Nationalist factions reunified under Redmond (elected leader of Irish Parliamentary Party, 6 Feb.).

July   First convention of reunified Clan na Gael, Atlantic City.

Sept.–Oct.   General Election confirmed Conservative Government under Salisbury; 81 nationalists (including 5 independents) elected in Irish constituencies.

1901
Jan. 22   Queen Victoria died; succeeded by Edward VII.

1902
July 12   Balfour succeeded Salisbury as Conservative Prime Minister.

1903
June 6   Griffith convened National Council.

1904
Jan.   HB and his brother Gerald enrolled in IRB, Dublin.

1905
Mar.   Ulster Unionist Council formed.

Dec. 5   Balfour replaced as Prime Minister by Campbell-Bannerman (Liberal).

1906
Jan.   General Election confirmed Liberal Government under Campbell-Bannerman; 82 nationalists (including 1 independent) elected in Irish constituencies.

1907
Dec.   HB elected to Dublin Co. Committee, GAA.

1908
Apr. 8   Asquith succeeded Campbell-Bannerman as Liberal Prime Minister.

Sept.   Sinn Féin founded, after merger (5 Sept. 1907) of Griffith's National Council and other separatist organisations.

Nov. 11   Irish Women's Franchise League formed.

Dec. 29   Larkin formed Irish Transport (and General) Workers' Union.

1909
Aug. 16   Fianna Éireann formed, under Constance de Markievicz.

1910
Jan.   General Election, following defeat of Lloyd George's budget (30 Nov. 1909), confirmed Liberal Government under Asquith; 81 nationalists (including 11 independents) elected in Irish constituencies, sharing balance of power.

Feb. 21   Carson elected leader of Irish Unionist MPs.

May 6   Edward VII died; succeeded by George V.

Dec.   General Election confirmed Asquith's minority Government; 83 nationalists (including 10 independents) elected in Irish constituencies.

1911

Aug. 18   Parliament Act curtailed powers of veto by House of Lords.

Oct. 22   HB elected President, Dublin Co. Committee, GAA.

1912

Apr. 11   Asquith's Government of Ireland Bill introduced, House of Commons.

Sept. 28   Ulster's Solemn League and Covenant against Home Rule administered to Unionists ('Ulster Day').

1913

Jan. 30   Government of Ireland Bill defeated, House of Lords, after first of three passages through Commons.

Jan. 31   Ulster Volunteer Force formed.

Aug. 26   Strike of tramwaymen in Dublin followed by lock-out (3 Sept.) and general strike led by Larkin (collapsed, Jan. 1914).

Sept. 24   Ulster Unionist Council authorised creation of Ulster Provisional Government under Carson upon enactment of Home Rule.

Nov. 19   Irish Citizen Army launched by Dublin Civic League.

Nov. 25   Irish Volunteers launched, Dublin (HB and Gerald Boland among those enlisted).

1914

Mar. 20   Cavalry officers at Curragh, Co. Kildare, solicited dismissal in preference to enforcing Home Rule in Ulster.

Apr. 2   Cumann na mBan inaugurated, Dublin.

Apr. 24–25   Rifles for Ulster Volunteers landed illegally at Larne, Co. Antrim, and elsewhere.

May 25   Government of Ireland Bill passed for third time by House of Commons.

July 10   Ulster Provisional Government convened, Belfast.

July 21–24   Unsuccessful search for compromise on Home Rule through Buckingham Palace Conference.

July 26   Rifles for Irish Volunteers landed illegally at Howth, Co. Dublin; 4 civilians killed by troops at Bachelor's Walk, Dublin.

Aug. 3   Redmond pledged Irish support for Britain against Germany, offering Irish Volunteers as coastal defence-force (war declared, 4 Aug.).

Aug. 8   Defence of the Realm Act facilitated censorship and emergency controls through executive order.

Sept. 18   Government of Ireland Act assented, with promise of future amendment to cater for Ulster (after Redmond had accepted its suspension and urged Irish nationalists to enlist for overseas service, 15 Sept.).

Sept. 24   Redmond's leadership of Irish Volunteers repudiated by

MacNeill's faction of executive, causing split and formation of Redmondite National Volunteers.

1915

Mar. 18   Defence of the Realm legislation amended to restore entitlement of civilians to trial by jury.

May 25   Coalition Government (including Carson) appointed under Asquith.

May, late   Military committee formed by IRB's Supreme Council to plan insurrection (expanded as military council, Dec.).

Aug. 6   10th (Irish) Division landed at Suvla Bay, Gallipoli.

Sept. 8   Gerald Boland married to Annie Keating, Dublin.

1916

Jan. 27   Ireland excluded from first Military Service Act, as from its successor (25 May).

Mar. 4–5   Irish Race Convention founded Friends of Irish Freedom, New York.

Mar. 17   MacNeill (Chief of Staff) reviewed Irish Volunteers in College Green, Dublin.

Apr. 21   Casement disembarked from submarine in Kerry and arrested; *Aud* scuttled after interception with cargo of German arms.

Apr. 22   MacNeill countermanded order for field manoeuvres by Irish Volunteers next day (Easter Sunday).

Apr. 24   Proclamation of Irish Republic at GPO, Dublin, by Pearse and IRB's military council; seizure of Dublin buildings by Irish Volunteers, followed by proclamation of Martial Law in Dublin (25 Apr.) and rest of Ireland (29 Apr.).

Apr. 27–29   16th (Irish) Division repulsed gas attack at Hulloch, in first major battle.

Apr. 29   Surrender of rebel forces, followed by internment in Britain (from 1 May), and Courts Martial leading to 15 executions (3–12 May) and imprisonment of 124 convicts.

May 9   HB sentenced to penal servitude for 10 years, remitted to 5 (removed to Dartmoor from Mountjoy, 16 May).

June 23   Northern nationalist convention, Belfast, accepted Lloyd George's proposals for immediate Home Rule with perhaps temporary exclusion of 6 counties (accepted by Ulster Unionist Council, 12 June).

July 1   Beginning of Somme offensive, decimating 36th (Ulster) Division at Thiepval (offensive ended, 13 Nov.).

July 24   Redmond repudiated Home Rule scheme as revised by Asquith.

Aug. 3   Casement hanged at Pentonville Prison, London.

Nov. 4   Maxwell replaced as army commander; Martial Law terminated.

Nov. 7	Wilson (Democratic Party) re-elected as American President.
Dec. 7	Asquith replaced by Lloyd George as Coalition Prime Minister.
Dec. 13	HB removed from Dartmoor to Lewes.
Dec. 22–23	Release of remaining internees (including Collins and Gerald Boland).

1917

Feb. 5	First of several by-election victories for separatist candidates (Count Plunkett, North Roscommon).
Apr. 7	USA declared war on Germany.
May 9	McGuinness (convict) returned for South Longford in by-election.
June 6	HB removed from Lewes to Maidstone (to Pentonville, 16 June).
June 17	Released convicts (including HB) welcomed in Dublin.
July 10	De Valera returned for East Clare in by-election.
July 25	Irish Convention opened at TCD (reports published, 12 Apr. 1918).
Sept. 9	HB secured lease for tailoring business at 64, Middle Abbey St., Dublin.
Oct. 26	HB elected to Executive, Sinn Féin; De Valera elected President (and of Irish Volunteers, 27 Oct.).

1918

Jan. 8	Wilson proposed '14 Points' for international peace.
Feb. 6	Representation of the People Act extended parliamentary suffrage to adult men and most women over 30.
Mar. 12	Dillon replaced Redmond (died, 6 Mar.) as leader of Irish Parliamentary Party.
Mar. 23	16th and 36th Divisions participated in retreat of 5th Army in face of German offensive, leading to heavy losses and effective collapse of these Divisions.
Apr. 9	Military Service Bill introduced by Lloyd George (assented, 18 Apr.), with provision for extension to Ireland by executive order.
Apr. 18	Anti-Conscription conference at Mansion House, Dublin, followed by meeting with Catholic bishops at Maynooth leading to co-ordinated declaration.
Apr. 21	Pledge to resist Conscription administered in Catholic churches.
Apr. 23	Token but effective general strike against Conscription.
May 17	HB replaced Stack (previously arrested) as joint Honorary Secretary, Sinn Féin.
May 17–18	Most republican leaders, including de Valera and McGarry (replaced as President of the IRB's Supreme Council by HB), interned as parties to 'German Plot'.
May 23	Gerald Boland arrested (imprisoned for 6 months by Court Martial, 4 June).
Nov. 11	Armistice between Germany and the Allies.

| Nov. 21 | HB appointed as Sinn Féin's acting chief election agent. |
| Dec. 14 | 'Coupon' general election resulted in new Coalition Government with Conservative majority under Lloyd George; 73 Sinn Féiners and 6 nationalists elected in Irish constituencies, including HB for South Roscommon (polls declared, 28 Dec.). |

1919

Jan. 18	Peace Conference convened, Paris.
Jan. 21	Dáil Éireann convened at Mansion House, Dublin, approving Declaration of Independence, appeal for international recognition of Irish Republic, and Democratic Programme (drafted by HB and others).
Feb. 3	De Valera rescued from Lincoln Prison by HB and Collins (returned secretly to Dublin, 20 Feb.).
Apr. 1	De Valera elected President of Dáil.
Apr. 4	Dáil authorised issue of republican Bonds within Ireland.
May 3	Irish-American delegation, fruitlessly seeking Irish representation at Peace Conference, visited Ireland.
May 4	HB left Liverpool for New York as envoy of IRB and Dáil (arrived, 16 May).
June 11	De Valera entered USA for campaign of propaganda and fund-raising (presented by HB to journalists, 23 June).
June 28	Treaty signed between Germany and the Allies, Versailles.
Oct. 1	De Valera and HB embarked on 'Grand Tour of America' (Philadelphia).
Oct. 7	Cabinet appointed committee to discuss Irish constitutional settlement.
Nov. 25	Membership of republican organisations proclaimed as illegal throughout Ireland, following proclamation of Dáil (12 Sept.).
Dec. 19	Unsuccessful ambush near Dublin's Phoenix Park of the Viceroy, Viscount French.

1920

Jan. 2	First enrolment in England of temporary constables to reinforce RIC ('Black and Tans').
Jan. 17	Prohibition given legal effect in USA. American Bond-Certificate Drive for Irish Republic launched under James O'Mara (replaced HB as chief organiser, Nov. 1919).
Feb. 6	De Valera's 'Cuban interview' drew parallel with Ireland's strategic dependency on Britain, alienating Devoy, Cohalan, and their Irish-American supporters.
Feb. 25	(Better) Government of Ireland Bill introduced, House of Commons.
Mar 18	American ratification of Versailles Treaty rejected by Senate

(majority in favour falling short of requisite two-thirds), after Irish-American and other opposition to Covenant of the proposed League of Nations.

Mar. 19	Temporary reconciliation between de Valera and Clan na Gael leaders, following confrontation arranged by HB.
Apr. 4	Destruction by IRA of almost 300 unoccupied RIC barracks around Easter Sunday.
Apr. 16	HB lent $20,000 to Russian envoy in USA, on security of 'Crown Jewels' (further loan, 29 Oct.).
Apr. 26	IRB's Supreme Council authorised HB to impose its supremacy over Clan na Gael.
May 15	HB embarked from New York (reached Dublin, 28 May).
June 5	HB reported on American mission to Dáil Ministry.
June, mid	HB visited Granard, evidently proposing marriage to Kitty Kiernan.
June 19	Disturbances in Derry, leading to 18 deaths.
June 26	HB embarked from Southampton (reached New York, 5 July).
July 13	'Third Party' presidential convention called for recognition of Irish Republic, following rejection of similar planks by Republican and Democratic Party conventions (8–12 June; 28 June–6 July).
July 21–24	Catholic and 'rotten Protestant' workers expelled from shipyards and engineering works, leading to fatal rioting in Belfast.
July 27	Formation belatedly sanctioned of force of ex-officers to assist RIC ('Auxiliary Division').
Aug. 6	Boycott of Belfast firms inaugurated by Dáil.
Aug. 9	Restoration of Order in Ireland Act maintained and expanded coercive powers under Defence of the Realm legislation.
Aug. 15	Temporary reconciliation between HB and Devoy's Clan na Gael.
Oct. 22	HB publicly severed link between Clan na Gael and IRB (sanctioned by Supreme Council, 18 Nov.).
Oct. 25	Terence McSwiney (Lord Mayor of Cork) died on hunger-strike in Brixton Prison, London.
Oct. 31	District Inspector Kelleher killed in Greville Arms, Granard, provoking destruction of Kiernans' hotel.
Nov. 1	First execution of rebel since 1916 (Kevin Barry). Recruitment commenced for (Ulster) Special Constabulary.
Nov. 2	Harding (Republican Party) elected as American President (inaugurated, 4 Mar. 1921).
Nov. 12	HB's circular initiated Clan na Gael Reorganized.
Nov. 16	De Valera launched AARIR.
Nov. 18	Inauguration of American Commission on Conditions in Ireland (organised by Committee of 150, formed 9 Oct.; final sitting, 21 Jan. 1921).

Nov. 21   Assassination of 14 British officers by IRA, followed by fatal reprisals at Gaelic football match in Croke Park, Dublin ('Bloody Sunday').

Dec. 10   Martial Law imposed in four south-western counties (extended to four adjacent counties, 4 Jan. 1921). De Valera secretly left USA, reaching Dublin, 23 Dec. (replaced by HB, as 'Special Envoy').

Dec. 16   American Committee for Relief in Ireland formed, New York.

Dec. 23   Government of Ireland Act assented, providing for separate parliaments in Northern and Southern Ireland and a Council for Ireland.

1921

Jan. 1   First 'authorised' military reprisals against property, Co. Cork.

Jan. 6   HB threatened 'race vendetta' at Madison Square Garden, New York.

Jan. 13   HB reported first order of Thompson sub-machine-guns.

Feb. 4   Craig succeeded Carson as leader of Ulster Unionists.

Mar. 20   Delegate conference of Clan na Gael Reorganized, New York (first convention in Philadelphia, 12 July).

Apr. 18–20 First convention of AARIR, Chicago, elected HB's slate of officers.

May 9   Resignation of James O'Mara as Fiscal Agent in USA (accepted, 25 May; replaced by brother Stephen).

May 13   All 124 Sinn Féin and 4 independent candidates returned unopposed for Southern House of Commons (HB elected for South Roscommon and South Mayo).

May 24   40 Unionists, 6 nationalists, and 6 Sinn Féiners elected for Northern House of Commons.

May 25   Dublin's Custom House destroyed by IRA.

June 7   Craig elected as first Prime Minister of Northern Ireland (Parliament opened by George V, 22 June).

June 13   495 Thompson guns seized at Hoboken, New Jersey (recovered by McGarrity, 1925).

July 9–15 Belfast disturbances caused over 20 deaths.

July 11   Truce implemented between British army in Ireland and IRA.

Aug. 13   HB embarked from New York (reached Dublin, 21 Aug.).

Aug. 16   Second Dáil convened by Sinn Féin MPs (TDs) at Mansion House, Dublin.

Aug. 25   Peace Treaty between Germany and USA.

Aug. 26   De Valera elected President of Irish Republic by Dáil.

Aug. 28–29 HB visited Granard with Collins, resulting in letter renewing proposal of marriage to Kitty Kiernan (1 Sept.).

Sept. 4   HB addressed Armagh meeting with Collins.

Sept. 13   HB and McGrath carried letter from de Valera to Lloyd George in Gairloch, Scotland, leading to temporary collapse of negotiations (resolved 30 Sept.).

Sept. 14	Dáil elected delegates to negotiate with Lloyd George and ministers.
Sept. 23	HB appointed by Dáil Ministry as salaried American Representative.
Oct. 2	HB embarked from Queenstown (reached New York, 10 Oct.; welcomed Madison Square Garden, 15 Oct.).
Oct. 11	Anglo-Irish Peace Conference opened, London, after further exchange of letters.
Oct., mid	Second American Bond-Certificate Drive launched.
Nov. 12	Naval Disarmament Conference opened, Washington (closed, 6 Feb. 1922).
Dec. 6	Articles of Agreement for a Treaty signed, London (welcomed by HB before reading text, 6 Dec.; denounced by de Valera, 9 Dec.).
Dec. 12	HB accepted Kitty Kiernan's three-month postponement of her response to his proposal of marriage.
Dec. 14	HB openly denounced Treaty after a week's public ambivalence.
Dec. 27	HB embarked from New York (reached Queenstown, 4 Jan. 1922).

1922

Jan. 6	HB spoke against Treaty in Dáil.
Jan. 7	Dáil narrowly approved Treaty, after acrimonious debate (opened 14 Dec.).
Jan. 10	HB congratulated Kitty Kiernan on her engagement to Collins (made public, early Mar.).
Jan. 14	Provisional Government appointed under Collins, in tandem with new Dáil Ministry under Griffith (replacing de Valera as President, 10 Jan.).
Jan. 16	Formation of Cumann na Poblachta (Republican Party), with HB as joint Honorary Secretary.
Jan. 20	HB reached Paris for Irish Race Congress (left for Dublin, 29 Jan.).
Jan. 21	Ineffectual Pact between Collins and Craig to end Belfast Boycott and protect northern Catholics.
Feb. 12	McGarrity reached Dublin, hoping to unify IRB (farewelled by HB and others, 22 Feb.).
Feb. 12–15	Belfast attacks causing 27 deaths, attributed to IRA, followed by four months of renewed sectarian rioting, sniping, and shooting.
Feb. 16	HB dismissed as American envoy by Gavan Duffy.
Feb. 21–22	Sinn Féin Ard Fheis, adjourned to 23 May to avoid irrevocable split.
Mar. 17	De Valera remarked, in Thurles, that republicans might have to 'wade through Irish blood'.
Mar. 26–27	IRA convention (attended by HB) established anti-Treatyist Executive Council under Traynor, in defiance of Mulcahy's army staff.

Mar. 30	Second futile Pact signed in London between Craig and Collins, with Churchill; Treaty given force of law in United Kingdom next day.
Apr. 7	Civil Authorities (Special Powers) Act allowed internment and other emergency measures in Northern Ireland for one year (periodically extended).
Apr. 14	O'Connor's faction of anti-Treatyist IRA established headquarters in Four Courts, Dublin.
Apr. 19	IRB convention postponed, signifying failure to reunify.
May 3	Dáil appointed Peace Committee (including HB) to seek collaboration between factions.
May 20	Collins and de Valera signed Pact, largely devised by HB, to maintain current balance of parties at forthcoming General Election and create Coalition Ministry (approved by Sinn Féin, 23 May).
May 23	Northern Government proscribed republican organisations.
June 16	58 Treatyist and 36 anti-Treatyist Sinn Féiners elected (with 34 others, mainly Treatyist) for Provisional Parliament to approve draft Constitution for the Irish Free State, following acceptance of British amendments and collapse of electoral Pact (HB retained seat, unopposed).
June 22	Sir Henry Wilson (military adviser to Northern Government) killed by IRA, London.
June 28	National army initiated Civil War by attacking O'Connor's garrison in Four Courts (surrendered, 30 June).
June 28–30	HB in Munster seeking reinforcements for Dublin IRA.
June 30	HB reached Blessington, Co. Wicklow, via Co. Wexford.
July 7	Brugha died of gunshot wounds (HB at funeral, 10 July).
July 8	Gerald Boland captured, Blessington (interned until July 1924); HB escaped from nearby mountains to Dublin.
July 17	HB appointed acting Quartermaster, Eastern Command, IRA.
July 30	HB with Griffin to Skerries; shot early next morning, Grand Hotel.
Aug. 1	HB died during evening, in St. Vincent's Hospital, Dublin (Inquest, 3 Aug.; funeral at Glasnevin, 4 Aug.).
Aug. 12	Griffith died of cerebral haemorrhage, Dublin.
Aug. 22	Collins killed in ambush, west Cork.
Sept. 9	Third Dáil (Provisional Parliament) convened; Cosgrave elected as President of Provisional Government.
Sept. 28	Dáil approved creation of military courts to try civilians.
Oct.	Kathleen Boland began 14-month-long campaign for anti-Treatyists, North America.
Oct. 10	Catholic bishops issued joint pastoral excommunicating active 'Irregulars'.

Oct. 23	Lloyd George replaced by Bonar Law (Conservative) as Prime Minister.
Oct. 25	Constitution approved by Dáil (ratified by British statute, 5 Dec.). Rival republican Government constituted under de Valera, with support from IRA.
Nov. 15	General Election, UK, confirmed Conservative Government under Bonar Law; 2 nationalists and 11 Unionists elected in Northern Irish constituencies.
Nov. 17	First of 77 anti-Treatyists executed (last, 2 May 1923).
Dec. 6	Irish Free State created; Cosgrave appointed as President of Executive Council.
Dec. 7	Northern Parliament voted to opt out of Free State (implementing Cabinet decision, 13 Mar.).

1923

May 23	Baldwin succeeded Bonar Law as Conservative Prime Minister.
May 24	De Valera instructed republicans to abandon armed resistance, following suspension of IRA offensive (27 Apr.).
June 11	Anti-Treatyist Sinn Féin reorganised at Mansion House, Dublin.
Aug. 15	De Valera arrested in Ennis, Co. Clare (interned until 16 July 1924).
Aug. 27	General Election for Dáil confirmed Cumann na nGaedheal Government under Cosgrave; 63 Treatyists and 44 republican Sinn Féiners elected (with 46 others).
Sept. 10	Irish Free State admitted to League of Nations (Anglo-Irish Treaty registered, 11 July 1924).
Dec.	Kathleen Boland married to Seán O'Donovan, Dublin.
Dec. 6	General Election resulted in appointment of MacDonald as first Labour Prime Minister (22 Jan. 1924); 2 Nationalists and 11 Unionists elected in Northern Irish constituencies.

Index

Abbreviations: APN (anti-Parnellite Nat.); AT (anti-Treatyist); CB (Cumann na mBan); D (Democratic); Gov. (Governor); Lab. (Labour); Lib. (Liberal); MC (Military Council); Min. (Minister); Nat. (National, Nationalist); PN (Parnellite Nat.); Rep. (Representative); R (Republican); SC (Supreme Council); SF (Sinn Féin); Sen. (Senator); T (Treatyist); U (Unionist). Distinctions attained after 1922 are not normally listed; positions and locations are selective and not given in detail.

Adams, Gerard (Belfast MP, SF leader; b. 1948), 326
Adamson, George (Cdant.-Gen. Nat. army; d. 1922), 291
Allan, Frederick James (Dublin, Pres. SC IRB; 1861–1937), 24, 25, 26, 27, 28, 29, 96
'Alpha' (IRB informer), 24, 26
Amalgamated Society of Engineers, 94
American Association for the Recognition of the Irish Republic, 190–1, 196, 199, 207, 248
   aims, 190, 201
   Anglo-Irish Treaty, 259, 273, 274
   HB and, 190–1, 200–3, 204, 205, 206, 245
   farewell banquet, 262–3
American Commission on Irish Independence, 143, 193, 206
American Committee for Relief in Ireland, 183, 184, 203
American Federation of Labor, 139, 200, 243
American Legion, 141
Ancient Order of Hibernians, 188, 230
Anderson, Samuel Lee (Crown Solicitor, Dublin Castle), 335
Anglo-Irish Treaty (1921)
   Dáil debates, 264, 265–70, 290–2O
   Dáil vote, 269–70
   HB and, 255–62, 263, 264–70, 275, 277, 288–9
   negotiations prior to
      HB and, 194, 222–3, 228–9, 230–1, 237, 238, 239, 241–3
      HB envoy to Lloyd George, 232–4
      Dominican option, 239, 240
   Pact following split, 296–8, 299–301, 307, 315–16
   public support for, 265, 268
Anglo-Irish War, 170–1, 181, 276
   truce, 210, 221, 223, 225, 246

Armistice (1918), 105, 107
arms-running, 147–8, 181–2, 212–17, 246–7, 263
Armstrong, Harry Gloster (b. Cavan, British Consul-Gen. NY; 1861–1938), 28, 157, 223–4, 262
Ashe, Thomas (b. Kerry, Lewes convict, Pres. SC IRB; 1885–1917), 45, 47, 52–3, 56, 57, 85, 89, 98, 99, 101, 348
Ashurst, Sen. Henry Fountain (Arizona, D; 1874–1962), 197
Asquith, Herbert Henry (Prime Min., Lib.; 1852–1928), 83
Aud (steamship), 38
Augustine, St. (d. 604), 62

ballads and songs
   'A Battle Hymn', 197
   'Comrades in Arms', 13
   'Danny Boy', 197
   'Eileen Aroon', 13
   'The Felons of our Land', 73
   'The Foggy Dew', 197
   'Galway Bay', 72
   'The Green Isle's Loved Emblem', 46
   'Hugh O'Donnell Roe', 72
   'Kelly and Burke and Shea', 236, 277
   'Little Mary Cassidy', 13
   'M'anan a Dhía, But There It Is', 58
   'The Mangy British Lion, Ha! Ha! Ha!', 162
   'Ode to Harry Boland', 13
   'Old Man's Town', 73
   'Out and Make Way for the Bold Fenian Men', 162
   'The Rising of the Moon', 31
   'A Soldier's Song', 197–8
   'The South Down Militia', 162
   'The Star-Spangled Banner', 173
   'To-Morrow', 13

'The West's Awake', 13, 277
Baltic (steamship), 179–80, 246
Banim, John (b. Kilkenny, novelist, 1798–1842), 62
Banim, Michael (b. Kilkenny, novelist, 1796–1874), 62
Barry, Leslie (née Price; b. Dublin, CB, AT; 1893–1984), 6, 225
Barry, Thomas Bernadine (Cork IRA, AT; 1897–1980), 225–6, 236, 281, 282, 283, 290, 293, 300
Beach, Rex Ellington (American novelist; 1877–1949), 62
Béaslaí, Piaras (Pierce Beasley; Kerry TD, T; 1883–1965), 1, 91, 92, 93, 104, 113, 320
Beatty, Admiral Sir David (1st Earl; 1871–1936), 252
Begley, Joseph (US mission), 13, 174, 241, 249, 262, 273, 281, 301, 306
Belfast Prison, 94–5, 104, 105, 108
Benjamin Franklin Bureau (Washington), 199–200
Bibby, Fr. Albert (Dublin Capuchin, AT), 325
'Black and Tans', 5, 170, 171, 276, 282
Bodkin, Matthias McDonnell (Roscommon MP, APN; 1850–1933), 31
Boer War, 102
Boland, Annie (Gerald's wife, née Keating; 1887–1970), 36, 38, 68–9
Boland, Catherine (Kate; HB's mother, née Woods; 1860?–1932), 168, 173, 275
background, 18, 19
businesses, 29–30
on Cait Fraher, 76–7
Easter Rebellion, 39
financial aid, 29, 68, 164
Gerald, dispute with, 68–9
HB and Civil War, 306, 317, 318–19
HB and Treaty, 241
HB's death, 3–4, 15, 324, 325
HB's imprisonment, 46, 48–9, 51, 54, 55–6, 61, 64, 65, 82, 87
house raided, 100, 164, 318–19
Kitty Kiernan, letter to, 251
World War I, 34
Boland, Edmund (Ned; HB's brother; 1893–1928), 125, 149, 167, 168, 169
Civil War, 309, 311
early life, 18, 30, 31, 67–8
Easter Rebellion, 38, 40, 41, 44, 49
Ena Shouldice and, 76
HB's death, 16
HB's imprisonment, 49, 51, 54, 64, 65, 66, 72, 75
IRB, 71
South Longford by-election, 85, 86, 87
travels, 94, 168, 365

Boland, Eliza (Patrick's wife, née Kelly), 18
Boland, Enda (Gerald's son; b. 1916), 64, 80
Boland, Gerald (HB's brother; 1885–1973), 233, 235
birth, 335–6
career, 30–1, 67–8, 94
childhood, 18, 24, 29, 30
Civil War, 309–10, 311–12, 313
build-up, 282
imprisonment, 311
de Valera's rescue from Lincoln Prison, 114
dispute with mother, 68–9
early nationalist organisations, 31
Easter Rebellion, 38–9, 40, 44–5
HB's death, 3, 5, 16–17, 324, 325
imprisonment (1918), 94–5, 100
internment, 44, 45, 50, 58, 61, 62, 64, 68
release, 82
IRB, 32, 34, 38, 81, 98
marriage, 36, 38
on Michael Collins, 92
religion, 62
Sinn Féin general election (1918), 112
South Longford by-election, 85, 86–7
Boland, Henry James (Harry; 1887–1922)
LIFE EVENTS AND WORK
background and family, 18–30
birth, 18
childhood, 18, 29
education, 30
early career, 30–1
first nationalist organisations, 31–2
IRB, 33–4, 38, 103, 108, 157, 228–9
arms-running, 147–8, 181–2
ascendancy in, 98–9
Clan na Gael split, 186, 187
enrols in 'Circle', 32
visit home from US, 169–70
GAA, 32–4, 38, 97–8
during imprisonment, 69–71, 74
hurling, 33, 63, 97, 234, 305
Irish Volunteers, 34, 35–6, 99, 102–3
World War I, 34–6
opposes conscription, 36
Easter Rebellion, 38–44, 101, 102
trial following, 45–6
visitors' tours, 276
imprisonment, 46–88
cheerfulness during, 45, 46, 48, 58, 59
correspondence, 65–8, 72, 78, 79–80
correspondence about girls, 73–8
correspondence censorship, 52, 59, 65–6, 79
Dartmoor, 46–51, 60
health, 59–60
hunger-strike, 53–4, 59
letter thrown during journey, 57–8
Lewes, 51–7, 59–88

Boland, Henry James (Harry; 1887–1922)
imprisonment (*Cont.*)
  Maidstone, 56, 57
  notebook, 52, 59
  Pentonville, 58
  reading and study, 47, 62–3
  release, 58, 87–8
  republicanism during, 79–88
  singing, 72–3
  skills acquired, 60
homecoming, 89–90
financial aid given to, 95–7
tailoring business, 96–7, 120, 225
as fugitive, 99–100
  disguises, 100, 104
Sinn Féin, 96, 99, 100–14, 117–20
  appeal as politician, 101
  Armistice celebrations, 105, 107
  draft manifesto, 109
  election (1918), 108, 109–12
  expounds strategy, 112–13, 130, 230
  Labour Party negotiations, 106–8, 114
  League of Nations, 118
  skills, 108–9, 118–19
  speeches, 101–2, 110
Peace Conference (Paris), 101–2, 106, 113,
  117–18
de Valera's rescue from Lincoln Prison,
  114–16
Irish Self-Determination League of Great
  Britain, 118
chosen envoy to America, 120
journey to America, 121, 122
in America
  aims, 120, 123, 135–6, 137, 147, 148–9,
    178–80, 242
  arms-running, 147–8, 181–2, 212–17,
    246–7, 263
  Bond Drives, 142–6, 153, 159, 183–4,
    203, 206, 242, 243–4
  Clan na Gael and, 120, 122, 132–3, 147,
    154–7
  Clan na Gael excommunication, 184–90
  Clan na Gael Reorganized, 207–10, 229,
    245, 248–9
  Cohalan and, 150–2, 153–4, 155–8, 170,
    184, 186, 199, 257, 262
  Collins and, 135, 157–60, 161, 210–11
  Cuban analogy, 153–4
  de Valera and, 123–6, 129, 132, 135,
    137, 153, 173–4, 192–3
  Devoy and, 122–3, 149–50, 152–7, 170,
    175, 184–6, 190, 199, 211–12
  Farmer-Labor (Third) Party, 178, 180
  fiscal control, 204, 205, 216
  fund-raising, 183, 199, 203–4, 244–6;
    see also Bond Drives
  health, 163, 250

loneliness and homesickness, 163–5, 193,
  220, 221
Nunan, shares digs with, 174
opposition to HB, 195
opposition to Irish nationalism, 140–2
passport, 239
'race vendetta', 194–6, 198, 247–8
recognition of Irish Republic, 196–203
Russian alliance, 138–9, 180–1, 200
salary, 235
social life, 160–3, 174–5, 220–1, 249–50
suffrage movement, 139–40, 197
tours and meetings, 130–5, 177, 197–8,
  240
versatility and skills, 128–30, 132–3,
  135–8, 146, 185, 193, 224
vision, 178–80, 194
visits home
  (first; 1920), 166–73
  (second; 1921), 206, 223–38
Anglo-Irish War, 170–1, 181
  truce, 225
Tom Barry's wedding, 225–6
Anglo-Irish Treaty, 255–62, 263, 264–70,
  275, 277, 288–9
  Dáil debates, 264, 265–70, 290–2
  Dominican option, 239, 240
  meets Lloyd George, 232–4
  negotiations, 194, 222–3, 228–9, 230–1,
    237, 238, 239, 241–3
  Roscommon constituents, 265
  Ulster expedition, 229–30
  returns to Ireland, 264
Irish Race Congress, 270–3
dismissed as envoy, 273–4, 286
continues contact with American associates,
  274–9
Civil War build-up, 279–85, 289–90,
  292–301
  diverts funds to IRA, 279–80
  Pact before, 296–8, 299–301, 307
  Peace Committee, 294–7
Sinn Féin, 286–9, 292, 297, 316
  election (1922), 298–9
Cumann na Poblachta, 286–7
Irish language debate, 290–1
Civil War, 306–24
  analysis of, 307–8
  Blessington, 309–12, 313
  Four Courts, 306, 307, 309
  good spirits during, 315–16
  Munster journey, 308–9
  organisational work, 313–15
  peace conference, 316–17
  pursuit of HB, 317–20
shooting of, 320–4
death, 1–4, 324–5
  effect on family, 15–17

funeral, 2, 5–7, 8
inquest, 1, 4–5
last words, 3–4, 8
martyr cult, 13
memorial ceremonies, 11–13
murder claims, 1, 2–3, 5, 11, 322
tributes, 6, 7–15
PERSONALITY
appeal of, 101
character, 92, 174–5
cheerfulness in prison, 45, 46, 48, 58, 59
description (Devoy's), 123
energy, 104, 123
hurling, enjoyment of, 33, 63, 97, 234, 305
loneliness and homesickness, 163–5, 193,
    220, 221
oratory, 101–2, 110, 130, 131, 133, 197–8,
    209, 230, 240
    Dáil speeches, 267, 268–9
    'race vendetta' speech, 194, 195
    repartee, 290–2
religion, 62
singing, 46, 58, 72–3, 162, 277
skills and versatility, 108–9, 118–19,
    128–30, 132–3, 135–8, 146, 185, 193,
    224
social life (US), 160–3, 174–5, 220–1,
    249–50
study and reading, 60–2
RELATIONSHIPS
Collins, Michael
    admiration for, 168, 169, 219
    in Civil War, 307–8, 314, 318, 322
    criticism from Collins, 277
    friendship, 92–3, 102, 158, 159, 172,
        237, 266, 273, 277–8, 300, 302
    horseplay, 119, 230
    mistrust, 253
    proposed US visit, 218–19
    Treaty split, 264–5, 294, 300, 301
de Valera, Eamon, 125–6, 135, 225
    loyalty towards, 10, 129, 191, 261, 269,
        277, 296, 300
    reliance on HB, 207
    Treaty split, 233–4, 295–6, 301–2
    wrestling bouts, 162–3
Kiernan, Kitty, 91–2, 164, 172, 221–2,
    226–7
    engagement, 236–7, 251
    HB's letters, 175–7, 226, 241, 252–5
    rejection by, 251–5, 265, 302–4
McGarrity, Joseph, 11, 14, 151–2, 163, 224
romances, 75–8; see also Kiernan, Kitty
    Fraher, Cait, 76–8, 91
    Fraher correspondence, 63, 65, 74, 75,
        77, 79, 87, 88
    O'Brien, Kate (Kitty), 250–1, 305
    Shouldice, Ena, 76, 90–1

Boland, James (Jim; HB's father; 1856–95),
    18–20, 21–7, 30, 122
Boland, John Patrick (Jack; HB's uncle;
    1862?–95), 20–1, 23, 25, 122, 330
Boland, Kathleen (HB's sister; 1889–1954),
    168, 230, 251, 264, 275
    career and work, 68, 164, 225
    Cohalan and HB, 151
    early life, 31
    Easter Rebellion, 39, 40–1, 45
        anniversary Mass, 80
    Gerald Boland and, 69
    HB and arms shipments, 246–7
    HB and Civil War, 307, 309, 313, 315,
        318
    HB's death, 3–4, 16, 322, 324–5
    HB's escape from raid, 100
    HB's imprisonment, 46, 50, 54, 58, 62, 64,
        65, 73, 88
    homecoming, 89
    HB's romances, 75–6, 77
    Irish Volunteers and, 34, 94, 120, 170, 221
    marriage, 73
    South Longford by-election, 86, 87
    Treaty split, 270
    World War I, 34
Boland, Kevin (Gerald's son; 1917–2001), 91,
    94
Boland, Michael (Kentucky Clan), 28
Boland, Nellie (HB's sister; 1884–98), 18, 30
Boland, Patrick (HB's grandfather), 18
Bolger, Joseph (Dublin), 336
Bolshevism, America, 138–9
Bond Drives, 142–6, 153, 159, 171, 173,
    183–4, 203, 206, 242, 243–4
Borah, Sen. William Edgar (Idaho, R;
    1862–1940), 150, 197
Brady, Joe ('Invincible'; d. 1883), 19
Brady, Nicholas Frederic (NY capitalist;
    1878–1930), 199, 244, 372
Brennan, Michael (Clare IRA, T; 1896–1986),
    414
Brennan, Robert (b. Wexford, Under-Sec.
    Foreign Affairs, AT; 1881–1964)
    HB and, 168–9, 219–20, 223, 224, 300
        during imprisonment, 46, 47, 53, 78, 116
    HB as fugitive, 100, 103–4, 221
    Michael Collins, 92, 119, 300
    Treaty, 234, 240, 242
    performance of Irish ballad, 341
    Sinn Féin, 78, 103, 109, 160, 171
Brett, Sgt. Charles (Manchester police; d.
    1867), 19
Briscoe, Robert (Dublin arms-smuggler, AT;
    1894–1969), 316
Browne, Dr. Patrick (de Brún; b. Tipperary,
    Maynooth scholar, AT; 1889–1960), 6,
    12

Brugha, Cathal (Charles William St. John
    Burgess; b. Dublin, Waterford TD,
    Min. Defence, AT; 1874–1922), 148
  American volunteers, 210
  arms-running, 181–2, 212, 215, 216, 246
  campaign against Collins, 217, 218
  Civil War build-up, 282, 283, 294, 296
  Cumann na Poblachta, 286
  death and tributes to, 2, 3–4, 8, 9, 11,
    313
  election (1918), 109
  HB, conflict with, 215–16, 219
  IRB, 98–9
  Labour Party and, 107, 108
  Speaker of Dáil, 114
Bruton, Sgt. John (DMP detective; b. 1870),
    119
Bulwer-Lytton, Edward Robert (1st Earl of
    Lytton; English poet; 1831–91), 224
Bureau of Investigation (Federal), 123, 138,
    195, 239
Burke, Mick (Tipperary IRA, AT), 312–13
Burke, Col. Ricard O'Sullivan (Cork Fenian,
    Chicago; 1838–1922), 149
Burke, Fr. Thomas Nicholas (b. Galway,
    Dominican polemicist; 1830–83), 62
Byrne, Vincent (Dublin 'Squad', T; 1900–92),
    276
Byron, George Gordon (6th Baron; English
    poet; 1788–1824), 62–3

Cahill, Fr. (Illinois AARIR), 116, 203, 244
Callaghan, Col. P. K. (Kentucky, Bonds
    organiser), 144
camogie, 74
Campbell, Seán P. (Dublin anti-
    Conscriptionist), 36
Cane, Dr. Robert (Mayor of Kilkenny, Nat.;
    1807–58), 149
Carey, James (IRB informer; 1845–83), 335
Carmelites (Calced), 5, 127, 162, 163, 174,
    214, 220, 262
Carroll, Mollie (NY), 262
Caruso, Enrico (b. Naples, tenor; 1873–1921),
    161
Catholic Truth Society of Ireland, 62
Ceannt, Éamonn (b. Galway, MC IRB;
    1881–1916), 80
Cecil, Lord Hugh Richard Heathcote (Oxford
    MP, U; 1869–1956), 102
Celtic Cross, 203, 245
Celtic Literary Society, 31
Central Council of the Liquor Trade for
    Ireland, 27
Chartres, John (Sec. Treaty delegation;
    1862–1927), 397
Childers, Robert Erskine (Wicklow TD, AT;
    1870–1922), 2, 171, 286, 397

Christensen, Parley Parker (b. Utah, 'Third
    Party' leader), 382
Christian Brothers, 30, 100
Christie, Peter (Dublin IRA, T), 319
Churchill, Winston Leonard Spencer (Dundee
    MP, Sec. War, Lib.; 1874–1965), 252,
    297, 301, 315, 319
Civil War, 306–24
  Blessington, 309–12, 313
  build-up, 279–85, 289–90, 292–301
    Pact, 296–8, 299–301, 307, 315–16
    Peace Committee, 294–7
  Four Courts, 306, 307, 309
  HB's analysis, 307–8
  HB's Munster journey, 308–9
  HB's organisational work, 313–15
  peace conference, 316–17
  pursuit of HB, 317–20
  shooting and death of HB, 1–4, 320–5
Clan na Gael, 120, 122, 188
  financial aid to Kate Boland, 15
  HB and, 120, 122, 124, 132–3, 147, 149
    conflict, 154–8, 169, 184–90
  HB's death, 2, 11–12
  James Boland and, 19, 28
  John Boland and, 20–1
  split, 157–8, 184–90
Clan na Gael Reorganized, 10, 12, 25, 188,
    211, 274, 275
  aims, 207–8, 209–10
  arms-running, 281, 315
  factions, 248
  HB and, 207–10, 229, 245, 248–9, 281,
    300
  diverts funds to IRA, 279–80
  military volunteers, 209–10, 247, 263
  recognition from IRB, 277, 278
  riot, 208–9
Clancy, John (Dublin Corporation), 24
Clancy, Peadar (Dublin IRA; 1886–1920), 181
Clark, Br. Albens (Holy Ghost missionary,
    Indiana), 132
Clark, Jim (Dublin bookmaker), 234
Clarke, Kathleen (née Daly; Dublin TD, AT;
    1878–1972), 86, 108, 170, 247, 294,
    295–6
  Civil War, 309–10, 311, 313, 317–18
  HB's death, 325
Clarke, Thomas James (b. Isle of Wight, SC
    IRB; 1857–1916), 43, 108
Cleary, Bishop Henry William (Auckland; b.
    Wexford; 1859–1916), 62
Clemenceau, Georges Eugène Benjamin
    (French Prime Min.; 1841–1920), 136
Clune, T. Conor (Clare Gaelic League; d.
    1920), 181
Cockran, William Bourke (ex-Rep. NY, D;
    1854–1923), 154, 244, 372

Codd, Bishop William (Ferns; 1864–1938), 3
Cohalan, Judge Daniel Francis (NY Clan;
        1865–1946), 12, 125, 137, 143, 145,
        149, 155, 162, 186, 206, 209, 223,
        256, 257
    HB and, 122, 126–7, 131, 140, 183
    Clan na Gael split, 184, 185, 186, 187,
        189
    conflict, 150–2, 153–4, 155–7, 170, 199,
        257, 262
    Treaty, 257, 258, 259
Colley, Harry (Dublin IRA, AT; 1891–1972),
        34, 40
Collins, Celia (Maurice's wife), 36, 73, 75, 88,
        170
Collins, Cornelius (Con; Limerick TD, AT;
        1881–1923), 120
Collins, Maurice J. (Mossy; b. Limerick,
        Dublin GAA, IRA, T)
    career and business, 65–6, 71–2
    billiards room, 65, 148
    GAA and, 69, 70–1, 98
    HB's imprisonment, 54–5, 65–6, 69, 87,
        88
    Home Rule, 83
    imprisonment, 170
    IRB and, 35, 36, 98, 157
    marriage, 73–4, 75
    tribute to HB, 7
Collins, Michael (Cork TD, Min. Finance,
        Pres. SC IRB, IRA GHQ, T;
        1890–1922), 152, 171, 173, 174, 178,
        223, 225, 226, 229, 234, 235, 326,
        327
    Anglo-Irish Treaty, 211, 228–9, 232, 256,
        259, 260, 261–2, 267
        split over, 276, 278–9
    Anglo-Irish War, 170, 181
        truce, 223
    Bond Drive, 144, 145, 146, 159, 183
    Civil War, 2, 306, 307–8, 313, 314, 315,
        316, 317, 318, 320, 322, 324–5
        build-up, 281, 284, 285, 293, 294,
        296–8, 302
        Pact before, 296–8, 299–300, 301, 307,
        315–16
    de Valera's rescue from Lincoln Prison,
        114–15
    de Valera's undermining of, 217–18
    Easter Rebellion, 43
        internment, 44, 58
    Fine Ghaedheal, 272–3
    fiscal control, 205, 216, 217
    as fugitive, 99, 159
    HB and, 101, 121, 176, 210–11, 227–8,
        302
        American campaign, 135, 157–60, 161,
        165, 187, 248, 263, 267

arms-running, 147–8, 182, 212–13, 214,
        247
    Civil War, 2, 307–8, 314, 318, 320,
        324–5
    criticism of HB, 277
    death of HB, 1, 7, 8, 9, 11, 12, 322
    friendship, 92–3, 102, 158, 159, 172,
        219, 266, 273, 277–8, 300, 302
    HB's admiration, 168, 169, 237
    horseplay, 119, 230
    letter from prison, 58
    mistrust, 253
    proposed US visit, 218–19
    Treaty split, 264–5, 293, 294, 300, 301
    IRB, 34, 81, 98, 103, 108, 210–11,
        228–9
    Irish language debate, 290–1
    Irish Volunteers, 99
    Kitty Kiernan and, 172, 222, 226, 227,
        228, 236, 253–4, 264, 265, 302,
        303–4
    McGarrity's visit, 275–6
    physical description, 93
    Sinn Féin, 103, 104–5, 113–14, 117–18,
        120, 287–8, 290, 298
    Tom Barry's wedding, 226
    Ulster expedition, 229–30
Colum, Pádraic (b. Longford, NY author;
        1881–1972), 370
Comyn, James Joseph (b. Clare, barrister, AT;
        d. 1953), 4
Comyn, Michael (b. Clare, KC, AT;
        1877–1952), 4–5
Condon, Mrs (Roscommon), 90
Conlon, Martin (Dublin IRB), 285
Connolly, James (b. Edinburgh, MC IRB, Lab.
        leader; 1868–1916), 40, 41, 42
Connolly, John (Dublin GAA), 49, 74
Connolly, Joseph (b. Belfast, Dáil Consul NY;
        1885–1961), 7, 250, 275
Conscription, Ireland, 36, 94, 103
Constitution, draft (Irish Free State), 297, 299,
        301, 307
Cooke, James (Dublin Corporation), 24–5
Coolidge, Pres. Calvin (R; 1872–1933), 141
Cooper, James Fenimore (American novelist;
        1789–1851), 134
Cope, Sir Alfred William (Andy; Ass. Under-
        Sec., Dublin Castle; 1877–1954), 235
Corcoran, Col. Michael (US army, NY; b.
        Sligo; 1827–63), 149, 374
Corrigan, Michael A. (Dublin solicitor), 345
Corrigan, William P. (Dublin solicitor, Lewes
        convict; b. 1888), 345
Cosgrave, William Thomas (Dublin
        Councillor, Kilkenny TD, Min. Local
        Govt., T; 1880–1965), 225, 329
Couch, Ralph F. (American journalist), 117

Coyne, Bishop Bernard (Elphin; 1854–1926), 106, 160
Craig, Sir James (Down MP, Prime Min. Northern Ireland, U; 1871–1940), 223, 284
Creel, George (American propagandist; 1876–1953), 117–18, 137
Crofts, Gerald (Dublin singer, Lewes convict, AT; b. 1888), 46, 73, 82, 89, 347
Cronin, Capt. Patrick (US army, Clan), 213, 415
Cronin, Dr. Philip Henry (Chicago Clan; d. 1889), 28
Crowe, Michael F. (Limerick GAA, IRB), 32, 33, 71, 81
Cullen, John F. (Lewes convict; b. 1896), 347
Cumann na mBan, 5, 6, 16
Cumann na Poblachta, 286–7, 292, 303, 317
Cummins, Canon T. H. (Roscommon), 361, 404
Curran, Fr. Michael J. (Sec. Archbishop Walsh; 1880–1960), 117
Curran, Miss (Begley's fiancée), 249
Cusack, Mrs Paul, 244–5
Cusack, Paul (Longford draper, IRA), 116, 164, 172, 176
Cussen, Dr. William Robert (Dublin surgeon), 418, 419

Dáil Éireann
convoked, 113–14
Treaty debates, 264, 265–70, 290–2
Dalton, Maj. James Emmet (British army; b. Dublin, IRA GHQ, T; 1898–1978), 226, 251–2, 255, 278
Daly, Paddy (Dublin 'Squad', T), 221
Dartmoor Prison, 46–51, 60, 64, 67
Daughters of the American Revolution, 195
Davis, Thomas Osborne (b. Cork, Young Irelander; 1814–45), 62, 79
Davitt, Michael (Mayo MP, APN; 1846–1906), 24, 25, 336
De Castro & Donner (NY), 19
De La Salle Brothers (of the Christian Schools), 30
de Lacy, Laurence (b. Wexford, IRB arms-smuggler), 207, 213
de Loughry, Peter (Mayor of Kilkenny, T), 115
de Valera, Eamon (b. NY, Clare TD, Dáil Pres., AT; 1882–1975), 199, 203, 204, 217, 221, 223, 224, 237, 249, 255, 291, 326
in America, 122, 123–6, 127, 130, 132–6, 141, 150, 151, 152, 160, 161, 171–2, 173–4, 177, 178, 181
arrival, 123–4
Bond Drives, 143, 144, 182, 183–4, 203
Clan na Gael conflict, 155–7, 186, 188, 189–90

Cuban analogy, 153–4
HB and, 120, 125–6, 129, 132, 135, 137, 153
Recognition Association, 184, 190, 191, 201
returns to Ireland, 191–3
Anglo-Irish Treaty, 256, 258–9, 260, 261, 265–7
negotiations, 194, 211, 222, 223, 228, 229, 233–4, 235, 238, 240, 243
split over, 233–4, 269–70, 276, 277, 279, 291, 292, 293, 294, 295–6
appeal of, 101, 102
Civil War, 313, 314, 316, 318
build-up, 282, 293, 294, 295–7, 299, 301–2, 304
Pact before, 296–7, 301
Collins, undermining of, 217–18
financial aid, 96–7
fiscal control of American budget, 204, 205, 216
HB, relationship with, 112, 125–6, 135, 225
HB's allegiance, 10, 92, 129, 191, 261, 269, 277, 296, 300
HB's death, 13–15, 322
reliance on HB, 207
Treaty split, 233–4, 291, 295–6, 301–2
wrestling bouts, 162–3
imprisonment, 46, 47, 50, 52, 53, 56, 78
description, 347
IRB and, 98, 103
Irish Race Congress, 271, 272
Irish Volunteers, 35, 99
McGarrity's visit, 276
'race vendetta', 247–8
rescue from Lincoln Prison, 114–16
Rockwell College, 71
Russian alliance, 200
Sinn Féin and, 103, 117, 119, 286, 287, 288, 290
elections, 90, 108, 109, 298
Tom Barry's wedding, 226
de Valera, Sinéad (née Flanagan; 1878–1975), 6, 97, 169, 191–2, 333
Deasy, Liam (Cork IRA, AT; 1896–1974), 282
Delaney, Patrick (IRB informer), 335
Denieffe, Joseph (b. Kilkenny, NY Fenian; 1833–1910), 150, 374–5
Derrig, Thomas (Mayo TD, AT; 1897–1956), 314
Devereux, Denis (Gaelic League), 31
Devlin, Joseph (Belfast MP, Nat.; 1871–1934), 86, 108
Devoy, John (b. Kildare, Fenian, NY Clan; 1842–1928), 12, 28, 51, 120, 124, 126–7, 128, 145, 150, 152, 153, 155, 163, 169, 186, 206, 209, 228, 261

Boland family and, 19, 20
HB and, 130, 135, 149–50
   Clan na Gael split, 184–6, 187, 188,
      189, 190, 207, 208, 211–12
   conflict, 152–3, 155–7, 170, 175, 199
   on HB's exploits, 100
   meets HB, 122–3
   tribute to HB, 10
Treaty, 278
Dillon, John (Mayo MP, APN, Nat. leader;
   1851–1927), 24, 105, 106, 117
Dillon, Luke (Philadelphia Clan), 10–11, 151,
   188, 209, 274, 277, 279, 280, 316
Dillon, Valentine Blake (Dublin solicitor, PN),
   29
Dineen, Frank Brazil (b. Limerick, Dublin
   GAA; d. 1916), 38
Dinneen, Maj. James (US army; Clan), 213,
   278, 400
Doheny, Edward Laurence (oil magnate;
   1856–1935), 197, 199, 259, 274, 388
Doheny, Michael (Tipperary Confederate, NY;
   1805–63), 149
Donegan, Mossy (Cork IRA, AT), 308–9
Donnelly, Patrick (Armagh MP, Nat.;
   1878–1947), 99
Doran, Kit (Dublin gardener), 64
Douglas, James Green (Dublin draper, White
   Cross, T; 1887–1954), 203, 241, 381
Dowd, Capt. (IRA, AT), 310
Downing, Rossa F. (Washington Clan), 138,
   140, 202
Downs, Barney (IRB seaman), 166, 182, 192
Doyle, J. C. (Dublin Telegraph Office), 90
Doyle, John (Dublin GAA), 49
Drury, Peter A. (Washington banker), 244, 400
Dublin Blue Terrier Club, 398
Dublin Corporation, 21, 31
Dublin County Board (GAA), 33, 34, 70
Dublin County Committee (GAA), 22
Duffy, George Gavan (b. France, Dublin TD,
   Min. Foreign Affairs, T; 1882–1951),
   56, 181, 272, 273–4, 281
Duggan, Bill (Todd, Burns)
   business with HB, 96, 120
   HB's imprisonment, 48, 59, 72, 79, 85, 88
Duggan, Edmund John (Eamon; Dublin
   solicitor, Meath TD, T; 1874–1936),
   53, 56, 57, 99, 187, 227, 294, 359
Dunlop, John Boyd (b. Ayrshire, Dublin tyre
   manufacturer; 1840–1921), 31
Dwyer, Mick (Dublin GAA), 36, 65
'Dynamiters', 28, 188

Eardley-Wilmot, Capt. Cecil Francis de Lys
   (Prison Commission; 1855–1916),
   46–7
East Side (steamship), 214–15

Easter Rebellion (1916), 38–44, 49
   anniversary Mass, 80
   HB's views, 101, 102
   visitors' tours, 276
Egan, Barry (Cork IRA), 236
Elder, Benedict (NY Bonds organiser), 144
elections
   general (1918), 108, 109–12, 128
   general (1922), 298–9
   South Longford by-election (1917), 84,
      85–7
Ellis, Fr. Michael (Skerries), 320, 322
Emmet, Robert (Dublin United Irishman;
   1778–1803), 81, 197
Emmet, Dr. Thomas Addis (b. Cork, United
   Irishman, NY barrister; 1764–1827),
   134
Emmet Monument Association, 149, 374
Enright, Fr. Dominick (Franciscan Provincial,
   Dublin), 3
Etchingham, Seán R. (Wicklow TD, AT;
   1870–1923), 51
Evans, Sam (Washington), 197

Fahy, Patrick (Galway Gaelic League, Lewes
   convict; 1879–1976), 52, 348, 353
Fairbairn & Co. (Manchester), 18
Farewell, J. R. (Prison Commission), 53, 116
Farmer-Labor (Third) Party, 178, 180
Farrell, Billy (Dublin socialist), 362
Farrell, Robert (IRB informer), 335
Faugh-a-Ballagh Hurling Club (Faughs;
   Dublin): see GAA; hurling
Fawsitt, Diarmuid (b. Cork, Dáil Consul, NY;
   1884–1967), 128, 148, 164, 184, 202,
   204, 206, 213
Ferguson, Capt. (Panhandle State), 262
Fianna (NY), 208–9
Fianna Fáil, 267
Field, Denis J. (Dublin stationer), 335
Field, William (Dublin MP, PN; 1848–1935),
   29, 36
Figgis, Darrell (Dublin TD, T; 1882–1925),
   119, 297, 358
Finan, Fr. John (Roscommon), 230
Fine Ghaedheal, 271–3
Finlay, Michael (Roscommon), 110
Fitzgerald, Dan (Kerry IRA, NY), 392
Fitzgerald, James (Manchester IRA), 363
Fitzgerald, P. N. (Dublin IRB), 338
FitzGerald, Thomas Joseph Desmond (b.
   London, Dublin TD, Director of
   Publicity, T; 1888–1947), 50, 56, 271
FitzGibbon, Fr. James (Dublin), 7
Fitzpatrick, John (b. Athlone, Lab. leader
   Chicago; 1870–1946), 178, 370
Fitzsimons, Anna (Dublin SF), 121, 164, 169,
   319

Flanagan, Catherine (Sec. Mary McSwiney),
    198
Flood, Rep. Henry de la Warr (Virginia, D;
    1865–1921), 137
Flood, James P. (Longford SF), 147
Fogarty, Bishop Michael (Killaloe; Dáil
    Trustee, T; 1859–1955), 145
Foley, Michael: see Ó Foghludha
Ford, Henry (Detroit automobile
    manufacturer; 1863–1947), 136
Fraher, Cait (Kathleen)
    correspondence with HB, 63, 65, 74, 75,
        77, 79, 87, 88, 176
    romance with HB, 76–8, 91
Fraher, Daniel (Waterford GAA), 76, 91, 98,
    109, 173, 351
Francis, Philip (Washington), 139
French, Field Marshal Sir John Denton
    Pinkstone (1st Earl of Ypres;
    1852–1925), 100
Friends of Irish Freedom, 120, 122, 127, 143,
    145, 149, 203, 258
    HB and, 123, 132, 144, 152, 155, 157,
        180, 183
    Clan na Gael split, 184, 186, 189–90
Friends of the Irish Free State, 12
Frongoch Internment Camp, 58, 82, 95, 127

Gaelic Athletic Association, 76, 78, 96, 281,
    291
    aims, 22, 23, 33, 70
    dissidence, 70–1
    HB and, 32–4, 38, 97–8, 123, 305
        death, 7
        during imprisonment, 69–71, 74
        hurling, 33, 63, 97, 234, 305
    James Boland and, 19, 22, 23, 27, 33
        funds for widow, 29
Gaelic League, 31, 76, 89, 103
Gallagher, Mr (New Jersey Clan), 149
Gallagher, Bishop Michael James (Detroit;
    1866–1937), 190
Gallivan, Sen. James Ambrose (Mass, D;
    1866–1928), 137
Garrity, Eamon S. (Mass. Clan), 385
Geddes, Sir Auckland Campbell (British
    Ambassador Washington;
    1879–1954), 197
Geraghty, Warder (Dartmoor Prison), 46
'German Plot' (1918), 98, 103
Ginnell, Alice (née King), 333
Ginnell, Laurence (Westmeath MP, TD, AT,
    Dáil envoy Argentina; 1854–1923),
    118, 179, 202
Gleeson, Tim (Faughs; 1877–1949), 71
Gloucester Prison, 116
Goff, Judge John William (NY Clan;
    1848–1924), 155, 190, 202, 402

Golden, Peter (b. Cork, NY Irish Progressive
    League; 1877–1926), 10, 13, 262
Gonne MacBride, Mme. Edith Maud (b.
    Aldershot, CB, AT; 1866–1953), 6
Gordon, Fr. (Wisconsin, Indian), 133
Gordon, Adam Lindsay (Australian poet;
    1833–70), 62
Gore, Sen. Thomas Pryor (Oklahoma, D;
    1870–1949), 136
Gosselin, Maj. Nicholas (Home Office
    Intelligence), 339
Grace, Joseph Peter (NY businessman;
    1872–1950), 372
Grace, John P. (Mayor of Charleston), 156,
    189
Great War, 34–6, 140–1
Griffin, Gerald (b. Limerick, novelist;
    1803–40), 62
Griffin, Joseph (Dublin IRA Intelligence, AT),
    4, 5, 313, 319–22, 323
Griffith, Arthur (Dublin, SF founder, Cavan
    TD, T; 1871–1922), 7, 11, 12, 27, 29,
        31, 34, 125, 164, 177, 182, 225, 289,
        304
    Dáil Pres., 270, 273, 275, 290, 291
    imprisonment, 99, 116
    Sinn Féin, 103, 288
    Treaty and split, 194, 265, 269–70, 277,
        291, 292, 293, 296, 307
Grigg, Sir Edward William Macleay (Sec.
    Lloyd George; 1879–1955), 232
Groves, John (Omaha INB), 28

Hall, Maj. Frank (b. Down, M.I.5; b. 1876),
    79, 367
Hand, P. (Washington), 138, 139
Hannigan, Donncadha (Cork IRA, AT), 414
Harding, Pres. Warren Gamaliel (R;
    1865–1923), 136, 197, 198, 240,
    243
Hardwick, Sen. Thomas William (Georgia, D;
    1872–1944), 138, 139
Harrigan, John F. (Mass. AARIR), 203
Harris, R. (IRA, AT), 415
Hart, Edward (Dublin pavior), 21
Hartnett, Lieut. Michael (British army), 34–5
Harty, Andrew C. (Faughs; 1880–1926),
    69–70, 74, 81, 86, 163, 350
Hayden, John Patrick (Roscommon MP, PN;
    1863–1954), 109, 110–11
Hayes, Dr. Richard Francis (Dick; Limerick
    TD, historian, T; 1882–1958), 50
Healy, Dr. Bernard (Skerries), 320
Healy, Timothy Michael (b. Cork, KC, Louth
    MP, APN; 1855–1931), 4, 21, 25,
    105, 233, 294
Hearn, John J. (Mass. AARIR), 202, 203, 274
Hearn, Mary (Mass.), 250

Hearst, William Randolph (NY press magnate; 1863–1951), 137–8, 200
Hearty, Edward J. (arms smuggler, NY to Louth), 246, 319
Henderson, Frank (Dublin IRA, AT; 1886–1959), 6, 34, 35, 81, 282, 331, 333
  Easter Rebellion, 40–1, 42, 44
Henderson, Leo (Dublin IRA Intelligence, AT), 9, 13, 41
Henry, Sgt. (British army instructor), 41, 45
Hobson, Bulmer (b. Down, Sec. Irish Volunteers; 1883–1969), 66, 342
Hogan, John J. (Dublin GAA), 70–1
Hogan, Paddy (Faughs), 59, 70, 71, 88
Hogan, Tom (Faughs), 74
Home Rule, 82–4, 86, 101, 102, 104, 105
Home Rule Confederation of Great Britain, 27
Hoover, John Edgar (Bureau of Investigation; 1895–1972), 195, 398
Hughes, Charles Evans (Sec. of State, R; 1862–1948), 240
Hughes, Katherine (Canadian, Irish Nat. Bureau Washington), 129
hunger-strikes, 53–4, 59
Hunter, Thomas (Lewes convict; b. 1884), 56
Hurley, John: see Ó Murthuile, Seán
hurling, 33, 63, 74, 163, 210, 234, 305, 378
Hylan, John Francis (Mayor of NY, D; 1868–1936), 404
Hyland, Joe (MC's driver), 168, 172

Indian Friends of Freedom, 138
International Socialist Congress (Berne, 1919), 114
Invincibles, Irish National, 19, 25, 26
'Irish Brigades', 27, 104
Irish Citizen Army, 40
Irish Emigrant Aid Society (NY), 149, 374
Irish National Aid Association, 58, 68, 70, 95–6
Irish National Alliance, 28
Irish National Amnesty Association, 24, 27
Irish National Brotherhood, 25, 27, 28
Irish National Bureau (Washington), 367–8
Irish National Club (Washington), 150
Irish National Foresters, 32, 34, 230, 284
Irish Parliamentary Party, 82–3, 109, 110, 112, 149
Irish Progressive League, 10
Irish Race Congress (Paris, 1922), 270–3
Irish Relief Fund, 183
Irish Republican Army, 170, 212, 226, 246, 263, 266, 285, 292, 293; see also Irish Volunteers
  arms agents, 281
  Civil War, 309–12, 313, 314, 316
    munitions, 315

  HB and, 281–3
  diverts funds, 279–80
Irish Republican Brotherhood, 81, 92, 120, 226, 262, 277, 278, 282, 284, 285, 292, 293, 315, 318, 324
  'Circles', 32, 98, 284
  Clan na Gael Reorganized and, 277, 278, 315
  growth after Rebellion, 98
  HB and, 33–4, 38, 103, 108, 156, 157, 158, 210–11, 228–9
  arms-running, 147–8, 246
  ascendancy, 98–9
  Clan na Gael split, 186, 187, 248, 277
  enrols, 32
  fund-raising, 183, 208, 245
  post-Treaty, 284–5
  visit home, 169–70
  James Boland and, 18–20, 22, 23–5
  John Boland and, 21
  Peace Conference, 84
Irish Republican Volunteers of America, 247
Irish Self-Determination League of Great Britain, 118
Irish Trades Union Congress, 106
Irish Victory Fund, 143, 144, 145, 147, 153, 184
Irish Volunteer Training Corps, 79
Irish Volunteers, 11, 34, 35–6, 99, 102–3, 112, 176, 230; see also Easter Rebellion, IRA
Irish Women's Franchise League, 112
Irwin, Dr. James Alexander Hamilton (Belfast Presbyterian minister; 1876–1954), 272
Ivers, Fr. Michael (Dublin), 27

Jenkinson, Sir Edward George (Dublin Castle Intelligence; 1835–1919), 21
Jennings, Samuel J. (Dublin landlord), 100
Johnson, Thomas Ryder (b. Liverpool, Dublin TD, Lab. leader; 1872–1963), 416
Joseph Holt '98 Club (Dublin IRB), 32, 98, 284

Kearns, Linda (Dublin CB, AT; 1888–1951), 16
Kelleher, Dist. Insp. Philip St. John Howlett (Longford RIC; 1897–1920), 176
Kelly, Dr. Gertrude B. (Irish Progressive League NY), 175
Kelly, Jack (Dublin GAA), 70
Kelly, Richard (Lewes convict; b. 1895), 52–3
Kelly, Col. Thomas J. (b. Galway, NY Fenian; 1833–1908), 18, 19, 23, 150, 374
Kelly, Tom (Dublin Alderman, TD, T), 36, 103, 105, 106, 107, 109
Kennedy, Dr. Denis (Dublin surgeon), 324

Kennedy, James Edward (Dublin clerk), 335
Kennedy, Mick (Dublin publican), 72
Kerr, Neil (Liverpool IRB), 167, 173
Kevans, Kitty (Todd, Burns), 352
Kickham, Charles Joseph (Tipperary novelist, Pres. SC IRB; 1828–82), 32, 185
Kickham, Charles J. (novelist's nephew; Dublin IRB), 32
Kiernan, Catherine Brigid (Kitty, m. Felix Cronin; 1891?–1945), 116, 174, 176, 177, 191, 237, 239, 240, 278, 412
    Collins and, 172, 222, 226, 227, 228, 236, 253–4, 264, 265, 302, 303–4
    HB's death, 8–9
    HB's romance with, 91–2, 164, 172, 221–2, 226–7
        engagement, 236–7, 251
        HB's letters, 175–7, 226, 241, 250, 252–5, 259
        Kitty changes affections, 251–5, 265, 302–4
Kiernan, Christine (Chrys, m. Tom Magee; 1889?–1953), 164, 172, 222
Kiernan, Helen (m. Paul McGovern; 1892?–1940), 92, 116, 148, 164, 172, 222, 226, 227, 251–2, 254–5
Kiernan, Lawrence Devlin (Larry, m. Peggy Sheridan; Longford publican; 1890?–1948), 164, 176, 303, 304
Kiernan, Maud (Mops, m. Gearóid O'Sullivan; 1893?–1940), 92, 164, 176, 227, 254–5, 303
King, Richard F. (Lewes convict; b. 1890), 53, 346
Kinkead, Maj. Eugene F. (US army; ex-Rep. New Jersey, D; 1876–1960), 154, 196, 202, 214, 215, 239, 240, 262, 274, 416
Kipling, Joseph Rudyard (b. India, English author; 1865–1936), 63, 80
Knights of Columbus, 160, 183

Labour Party, 106–8, 114, 298, 316
La Follette, Sen. Robert Marion (Wisconsin, R; 1855–1925), 197
La Guardia, Fiorello Henry (ex-Rep. NY, R; 1882–1947), 160
Lamie, William (IRB informer), 335
Langan, Peter (Dublin IRB), 149
Laverty, Mr (New Jersey Clan), 149, 162
Lavery, Hazel, Lady (née Martyn; b. Chicago; 1880–1935), 315
Lawless, Francis J. (Dublin TD, T; 1871?–1922), 291
Lawless, James (Lewes convict; b. 1879), 51, 360
Lawless, Louis (Dublin Corporation), 20, 21

Lazenby, Elizabeth Annie (née Tottie, Unitarian minister's wife; Manchester and Mass.), 405
League of Nations, 118, 135, 136, 191
League of Oppressed Peoples, 138
Leahy, Tom (Dublin IRA), 42, 43
Lee, J. C. (NY), 162
Leech, Peter (Dublin publican), 65, 83
Lehane, Seán (Donegal IRA, AT), 308–9
Lemass, John Francis (Seán; Dublin IRA, AT; 1899–1971), 309, 310, 314, 320
Levinson, Solomon (Salmon) Oliver (b. Indiana, peace advocate; 1865–1941), 138
Lewes Prison, 51–7, 59–88, 176
Liddy, Martin Joseph (Indiana Clan), 385
Limerick, 'Siege' of (1922), 293
Lincoln Prison, 92, 114–16
Little, Patrick John (Dáil envoy S. America; b. 1884), 410
Lloyd George, David (Carnarvon MP, Prime Min., Lib.; 1863–1945), 83, 118, 179, 197, 353
    Treaty and, 222, 223, 228, 229, 243, 307
        HB envoy to, 232–3, 234
Loyal Orange Institution, 230
    of the United States, 141
Lydon, Patrick (Kentucky), 248
Lyman, William (NY INB), 28
Lynam, William Francis (Dublin comic writer; 1845?–94), 67
Lynch, Col. Arthur Alfred (South African, British armies; b. Australia, Clare MP, PN; 1861–1934), 104
Lynch, Diarmuid C. (Jeremiah; SC IRB, Cork TD, T; 1878–1950), 93, 99, 103
    in America, 122, 126, 145, 149
    Easter Rebellion, 42–3
    HB and, 152, 183, 185, 256, 257, 258
    resigns from Dáil, 189
Lynch, Fionán (Finian; Kerry TD, T; 1889–1966), 8, 397
Lynch, Liam (William Fanaghan; SC IRB, Cork IRA, AT Chief of Staff; 1893–1923), 169, 261
    Civil War, 308, 310, 315, 323
        build-up, 280, 281, 282, 283, 284, 293
    tribute to HB, 9
Lynch, Michael (Dublin IRA), 358
Lynch, Mrs M. (Dublin), 189
Lynch, Patrick G. (KC, Nat. ; 1863–1947), 4
Lyster, Lionel (KK's fiancé), 221

McAllister, Bernard (Dublin IRA, interned Frongoch, Capt. Nat. army; b. 1895?), 323–4
McArdle, John (Lewes convict; b. 1877), 50
McBride, Mr (Washington), 138

MacBride, Maj. John (South African army; b.
    Mayo, IRB; 1865–1916), 27, 28, 44
McCabe, Alex (Sligo TD, SC IRB, T;
    1886–1972), 76
McCann, Pierce (Tipperary TD; 1882–1919),
    116
McCarney, Harry (New Jersey Clan), 149,
    162
McCartan, Dr. Patrick (b. Tyrone, IRB, Offaly
    TD, T; 1878–1963)
  American envoy, 84, 122, 124, 138, 139,
    151
  arms-running, 147
  Russian alliance, 180–1, 200
  Armagh by-election, 99
  Civil War, 308, 314
  description, 126
  HB and, 126–7, 161, 189
  HB's death, 7–8, 11, 323, 325
  Treaty and split, 270, 275, 277, 282, 293,
    294, 299
McCarthy, Dan (Dublin GAA, TD, T;
    1883–1957), 85–6, 87
MacCarthy, Seán (Cork GAA), 331
McCormack, John (b. Athlone, tenor;
    1884–1945), 165, 270
MacCrainn, Liam (Roscommon, AT), 332
McCullough, Denis (b. Belfast, Pres. SC IRB;
    1883–1968), 98
McDermott, Fr. Francis (Roscommon), 404
McDermott, James ('Red Jim'; b. Dublin, IRB
    informer; d. 1885), 25
McDermott, Seán (b. Leitrim, MC IRB;
    1883–1916), 42, 66
McDevitt, Danny (Belfast tailor), 32
MacDonagh, Thomas (b. Tipperary, MC IRB;
    1878–1916), 38, 39, 44
McDonald, Fr. Walter (Dublin), 88
McDonnell, Andrew (Dublin IRA, AT), 309,
    310, 311, 312
McElligott, Thomas Joseph (ex-Sgt. RIC, AT;
    1888–1961), 401
McEntee, Seán Francis (Monaghan TD, AT;
    1889–1984), 100
McGarrity, Joseph (b. Tyrone, Philadelphia
    Clan; 1874–1940), 137, 151–2, 155,
    229, 240
  arms-running, 214, 215, 216
  Civil War, 306–7, 315, 317
  Clan na Gael Reorganized, 207–8, 245, 248
  HB and, 127, 163, 173, 177, 178, 183,
    184, 192, 194, 202, 220, 274, 322
  Clan na Gael split, 154, 155, 184, 186,
    187, 188
  friendship, 11, 14, 151–2, 163, 224
  funds diverted, 280
  HB's death, 4, 8, 11–12, 14, 323
  life profile, 124, 151–2

Treaty and split, 242, 258, 259, 275, 288,
    293, 294, 297, 299
  visits Ireland, 275–9, 304
McGarry, John A. (Chicago Clan), 155, 156,
    200
McGarry, Seán (Lewes convict, Pres. SC IRB,
    Dublin TD, T; 1886–1924), 57, 96,
    98, 99, 104, 114–15, 169, 296
MacGearailt, Seumas (James Fitzgerald; Cork
    TD, AT), 291
McGee, James (NY Clan), 166, 208, 214
McGovern, Paul (Fermanagh solicitor), 226
McGrath, John (Dublin journalist), 100
McGrath, Joseph (Dublin TD, Min. Labour, T;
    1888–1966), 232–4, 269, 273, 291
McGreal, Michael B. (Connecticut Clan), 385
McGuinness, Francis (Longford TD, T; d.
    1934), 99, 354
McGuinness, James Martin (Londonderry MP,
    SF; b. 1950), 326
McGuinness, Joseph (Lewes convict, Longford
    TD, T; 1876–1922), 85, 86, 87
McGuire, Mrs Frances G., 220
McGuire, James K. (Virginia Clan), 125, 154,
    161, 162, 184, 185, 188, 210, 214,
    220, 274–5, 279, 297
McGuire, John (Dublin IRA, Vice-Cdant. Nat.
    army; b. 1899), 323–4
MacHale, Archbishop John (Tuam;
    1791–1881), 62
McHugh, Mr (Clan emissary), 211–12
McKee, Dick (Dublin IRA, GHQ;
    1892–1920), 181
McKelvey, Joseph (SC IRB, Belfast IRA, AT
    Executive; 1900?–22), 280
McKenna, Patrick (Longford Nat.), 86
McKeown, John Joseph (Seán MacEoin;
    Longford TD, SC IRB, T; 1893–1973),
    197, 225, 226, 229, 231, 234, 242,
    294, 295, 297, 314
MacLaverty, Dr. Robert A. (Dublin surgeon),
    277
MacLaverty, Mrs Madge, 277
MacLysaght, Edward Anthony Edgeworth
    (formerly Lysaght; b. Bristol, Clare
    polymath; 1887–1986), 353
MacMahon, James (PC, Under-Sec., Dublin
    Castle; 1865–1954), 398
McMahon, Liam W. (Manchester IRB), 377
McMahon, Seán (Dublin IRA, GHQ, SC IRB,
    T), 213
McNabb, Mr (Delaware), 140
MacNeill, Prof. Eoin (b. Antrim, historian,
    Chief of Staff Volunteers, Nat.
    University TD, T; 1867–1945), 35,
    103, 107, 292, 342
  Easter Rebellion, 38, 39, 349
  imprisonment, 47, 52, 53

MacNeill, Hugo (Nat. army; 1900–63), 312
McSweeney, Edward F. (Boston banker, Bonds
    organiser), 144
McSwiney, Annie, 236, 237
McSwiney, Mary Margarite (Min; b. London,
    Cork TD, AT; 1872–1942), 11, 226,
    249
    in America, 177–8, 194, 197, 198–9, 202,
        206, 218, 224, 242
    popularity, 198
    HB and, 198–9, 223, 224, 231–2, 236, 242
    Treaty and split, 270, 271, 286, 294
McSwiney, Muriel (née Murphy, Terence's
    widow; AT; 1892–1982), 16
McSwiney, Peter J. (b. London), 11, 275, 306
McSwiney, Seán (Cork TD, AT; d. 1934), 236,
    301, 416
McSwiney, Terence J. (Lord Mayor of Cork,
    IRA; 1879–1920), 175, 177, 181, 200,
    241
MacWhite, Michael (Dáil envoy Geneva, T;
    1883–1958), 271
McWhorter, Mrs Mary F. (Chicago AOH), 16,
    188, 203, 245, 283, 302
    Civil War, 307, 313, 314, 317, 318
    HB's death, 322, 324, 325, 418
Madden, Miss (Ohio AARIR), 198
Magennis, Fr. Peter E. (b. Armagh, Carmelite
    NY, Rome; 1868–1937), 6, 10, 123,
    127, 190
Maguire, Samuel (b. Cork, London GAA, IRB;
    1879–1927), 342
Maguire, Tom (Mayo TD, AT; 1892–1993),
    412
Mahmud, Muhammad (Pasha; Egyptian
    revolutionary; 1877–1941), 163
Maidstone Prison, 56–7, 58
Mallon, Supt. John (DMP detective;
    1839–1910), 23, 26–7, 336, 337
Malone, Dudley Field (NY maverick reformer;
    1882–1950), 138
Maloney, J. T. (NY Clan), 155
Maloney, Dr. William Joseph Marie Alais (b.
    Edinburgh, British army, NY
    neurologist; 1882–1952), 11, 183,
    189, 196, 274, 293, 370
    HB and, 162, 163, 223, 235, 244, 262, 270
    HB's death, 10
    life profile, 152
'Manchester Martyrs' (1867), 18–19, 22, 23,
    24
Mannix, Archbishop Daniel (Melbourne; b.
    Cork, AT; 1864–1963), 177, 178,
    179–80, 373
Mannix MacSwiney Marine Protest
    Committee, 180
Markievicz, Mme. Constance Georgina de (née
    Gore-Booth; b. London, Dublin TD,

Min. Labour, AT; 1868–1927), 2, 6,
    13, 90, 242, 271, 273, 286, 309
Marley, Mr (Washington), 197
Marriott, Maj. R. A. (Gov. Lewes Prison),
    52–3, 55, 63
Marshall, Thomas Riley (Vice-Pres., D;
    1854–1925), 141
Martens, Ludwig Christian Alexander
    Karlovich (Soviet envoy NY;
    1874–1948), 138–9, 181, 200
Mason, Rep. William Ernest (Illinois, R, ex-
    Sen.; 1850–1921), 137
Mathew, Fr. Theobald (b. Tipperary, Capuchin
    Temperance advocate; 1790–1856), 3
Maunsell, Mother M. Thecla (Dublin Sister of
    Mercy), 330
Maxwell, Gen. Sir John Grenfell (British army,
    Irish command; 1859–1928), 45, 97
Meagher, Mary O'Connor (Mass.), 369
Mellows, Liam (Galway TD, AT; 1892–1922),
    235, 249, 279, 282
    in America, 126, 127, 132–3, 135, 141,
        184, 198, 206
    arms-running, 147, 181–2, 246, 281
    HB's 'race vendetta', 247–8
    Anglo-Irish Treaty, 262, 270
    split, 282, 283, 286, 294, 295
    Civil War, 308, 316
    description, 126
Merrick, Joseph (Manchester), 340
Metcalfe, Fr. R. A. (NY Carmelite), 162
Midland and Great Western Railway Co., 30
Milholland, John Elmer (NY journalist;
    1860–1925), 137, 138, 139, 140, 142,
    178, 196, 240, 262
Mills, Insp. John (DMP; 1866–1917), 347
Mills, Supt William B. (Philadelphia police),
    332
Milroy, Seán (Cavan TD, T; 1877–1946), 114,
    247, 296, 373
Mitchel, John (b. Newry, Confederate exile,
    Tipperary MP, Nat.; 1817–75), 81
Mockler, John Bob (Faughs; 1886–1966), 71
Molloy, Fr. Gerald (author) 62
Molloy, Patrick (Dublin IRB), 335, 337
Montague, Hugh (NY Clan), 184, 416
Moore, Col. Maurice George (British army; b.
    Mayo, Nat. Volunteer leader;
    1854–1939), 309
Moore, Theodore Conyngham Kingsmill
    (Dublin KC; 1894–1979), 118
Moore & McCormack (NY shipping line),
    148, 213
Moran, Cardinal Patrick (Archbishop of
    Sydney; b. Carlow; 1830–1911), 62
Moran, Linus (AARIR), 203
Morgan, John Pierpont (American financier;
    1867–1943), 370

Morrison, Robert (Todd, Burns), 64, 79
Morse, Canon J. W. (NY), 138
Mountjoy Glee Singers, 13
Mountjoy Prison, 6, 16, 18, 46, 68, 94,
    116–17, 325
Moylan, Seán (Cork, TD, AT; 1888–1957),
    265, 282, 294
Moylett, Patrick (b. Mayo, Pres. SC IRB,
    Dublin importer), 98
Moynihan, Fr. John Senan (Capuchin; b.
    1900), 330
Mulcahy, Mary Josephine (Min, née Ryan;
    1884–1979), 15, 294, 418
Mulcahy, Richard (b. Waterford, Dublin TD,
    IRA Chief of Staff, Min. Defence;
    1886–1971), 103
    Civil War, 313
    build-up, 280, 282, 283, 293–4, 296, 298
    IRB, 99, 108, 109, 210, 246, 266
Muldoon, Malachi (Mayo solicitor), 330
Mulholland, Rosa (Lady Gilbert; b. Belfast,
    novelist; 1841–1921), 62
Mullett, Joseph (Dublin IRB), 335
Mulrean, Mr (Delaware), 140
Mulvena, Mr (Delaware), 140
Murphy, Fintan (b. London, interned
    Frongoch), 231
Murphy, Fr. Austin (Dublin Vincentian), 97
Murphy, John Archdeacon (Buffalo, NY
    Clan), 185, 384
Murray, Fr. P. J. (Roscommon), 160
Mythen, Revd. Patrick James Grattan
    (Orthodox convert, NY), 142

Nally, Bébé (Patrick's sister), 23, 28
Nally, Patrick William (Mayo IRB; 1857–91),
    22–3
Nally Clubs, 23, 27, 28
National army, 280–1, 301
National Association of Gaelic and Athletic
    Clubs, 350
National Club (Dublin), 25, 27, 28, 29
National Committee of the Motion Picture
    Industries, 203
National Woman Party, 196–7
Naval Disarmament Conference (Washington,
    1921–2), 197, 243, 249
'Nero' (IRB informer), 24
Nevinson, Henry Woodd (English journalist;
    1856–1941), 257, 258, 260, 399–400
Newman, Cardinal John Henry (English
    Catholic convert; 1801–90), 62
Newton, Rep. Cleveland Alexander (Missouri,
    R; 1873–1945) or Rep. Walter Hughes
    (Minnesota, R; 1880–1941), 137
Nolan, John (Dublin IRB; d. 1920), 26
Norris, Sen. George William (Nebraska, R;
    1861–1944), 197

Nowlan, James (Kilkenny Alderman, Pres.
    GAA), 98
Nugent, John Dillon (b. Armagh, Dublin MP,
    Nat.; 1869–1940), 86
Nunan, Seán (b. London, IRB, Sec. EdeV, T;
    1890–1981), 126, 127, 132, 135, 145,
    158, 162, 166, 177, 192, 239, 240,
    262, 360
    HB and, 132, 152, 158, 161, 195, 252,
        253, 262, 264, 380
    arms-running, 246
    Bond Drive, 184
    clothes, 159
    friendship, 127, 129, 158, 162, 174, 220,
        224, 234, 270
    tribute to HB, 7
Nuorteva, Santeri (Soviet envoy NY), 138,
    139, 181

O'Brien, Art (Dáil envoy London, AT;
    1872–1949), 225, 405
O'Brien, Ellen Lucy (Nellie; Dublin Gaelic
    League; 1864–1925), 31
O'Brien, Kate (Kitty; b. Limerick, novelist;
    1897–1974), 250–1, 305
O'Brien, Judge Morgan Joseph (NY, D;
    1852–1937), 199
O'Brien, Patrick (Kilkenny MP, PN;
    1853?–1917), 27, 29, 30
O'Brien, Richard Barry (b. Clare, historian;
    1847–1918), 62
O'Brien, William (b. Cork, Dublin TD, Lab.;
    1881–1968), 24, 36, 106, 114
O'Brien Institute for Destitute Children
    (Dublin), 30
O'Callaghan, Donal (Lord Mayor of Cork,
    TD, IRB, AT), 200, 202, 220, 225,
    236, 270, 271, 274
O'Casey, Sean (Dublin playwright;
    1881–1964), 256
O'Clohessy, John 'Shehan' (Dublin Fenian), 26
O'Connell, Fr. (NY), 163
O'Connell, Daniel (b. Kerry, MP, Repeal
    leader; 1775–1847), 102
O'Connell, Capt. Daniel T. (US army; Boston
    lawyer, Irish Nat. Bureau Washington),
    161
O'Connell, James (Dublin IRA, interned
    Frongoch, Cdant. Nat. army; b. 1891),
    323–4
O'Connell, Kathleen (b. Kerry, Sec. EdeV;
    1888–1956), 264, 295, 301, 380,
    402
    HB and, 129, 174, 227–8, 231, 286–7
    HB's death, 13–14
O'Connor, Arthur John Kickham (Kildare TD,
    Min. Agriculture, AT; 1888–1950),
    265

O'Connor, Bartholomew (Batt; IRB, T; 1870–1935), 92–3, 98, 168, 294
O'Connor, Fr. Denis (NY Carmelite), 145, 385
O'Connor, Fr. Dominic (Cork Capuchin, AT), 419
O'Connor, John (Tipperary MP, PN; 1850–1928), 24
O'Connor, Roderick (Rory; Dublin IRA, GHQ, AT Executive; 1883–1922), 282, 283, 306, 308, 414
O'Connor, Tommy (alias Walsh; IRB courier, imprisoned Atlanta), 207
O'Connor, Thomas Power (b. Athlone, Liverpool MP, APN; 1848–1929), 82, 353
O'Conor, Owen Phelim ('the O'Conor Don'; High Sheriff, Roscommon; 1870–1943), 361
O'Doherty, Joe (Dublin, Pres. SC IRB, Philadelphia Clan), 412–13, 416
O'Doherty, Mrs Kitty (Clan courier), 312, 315, 318–19, 416
O'Donoghue, Thomas (Kerry TD, AT), 304, 414
O'Donovan, Cornelius (Con; Lewes convict; b. 1888), 36, 45, 46, 94, 170, 173, 310
O'Donovan, Peter (Cork hunger-striker), 170
O'Donovan, Mrs Seán: see Boland, Kathleen
O'Donovan, Seán (Cork GAA, IRA, AT; b. 1893), 16, 319, 264
O'Donovan Rossa, Jeremiah (Cork Fenian, NY; 1831–1915), 21, 23, 28
O'Duffy, Eoin (Owen; Monaghan TD, SC IRB, IRA Chief of Staff, T; 1890–1944), 229–30, 231, 261, 285, 299, 313, 316
O'Flaherty (Galway seaman), 122, 124
O'Flanagan, Fr. Michael (Roscommon, SF, AT; 1876–1942), 103, 105, 106, 109, 160, 172, 242
Ó Foghludha, Mícheál (Foley; Dublin stationer, Gaelic League; 1879–1952), 36, 314
O'Geary, Colm (Ó Gaora; Lewes convict; 1887–1954), 348
O'Growney, Fr. Eugene (b. Meath, Maynooth Gaelicist; 1863–99), 47
O'Hanrahan, Henry (Lewes convict; b. 1876), 78
O'Hegarty, Diarmuid (b. Cork, Sec. Dáil Min., SC IRB, T; 1892–1958), 159, 160, 169, 278
O'Hegarty, Patrick Sarsfield (b. Cork, historian, IRB, T; 1879–1955), 119, 278
O'Higgins, Kevin Christopher (Laois TD, Min. Economic Affairs, T; 1892–1927), 6, 290, 291, 325, 397

O'Keefe, Mary (Todd, Burns), 79, 352
O'Keeffe, Paudeen (Pádraig Ó Caoimh; Cork TD, SF Gen. Sec., T; 1881–1973), 297, 359, 409, 416
O'Kelly, James J. (Roscommon MP, PN; 1845–1916), 24
O'Kelly, John Joseph ('Sceilg'; Louth TD, Min. Education, AT; 1872–1957), 171, 360
O'Kelly, Marie (Sec. EdeV), 322
O'Kelly, Mary Kate (Nan, née Ryan; 1878–1934), 220, 294, 318, 367
O'Kelly, Seán Thomas (Dublin TD, Dáil envoy Paris, AT; 1882–1966), 109, 112, 113–14, 116, 273, 283, 294, 349
   Civil War, 315, 316, 317–18, 323
   Sinn Féin, 286, 287
   Treaty and split, 260, 265, 266, 271, 296, 297, 299–301
Old Guard Benevolent Society, 25–6, 29
O'Leary, Jeremiah A. (NY Clan; b. 1881), 209, 248
O'Leary, John (Tipperary Fenian, Pres. SC IRB; 1830–1907), 28, 34
O'Leary, John Stratton (NY Clan), 209
O'Loughlin, Fr. A. (Chaplain, Lewes Prison), 62
Olympic (steamship), 223, 224, 231
O'Mahony, Timothy L. (Todd, Burns), 60, 61, 63, 65, 66–7, 68, 71, 73, 78, 80, 83, 88
O'Malley, Earnán (Ernie; b. Mayo, Dublin IRA, AT Executive; 1897–1957), 283, 309, 310, 314, 319, 323, 331
O'Mara, Agnes (née Cashel, James's wife), 174, 202
O'Mara, James (b. Limerick, Kilkenny MP, TD, Dáil fiscal envoy US, T; 1873–1948), 213
   Bond Drives, 144, 145, 182, 183–4, 203, 204, 242, 244
   HB and, 125, 127–8, 139, 155, 158, 161, 166, 173, 174, 180, 189, 195, 206, 207, 208, 221
   tribute to HB, 7
   profile, 127–8
   recognition of Irish Republic, 191, 196, 198, 200, 201, 202–3
   resignations, 128, 204–5, 218
   Treaty and split, 264, 274
O'Mara, Nance (née O'Brien, Stephen's wife), 174, 250
O'Mara, Patricia (James's daughter), 174–5
O'Mara, Stephen (fiscal envoy US, Mayor of Limerick, AT; 1885–1926), 206, 223, 224, 239, 241, 242, 245, 249
   Civil War build-up, 281, 292–3, 299
   friendship with HB, 234, 243, 250, 331

Treaty and split, 257, 258, 259, 263, 274, 280
Ó Murchadha, Colm (Gov. Mountjoy Prison, T), 325
Ó Murthuile, Seán (John Hurley; b. Cork, SC IRB, T; 1881–1941), 229, 278, 283
IRB, 93, 98, 99, 104, 120, 121, 159, 169
Treaty split, 187, 277, 278, 284
Ó Murthuile, Mrs Seán, 227
O'Neill, Charles (Lewes convict; b. 1896?), 353
O'Neill, Laurence G. (Lord Mayor of Dublin, TD, Independent; 1874–1943), 89, 105, 119
O'Neill, Moira (pseud. Agnes Nesta Shakespeare Skrine, née Higginson; b. Antrim, novelist; 1865–1955), 62
O'Rahilly, Michael Joseph ('the O'Rahilly'; b. Kerry, Treasurer Volunteers; 1875–1916), 39, 41, 349
Orangeism: see Loyal Orange Institution
O'Shannon, Cathal (b. Antrim, Louth TD, Lab.; 1893–1969), 106, 107
O'Shiel, Kevin Roantree (b. Tyrone, Dáil Land Commissioner; 1891–1970), 330
O'Sullivan, Gearóid (George; b. Cork, Carlow TD, GHQ IRA, T; 1891–1948), 34, 169, 227, 255, 261, 325
O'Toole, Luke (Dublin, Sec. GAA; 1873–1929), 65, 70, 71, 72, 93, 97, 163

Page, Robert (Dublin IRB), 342
Panhandle State, (steamship), 262, 263, 264
Parnell, Charles Stewart (b. Wicklow, Cork MP, Nat. leader; 1846–91), 19, 22, 102, 307
Patrick, St. (d. 490?), 62
Partridge, William P. (Dublin Councillor, Lab., Lewes convict; 1874?–1917), 54, 55, 347
Paterson, Andrew Barton ('Banjo'; Australian poet; 1864–1941), 348
Paul, Dr. Alice (b. New Jersey, suffragist; 1885–1977), 138, 139–40, 196
Paviors' Society (Dublin), 21, 27
Peace Conference (London, 1921): see Anglo-Irish Treaty
Peace Conference (Paris, 1919), 84, 101–2, 106, 113, 117–18, 136
Pearse, Margaret (née Brady; St. Enda's school, Dublin TD, AT; 1856?–1932), 307, 308, 312–13
Pearse, Patrick Henry (b. Dublin, MC IRB; 1879–1916), 3, 35, 39, 41, 42, 44, 80, 81, 102, 114, 268
Pedlar, Liam (b. Down, Dáil military attaché NY; b. 1884), 151, 274

arms-running, 214, 246, 280, 281
Civil War, 306, 315, 317, 318, 319
HB and, 173, 224, 234, 249, 250, 262, 264
HB's death, 5
Treaty split, 270, 301
Pentonville Prison, 58
Peppard, Thomas (Lewes convict, Dublin IRA Intelligence, Capt. Nat. army; b. 1894), 52, 96, 323–4
Phelan, Bishop Patrick (Sale, Victoria; b. Kilkenny; 1860–1925), 238
Philadelphia (steamship), 172
Phillips, Mrs (Ohio), 220
Phoenix Park murders (1882), 19
Pinchot, Amos R. E. (NY lawyer), 240
Plunkett, George Noble, Count (b. Dublin, Roscommon TD, AT; 1851–1948), 90, 91, 112, 384
Plunkett, Josephine, Countess (née Cranny; d. 1944), 86
Plunkett, Joseph Mary (b. Dublin, MC IRB; 1887–1916), 38
Plunkett, St. Oliver (Archbishop of Armagh; 1625–81), 62
Poole, Vincent (Lewes convict; b. 1881), 40, 41–2, 43, 44, 56, 57
Porter, Rep. Stephen Geyer (Pennsylvania, R; 1869–1930), 137
Power, Fr. James W. (NY), 209
Power, Jennie Wyse (née O'Toole; CB, SF, T; 1858–1941), 226, 237, 287, 316
Power, Nancy Wyse (Anne; CB, T; 1889–1963), 358
Protestant Friends of Ireland, 142
Pulitzer, Miss (Washington), 138

Quinlisk, H. W. (alias Quinn; double agent; d. 1920), 158
Quinn, John (Lewes convict; b. 1874), 52, 56

Reade, Maj. E. R. (Gov. Dartmoor Prison), 46, 50
Redmond, John Edward (Waterford MP, PN, Nat. leader; 1857–1918), 29, 35, 67, 83, 87, 89, 106, 353
Redmond, Capt. William Hoey Kearney (British army; b. Liverpool, Clare MP, PN; 1861–1917), 82
Reed, John (American radical journalist; 1887–1920), 370
Reid, Pat (Dublin IRB; d. 1893), 25, 26
Reilly, Col. (AARIR), 203
Reilly, James J. (Chicago Clan), 332
Rice, Laurence J. (NY Clan), 153, 154
'Richmond' (IRB informer), 24, 28
Ridgeway, Francis R. (Dublin merchant), 45
Robins, Raymond (American peace advocate; 1873–1954), 139

Robinson, Séamus (Tipperary IRA, AT; 1890–1961), 281, 293
Roche, Mr (Boston journalist), 142
Roche, Mr (NY Fenian), 150
Rooney, William (Dublin Irish-Irelander; 1872–1901), 31
Rorke, George Gordon (Washington arms dealer), 212, 213, 315, 383
Rosser, Miss (Washington), 129
Royal Black Institution, 230
Royal George (steamship), 121, 122, 124
Russell, George William ('AE'; b. Armagh, poet, journalist; 1867–1935), 353
Russell, Seán (Dublin IRA, AT; 1893–1940), 42
Russian-Irish alliance, proposed, 138–9, 180–1, 200
Russian Soviet Government Information Bureau (NY), 138
Ruttledge, Patrick Joseph (Mayo TD, AT; 1892–1952), 294
Ryan, Mrs A. (Ohio), 221
Ryan, Dr. James (Wexford TD, AT; 1892–1970), 318
Ryan, John D. (Montana mining magnate, banker; 1864–1933), 199, 372
Ryan, John T. (Buffalo, NY Clan), 10, 242, 376, 384
Ryan, Michael J. (Philadelphia lawyer, Pres. United Irish League; 1862–1943), 155
Ryan, Miss (Waterford), 74

Samuel, Sir Herbert Louis (Yorkshire MP, Home Sec., Lib.; 1870–1963), 53
Saurin, Charles (Dublin IRA), 34
Scaevola, Gaius Mucius (Roman soldier), 67
Seymour, Joseph (Dublin), 334
Shahan, Fr. Thomas Joseph (b. New Hampshire, Rector Cath. Univ. Washington; 1857–1932), 244, 400
Shanahan, Phil (Dublin publican, AT), 318
Shanley, Fr. Timothy H. (NY, b. Leitrim), 10, 224, 236–7, 271
Shanley's restaurants (NY), 175, 381
Shaw, Mr (NY), 180
Sheehan, Michael (Tipperary IRA, AT), 309, 310
Sheehan, Paddy (SF, journalist), 344, 416
Sheehy-Skeffington, Joanna M. (Hanna; suffragist, SF, AT; 1877–1946), 16, 112, 120, 410
Sheridan, Peggy (m. Larry Kiernan; b. Cavan), 303
Shields, Arthur (Dublin actor, interned Frongoch; 1896–1970), 34
Shouldice, Christina (Ena; b. Roscommon, Dublin telegraphist), 50, 82, 86, 88, 90

romance with HB, 76, 90–2
Shouldice, Frank J. (Roscommon IRA, interned Frongoch), 39, 76, 81, 82
Shouldice, John Francis (Jack; b. Roscommon, Lewes convict; b. 1881?), 35, 39, 76, 91, 331, 346
as fugitive, 100
GAA and, 97–8
imprisonment, 45, 46, 62, 72, 78, 80, 82
homecoming, 89–90, 96
Sinn Féin and, 101
Sinn Féin, 147, 168, 244, 265
Ard Fheis (1922), 273, 278, 287–8
election (1918), 108, 109–12, 128
election (1922), 298–9
growth of, 81, 82, 85, 100–1
HB and, 89, 96, 99, 100–14, 117–18
draft manifesto, 109
expounds strategy, 112–13, 130, 230
post-Treaty, 286–9, 292, 297, 298–9, 316
Labour Party negotiations, 106–8, 114
Mansion House convention (1917), 103
principles, 101
recruitment, 207
South Longford by-election (1917), 84, 85–7
Treaty, 222
US suspicion, 142
Smiddy, Prof. Timothy A. (Cork economist, US envoy; 1875–1962), 279, 281
Smyth, Tom (Dublin GAA), 65
Society of Technical Assistance to Soviet Russia (NY), 138
Stack, Augustine Mary Moore (Austin; Kerry TD, Min. Home Affairs, AT; 1879–1929), 169, 234, 274, 279
Civil War, 313, 314, 319
build-up, 284, 285, 287, 288, 297, 298, 300–1
HB's death, 4, 5
imprisonment, 45, 103, 104, 105, 108, 119
Staines, Michael Joseph (Dublin TD, T; 1885–1955), 58
Stephens, James (Kilkenny Fenian; 1825–1901), 18, 25
Stoker, Abraham (Bram; b. Dublin, novelist; 1847–1912), 30
Stone, Warder Tom (Dartmoor Prison), 46
Stritch, Honoria (Dublin), 334
Stritch, James (Dublin IRB), 27, 28, 32, 34, 336
suffrage movement (US), 139–40, 197
Sullivan, Alexander (Chicago Clan; 1847–1913), 28
Sullivan, Timothy (Dublin KC; 1874–1949), 330

Sweeney, Michael (Dublin IRA, AT; 1900?–22), 291
Sweeney, Patrick (Lewes convict; b. 1878), 81
Synge, John Millington (Dublin playwright; 1871–1909), 151
Synnott, Const. Patrick (DMP detective; d. 1892), 25

Tally, Judge Alfred E. (NY), 240
Talty, Kathleen (b. Clare, Manchester teacher), 362–3
Tammany Hall (NY), 150, 266, 267
Taylor, Thomas (Dublin publican, T), 319
Third (Farmer-Labor) Party, 178, 180
Thomas, Revd. Norman M. (American Presbyterian pacifist, socialist; 1884–1968), 142
Thompson, Lieut.-Col. Marcellus Hagans (New Jersey arms manufacturer), 182, 212
Thornton, Frank (Dublin IRA Intelligence, T), 116
Thornton, Fr. Walter (St. Vincent's Hospital Chaplain), 324
Tierney, Fr. (NY), 385
Tobin, Patrick (Dublin IRB), 21, 23, 28
Todd, Burns & Co. (Dublin), 31, 48, 54, 55, 60, 63, 66, 75, 79, 87, 90, 95, 96
Tone, Theobald Wolfe (Dublin United Irishman; 1763–98), 70, 102, 369
Total Abstinence Association, 36
Tracey, Mrs (Dublin), 64
Traynor, Annie (née Coyne), 16, 319
Traynor, Oscar (Dublin IRA, T; 1886–1963), 34, 35, 81, 279
  Civil War, 308, 309, 311–12, 313, 319
  build-up, 281, 283, 293
  Easter Rebellion, 38, 39, 40, 41–2, 43, 44
Treacy, Mick (Dublin GAA), 345
Treaty: see Anglo-Irish Treaty (1921)
'Triangle' (Clan na Gael), 28
Turner, Bishop William (Buffalo, NY; b. Limerick; 1871–1936), 155, 156, 190
Twomey, Maurice (Moss; Cork IRA, AT; 1896–1978), 357, 408
Tynan, Patrick J. P. ('Invincible' leader), 28
Tynan, Thomas and Anna (Laois), 30

Ulster Delegation (to US), 141–2
Ulster Volunteer Force, 34, 230
United Irish League, 110
United Irishmen, 18, 31, 109
  clubs, 32, 109
United Labourers of Ireland, 29
United Press of America, 117
United States Mail Steamship Co. (NY), 214, 223

Vaughan's Hotel (Dublin), 85, 121, 127, 225, 283, 305, 306
Versailles Treaty (1919), 136–7
Victoria, Queen Alexandrina (1819–1901), 23, 149
Villard, Oswald Garrison (NY journalist; 1872–1949), 138, 195

Walsh, Billy (Dublin IRA, AT), 309
Walsh, Celia (Frank's daughter), 160, 162
Walsh, Sen. David Ignatius (Mass., D; 1872–1947), 197
Walsh, Frank Patrick (b. Kansas, NY radical lawyer; 1864–1939), 136, 154, 198, 224, 240, 248, 262
  HB and, 137, 160, 162, 163, 173, 174, 221, 230, 252, 274
  Bond Drive, 143–4, 145, 203, 204
  Legal Counsel, 196–7, 206, 406
Walsh, James (Frank's son), 160, 162
Walsh, James Joseph (Cork TD, GAA, T; 1880–1948), 33, 113, 159, 247, 275, 397
Walsh, Joseph Cyrillus (Canadian journalist, AARIR; 1870–1955), 191, 199, 201, 202, 204, 276–7, 356, 366
Walsh, Katharine M. (née O'Flaherty, Frank's wife), 160, 224
Walsh, Sen. Thomas James (Montana, D; 1859–1933), 244
Walsh, Virginia (Frank's daughter), 160, 162, 224
Walsh, Archbishop William Joseph (Dublin; 1841–1921), 106, 117
'War of Independence', Irish, 170–1, 181, 276
  Truce (1921), 221, 223, 225, 246
Ward, Gilbert (US mission, NY), 174, 224, 262, 280, 301, 306, 380
Washington Disarmament Conference (1921–2), 197, 243, 249
Weafer, Thomas (Dublin IRA), 39, 40
Wharton, Const. Thomas (DMP detective), 119
Wheeler, Charles N. (NY Bonds organiser), 131, 136, 143, 144
Wheeler, Capt. Harry de Courcy (British army; b. Kildare), 43
Wheelwright, Catherine (née Coll, EdeV's mother; b. 1856), 125
Wheelwright, Charles (Rochester, NY), 125
Whelan, Bill (Dublin), 64
White Cross, 183, 203–4, 214, 225, 244–5
Wilson, Pres. Thomas Woodrow (D; 1856–1924), 117–18, 137, 138, 141
Winn, Lieut.-Col. J. (Prison Commission), 57, 116
Wolfe Tone clubs, 32

Wolsey, Cardinal Thomas (Archbishop of Canterbury; 1475?–1530), 62
Women's Auxiliary Army Corps, 105
Woods, James (Louth United Irishman; d. 1820?), 18
Woods, Philip (Kate Boland's father), 18
Workmen's Club (Dublin), 31, 36
World War I: see Great War
Worthington, Robert (Dublin contractor; 1841?–1922), 19

Worthington, Samuel E. (Dublin contractor), 19

Yeats, Jack Butler (b. London, artist; 1871–1957), 6–7
Yeats, William Butler (b. Dublin, poet, INB; 1865–1939), 272, 301
Young Ireland League, 29
Young Scotland, 200